# CLASSIC MILITARY AIRCRAFT

# CLASSIC MILITARY AIRCRAFT
## THE WORLD'S FIGHTING AIRCRAFT: 1914–1945

GENERAL EDITOR: JIM WINCHESTER

amber
BOOKS

This edition first published in 2010 by
Amber Books Ltd
Bradley's Close
74–77 White Lion Street
London N1 9PF
United Kingdom
www.amberbooks.co.uk

ISBN 978-1-907446-39-9

Printed and bound in China

10 9 8 7 6 5 4 3 2 1

This material was originally published as part of the reference set *Aircraft of the World*

# Contents

# Introduction

Military aircraft began before World War I as trainers and unarmed observation platforms, but before long they evolved into fighting machines and bombers able to take the war well beyond the front lines. The air battles over the Western Front set the template for air combat to follow until the missile age. Contrary to the chivalrous 'knights of the air' image, success usually meant sneaking up and shooting one's opponent in the back.

*Above: Beginning as reconnaissance platforms with ad hoc armament, fighters evolved into specialised killing machines like the Fokker Dr 1. The Dr 1 had its limitations, but gained fame through the exploits of a handful of highly skilled pilots.*

Biplanes stayed in fashion for many years after the war, only slowly adding refinements such as metal structure, radios and inline engines. Guns moved from the pilot's reach into the wings. Bombers developed enclosed turrets. Interwar fighter pilots were members of elite flying clubs until the threat of war and modern fast bombers grew and rearmament began in earnest. Theories that the bomber would always get through were prevalent and some 1930s bombers were faster and higher-flying than contemporary fighters.

In the last years of peace, truly modern fighters emerged, including the Spitfire, Bf 109, and A6M 'Zero'. During the war, Germany managed to field no completely new types in large numbers other than the Fw 190. The Bf 109 remained in production until the war's end. The 'war-winning' jets such as the Me 262 appeared to late to have any great impact on events. Germany also failed to develop an effective strategic bomber, concentrating on medium and dive-bombers.

Nearly 800,000 aircraft were produced by the main combatants during the war, but no country could match the industrial might of the USA, whose factories built over 300,000 from 1940-45. For every two American fighters or bombers it should be remembered there was also a trainer, a transport or a liaison aircraft. The major US combat types introduced after 1942, notably the P-51 and F6F fighters and the B-29 bomber, were able to incorporate the lessons of the early war years.

Change came faster after 1945 than it did after 1918. Piston engines and propellers were on their way out and a new era of jets, swept wings and

*Below: The Allies hoped that strategic bombing would hasten the end of the war without prolonged ground fighting. The limitations of technology meant that few attacks were as accurate as the October 1943 Eighth Air Force strike on the Focke Wulf Plant at Marienburg.*

missiles began. Today, the warplanes of the 1914-45 era are regarded as the classics upon which the subsequent generations of military (and civil) aircraft were built.

# AICHI

# D3A 'VAL'

● Naval dive-bomber ● Influenced by the He 70 ● Highly manoeuvrable

▲ When the 'Val' entered service, Japanese crews originally found themselves with a highly competent aircraft. Unfortunately, it was to become increasingly vulnerable.

**H**aving dropped the first Japanese bombs to fall on American targets during World War II, the D3A went on to sink more Allied warships than any other Axis aircraft. It was given the Allied codename 'Val' and its early success gave no hint of its troubled design history or the terrible losses that were to be suffered later in the war. During the initial stages of hostilities against America, the D3A was feared as a formidable dive-bomber.

◀ **Attack on Pearl Harbor**
This dramatic photograph depicts a D3A1 in action during the Japanese attack on Pearl Harbor. Exploding anti-aircraft shells surround this machine, but losses were comparatively light.

▼ **'Val' in plan**
A near-perfect plan view shows the He 70-inspired elliptical wing of the D3A. The dive brakes and undercarriage may also be seen.

▲ **Navy Type 99**
Known to the Japanese as the Navy Type 99 Carrier Bomber Model 11, the D3A1 was a highly accurate delivery platform, especially effective in diving attacks on ships. Later in the war, both D3A1 and D3A2 aircraft were used in desperate kamikaze attacks.

▲ **Second prototype**
Aichi produced two prototypes of the 11-Shi Navy Experimental Carrier Bomber, which was to become the D3A. This was the much-modified second aircraft.

◀ **Distinctive features**
This US Naval Intelligence photograph clearly shows the retracted dive brakes and tail-mounted arrester hook.

## FACTS AND FIGURES

➤ An undesirable feature of the D3A prototype was its tendency to snap roll during tight turns.

➤ The 'Val' was the last Japanese carrier-based aircraft with spatted landing gear.

➤ Because of its agility, the D3A was sometimes flown as a fighter.

➤ During attacks on British ships in the Indian Ocean, 'Vals' placed 82 to 87 per cent of their bombs on target.

➤ Some aircraft were modified as D3A2-K Bomber Trainer Model 12s.

➤ With its extra fuel, the D3A2 could fly long-range missions over the Solomons.

**PROFILE**

# 'Val' in force over Pearl Harbor

Having identified a requirement for a new carrier-capable dive-bomber to replace its Aichi D1A2 biplanes, the Imperial Japanese Navy (IJN) issued a specification to Japanese industry during 1936.

Aichi answered with a monoplane design featuring a fixed, spatted undercarriage and a wing inspired by that of the He 70. Research had shown that the extra weight and complexity of retractable landing gear was not justified by the corresponding small increase in overall performance.

Initial flight tests revealed a number of serious problems, but after a major redesign, which included an increase in power, the aircraft was chosen over the Nakajima D3N1. At this stage a dorsal fin was added to rectify persistent directional stability problems, before carrier qualification began in 1940.

Involved in a number of naval actions, including the attacks on Pearl Harbor and the sinking of the British carrier HMS Hermes, the D3A1 was replaced from June 1942 by the D3A2, which featured increased fuel capacity, a propeller spinner and modified canopy. As World War II progressed, the 'Val' began to suffer horrendous losses and all but the smallest carriers had their aircraft replaced by the Yokosuka D4Y Suisei. In the final year of war, many D3As were expended in suicide attacks.

*Externally, the main difference between the D3A1 and D3A2 was the use of a propeller spinner on the latter.*

*Belonging to the 33rd Kokutai, this D3A1 has its rear canopy removed, allowing the rear-seater a greater field of fire. This was a typical in-service configuration.*

## D3A2 Model 22 'Val'

**Type:** two-seat, carrier-based dive-bomber

**Powerplant:** one 969-kW (1,300-hp.) Mitsubishi Kinsei 54 14-cylinder, air-cooled radial engine

**Maximum speed:** 430 km/h (267 m.p.h.) at 6200 m (20,000 ft.)

**Range:** 1352 km (840 mi.) with bombload

**Service ceiling:** 10,500 m (34,500 ft.)

**Weights:** empty 2570 kg (5,654 lb.), maximum take-off 3800 kg (8,360 lb.)

**Armament:** two fixed forward-firing 7.7-mm (.303 cal.) Type 97 machine-guns and one flexibly-mounted 7.7-mm Type 97 machine-gun in the rear cockpit, plus 370 kg (814 lb.) of bombs

**Dimensions:**
| | |
|---|---|
| span | 14.37 m (47 ft. 2 in.) |
| length | 10.20 m (33 ft. 6 in.) |
| height | 3.85 m (12 ft. 8 in.) |
| wing area | 34.90 m² (373 sq. ft.) |

---

A prominent tubular sight mounted ahead of the windscreen enabled the pilot to aim the forward-firing machine-guns. They were useful weapons for ground-strafing but limited in air-to-air combat.

A further modification introduced on the D3A2 was a revised canopy profile. Even longer than the 'greenhouse' canopy of the D3A1, the new glazing featured an elongated rear section which was faired neatly into the rear fuselage. The frequent removal of this section in use meant that the canopy was not a reliable recognition feature of the D3A2.

## D3A2 MODEL 22 'VAL'

Built by Showa Hikoki Kogyo, this late-production D3A2 was flown by the Meikoya Kokutai. Later in the war, 'Vals' flew only from the smaller carriers denied to the D4Y by its high landing speed.

Persistent problems with directional stability led Aichi to fit a dorsal fin to the 'Val'. This cured the stability problem, while cambered outer-wing leading edges cured an early tendency to snap roll in small radius turns.

An engine of increased power gave the D3A2 generally improved performance compared to the D3A1. Take-off power was 969 kW (1,300 hp.).

Mounted on a hinged crutch beneath the centre fuselage, the 250-kg (550-lb.) bomb was swung forwards and downward on release. Two 60-kg (132-lb.) bombs could be carried beneath the wings.

## COMBAT DATA

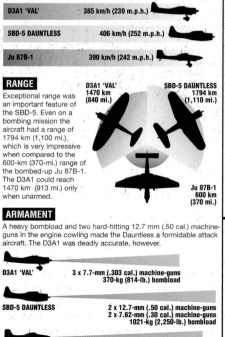

### MAXIMUM SPEED

Although it was carrier-based like the Douglas SBD-5 Dauntless, the D3A1 was very close to the Junkers Ju 87B-1 in overall design philosophy. With its fixed undercarriage, the 'Val' offered similar performance to the German design.

| | |
|---|---|
| D3A1 'VAL' | 385 km/h (239 m.p.h.) |
| SBD-5 DAUNTLESS | 406 km/h (252 m.p.h.) |
| Ju 87B-1 | 390 km/h (242 m.p.h.) |

### RANGE

Exceptional range was an important feature of the SBD-5. Even on a bombing mission the aircraft had a range of 1794 km (1,100 mi.), which is very impressive when compared to the 600-km (370-mi.) range of the bombed-up Ju 87B-1. The D3A1 could reach 1470 km (913 mi.) only when unarmed.

D3A1 'VAL' 1470 km (840 mi.)
SBD-5 DAUNTLESS 1794 km (1,110 mi.)
Ju 87B-1 600 km (370 mi.)

### ARMAMENT

A heavy bombload and two hard-hitting 12.7 mm (.50 cal.) machine-guns in the engine cowling made the Dauntless a formidable attack aircraft. The D3A1 was deadly accurate, however.

D3A1 'VAL' — 3 x 7.7-mm (.303 cal.) machine-guns, 370-kg (814-lb.) bombload

SBD-5 DAUNTLESS — 2 x 12.7-mm (.50 cal.) machine-guns, 2 x 7.62-mm (.30 cal.) machine-guns, 1021-kg (2,250-lb.) bombload

Ju 87B-1 — 3 x 7.9-mm (0.31-in.) machine-guns, 700-kg (1,540-lb.) bombload

---

## Naval Aichis

**B7A RYUSEI 'GRACE':** A powerful torpedo and dive-bomber, the B7A suffered a protracted development period and, by the time it was ready for service, all the IJN's carriers had been lost.

**D1A 'SUSIE':** Relying heavily on Heinkel's He 66 design, the D1A was the IJN's principal dive-bomber before the D3A entered service. Some 68 D1As were serving as trainers in 1941.

**E13A 'JAKE':** Designed as a reconnaissance floatplane, the E13A developed into a useful multi-role type and flew from land and shore bases throughout World War II.

# AIRCO

# DH.2

● Single-seater ● Pusher-engined fighter ● Fully aerobatic

▲ Both the two-seat DH.1 and single-seat DH.2 used a pusher propeller layout, which allowed a clear field for forwards fire. By dispensing with the observer, the DH.2 became a fast and agile fighter.

**A** rotary engine mounted in the pusher position drove the propeller of the DH.2. This was the second pusher fighter designed by Geoffrey de Havilland and built by Airco. The pusher concept has been tried a number of times in aviation history, but has rarely produced a combat aircraft on par with a 'tractor'-engined equivalent. The DH.2 was an interesting design, but it never became one of the great fighters of World War I.

---

## AIRCO DH.2

**Exposed engine position ▶**
The DH.2's engine and propeller were installed inside the open fuselage structure of the aircraft.

**▼ 'Fly-by-wire'**
A mass of control wires and rigging cables characterised the DH.2. A number of early aircraft were lost when their rotary engines broke-up in flight and flying fragments damaged the vulnerable wing and fuselage structure.

**▲ Royal Flying Corps fighters**
No. 24 Squadron took the DH.2 to war in early 1917, but by August 1918 there was none left in service. This collection of replicas includes the contemporary Bristol Scout, Bristol M.1C and SE.5a.

**▲ No Lewis gun**
A single Lewis machine-gun was normally mounted in the position shown by the white fairing mounted on the cockpit lip.

**Fabric covering ▶**
Sunlight shining through the fabric covering reveals the wooden structure of the wings.

---

## FACTS AND FIGURES

➤ Geoffrey de Havilland was forced to choose a pusher layout because British interrupter gear was not available.

➤ Many of the DH.2's components were simply scaled down from the DH.1.

➤ No. 29 Squadron lost four out of 16 DH.2s when flying to France in a snowstorm.

➤ Oswald Boelcke was killed in a flying accident when engaging a DH.2.

➤ In the prototype a ballast weight of 13.6 kg (30 lb.) was needed in the nose as the DH.2 was tail heavy without its machine-gun.

➤ In April 1916 the DH.2 was found to be a match for the Fokker monoplanes.

# Fighting the Fokkers

A smaller version of Geoffrey de Havilland's earlier DH.1 fighter, the DH.2 retained the pusher configuration of its predecessor to create a clear field of fire for its Lewis gun. In 1915, British aeronautical engineers had not yet designed a practical 'interrupter' to enable a machine-gun to fire through the propeller.

Although the Lewis gun did not endanger the propeller, its initial installation in the DH.2 provided a host of problems for the pilot. A mounting was provided on each side of the cockpit and the pilot was expected to set up the gun on whatever side would give him the best chance of hitting the target. The pilot was challenged to maintain control of the aircraft while struggling to move the gun from side to side.

The DH.2 was never easy to fly or to shoot from, but it gave British pilots a fighter with which to seize the advantage against Germany's Fokker monoplanes. Eventually, the Lewis gun was mounted in the centre in front of the pilot, and the DH.2 held its own in battle until more modern German types appeared.

*Below: Pilots were completely exposed to the elements in the DH.2, but the field of view was excellent. Pilots soon began to use the gun as a fixed weapon, moving the whole aircraft to aim it.*

*Above: With its Lewis gun in place, a DH.2 comes in to land at the end of a patrol.*

## DH.2

**Type:** single-seat scout fighter

**Powerplant:** one 75-kW (100-hp.) Gnome Monosoupape rotary piston engine or one 82-kW (110-hp.) Le Rhône rotary engine (late models)

**Maximum speed:** (Gnome engine) 150 km/h (93 m.p.h.) at sea level

**Cruising speed:** 126 km/h (78 m.p.h.)

**Endurance:** 2 hours 45 min

**Service ceiling:** 4265 m (14,000 ft.)

**Weights:** empty 428 kg (942 lb.); maximum take-off 654 kg (1,441 lb.)

**Armament:** one forward-firing 7.62-mm Lewis machine-gun with canisters holding 47 rounds

**Dimensions:**
| | | |
|---|---|---|
| span | 8.61 m | (28 ft. 3 in.) |
| length | 7.68 m | (25 ft. 2 in.) |
| height | 2.91 m | (9 ft. 6 in.) |
| wing area | 23.13 m² | (249 sq. ft.) |

## DH.2

Towards the end of 1915 No. 24 Squadron began receiving its first DH.2s. This aircraft was one of the first batch to join the unit, which pioneered operations with the DH.2.

Once pilots had adopted the tactic of aiming the aircraft and not the gun, the gun was fixed in position. Some movement up and down was allowed for minor aiming corrections, however.

Although they looked fragile, the tubular-steel tailbooms were comprehensively rigged, which made them strong yet flexible.

The DH.2 had a single fin and rudder and an unusually large tailplane.

Not only was the pilot expected to juggle his Lewis gun from side to side while maintaining control of the aircraft during combat, but he also had to change the heavy 47-round ammunition drums.

Both the top and bottom wings were fitted with ailerons. Once initial structural problems had been overcome and pilots had mastered its tricky handling, the DH.2 proved to be a manoeuvrable fighter.

Most DH.2s were powered by the Gnome Monosoupape rotary engine, but some of the later aircraft featured the 82-kW (110-hp.) Le Rhône engine.

A steerable tailskid aided ground handling, which was also improved, together with flight performance, by a larger rudder on production machines.

## COMBAT DATA

### MAXIMUM SPEED

Airco DH.2s were able to prevent air-superiority by the all-conquering Fokker monoplanes by virtue of their forward-firing gun, good manoeuvrability and high speed. Nieuport's Type 11 was faster still, but saw comparatively little service.

| | |
|---|---|
| DH.2 | 150 km/h (93 m.p.h.) |
| E.III | 140 km/h (87 m.p.h.) |
| TYPE 11 | 155 km/h (96 m.p.h.) |

### MAXIMUM POWER

Most aero-engines of the period produced a similar power output. More powerful engines were larger and therefore heavier. It was down to the aircraft designer to produce a light, efficient airframe to maximise available power, thereby giving optimum performance.

| DH.2 | E.III | TYPE 11 |
|---|---|---|
| 75 kW (100 hp.) | 75 kW (100 hp.) | 60 kW (80 hp.) |

### ENDURANCE

Escort missions were sometimes flown by fighting scouts such as these, but the majority of air-to-air victories were gained when pilots set out to find and engage enemy fighters. Long endurance gave a pilot more time to find targets and greater combat persistence.

| DH.2 | E.III | TYPE 11 |
|---|---|---|
| 2 hours 45 min | 1 hour 30 min | 2 hours 30 min |

## British pusher-engined fighters

**■ VICKERS F.B.5 GUNBUS:** This 1914 design represents the first British aircraft intended from the outset for air-to-air fighting.

**■ GRAHAME-WHITE TYPE 11:** The Type 11 was an unsuccessful attempt at producing a fighter in the 1915/16 period.

**■ BLACKBURN TRIPLANE:** Designed as a Zeppelin airship killer, the Triplane did not perform well and only one was built.

**■ VICKERS TYPE 161 COW GUN FIGHTER:** Built to carry the 37-mm COW gun, this 1931 fighter was the ultimate in pusher designs.

# AIRCO

# DH.4

● Day bomber ● British and US production ● Powerful engines

▲ After their success in France during World War I, British-built DH.4s and American-built DH.4s found further service in foreign air forces, including those of Belgium, Greece, Japan and Nicaragua.

O ne of the most successful aircraft of World War I, the DH.4 was the first British bomber designed for the role. After its first flight in August 1916, the DH.4 was transformed by the Rolls-Royce Eagle engine, which enabled the aircraft's performance to match that of contemporary fighters. Nearly 7,000 were built, more than half of these in the US. Production continued after World War I, when several air forces, together with early airlines, retained the DH.4.

## AIRCO DH.4

▲ DH-4B air mail pioneer
Surplus DH-4s were converted for the US Postal Department to establish an air mail service; the front cockpit held mail bags. This aircraft has wingtip landing lights.

▲ 'Liberty Plane'
With hundreds of surplus DH-4s available after World War I, many found their way into civil operation. DH-4s were used not only as mail carriers, but also as airliners and crop-dusters.

▲ Steel-framed DH-4M-1
A.S.23007 was one of a number of American-built DH-4s rebuilt by Boeing and Atlantic Aircraft during the 1920s, with steel-tube fuselages. These aircraft were designated DH-4M-1s and -2s, respectively.

▲ Cabin-equipped DH-4A
DH-4As carried a pilot and two passengers. Nine were converted from DH-4s, serving with the RAF and on early routes across the English Channel.

Army air ambulance ▶
Among numerous DH-4 variants to enter US military service were a number of DH-4Amb-2s which were able to carry two stretcher cases.

## FACTS AND FIGURES

➤ A total of 30 aircraft were built for the US Postal Department, with increased-span wings and two 149-kW Hall-Scott engines.

➤ DH.4s were fitted with engines ranging in power output from 149 kW to 391 kW.

➤ Total US DH-4 production reached 4,846; 15 were built in Belgium; 1,449 in the UK.

➤ A DH.4 shipped to New Zealand became the first aircraft to fly over that country's highest mountain, 3760-m (12,330-ft.) Mount Cook.

➤ The Airco DH.4 prototype flew in August 1916 from its base at Hendon, London.

➤ For coastal patrol tasks, the RNAS fitted floats to at least one DH.4.

**PROFILE**

# de Havilland's day bombing master

Staggered wings were used on the DH.4 to give the pilot a good view of the ground for bombing. One or two Lewis guns were fitted in the observer's cockpit, and one or two forward-firing Vickers guns were mounted on the fuselage sides. In this form the DH.4 made an immediate impression over the Western Front in 1917.

Nearly 1,500 were built in the UK, and almost 5,000 with 298-kW (400-hp.) Liberty 12

engines, in the United States, where the US Army used DH-4s until 1932. The US Navy and Marine Corps also used the type.

After the war, RAF aircraft were retired, and many were transferred to other countries. More than 1,500 of the American aircraft were modified as DH-4Bs, while Boeing and Fokker Atlantic built 285 modernised DH-4Ms with steel-tube fuselages. There were more than 60 modified versions, including single-seaters, dual-

control trainers and air ambulances. A total of 100 DH-4Bs were also used to establish the US air mail service, the aircraft serving until 1927.

*Above: In 1923, USAAC DH-4s conclusively demonstrated air-to-air refuelling for the first time. The receiver was aloft for over 37 hours.*

*Above: The DH.4 was operational from April 1917. On 6 April, No. 55 Squadron flew from Fienvilliers on a mission to bomb Valenciennes. Its performance matched that of fighters of the time.*

## DH.4

N5977 was one of a batch of 50 DH.4s built by Westland Aircraft with Rolls-Royce Eagle engines. It carries the markings of No. 2 Squadron, RNAS, immediately prior to its redesignation in 1918 as No. 202 Squadron, RAF.

### DH.4

**Type:** light day bomber

**Powerplant:** one 280-kW (375-hp.) Rolls-Royce Eagle VIII water-cooled 12-cylinder engine

**Maximum speed:** 230 km/h (143 m.p.h.) at sea level

**Endurance:** 3 hours 45 min

**Range:** 700 km (435 mi.)

**Service ceiling:** 6705 m (22,000 ft.)

**Weights:** empty 1083 kg (2,383 lb.); maximum take-off 1575 kg (3,465 lb.)

**Armament:** (RNAS aircraft) two forward-firing 7.7-mm (.303 cal.) Vickers machine-guns and one or two 7.7-mm Lewis machine-gun(s) in the rear cockpit, plus up to 209 kg (460 lb.) of bombs

**Dimensions:**
| | |
|---|---|
| span | 12.92 m (42 ft. 4 in.) |
| length | 9.35 m (30 ft. 8 in.) |
| height | 3.05 m (10 ft.) |
| wing area | 40.32 m² (434 sq. ft.) |

American interest in the DH.4 was high; almost 5,000 were built with 298-kW (400-hp.) Liberty 12 engines fitted. In all, 1,885 were shipped to France.

The placement of the main fuel tank between the pilot and the gunner proved a disadvantage as it hampered in-flight communication. It was also prone to catching fire if hit by enemy guns, earning the aircraft the nickname 'The Flaming Coffin'.

DH.4s were defensively and offensively well-armed. RNAS aircraft carried two forward-firing 7.7-mm (.303 cal.) Vickers machine-guns above the engine (RFC machines carried only one) and one or two 7.7-mm Lewis machine-guns in the rear cockpit.

The DH.4 was a conventional two-bay biplane with a wood and fabric structure, although its forward fuselage was skinned with plywood for strength. The tailplane was adjustable, allowing the pilot to trim the aircraft in flight.

Originally intended to be powered by an uprated Beardmore engine of 119 kW (160 hp.), the first DH.4 actually flew with a 172-kW (230-hp.) BHP powerplant. However, it was Rolls-Royce's 186-kW (250-hp.) Eagle 12-cylinder engine that took the DH.4 to fame.

Underfuselage/wing bomb racks on the DH.4 had a 209-kg (460-lb.) capacity. As No. 55 Squadron, Royal Flying Corps received its first aircraft, Royal Naval Air Service examples were also being delivered. These aircraft undertook bombing, gun ranging (for ships), reconnaissance and photographic tasks.

### COMBAT DATA

#### ENDURANCE

The DH.4 had a good range and endurance performance compared to the contemporary Albatros C.V/16. The post-war American-built DH-4M retained this ability.

| DH.4 | C.V/16 | DH-4M |
|---|---|---|
| 3 hrs 45 mins | 3 hrs 15 mins | 3 hrs 45 mins |

#### ARMAMENT

While RFC DH.4s were equipped with three machine-guns, RNAS aircraft used four, like the later US-built DH-4M. The Albatros was lightly-armed by comparison, although it could carry a 'light bombload'.

| | |
|---|---|
| DH.4 | 3 x 7.7-mm (.303 cal.) machine-guns / 209-kg (460-lb.) bombload |
| C.V/16 | 2 x 7.92-mm machine-guns |
| DH-4M | 4 x 7.63-mm (.30 cal.) machine-guns / 209-kg (460-lb.) bombload |

#### POWER

The chief benefits of the post-war DH-4M were its more powerful engine and more robust steel-tube fuselage structure. With the Liberty 12 installed, it had twice the power of the C.V/16.

| DH.4 | C.V/16 | DH-4M |
|---|---|---|
| 280 kW (375 hp.) | 164 kW (220 hp.) | 313 kW (420 hp.) |

## British land-based bombers of World War I

**AVRO 504:** In November 1914, four modified RNAS 504 trainers from a base in France made a raid on Zeppelin sheds at Friedrichshafen.

**ROYAL AIRCRAFT FACTORY BE.2:** This two-seat reconnaissance type was adapted as a bomber, but was vulnerable to enemy fighters.

**SHORT BOMBER:** A land-based version of the Short 184 floatplane, the Bomber flew missions with the RNAS from late 1916.

**SOPWITH 1½ STRUTTER:** Armed with a forward-firing gun, this Sopwith design equipped RNAS and RFC units as a bomber and escort.

# AIRCO

# DH.9 AND DH.9A

● Two-seat bomber ● World War I ● Popular civilian aircraft

**▲ Post-war versatility**
*After World War I, many DH.9s were sold on the civilian market; some were exported, including this floatplane conversion which was sold to the British and Egyptian Tea Co. Ltd.*

**▲ Large wing**
*The later versions of the DH.9 and DH.9A had a very good service ceiling, made possible by the large wing area.*

**Civil service ▼**
*Belgian airline SNETA's DH.9C flew between Croydon and Brussels, with wing-mounted luggage racks and a DH.4 cabin.*

**Flexible load ▲**
*During World War I the DH.9 was used to distribute propaganda leaflets behind enemy lines – one of the earliest examples of psychological warfare. DH.9s of No.110 Squadron dropped over 10 tons of bombs on German cities in 1918.*

**▲ Close formation**
*In 1923 the DH.9A was a state-of-the-art day-bomber; crews from No. 39 Squadron are seen here practising formation flying.*

**Mock attack ▶**
*At the Hendon Pageant in 1929 No. 208(AC) Sqn conducted bombing demonstrations with their DH.9As against a mock fort and tanks.*

A n ambitious attempt to improve the DH.4, the Airco DH.9 was a bomber expected to play a major role in the Great War. It had the advantage of using wings, tail and landing gear similar to those of the DH.4, which made it easy to produce, but the type suffered from having inadequate engines and remained inferior to the plane it was meant to replace in the newly-established Royal Air Force. The DH.9A, however, was a much improved model.

*▲ Serving briefly in the day-bomber role at the end of World War I, the DH.9A, known as the 'Nine-Ack', stayed in production after 1918 and in the 1920s served as an army co-operation aircraft in Iraq and on the North-West Frontier. UK-based bomber and auxiliary squadrons were also equipped with the DH.9A.*

## FACTS AND FIGURES

➤ The DH.9 was introduced to combat service in France with British squadrons in April 1918, and the DH.9A in June.

➤ The prototype for this series began flight tests in July 1917.

➤ The total production of the DH.9 exceeded 3,200 aircraft.

➤ War surplus DH.9 and DH.9As served in many countries, including Afghanistan, Canada, Estonia, Greece and Latvia.

➤ Hispano-Suiza manufactured about 500 DH.9s for the Spanish air force.

➤ Ultimately, DH.9s were produced at the rate of one every 40 minutes.

# PROFILE

# The nine and the 'Nine-Ack'

The DH.9 was produced because of the concern about daylight attacks on London by German bombers. Seeking to improve its own bomber force, the Royal Flying Corps invested heavily in the DH.9, a handsome but under-powered aircraft based on the proven (and famous) DH.4.

Flown with several engine types, the DH.9 was always hamstrung by inadequate power. Intrepid British crews, flying with squadrons in France, achieved some success against

the Kaiser's forces, but suffered heavy losses which were blamed on the flaws of this promising but disappointing biplane.

DH.9s were more effective in Macedonia, Palestine and at home in the United Kingdom, where they flew coastal defence and anti-Zeppelin patrols. The last RAF DH.9s were used as ambulances in Somaliland, but these were withdrawn by July 1919.

The DH.9A, however, was one of the most successful

strategic bombers of the period. Considerably more powerful engine types and a larger wing area ensured much improved performance. Though used only briefly before the Armistice, the DH.9A was standard equipment in the RAF until 1931.

*Above: Despite its ungainly appearance the DH.9A gave valuable service in India, the Middle East and North Africa. Reconditioned in 1925, this aircraft enjoyed a very long service life.*

*Above: After the war some DH.9As were 'tropicalised' for service in Iraq and on the North-West Frontier. This aircraft has an extra radiator under the nose and an overload fuel tank under the starboard upper wing.*

## DH.9A

**Type:** two-seat light day-bomber

**Powerplant:** one 298-kW (400-hp.) Liberty 12 inline piston engine

**Maximum speed:** 193 km/h (120 m.p.h.) at 3048 m (10,000 ft.)

**Endurance:** 5 hours 45 min

**Range:** 1000 km (620 mi.)

**Service ceiling:** 5105 m (16,750 ft.)

**Weights:** empty 1012 kg (2,226 lb.); maximum take-off 1508 kg (3,310 lb.)

**Armament:** one fixed forward-firing 7.7-mm (.303 cal.) Vickers machine-gun and one or two 7.7-mm Lewis guns fitted on a Scarff ring in the aft cockpit, plus up to 299 kg (660 lb.) of bombs

**Dimensions:**
span 14.02 m (46 ft.)
length 9.14 m (30 ft.)
height 3.44 m (11 ft. 3 in.)
wing area 40.32 m² (434 sq. ft.)

Most DH.9s were powered by the Rolls-Royce Eagle or the slightly more powerful Liberty 12 engine built in the United States.

In the DH.9 the pilot no longer sat in the potentially dangerous position between the engine and fuel tank, as in the DH.4. With the cockpit set further back, he could also communicate with the gunner far more easily.

## DH.9A

J7832 was operated by No. 45 Squadron, RAF, based at Helwan, Egypt, in 1928. It was tasked with aerial policing in co-operation with the army.

The silver colour scheme carried by this 'Nine-Ack' is typical of RAF army co-operation aircraft in the Middle East during the 1920s.

The 'winged camel' symbol on the nose of this aircraft is that of No. 45 Squadron, RAF. This symbol formed part of their official squadron badge, alluding to colonial policing duties in the Middle East.

Armament consisted of two machine-guns: the pilot's 7.7-mm (.303 cal.) Vickers firing through the propeller and the observer's single or twin 7.7-mm Lewis gun.

Initially fitted with a 171-kW (230-hp.) engine, the DH.9 was unable to climb above 3962 metres (13,000 ft.) with a full military load of fuel, oil, water and armament.

## ACTION DATA

### MAXIMUM SPEED

The DH.9A was designed to have a superior service ceiling rather than a high top speed. The other two types were fitted with more powerful engines.

| | |
|---|---|
| DH.9A | 193 km/h (120 m.p.h.) |
| ANT-3 | 207 km/h (128 m.p.h.) |
| Bre.19A2 | 235 km/h (146 m.p.h.) |

### SERVICE CEILING

In action from bases the DH.9A was able to elude enemy fighters with its altitude capability, which was exceptional for the period.

| DH.9A | ANT-3 | Bre.19A2 |
|---|---|---|
| 5105 m (16,750 ft.) | 4950 m (10,900 ft.) | 5000 m (16,400 ft.) |

### ARMAMENT

Compared to other light day-bombers of the era, the DH.9A had a comparable gun armament, but a relatively light bombload. The Breguet 19 had superior defensive armament.

| DH.9A | ANT-3 | Bre.19A2 |
|---|---|---|
| 299 kg (660 lb.) bombs and 2 x 7.7-mm (.303 cal.) MGs | 500 kg (1,100 lb.) bombs and 2 x 7.62-mm (.30 cal.) MGs | 400 kg (880 lb.) bombs and 3 x 7.7-mm (.303 cal.) MGs |

# Early Airco/de Havillands

■ **DH.2:** When the first DH.2 flew in 1915 the British had yet to develop interrupter gear to allow a gun to be fired forwards through the propeller arc. The DH.2 was a successful single-seat fighter with a pusher propeller and armed with a Lewis machine-gun.

■ **DH.4:** One of the outstanding designs of World War I, the DH.4 had handling and performance that made it almost impossible to intercept when it entered service in France in March 1917. Thousands were built in the United States after the war.

■ **DH.10 AMIENS:** A twin-engined bomber based on the smaller DH.3, the Amiens was just too late to see war service. Peacetime duties included an airmail service between England and occupied Germany; others served on the North-West Frontier.

# ALBATROS

# C.I-C.XII

● Artillery observation ● Bomber ● Long service history

▲ *Pilots came to respect the C Series aircraft as they built up a reputation for viceless handling and the ability to bring their crews home despite suffering considerable damage.*

**T**o take advantage of the more powerful engines available to the Germans in 1915, Albatros designed a two-seat general-purpose aircraft named the C.I. The design was so good that it spawned a number of successors which served until the conclusion of World War I. With a sturdy wooden fuselage the C Series aircraft could take a considerable amount of punishment. Several of Germany's most famous pilots started their operational careers in the type.

▼ **Production milestone**
*In 1917 Albatros celebrated the construction of their 2,500th aircraft by decorating this C.V. This version was powered by a 164-kW eight-cylinder Mercedes engine.*

▲ **Modified C.I**
*This aircraft has a modified fin and rudder with a vertical trailing edge. Unusually, the aircraft is being flown from the rear cockpit.*

**Restricted view** ▶
*The large engine, with its vertical exhaust, gave C.III pilots very restricted forward vision.*

▲ **Heavily braced**
*The biplane wings were supported by wooden wing struts and a multitude of bracing wires.*

**Versatile aircraft** ▶
*The Albatros C.III was the most important general-purpose German aircraft of 1916.*

## FACTS AND FIGURES

➤ The world's most famous ace, Baron Manfred von Richthofen, flew as an observer in a C.I on the Russian Front.

➤ The C.Ib dual-control trainer version was built mainly by Mercur Flugzeugbau.

➤ The Albatros series was identifiable by the distinctive 'chimney' exhausts.

➤ Although initially regarded as a 'stop-gap' machine, 350 C.VIIs were still serving with front-line units as late as February 1917.

➤ Serving in all battle areas, the C.VII was often used as a light tactical bomber.

➤ The C.X was fitted with oxygen equipment, allowing high-altitude reconnaissance.

**PROFILE**

# Germany's multi-role master

Designed at a time when the full capabilities of the aeroplane were not fully appreciated, the Albatros C.I was an advanced aircraft for its day. Entering service in 1915, the Albatros was used for reconnaissance, bombing, photography, artillery observation and, for a brief period, as an escort.

One reason for the C.I's popularity with crew was its excellent rearward-firing gun

on a moveable mounting, which, for the first time, allowed the observer to take defensive action against hostile aircraft.

Among the famous pilots who flew the C.I was Oswald Boelcke, who developed the technique of positioning his aircraft to enable the observer to fire at enemy aircraft.

The C.I was followed in production by the C.III, which became the most prolific of all Albatros two-seaters. Similar in

form to the C.I, this aircraft featured a more powerful engine and revised tail surfaces which increased agility. The less successful C.V and C.VI designs were followed by the C.VII, which again featured a more powerful engine and control improvements. The last two major types, the C.X and C.XII, were highly capable machines but they retained many features from the original C.I.

*Left: To help prevent noxious fumes from the engine reaching the cockpit, this C.I featured extended exhausts which released fumes over the wing.*

*Above: This Swedish version of the Albatros C.I was designated SK 1 and was used as a trainer in the 1920s. It is seen here preserved at the Malmslatt Museum in Sweden.*

## C.III

**Seen in a typical factory-finish colour scheme, this C.III was delivered in early 1917. The type commanded great respect from Allied pilots who found it very difficult to shoot down.**

The pilot, seated in the front cockpit, flew the aircraft using wheel and rudder-bar type controls. Instrumentation was comprehensive for the period and included altimeter, fuel gauges, tachometer, clock and compass.

The trainable Parabellum machine-gun of the C.III was a very useful weapon and allowed the observer to fire at attackers approaching from behind.

Although similar to its C.I predecessor, the C.III featured completely revised tail surfaces. The new, more rounded unit was a hallmark of subsequent C Series Albatros aircraft.

The majority of C.IIIs were fitted with a Mercedes D III engine, which was mounted on stout wooden bearers. A short chimney-type manifold exhausted the engine fumes vertically. Later versions were fitted with a fixed forward-facing machine-gun which fired through the propeller arc.

The vee-type main undercarriage was constructed of steel tube. A 'claw'-type brake was fitted in the centre of the axle and was operated by a lever in the cockpit.

The C.III's great strength was due to the construction of the fuselage. This comprised four main fuselage longerons covered with plywood panels which did not need internal bracing.

*C III 5403/16*

### COMBAT DATA

**POWER**

Developed before the outbreak of World War I, the B.I was relatively underpowered compared to the later C Series. The ultimate C.XII had excellent performance thanks to its powerful engine.

| B.II | C.I | C.XII |
|---|---|---|
| 74 kW (100 hp.) | 119 kW (160 hp.) | 194 k|W (260 hp.) |

**SERVICE CEILING**

As engines and aerodynamics improved during World War I so did the service ceiling of Albatros designs. The 5000-m (16,400-ft.) ceiling of the C.XII helped it to stay out of reach of Allied fighters, as well as increasing its reconnaissance capabilities.

| B.II 3000m (9,840 ft.) | C.I 3353 m (11,000 ft.) | C.XII 5000 m (16,400 ft.) |
|---|---|---|

**ENDURANCE**

The B.I was one of the best observation aircraft of 1914/15. One of its main assets was its excellent endurance, allowing it to cover a large area during reconnaissance missions. Later C Series aircraft generally had poorer endurance because of their 'thirsty' engines.

| B.II 4 hours | C.I 2 hours 30 min | C.XII 2 hours 15 min |
|---|---|---|

## Albatros family

■ **D SERIES:** The D Series of fighting scouts were highly respected by the Allies and saw action from 1916 until the end of the war.

■ **G SERIES:** Albatros produced three bomber designs during World War I. This example, a G.II, was built only in prototype form.

■ **L SERIES:** Post-war Albatros aircraft were given L prefixes. This example is a L.72 biplane which transported freight between German cities.

■ **W SERIES:** Fitted with twin floats, the W.1 was basically an unarmed reconnaissance seaplane version of the B.II landplane.

# ALBATROS

# D.VA

● Single-seat biplane fighter ● Wooden fuselage

R ight to the end of World War I, the name Albatros could strike fear into the hearts of Allied flyers. The D.V could be a tough adversary and many were flown by the German aces of the day. An Achilles heel of the D.V, however, was a weakness in the wing struts, which was never fully overcome. As Allied air superiority increased, the greatly improved D.Va was introduced and hundreds of examples entered service before November 1918.

▲ Introduced in the mid-summer of 1917, the Albatros D.V was the German air service's answer to the Allies' SE.5a and Spad, both of which had gained the upper hand against the earlier D.III.

## ALBATROS D.VA

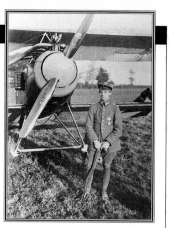

◄ **Fighter pilot Göring**
Lieutenant Hermann Göring, later the infamous head of the Luftwaffe, led Jasta 27 in an Albatros D.V similar to this, but black with a white nose and tail.

▲ **Proud pilot and his D.I**
A young pilot in the German Imperial Air Service poses next to his Albatros D.I. The positioning of the upper wing on the D.I impaired the pilot's upward forward vision – a problem rectified on the later D.II by lowering the wing. D.IIs also had a modified radiator system.

▲ **Captured Albatros**
The occasional capture of enemy aircraft allowed Allied pilots to test fly and assess the machines they would meet in hostile skies.

▼ **Albatros D.IIIa**
The D.V was developed from the earlier D.III, but with a deeper, more elliptical fuselage and a modified rudder, among other changes.

▲ **Albatros D.I**
The Albatros D.I of 1916 was the earliest ancestor of the D.V, designed to meet the threat of the Allied DH.2s and Nieuports. Note the flat fuselage sides compared to the D.V. Though not very manoeuverable, the D.I was relatively fast.

## FACTS AND FIGURES

➤ Total production of the Albatros D.V was 900 aircraft, followed by 1,612 examples of the D.Va.

➤ The D.Va took just 17 minutes to reach a height of 3658 m (12,000 ft.).

➤ The D.Va was the last Albatros design to see action in World War I.

➤ In April 1918, D.V and D.Va aircraft made up more than 54 per cent of the total number of German fighters available for action.

➤ The 'Red Baron', Manfred von Richthofen, was shot down in a D.V on 6 July 1917.

➤ Albatroses of Jasta 21 shot down 41 French aircraft in September 1917.

## PROFILE

# Imperial Germany's bird of prey

The intended successor to the Albatros D.III, the D.V fighter was something of a compromise design that entered service without adequate testing. German engineers overlooked a dangerous flaw in the wing-fuselage attachment points and one that, despite modifications, was never completely cured. No less a personality than Baron Manfred von Richtofen was scathing about the flying and fighting qualities of the D.V. In a letter written in July 1917 he called it 'so obsolete and so ridiculously inferior to the English that one can't do anything with this aircraft'. But such was the strength of the opposition on the Western Front at that time that the German air service had little choice.

Timely testing of the suspected weak areas of the D.V airframe helped save the situation, as did the availability of the Mercedes D.IIIa engine. This powerplant gave back what the D.Va had lost to increased weight as a result of wing and strut modifications.

Albatros D.Va fighters were ordered in quantity and began to reach operational units in October 1917 in time for the Spring Offensive the following year. They soon represented over half the fighters available to the Germans during the last months of the war.

*Above: The need for aircraft was so great that the D.V was produced in large numbers despite its inferior performance.*

*Left: With the success of such aircraft as the Fokker Triplane, Albatros flew an unsuccessful triplane version of the D.V.*

## D.Va

This Albatros D.V flew with Jasta 5, one of the Imperial Air Service's elite fighter units on the Western Front. The multi-point star emblem was the personal marking of its pilot, Lietenant Klein.

Typical of fighters of the period, the aircraft's machine guns fired through the arc of the propeller, with the aid of interrupter gear.

A strong monocoque plywood fuselage and smoothly faired engine made the Albatros one of the most streamlined aircraft of the period.

Many Albatros Scouts in service with the German Air Corps flew with their plywood fuselages largely unpainted.

The large spinner on the Albatros's propeller was designed to reduce drag, increasing performance.

Sustained diving maneuvers resulted in vibrations in the lower wing and its eventual failure. A design flaw was to blame. Strengthened wing struts solved the problem temporarily.

The elliptical fuselage cross-section of the D.V and D.Va contrasted with the flat fuselage sides of the earlier D.I.

---

### ACTION DATA

**SPEED**

A major area in which the Albatros D.V was deficient compared to the Allied fighters of the closing years of World War I was speed. Aircraft like the SE.5a and Spad VII were capable of speeds in excess of 200 km/h (124 m.p.h.).

| | |
|---|---|
| SE. 5A | 222 km/h (138 m.p.h.) |
| ALBATROS D.V | 185 km/h (115 m.p.h.) |
| SPAD VII | 211 km/h (131 m.p.h.) |

**WEAPONS**

The twin Maxim machine gun armament of the Albatros was introduced first on the D.I of 1916 and took a major toll on Allied aircraft. By 1917, however, guns of this type and caliber were more common, and the advantage became nil.

| | |
|---|---|
| SE. 5A | 2 x 7.7-mm (.303 cal.) MGs |
| SPAD VII | 1 x 7.7-mm (.303 cal.) MG |
| ALBATROS D.V | 2 x 7.92-mm MGs |

**CEILING**

Once again, the dated design of the D.V was reflected by its service-ceiling. Wing problems led to pilots being advised not to over-dive their aircraft. This restriction had obvious effects on morale.

| SE. 5A 6703 m (21,990 ft.) | SPAD VII 6553 m (21,500 ft.) | ALBATROS D.V 6095 m (20,000 ft.) |

---

## Multi-coloured wooden dogfighters

■ **JASTA 4:** In service the yellow tail of this D.V signifies an aircraft of Jasta 4. The plywood fuselage of this aircraft has been varnished to a high degree.

■ **JASTA 5:** With the green fin of Jasta 5, this D.V adorned with a edelweiss symbol was flown by Obltn Paul Baümer (43 kills) and later Lt. Wilhelm Lehmann, Jastafuhrer.

■ **JASTA 5:** This aircraft, with its entire fuselage in green, was seen at Boistrancourt in the summer of 1917. A black chevron was painted on the upper wing.

■ **JASTA 5:** Another Jasta 5 aircraft featuring an elaborate blue and white diamond colour scheme; the upper surfaces of the wings are a more conventional green.

# AMIOT

# 143

● **Twin-engined bomber** ● **1930s design** ● **World War II service**

In 1928 the Armée de l'Air announced its *Multiplaces de Combat* requirement for a new class of day- and night-bomber, reconnaissance and escort aircraft. In a competition to find a suitable design to fill the requirement, Amiot, Blériot, Breguet and SPCA built prototypes, from which Amiot's 140 was chosen. Placed in service as the 143 and 143M from the mid-1930s, the design was obsolete by 1939, but was active in the bombing role as late as 1941.

▲ *An undoubtedly apocryphal story relates that the Amiot 143 was chosen for production by the Armée de l'Air because it was the ugliest of the four competing designs.*

◄ **Amiot 150BE**
*One of the final derivatives of the 143 was the 150BE scout/torpedo-bomber aircraft for the Aéronavale. The sole example crashed in 1939.*

▲ **North African transport**
*After France's defeat and the retirement of Amiot 143s from the bombing role, the aircraft were converted to transports by the Vichy air force and transferred to North Africa.*

◄ **First in service**
*These aircraft were attached to the 1er Groupe, 22e Escadre at Chartres, the first unit to be equipped with 143s.*

▼ **Vichy transport**
*Bearing the distinctive red and yellow striped tail markings of a Vichy aircraft, this 143M was operated in Morocco by GT III/15 in 1942.*

▲ **Early production**
*The first 30 aircraft had a 17.95-m (59-ft.) fuselage which was shorter than that of subsequent aircraft. From the 41st aircraft, Lewis 7.7-mm (.303 cal.) machine-guns were replaced by MAC 1934 7.5-mm (0.3-in) guns.*

## FACTS AND FIGURES

➤ During 1936 one 143M was fitted with Gnome-Rhône 14N radials for high-temperature trials in Indo-China.

➤ An Amiot 142, powered by two liquid-cooled Hispano-Suiza engines, was built.

➤ As well as home-based units, a bomber group in Marrakesh had 143Ms in 1939.

➤ One daylight raid was made by 143s, when 12 aircraft attacked bridges at Sedan on 14 May 1940; most were lost.

➤ During night operations GB I/38 and II/38 lost just four 143s in 197 sorties.

➤ The last Amiot 143s were grounded in North Africa in February 1944.

**PROFILE**

# Armée de l'Air's valiant defender

*Left: Amiot 143-01, the first prototype, flew in August 1934 and was engaged in bombing and firing trials the following year.*

Amiot's less-than-attractive aircraft was a typical example of an interim monoplane bomber design of the 1930s, which was rendered obsolete by the rapid advances in aircraft design brought about by the onset of war.

Initially, an order for 40 Amiot 140s was placed, but the advent of a more powerful, supercharged Gnome-Rhône 14Kdrs/Kgrs engine meant that this was amended to a similar number of the improved 143. From the 41st example

production switched to the 143M, which had further improved 649-kW (870-hp.) 14 Kirs/Kjrs engines, a lengthened fuselage and different machine-guns. The last 25 examples were built to 143 BN4 night-bomber and 143 B5 day-bomber standard. Production of 140/143/143Ms amounted to 178 aircraft, and deliveries to the Armée de l'Air were complete by 1939.

From 3 September 1939 the type was used for night reconnaissance and leaflet-dropping raids over enemy

territory. Apart from the equally antiquated Farman 222, the air force had no other aircraft with sufficient range. Even after the German invasion of France in May 1940, 143s were making bombing sorties over targets such as bridges and railway marshalling yards in Belgium, France and Germany.

From 1941, the Vichy government made use of the type in the transport role and mainly in North Africa, where 143s continued flying until the Axis was defeated in Tunisia in 1943.

*Above: Amiot 143M No. 118 belonged to the 4e Escadrille, 35e Escadre based at Bron. Although outdated, the Amiot 143 had a useful range compared to other French bombers.*

## 143M

On 3 September 1939, 143M No. 78 was serving with GB II of the 35e Escadre de Bombardement, which undertook night reconnaissance operations from Pontarlier. By 10 May 1940, when France was invaded, GB II/35 had re-equipped with Breguet 691s.

While the Amiot 140, 143 and 143M production standard aircraft were powered by versions of the Gnome-Rhône 14K Mistral Major, various versions were proposed with alternative powerplants. Principal among these was the Hispano-Suiza-engined 142, which used the supercharged, liquid-cooled 12-cylinder Hispano-Suiza 12Y.

The 143 had an all-metal fuselage. The thick-section wing comprised five sections built up on three Duralumin tube girder spars with tube girder ribs. Duralumin sheet was rivetted to this to form the skin. The outermost wing sections contained six fuel tanks (from the 41st aircraft) with a total capacity of 2719 litres (718 gal.). In earlier aircraft, fuel tanks were jettisonable.

The rectangular-section fuselage was made up of open-sectioned formers with fore and aft stringers covered with Duralumin sheet.

Originally envisaged with a crew of four, the 143M had a fifth crewmember for the night–bomber role. The navigator/bombardier and radio operator were situated in the ventral gondola.

Bombload capacity was limited to 800 kg (1,760 lb.) internally, in varying combinations from four 200-kg (440-lb.) to 64 12.5-kg (27.5-lb.) bombs. A further 800 kg (1,760 lb.) could be carried on external outer wing racks.

Although lightly armed by the standards of World War II, the 143 had a defensive armament which was arranged to protect the aircraft from attack from every direction. Apart from nose and dorsal turrets and a flexible ventral mounting, 143s often carried a fourth 7.5-mm (0.3-in.) MAC 1934 machine-gun which fired through the floor of the forward fuselage.

### 143M

**Type:** five-seat night-bomber and reconnaissance aircraft

**Powerplant:** two 649-kW (870-hp.) Gnome-Rhône 14Kirs/Kjrs Mistral Major 14-cylinder radials

**Maximum speed:** 310 km/h (192 m.p.h.) at 4000 m (13,000 ft.)

**Climb rate:** 14 min 20 sec to 4000 m (13,000 ft.) at 8610-kg (18,942-lb.) weight

**Normal range:** 1200 km (745 mi.)

**Service ceiling:** 7900 m (26,000 ft.)

**Weights:** empty 6100 kg (13,420 lb.); maximum take-off 9700 kg (21,385 lb.)

**Armament:** four 7.5-mm (0.3-in.) MAC 1934 machine-guns, plus up to 800 kg (1,760 lb.) of bombs on external racks and 800 kg (1,760 lb.) of bombs in an internal bomb-bay

**Dimensions:**
| | |
|---|---|
| span | 24.53 m (80 ft. 5 in.) |
| length | 18.26 m (59 ft. 10 in.) |
| height | 5.68 m (78 ft. 6 in.) |
| wing area | 100 m² (1,076 sq. ft.) |

### ACTION DATA

**MAXIMUM SPEED**

By 1939 the obsolescence of the Amiot 143 had become increasingly apparent. Although its maximum speed was not far short of that of the Dornier Do 17, the 143's cruising performance when carrying a load was considerably less and made it vulnerable to fighter attack.

| | |
|---|---|
| 143M | 310 km/h (192 m.p.h.) |
| H.P.54 HARROW Mk II | 322 km/h (200 m.p.h.) |
| Do 17E-1 | 347 km/h (215 m.p.h.) |

**SERVICE CEILING**

In terms of its range and altitude ability, the 143M was one of the Armée de l'Air's better bomber types. This led to the type's use in raids on the Rhine during 1939.

| 143M | H.P.54 HARROW Mk II | Do 17E-1 |
|---|---|---|
| 7900 m (26,000 ft.) | 6950 m (22,800 ft.) | 5100 m (16,700 ft.) |

**ARMAMENT**

Although the Amiot had a useful bombload – better than that of the contemporary Handley Page Harrow and over twice that of the Do 17 – it was a far more vulnerable aircraft. The Do 17 was able to use its speed to good effect in the early years of the war.

| | |
|---|---|
| 143M | 4 x 7.5-mm (0.3-in.) machine-guns 1600-kg (3,520-lb.) bombload |
| H.P.54 HARROW Mk II | 4 x 7.7-mm (.303 cal.) machine-guns 1361-kg (3,000-lb.) bombload |
| Do 17E-1 | 2 x 7.92-mm (0.31-in.) machine-guns 750-kg (1,650-lb.) bombload |

## Amiot's inter-war designs

**110C.1:** A single-seat design, the 110 was built to a French lightweight fighter requirement. Two were produced; one later became a racer.

**122-BP3:** This large biplane bomber/escort had a crew of three and entered service in 1929. Eighty were built for the Armée de l'Air.

**340:** Based on the long-range postal 341, the 340 was a three-seat bomber flown in 1937. It featured an all-metal fuselage.

**351:** The 350 series bombers were derived from the 340. By June 1940, 86 Amiot 351s and 354s had been completed for the Armée de l'Air.

# ARADO

# AR 68

● Biplane fighter ● Superseded by the Bf 109 ● Combat proven

▲ With its sleek lines and outstanding handling, the Ar 68 should be considered, along with the Polikarpov I-153 and Fiat CR.42, one of the finest biplane fighters.

**W**hen German authorities approved production of the Arado Ar 68 in 1936, they were ordering the Luftwaffe's last biplane fighter. The Ar 68, like so many similar aircraft of its era, was destined to spend only a brief time as a front-line fighter. However, when fitted with early Junkers Jumo engines, the Ar 68 gave excellent performance which was not surpassed until the introduction of the Bf 109 into squadron service.

## ARADO AR 68

▼ Arado's last attempt
Convinced that the biplane fighter was still viable in 1937, Arado built a single Ar 68H, with an enclosed cockpit and a radial engine.

▲ Luftwaffe service
One of the earliest Ar 68Es shows its clean and aerodynamic lines.

▼ Supercharged Jumo
With its Jumo 210Da engine, the Ar 68e marked a departure from the BMW engine of the Ar 68d.

▲ Third prototype
The second of the Jumo-engined prototypes, the Ar 68c featured a cleaner radiator installation than that of the similarly engined Ar 68b.

Inferior fighter ▶
Problems in supplying the Jumo engine led to an initial order for Ar 68F-1s powered by the BMW VId engine of the Ar 68a and d prototypes. Very poor performance meant that only a few Ar 68F-1s were built.

## FACTS AND FIGURES

➤ The Ar 68 followed on from the unsuccessful Arado Ar 67, which had first flown in late 1933.

➤ By the outbreak of World War II only a few Ar 68s were left on the front line.

➤ The Ar 68a prototype made its initial flight early in the summer of 1934.

➤ Arado used the distinctive fin seen on the Ar 68 on all its subsequent single-engined designs.

➤ Arado was producing He 51 fighters while it designed the Ar 68.

➤ Early in 1938 the Ar 68 equipped the majority of German fighter units.

## PROFILE

# Germany's finest biplane fighter

As the Luftwaffe's principal fighter aircraft in the late 1930s, the Arado Ar 68 was flown by a generation of German aviators who later used their skills in war.

The Ar 68, with its metal airframe covered by plywood skinning and fabric, was very much up to early-1930s standards of advanced biplane design. Some pilots were initially concerned about the Ar 68,

however. Attrition rates of the earlier He 51 had been high because of its comparatively high weight and fast landing speeds, characteristics which were even more pronounced in the Arado fighter. To dispel any doubts, Ernst Udet, who was then Inspector of Fighter and Dive-Bomber Pilots, arranged for a mock combat between himself, in a Jumo-engined Ar 68, and one of the Luftwaffe's top fighter

*Above: Arado initially fitted the Ar 68a with the BMW VI engine, even though it was limited in performance.*

*Left: This Ar 68F-1 shows the troughs for the twin MG 17 machine-gun installation in the top of the engine cowling. The upper wing ailerons were almost full span.*

pilots in an He 51. Udet's decisive victory proved the exceptional manoeuvrability and ruggedness of the Ar 68, which immediately entered squadron service.

A few Ar 68s were in service as night-fighters during the winter of 1939/40, but most saw wartime service as trainers.

### AR 68E-1

This aircraft was the personal mount of Leutnant Riegel, the Gruppe adjutant of III/JG 141. The unit was based at Fürstenwalde during 1938. Most Ar 68s were operated by fighter pilot training schools by the time war broke out.

This highly distinctive tailfin design became something of an Arado trademark. It was also used on types such as the Ar 95, Ar 96 and Ar 196. Unusually placed vee-struts connected the tailplane to the vertical fin. Like the fuselage, the tail surfaces had a steel framework and metal skinning.

A small windscreen protected the pilot from the worst of the slipstream. Pilots of early aircraft complained that exhaust fumes entered the cockpit.

A rectangular welded steel-tube framework made up the basic structure of the aircraft. A great deal of the fuselage and wings was plywood covered with some fabric.

Powered by the excellent Junkers Jumo 210 powerplant, the Ar 68E-1 had an exceptionally neat engine installation. Twin machine-guns were mounted in the upper fuselage.

Unusually for an aircraft with a spatted undercarriage, the Ar 68E-1 appears to have retained its spats while in service. The cantilever main undercarriage legs were also aerodynamically faired.

The upper wing had large ailerons and the lower wing had flaps fitted. A single set of interplane struts braced the wings on each side. They were of N-type and canted outwards.

Even the tailwheel was faired by a spat. The unit was free swivelling, giving improved ground handling. The landing speed of the Ar 68 was comparatively high.

### Ar 68E-1

**Type:** single-seat biplane fighter

**Powerplant:** one 515-kW (690-hp.) Junkers Jumo 210Da 12-cylinder inverted-vee liquid-cooled piston engine

**Maximum speed:** 305 km/h (189 m.p.h.) at sea level

**Cruising speed:** 281 km/h (174 m.p.h.) at sea level

**Range:** 415 km (260 mi.)

**Service ceiling:** 8100 m (26,500 ft.)

**Weights:** empty 1840 kg (4,048 lb.); maximum take-off 2475 kg (5,445 lb.)

**Armament:** two fixed forward-firing 7.92-mm MG 17 machine-guns with 500 rounds per gun and six 10-kg (22-lb.) SC 10 fragmentation bombs in an optional underfuselage magazine

**Dimensions:**
| | | |
|---|---|---|
| span | 11.00 m | (36 ft. 1 in.) |
| length | 9.50 m | (31 ft. 2 in.) |
| height | 3.28 m | (10 ft. 9 in.) |
| wing area | 27.30 m² | (294 sq. ft.) |

### COMBAT DATA

**POWER**

In the UK the Gloster Gladiator represented the last service biplane fighter. It had the most powerful engine of these three aircraft, but was only a development of the Gauntlet and represented no real advance in fighter design.

Ar 68E-1    515 kW (690 hp.)
GLADIATOR Mk II   619 kW (830 hp.)
I-15BIS CHAIKA   578 kW (775 hp.)

**RANGE**

Again the Gladiator Mk II was the superior aircraft. If a fighter is to be useful on patrol missions during which it is expected to spend some time on station, then range is important. The I-15bis had only marginally shorter range and was probably a better fighter.

Ar 68E-1 415 km (260 mi.)
I-15BIS CHAIKA 550 km (330 mi.)
GLADIATOR Mk II 708 km (440 mi.)

**ARMAMENT**

In service the Ar 68E-1 rarely carried fragmentation bombs because of the excessive drag associated with the magazine installation. In air-to-air combat the I-15bis has the edge with its four-gun armament and good performance.

Ar 68E-1
2 x 7.92-vmm machine-guns
60-kg (132-lb.) bombload

GLADIATOR Mk II
4 x 7.7-mm (.303 cal.) machine-guns

I-15BIS CHAIKA
4 x 7.62-mm (.30 cal.) machine-guns
150-kg (330-lb.) bombload

## Wartime Arados

**Ar 95:** Having first flown in 1937, the Ar 95 was combat tested in the Spanish Civil War and served the Luftwaffe early in World War II.

**Ar 96:** Although designed by Arado, the majority of these advanced trainers were built by other companies; 11,546 were completed.

**Ar 196:** Respected for its excellent sea performance, good flying qualities and heavy armament, the Ar 196 was a classic floatplane.

**Ar 234:** Arado pioneered the twin-jet bomber with the Ar 234. Many of them were used on daylight raids and reconnaissance over the UK.

# ARADO

# AR 95

● Limited service ● Small numbers built ● Biplane floatplane

**D**esigned to fly from Germany's aborted aircraft-carrier, the Ar 95 was a torpedo-bomber with floats or wheeled landing gear. It flew for the first time in 1936 and served briefly in the Spanish Civil War, but the aircraft-carrier was never completed and only a small number of Ar 95s were built. A handful went to Chile and a batch was supplied to the Luftwaffe, while three Ar 95s served with the Spanish air force until 1948.

▲ The Ar 95 served reliably in combat over Spain and in northern Europe. The Luftwaffe only operated the type until 1941, when the BV 138 was introduced.

## ARADO AR 95

◀ **Production prototype**
*Both the Ar 95 V3 and V5 were finished as three-seat floatplanes and were regarded as prototypes of the production Ar 95A.*

▼ **Distinctly Arado**
*Arado retained several features of the Ar 95 in later designs, including the Ar 196.*

▼ **Torpedo bomber**
*In its original form the Ar 95 was to be a carrier-based torpedo aircraft. A 700-kg (1,760-lb.) weapon could be carried between the float struts.*

▼ **Trousered undercarriage**
*Serving as the Ar 95B prototype, the Ar 95 V4 featured large trouser-type fairings on its main undercarriage. Three aircraft of this type were ordered by the Chilean government.*

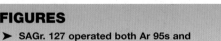

◀ **Grupo 64**
*Based at Pollensa, Majorca, the six Ar 95A-0s were flown by Grupo 64 of the Condor Legion.*

### FACTS AND FIGURES

➤ Early trials showed that the Ar 95A fell short of the required performance, and the Ar 95B was obsolescent by 1937.

➤ Grupo 64 disbanded in 1939 and passed its Ar 95s to the Spanish Nationalists.

➤ Luftwaffe unit 3./SAGr. 125 gave up its Ar 95s at Constanza, Romania, in 1941.

➤ SAGr. 127 operated both Ar 95s and He 60s; it retained the Arado floatplanes until 1944.

➤ Turkey ordered Ar 95s, but its aircraft were diverted to the Luftwaffe.

➤ Arado built the unsuccessful Ar 195 as a potential replacement for the Ar 95B.

# Fighting floatplane from Arado

*It was clear that the Ar 95B would be obsolescent by the time Germany's aircraft carrier was completed.*

There were both two- and three-seat prototypes of the Ar 95, and one was temporarily fitted with a liquid-cooled Junkers Jumo engine. Production aircraft had three seats under a single, long canopy and used the more powerful BMW 132 radial.

All six pre-production Ar 95A-0s went to Majorca in 1938 as part of a Condor Legion reconnaissance unit supporting the Nationalist forces in the Spanish Civil War. They saw only limited service during the conflict, but three of the aircraft were transferred to the Nationalists in 1939 and served until 1948.

Only 14 production aircraft were built – 11 Ar 95A floatplanes and three Ar 95B landplanes. Three of each were delivered to Chile in 1939 and remained in service until after World War II.

One squadron of the Luftwaffe's 125 maritime reconnaissance wing (3./SAGr. 125) was equipped with eight Ar 95A-1s. This unit was stationed in the Baltic in June 1942, when Germany invaded the Soviet Union. Ar 95s were involved in the occupation of islands off the coast of Estonia in October 1941, before ending their service career in the Gulf of Finland.

## AR 95A-1

Luftwaffe Ar 95A-1s served with only two units, the second unit receiving aircraft retired by the first. The aircraft were initially delivered to 3./SAGr. 125, one of whose machines is seen here in the summer of 1941.

Two 7.9-mm machine-guns were fitted as standard. The forward-firing MG 17 was supplied with 500 rounds, while the flexibly-mounted MG 15 in the rear cockpit had 600 rounds stored in eight 75-round ammunition drums.

A reliable and well-tested BMW 132 engine was fitted to the Ar 95. Take-off power was 656 kW (880 hp.), falling to 634 kW (850 hp.) at 2500 metres (8,000 ft.). The performance of the Ar 95 fell short of official expectations.

This four-bomb rack was commonly fitted to the Ar 95. Alternative loads included a 700-kg (1,540-lb.) torpedo or a 375-kg (825-lb.) bomb beneath the fuselage, with six 50-kg (110-lb.) bombs beneath the wings.

The Ar 95 had an all-metal fuselage of semi-monocoque construction and aft folding metal framed wings. The wing upper surfaces were metal-covered, with fabric lower surfaces.

The floats were of light metal, giving buoyancy and stability on the water. A small rudder was attached to the rear of each, providing directional control during taxiing.

### COMBAT DATA

**ARMAMENT**

At the beginning of World War II, the Fairey Seafox was already obsolescent since it was an old design. The Ar 95 was also dated, although it was more heavily armed. Arado produced its best seaplane in the Ar 196, sacrificing bombload for heavy gun armament.

| | |
|---|---|
| Ar 95A-1 | 2 x 7.92-mm machine-guns 800-kg (1,760-lb.) bombload |
| Ar 196A-3 | 2 x 20-mm cannon 2 x 7.92-mm machine-guns 100-kg (220-lb.) bombload |
| SEAFOX | 1 x 7.7-mm (.303 cal.) machine-gun |

**RANGE**

The Ar 95 had long range, which was particularly important in the torpedo-bombing and reconnaissance roles. It also allowed long coastal patrols and even search and rescue missions to be undertaken. The Ar 196 had shorter range but excellent handling.

SEAFOX 700 km (435 mi.)
Ar 95A-1 1100 km (680 mi.)
Ar 196A-3 800 km (500 mi.)

**CRUISING SPEED**

Although the Ar 196 used a more powerful BMW 132 engine than the Ar 95, it was only marginally faster. The Seafox was a considerably less powerful aircraft but gave useful service, including confirming the fate of the *Graf Spee*.

| | |
|---|---|
| Ar 95A-1 | 255 km/h (158 m.p.h.) |
| Ar 196A-3 | 267 km/h (166 m.p.h.) |
| SEAFOX | 171 km/h (106 m.p.h.) |

## Biplane floatplanes in World War II

■ **DE HAVILLAND DH.82 TIGER MOTH:** Many examples of this ubiquitous trainer were mounted on floats.

■ **FAIREY SWORDFISH:** Usually launched from a ship's catapult, Swordfish floatplanes saw widespread Fleet Air Arm service.

■ **HEINKEL He 59:** Used extensively on search and rescue missions during the Battle of Britain, the He 59 was retired in 1943.

■ **IMAM Ro 44:** Thirty Ro 44s were in service with the Italian navy at the outbreak of World War II. A few survived the Armistice.

# ARADO
# AR 196

● **Catapult-launched reconnaissance floatplane** ● **Eyes of the fleet**

▲ *Most Ar 196 floatplanes served from land bases in occupied Norway, France and Denmark, but the aircraft is best remembered as the catapult-launched light spotter of the German navy.*

**A** highly successful design, the little Arado 196 was the eyes of the Kriegsmarine. Not only did it perform the hazardous role of spotting for the guns of the fleet, it performed daring air–sea rescues in the English Channel and lonely coastal patrols over Biscay. The Ar 196 served on Germany's capital ships and cruisers and in all European maritime theatres of war. It was one of the finest floatplane designs of its time.

## ARADO AR 196

**Trials on the water ▶**
*The prototypes of the Ar 196 were recognisable by the twin-bladed propeller. This was replaced by a variable-pitch three-bladed type, and the airframe was slightly modified in production aircraft.*

**Lone patrol ▶**
*Although designed to spot for the fleet's guns, the Ar 196 was used for many tasks, such as dropping agents and attacking Allied maritime patrol planes.*

**▲ Seal hunter**
*One of the Ar 196's great moments was the capture of HMS Seal in 1940. The British submarine had been damaged by a mine during a patrol off the coast of Norway. Two Ar 196s, operating from Aalborg in Denmark, attacked the crippled submarine and managed to inflict enough damage to prevent it submerging. It was then captured by the Kriegsmarine.*

**▲ Plane sailing**
*Most Ar 196s had twin floats, as trials of a single-float version with small outrigger floats had proved it to be tricky to operate on water.*

**◀ On the slipway**
*This Ar 196 served with 2./SAGr 125, and was moored in Suda Bay, Crete. The unit carried out anti-submarine patrols against the Royal Navy.*

## FACTS AND FIGURES

➤ The Arado beat a rival Focke-Wulf design in the competition to replace the Heinkel He 50 as the fleet floatplane.

➤ Ar 196s also served in coastal units with Bulgaria, Finland and Romania.

➤ Twin floats were chosen because pilots liked the stability given during taxiing.

➤ The Ar 196 was almost used in a floatplane record-breaking attempt, but the Reich Air Ministry banned it.

➤ *Bismarck* launched its Ar 196 to drive off a shadowing RAF Catalina in 1941.

➤ Ar 196 operations ranged from the Arctic Circle to the Black Sea.

# PROFILE

# Eyes of the German fleet

Arado began designing the Ar 196 in 1936, to replace the obsolete Heinkel He 50 reconnaissance floatplanes then in service with the fleet. Unlike the floatplanes of most navies, the Ar 196 was a thoroughly modern design, with metal frame construction for most of the aircraft. It also packed a very powerful punch; two Ar 196s even managed to

capture a Royal Navy submarine in 1940 after blasting it with their cannon and machine-guns.

The Ar 196 completed trials just as the war was beginning. The first warship to take the aircraft to sea was the *Admiral Graf Spee*, and all the other Kriegsmarine capital ships and heavy cruisers subsequently received them, including the

*The Arado was the last fighting floatplane to be built in Europe. This example was captured by the Royal Navy and was evaluated by the Marine Aircraft Experimental Establishment.*

*Bismarck.* The Ar 196 was produced in several variants, and was built by Fokker and SNCA for Germany.

The wing was of very modern construction for a floatplane, being all-metal except for the fabric-covered control surfaces.

Bomb racks were installed under the wings.

## Ar 196A-3

**Type:** two-seat shipboard and coastal patrol aircraft

**Powerplant:** one 716-kW (960-hp.) BMW 123K nine-cylinder radial

**Maximum speed:** 310 km/h (193 m.p.h.) at 4000 m (13,120 ft.)

**Combat radius:** 1070 km (665 mi.)

**Service ceiling:** 7000 m (23,000 ft.)

**Weights:** empty 2990 kg (6,592 lb.); loaded 3730 kg (8,223 lb.)

**Armament:** two 20-mm (0.79-in.) cannon in the wings; one or two 7.92-mm (0.31-in) guns in the rear cockpit and front fuselage; two 50-kg (110-lb.) bombs

**Dimensions:**
| | |
|---|---|
| span | 12.40 m (40 ft. 8 in.) |
| length | 11.00 m (36 ft. 1 in.) |
| height | 4.45 m (14 ft. 7 in.) |
| wing area | 28.40 m² (306 sq. ft.) |

## AR 196A-5

This aircraft served with 2./Seeaufklärungsgruppe 125 which operated from shore bases in the eastern Mediterranean and the Aegean Seas during 1943.

Power was provided by a 716-kW (960-hp.) BMW radial engine. The mounts were one of the aircraft's weak spots – engines were known to break off when moving across choppy water.

The cannon armament was unusually powerful for a floatplane, enabling it to take on RAF Whitley bombers over the Bay of Biscay or shoot up enemy ships.

Final production versions carried two MG 81 machine-guns in the rear cockpit, but most versions carried a single 7.92-mm (0.31-in.) MG 15.

The Arado had a roomy, modern, enclosed cockpit, in contrast with its British opponents, which were generally open to the elements and far more uncomfortable for their crews.

The Ar 196 had a conventional steel tube frame with a forward metal skin covering and a fabric covering for the rear fuselage. The airframe was a sound design, and was barely changed after completing prototype trials.

To ease handling on the water the floats were equipped with rudders. They also contained fuel tanks, and could store emergency survival kit.

### COMBAT DATA

#### MAXIMUM SPEED

Floatplanes are not very fast, since their huge floats create immense amounts of drag in flight. However, the Arado's clean, modern design meant that it was one of the fastest of its type, with considerably more performance than its British and American equivalents.

| | |
|---|---|
| Ar 196 | 310 km/h (193 m.p.h.) |
| OS2U KINGFISHER | 265 km/h (165 m.p.h.) |
| SEAFOX | 200 km/h (125 m.p.h.) |

#### RANGE

Scout planes were designed to extend the horizon of the mother ship out to 100 or 200 km (62 to 125 mi.). The ability to loiter for long periods was more important than out-and-out range, and the Ar 196 could remain on station for more than four hours.

OS2U KINGFISHER 1300 km (808 mi.)
Ar 196 1070 km (665 mi.)
SEAFOX 700 km (435 mi.)

#### SERVICE CEILING

The Arado could climb much higher than either the American Kingfisher or the British Seafox. This was of inestimable advantage when searching for ship-sized targets, as the crew of the German machine could keep watch over a greater area of sea than observers in either of their opponents.

OS2U KINGFISHER 4000 m (13,120 ft.)
SEAFOX 3000 m (9,840 ft.)
Ar 196 7000 m (22,965 ft.)

## Prowling the oceans

**SCOUTING FOR THE FLEET:** The Arado Ar 196 was designed to scout for raiders like the battlecruiser *Gneisenau*. In effect, it gave the warship's lookouts the ability to search for targets at distances of several hundred kilometres.

**COMMERCE RAIDING:** The Kriegsmarine's main task was to interrupt Britain's seaborne trade. Battleships, cruisers and disguised commerce raiders used their Arados to locate Allied convoys or individual merchant ships, checking to see if they were escorted. The location of a target would be transmitted to the mother ship, which would then steam to intercept, sinking the hapless merchantman by gunfire.

# ARADO

# AR 232

● Heavy transport ● Two sets of undercarriage ● Unique design

▲ Even though the Ar 232 had two sets of undercarriage and rough-field capability, landing supplies at the front line was always dangerous. This one has crashed on a supply flight late in the war.

**B**y the autumn of 1938, it was clear that the Luftwaffe needed a new medium transport aircraft to replace its ageing Ju 52/3ms. Both Arado and Henschel received specifications for an aircraft capable of raising and lowering itself to truck-bed height for loading. Henschel's twin-boom machine proved unsuccessful, allowing Arado to go ahead with production of one of the most distinctive transport aircraft of World War II.

## ARADO AR 232

**▼ Rough landing**
The 11 pairs of wheels were designed to cope with ditches up to 1.5 m (5 ft.) wide.

**▲ Engine shortage**
Flown for the first time in the summer of 1941, the Ar 232 V1 was powered by two BMW 801 engines, the same powerplant as in the Fw 190. The priority given to fighters saw them replaced with four less-powerful BMW 323 nine-cylinder radials.

**Last plane out ▶**
The Ar 232's finest hour was in the winter of 1942/43, when it flew supply missions to support the beleaguered Sixth Army in Stalingrad. This aircraft gained the distinction of being the last transport to fly out of the city before the garrison surrendered to Soviet forces.

**◀ Sole survivor**
Having survived the war, this Ar 232 was brought from Flensburg to the Royal Aircraft Establishment at Farnborough and test flown. Pilots found the handling qualities were good.

**Post-war service ▶**
Because of the carrying capacity of the four-engined variant, immediately after the war the sole surviving Ar 232 was pressed into service repatriating prisoners of war from both sides.

### FACTS AND FIGURES

➤ Ar 232B-08 (V11) operated in Norway with its under-fuselage wheels replaced by an 8-metre long ski.

➤ During the early summer of 1941, the Ar 232 V1 flew for the first time.

➤ Performance of the twin- and four-engined aircraft was very similar.

➤ Arado used an Ar 232 during the Ar 234 test programme and passed the aircraft on to the RAF at the end of World War II.

➤ During 1942, both the V1 and V2 aircraft saw extensive service over the USSR.

➤ All but one of the Luftwaffe's Ar 232s were destroyed by enemy action.

## PROFILE

# The military 'Millipede'

*Left: One of eight Ar 232B-0 pre-series transports which equipped the 'Arado Staffel' transport wing.*

No more than 30 Ar 232s seem to have been completed and the type saw only limited service.

Both the Ar 232 V1 and V2 prototypes were fitted with two BMW 801 radial engines as demanded by the original specification. It was immediately apparent, however, that Fw 190 production would place huge, more urgent demands on the limited supply of this powerplant. Hence, Arado was instructed to complete the V3 and subsequent aircraft with four lower-powered BMW-Bramo 323R engines.

A unique feature of the Ar 232 was its multi-wheel undercarriage arrangement. Normal operations were carried out with the tricycle main gears, but for loading and taxiing over rough ground, these units were partially retracted, allowing the aircraft to be loaded directly from a truck-bed and manoeuvred on its 11 pairs of under-fuselage wheels.

Eight pre-series Ar 232B-0 aircraft were completed, the first of them also being known as the Ar 232 V4. Four B-0s joined the surviving Ar 232As in special missions over the Soviet Union, flying from bases in Finland and Norway during 1944. One aircraft crashed near Moscow while on a covert mission.

Ironically, the Allies made extensive use of the one surviving Ar 232 in transporting personnel and captured aircraft to the UK, immediately after the cessation of hostilities.

*Above: The twin-engined Ar 232 V2 is seen in flight. This aircraft served until late 1944, before being lost in action.*

### Ar 232B-0

**Type:** heavy transport aircraft

**Powerplant:** four 895-kW (1,200-hp.) BMW-Bramo 323R-2 radial piston engines.

**Maximum speed:** 340 km/h (211 m.p.h.) at 4600 m (15,100 ft.)

**Range:** 1060 km (660 mi.)

**Service ceiling:** 8000 m (26,250 ft.)

**Weights:** empty 12,802 kg (28,164 lb.); loaded 21,135 kg (46,595 lb.)

**Armament:** one 13-mm (0.51-in.) MG 131 machine-gun in the nose; one or two similar weapons at the rear of the fuselage; one 20-mm (0.79-in.) cannon in a power-operated dorsal turret

**Dimensions:** span 33.50 m (109 ft. 11 in.)
length 23.52 m (77 ft. 2 in.)
height 5.69 m (18 ft. 8 in.)
wing area 142.60 m² (1,535 sq. ft.)

Extensive glazing in the nose offered the pilots excellent visibility on approach to landing zones. This was a major advance over previous designs, although the aircraft was vulnerable to attack. A single forward-firing 13-mm (0.51-in.) machine-gun was located in the extreme nose, with 500 rounds, and above the cockpit a power-operated turret housed one 20-mm (0.79-in.) cannon.

The Ar 230 was designed for twin-engined layout, but demand for the Fw 190 fighter meant that there were insufficient powerplants to allocate. Four lower-powered BMW-Bramo 323R-2 Fafnir engines were fitted instead. Moving from a two- to a four-engined layout required a larger wing span, although handling characteristics were found to be unaffected by the change.

The semi-monocoque fuselage pod was attached to a shoulder-mounted wing and the tail surfaces were carried on a single circular-section boom which projected from the upper fuselage. This design proved highly successful and allowed unrestricted loading around the rear of the airframe. The rear loading ramp could not be opened in flight to drop supplies.

Although few Arado 232s reached operational service, their contribution to airlift operations was significant. Their missions ranged from evacuation of wounded to transporting special operations troops across Russia.

The main undercarriage was of the tricycle type and was used during normal ground operations and take-offs and landings. During loading and unloading the gear retracted upwards, thereby lowering the fuselage.

The 11 pairs of idler wheels were fitted with low-pressure tyres and mounted on independently-sprung suspension legs. They could cope with soft, rough terrain and ditches up to 1.5 m (5 ft.) across.

A rear loading ramp offered sufficient clearance to permit direct loading onto trucks, thereby reducing the loading and unloading times. Defence at the rear was provided by a single machine-gun.

### AR 232A-0

The Luftwaffe required a large transport aircraft almost as soon as World War II started. Although it was a successful design, events prevented the Ar 232 from achieving its full operational potential.

## COMBAT DATA

### MAXIMUM SPEED

Because of their slow speed, the Me 323 and Ar 232 often required an escort of fighters to support any supply mission. Although faster, the C-47 carried far less cargo so more aircraft were needed to deliver the equivalent payload.

| | |
|---|---|
| Ar 232B-0 | 340 km/h (211 m.p.h.) |
| Me 323E-2 | 253 km/h (157 m.p.h.) |
| C-47A | 365 km/h (226 m.p.h.) |

### RANGE

Based on a pre-war airliner, the C-47 featured exceptional range. Because of its wartime design – and complications that arose during its manufacture – the Ar 232 had poor range when compared to other Allied and German transports.

Ar 232B-0 1060 km (660 mi.)
C-47A 2575 km (1,600 mi.)
Me 323E-2 4500 km (682 mi.)

### PAYLOAD

The Luftwaffe's transport fleet at the start of the war was regarded as the largest in the world. Later designs of transport were capable of carrying small tanks and troops; the Arado proved to be more suitable than the C-47 for moving outsized loads.

| Ar 232B-0 | Me 323E-2 | C-47A |
|---|---|---|
| 21,135 kg (18,000 lb.) | 45,000 kg (35,000 lb.) | 11,794 kg (8,000 lb.) |

## German World War II transports

**Fw 200 CONDOR:** Developed from the maritime patrol aircraft, the Condor transport had turrets and bomb equipment removed.

**Ju 52:** Designed as a pre-war airliner, the Ju 52 was the main transport aircraft for the Luftwaffe and served on every major front.

**Ju 290:** A late-war design which was pressed into service as a transport despite being designed as an patrol bomber.

**Me 323:** Basically a powered version of the 321 glider, the Gigant was capable of carrying small tanks but proved extremely vulnerable.

# ARADO

# AR 234

● First jet bomber ● Fast reconnaissance aircraft ● Brief success

▲ The first operations by
Ar 234s were reconnaissance sorties by two
aircraft based in France in 1944. These were
judged a success and bombing missions
followed in the Ardennes later in the year.

**T**he Arado Ar 234 'Blitz' (Lightning)
was the world's first jet bomber,
although initially it was conceived
as a fast reconnaissance aircraft. When it
appeared in 1943 this advanced aircraft
was unique in the aviation world. However,
while it possessed speed and versatility,
it was far from viceless and, although
early operations showed promise, this
potentially devastating new weapon was
'too little, too late' for the Third Reich.

## ARADO AR 234

### ▼ Rocket assistance
Two Walter rocket-assisted take-off (RATO) units
were fitted to improve performance. These were
used on the first reconnaissance missions in 1944.

### ▲ Parachute malfunction
The RATO units were jettisoned
after take-off, although their
landing parachutes had a
tendency to malfunction.

### Trolley undercarriage ▶
The trolley undercarriage
generally worked well, only rarely
refusing to detach on take-off.
A major disadvantage, however,
was the aircraft's vulnerability
after a skid landing.

### ▼ Night-fighter version
Some of the least-known sorties
were the night-fighter missions
flown experimentally by
Kommando Bonow with two
Ar 234s from March 1945.

### ▲ Four-engined 'Blitz'
The 13th prototype, with four BMW 003A-1 engines,
was the basis for the stillborn Ar 234C version.

## FACTS AND FIGURES

➤ Development of the Jumo engines was
slow, so the prototype 'Blitz' did not fly
until 15 June 1943.

➤ The 'Blitz', with conventional landing gear,
made its maiden flight on 10 March 1944.

➤ At least a third of the 210 Ar 234Bs built
failed to reach operational units.

➤ Ar 234s were operational for six months
before one was shot down by an RAF
Tempest pilot.

➤ Twin- and four-engined versions were built
using Junkers and BMW engines.

➤ Ar 234s were the first combat aircraft to
use rocket-assisted take-off, or RATO.

# PROFILE

# The world's first jet bomber

On the cutting edge of aircraft design when it appeared in 1943, the Ar 234 'Blitz' was intended to fulfil a Luftwaffe requirement for a high-speed reconnaissance aircraft. Delivered during the winter of 1941/42, the prototype's first flight was delayed by the slow arrival of its Junkers turbojets.

The first reconnaissance sorties were flown in late-1944, many taking the 'Blitz' over the United Kingdom. Its speed made the evasion of enemy fighters straightforward.

Production examples were designated Ar 234B. Bombing duties began on Christmas Eve 1944 when a successful raid took place on Allied supplies in the Belgian town of Liege. Perhaps the type's most vital missions were against the Allied assault on the Ardennes, especially during the battle for Remagen in 1945.

However, 'Blitz' operations had ceased by March, the Ar 234 having arrived too late and in too small numbers to have the impact which the Luftwaffe had desired.

*A number of Ar 234s were captured by the Allies in the closing stages of the war in Europe.*

For level bombing the pilot used an autopilot system. This allowed him to disconnect the control stick and use a bombsight between his feet. Though very advanced, this was a risky manoeuvre if there were enemy fighters in the area.

Although it had the straight-line speed to outrun the Allies' piston-engined fighters, the Ar 234 was unmanoeuvrable at low speeds.

Plans and actual prototypes for several experimental Ar 234s existed at the end of World War II. One involved fitting a swept 'crescent' wing to a 'Blitz' to improve performance. This design was adopted by the British company Handley Page and fitted to the Victor bomber in the 1950s.

## Ar 234B-2

**Type:** single-seat twin-turbojet tactical reconnaissance bomber

**Powerplant:** two 8.8-kN (1,975-lb.-thrust) Junkers Jumo 004B-1 Orkan turbojet engines

**Maximum speed:** 742 km/h (460 m.p.h.) at 6000 m (20,000 ft.)

**Range:** 1630 km (1,010 mi.)

**Service ceiling:** 10,000 m (33,000 ft.)

**Weights:** empty 5200 kg (11,440 lb.); maximum take-off 9800 kg (21,560 lb.)

**Armament:** up to 1995 kg (4,400 lb.) of bombs

**Dimensions:**
| | | |
|---|---|---|
| span | 14.44 m | (46 ft.) |
| length | 12.64 m | (41 ft.) |
| height | 4.29 m | (14 ft.) |
| wing area | 27.3 m² | (294 sq. ft.) |

## AR 234B-2

**Delivered to KG76 in 1944, this Ar 234 undertook bombing missions in the Ardennes over the winter. It was captured by the Allies at Achmer in May 1945.**

For shallow diving attacks a periscope sight was fitted above the pilot's seat.

Although the prototype first flew with BMW engines, these proved less reliable than the Junkers Jumos fitted to production aircraft. These early turbojets had a life of just 25 hours. A lack of fuel hampered operations in the closing stages of the war.

The Ar 234 was reportedly pleasant to fly, though its directional stability was poor. Fully laden and without RATO gear, it required up to 380 m (1,250 ft.) to become airborne.

A primitive but effective ejection seat was fitted in the cockpit.

This 'Blitz' carries an SC1000 'Hermann' 907-kg (2,000-lb.) bomb under the fuselage.

Prototype Ar 234s used a trolley undercarriage because of a lack of room in the fuselage – fuel tanks were more important. Later variants were redesigned to include landing gear.

Two fixed aft-firing Mauser MG151/20 20-mm (0.79-in) cannon were fitted to some aircraft. These were aimed with the dive-bombing periscope which could be turned aft.

## COMBAT DATA

### MAXIMUM SPEED

At Hitler's insistence a bomber version of the new Messerschmitt jet fighter was built to assist the attempts to stop the Allied advance through Europe. As a fighter design it was faster than the Arado. The piston-engined Mosquito was the Allies' fastest bomber.

| | |
|---|---|
| Ar 234B-2 | 742 km/h (460 m.p.h.) |
| Me 262A-2a | 870 km/h (540 m.p.h.) |
| MOSQUITO B.Mk IV | 612 km/h (380 m.p.h.) |

### RANGE

The Mosquito was conceived as a long-range reconnaissance aircraft and its size gave it good range performance. Similarly, the 'Blitz' was a reconnaissance aircraft modified for the bombing role. The smallest of the three was the Me 262. While its range compared well with other fighters like the P-51 Mustang, as a bomber it was lacking. The early jet engines used by the Ar 234 and the Me 262 had very high fuel consumption and were unreliable.

| Ar 234B-2 | Me 262A-2A | MOSQUITO B.Mk IV |
|---|---|---|
| 1630 km (1,010 mi.) | 845 km (524 mi.) | 1963 km (1,217 mi.) |

### BOMBLOAD

As a light bomber the Ar 234 could deliver around two tons of bombs. Later versions of the Mosquito could match this load in an enlarged bomb-bay, at the expense of top speed. Had the war continued, plans for larger versions of the 'Blitz' would undoubtedly have been manufactured.

| Ar 234B-2 | Me 262A-2A | MOSQUITO B.Mk IV |
|---|---|---|
| 2000 kg (4,400 lb.) | 500 k (1,100 lb.) | 907 kg (2,000 lb.) |

## Arado 'Blitz' take-off

**TROLLEY UNDERCARRIAGE:** Early Ar 234 prototypes were not fitted with conventional undercarriages and used a three-wheeled trolley. On the first flights this was jettisoned once the aircraft was 60 m (200 ft.) off the ground.

**PARACHUTE BRAKE:** Unfortunately, parachute problems resulted in a number of trolleys being destroyed. Instead it was decided to jettison the trolley on take-off, but still using a parachute to bring it to a stop.

**LANDING SKID:** On landing, retractable skids were deployed. One was fitted under the fuselage, the others being outriggers; one each under the engine nacelles. These prevented the wings from touching the ground on landing.

# ARADO

# AR 240

● Multi-role ● Remotely controlled armament ● Advanced design

▲ As the subject of a comprehensive redesign, the Ar 240 suffered from so many problems that the entire project was scrapped. The design was highly advanced, however.

**R**enowned for its advanced and unusual aircraft designs, Arado was quick to draw up a proposal to satisfy a new Reichsluftfahrtministerium (RLM) development order. This called for a multi-role machine, armed with a new weapons system consisting of machine-guns firing from remotely-controlled barbettes. The resulting Ar 240 was plagued by problems, however, and was eventually cancelled.

## ARADO **AR 240**

▲ **Pre-production aircraft**
Ar 240A-01 (V5) is the central aircraft of this group of three pre-production machines.

▲ **Operational reconnaissance**
Both the Ar 240A-01 (illustrated) and the A-02 were issued to JG 5 in Finland. Three more pre-production aircraft were built, all of which flew operationally.

▲ **New aerodynamics**
Even at the pre-production stage fundamental problems were being tackled. Both the V5 and V6 aircraft featured an entirely new wing of revised section but similar planform.

▲ **Third prototype**
V3 was an attempt to solve the problems of the initial prototypes and was radically altered.

**Finnish combat trials** ▶
Finland's harsh climate served to accentuate the shortcomings of the basic Ar 240 design.

## FACTS AND FIGURES

➤ After cancellation of the Ar 240, Arado nonetheless continued development with the Ar 240 V7 to V12.

➤ Reconnaissance, dive-bomber and anti-bomber versions were planned.

➤ All Ar 240s flew badly and suffered innumerable minor problems.

➤ AGO Flugzeugwerke was to have been responsible for building a series of pre-production Ar 240A-0 machines.

➤ Ar 240A-02 and -01 flew reconnaissance missions over the Murmansk railway.

➤ The Ar 240Cs were intended to be high-speed bombers and night-fighters.

# Germany's misguided Kampfzerstörer

Early in 1938, Arado began work on its E 240 project. A highly advanced machine, the E 240 not only used a new weapons system, but also utilised the latest aerodynamic devices, cockpit pressurisation and a unique tail-mounted airbrake which acted a little like an umbrella.

Flown initially as the Ar 240 V1 and V2, the aircraft proved impossibly unstable and emerged after a major redesign in V3 form.

Although not entirely devoid of the evil handling

characteristics of the earlier machines, the V3 was used on operational trials in a reconnaissance role. Several missions were flown at high speeds and altitudes over Britain. The Ar 240 V4 followed, equipped for dive-bombing and with the dive brake which had been deleted from the V3 reinstated. Successful trials of the V4 were completed, but it was felt that the reconnaissance aircraft was most important. The V5 and V6 prototypes were completed as Ar 240A-01 and -02 pre-production aircraft.

*Below: Among the changes intended to make the Ar 240 V3 a workable aircraft was the deletion of the dive brake and repositioning of the pressure cabin to the extreme nose.*

*Above: Complex aerodynamics and unreliable, fragile systems served to make the Ar 240 a failure.*

Again, service trials were performed, but the programme was halted in December 1942. Arado doggedly continued development, however, testing the Ar 240C-01 as late as 1943.

## Ar 240A-01

**Type:** high-speed reconnaissance aircraft

**Powerplant:** two 877-kW (1,176-hp.) Daimler-Benz DB 601E 12-cylinder inverted, in-line piston engine

**Maximum speed:** 620 km/h (384 m.p.h.) at 6000 m (20,000 ft.)

**Climb rate:** 11 min to 6000 m (20,000 ft.)

**Range:** 2000 km (1,240 mi.) maximum, with 600-litre (159-gal.) auxiliary fuel tank

**Service ceiling:** 10,500 m (34,400 ft.)

**Weights:** empty 6200 kg (13,640 lb.), maximum take-off 9450 kg (20,790 lb.)

**Armament:** two fixed forward-firing 7.92-mm (0.31-in.) MG 17 machine-guns and four 7.92-mm machine-guns in remotely controlled barbettes

**Dimensions:**
| | | |
|---|---|---|
| span | 13.33 m | (43 ft. 9 in.) |
| length | 12.80 m | (42 ft.) |
| height | 3.95 m | (12 ft. 11 in.) |
| wing area | 31.30 m² | (337 sq. ft.) |

---

Although apparently similar to the wings used previously, the flying surfaces of the Ar 240A-0 were entirely new and of laminar flow section.

## AR 240A-02

**Both the Ar 240A-01 and -02 were issued to Jagdgeschwader (JG) 5 and based in the Petsamo area in North Finland. They were used on operational reconnaissance missions.**

Originally, the Ar 240 project hinged around a system of remotely-controlled gun barbettes and their potential for bomber-destroying.

When the pre-production aircraft were built, Arado again deleted the unique 'umbrella' dive brake. Reconnaissance was considered a more important mission than dive-bombing, hence the completion of the A-0 aircraft for the former role.

In an attempt to cure the appalling handling of the Ar 240 V1 and V2, the cockpit section was moved forward from its original, more conventional position.

As reconnaissance machines, each of the Ar 240A-0 aircraft carried a vertically-mounted Rb 50/30 camera in the rear of each engine nacelle. Annular cooling intakes were fitted in place of the conventional spinners used on earlier machines.

Arado made many attempts to solve the Ar 240's inherently poor flying qualities. This included auxiliary fins above and below the tailcone of the A-0s.

## COMBAT DATA

### MAXIMUM SPEED

Arado's Ar 240 was fast enough to avoid interception by Allied fighters during its limited operational career, but could not match the later Mosquito PR.Mk 34 or Lockheed F-5G.

| | |
|---|---|
| Ar 240A-0 | 620 km/h (384 m.p.h.) |
| MOSQUITO PR.Mk 34 | 684 km/h (424 m.p.h.) |
| F-5G LIGHTNING | 673 km/h (417 m.p.h.) |

### SERVICE CEILING

Both the Ar 240A-0 and Mosquito PR.Mk 34 had similar altitude capabilities, but were not as high-flying as the Lightning. Reconnaissance types often relied on their altitude for safety.

F-5G LIGHTNING 13,565 m (44,500 ft.)

Ar 240A-0 10,500 m (34,400 ft.)

MOSQUITO PR.Mk 34 10,973 m (36,000 ft.)

### MAXIMUM RANGE

Ar 240A-0 2000 km (1,240 mi.)

MOSQUITO 5633 km (3,500 mi.)

F-5G LIGHTNING 4185 km (2,600 mi.)

Even with auxiliary fuel the Ar 240A-0 was short-ranged by comparison with the Mosquito and Lightning. Had further operational use been made of the Arado this would have limited the type's usefulness to tactical reconnaissance missions, further adding to the problems that the design presented to its crews.

---

## Reconnaissance in World War II

■ **DE HAVILLAND MOSQUITO PR:** Successive marks of photo-reconnaissance (PR) Mosquito, such as the PR.Mk XVI, offered increased performance and capability.

■ **MITSUBISHI Ki-46-II 'DINAH':** This PR version of the Ki-46 initially proved immune to Allied interception, but as improved fighters were introduced losses mounted.

■ **NORTH AMERICAN P-51 MUSTANG:** PR conversions of most P-51 variants were completed, as well as many new-build aircraft. The RAF used its Mk IAs for low-altitude work.

■ **SUPERMARINE SPITFIRE PR:** Spitfires were used by the RAF and US Army Air Force for both high- and low-altitude missions. This PR.Mk XIX has a long-range fuel tank.

# ARMSTRONG WHITWORTH

# ALBEMARLE

● Bomber design ● Wood/metal construction ● D-Day glider-tug

▲ Based on a
Bristol design intended to meet
an RAF bomber requirement, the Albemarle
entered service as a transport and glider-tug
for British special forces.

**D**esigned by Bristol and manufactured by A.W. Hawkesley Ltd, the Albemarle evoked little enthusiasm when it first appeared as a medium bomber. Constructed at a time when a shortage of light alloy was anticipated and when fears that Britain's aircraft factories would be devastated by the Luftwaffe were at their height, the Albemarle used steel and wooden components provided by small sub-contractors outside the aircraft industry.

## ARMSTRONG WHITWORTH ALBEMARLE

▼ Glider-towing over Sicily, 1943
No. 297 Squadron, RAF, was one of two units to make the first use of the Albemarle as a glider-tug.

▼ Bristol design
The Albemarle began life as the Bristol Type 155, designed to Spec. B.18/38.

▲ Special Transport Mk I
The last Mk I built became the ST.Mk I prototype. Principal changes included deletion of the rear fuselage fuel tank and bomb release gear to make space internally, and a reduction in armament.

▼ Easily dismantled and transported
The Albemarle was easily dismantled and moved aboard 18.3-m (60-ft.) 'Queen Mary' road trailers.

▲ Production
Production of the Albemarle ended in December 1944, after 602 aircraft had left the Brockworth factory of A.W. Hawkesley Ltd.

### FACTS AND FIGURES

➤ Production of Albemarle sub-assemblies was entrusted to numerous contractors, including car and furniture makers.

➤ Russia took delivery of 10 RAF Albemarles for the transport role.

➤ The first Albemarle flew in 1939 but crashed before the second aircraft flew.

➤ Vickers 'K' guns of 7.7-mm (.303 cal.) calibre were employed; either four in a Boulton Paul turret, or two under a sliding hood.

➤ The Albemarle's tricycle undercarriage was of Lockheed design.

➤ As many as 1000 sub-contractors were employed on the Albemarle project.

**PROFILE**

# Wood and metal special transport

Bomber design had advanced at such a pace during the years of the Albemarle's development that the aircraft was destined never to enter service as a bomber.

Instead it was found to be more useful in transport and glider-tug duties for Britain's special forces. The Albemarle's first action came in 1943 with the invasion of Sicily, when it was used to tow gliders full of troops to the battlefield.

Another famous episode for the RAF's Albemarles came in

June 1944, when four squadrons of the aircraft towed the Horsa gliders that took Allied airborne troops to France for the first time during Operation Overlord, the invasion of occupied Europe. Later the same year, two squadrons provided glider-tugs during the assault on the Rhine bridges at Arnhem.

The anticipated light alloy shortage did not occur and Britain's aircraft factories escaped relatively unscathed by German attack. Thus the

Albemarle 'experiment' was not to have the significance it might otherwise have had.

The Soviet Union was the only other Albemarle operator, although it has been suggested that the country was only interested in the aircraft's engines, which, it is thought, were later copied for local use.

Albemarle production ended in December 1944 after 602 of an ordered 1060 had been built.

*Left: The first Albemarles were operational with No. 295 Squadron, RAF, in 1942. Nos 296 and 297 followed in 1943.*

*Above: Although the alloy shortage failed to materialise, Albemarle production soon proved justified in the type's role.*

## ALBEMARLE ST.Mk V

On the night before D-Day, 6 June 1944, No. 297 Squadron dropped troops and supplies behind enemy lines. The following day, Albemarles from No. 297 towed Horsa gliders across the Channel.

Test pilot John Grierson described the Albemarle as an average aircraft, '… with no virtues and no vices'. The first 32 built were intended for use as reconnaissance bombers, with a crew of two pilots, a navigator and a radio operator. However, the Albermarle was never operated in this role.

The only defensive armament fitted to the Albemarle was four 7.7-mm (.303 cal.) machine-guns in a Boulton Paul turret. When firing forwards, a fairing in front of the turret lowered automatically. Some aircraft modified as special forces transports dispensed with the turret in favour of a two-gun armament covered with a sliding hood.

Albemarles often wore standard Bomber Command markings. The black and white striping on the fuselage and wings was an identification aid for Allied aircraft during the D-Day landings.

Most Albemarles were powered by two 1186-kW (1,590-hp.) Bristol Hercules XI two-row radial engines. Two aircraft, a GT.Mk II and a Mk IV, were fitted with American Wright Double Cyclones. When the Soviet air force acquired Albemarles, it is believed they were valued mostly for their engines, which are thought to have been copied later.

The Albemarle consisted of a steel structure with spruce formers and plywood covering. Much of the wing structure was wooden with a plywood covering. The wing centre-section was also covered in plywood.

For glider-towing a Malcolm-type quick-release hook was fitted to the extreme rear of the fuselage. The release mechanism was controlled by the pilot.

### COMBAT DATA

**ENGINE POWER**

Heinkel's He 111Z was specially designed as a glider-tug and effectively consisted of two He 111 bombers joined together with an extra engine added. This gave it a huge power advantage over other glider-tug types.

| ALBEMARLE ST.Mk V | He 111Z-1 ZWILLING | C-47A SKYTRAIN |
|---|---|---|
| 2372 kW (3,180 hp.) | 5033 kW (6,750 hp.) | 1790 kW (3,940 hp.) |

**MAXIMUM TAKE-OFF WEIGHT**

The comparatively massive He 111Z Zwilling weighed almost twice as much as other glider-tug types. The C-47 and Albemarle were of similar size, although the Albemarle, as a bomber design, was the heavier aircraft.

| ALBEMARLE ST.Mk V | He 111Z-1 ZWILLING | C-47A SKYTRAIN |
|---|---|---|
| 16,556 kg (36,423 lb.) | 28,600 kg (62,920 lb.) | 11,793 kg (25,945 lb.) |

**ARMAMENT**

The C-47 carried no defensive armament, while the Albemarle retained part of its defensive machine-gun fit as installed in the original bomber design. The He 111Z carried no fewer than eight cannon and machine-guns.

ALBEMARLE ST.Mk V — 4 x 7.7-mm (.303 cal.) machine-guns

He 111Z-1 ZWILLING — 4 x 7.9-mm (0.31-in.) machine-guns / 1 x 20-mm (0.79-in.) cannon, 3 x 13-mm (0.51-in.) cannon

C-47A SKYTRAIN — none

## RAF special forces transports and tugs

■ **ARMSTRONG WHITWORTH WHITLEY:** Employed as a paratroop trainer from 1940, this bomber design saw action in 1941, dropping troops over Malta. Although not used operationally as glider-tugs, Whitleys equipped a glider training unit.

■ **DOUGLAS DAKOTA:** The Allies' standard transport throughout World War II, the C-47/Dakota also filled a Horsa glider-tug role, especially with the RAF and USAAF during the D-Day landings in 1944.

■ **SHORT STIRLING:** By 1944 this, the first of the RAF's four-engined bombers, had been relegated to transport and glider-towing duties. First used on D-Day, Stirlings were active in these roles until March 1945.

# ARMSTRONG WHITWORTH

# WHITLEY

● Early heavy bomber ● Maritime patrol and special operations

*▲ Having been designed as a heavy bomber, the Whitley found success flying in the maritime patrol role, towing gliders, dropping paratroops and special agents and as a civilian freighter.*

**A**long with the Vickers Wellington and Handley Page Hampden, the Whitley was one of the RAF's three principal bomber types at the start of World War II. Though the oldest of the three, it was to become the first British aircraft to drop bombs over both Germany and Italy. It was also the first to be equipped with radar for submarine hunting. It also went on to fill several other roles, including paratrooping aircraft on special operations.

**▼ Maritime operations**
*The Mk VII was slightly slower than the bomber versions because of its higher weight and the drag from its ASV Mk II radar antennas.*

**▲ On the flightdeck**
*There were a few initial criticisms of the Whitley and most of these centred on the cockpit layout. Some controls were difficult to operate.*

**▲ Engine testbed**
*This Mk I was used without armament to test the Rolls-Royce Merlin for later versions.*

**▲ Glider tug**
*Whitley Mk Vs were used for the training of glider tug pilots. Three squadrons served operationally.*

**Night bomber ▶**
*With docile landing characteristics and long range, the Whitley was an ideal night bomber.*

## FACTS AND FIGURES

➤ Ordered from the drawing board in June 1935, the prototype first flew on March 17, 1936 from Whitley Aerodrome.

➤ A box-like shape was chosen for the fuselage to make manufacture simple.

➤ A new wooden wing was designed to save materials, but was never flown.

➤ On the first night of World War II during the so-called Phony War, 10 Whitleys flew over Germany, dropping propaganda leaflets.

➤ As initially fitted, the Merlin engines were unusually noisy and needed modification.

➤ A four-gun rear turret improved rearward defence from the Mk IV onwards.

**PROFILE**

# The right Mark for the right job

*Left: Obvious on this Whitley Mk V is the flat glass panel for the bombardier. Less apparent is the extended rear fuselage.*

Designed to a 1934 requirement and first flown in March 1936, the Whitley was originally powered by Armstrong Siddeley Tiger radial engines. These were used on the 160 Mks I, II and III; later models switched to Merlin in-line engines, which boosted top speed by 84 km/h (52 m.p.h.).

There were only 40 Mk IVs, but nearly 1500 of the Mk V, which remained in production from 1939 until 1943. The Mk IV had introduced a powered tail turret with four machine guns,

and the Mk V had a slightly longer fuselage to extend the tail gunner's field of fire.

Whitleys carried out the majority of the controversial leaflet raids during the first year of the war and joined the night bombing offensive in 1940, taking part in the first raid on Berlin in August. The Whitley remained in front-line service with Bomber Command until the spring of 1942.

Some Mk Vs had been transferred to Coastal Command early in the war for use in maritime

patrol and another 146 were built as Mk VIIs with long-range search radars capable of detecting submarines. These were active from March 1941 over the Atlantic; a Whitley crew made the first U-boat kill with ASV radar in November. They remained in service until early 1943.

Whitleys were used as paratroop trainers and glider tugs from 1940, while 12 Mk Vs were converted to freighters in 1942 and used by British Airways.

*Above: With long range and search radar, the Whitley joined coastal command in 1942. No. 502 Squadron had previously sunk U-206 with a Mk VII on 30 November 1941.*

## Whitley Mk V

**Type:** bomber, reconnaissance and anti-submarine aircraft

**Powerplant:** two 895-kW (1,200-hp.) Rolls-Royce Merlin X inline piston engines

**Maximum speed:** 367 km/h (228 m.p.h.) at 5395 m (17,700 ft.)

**Range:** 2540 km (1,500 mi.)

**Initial climb rate:** 244 m/min (800 f.p.m.)

**Service ceiling:** 5395 m (17,700 ft.)

**Weapons:** five 7.7-mm (.303 cal.) machine guns; up to a 3168-kg (6,985-lb.) bomb load (usually fourteen 227-kg/500-lb. bombs).

**Weights:** Empty 8759 kg (19,310 lb.); maximum take-off 15,164 kg (33,431 lb.)

**Dimensions:**
span 25.60 m (84 ft.)
length 22.10 m (72 ft. 6 in.)
height 4.57 m (15 ft.)
wing area 105.63 m² (1,137 sq. ft.)

## WHITLEY MK IV

Serving with No. 10 Squadron in the summer of 1939, this Mk IV shows the higher visibility of pre-war markings. Before going into action the underwing serial numbers were removed.

Problems with the change to Merlin engines included a drop in the efficiency of the cabin heater. This had to be rectified for long-range, high-altitude night missions.

Rolls-Royce worked with the Royal Aircraft Establishment to solve the problem of noisy engines. Investigation of the propellers and exhausts was necessary.

The first prototype had straight wings, but the second prototype and all production aircraft had a small amount of dihedral on the outer wing panels.

Rolls-Royce Merlin IV engines gave a 84 km/h (52 m.p.h.) speed improvement over the Whitley Mk I.

A bombardier and nose-gunner occupied the extreme end of the nose, which contained a single 7.7-mm (.303 cal.) Browning machine gun.

A limited field of fire was presented to the rear gunner by the twin tailfins. From the Mk V onward the rear fuselage was extended to solve this problem.

When retracted, the main wheels protruded below the level of the undercarriage doors. This minimised damage in the event of a wheels-up landing.

Unsure of the effect of flaps, the manufacturer fitted the wing at a high angle to the fuselage. This gave a low landing speed and distinctive nose-down flying attitude.

The power-operated Nash and Thompson rear turret, introduced on the Mk IV, relieved the gunner from having to manually turn the turret when tracking a target.

## World War II Whitley actions

**ANTI-SUBMARINE WARFARE:** Using its ASV search radar the Whitley Mk VII was able to detect any part of the submarine above the surface.

**LEAFLET DROPPING:** Early Whitley raids were used to distribute propaganda leaflets, known as 'nickelling'.

**AGENT INSERTION:** Whitleys were often used for air dropping agents behind enemy lines.

**ACTION DATA**

**BOMB LOAD**

As the Luftwaffe's most important bomber, even the most developed forms of the He 111 suffered from limited bomb load. With the B-18 not seeing combat, the large bomb load of the Whitley so early in World War II was impressive.

| WHITLEY Mk V | He 111H-16 | B-18 BOLO |
|---|---|---|
| 3168 kg (6,985 lb.) | 2495 kg (5,500 lb.) | 2942 kg (6,485 lb.) |

# ARMSTRONG WHITWORTH

# SISKIN

● All-metal fighter ● Highly manoeuvrable ● King's Cup winner

▲ *Although it was not beautiful to look at, the Siskin was a delight to fly and had none of the vices that were so apparent in early biplane fighters. The unequal span wings and the uncowled radial engine were distinctive features.*

**F**ighter development slowed almost to a halt after the end of World War I. It was five years before the RAF started to replace its wartime Sopwith Snipes, even though one of its two new fighters, the Siskin, had flown for the first time in early 1919. Despite its slow start, the Siskin developed into a capable combat aircraft and went on to become the RAF's standard fighter of the late 1920s serving with a total of 11 UK-based squadrons.

## ARMSTRONG WHITWORTH SISKIN

▼ **Canadian service**
Canada acquired 12 Siskins, including this IIIA which took part in the 1931 Trans-Canada Air Pageant.

▲ **Squadron service**
The most famous Siskin squadron was No. 43, which regularly thrilled crowds at the RAF Display, Hendon.

▼ **Learning to fight**
The RAF operated more than 40 two-seat Siskin IIIDC trainers until their retirement in 1932.

▲ **Civilian Siskin**
The second Siskin II, G-EBHY, was exported to Sweden where it was equipped with skis.

◄ **Ultimate Siskin**
By 1931 the 142 Siskin IIIAs were showing their age and the RAF sought a replacement. Armstrong Whitworth submitted the Siskin IIIB, which had better speed and climb performance. However, testing revealed inadequate handling and range and the IIIB was not selected.

## FACTS AND FIGURES

➤ The Siskin III entered RAF service in May 1924 with No. 41 Squadron based at Northolt aerodrome.

➤ The Siskin was designed by Siddeley Deasy and was originally called the S.R.2.

➤ Siskins became famous for their tied-together aerobatic routines.

➤ S.R.2 test pilot Oliver Stewart said: 'The Siskin was gentle, easy-going, calm and good-tempered.'

➤ By June 1931 there were 179 Siskins in service with the RAF.

➤ Altogether, 485 Siskins of all marks, including the S.R.2, were built.

## PROFILE

# Britain's famous inter-war fighter

A Dragonfly engine powered the original Siskin, and one of a pair built as civil aircraft won the 1923 King's Cup air race at an average speed of 240 km/h (149 m.p.h.). The original prototype was rebuilt with a steel fuselage frame and wing spars, and was fitted with a Jaguar radial engine. The result was the Siskin III, which entered service in May 1924 and equipped two squadrons. A dozen of the 62 Mk IIIs were built as two-seat fighter trainers before the first IIIA flew in October 1925.

With its supercharged Jaguar engine, the IIIA was 35 km/h (22 m.p.h.) faster at sea level than the earlier model and had a higher service ceiling. It also had minor airframe changes, and the twin nose guns were enclosed by the forward fuselage. As well as serving with the RAF until 1932, the Siskin became the standard fighter of the Royal Canadian Air Force. Some of the Mk IIIAs supplied to Canada were still in service in 1939. Total production reached 382, including one fitted with a ski undercarriage for the Swedish air force in 1925.

After the failure of the Dragonfly engine subsequent Siskins were powered by the very reliable and powerful Armstrong Siddeley Jaguar radial engine.

Above: The Siskin prototype first flew in 1919 as the Siddeley S.R.2, powered by the ill-fated A.B.C. Dragonfly engine. In 1921 a Jaguar radial was fitted and the Siskin name was adopted.

Above: The Romanian government ordered the Siskin V, but after a fatal accident the order was cancelled.

### SISKIN IIIA

This Siskin IIIA is in the markings of No. 43 Squadron in 1929. Famous for their aerobatic displays at the Hendon pageants, the unit operated the type until 1932.

The pilot sat just behind the top wing with his eyes roughly level with the trailing edge; his view upward and forward was therefore good.

The Siskin IIIA had a raised tailplane and did not have the ventral fin that was fitted to earlier marks. The control surfaces were well balanced and gave the aircraft excellent agility.

No. 43 Squadron's black and white checkerboard markings on the fuselage and tail were highly distinctive.

The V-type undercarriage featured telescopic legs consisting of steel tubes forming an oil dashpot which damped the action of the rubber shock-absorber cords.

The short-span, narrow single-spar lower wing contrasted sharply with the broad overhanging top wing. The wings were supported by V-shaped interplane struts and bracing wires.

Although the initial Siskin variants were of wood and fabric construction, the production variants were the first all-metal framed aircraft to be built in quantity for the RAF.

J-8959

### Siskin IIIA

**Type:** metal-framed biplane fighter

**Powerplant:** one 336-kW (450-hp.) Armstrong Siddeley Jaguar IVS 14-cylinder radial engine

**Maximum speed:** 251 km/h (156 m.p.h.)

**Range:** 450 km (280 mi.)

**Service ceiling:** 8260 m (27,100 ft.)

**Climb rate:** to 3048 metres (10,000 ft.) in 6 min 35 sec

**Weights:** empty 935 kg (2,057 lb.); loaded 1366 kg (3,000 lb.)

**Armament:** two 7.7-mm (.303 cal.) machine-guns and four 9-kg (20-lb.) bombs

**Dimensions:** span 10.11 m (33 ft. 2 in.)
length 7.72 m (25 ft. 4 in.)
height 3.10 m (10 ft. 2 in.)
wing area 27.22 m² (293 sq. ft.)

### COMBAT DATA

#### MAXIMUM SPEED

Aircraft were not a priority during the 1920s and fighters of this period were not much faster than World War I dogfighters. The Siskin is the slowest of the three designs, but is also the earliest.

| | |
|---|---|
| SISKIN IIIA | 251 km/h (156 m.p.h.) |
| P-1A HAWK | 257 km/h (159 m.p.h.) |
| CR.1 | 272 km/h (169 m.p.h.) |

#### SERVICE CEILING

The Siskin had excellent performance at altitude, mainly due to its supercharged engine. One RAF squadron even used the Siskin as a specialised high-altitude fighter.

SISKIN IIIA 8260 m (27,100 ft.)
P-1A HAWK 6157 m (20,200 ft.)
CR.1 7450 m (24,450 ft.)

#### ENGINE POWER

The Siskin's powerful Jaguar engine gave it an excellent service ceiling and an impressive rate of climb. Although the CR.1 had less power, its streamlined shape gave it good performance.

SISKIN IIIA 336 kW (450 hp.)
P-1A HAWK 324 kW (435 hp.)
CR.1 224 kW (300 hp.)

## Armstrong Whitworth family

■ **F.K.8:** The excellent F.K.8 reconnaissance aircraft was produced in considerable numbers during the last two years of World War I.

■ **F.K.10:** This amazing quadruplane design first flew in 1917, but it was not successful and only a small number were eventually delivered.

■ **APE:** The ugly Ape had an adjustable incidence tail and was built as an experimental aircraft for the Royal Aircraft Establishment.

■ **STARLING:** Based on the highly successful Siskin, the Starling was intended to be a day- and night-fighter, but was never put into production.

# AVIA

# B.534

● Biplane fighter ● Outstanding performance ● Ground attack

▲ A sturdy and agile machine with adequate performance, the Avia B.534 also had relatively powerful armament, consisting of four 7.7-mm (.303 cal.) machine-guns.

**P**roduced by the Czechoslovakian Avia company, the Hispano-Suiza-engined B.534 was widely considered to be the finest biplane fighter of its time and was the most important Czech aircraft built between the two world wars. Production totalled 566 and a number were exported. After the occupation of Czechoslovakia by Germany in 1939, B.534s equipped the Slovak 'puppet' regime and were sold to Bulgaria.

## AVIA B.534

▼ **Reliable power**
After the failure of the Avia Rr 29 nine-cylinder radial engine, the B.34/2 prototype was re-engined with the 12-cylinder Hispano-Suiza 12Ybrs and became known as the B.534/1 after official trials.

▲ **Front-line strength**
The majority of B.534s were supplied to the Czechoslovakian air force and by the time of the Munich crisis in September 1938, they equipped 21 front-line fighter squadrons.

**Modern replica** ▶
As a tribute to the B.534 and the airmen who flew it, this full-scale replica, accurately painted with Czechoslovakian markings, was completed in 1975. It is on display at the Air Force and Army Museum in Prague-Kbely.

▼ **Fine performance**
The B.534 was a sturdy fighter, with outstanding climb and dive capabilities. Its enclosed cockpit was a modern feature for the era.

◀ **Winter operations**
B.534s were often equipped with skis to cope with the harsh operating conditions of Eastern Europe.

## FACTS AND FIGURES

➤ A refinement of the B.34, the B.534 entered service with the Czechoslovakian air force in 1935.

➤ A number of B.534s were exported – six to Greece and 14 to Yugoslavia.

➤ The most-produced version was the B.534-IV, of which 272 were built.

➤ The B.534 proved to be the outstanding biplane fighter at the Zurich international flying meet in July 1937.

➤ Bulgarian B.534s were flown in combat against USAAF B-24 Liberators.

➤ Three Slovak fighter squadrons operated B.534s on the Russian Front in 1941.

# PROFILE

# Czech biplane warrior

Nearly 500 B.534s were built in four series. The first 100 had two machine-guns, but later models had four guns with the 272 Series IV aircraft also having cockpit canopies and metal propellers. In addition, 54 Bk.534s were built, armed with a 20-mm cannon firing through

the propeller, plus two 7.7-mm (.303 cal.) machine-guns.

Some B.534s were used by the Luftwaffe, both as fighter trainers and as tugs for troop-carrying gliders. A few, previously supplied to Greece, were used in combat during the Italian invasion of 1940.

Around 65 were used to equip the Slovak air force. Some were shot down by Hungarian C.R.32s, and one squadron

fought alongside the Germans during the invasion of Poland. Three Slovak B.534s even survived to take part in the 1944 uprising against the German occupation.

The B.534 was an unequal-span, staggered-wing biplane, with ailerons on both upper and lower wings. The wings and aft fuselage were fabric covered, with detachable metal panels on the forward fuselage.

*Above: Early versions of the B.534 flew without the wheel spats that were later incorporated on the definitive B.534-IV.*

*Below: This was one of several B.534-IVs operated by the Czechoslovakian air police in 1938. The Avia emblem is on the fin next to the national insignia.*

## B.534-IV

This aircraft carries the markings of a Slovak air force unit at Zitomir-Kiev, Ukraine, during the invasion of the USSR in 1941/42.

Some 450 B.534s and Bk.534s were on strength with the Czechoslovakian forces when the country was occupied by the Germans in March 1939. Of these, a number were absorbed into the newly created Slovak air force and the Luftwaffe. Five squadrons of the Bulgarian air force also received 78 examples.

B.534-IVs had an aft-sliding cockpit canopy with raised fuselage rear decking. Earlier versions had an open cockpit.

Development of the earlier B.34 fighter led to the B.34/2 prototype being re-engined with a Hispano-Suiza 12Ybrs 12-cylinder Vee liquid-cooled piston engine after the failure of the planned Avia Rr 29 nine-cylinder radial. This became the B.534/1 and the final version, the B.534-IV, was fitted with the 634-kW Avia-built 12Ydrs, giving it a maximum speed of almost 400 km/h (250 m.p.h.).

Four 7.7-mm (.303 cal.) machine-guns armed the B.534 – two in the fuselage and two in the wings – but excessive wing vibration led to all four being fuselage-mounted after the 48th aircraft. The Bk.534 was fitted with an engine-mounted 20-mm Oerlikon cannon and two 7.7-mm guns, but problems with the cannon meant that it was replaced by a third 7.7-mm weapon.

## COMBAT DATA

### MAXIMUM SPEED

The last biplane fighter designs of the late-1930s were capable of around 400 km/h (250 m.p.h.). This performance was soon surpassed by the new monoplane designs, but biplanes were still able to harass unescorted bombers.

**B.534-IV** 395 km/h (245 m.p.h.)
**GLADIATOR Mk I** 407 km/h (252 m.p.h.)
**CR.42 FALCO** 420 km/h (260 m.p.h.)

### ARMAMENT

The Avia B.534-IV had the versatility of a light bombload in addition to its four machine-gun armament. The CR.42, which was widely used in World War II, was relatively lightly armed with two larger calibre guns.

**B.534-IV** 4 x 7.7-mm (.303 cal.) machine-guns 120 kg (270 lb.) of bombs
**GLADIATOR Mk I** 4 x 7.7-mm (.303 cal.) machine-guns
**CR.42 FALCO** 2 x 12.7-mm (.50 cal.) machine-guns

### RANGE

A range of around 600 to 700 km was typical of fighters of this period. The earliest monoplane fighters did not improve on this by a significant amount. The war soon spurred designers to increase range, however.

**B.534-IV** 580 km (373 mi.)
**GLADIATOR Mk I** 547 km (439 mi.)
**CR.42 FALCO** 780 km (484 mi.)

## B.534 during World War II

**LUFTWAFFE GLIDER TUG:** Several B.534s in Luftwaffe service were given raised canopies and were used as glider tugs. Although operational use was limited, they were used extensively for training, usually towing the DFS 230 assault glider.

**FIGHTING THE LIBERATOR:** Bulgaria operated its B.534s against US Army Air Force B-24 bombers which entered Bulgarian airspace while returning from the 'Tidal Wave' bombing raid against the Ploesti oilfields.

**SLOVAK INSURGENTS:** During the Slovak national rising of the summer of 1944, three B.534s were flown from Tri Duby airfield by insurgents. The Luftwaffe destroyed two on the ground and the third was eventually burned to prevent it being captured.

# AVRO

# ANSON

● Airliner design ● Maritime reconnaissance ● Training

▲ The prone bomb-aimer's position in the nose of the Anson Mk I had a sliding panel in the floor for operation of the Wimperis Mk VIIB bombsight.

**D**eveloped to meet an RAF Coastal Command requirement for a land-based reconnaissance aircraft, the Anson was derived from the Avro 652 six-seat airliner. Flown for the first time in March 1935, it entered service a year later. Although the Hudson had started to replace it by the start of World War II, the Anson continued to carry out reconnaissance missions until 1942. It also became one of the Allies' most widely used trainers.

## AVRO ANSON

### ▼ Radar training
In 1944 the Royal Navy received Ansons, fitted with radar scanners, for training observers to use radar.

### ▲ Cadet gunners
By 1943 the Anson's primary task was training. Prospective air gunners were taught day and night gunnery skills using the Boulton Paul turret.

### Trainer for Rhodesia ▶
The post-war Anson Mk 20 was built as a trainer for Rhodesia. The RAF also used a small number.

### ◀ Pre-war exports
The RAF was not the only armed force to realise the potential of the Anson. This example was one of three acquired by Finland in 1938. Other export users of the Mk I included Australia, Estonia, Ireland and Greece.

### Dutch survivors ▶
No. 321 was one of two RAF squadrons manned by Dutch aircrew who escaped during the German invasion. The aircraft has a Dutch insignia on the fin.

## FACTS AND FIGURES

➤ Avro's Anson was based on the Avro 652 six-seat airliner for Imperial Airways which first flew on 7 January 1935.

➤ The Anson beat the competing DH.89M Rapide for the RAF order.

➤ On 5 September 1939 the Anson first saw combat, attacking a German U-boat.

➤ During the Dunkirk evacuation an Anson of No. 500 Squadron shot down two of three attacking Bf 109 fighters.

➤ Retired in 1968, after 32 years, the Anson was the longest-serving RAF type.

➤ Anson production totalled 11,020 airframes, including licence production.

# PROFILE

# From maritime patroller to trainer

When it first entered service in 1936, the Anson was the RAF's fastest twin-engined aircraft and the force's first monoplane with a retractable undercarriage. For military service a forward-firing machine-gun, one in a dorsal turret, plus a bomb-bay for two 45-kg (100-lb.) and eight 9-kg (20-lb.) bombs, were added.

Although its performance was rather tame by the standards of 1940, the type could turn inside the Bf 109 and continue turning for much longer. This ability enabled Anson crews to claim six of the German fighters in combat. From 1941 it was also used by a number of air-sea rescue squadrons.

In addition, the Anson was used as a trainer from an early stage in its career, and in 1940 it was chosen as the standard twin-engined aircraft for training pilots in Canada.

The Anson was used by at least 20 air forces, and after the war many were converted to civil transports. More than 11,000 were built, nearly 3000 of them

*Below: Demand for the Anson was so great that licence production, supervised by Federal Aircraft Ltd, was set up in Canada The 50 . purchased by the US Army Air Force were designated AT-20s. They differed from British Mk Is in having Jacobs L-6BM engines and Canadian equipment.*

*Above: Tasked with land-based maritime reconnaissance of the English Channel, North Sea and the Western Approaches, the Mk I was a vital tool in protecting British shipping.*

in Canada with Wright, Jacobs or Pratt & Whitney engines. Production continued until 1952, and the type remained in RAF service until 1968.

## Anson Mk I

**Type:** advanced trainer

**Powerplant:** two 261-kW (350-hp.) Armstrong Siddeley Cheetah IX seven-cylinder air-cooled radial engines

**Maximum speed:** 303 km/h (188 m.p.h.) at 2130 m (7,000 ft.)

**Climb rate:** 229 m/min (750 f.p.m.) at sea level

**Range:** 1270 km (787 mi.)

**Service ceiling:** 5790 m (19,000 ft.)

**Weights:** empty 2438 kg (5,361 lb.); maximum take-off 3629 kg (7,984 lb.)

**Armament:** two 7.7-mm (.303 cal.) machine-guns and up to 163 kg (360 lb.) of bombs

**Dimensions:**
| | | |
|---|---|---|
| span | 17.22 m | (56 ft. 6 in.) |
| length | 12.88 m | (42 ft. 3 in.) |
| height | 3.99 m | (13 ft. 1 in.) |
| wing area | 43.00 m² | (463 sq. ft.) |

## ANSON MK I

Carrying the training colour scheme of temperate land upper camouflage and trainer yellow lower surfaces, this Mk I was one of 850 from the sixth RAF production batch.

During the bomb run, the bomb aimer would move to a prone position in the nose. A sliding panel in the floor allowed the bombsight to be operated.

With a normal crew of three, the cockpit was fairly spacious. The pilot had solo controls and a Reid and Sigrist Mk I blind flying panel. A navigator/bomb aimer, with a plotting table and instrument panel, sat behind the pilot. The wireless operator/gunner sat at the rear of the cabin.

The only major design changes from the prototype were a 25 per cent increase in tailplane span and a reduction in elevator area. After stability trials in January 1936, the rudder area was also increased.

Defensive armament included a manually-operated Armstrong Whitworth turret fitted with a 7.7-mm (.303 cal.) Lewis Mk 3A machine-gun and five drums of ammunition. When not in use, the gun barrel was lowered into a slot in the top of the fuselage.

N9765

Power for the Mk I was provided by two Armstrong Siddeley Cheetah IX engines within seven-lobed NACA cowlings.

Originally designed as a low-wing airliner, the Anson had a welded steel tube fuselage covered with fabric and wooden wings.

The Anson Mk I had a fixed tailwheel and retractable main undercarriage. The manually-operated mainwheels, which required 164.5 turns of a handle to raise, were replaced by hydraulically-operated gear on later models.

## COMBAT DATA

### CRUISING SPEED

As it was derived from a small airliner of the mid-1930s, the Anson had a respectable, though not particularly fast, top speed. The Si 204 was equipped with more powerful engines than both the Anson and Ki-54.

| | |
|---|---|
| **ANSON Mk I** | 254 km/h (188 m.p.h.) |
| **Si 204D** | 340 km/h (210 m.p.h.) |
| **Ki-54a 'HICKORY'** | 240 km/h (148 m.p.h.) |

### ARMAMENT

Although the reconnaissance variants of the Siebel Si 204 were often fitted with radar, they were generally unarmed. The Anson and Tachikawa Ki-54 were both armed, and the latter could carry twice the load and defensive armament of the British aircraft.

| | |
|---|---|
| **ANSON Mk I** | 2 x 7.7-mm (.303 cal.) machine-guns / 163-kg (360-lb.) bombload |
| **Si 204D** | none |
| **Ki-54a 'HICKORY'** | 4 x 7.7-mm (.303 cal.) machine-guns / 408-kg (900-lb.) bombload |

### RANGE

The Anson's range made it suitable for maritime reconnaissance until it was replaced by the Lockheed Hudson, another type derived from an airliner. The 'Hickory' had the least range, although it carried a larger weapons load. This aircraft was developed initially as a trainer; a maritime version entered service later.

ANSON Mk I 1270 km (787 mi.)

Si 204D 1800 km (1,118 mi.)

Ki-54a 'HICKORY' 960 km (595 mi.)

## RAF World War II trainers

■ **AIRSPEED OXFORD:** As the first twin-engined monoplane advanced trainer in RAF service, the Oxford was used for all aspects of aircrew training, including gunnery.

■ **DE HAVILLAND TIGER MOTH:** As the most numerous and famous British elementary trainer during World War II, the Tiger Moth equipped 44 Flying Training Schools in 1939.

■ **MILES MAGISTER:** Known as the 'Maggie', this classic Miles design was the first monoplane trainer to be used by the RAF. Employed in elementary training, it was fully aerobatic.

■ **MILES MASTER:** In 1938 the Master gained the largest ever contract for a trainer at the time. Used for advanced training, the Master had a top speed of 364 km/h (226 m.p.h.).

# AVRO

# MANCHESTER

● Night bomber ● Father of the Lancaster ● Maritime patrol

▲ *The Manchester might have been a useful design, having a potent defensive and offensive armament, but the Vulture engine spent more time under repair than in service.*

**O**vershadowed by the immortal Lancaster that replaced it in service, the Manchester was plagued by the unreliability of its Rolls-Royce Vulture engine. First flown in 1940, the Manchester had a brief operational career, and the aircraft's last combat mission was flown in mid-1942. The real fame of the aircraft was that, with the marriage of its airframe and four Rolls-Royce Merlin engines, it became the Avro Lancaster.

▼ **Night raider**
*A Manchester Mk IA from No. 207 Squadron, which was based at RAF Waddington.*

▲ **First of the few**
*This Manchester is a Mk I with a central tail fin. The fin was later deleted and the tail span increased by another 3 m (10 ft.), as in the Lancaster.*

▲ **Short span**
*Like many of the first RAF night bombers, the Manchester had a short wing span to fit pre-war hangars.*

▲ **Son of Manchester**
*With four reliable and powerful Merlin engines, most of the Manchester's ills were cured. The Lancaster immediately replaced its ancestor in squadron service.*

▲ **Waiting for the night**
*A Mk IA Manchester awaits another night of bombing operations. A Westland Lysander army co-operation aircraft is parked behind it.*

◄ **Well protected**
*One of the best points of the Manchester was the good coverage of its defensive armament, with tail, nose and dorsal gun turrets.*

## FACTS AND FIGURES

➤ Flying Officer L. T. Master of No. 50 Squadron won a Victoria Cross while flying a Manchester.

➤ Manchesters took part in the first ever 1000-bomber raid, against Cologne.

➤ The first Lancaster was in fact a Manchester III with four Merlin engines.

➤ The first 13 Manchesters built were destroyed in a German air raid on the Metropolitan Vickers factory.

➤ Manchesters dropped 1855 tonnes (1,825 tons) of bombs and incendiaries.

➤ The original company designation of the Manchester was the Avro 609.

## PROFILE

# Killed by the Vulture engine

Had the Manchester been powered by a viable engine, its career might have been far longer. However, it was stuck with the dubious Rolls-Royce Vulture, a mighty V-24 in-line engine that failed to deliver the power intended, and also suffered from chronic reliability problems. The engine was also intended for a rival Handley Page design which was later cancelled.

The first Manchester prototype flew in July 1939, and a second in 1940. The Air Ministry ordered 200, and then 400. After flight trials, the wing span was increased by three metres and a central fin was added between the two endplate fins (later deleted in the Mk IA). The first squadron, No. 207, was formed in November 1940 and carried out its first mission in February 1941. Nine bomber squadrons received the aircraft, and one flight of Coastal Command. The Manchester was not really a success in combat, suffering from a number of airframe faults as well as endless failures of the Vulture engine. The last

Bomber Command operation with the aircraft took place over Bremen on 25/26 June 1942. Only 202 Manchesters had been built, of which about 40 per cent were lost on operations and 25 per cent in accidents.

Were it not for the Manchester, Avro might not have built the Lancaster, probably the best night bomber of the war. The type also gave Bomber Command useful ideas about how its future bomber aircraft should look.

*Left: No. 207 Squadron had the dubious privilege of first taking the Manchester to war, over Brest harbour on 25 February 1941.*

*Above: The first Manchester bomber is seen in December 1940. Unfortunately, this example and several others were destroyed in an enemy air raid a few days later.*

### Manchester Mk I

**Type:** twin-engined medium bomber

**Powerplant:** two Rolls-Royce Vulture 24-cylinder engines rated at 1312 kW (1,760 hp.)

**Maximum speed:** 426 km/h (264 m.p.h.) at 5180 m (17,000 ft.)

**Combat radius:** 2623 km (1,625 mi.) with 3674-kg (8,100-lb.) load

**Service ceiling:** 5850 m (19,200 ft.)

**Weights:** empty 13,350 kg (29,370 lb.); loaded 25,401 kg (55,880 lb.)

**Armament:** two 7.7-mm (.303 cal.) machine-guns in the nose turret and mid-upper turret, four 7.7-mm machine-guns in the rear turret; 4695 kg (10,330 lb.) of bombs or incendiaries

**Dimensions:**
| | |
|---|---|
| span | 27.46 m (90 ft 1 in.) |
| length | 21.13 m (69 ft. 4 in.) |
| height | 5.94 m (19 ft. 6 in.) |
| wing area | 105.63 m² (1,137 sq. ft.) |

## MANCHESTER MK IA

One of the first Manchesters into action, this No. 207 Squadron aircraft enjoyed a brief operational career. The RAF roundel with its white band was abandoned later in the war as it was too visible at night.

The nose of the Manchester was almost identical to that of the later Lancaster, and was one of the better parts of the design. The pilot and flight engineer sat side by side in the cockpit, with an astrodome behind for the navigator to take measurements of the stars for astro-navigation. The controls were well laid out, and the aircraft was not hard to fly.

All operational Manchesters were painted in the standard matt black lower (to reduce detection by enemy searchlights) and camouflage upper (to blend in with the terrain when viewed from above).

EM was the marking for No. 207 Squadron, the first Manchester operator. Later in the war the squadron flew Lancasters, and then their replacement, the Avro Lincoln.

The nose gunner/bomb aimer sat in a powered turret with a pair of Browning 7.7-mm (.303 cal.) machine-guns. At night, the nose gunner rarely had to use his guns.

After flight trials, wing span was increased by 3.05 m (10 ft.). This wing was a sound design, being well able to accept a new engine configuration and absorbing massive battle damage.

The capacious bomb bay was one of the most useful Manchester features. It could accept the large RAF 1818-kg (4,000-lb.) 'Cookie' bomb that became a standard load for British bombers at night.

The rear gunner fired four Browning machine-guns. He was usually the most vital gunner, as night-fighters tended to attack from below and behind. He would call out evasive actions to the pilot if the aircraft came under attack.

### COMBAT DATA

**BOMB LOAD**

The Manchester's ability to deliver a respectable bomb load came at a cost to its performance. It could carry more than the Vickers Wellington, however. The Lancaster, which is widely regarded as the best four-engined night bomber of World War II, corrected all the mistakes of its Manchester forebear.

MANCHESTER Mk I
4695 kg (10,330 lb.)

WELLINGTON Mk III
2041 kg (4,490 lb.)

LANCASTER Mk I
6350 kg (13,970 lb.)

**MAXIMUM SPEED**

Though the Manchester was capable of a high speed compared to similar twin-engined bombers, its Vulture powerplants were unreliable and often resulted in the aircraft being lost because of mechanical failure. Rapid progress in engine development led to Bristol powerplants being installed in the Wellington.

MANCHESTER Mk I 426 km/h (264 m.p.h.)
WELLINGTON Mk III 378 km/h (234 m.p.h.)
LANCASTER Mk I 462 km/h (286 m.p.h.)

**RANGE**

Bombing missions during the war required that RAF aircraft be capable of crossing Europe to attack targets in Germany. Although the Manchester could reach these objectives, many were lost. The Lancaster, which improved the striking power of Bomber Command, owed much of its design to the earlier Manchester.

MANCHESTER Mk I 2623 km (1,625 mi.)
WELLINGTON Mk III 2478 km (1,535 mi.)
LANCASTER Mk I 4072 km (2,525 mi.)

## RAF bombers of 1939

■ **HAMPDEN Mk I:** The only RAF medium bomber at the start of the war, its poor defensive armament saw the aircraft reduced to second-line duties with Coastal Command squadrons.

■ **HARROW Mk II:** The first monoplane bomber to enter service with the Royal Air Force, the Harrow was introduced before World War II, but was quickly replaced by the Wellington.

■ **WELLINGTON Mk IC:** One of the first aircraft capable of bombing Germany, the Wellington was the work-horse of Bomber Commands during the raids early in World War II.

# AVRO
# LANCASTER

● Heavy bomber ● Dam-buster ● Delivered largest bomb of WWII

**B**ritain's greatest bomber of World War II was the Avro Lancaster, providing the backbone of the RAF's night assault on Germany. This four-engined heavy bomber carried and delivered a bigger bombload than any other bomber in the European theatre. From its first minelaying mission in 1942 to its final bombing sortie of 1945, the 'Lanc' was a formidable fighting machine. One aircraft even survived 140 combat missions over Germany.

▲ *Lancaster crews liked their aircraft, considering it superior to the previous Halifaxes and Stirlings. A total of 59 Royal Air Force squadrons flew the Lancaster on 156,000 combat sorties.*

## AVRO LANCASTER

◀ **'Window'**
*An electronic warfare Lancaster drops metal strips known as 'Window' to jam German radar.*

**Tail-end Charlie ▶**
*Usually the first victim of a night-fighter, rear gunners had an unenviable task and low survival rate.*

◀ **Low level**
*The Lancaster was not just a night-bomber. One of the first Lancaster missions was a daylight raid on the MAN works at Augsburg, flown at low level.*

▼ **Power turrets**
*The RAF fitted fast-acting power turrets to enable its bombers to defend themselves. Apart from an underside blindspot, the Lancaster was no easy meat for a fighter.*

▲ **Bridge buster supreme**
*The tough Bielefeld Viaduct survived many RAF attacks, but was finally smashed by Lancasters of the famous No. 617 Squadron, using 9979-kg (10-ton) 'Grand Slam' bombs.*

## FACTS AND FIGURES

➤ The Lancaster on display at the RAF Museum at Hendon near London flew 137 combat missions over Europe.

➤ The first Lancaster, a rebuilt Manchester, flew on 9 January 1941.

➤ The Lancaster could drop the massive 9979-kg (10-ton) 'Grand Slam' bomb.

➤ To bomb Japan, a long-range version with a 5455-litre (1,360-gal.) 'saddle' fuel tank atop its fuselage was tested but not needed.

➤ One 'Lanc' was rebuilt with the Bristol B.17 dorsal gun turret.

➤ France's Aeronavale was still flying maritime Lancasters into the 1950s.

# Britain's finest night-bomber

The Lancaster won immortality with the 'Dambusters'. Royal Air Force No. 617 Squadron, under Wing Commander Guy Gibson, used the new bomber for their 21 March 1943 low-level attacks on German dams using drum-like 4196-kg (9,230-lb.) bombs designed by Sir Barnes Wallis.

But the Lancaster was much more than a one-mission wonder. Developed from the unsatisfactory twin-engined Avro Manchester, it was one of the few warplanes in history to be 'right' from the start. It was so well-designed that only minor changes were made as production surged ahead through World War II. While Flying Fortresses and Liberators pounded Hitler's 'Fortress Europe' during the day, the Lancaster ruled the night. It was vulnerable to German fighters from below, but it was also fast and heavily armed, and it usually got through to the target.

The Lancaster served well in post-war years, sometimes in civil duties. The final military user was Canada. Today, the Royal Air Force still maintains one flying Lancaster, alongside Spitfires and Hurricanes, in the Battle of Britain Memorial Flight.

*The Lancaster possessed all the features desired by the RAF. It had a good ceiling, long range and enormous load capacity. And combat experience showed that it was tough, reliable and had reasonable defensive armament.*

## Lancaster B.Mk I

**Type:** seven-seat heavy bomber

**Powerplant:** four 1223-kW (1,750-hp.) Merlin 24 inverted inline piston engines

**Maximum speed:** 462 km/h (286 m.p.h.) at 3500 m (11,480 ft.)

**Range:** 2700 km (1,674 mi.) with 6350-kg (13,970-lb.) bombload

**Service ceiling:** 7467 m (24,492 ft.)

**Weights:** empty 16,783 kg (36,923 lb.); loaded 30,845 kg (67,859 lb.)

**Armament:** early production model, nine 7.7-mm (.303 cal.) Browning machine-guns plus up to 6350 kg (14,000 lb.) of bombs

**Dimensions:**
| | |
|---|---|
| span | 31.09 m (102 ft.) |
| length | 21.18 m (69 ft.) |
| height | 6.25 m (20 ft.) |
| wing area | 120.49 m² (1,296 sq. ft.) |

## LANCASTER B.MK I

'S-Sugar' served with No. 83 Squadron during 1942. It went on to fly 137 combat missions and is preserved in the Royal Air Force Museum.

The crew consisted of pilot, navigator, flight engineer, bomb-aimer/nose gunner, mid-upper gunner/radio operator and rear gunner.

The Lancaster's undercarriage retracted backwards into the inner engine nacelles. It was of simple but immensely tough construction.

The radio operator doubled as the mid-upper gunner, firing a pair of Browning 7.7-mm (.303 cal.) machine-guns from a powered turret.

The twin-tail layout gave the Lancaster great stability. The extra control surfaces could take massive damage and still leave the bomber flyable enough to get home.

The sting in the tail was provided by a four-gun turret. The tail gunner was the most isolated and vulnerable member of the crew.

The key to the Lancaster's success was its capacious bomb-bay, which could hold up to seven tons of bombs and, with modification, could house the massive 10-ton 'Grand Slam' semi-recessed under the fuselage.

Most Lancasters were powered by the same kind of Merlin engines as used in Spitfires, Hurricanes, Mosquitoes and Mustangs.

## COMBAT DATA

### CRUISING SPEED

| | |
|---|---|
| **LANCASTER** | 340 km/h (211 m.p.h.) |
| **B-17 FLYING FORTRESS** | 400 km/h (248 m.p.h.) |
| **B-24 LIBERATOR** | 350 km/h (217 m.p.h.) |

Since American bombers were expected to operate by day they were much more vulnerable to enemy defences than the Lancaster. Every step was taken to reduce that vulnerability, from heavy armour and armament to a higher speed than their British equivalents.

### RANGE

**LANCASTER**
4000 km (2,480 mi.) with 2000-kg (4,400-lb.) load
**B-17 FLYING FORTRESS**
5000 km (3,100 mi.) with 1000-kg (2,200-lb.) load
**B-24 LIBERATOR**
3500 km (2,170 mi.) with 2500-kg (5,500-lb.) load

The Lancaster had exceptional range when carrying a heavy load. The B-17 could go farther, but could not deliver as powerful a punch. A 'bombed-up' B-24 could not match the other two four-engined aircraft. However, with a light load and extra fuel it could go the farthest of them all, regularly mounting anti-U-Boat patrols into the middle of the Atlantic.

### NORMAL BOMBLOAD

| **LANCASTER** | **B-17 FLYING FORTRESS** | **B-24 LIBERATOR** |
|---|---|---|
| 6350 kg (13,970 lb.) | 2725 kg (5,995 lb.) | 3629 kg (7,984 lb.) |

Lancasters routinely operated with heavier bombloads than their contemporaries, and could carry the massive 9979-kg (21,954-lb.) 'Grand Slam' bomb. The B-17 Flying Fortress had a maximum bombload almost as high as the Lancaster, but rarely carried such weight, the USAF preferring to use surplus power to lift extra armour and defensive guns.

## The Dambusters Raid

It was one of the most spectacular missions of World War II. By the dead of night, RAF bombers mounted an attack on the Ruhr dams, whose associated power stations served Germany's greatest industrial complex. Smashing the Möhne and Sorpe Dams with the revolutionary bouncing bomb, designed by Sir Barnes Wallis, the chosen crews of No. 617 Squadron performed a low-level night attack of unbelievable precision. But although it disrupted German war production for some months, the raid had little permanent effect, and it cost the lives of 56 of the cream of British and Commonwealth aircrew.

The bomb used to attack the dams was a rotating cylinder, 127 cm (50 in.) in diameter and weighing 4196 kg (9,231 lb.). Bouncing across the water to hit the dam, the bomb then sank down the inner side of the structure, detonating well below the surface of the lake.

Precision flying was essential. The aircraft had to release its weapon between 370 and 410 m (1,214 and 1,345 ft.) from the target, while flying at exactly 402 km/h (249 m.p.h.) and at a height of 18.3 m (60 ft.) above the water.

# BACHEM
# BA 349 NATTER

● Rocket-powered ● Wooden construction ● Point defence

▲ After a number of pilotless Natter launches, the first manned flight took place on 28 February 1945. It ended fatally, but was followed by three successful tests.

**B**y the spring of 1944 the mounting pressure placed on the Luftwaffe's fighter force by the continuous stream of Allied bombers had reached a critical point. Germany could not survive unless the effect of these raids was rapidly reduced. A radical solution was sought, and the German air ministry issued a request for a machine which combined the capabilities of an interceptor aircraft and a missile. Bachem proposed the rocket-powered Ba 349 Natter (Adder).

## BACHEM BA 349 NATTER

**Museum piece ▶**
One Ba 349 survived Allied evaluation after the war. It is now in the Smithsonian in Washington, DC.

**▼ Fifty prototypes built in three months**
Unpowered gliding trials began in November 1944. They were so successful that powered launching began the following month.

**▼ On the gantry**
Natters blasted off from a 6-m (20-ft.) vertical gantry. Three channelled rails guided the wings and the lower fin.

**First manned flight ▶**
Oberleutnant L. Siebert died during the first manned flight. After launch the canopy blew off, probably knocking him out.

**▼ Rocket armament**
The Ba 349's primary weapons were the 24 Hs 217 rockets housed in the nose.

## FACTS AND FIGURES

➤ Erich Bachem had first proposed his rocket-powered interceptor in 1939 but received little official encouragement.

➤ For the first unpowered flight, the Natter was carried to 5500 m (18,000 ft.) beneath an He 111.

➤ Unmanned test launches were carried out with a dummy pilot in the cockpit.

➤ The improved Ba 349B had a rocket motor of increased endurance, but only three were produced before VE Day.

➤ To fire the salvo of unguided rockets the pilot ejected the Natter's nosecone.

➤ To prevent them falling into Allied hands all but four of the Ba 349s were blown up.

## PROFILE

# Germany's desperate defender

Four companies submitted designs to meet the German air ministry's demand for a small point interceptor and Bachem's Ba 349 was eventually chosen for evaluation. This was mainly due to the intervention of SS leader Heinrich Himmler, who was looking for ways to increase his influence in the armed forces.

With Germany's industry suffering from Allied raids it was necessary for the Natter to be built from wood and be of simple construction, allowing rapid and economical production.

The final Ba 349 design was essentially that of a manned surface-to-air missile. Launched from a vertical rail, the Natter would continue to climb vertically, controlled by an autopilot, using its main rocket engine and additional power from rocket boosters. As the aircraft reached a bomber formation, the pilot would resume control and make a firing pass using unguided rockets. The aircraft would then descend to an altitude of 1400 m (4,600 ft.) and the nose section would separate from the fuselage. The pilot would release

*Left: A pilotless Ba 349 is prepared for the first vertical launch on 18 December 1944.*

himself and descend, along with the fuselage, by parachute.

Of 36 airframes built, only 10 reached operational status. These never saw combat, however, but were blown up as American land forces approached their base.

*Above: This Ba 349A is mounted on a trailer which was used to transport the aircraft to the launching ramp. In the foreground is one of the Schmidding solid-fuel booster rockets, four of which were attached to the rear fuselage.*

Above the nose was a ring sight for the nose-mounted rocket armament, which was covered by a jettisonable plastic fairing before launch. Twin 30-mm (1.18-in.) MK 108 cannon were proposed but never fitted.

Protection for Natter pilots was of major importance, with sandwich-type armour being fitted on all four sides. Instrumentation in the cockpit was spartan. Plans to fit an ejection seat were rejected because of space constraints.

The main engine was a variant of that fitted to the Messerschmitt Me 163 interceptor. For vertical launch four booster rockets were added, which burned during the first 10 seconds of flight.

Cruciform fins on the rear fuselage carried the control surfaces. Elevators and rudders, operating differentially, provided roll control.

The fuselage was constructed of wood. The only metal parts were control push rods, hinges and load-supporting attachment points.

Originally it was envisaged that the Natter would make ramming attacks on bomber formations once it had expended its rockets. This would have necessitated fitting an ejection seat for the pilot, but the idea was abandoned and a jettisonable nose was fitted instead.

### BA 349A NATTER

This example is one of an estimated 20 Ba 349As completed by early 1945. Ten of these aircraft were set up for operations at Kirchheim, close to the Wolf Hirth production factory.

---

### Ba 349A Natter

**Type:** single-seat semi-expendable interceptor

**Powerplant:** one 19.62-kN (3,748-lb.-thrust) Walter HWK 509C-1 bi-fuel rocket motor, plus four 4.9-kN (2,640-lb.-thrust) Schmidding 109-533 solid-fuel rockets

**Maximum speed:** 998 km/h (619 m.p.h.) at 5000 m (16,400 ft.)

**Initial climb rate:** 11,400 m/min (36,415 f.p.m.)

**Combat radius:** 40 km (25 mi.) at 12,000 m (39,400 ft.)

**Weights:** loaded 2200 kg (4,850 lb.)

**Armament:** 24 x 73-mm (2.9-in.) Hs 217 Föhn rockets

**Dimensions:**
| | | |
|---|---|---|
| span | 3.60 m | (11 ft. 10 in.) |
| length | 6.10 m | (20 ft.) |
| wing area | 2.75 m² | (30 sq. ft.) |

---

### COMBAT DATA

#### MAXIMUM SPEED

Powered by the same engine as the Messerschmitt Me 163, the Natter's lighter and more streamlined form gave it an edge in performance, pushing the aircraft close to the sound barrier. The Bolkhovitinov BI was the world's first rocket-powered fighter and had startling performance.

| | |
|---|---|
| Ba 349B-1a NATTER | 998 km/h (619 m.p.h.) |
| Me 163B-1a KOMET | 960 km/h (595 m.p.h.) |
| BI | 1000 km/h (620 m.p.h.) |

#### CLIMB RATE

With its main rocket engine plus booster rockets the Natter had an amazing rate of climb from the vertical position. The g forces sustained were so great that the aircraft had to be controlled by autopilot during the ascent.

| Ba 349B-1a NATTER | Me 163B-1a KOMET | BI |
|---|---|---|
| 11,400 m/min (36,415 f.p.m.) | 5000 m/min (16,400 f.p.m.) | 4980 m/min (16,335 f.p.m.) |

#### ENDURANCE

Both the Natter and the Me 163 were designed as point interceptors and had exceptionally short endurance. This meant that they were only capable of making one firing pass on an enemy formation.

| Ba 349B-1a NATTER | Me 163B-1a KOMET | BI |
|---|---|---|
| 4 min 22sec | 7min 30sec | 15 min |

---

## Operational Natter missions

**1 LAUNCH:** If the Natter had ever been used operationally it would have been launched from a vertical rail to accelerate rapidly to its operational height guided by an autopilot.

**2 INTERCEPTION:** On reaching the enemy bomber formation the Natter pilot would eject the nose cone and fire a salvo of unguided rockets.

**3 DESCENT:** When the rocket fuel was exhausted the Natter would make an unpowered descent to 1400 m (4,600 ft.).

**4 TOUCHDOWN:** The pilot would then jettison the nose section using explosive bolts and release himself from the fuselage. Both the pilot and the rear fuselage would then descend to the ground by parachute.

# BELL

# P-39 AIRACOBRA

● **Tricycle undercarriage** ● **Mid-engined design** ● **Soviet service**

▲ *The most remarkable feature of the P-39 was its mid-mounted engine, which drove the propeller via a long driveshaft. The main reason for adopting this layout was so that the aircraft could carry the massive 37-mm (1.46-in.) cannon.*

**A** revolutionary design, the Airacobra had its engine located behind the pilot and was one of the world's first single-seat fighters to feature a tricycle landing gear. But due to the pace of fighter development in the early 1940s the P-39 was rapidly outclassed. It fought well against heavy odds in the early days of World War II in the Pacific and later won high praise from Russia, which used its cannon to destroy German ground targets.

---

## BELL P-39 AIRACOBRA

### BELL P-39 AIRACOBRA

**P-39 in the Pacific ▶**
*The Airacobra performed well in the Pacific against Japanese opposition. It was mainly used for ground-attack missions.*

**▼ Car door**
*Another unusual feature of the P-39 was the side-opening, car-style door.*

**◀ Cannon armed**
*The barrel for the mighty 37-mm (1.46-in) cannon protruded through the propeller spinner.*

**▼ Post-war racer**
*At the end of World War II, several P-39s were snapped up at rock-bottom prices and modified for air racing.*

**▲ USAAF fighter**
*When the US entered the war in 1941, the P-39 was the best fighter they had available. A few flew in Europe with the USAAF, but they were outclassed by German fighters and were replaced by Spitfires.*

---

## FACTS AND FIGURES

➤ The Airacobra was the first US single-seat fighter with a nosewheel to enter service.

➤ The prototype Bell XP-39 made its first flight on 6 April 1939.

➤ Russian forces took delivery of about 5000 P-39s during World War II.

➤ Although designed as a fighter, Soviet forces used the P-39 for ground attack, with great success.

➤ The RAF ordered 675 Airacobras, but only one squadron was ever equipped.

➤ P-39s were operated by the Italian Co-Belligerent Air Force during 1944.

**PROFILE**

# Mid-engined attacker

One of many pre-war innovations explored by the Bell Aircraft Company, the Airacobra appeared to be fast and heavily armed when it was first produced. Its engine, 'buried' in the fuselage behind the pilot's seat, was fitted with an extension shaft to the propeller running under the cockpit. A tricycle undercarriage and a 37-mm (1.46-in.) cannon were also incorporated.

When war came in 1939, RAF tests revealed that the P-39's overall performance did not match that of British fighters. This and the fact that the Airacobra's unusual systems could prove unreliable caused it to be rejected for service.

In the Pacific, the USAAF had to use any available fighters and the outclassed Airacobras were thrown into war sorties against the Japanese during 1942/43. American pilots also flew it during the early combat operations in the Middle East.

Bell improved the aircraft, and when US fighter groups re-equipped with other types many Airacobras were passed to the Red air force, where the 'Little Shaver' proved very popular. 'Shaving' was Russian pilot slang for ground strafing, and the P-39 soon earned great respect as a destroyer of German tanks and vehicles.

Airacobra pilots stencilled dozens of tiny stars on their machines to show how adept the 'Lend-Lease' American fighter was at this deadly and dangerous task. The P-39 was also flown by Italian and French pilots during the war.

*Above: Although its performance could not match that of fighters such as the Spitfire, the P-39 had respectable figures and good manoeuvrability.*

*Left: If the RAF had only retained the P-39 with its original turbocharged engine, it might have found a winner. Instead, it was discarded due to chronic unreliability.*

Chief armament of the P-39 was the 37-mm (1.46-in.) M4 cannon, fed by a belt-type magazine holding 30 rounds. British Airacobras had a 20-mm (0.79-in.) cannon instead.

The pilot sat in an extremely well-protected cockpit, surrounded by armour to protect him from bullets. This was especially useful in the ground-attack role.

A large percentage of the 9,558 Airacobras built wore the Soviet red star. These were usually assigned to the elite Guards regiments.

The engine was mounted immediately behind the pilot's seat, and a long shaft ran under the seat, through the cockpit to a gearbox below the propeller shaft.

In addition to the main cannon, the Airacobra had a pair of 12.7-mm (.303 cal.) machine-guns in the top of the forward fuselage. The P-39Q could carry two more 12.7-mm guns in underwing pods.

Due to the cannon and engine installation, Bell had to design a tricycle undercarriage, the first in an operational fighter.

## P-39N AIRACOBRA

The Airacobra played an important part in World War II, notably in the hands of Soviet pilots. The Soviet air force not only found the type ideal for tank busting but also in the air-to-air role.

## COMBAT DATA

### MAXIMUM SPEED

The late-model P-39N restored some of the lost performance of the early P-39s by having a more powerful engine. It was no better than a Bf 109, however, and grossly inferior to the excellent Yak 9.

| | |
|---|---|
| P-39N AIRACOBRA | 642 km/h (400 m.p.h.) |
| Bf 109G | 623 km/h (386 m.p.h.) |
| Yak 9 | 700 km/h (434 m.p.h.) |

### SERVICE CEILING

Soviet fighters were almost invariably better at low altitude, and the P-39 was thus markedly superior to the Yak 9 at altitude. It was equivalent to the Bf-109G, which was a good performer at height.

| P-39N AIRACOBRA | Bf 109G | Yak 9 |
|---|---|---|
| 11,735 m (38,500 ft.) | 11,750 m (38,550 ft.) | 10,950 m (35,900 ft.) |

### ARMAMENT

The P-39's cannon was a single-shot killer, even to tanks. The use of a single, large cannon and two smaller guns was popular with Soviet and German designers but not the British or Americans.

P-39N AIRACOBRA
4 x 7.62-mm (.30 cal.) MGs
2 x 12.7-mm (.50 cal.) MGs
1 X 37-mm (1.46-in.) cannon

Bf 109G
2 x 7.92-mm (0.31-in.) MGs
2 x 20-mm (0.79-in.) cannon
1 x 30-mm (1.18-in.) cannon

Yak 9
2 x 12.7-mm (.50 cal.) MGs
1 x 23-mm (0.9-in.) cannon

## Modified Airacobras

■ **NAVAL XFL-1:** The XFL-1 Airabonita was a naval variant with a tailwheel, strengthened fuselage and arrester hook. It was not adopted by the US Navy due to unsuccessful trials.

■ **V-TAIL:** An experimental trial of tail surfaces combining elevator and rudder functions was not used in service, as it reduced the P-39's excellent handling.

■ **SQUARE TAIL:** This trials XP-39E's square-cut wing and tailfin was also not adopted. Powered by an Allison V-1710-47, its tail bore a strong resemblance to that of a Mustang.

■ **AIR RACER:** This P-39, registration N40A, was owned privately and based in Orange County, California. It was painted red and white with blue trim, and flew frequently.

# BELL

# P-63 KINGCOBRA

● Close-support fighter ● Huge exports ● Airacobra development

▲ Although not one of the most successful wartime fighters, the Kingcobra operated successfully in the close-support and attack roles. It saw most service with Soviet forces and was formidably armed and armoured.

**C**reated as an improved version of the Bell P-39 Airacobra, the P-63 Kingcobra retained the tricycle landing gear of the earlier type, a nose cannon and an engine mounted behind the pilot driving the propeller through a long shaft. Like the P-39, it also had a car-type door for access to the cockpit. Unfortunately, the P-63 never measured up to the top wartime fighters, like the P-51, Bf 109 and Zero.

## BELL P-63 KINGCOBRA

### ▼ Silver Kingcobra
Of the few P-63s which remained in the United States, some were used for test and training duties. The majority of the rest went to the USSR.

### ▲ Nose guns
Most P-63s had twin 12.7-mm (.50 cal.) machine-guns installed in the upper engine cowling.

### ▼ Experimental variants
Two XP-63Ns were flown with 'butterfly' tails. One was modified after the war to L-39-1 standard and flew swept-wing tests for the US Navy.

### ▲ Lend-Lease to Russia
Fitted with underwing drop-tanks, this P-63A flying with the Soviet air force is typical of the 2400, or more, delivered under the Lend-Lease programme.

### Allison power ▶
Removal of the engine access panels from this preserved P-63A reveals the 12-cylinder Allison V-1710 engine mounted behind the cockpit.

## FACTS AND FIGURES

➤ A Kingcobra on display in San Antonio, Texas, survived use as a frangible bullet target during 1946.

➤ More than 3300 Kingcobras, in half a dozen versions, were produced.

➤ The first Kingcobra prototype made its initial flight on 7 December 1942.

➤ During the Korean War, some American pilots said that they had encountered P-63s flown by North Koreans.

➤ Both prototypes were lost in mishaps early in the flight test programme.

➤ About 2400 Kingcobras were turned over to the Soviet Union.

## PROFILE

# Close-support over Europe

A US Army Air Force (USAAF) order for two prototypes in June 1941 launched the P-63 Kingcobra. Further prototypes followed before deliveries of the first production version began in October 1943.

It quickly became clear that the P-63 was not advanced enough for front-line service, and the majority of Kingcobras were delivered to the Soviet Union under the Lend-Lease programme. A significant number also went to Free French forces, and a single example was delivered to the RAF. Several were used as flying testbeds.

The P-63 was a low-wing design which served American forces well in a training capacity but was never used by them in combat. The Kingcobra was not an easy aircraft to fly, however, especially in the circuit pattern around an airfield, and pilots never bestowed on it the affection they extended to the Mustang, Thunderbolt and Hellcat.

Kingcobras were given a variety of second-line duties. In one of the most unusual, known as Project Pinball, modified, armoured Kingcobras acted as manned targets for gunnery exercises by fighters shooting frangible bullets.

*Above: At least 300 P-63s were delivered to the Free French Armée de l'Air. This is a P-63C with its distinctive ventral fin.*

*Below: All aircraft up to the P-63A-5 were fitted with a centre-section rack but had no wing racks. The four 12.7-mm (.50 cal.) machine-guns were supplemented by a 37-mm (1.46-in.) cannon in the nose.*

## P-63A KINGCOBRA

One of a large number of P-63A and P-63C Kingcobras supplied to the Soviet air force during World War II, this P-63A-9 was fitted with an M10 (instead of an M4) hub cannon and additional armour.

### P-63A Kingcobra

**Type:** fighter and ground attack aircraft

**Powerplant:** one 988-kW (1,325-hp.) Allison V-1710-93 liquid-cooled 12-cylinder Vee piston engine driving a four-bladed propeller

**Maximum speed:** 660 km/h (409 m.p.h.) at 7620 m (25,000 ft.)

**Cruising speed:** 608 km/h (377 m.p.h.)

**Range:** 724 km (450 mi.)

**Service ceiling:** 13,106 m (43,200 ft.)

**Weights:** empty 2892 kg (6,932 lb.); maximum take-off 4763 kg (10,479 lb.)

**Armament:** one 37-mm (1.46-in.) cannon and four fixed forward-firing 12.7-mm (.50 cal.) machine-guns, plus up to three 237-kg (520-lb.) bombs or six rocket projectiles dependent on the sub-variant

**Dimensions:**
| | | |
|---|---|---|
| span | 11.68 m | (38 ft. 4 in.) |
| length | 9.96 m | (32 ft. 8 in.) |
| height | 3.84 m | (12 ft. 7 in.) |
| wing area | 23.04 m² | (248 sq. ft.) |

Unlike other fighters, the P-63 did not have a hinged or sliding canopy. The pilot entered the cockpit via a car-type door on the port side.

An Allison V-1710 engine drove the four-bladed propeller of the P-63A via a long extension shaft. This ran forwards through the cockpit and between the pilot's legs.

This large intake above the rear fuselage fed air to the carburettor. Placing the engine behind the pilot seemed, on paper, to offer many advantages. Instead it created a number of engineering problems and did not provide the hoped-for performance benefits.

Twin 12.7-mm (.50 cal.) machine-guns were mounted in the upper nose.

The powerful nose armament was completed by the 37-mm (1.46-in.) cannon, which fired through the spinner. Sub-types up to the P-63A-8 carried only thirty 37-mm rounds.

Streamlined fairings covered the underwing machine-guns. Starting with the P-63A-6, underwing hardpoints were fitted.

Aircraft fitted with only the centreline hardpoint could carry a single 237-kg (520-lb.) bomb. Alternatively, a 341-litre (90-gal.) or 796-litre (200-gal.) fuel tank could be fitted. Later aircraft carried more weapons; the A-9 and A-10 variants complementing this with 28 extra rounds of 37-mm (1.46-in.) ammunition.

The P-63 had a taller, more angular tail than the P-39 Airacobra. The P-63's configuration, including its laminar flow wing, was largely tested on the experimental XP-39E.

### COMBAT DATA

#### MAXIMUM SPEED

The P-63A was much faster than the P-40N Warhawk, since the Curtiss fighter was nearing the end of its development potential. The P-63 was much slower than, arguably, the greatest US fighter of World War II, the North American P-51D Mustang.

| | |
|---|---|
| P-63A KINGCOBRA | 660 km/h (409 m.p.h.) |
| P-51D MUSTANG | 721 km/h (447 m.p.h.) |
| P-40N WARHAWK | 609 km/h (378 m.p.h.) |

#### RANGE

North American achieved exceptional range with the P-51, while Curtiss always struggled with the P-40 design. The P-63 was optimised for the ground attack role and, as such, was unlikely to be required to fly long-range escort or fighter missions. It had adequate range for the close-support role.

P-63A KINGCOBRA 724 km (450 mi.)
P-51D MUSTANG 2092 km (1,297 mi.)
P-40N WARHAWK 386 km (250 mi.)

#### ARMAMENT

Both the P-40 and P-51 adopted ground attack as a secondary role and were therefore able to carry fewer bombs than the P-63A. The Kingcobra also featured a powerful spinner-mounted cannon.

| P-63A KINGCOBRA | P-51D MUSTANG | P-40N WARHAWK |
|---|---|---|
| 1 x 37-mm (1.46-in.) cannon 4 x 12.7-mm (.50 cal.) machine-guns | 6 x 12.7-mm (.50 cal.) machine-guns | 6 x 12.7-mm (.50 cal.) machine-guns |
| 681-kg (1,500-lb.) bombload | 454-kg (1,000-lb.) bombload | 227-kg (500-lb.) bombload |

## Bell fighters of the 1940s

■ **P-39 AIRACOBRA:** Designed as a highly manoeuvrable fighter, the radical P-39 proved to be a disappointment. It matured into an effective ground attack aircraft, however.

■ **P-59 AIRACOMET:** Planned as a contemporary of the Gloster E.28/39 and He 178, the P-59 did not in fact fly until after the Me 262 and Meteor. It was America's first jet fighter.

■ **XP-77:** Using pre-war racing aircraft design as a basis, Bell produced this lightweight wooden fighter prototype. It failed to achieve acceptable performance.

# BLOHM UND VOSS

# BV 138

● Flying-boat ● Air-sea rescue ● Maritime patrol

**T**he Blohm und Voss BV 138 was crucial to Germany's naval war effort. It was the brainchild of Dr Ing Richard Vogt, and although it suffered from initial structural weaknesses the BV 138 had a successful career as a maritime patrol aircraft and anti-ship bomber. Despite extensive problems with the initial design, the BV 138 eventually proved to be a capable machine and was later adapted for minesweeping.

▲ Although it finally emerged as a useful design, the BV 138 had a problematic start and came close to being abandoned. It served from the Black Sea to the fringes of the Arctic Circle.

# BLOHM UND VOSS **BV 138**

**▲ Sweeping circle**
With its guns removed, the BV 138MS (nicknamed the mouse-catching aircraft) was used to sweep canals for mines.

**▲ Water jump**
Early BV 138s had alarming handling on water. Hull drag was excessive, making take off a prolonged business.

**▼ First missions**
The Luftwaffe was so short of floatplanes that it impressed the first two BV 138s into service for the Norwegian campaign.

**▲ Black Sea patrol**
BV 138s flew patrols in the Black Sea as late as 1944 from bases in Romania, with protection from Romanian escort fighters.

**Back to the drawing board ▶**
The Ha 138V2 was the second prototype. With enlarged tail surfaces it handled better than the original aircraft but still suffered from vibration problems. A complete redesign was recommended by the Air Ministry technical office.

## FACTS AND FIGURES

➤ A BV 138 was one of the last planes to leave Berlin on 1 May 1945, taking off from a lake with wounded troops.

➤ In 1941 a BV 138 shot down an RAF Catalina over the North Sea.

➤ Convoy PQ-18 was the first to fight off shadowing BV 138s with Sea Hurricanes.

➤ This seaplane was nicknamed 'Der Fliegende Holzschuh' (The Flying Clog) when it appeared as a prototype in 1937.

➤ The prototype, known then as the Ha 138, first flew on 15 July 1937.

➤ As late as the summer of 1944 BV 138s flew anti-ship missions in the Black Sea.

# PROFILE

# Germany's hunchback

The BV 138 was handicapped by not being strong enough to withstand the battering of prolonged operation on the open seas, and the prototype had to be extensively redesigned after showing severe instability on the water. After major modifications, the aircraft entered squadron service in 1940, initially proving unreliable. However, the aircraft's problems were later solved and it went on to provide good service, flying important naval reconnaissance missions against Allied convoys, especially in the Atlantic and Barents Sea. Two

BV 138s even operated from the frozen wastes of Novaya Zemlya with the support of U-boats.

In addition to shore bases, BV 138s flew from seaplane tenders, some modified with catapults for launch. All BV 138s were able to use assisted take-off rockets and some carried FuG 200 Hohentwiel radar for shadowing convoys. The BV 138 could even fight off Allied fighters, as one crew showed by downing a Blenheim over Norway. The final version was fitted with a giant electromagnetic ring for triggering magnetic mines.

*One of the BV 138's main problems was the centrally mounted engine which suffered exhaust blockages.*

Although its enclosed cockpit was an improvement on rival designs, the prototype's crew stations were criticised as being inadequate for long patrols.

With the increases in weight caused by structural modifications, the BV 138 was considered somewhat underpowered. This was remedied in the BV 138B-1 by the installation of Jumo 205D engines.

Wing construction was all-metal with a tubular main spar. It was built in three sections.

## BV 138C-1

The BV 138 equipped the Luftwaffe's See Aufklarungsgruppen, serving in the coastal patrol and reconnaissance role.

Nose armament was especially effective, with a power-operated turret mounting a 20-mm (0.79-in.) MG FF cannon. The BV 138B-1 used the faster firing MG 151 cannon.

One of the BV 138's best features was its flying controls. These were hydraulically operated and fabric covered, making the aircraft easy to fly.

Production aircraft had rectangular section stressed-skin metal tail booms replacing the earlier tubular booms. They suffered from vibration problems, which in turn caused crew fatigue.

The biggest fault was the hull design, which was not sufficiently strong to withstand the stresses imposed by rough seas at maximum load.

## BV 138C-1

**Type:** reconnaissance flying-boat

**Powerplant:** three 656-kW (880-hp.) Junkers Jumo 205D inline piston engines

**Maximum speed:** 285 km/h (177 m.p.h.) at sea level

**Cruising speed:** 235 km/h (146 m.p.h.)

**Range:** 5000 km (3,107 mi.)

**Service ceiling:** 5000 m (16,400 ft.)

**Weights:** empty 11,770 kg (25,948 lb.); maximum take-off 17,650 kg (38,912 lb.)

**Armament:** one 20-mm (0.79-in.) MG 151 cannon in the bow turret, one 13-mm (0.51-in.) MG 131 machine-gun at the rear centre engine nacelle and one 7.92-mm (0.31-in.) MG 15 firing through starboard hatch; three 50-kg (110-lb.) bombs under starboard wingroot, or six 50-kg (110-lb.) bombs or four 150-kg (330-lb.) depth charges (BV 138C-1/U1)

**Dimensions:**
| | | |
|---|---|---|
| span | 27.00 m | (88 ft. 7 in.) |
| length | 19.90 m | (65 ft. 3 in.) |
| height | 5.90 m | (19 ft. 4 in.) |
| wing area | 112 m² | (1,206 sq. ft.) |

## COMBAT DATA

### ARMAMENT

Cannon armament made attacking a BV 138 a hazardous task, as the nose gunner occupied a powered turret and had an excellent field of fire. In comparison the He 115 and the Walrus were easy targets for a fighter pilot and neither usually carried bombs.

**BV 138C-1** — 1 x 20-mm (0.79-in.) cannon, 1 x 7.92-mm (0.31-in.) MG, 1 x 13-mm (0.51-in.) MG, 4 x 150-kg (330-lb.) bombs

**He 115** — 2 x 7.92-mm (0.31-in.) MGs, 2 x 250-kg (550-lb.) bombs

**WALRUS** — 2 x 7.7-mm (.303 cal.) MGs, up to 345 kg (760 lb.) of bombs

### RANGE

The BV 138 was much larger than the He 115 or the Walrus, and its capacious if ungainly fuselage held a large amount of fuel. The Walrus was a short-range aircraft, used for coastal air-sea rescue duties or for launching from warships for spotting the fall of gunfire. This range was for unladen aircraft; the weight of the minesweeping ring made the BV 138MS version less capable.

**BV 138C-1** 5000 km (3,107 mi.)

**He 115** 2000 km (1,240 mi.)

**WALRUS** 1000 km (621 mi.)

## BV 138 missions

**AIR-SEA RESCUE:** At the start of the war the Luftwaffe was notably more efficient than the RAF at rescuing its shot-down aircrew. Pilots had excellent survival equipment.

**PICK-UP:** One of the last BV 138 sorties of the war was to a lake in Berlin. The pilot picked up 10 wounded soldiers and escaped back to Denmark.

**CONVOY PATROL:** BV 138s spotted the location of Allied convoys, giving position reports to U-boat Wolf Packs. The British replied by using Sea Hurricanes in defence, rocket-launched from ships.

**MINE SWEEP:** Using a powerful magnetic signal, the BV 138MS could set off enemy mines which were often dropped in canals.

# BLOHM UND VOSS

# BV 222 WIKING

● Airliner design ● Huge capacity ● Transport and patrol service

▲ During 1942 BV 222s were engaged on supply missions to North Africa. From Greek and Italian bases the aircraft flew to Tobruk or Derna, and often returned carrying casualties.

**D**eutsche Lufthansa (DLH) ordered three Blohm und Voss BV 222 Wiking (Viking) aircraft in September 1939 to fill a requirement for a new 24-berth transatlantic airliner. The first of these made its initial flight in September 1940; by then World War II had started and DLH no longer had a use for the type. Possible military roles were investigated and the following July BV 222 V1 made its first supply flight, the first of many sorties for the Luftwaffe.

## PHOTO FILE

## BLOHM UND VOSS BV 222 WIKING

**Responsive controls ▶**
Flight tests proved that the BV 222 handled well in flight. The only drawbacks were slight directional instability and a tendency to porpoise whilst taxiing.

**▲ Diesel power**
The long-range reconnaissance BV 222C was powered by six Jumo 207C diesel engines.

**▼ Submarine support**
In May 1943 BV 222 V5 was transferred to south-west France for U-boat support duties.

**▲ Defensive sting**
After two BV 222As were lost to Allied fighters in 1942, the bow gun position (seen here) was removed and more powerful armament installed including unusual wing-mounted turrets.

**Diverted to the Luftwaffe ▶**
Rolled out in August 1940, the prototype BV 222 carried a civilian registration. The aircraft was acquired by the Luftwaffe and began operations in July 1941.

## FACTS AND FIGURES

➤ Production time of a complete BV 222 airframe (less engines and equipment) totalled 35,000 man hours.

➤ Slow and vulnerable, a number of BV 222s were shot down by RAF fighters.

➤ Towards the end of World War II, Wikings reverted solely to transport roles.

➤ By the end of 1942 Wikings had carried more than 1400 tonnes (1,377 tons) of cargo, 17,000 troops and 2400 casualties in the Mediterranean.

➤ Seven BV 222s survived the war; two were flown to the US for evaluation.

➤ In October 1943 a Wiking shot down an RAF Lancaster bomber over the Atlantic.

## PROFILE

# Giant German flying boat

Powered by six BMW-Bramo Fafnir 323R radial engines, the giant Wiking was the largest flying-boat to see service during the war.

The first prototype (BV 222 V1) made its first cargo flight to Norway in July 1941 and later flew supplies to the Afrika Korps in North Africa. The subsequent V2 and V3 were armed with machine guns in various positions on the fuselage and wings for defence. By late 1942, five more pre-production Wikings had entered service

and, with the first three aircraft, equipped the specially-formed Luft-Transportstaffel (See) 222.

With interest in the BV 222 as a long-range reconnaissance aircraft growing, a number of the flying-boats were refitted, receiving search and rear-warning radar equipment and powered gun turrets. Soon they were in service from bases in the Bay of Biscay, for Atlantic U-boat co-operation flights.

Meanwhile, in April 1943, BV 222 V7 made its first flight, powered by six Junkers Jumo

207C diesels. This became the prototype for the BV 222C, which entered production at the Blohm und Voss plant near Hamburg. Five were delivered to maritime patrol units in 1943; four others remained uncompleted.

*Above: The stabilising floats retracted to lie flush with the outer wing panel. This example has its floats lowered in preparation for landing.*

*Above: BV 222A-0 V8 is seen here testing its engines on a launching ramp. It was shot down by RAF Beaufighters on 10 December 1942.*

---

The flight crew consisted of two pilots, two flight engineers, a navigator and a wireless operator. To help the pilot on longer missions an autopilot system was fitted to a three-section elevator. The pilot controlled the outer and inner sections with the autopilot controlling the central section.

Armament was upgraded a number of times although, even with its most powerful arrangement, the aircraft was still vulnerable to fighters. Upgraded BV 222As had the unusual arrangement of two turrets mounted in the wings aft of the outer engine nacelle each armed with a single 20-mm (0.79-in) cannon.

The main passenger/cargo portion of the hull was very spacious thanks to the lack of bulkheads. The bulkheads were fitted between the keel and the floor.

### BV 222A-0 WIKING

This BV 222 flew transport sorties from Petsamo, Finland during the early months of 1943. The yellow bands signify that the aircraft was operating in the Eastern Front theatre.

Of all-metal construction, the two-step hull was covered by corrosion-resisting alloy sheet which varied from 3 mm to 5 mm (⅛ to ¼ in.) in thickness. It was divided into two sections, the lower for passengers/cargo and the upper for the flight crew.

The all-metal wings were supported by a single, immensely strong, wing spar measuring 145 cm (4 ft. 9 in.) in diameter. The spar was sub-divided to contain six fuel tanks.

The fin and rudder were large and, after initial problems, provided good directional stability. The rudder was operated by two interconnected tabs driven by the main circuit. The elevator was mounted near the base of the fin.

## COMBAT DATA

### MAXIMUM SPEED

With six engines, the BV 222 was by far the most powerful of the German World War II seaplanes. This power translated into a healthy maximum speed for an aircraft of this type. It was faster than the RAF's closest equivalent, the Short Sunderland.

| | |
|---|---|
| BV 222C WIKING | 390 km/h (242 m.p.h.) |
| BV 138B | 289 km/h (180 m.p.h.) |
| Ju 52/3mW | 262 km/h (163 m.p.h.) |

### OPERATIONAL RANGE

Designed for the long-range maritime patrol role, the BV 222C had much greater range than the BV 138 and Ju 52 floatplane which were intended to patrol coastal waters. The BV 222C actually had a shorter range than the BV 222A as fuel capacity was decreased with the installation of the Junkers Jumo diesel-powered engines.

BV 222C WIKING 6095 km (3,787 mi.)

BV 138B 3878 km (2,410 mi.)

Ju 52/3mW 1496 km (930 mi.)

### CREW CAPACITY

As the largest flying boat to reach operational status in any country during World War II, the BV 222 was capable of carrying a large crew. Eight of the crew were gunners.

BV 222C WIKING 14

BV 138B 5

Ju 52/3mW 3

## Blohm und Voss seaplanes

■ **BV 138:** The first flying-boat design to be built by the company, the BV 138 was used in a variety of roles during World War II including reconnaissance and mine-sweeping.

■ **Ha 139:** Designed to meet a requirement for a transatlantic mailplane, the Ha 139 was pressed into Luftwaffe service late in 1939. Three examples were operated until 1942.

■ **Ha 140:** In 1935 design work began on the Ha 140 which was to compete directly with the Heinkel He 115 as a torpedo and reconnaissance floatplane. It did not win the orders.

■ **BV 238:** The giant BV 238 was to have been built in both sea and landplane versions. Only one example flew and this was sunk at its moorings by USAAF P-51 Mustangs.

# BOEING

## B-17 FLYING FORTRESS (EARLY)

● Heavy bomber ● Maritime defence ● Early wartime service

**R**olled out in 1935, the B-17 Flying Fortress represented something very new at a time when many bombers in service with the world's air forces were either biplanes, twin-engined monoplanes or slow, lumbering types. The B-17 was sold to the US Congress as a coastal patrol aircraft to guard approaches to isolated North America. However, America was not isolated for long and the B-17 was soon to develop into a crucial weapon.

▲ *The B-17 was designed to meet an exacting USAAC specification calling for an aircraft which was capable of 400 km/h (250 mph) over a range of 3540 km (2000 miles) when carrying a 907-kg (2000-lb) bombload.*

## BOEING B-17 FLYING FORTRESS (EARLY)

▼ **In war paint**
*From March 1941 army depots applied olive drab and grey paint to their B-17Cs and Ds. By the time the US entered World War II, all the aircraft been painted. These early versions were relegated to training duties by 1944.*

▲ **The $432,034 gamble**
*For Boeing, a company of just 600 employees, the money spent in building the revolutionary Model 299 prototype represented a huge gamble.*

◄ **Flying Fortresses over the 'Big Apple'**
*Six of the 13 YB-17 (later redesignated Y1B-17) test airframes are seen here over New York. Although similar to the Model 299 prototype, they had different engines and carried six crew.*

▼ **Newly delivered D-model**
*The third B-17 production model was the B-17D, which differed from the B-17C only in having engine cowling flaps and an extra crewmember. Forty-two were built in all.*

◄ **RAF Fortress Mk I**
*This RAF Fortress carries the serial AM528, erroneously applied in place of the intended AN528. Twenty of 38 Fortress Mk Is, which were ordered as training aircraft, were delivered in 1941.*

### FACTS AND FIGURES

➤ RAF Fortresses later flew anti-shipping missions in the Middle East and with Coastal Command in the UK until 1943.

➤ The first B-17s were delivered to the 2nd Bomb Wing at Langley Field in 1937.

➤ RAF experience over Europe resulted in better armament on later variants.

➤ On 8 December 1941, 30 B-17Ds were wrecked on the ground in the Philippines by Japanese bombers.

➤ A famous early B-17, *Swoose* ('half swan, half goose'), is preserved in Washington.

➤ Total Fortress production amounted to 12,731 aircraft.

## PROFILE

# First Fortresses for the Air Corps

When Boeing unveiled its Flying Fortress, critics argued that the world was not ready for such a big bomber. Despite its lofty name and good flight performance, the B-17 was not equipped for modern warfare. Early models, with their smooth lines and smaller fin, did not have a tail gunner.

In 1940 the Army Air Corps began receiving aircraft with a broader fin and tail gun position, although newly delivered B-17s on the West Coast in 1941 lacked guns or ammunition.

To deter Japanese aggression, America planned to add four bomber groups to the one that was already in the Philippines by April 1942. Had the plan been implemented, the Pacific war could have been a very different story.

The first dozen B-17s detailed by the plan departed California for a stop in Hawaii on the night of 6 December 1941, and arrived 12 hours later during the Japanese attack on Pearl Harbor.

Many of the aircraft in the Philippines and Hawaii were destroyed on the ground.

The survivors of the Pearl Harbor attack became the first US aircraft in offensive action in World War II, attacking Japanese shipping from 10 December. The following month, the better armed B-17E started to enter service. No. 90 Squadron, RAF, took the B-17C to war (as the Fortress Mk I) over Germany in 1941 and later in the Mediterranean, but with little success.

*The Flying Fortress was so-named for its original intended role – protecting North America's coast lines from maritime attack.*

Many of the USAAC's B-17Cs were later modified to B-17D standard. The RAF was supplied with 20 C-models in 1941 on the understanding that the USAAC would be supplied with complete information on its combat performance.

### Fortress Mk I

**Type:** heavy bomber and maritime patrol aircraft

**Powerplant:** four 895-kW (1200-hp) Wright R-1820-G205A Cyclone radial piston engines

**Maximum speed:** 515 km/h (320 mph)

**Cruising speed:** 373 km/h (232 mph) at 4267 m (14,000 ft)

**Range:** (normal) 3380 km (2100 miles); (maximum) 5085 km (3160 miles)

**Initial climb rate:** 396 m/min (1300 fpm)

**Weights:** empty 14,129 kg (31,149 lb); loaded 20,624 kg (45,468 lb)

**Armament:** one 7.62-mm (.30-cal.) machine gun in the nose, two 12.7-mm (.50-cal.) machine guns in each of the dorsal and ventral positions and two 12.7-mm machine guns through waist positions, plus up to 4761 kg (10,496 lb) of bombs

**Dimensions:**
| | |
|---|---|
| span | 32.23 m (105 ft 9 in) |
| length | 20.97 m (68 ft 10 in) |
| height | 4.68 m (15 ft 4 in) |
| wing area | 125.45 m² (1350 sq ft) |

## B-17C FLYING FORTRESS

Aircraft 10 of the 7th Bomb Group carries the olive drab and grey camouflage scheme applied to USAAC aircraft after the US entered World War II.

The nose position had three gun sockets, one on either side and one in the centre, for a single 7.62-mm (.30-cal) machine gun. The 12.7-mm (.50-cal.) gun was said to break the Plexiglass if used from the nose positions.

Both the dorsal and ventral gun positions on the B-17C were equipped with twin 12.7-mm (.50-cal.) machine guns. The bomb-bay, situated below the wing centre section, carried a typical load of 2177 kg/4800 lb (eight 272-kg/600-lb bombs).

In place of the fuselage blisters on previous models, the B-17C had a simple oval opening for the twin waist gun positions. Each was usually equipped with a 12.7-mm (.50-cal.) machine gun.

Apart from the B-299 prototype, which used four Pratt & Whitney Hornet engines, four Wright Cyclones were the standard B-17 powerplants. The C-model's four R-1820s produced 895 kW (1200 hp) each.

Self-sealing wing fuel tanks were among the improvements introduced on the B-17C. Armour protection for the crew was also fitted.

The B-17C and D featured the so-called 'tin bathtub' beneath the fuselage in place of the ventral 'blister' gun position.

### ACTION DATA

**SERVICE CEILING**

The USAAC's bomber specification was a demanding one, which required better speed, range and armament than that possessed by twin- and four-engined types then in service. Its service ceiling requirement, for example, was greatly increased.

B-17 FLYING FORTRESS 10,973 m (36,000 ft)

He 111E-3 7500 m (24,600 ft)

WHITLEY Mk V 7925 m (26,000 ft)

**RANGE**

Range was an important attribute of the Fortress, given its role as a maritime bomber designed to defend the US from attack. The RAF's bomber force was not able to reach distant targets until four-engined types entered service.

B-17C FLYING FORTRESS 3862 km (2400 miles)

WHITLEY Mk V 2414 km (1500 miles)

He 111E-3 1500 km (932 miles)

**ARMAMENT**

The Flying Fortress was well armed compared to other bombers of the period. However, its lack of rearward-facing guns proved to be a handicap, and was addressed on later versions. Its four engines allowed a bigger bombload to be carried than the others.

| | |
|---|---|
| B-17C FLYING FORTRESS | 6 x 12.7-mm (.50-cal.) machine guns, 1 x 7.62-mm (.30-cal.) machine gun, 4761-kg (10,496-lb) bombload |
| He 111E-3 | 3 x 7.9-mm machine guns, 2000-kg (4400-lb) bombload |
| WHITLEY Mk V | 5 x 7.7-mm (.303-cal) machine guns, 3175-kg (7000-lb) bombload |

## Early bomber types of World War II

**■ AVRO MANCHESTER:** The Manchester of 1940 was judged to be a failure, thanks to its unreliable engines, but was developed into the RAF's most successful four-engined bomber, the Lancaster.

**■ JUNKERS Ju 86:** The Luftwaffe did not field a true four-engined bomber during World War II. The Ju 86 was an early twin-engined type, which was later used for high-altitude reconnaissance.

**■ VICKERS WELLINGTON:** This twin-engined aircraft was in RAF service when war broke out in 1939 and formed the backbone of Bomber Command until 1943.

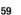

# BOEING

# B-17 FLYING FORTRESS

● Long-range heavy bomber ● Backbone of the US 8th Air Force

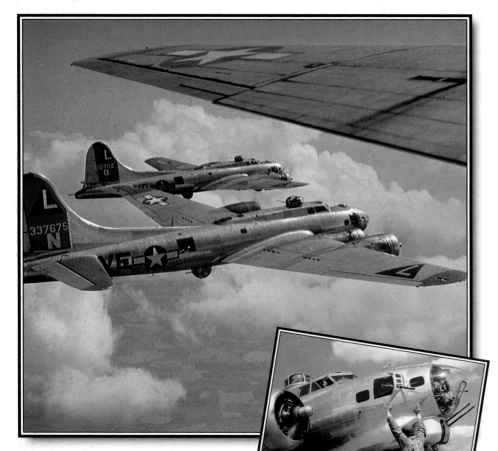

**B**oeing's Flying Fortress was one of the most important bombers in history. B-17s fought in every theatre of World War II, but won immortality in their epic daylight battles against the Luftwaffe in which thousands of young American flyers lost their lives transforming the impotent United States Army Air Force of early 1943 into a force of devastating, destructive power just 12 months later.

▲ The Flying Fortress was America's main strategic weapon in Europe during World War II. From the summer of 1943, huge numbers of Boeing's great silver bird were to be found on English airfields.

## BOEING B-17 FLYING FORTRESS

◀ **Mass production**
Nowhere was America's huge industrial might more visible than in the aircraft factories which turned out hundreds of B-17s each month.

**Daring missions ▶**
During the long bomb-run into the target area the bomb-aimer controlled the B-17. Losses were extremely high as the aircraft was forced to fly straight and level.

▼ **A hard-fought battle**
The Fortress was tough, but over Germany it was pitted against some of the most experienced fighter pilots in the world, and losses were heavy.

◀ **The young man's war**
It was a rare B-17 pilot who was older than 30: most of the men who took the big bombers into battle were barely into their 20s.

▲ **Silver machines**
The B-17 soldiered on after World War II in some oddball roles. This is a rescue aircraft with a lifeboat carried under the fuselage.

### FACTS AND FIGURES

➤ A B-17 shot down by Japanese Zeroes on the way to Pearl Harbor was the first American combat loss in World War II.

➤ The Boeing 299, the Flying Fortress prototype, first flew on 28 July 1935.

➤ 12,731 B-17s were built, with production of the B-17G model reaching 8680.

➤ At the height of the war in Europe, B-17s occupied more than 25 airfields in the south and east of England.

➤ More than 47,000 US 8th Air Force crew died in daylight raids over Germany.

➤ A search and rescue SB-17 flew the first American sortie of the Korean War.

## PROFILE

# Castles in the sky

*Right: B-17s were used to make precision daylight attacks on German industrial centres.*

In the mid-1930s, Boeing engineers suggested a big bomber to the US Army Air Corps. The best American bomber at the time was an inadequate, twin-engined adaptation of the DC-3 transport. The decision to go ahead with the B-17 Flying Fortress was a courageous leap forward: it gave the United States an embryonic bomber

force by the time of the attack on Pearl Harbor. Early B-17s did not have enough guns and were not available in sufficient numbers, but as the war progressed the Flying Fortresses took command of the skies.

B-17 crews faced unspeakable horror, pressing ahead into Luftwaffe fighters and flak while blinded by smoke, beaten by turbulence,

plagued with mechanical mishaps and paralysed by numbing cold. On the first Berlin mission, B-17 crewmen killed in the air numbered the same as Germans killed on the ground by bombs (about 400). As the bombing campaign wore on casualties aboard the B-17s remained high, but the bombing became more effective.

*Left: Hit by flak, a burning B-17 falls away from the protection of its fellows.*

The 'Mighty Eighth' Force was the premier user of the B-17 Flying Fortress.

## B-17F 'FAST WOMAN'

'Fast Woman' was one of the first American B-17s to arrive in Britain during World War II. Attached to the 359th Bomb Squadron of the 303rd Bomb Group, it was based at Molesworth in Huntingdonshire.

The Norden bombsight with which the B-17 was equipped was reputed to be able to 'drop a bomb into a pickle barrel' from 4000 m (13,125 ft.).

Boeing were among the pioneers of stressed-skin design, and the B-17 was among the earliest all-metal monoplane heavy bombers to enter service.

Fortresses were defended by as many as 13 heavy machine-guns. The vulnerable undersides were covered by a ball turret and by the two waist gunners.

The B-17 was immensely strong. Aircraft managed to return to base with severe battle damage, and the big bomber could still fly even with large sections of the huge vertical tail shot away.

The B-17 was powered by reliable Wright Cyclone radial engines. They were turbocharged, which enabled the Fortress to operate at higher altitudes than its European contemporaries.

The bomb-bay was relatively small, and although the B-17 could fly with an eight-tonne bombload it generally carried a quarter of that amount on operations.

B-17s were not originally fitted with tail guns. A tail gunner's position was added to the B-17E and all subsequent models.

## COMBAT DATA

### RANGE

Designed at a time when other air forces still thought twin-engine machines were heavy bombers, the B-17 was revolutionary with its ability to carry more bombs over much greater distances than its contemporaries.

**B-17 FLYING FORTRESS**

STIRLING
3200 km (1,988 mi.) with 1600-kg (3,527-lb.) bombload

3300 km (2,050 mi.) with 2500-kg (5,512-lb.) bombload

B-24 LIBERATOR
3000 km (1,864 mi.) with 2300-kg (5,071-lb.) bombload

### DEFENCES

Originally relatively lightly armed, the Flying Fortress entered combat in armour plate and with an all-round machine-gun fit. A box of 18 bombers could bring tens or even hundreds of guns to bear on an attacker coming from any direction.

STIRLING
8 x 7.7-mm (.303 cal.) machine-guns

B-17 FLYING FORTRESS
13 x 12.7-mm (.50 cal.) machine-guns

B-24 LIBERATOR
10 x 12.7-mm (.50 cal.) machine-guns

## Layered defences

Every B-17 aircraft contributed to the defence of the whole formation. Each squadron of six aircraft moved in unison in formations called boxes, and squadrons were layered and staggered horizontally and vertically, to allow simultaneous release of bombs.

■ PLAN VIEW

■ SIDE VIEW

**3rd COMBAT BOX (7900 m/25,920 ft.))**
Each box contained 18 bombers, which could amass more than 200 heavy machine-guns.

**LEAD COMBAT BOX (7600 m/24,934 ft.))**
The formation commander flew in the lead bomber, with responsibility for navigation and ordering simultaneous release of bombs.

**2nd COMBAT BOX (7300 m/23,950 ft.))**
Combat boxes manoeuvred in unison, always keeping in close formation for mutual support against fighters.

# BOEING

# B-29 SUPERFORTRESS

● Long-range bomber ● Largest of World War II ● Assault on Japan

▲ Sting in the tail: in Korea, B-29 gunners were so good at shooting down enemy aircraft that it became the second highest-scoring Allied type, after the F-86 Sabre.

**B**oeing's talent for turning out huge aircraft paid a super dividend with the Superfortress: the B-29 became the 'big stick' of the final campaign of World War II. Feared by those who fell beneath its shadow, this giant brought war home to Japan's cities and people and ushered in the atomic age. The B-29 also fought in Korea, it was converted into a key post-war transport and tanker, and was even copied without permission by the Russians.

---

## BOEING B-29 SUPERFORTRESS

◀ Fire from the sky
In the last days of World War II B-29s poured a deluge of incendiary bombs onto Japanese cities, which were built largely of wood. The resulting conflagration consumed most of the residential areas.

◀ The bomb ends the war
Dropping the atomic weapons brought the war to a swift conclusion, saving many lives in the process.

X-plane ▶
mother ship
Several B-29s and the improved B-50 were modified for special missions. Among the most important was carrying early supersonic X-planes to altitude.

▲ Bomber over Korea
Just as the B-29 had flattened Japan, the Superfortress relentlessly crushed Communist resistance in Korea.

▼ Atomic bomber
Immortalised in song, 'Enola Gay' was the Superfortress which dropped the first atomic bomb on Japan, hitting the port city of Hiroshima on 6 August 1945.

▲ Flying gas station
In its KB-29 form the Superfortress was the world's first true service tanker aircraft, pioneering the inflight refuelling that has become vital to modern air combat.

### FACTS AND FIGURES

➤ On the night of 9-10 March 1945, 324 B-29s attacked Tokyo at low level in the most destructive air raid in history.

➤ $3 billion had been invested in the B-29 before the first aircraft flew – more than any other aircraft project to that time.

➤ Russia's Tupolev design bureau copied the B-29 as the Tu-4 bomber.

➤ After the war, KB-29s were the USAF's first aerial refuelling tankers.

➤ Crew members travelled from nose to tail of the B-29 through a 'personnel tunnel' above the bomb-bay.

➤ B-29s were used to drop the first atomic bombs on Japan, and in post-war tests at Bikini atoll.

# The first strategic bomber

The B-29 was the first pressurised bomber to enter service, and was therefore able to operate over vast distances and at safe heights to deliver huge bombloads onto the enemy.

Originally designed to bomb Germany from America during World War II, the B-29 entered service only at the end of the European war. This massive, revolutionary bomber was transferred to the fight against Japan, where it devastated cities in huge firebomb raids.

Without the reach of the B-29, America would have had to fight for much longer to recover the Pacific islands from Japan. And it was the B-29 that delivered the final, catastrophic blow in the form of two atomic bombs, dropped onto the cities of Hiroshima and Nagasaki.

Post-war, the B-29 joined the Royal Air Force as the Washington, and inspired the Russian Tu-4. Its final battle was in Korea, where it carried out night bombing raids and shot down many enemy aircraft.

In RAF service the B-29 served as a nuclear bomber, and as a secret reconnaissance aircraft which probed Soviet airspace for electronic signals.

*The Superfortress represented one of the biggest technological leaps ever achieved by one aircraft type. Even today, its technology turns up in Russia's nuclear bombers.*

It took 11 men to fly the B-29 on operations. There were two pilots, a bombardier, navigator, flight engineer, radio operator, radar operator, central fire control gunner, left gunner, right gunner and tail gunner.

Most B-29s had a sophisticated radar under the belly which allowed them to bomb accurately even through cloud.

### B-29 Superfortress

**Type:** 10-/11-seat long-range strategic bomber

**Powerplant:** four 1641-kW (2,200-hp.) Wright R-3350 Cyclone 18 turbocharged radial piston engines

**Maximum speed:** 576 km/h (358 m.p.h.)

**Range:** 5230 km (3,250 mi.)

**Service ceiling:** 9170 m (30,085 ft.)

**Weights:** empty 31,815 kg (70,140 lb.); loaded 56,245 kg (123,999 lb.)

**Armament:** two 12.7-mm (.50 cal.) machine-guns in each of four remotely-controlled turrets and three 12.7-mm guns or two 12.7-mm guns and one 20-mm cannon in the tail; bombload 9072 kg (20,000 lb.)

**Dimensions:** span 43.05 m (141 ft. 3 in.)
length 30.18 m (99 ft. 2 in.)
height 9.02 m (29 ft. 7 in.)
wing area 161.27 m² (1,736 sq. ft.)

## WASHINGTON B.Mk 1

The mighty Superfortress was a war-winning weapon, and went on to become one of the main forces in the Cold War. The RAF operated the type in the late 1940s and early 1950s, calling it the Washington.

The gunners all sat in the rear compartment, looking out for enemy fighters through domed windows and firing the guns via an early computer system.

The forward cabin was connected to the rear cabin by a crawlway. In the back sat the gunners, and there were also bunks for resting on long missions.

Two enormous weapons bays carried the B-29's bombload. Each bay had winches inside to hoist the bombs up into the aircraft.

Under its tail the Superfortress had a retractable tail bumper, which protected the rear fuselage when the aircraft took off.

Sitting alone in the tail compartment, the tail gunner had two machine-guns and a 20-mm (0.79-in) cannon at his fingertips.

## Superfortress superbomber

**B-29 SUPERFORTRESS:** The B-29's two bays held over 9000 kg (19,842 lb.) of bombs, the biggest standard load of any wartime bomber.

**B-17 FLYING FORTRESS:** Although it theoretically could carry 7900 kg (17,417 lb.) of bombs, the B-17 rarely flew combat missions with more than 2300 kg (5,071 lb.).

**AVRO LANCASTER:** The RAF's main bomber had a normal combat load of about 6300 kg (13,889 lb.).

**HEINKEL He 177:** In theory, Germany's heaviest bomber could carry 6000 kg (13,230 lb.), but in practice 2000 kg (4,400 lb.) was a more realistic load.

### COMBAT DATA

#### MAXIMUM SPEED

The Boeing B-29 was a revelation when it first flew. Easily the biggest bomber of World War II, it flew faster than any of its predecessors, and at altitude it could outpace most of the Japanese fighters which were its principal foes.

| | |
|---|---|
| B-29 SUPERFORTRESS | 576 km/h (358 m.p.h.) |
| LANCASTER | 462 km/h (287 m.p.h.) |
| B-24 LIBERATOR | 467 km/h (290 m.p.h.) |

# BOEING
# F4B/P-12

- Biplane fighter ● Inter-war defender of the US Fleet

▲ Pilots loved the F4B for its superb manoeuvrability, massive strength and impressive performance. But by the end of the 1930s the days of open-cockpit biplane fighters were numbered.

**S**erving the US Navy at the end of the biplane era, the classic F4B was the star of a family of famous Boeing fighters which included the US Army Air Corps' P-12 and the export Model 100. The F4B was a super ship to fly and was the most capable carrier-based fighter of its time. For all its elegance and manoeuvrability, the F4B triumphed successfully for only a brief time before being eclipsed by the arrival of the monoplane in the late 1930s.

## BOEING F4B/P-12

▲ **Last of the line**
A late-model P-12F above Hensley Field, Texas. This model was the equivalent of the Navy's F4B-4, and often had radio fitted.

▲ **Still going strong**
This P-12C is a rare survivor of the 568 built. A Boeing F4B-4 that also survived is on display at the Naval Aviation Museum at NAS Pensacola, Florida.

▲ **Line abreast**
P-12Es of the 27th Pursuit Group practise their immaculate precision formation flying above Selfridge Field, Michigan.

▲ **Fabric fighter**
Early P-12s had a fabric-covered fuselage, but by 1930 Boeing was building P-12Es with a stressed metal skin for better strength.

**Streamlining ▶**
Early P-12 models had uncowled Wasp engines. The Townend ring cowling fitted to later models streamlined the engine and helped increase speed.

## FACTS AND FIGURES

- ➤ The first F4B-1 went on duty aboard the carrier *Lexington* on 8 August 1929.

- ➤ A special F4B-1A served as a 'taxi' for Assistant Secretary of the US Navy Douglas Ingalls.

- ➤ The first protoype in this great fighter series flew on 25 June 1928.

- ➤ The F4B landed on a carrier deck at about 60 km/h, or about one-third the speed of the modern F-14 Tomcat.

- ➤ Many F4B-4 fighters served as unmanned target drones during World War II.

- ➤ The F4B was the favourite aeroplane of stunt pilot hero Frank Tallman.

## PROFILE

# Boeing's great Navy biplane

In early days of carrier aviation, the F4B was the hottest thing with wings. Boeing's Model 83 and 89 prototypes led to four principal versions of this superb biplane fighter, numbered F4B-1 through F4B-4; the final version is the best remembered among the 200 or so of these aircraft which saw active service with the Navy between 1930 and 1938.

These great fighters were exciting and colourful: most had grey fuselage and wings, a brilliant yellow upper wing surface, and squadron colours on fuselage and cowling.

Part of the success of the F4B belongs to the Wasp engine, or R-1340, which was this period's finest technical achievement. But the real measure of the F4B was its prowess as a fighting plane.

*Touchdown landing on the wooden deck of the USS Lexington. Landing and take-off accidents were common.*

In the heyday of the biplane, this air-to-air dogfighter could not be defeated. Unfortunately, the romance of this era was all too brief. By the late 1930s, faster monoplane fighters had consigned biplanes to history.

US military aircraft generally sported bright colour schemes in the inter-war period. The vivid yellow wings aided recognition over the sea.

### F4B-4

**Type:** single-seat carrier-based fighter

**Powerplant:** one 410-kW (550-hp.) Pratt & Whitney R-1340-16 radial piston engine

**Maximum speed:** 300 km/h (186 m.p.h.) at 1830 m (6,000 ft.)

**Range:** 600 km (375 mi.)

**Service ceiling:** 8200 m (29,600 ft.)

**Weights:** empty 1068 kg (2,350 lb.); loaded 1638 kg (3,600 lb.)

**Armament:** two 7.62-mm (.30 cal.) fixed forward-firing Browning machine-guns or one 7.62-mm and one 12.7-mm (.50 cal.) Browning machine-guns, five 12-kg (25-lb.) bombs or one 227-kg (500-lb.) bomb or one 208-litre (50-gal.) drop tank

**Dimensions:**
| | |
|---|---|
| span | 9.14 m (30 ft.) |
| length | 6.12 m (20 ft. 1 in.) |
| height | 2.84 m (9 ft. 4 in.) |
| wing area | 21m² (228 sq. ft.) |

A compartment in the headrest housed a dinghy in case the pilot was forced to crash-land in the sea. This version also had a radio fitted.

**F4B-4  9026**

**6-F-10**  **NAVY**

The 'Felix the Cat' insignia was the squadron badge of fighter squadron VF-6, operating from USS *Saratoga* in 1935. The badge is still being used today on the F-14 Tomcats of VF-31.

### F4B-4

This F4B-4 was one of about 200 used by the US Navy between 1929 and 1938. The F4B-4 was similar to the Army's P-12E, with a 410-kW Wasp engine but with the essential arrester hook and wing bomb racks.

The fuselage frame of all F4Bs was built of welded steel tube for strength. Stressed metal skins replaced fabric on the fuselage of the later versions, but all F4Bs retained a fabric-covered wing.

The undercarriage of the F4B needed to be strong. Even with the low speeds of biplane fighters, landings on carrier decks were often very hard.

The nine-cylinder Pratt & Whitney Wasp radial was the forerunner of a family of engines that would power US Navy fighters throughout World War II.

### COMBAT DATA

**RANGE**

Even in the early days of carrier aviation, naval aircraft were expected to operate over greater distances than their land-based equivalents – after all, emergency landing fields are few and far between in the vast ocean spaces – and the F4B comfortably outranged the British Bulldog.

**BULLDOG** 475 km (295 mi.)
**F4B** 600 km (375 mi.)
**FLYCATCHER** 500 km (310 mi.)

**MAXIMUM SPEED**

**BULLDOG** 280 km/h (174 m.p.h.)
**F4B** 300 km/h (186 m.p.h.)
**FLYCATCHER** 214 km/h (135 m.p.h.)

The F4B was one of the fastest fighters around when it went into service in the late-1920s. It had the edge on land-based machines like the Bristol Bulldog and was much quicker than the Fairey Flycatcher, the standard British carrier fighter of the time.

**ARMAMENT**

Aircraft armament in the biplane era had not advanced much in the decade since the end of World War I. Two forward-firing machine-guns was the norm for most fighters of the early 1930s. However, the F4B's powerful radial engine meant that it could carry a fairly heavy bombload for a fighter.

**BULLDOG** 2 x 7.7-mm (0.303 cal.) machine-guns, 4 x 10-kg (25-lb.) bombs
**FLYCATCHER** 2 x 7.7-mm (0.303 cal.) machine-guns, 4 x 10-kg (25-lb) bombs
**F4B** 2 x 7.62-mm (0.30 cal.) machine-guns, 1 x 227-kg (500-lb.) bomb

## Carrier Air Power – then and now

■ **USS KITTYHAWK** has been in service since 1961 and displaces more than 91,500 tonnes (90,000 tons). It carries an air wing of 85 advanced combat jets, and with its nuclear arsenal deploys more firepower than the entire US Navy of the 1930s, and is able to project power on a global basis.

■ **USS RANGER** was laid down in 1931. It displaced only 14,500 tonnes (14,732 tons), but it too could carry more than 80 aircraft. Most were tiny biplanes, however, and five or six could be stored in the space a single modern F-14 Tomcat occupies.

# BOEING

# P-26 PEASHOOTER

● Pioneering all-metal monoplane ● China war veteran ● Dogfighter

▲ The P-26 was a major advance in fighter design, blending old features like fixed undercarriage and open cockpit with modern metal construction and powerful engine, including fuel injection.

**T**he Boeing P-26 Peashooter was an incredibly bold new venture: the first all-metal fighter, and the first monoplane fighter to enter squadron service. Progress was rapid in the 1930s, however, so the P-26 enjoyed glory only briefly. When Pearl Harbor was attacked a decade after the P-26 was conceived, Peashooters remaining in the hands of a few Filipino pilots became easy pickings for the Japanese Zero.

## BOEING P-26 PEASHOOTER

▲ Open cockpit
The P-26 was the last open fighter in US service. The roomy cockpit was well liked by pilots.

▲ Fastest fighter
For a short time, the P-26 was the fastest fighter in service. The P-26s of the Philippine Army Air Corps even managed to shoot down some faster Japanese fighters in December 1941.

◀ In stripes
This P-26 wears a typical inter-war colour scheme, with yellow wings and stripes. This type of scheme was abandoned before the start of World War II, when less visible toned-down colours were adopted.

▲ Echelon formation
Stepped upwards away from the photographer, a P-26 pursuit squadron poses for the camera.

◀ On parade
Pilots and ground crew of the 17th pursuit group on review at their base in March Field, California.

## FACTS AND FIGURES

➤ The XP-936 prototype for the P-26 series first flew on 20 March 1932.

➤ Boeing in Seattle manufactured 136 Peashooters of all versions.

➤ On 12 December 1941, six Philippine P-26s battled 54 Japanese aircraft, shot down three, and suffered three losses.

➤ Twelve Boeing Model 281s, identical to the P-26, were built for export to China.

➤ The last flight of a P-26 occurred in 1964 when a restored 'warbird' went aloft in the United States.

➤ The modern Boeing 747-400 weighs as much as 300 'Peashooters'.

# PROFILE

# Last of the old, first of the new

The P-26 had fixed landing gear with heavy, high-drag wheel pants, and was festooned with bracing wires. So although it was modern when introduced in 1931, it also marked the end of an era; it was the last open-cockpit fighter accepted by the US Army, the last with a fixed undercarriage, and the last with an externally braced wing. The P-26 was also

the final production fighter from Boeing.

Based on three XP-936 prototypes, the P-26A, B and C served with all US Army fighter groups in the 1930s. Variants were employed overseas by Guatemala, China and the Philippines (which employed a few P-26s in early days of World War II). In one of its few combat engagements Philippine P-26s

managed to down three Japanese aircraft despite being outclassed in every area of performance. American P-26s also put up futile resistance at Pearl Harbor.

Called a 'sport roadster' by Army pilots, the P-26 went into production in 1932. The last ship built was delivered in 1936. The last American Peashooter left service in 1943, but P-26s flew in Guatemala until 1957.

## P-26A PEASHOOTER

This P-26A carries the badge of the 95th Pursuit Squadron, known as the 'Kicking Mules'. The squadron used the P-26 in the ground-attack role.

The nickname 'Peashooter' came from the aircraft's tubular gunsight.

The headrest helped protect the pilot if the aircraft rolled over on the ground.

The wide-chord wing and chunky tail of the P-26 were reminiscent of earlier Boeing designs such as the P-12.

*The P-26B of 1935 featured a fuel-injected engine, revised controls and landing flaps. The flaps were fitted to reduce the landing speed, which had been excessively high in the P-26A.*

The P-26's major contribution to aviation technology was its sturdy, all-metal construction.

The P-26 used the Pratt & Whitney radial engines common to most US fighters. They were strong and powerful, but had a large frontal area, which meant high drag.

The fairing over the undercarriage reduced drag. Fixed undercarriages were vanishing by the late 1930s.

The bracing wires showed that the P-26 was still halfway between the days of biplanes and more modern monoplanes.

## Monoplane fighters of the 1930s

**DEWOITINE D.510:** Developed from the D.500 of 1932, the D.510 was the mainstay of French fighter strength in the mid 1930s.

**MITSUBISHI A5M 'CLAUDE':** This Japanese carrier fighter first flew in 1935. It was one of the most manoeuvrable fighters ever built.

**POLIKARPOV I-16:** Flying only two years after the P-26 entered service, the Soviet I-16 was the true herald of fighters to come. A powerful engine and retractable undercarriage made it at least 100 km/h (60 mph) faster than the P-26.

---

### P-26A Peashooter

**Type:** single-seat pursuit aircraft

**Powerplant:** one 373-kW (500-hp) Pratt & Whitney R-1340-27 Wasp nine-cylinder air-cooled radial engine driving a two-bladed propeller

**Maximum speed:** 377 km/h (234 mph) at 2250 m (7382 ft)

**Range:** 580 km (360 miles)

**Service ceiling:** 8500 m (27,887 ft)

**Weights:** empty 996 kg (2196 lb); loaded 1340 kg (2954 lb)

**Armament:** one 7.62-mm (.30-cal.) and one 12.7-mm (.50-cal.) or two 12.7-mm machine guns; provision for two 45-kg (100-lb) or five 13.60-kg (30-lb) bombs

**Dimensions:**
| | | |
|---|---|---|
| span | 8.52 m | (27 ft 11 in) |
| length | 7.19 m | (23 ft 7 in) |
| height | 3.07 m | (10 ft 1 in) |
| wing area | 13.89 m² | (150 sq ft) |

---

## COMBAT DATA

### RANGE

The P-26 was smaller than contemporary canvas and wire biplanes, and as a result could not carry as much fuel. This, allied to the high drag caused by its bulky radial engine, had a slightly adverse effect on the Peashooter's range. Even so, it was more than enough for the short range interception missions it was designed for. The bigger Gauntlet could carry a much larger fuel load, increasing its range.

400 km (249 miles) — He 51

580 km (360 miles) — P-26 PEASHOOTER

740 km (460 miles) — GAUNTLET

### MAXIMUM SPEED

**GAUNTLET** 370 km/h (300 mph)

**P-26A PEASHOOTER** 377 km/h (234 mph)

**He 51** 330 km/h (205 mph)

Although fast for the time, the P-26 had only a slight speed advantage over the best of contemporary biplanes. It was tough and manoeuvrable, however, and gave the US Army Air Corps valuable monoplane experience.

### ARMAMENT

By the 1930s aircraft armament had not progressed beyond World War I levels, with two forward-firing machine guns as a standard fit. The P-26 had a slight advantage over its contemporaries in being armed with a pair of the classic Browning '50-calibre' heavy machine guns, which packed a hefty punch. It could also carry two 45-kg (100-lb) bombs.

**P-26A PEASHOOTER** 2 x 12.7-mm (.50-cal.) machine guns

**GAUNTLET** 2 x 7.7-mm (.303-cal.) machine guns

**He 51** 2 x 7.92-mm machine guns

# BOULTON-PAUL

# SIDESTRAND/OVERSTRAND

● Biplane medium bomber ● Powered turret ● Speed and agility

▲ Both types shared
an all-metal structure with fabric
covering. Although representing the peak of
British biplane bomber design, they were
destined for a short service life.

**I**ntended to complement the Fairey Fox, the Sidestrand was the RAF's first medium bomber. Initially flown in 1926, it served with only one squadron, No. 101, from 1928 until 1936. The Overstrand (both types were named after villages near the Boulton and Paul factory in Norwich) was a developed version of the Sidestrand and replaced it from 1937. The Overstrand was notable as the first RAF aircraft to be equipped with a powered gun turret.

## BOULTON-PAUL SIDESTRAND/OVERSTRAND

▼ Outstanding platform
In bombing and gunnery exercises, No. 101 Squadron's Sidestrands broke all RAF records for accuracy. They were limited to a 476-kg (1,050-lb.) bombload.

▲ Exposed to the elements
The Sidestrand's crew were at the mercy of the elements. Yet the Overstrand represented a huge improvement in crew comfort, with its enclosed cockpit and nose turret and shielded mid-upper gun position.

▲ On exercises
On air exercises the Sidestrand demonstrated that it was as fast and agile as a single-engined bomber.

▲ Gunnery training
Superseded as a first-line bomber in 1937, the Overstrand was relegated to gunnery training. It served in this role until 1941.

No. 101 Squadron, RAF ▶
The unit most associated with the Sidestrand Mk III and Overstrand was No. 101, which was based at three different RAF stations while flying the types.

### FACTS AND FIGURES

➤ Part of No. 101 Squadron's badge consisted of a castle tower – a reference to the Overstrand's powered turret.

➤ After an Overstrand fell apart in mid-air in 1940 flying was severely curtailed.

➤ The Overstrands of No. 101 Squadron were the last new RAF biplane bombers.

➤ At the outbreak of World War II the RAF had 11 Overstrands on charge, six of which were flying with training units.

➤ At the 1937 RAF display an Overstrand demonstrated air-to-air refuelling.

➤ Although innovative, the Overstrand was reliable and popular with ground crew.

## PROFILE

# RAF's first medium bombers

Like the two prototypes, the 18 production Mk II Sidestrands were powered by 317-kW Jupiter VI engines. These aircraft were later modified with geared Jupiter VIIFs to become Mk IIIs. They had both dorsal and ventral gun mountings, although only a single gunner was carried in the fuselage. The choice of installation was intended to be made according to the individual aircraft's position in the attack formation.

One of the Mk IIIs was re-engined again with Bristol Pegasus IM3s. Originally designated Sidestrand Mk IV, it became the prototype for the Overstrand. The most obvious change introduced by the new type was a powered nose turret, although the structure was also strengthened and the crew's accommodation, protection and the bomb installation were all improved.

The turret itself used pneumatic motors for rotation,

while hydraulic rams helped the gunner to elevate or depress the Lewis machine-gun. Two 227-kg (500-lb.) and two 113-kg (250-lb.) bombs could be carried beneath either the wings or the fuselage.

From 1936 the 24 production Overstrands were used by No. 101 Squadron (which had operated the Sidestrand) and, briefly, by No. 144 Squadron until they were replaced by Blenheims in 1938. A projected development with a retracting undercarriage, the Superstrand, was abandoned.

*Left: J9181 was the fifth production Sidestrand Mk II. The type entered RAF service in 1928.*

*Above: Originally intended to be fitted with Napier Lion in-line engines, the Sidestrand Mk I was powered by Jupiter VIs.*

### OVERSTRAND MK I

**No. 101 Squadron was one of two squadrons to be equipped with the Overstrand. Production totalled 24, K4546 being the first of the initial batch of 19 aircraft. An overall silver finish was typical of the period.**

### Sidestrand Mk III

**Type:** medium day-bomber

**Powerplant:** two 343-kW (460-hp.) Bristol Jupiter VIIF nine-cylinder air-cooled radial engines

**Maximum speed:** 225 km/h (140 m.p.h.) at 3050 m (10,000 ft.)

**Climb rate:** 4572 m (15,000 ft.) in 19 min

**Range:** 805 km (500 mi.)

**Service ceiling:** 7300 m (24,000 ft.)

**Weights:** empty 2726 kg (6,000 lb.); loaded 4627 kg (10,179 lb.)

**Armament:** three 7.7-mm (.303 cal.) Lewis machine-guns, plus up to 476 kg (1,050 lb.) of bombs

**Dimensions:**
| | | |
|---|---|---|
| span | 21.92 m | (71 ft. 11 in.) |
| length | 14.02 m | (46 ft.) |
| height | 4.52 m | (14 ft. 10 in.) |
| wing area | 91 m² | (979 sq. ft.) |

Overstrands were the first RAF bombers to be fitted with a power-operated gun turret. While later aircraft had electrically-actuated turrets, the Overstrand's used pneumatic rotation. In air-to-air fighting gunners were able to improve their accuracy five-fold.

As well as the powered nose turret, the Overstrand had a more traditional Scarff ring-mounted Lewis gun in the dorsal position. One innovation was a protective windscreen for the gunner.

For a bomber the Overstrand was highly manoeuvrable and immensely strong. This was demonstrated at the 1936 air display at RAF Hendon during which the aircraft performed half-rolls and loops.

Bristol supplied the radial engines for both the Sidestrand and Overstrand; Jupiters in the former and early versions of the Pegasus in the latter.

During the 1930s RAF bomber squadron aircraft often carried their numbers on the fuselage. Individual aircraft were identified by a code letter, in this case 'W' on the aircraft's nose.

A ventral gun position mounted the third 7.7-mm (.303 cal.) machine-gun. A 227-kg (500-lb.) capacity bomb rack was fitted beneath each wing inboard of the engine. Fuselage racks under the cockpit and mid-upper gun position could each carry four 9-kg (20-lb.) bombs.

The Overstrand continued the good reputation of its predecessor. With a top speed of above 240 km/h (150 m.p.h.), it was able to 'hold its own' against many fighters of the day, with its defensive armament covering most 'blind' spots.

### ACTION DATA

#### ARMAMENT
The Overstrand had a more limited bombload than contemporary bombers from France and the USA. Its defensive armament was on a par with other top bombers, but it did not form a successful basis for further bomber development.

**OVERSTRAND Mk I** — 3 x 7.7-mm machine-guns 726-kg (1,600-lb) bombload

**MB.200B.4** — 3 x 7.5-mm machine-guns 1200-kg (2,650-lb.) bombload

**B-10B** — 3 x 7.62-mm (.30 cal.) machine-guns 1025-kg (2,250-lb.) bombload

**SPINNING:** Few modern combat aircraft are cleared for regular spinning manoeuvres, but Boulton-Paul's Overstrand accomplished them with ease.

**SPIRALLING EARTHWARDS:** As the aircraft descends at a shallow angle, the nose revolves slowly around the vertical. At the same time the tail rotates at a faster rate around the nose, causing the aircraft to spin as it slowly spirals down.

## Aerobatic Overstrand

**ROLLING:** Thanks to the Overstrand's manoeuvrability and structural integrity crews found that it was possible to perform aerobatics in the aircraft. Rolls could be carried out quite easily – an impressive accomplishment for such a large aircraft.

**LOOPING:** The Overstrand could also perform loops. It was the first, and one of the very few, RAF bombers able to perform such manoeuvres with regularity.

# BREDA

# BA.65

● Attack aircraft ● Spanish Civil War service ● North African use

▲ Flown for the first time
in 1935, the Ba.65 was one of a number
of Italian designs that were outmoded
and unsuitable for combat tasks by the
time Italy entered World War II in 1940.

**D**espite its heavy armament, the Ba.65 was not a success in the ground-attack role for which it was intended. Although comparable in size, weight and power to the earliest Spitfires, it was much slower and far less manoeuvrable. In service from the late 1930s, the Ba.65 found a few export customers, but was used principally by the Regia Aeronautica assisting Nationalist forces in Spain and fighting British forces in North Africa.

# BREDA BA.65

▼ **Nationalist Spanish Ba.65**
Thirteen Ba.65s equipped the
65ª Squadriglia of the Aviazione
Legionaria, the Italian air
contingent supporting the Fascist
forces in the Spanish Civil War.

▲ **Engine problems in the desert**
After Italy's entry into World War II, Ba.65s were committed to the
North African campaign, where they came up against British forces.
Serviceability, or lack of it, in the sandy desert conditions proved to
be the type's biggest problem.

▲ **Natural metal**
This Ba.65bis, seen at the factory, has been
fitted with a hydraulically-operated turret of
unusual design, mounting a single 12.7-mm
(.50 cal.) machine-gun. The Ba.65 was a
descendant of the Ba 64 two-seat ground-
attack type.

▲ **First batch**
The 81 aircraft for Italy
were powered by 522-kW
Gnome-Rhône radials.

◄ **101ª Squadriglia**
This Ba 65 carries 101ª
Squadriglia markings. Eight
squadrons were equipped
with the aircraft in 1939.

## FACTS AND FIGURES

➤ The last operational Italian Ba.65s
were lost during the British offensive
in Cyrenaica in early 1941.

➤ Iraqi Ba.65s saw limited action against
the British during the 1941 insurrection.

➤ In June 1937 one Ba.65 was flown with
a Pratt & Whitney R-1830 engine.

➤ Regia Aeronautica Ba.65s made
reconnaissance flights during the
invasion of Abyssinia.

➤ Caproni-Vizzola built 57 of a batch of
137 aircraft for the Regia Aeronautica.

➤ Ba.65s in Fascist service were used over
Santander, Teruel and the River Ebro.

# PROFILE

# Civil War and desert veteran

Derived from the earlier Ba 64 and flown for the first time in 1935, the Ba.65 was produced in both single- and two-seat versions. Most were two-seaters, and some had a Breda L turret and 7.7-mm (.303 cal.) machine-gun fitted at the rear of the cockpit, in addition to the four wing-mounted weapons. The final Ba.65bis variant had an open cockpit-mounted gun.

The first Ba.65s, powered by Fiat engines, were supplied to the Iraqi air force in 1937. The first aircraft for the Italian air force were Gnome-Rhône-powered. Other exported Ba.65s were delivered to Chile, Hungary, Portugal and Paraguay, but plans to sell a Pratt & Whitney-powered version to Nationalist China foundered.

From August 1937 the Ba.65 served in substantial numbers with the Italian legionary air force fighting alongside the Nationalists in the Spanish Civil War. However, it was used only for reconnaissance missions during that conflict.

By the time Italy joined World War II in June 1940, the Italian air force had 154 Ba.65s in front-line service. They were used mainly in North Africa, but their poor manoeuvrability and lack of speed made them easy prey for Allied fighters.

Left: Portugal took delivery of 10 two-seat Ba.65s, powered by Fiat radials and fitted with the Breda L turret, in November 1939.

Above: The basic Ba.65 was a single-seater, and was intended for interceptor, light bomber and attack/reconnaissance roles.

## Ba.65/A.80

**Type:** single-seat ground-attack aircraft

**Powerplant:** one 746-kW Fiat (1,000-hp.) A.80 RC41 18-cylinder air-cooled radial engine

**Maximum level speed:** 430 km/h (267 m.p.h.)

**Range:** 550 km (340 mi.)

**Service ceiling:** 6300 m (20,660 ft.)

**Weights:** empty equipped 2400 kg (5,280 lb.); maximum take-off 2950 kg (6,490 lb.)

**Armament:** two 12.7-mm (.50 cal.) and two 7.7-mm (.303 cal.) machine-guns, plus up to 500 kg of bombs in the internal bomb-bay and on wing racks

**Dimensions:**
| | | |
|---|---|---|
| span | 12.10 m | (36 ft. 8 in.) |
| length | 9.30 m | (30 ft. 6 in.) |
| height | 3.20 m | (10 ft. 6 in.) |
| wing area | 23.50 m² | (253 sq. ft.) |

---

Initial examples of the Ba.65 were single-seaters, but most were two-seaters with an observer/gunner and machine-gun in the rear cockpit.

An internal fuselage bomb-bay usually carried 300 kg (660 lb.) of bombs; an additional 200 kg (440 lb.) was carried on wing racks. A maximum load of 1000 kg (2,200 lb.) was theoretically possible.

## BA.65

No. 5 (Fighter) Squadron of the Iraqi air force, formed in 1938, was equipped with Ba.65s. They were among a number of Italian aircraft delivered in the late 1930s, including Savoia-Marchetti SM.79s.

This Ba.65 is a Fiat-engined example, like the bulk of production aircraft. The first 81 delivered to the Regia Aeronautica employed 522-kW (700-hp.) French Gnome-Rhône K-14 radials. Chile's 20 examples were powered by Piaggio P.XI C.40s.

A conventional cantilever low-wing monoplane, the Ba.65 had a fuselage and wing structure of chrome-molybdenum steel alloy tubing covered with Duralumin sheet, except for the trailing edges of the wing which were fabric-covered. The wing incorporated trailing-edge flaps and Handley Page leading-edge slats. The single fin and rudder were strut- and wire-braced.

## ACTION DATA

### MAXIMUM SPEED

Although the Ba.65 was appreciably faster than similar types like the Ju 87 (by more than 100 km/h/60 m.p.h.) and was able to carry heavier bombloads, it suffered at the hands of more agile Allied fighters in the North African campaign.

| | |
|---|---|
| BA.65/A.80 | 430 km/h (267 m.p.h.) |
| Ju 87A-1 | 320 km/h (198 m.p.h.) |
| Hs 123A-1 | 341 km/h (211 m.p.h.) |

### RANGE

Breda Ba.65s lacked the range of the Junkers Ju 87 and Henschel Hs 123. This limited their operational usefulness when deployed against British and Allied forces in North Africa. However, the type could carry a much larger load.

BA.65/A.80 550 km (340 mi.)

Ju 87A-1 1000 km (952 mi.)

Hs 123A-1 860 km (535 mi.)

### ARMAMENT

Compared to contemporary attack types, the Ba.65/A.80 was defensively well-armed, with four forward-firing machine-guns. To defend the rear of the aircraft, later versions had a rearward-facing gun. This was turret-mounted in some examples.

| | |
|---|---|
| BA.65/A.80 | 2 x 12.7-mm (.50 cal.) machine-guns<br>2 x 7.7-mm (.303 cal.) machine-guns<br>500-kg (1,100-l.b) bombload |
| Ju 87A-1 | 2 x 7.9-mm (0.31-in.) machine-guns<br>250-kg (550-lb.) bombload |
| Hs 123A-1 | 2 x 7.9-mm (0.31-in.) machine-guns<br>200-kg (440-lb.) bombload |

# Breda designs of the 1920s, 1930s and 1940s

■ **A 7:** This two-seat, parasol-winged monoplane served in small numbers with Italian air force reconnaissance units from 1929.

■ **Ba 27:** This fighter, which resembled the Boeing P-26, flew in 1934. Its metal structure led to the nickname *Metallico* (Metal One).

■ **Ba 88 LINCE:** Originally a speed record-breaking aircraft, the Lince (Lynx) suffered severely impaired performance in military trim.

■ **Ba 201:** Evaluated during 1941, the Ba.201 single-seat dive-bomber was first thought to be a licence-built Junkers Ju 87.

# BREGUET
# 14

● Famous World War I bomber ● Built in large numbers

▲ *Not one of
the prettiest aircraft to emerge
from the Breguet Velizy-Villacoublay works,
the model 14 nevertheless became one
of the most important types of World War I.*

**B**uilt in greater numbers than any
other French aircraft of its vintage,
the Breguet 14 flew for the first time,
with Louis Breguet himself at the controls,
in November 1916. More than 5,500 had
been ordered by the end of the war, and
production continued until 1926 to bring the
total built to more than 8,000. The type was
used by the French, Belgian and US air
forces during the war itself, and afterwards
served with a dozen other countries.

## BREGUET 14

**▲ Longevity**
*A very sound basic design
ensured that the Breguet 14
remained in production for many
years after World War I. It also
spawned a number of successors
which shared many components
with this excellent aircraft.*

**▲ Service pioneer**
*First version to see action was
the A2 reconnaissance variant
which entered service in 1917.*

**Exclusive power ▶**
*Only one engine, a Renault 12 Fe
powered the Breguet 14 series,
though others were evaluated.*

**◀ Sturdy design**
*Like several other late-war
French aircraft, such as the SPAD
VII, the Breguet 14 was a sturdy
machine and featured ailerons on
both the upper and lower wings.*

**Tending to the injured ▶**
*In addition to its primary roles as
a bomber, reconnaissance and
artillery support aircraft, the
Breguet 14 was also used by the
Armée de l'Air as a flying
ambulance, evacuating casualties
from the front line.*

### FACTS AND FIGURES

➤ Known as the Breguet AV (*avant*, or
forward), the prototype was the first
Breguet biplane with a tractor engine.

➤ In 1923 Breguet 14 air ambulances
evacuated 870 casualties in Morocco.

➤ The United States Air Service used
model 14s on the Western Front in 1918.

➤ In 1919 French airmen, Captain Coli and
Lieutenant Roget, flew a record distance
of 1609 km in a Breguet model 14.

➤ A small number of aircraft were built
post-war to keep the company in being.

➤ By the end of its production run, at least
five firms had built Breguet 14s.

## PROFILE

# France's famed World War I bomber

The initial production version of the Breguet 14 was the B2 day bomber. In addition to a forward-firing Vickers machine-gun, it carried a pair of Lewis guns on a ring mounting for the observer and some later examples had a third Lewis firing downward to the rear. The B2 was soon joined in service by the A2 reconnaissance bomber, which had wings of reduced span and did not have the B2's rear-cockpit side windows. Other variants included the E2 trainer

and B1 single-seat bomber. Many different engines were also tested. The type was manufactured by at least three other French firms during the war and was later built under licence in Japan and Spain.

The B2 equipped French units in Greece, Macedonia, Morocco and Serbia as well as serving in large numbers on the Western Front. It was also used in smaller numbers by the American Expeditionary Force and two Belgian air force units. Post-war users of the military

Breguet 14 included Brazil, China, Czechoslovakia, Denmark, Finland, Greece, Japan, Poland, Portugal, Romania, Siam (Thailand) and Spain. There was also a passenger transport version called the Salon.

*Left: A civil registration and the modern cityscape below betray this particular aircraft as a Breguet 14 replica. Such machines allow the legacy of early aircraft to live on today.*

### Bre. 14B2

**Type:** two-seat bomber and reconnaissance aircraft

**Powerplant:** one 224-kW (300-hp.) Renault 12 Fe liquid-cooled V-12 engine

**Maximum speed:** 177 km/h (110 m.p.h.) at 2000 m (6,600 ft.)

**Endurance:** 2 hr 45 min

**Service ceiling:** 5750 m (18,850 ft.)

**Weights:** empty 1040 kg (2,288 lb.); loaded 1765 kg (3,883 lb.)

**Armament:** three or four 7.7-mm (.303 cal.) machine-guns plus up to 320 kg (704 lb.) of bombs

**Dimensions:**
| | | |
|---|---|---|
| span | 14.36 m | (47 ft. 2 in.) |
| length | 8.87 m | (29 ft. 1 in.) |
| height | 3.03 m | (9 ft. 11 in.) |
| wing area | 51 m² | (549 sq. ft.) |

---

## BREGUET 14A2

This Breguet 14 is in fact a post-war variant, which served with 15e Escadrille, 5e Groupe, 33e Regiment Aerien d'Observation, French air force, during 1920-21. The last of the Bre. 14s was retired in 1932.

*Above: Breguet 14s remained in production after World War I. This is a Bre. 14T bis, identified by the four large cabin windows on each side, which first appeared in 1921.*

Protruding from the top of the engine cowling was the exhaust, which deflected fumes away from the pilot.

An excellent feature of the Bre. 14 was its cockpit layout, with both pilot and gunner/observer in proximity to each other. Twin Lewis 7.7-mm (.303 cal.) machine-guns were mounted in the rear cockpit.

Although the aircraft did not have severe handling vices, horn-balanced elevators were introduced in 1918 to improve control further.

Housed under the metal panelling was a 12-cylinder Renault 12 Fe in-line piston engine. Although a fairly bulky powerplant, this engine performed admirably and few problems were encountered. Derivatives of this engine powered later Breguet designs.

By World War I standards, the Breguet was a relatively large aeroplane with a deep fuselage. On the Bre. 14A2 variant, twin windows were fitted on each side for the reconnaissance role.

In common with the vast majority of aircraft of the time, the Bre. 14 was fitted with a tail skid. A rather crude bungee cord provided suspension for the skid.

---

## COMBAT DATA

### MAXIMUM SPEED

Faster than the renowned LVG C.V, the French Breguet proved itself to be one of the best aircraft of World War I. It was slightly slower than the Airco DH.4, a somewhat heavier and more advanced type which also remained in service after the war.

| | |
|---|---|
| 14A2 | 184 km/h (114 m.p.h.) |
| DH.4 | 230 km/h (143 m.p.h.) |
| C.V | 164 km/h (102 m.p.h.) |

### ENDURANCE

By the summer of 1917, aircraft had become larger, more powerful and had greater endurance. This enabled them to roam further and to operate deep into enemy territory. Both the LVG C.V and Airco DH.4 could stay up for slightly longer than the Breguet 14.

| 14A2 | D.H.4 | C.V |
|---|---|---|
| 3 hr | 3 hr 40 min | 3 hr 30 min |

### ARMAMENT

With air power becoming more important as a ground-support asset, plus the growing number of effective combat aircraft on both sides, sufficient armament was a necessity. The British DH.4 in particular had a heavy arsenal of four machine-guns, though the LVG C.V and Breguet were by no means easy victims in combat.

**14A2** 3 x 7.7-mm (.303 cal.) machine-guns

**DH.4** 4 x 7.7-mm (.303 cal.) machine-guns

**C.V** 2 x 7.92-mm machine-guns

---

## Breguet biplane designs

■ **BREGUET 16:** An enlarged Bre. 14, this aircraft was a two-seat night bomber which served in this role until the mid-1920s.

■ **BREGUET 17:** This was a down-sized version of the Breguet 14 and had a more powerful engine for better performance.

■ **BREGUET 19:** Perhaps even more famous than the Bre. 14, these aircraft were widely exported and were built under licence abroad.

■ **BREGUET 410:** One of the company's last biplane designs, this was a twin-engined machine which entered service in the late 1920s.

# BREGUET
# MODEL 19

● Day-bomber ● Reconnaissance ● Long-range record breaker

**F**rance introduced the Breguet 19 day-bomber and reconnaissance aircraft in 1922. This practical biplane was built in larger numbers than any other inter-war type and excelled in tough conditions during colonial operations in Africa and Asia. The Breguet was also manufactured abroad and reached users as diverse as Persia and Japan. Pilots greatly admired the two-seat aircraft, which kept pace with advances in aviation during its era.

▲ Aviation Militaire
(French air force) personnel pose proudly by a 15ᵉ Escadrille Bre.19 A.2. The type was built in two main variants, the A.2 for reconnaissance and the B.2 bomber.

## BREGUET MODEL 19

◀ **Spanish special**
Named Cuatro Vientos, this was a long-range special built by CASA. It flew from Seville to Cuba non-stop, but was then lost flying on to Mexico.

▲ **Civil War in Spain**
Breguet 19s were licence-built by CASA in Spain, and both sides used the type during the Spanish Civil War. This aircraft carries Nationalist markings.

**French bomber** ▶
Many French bomber squadrons were equipped with the Bre.19 B.2 between 1926 and 1933. The aircraft served reliably in overseas colonies, seeing action in several small wars.

▲ **Pride of France**
The prototype A.2 version was displayed at the 1921 Paris Air Show before it had flown.

▼ **Balkan warrior**
Greece bought 30 Bre.19s in 1930 and the survivors saw action in World War II, attempting to fend off the Italian invasion.

▲ **Export success**
Large numbers of Breguet 19s were sold overseas. In South America it served with Argentina (illustrated), while Bolivia and Paraguay took their aircraft to war. It also flew with Brazil and Venezuela.

## FACTS AND FIGURES

➤ The prototype Breguet 19 first took to the air in March 1922.

➤ Test pilot Pierre Messerli referred to the Breguet 19 as 'a love affair – the way you love your mother'.

➤ More than 1,000 of these fine aircraft were built for the French air arm.

➤ A Breguet 19 flew a record-breaking 7905 km from Paris to Manchuria in 1929.

➤ Spain's CASA completed 203 Breguet 19s, some with Spanish engines.

➤ The last Bre.19s to be completed were 48 Kraljevo-built machines delivered to the Yugoslav air force in 1937.

## PROFILE

# Backbone of the French air force

Breguet's chief engineer Louis Vuillerme put his considerable experience with earlier, successful aircraft into the Breguet 19. The result was a metal warplane with fabric-covered wings of unequal span, fixed landing gear and open cockpits. It had a very long range for the period, and the aircraft was used on many record flights in the 1920s.

The Breguet 19 was one of the best bombers of its time and proved extremely reliable. It was manufactured in huge numbers, with close to 2,500 being built in 15 years of production in Belgium, France, Spain and Yugoslavia.

France used the Breguet 19 against Druze tribesmen in Syria and Riff insurgents in Morocco. Spain became a major operator in its colonial wars of the 1930s. Others went to Belgium, Bolivia, Britain, Italy, Poland and Paraguay. Two were delivered

to Japan, where the Japanese Nakajima company eventually decided not to proceed with production plans.

Yugoslavian aircraft saw action against the Wehrmacht in 1941, and were later used by Croat forces. Two survived to be captured by Tito's partisans in 1945.

*Left: The ultimate long-range Breguet 19 was the one-off 'Super Bidon', seen here in 1929, the year of its record-breaking flight.*

*Right: Named Nungesser-Coli, this Breguet 19 made the first non-stop flight across the South Atlantic on 14/15 October 1927. It flew from St Louis, Senegal, to Port Natal in Brazil.*

### Breguet 19 B.2

**Type:** two-seat reconnaissance bomber

**Powerplant:** one 336-kW (450-hp.) Lorraine 12Ed inline piston engine

**Maximum speed:** 214 km/h (133 m.p.h.) at sea level

**Range:** 800 km (500 mi.)

**Service ceiling:** 7200 m (23,600 ft.)

**Weights:** empty equipped 1387 kg (3,051 lb.); maximum take-off 2500 kg (5,500 lb.)

**Armament:** one fixed forward-firing 7.7-mm (.303 cal.) Lewis machine-gun and two Lewis guns mounted in the rear cockpit, plus provision for 30 10-kg (22-lb.), eight 50-kg (110-lb.) or two 200-kg (440-lb.) bombs

**Dimensions:**
| | | |
|---|---|---|
| span | 14.83 m | (49 ft.) |
| length | 9.61 m | (32 ft.) |
| height | 3.69 m | (12 ft.) |
| wing area | 50 m² | (538 sq. ft.) |

The 'Super Bidon' was powered by a Hispano-Suiza 12Lb engine for its distance record-breaking flight. Earlier it had featured a Lorraine-Dietrich 12Db.

The upper wings and the raised forward fuselage severely restricted the pilot's view making taxiing the aircraft especially dangerous. The guns fitted in the rear cockpit were removed to save weight.

The 'GR' on the fin stood for 'Grand Raid' – literally 'long range'. The 'Super Bidon' was the last in a series of special 'GR' aircraft built by Breguet.

A feature of the Breguet 19 was its protruding radiator below the engine cowling.

The 'Super Bidon' special aircraft was given extra fuel tankage in the upper wings, in the lengthened fuselage and in the underwing slipper tanks. The word *bidon* is French for petrol can.

The 'Super Bidon' carried a large question mark and was called the *Point d'Interrogation*. The cigognes (stork) badge was from a famous World War I fighter squadron.

## BREGUET 19 'SUPER BIDON'

The most famous of the 'Grand Raid' aircraft, *Point d'Interrogation*, undertook a failed attempt to cross the Atlantic, only reaching the Azores. It was later used to gain the world distance record.

## COMBAT DATA

### MAXIMUM SPEED

Throughout the 1920s, the speed of warplanes showed no dramatic improvement over those of World War I. The Breguet 19 was not a streamlined design, but did have a powerful engine and its drag was minimised by having a very short lower wing.

| | |
|---|---|
| BREGUET 19 B.2 | 214 km/h (133 m.p.h.) |
| DH.9A | 198 km/h (123 m.p.h.) |
| O-1E | 227 km/h (140 m.p.h.) |

### ARMAMENT

For observation and light bomber aircraft of the 1920s, defensive armament was fairly standard, comprising one forward-firing machine-gun and two on a ring mount in the observer's cockpit. Most used the World War I-vintage Vickers and Lewis guns.

| BREGUET 19 B.2 | DH.9A | O-1E |
|---|---|---|
| 3 x 7.7-mm MGs | 3 x 7.7-mm MGs | 2 x 7.7-mm MGs<br>1 x 7.62-mm MG |

### RANGE

Thanks to its 'Grand Raid' special variants, the Breguet 19 has a reputation for long range, but in its mainstream service versions it was at the lower end of the league compared to its competitors. The range was respectable for its day, and was more than adequate for the tasks it was used for.

DH.9A 850 km (525 mi.)
BREGUET 19 B.2 800 km (500 mi.)
O-1E 1014 km (630 mi.)

## Breguet's early dynasty

■ **BREGUET G.3:** The company of Louis Breguet was active before the start of the war. The G.3 was a typical product, with a 97-kW (130-hp.) engine driving a four-bladed propeller.

■ **BREGUET 5:** A handful of Breguet 5s served as fighters during World War I, armed with a 37-mm Hotchkiss cannon. There was also a bomber version armed with six light bombs.

■ **BREGUET 14:** One of France's best-known warplanes, the Bre.14 was built in huge numbers. It served from 1917 until 1932 in many roles, including bomber and air ambulance.

■ **BREGUET 17:** Essentially a scaled-down but up-engined Bre.14, the Breguet 17 was intended as a fighter, and a few saw service in the last months of World War I.

■ **BREGUET XX:** Known as the Léviathan, the Bre.XX was an attempt to provide an early airliner. The Breguet-Bugatti powerplant consisted of four engines driving one propeller.

# BREGUET

# 690

● Little-known World War II bomber ● Early Breguet monoplane

I n October 1934 the French air ministry issued a specification for a new fighter. As well as serving as a two-seat day or night-fighter, it was to be capable of carrying the commander of a fighter formation. The Breguet 690 prototype was rejected because it was more than 1000 kg (2,200 lb.) heavier than the maximum 3500 kg (7,700 lb.) specified. Despite its weight, though, it was faster than its rivals and was subsequently developed as the 691 two-seat attack aircraft.

▲ One of the best French aircraft at the outbreak of World War II, the Breguet 690, originally designed as a fighter, ended up as an attack aircraft. Built in three major versions, its operational career was cut short by the Nazi occupation of France.

# BREGUET 690

### Quick into service ▶
By May 1940 several units, mainly belonging to Groupement 18, were equipped with the Bre. 693.

### ▼ Beaufighter forerunner
A trio of Bre. 693s in flight illustrate the distinctive lines, reminiscent of the later Bristol heavy fighter.

### ▼ Franco-American Breguet
More powerful Pratt & Whitney Twin Wasp radials marked the Breguet 695. This variant was the last major production version and entered service in 1940. In all 50 were built and they ended up being operated by GBA 151 of the Armée de l'Air Armistice (Vichy French Air Force) until late 1942.

### ▲ Italian trainers
In 1943 the few 690s that remained were transferred to the Regia Aeronautica in Italy for use as operational trainers.

### Rush order ▶
Built to a Triplace de Chasse (three-seat fighter) specification, the first Breguet 690 was a very clean-looking aircraft when it was rolled out in April 1938. Before it had even flown, a production order for 100 examples was given by the French air ministry.

## FACTS AND FIGURES

➤ Although design of the 690 began in 1935, the prototype did not fly until 1937, because of a lack of suitable engines.

➤ The change from the fighter to ground attack role resulted in the 691.

➤ Engines could be removed, overhauled and replaced in one hour 30 minutes.

➤ The second major variant, the 693, was powered by Gnome-Rhône engines instead of Hispano Suizas fitted to 691s.

➤ Production ceased when German forces over-ran the factory at Villacoublay.

➤ Breguet 695s, despite more powerful engines, were not popular with pilots.

# PROFILE

# Promising attack bomber

After making its first flight in March 1938, the Breguet 690 was ordered for the French air force as the 691-AB2 attack bomber. Early models had 522-kW (700-hp.) Hispano-Suiza 14AB10/11 engines, but later aircraft of the 78 production run had 597-kW (800-hp.) 14AB12/13s.

In 1940 the 691 version was superseded in production by the 693, which was fitted with 522-kW (700-hp.) Gnome-Rhône 14M6/7 engines. About 130 were built before the German occupation, along with 33 examples of the 695, which was powered by 615-kW (825-hp.) Pratt & Whitney Twin Wasp Juniors. Breguet had also

produced a new fighter design, the 692, to meet a two-seat fighter specification issued at the end of 1936. This was then developed as the 697 and the intended production version, designated the Breguet 700, would have been armed with two cannon and two or four machine-guns.

Two prototypes were ordered, and there were plans to start production of the 700 alongside the 693 and 695 attack aircraft, but these were halted by the German invasion of May 1940. Subsequently, some of the 693s and 695s captured by the Germans were transferred to Italy and used by the Italian air force as crew trainers.

*Above: A clean, squat fuselage, mid-mounted wing and twin tails were distinctive 690 features.*

Fabric-covered metal control surfaces were a feature of the 690. In flight the aircraft had pleasant handling and was quite agile for its size.

An endearing feature of the 693, especially to the technicians, was its ease of maintenance. An entire engine could be removed, overhauled and quickly replaced.

A simple and rugged structure meant that the Bre. 693 could sustain heavy battle damage and still return to base. This was demonstrated on several occasions.

## Bre.693

**Type:** two-seat attack bomber

**Powerplant:** two 522-kW (700-hp.) Gnome-Rhône 14M-6/7 radial engines

**Maximum speed:** 490 km/h (304 m.p.h.)

**Cruising speed:** 299 km/h (185 m.p.h.)

**Range:** 1350 km (837 mi.)

**Service ceiling:** 5000 m (16,400 ft.) (est.)

**Weights:** empty 3010 kg (6,622 lb.); loaded 4900 kg (10,780 lb.)

**Armament:** one 20-mm (0.79-in.) Hispano Suiza cannon and three 7.5-mm (0.3-in.) Darne machine guns plus up to 400 kg (880 lb.) of bombs

**Dimensions:**
span 15.73 m (51 ft. 7 in.)
length 9.67 m (31 ft. 9 in.)
height 3.19 m (10 ft. 5 in.)
wing area 29.20 m² (314 sq. ft.)

## BRE 693

This aircraft belonged to GBA (Groupe Bombardement d'Assaut) II/54. Based at Roye during May 1940, this unit flew sorties against the advancing Germans in the Tongeren area.

A single-seat cockpit was located in the nose. Pilots enjoyed flying the 693 which was remarkably capable in the air, especially at low level. This performance was improved by the substitution of more reliable engines.

Production attack bombers had the navigator's station replaced by a small internal bomb bay which could accommodate 50-kg (108-lb.) bombs.

Located just behind the wing was a second cockpit for a gunner/radio operator who had a single 7.5-mm (0.3-in.) MAC machine-gun for defence. The two fuselage mainframes separated the crew compartments.

Aircraft flying with the Armée de l'Air carried their unit colours on the rear fuselage. Breguet 693 No. 1013 of GBA II/54 wore these very distinctive markings in June 1940.

## COMBAT DATA

### MAXIMUM SPEED
Despite the excellent performance of the Breguet 690, the French air ministry selected the Potez 63 instead; the latter aircraft proved less effective in combat although it was marginally faster. The Messerschmitt Bf 110 was primarily a fighter and thus quicker.

BREGUET 693 — 490 km/h (304 m.p.h.)
POTEZ 63 — 440 km/h (273 m.p.h.)
MESSERSCHMITT Bf 110C — 562 km/h (348 m.p.h.)

### RANGE
A problem that plagued the Luftwaffe was the inadequate range of its fighters, including the Bf 110. This gave them little combat time over enemy territory. French aircraft such as the Breguet 690 and Potez 63 had a much greater radius of action.

BREGUET 693 1350 km (837 mi.)
POTEZ 63 1500 km (930 mi.)
Bf 110C 850 km (527 mi.)

### ARMAMENT
Armament was crucial to the survivability of bombers during World War II. The Potez 63 had no hard-hitting cannon and many of these aircraft were easily shot down by German fighters in 1940. Bre. 690s proved to be tougher opposition.

BREGUET 693 1 x 20-mm (0.79-in.) cannon 4 x 7.5-mm (0.3-in.) MG
POTEZ 63 8 x 7.5-mm (0.3-in.) MG
BF 110C 2 x 20-mm (0.79-in.) cannon, 5 x 7.92-mm (0.31-in.) MG

## Breguet 690 operators

■ **ARMÉE DE L'AIR:** Belonging to Groupement 18, this was one of many 690s on strength that braved the German onslaught in May 1940. These aircraft were based at La Ferte Gaucher.

■ **ARMÉE DE L'AIR ARMISTICE:** Remaining aircraft were assigned to newly formed Vichy units in late 1940. This Pratt & Whitney engined Bre. 695 flew with GBA 1/51 at Lezignan.

■ **REGIA AERONAUTICA:** When the Germans took total control of France in 1942, the few remaining Bre. 690s were transferred to Italy. These only served until the armistice in 1943.

# BRISTOL

# BEAUFIGHTER

● Rocket-armed fighter ● Anti-shipping ● Torpedo strike

▲ Beaufighter crews had great confidence in their aircraft, which had a combination of long range, fair speed, massive strength and the heaviest gun armament of any Allied fighter.

**D**ubbed 'Whispering Death' by the Japanese, the heavily-armed Bristol Beaufighter could be tricky to handle, especially in low-speed flight. It was nevertheless one of the most lethal warplanes of its era and was a Royal Air Force stalwart in the battle against Germany's night offensive over Britain. The powerful, slab-winged Beaufighter went on to become one of the most potent anti-shipping strike aircraft of the war.

---

## BRISTOL BEAUFIGHTER

▲ **New tail**
The early Beaufighters experienced some instability when carrying a torpedo, but this was corrected by fitting a dihedral tailplane. The Beaufighter proved to be a very stable weapon launching platform.

▲ **Rocket raid**
Armed with eight rockets, the Beaufighter blasted coastal targets throughout Norway.

▲ **Bristol factory**
Over 5500 Beaufighters were built, not only by the Bristol Aeroplane Company, but also at factories in Australia.

**Radar nose ►**
The TF.Mk X version carried a nose thimble centimetric radar for detecting surface ships. It was the first radome fairing ever fitted to an aircraft.

▲ **Torpedo bomber**
By 1944, many Beaufighters were used as anti-shipping torpedo aircraft. They brought German coastal shipping in Europe to a standstill.

### FACTS AND FIGURES

➤ The first 50 Beaufighters built claimed 60 aerial victories in night battles over Britain in 1941.

➤ The Beaufighter prototype's maiden flight took place on 17 July 1939.

➤ First flight of a Merlin-powered Beaufighter occurred on 26 July 1940.

➤ RAF Beaufighters attacked Japanese forces at Myitkyina in occupied Burma on the Emperor's birthday.

➤ Australian Beaufighters sank more than 700 Japanese vessels in 1945.

➤ Between 1939 and 1944, a total of 5564 Beaufighters were manufactured.

## PROFILE

# The 'Whispering Death'

A snub-nosed battleship of a plane which first appeared in 1939, the twin-engined Beaufighter was immensely strong and surprisingly manoeuvrable. Although early Hercules-engined Beaufighters were a little underpowered, the more powerful engines of later models made them fast and snappy.

The Beaufighter was roomy enough to carry the bulky first generation of AI (airborne intercept) radar, and when radar-equipped fighters joined the RAF, they became a strong reason for the Luftwaffe abandoning its night assaults on London.

Eventually, the 'Beau' fought on all fronts. Rockets were added to the type's potent gun armament in 1943 and in combination with air-launched torpedoes made the beefy aircraft a superb long-range fighter, fighter-bomber and anti-shipping machine. Beaufighters

*Left: When all eight rockets were fired at once, the effect was devastating. A rocket salvo was equivalent to the broadside from a cruiser's main guns.*

destroyed German shipping running down the coast from Norway. Australian Beaufighters did a similar job with Japanese shipping, and it was their victims that gave the aircraft the name 'Whispering Death', a reference to the distinctive noise made by the sleeve-valve radial engine.

*Above: Beaufighters were formed into specialised strike wings, with a mixture of torpedo- and rocket-armed aircraft able to destroy any target at sea.*

### Beaufighter TF.Mk X

**Type:** two-seat low-level strike fighter

**Powerplant:** two 1320-kW (1,770-hp.) Bristol Hercules XVIII radial piston engines

**Maximum speed:** 488 km/h (330 m.p.h.) at 400 m (1,312 ft.)

**Range:** 2366 km (1,470 mi.)

**Service ceiling:** 4570 m (29,000 ft.)

**Weights:** empty 7076 kg (15,507 lb.); loaded 11,431 kg (25,200 lb.)

**Armament:** six forward-firing 7.7-mm (.303 cal.) machine-guns and one flexible 7.7-mm Vickers 'K' machine-gun in dorsal position, four forward-firing 20-mm (0.79-in.) cannon, plus one torpedo and two 113-kg (230-lb.) bombs or eight 41-kg (90-lb.) air-to-surface rockets

**Dimensions:**
| | | |
|---|---|---|
| span | 17.63 m | (58 ft.) |
| length | 12.70 m | (42 ft.) |
| height | 4.83 m | (16 ft.) |
| wing area | 46.73 m² | (503 sq. ft.) |

## BEAUFIGHTER MK VI

**The Beaufighter Mk VI was the first of the type to be supplied to the US Army Air Force (USAAF), serving in the Middle East and Mediterranean with the 1st Tactical Air Command.**

The observer's rear bubble could mount a single Vickers 'K' machine-gun for defence. The rear fuselage contained a store of food and water for emergency survival.

The tail was modified in the Beaufighter Mk II because the liquid-cooled Merlin engine caused the aircraft's centre of gravity to change, leading to instability problems.

KV912

The Hercules radial was a solid and reliable design, which had 'sleeve valves' that were built around the sides of the engine cylinders.

A tough wing was another great strength of the Beaufighter design, which was able to carry rocket rails or a 113-kg (250-lb.) bomb. It could also survive heavy combat damage.

Crew entered the Beaufighter through hatches in the underside of the fuselage. These could also be used as an emergency exit, in addition to a knock-out window in the canopy.

## COMBAT DATA

### RANGE

The Ju 88 was designed as a bomber and had long range. The Pe-2 was originally intended as a long-range fighter like the Bf 110; it could fly further than most single-seat fighters but not as far as dedicated long-range strike aircraft. The Beaufighter's performance was somewhere between the two, with good range for a strike aircraft.

BEAUFIGHTER TF.Mk X 2366 km (1,470 mi.)

Ju 88A-4 2730 km (1,693 mi.)

Pe-2 bis 1160 km (719 mi.)

### MAXIMUM SPEED

The Beaufighter was not powerful enough to outrun single-engined fighters, but it could hold its own with a Bf 110 or Ju 88. The Pe-2 was a much faster machine, but mainly because it carried less fuel and had a sleeker design.

BEAUFIGHTER TF.Mk X — 488 km/h (330 m.p.h.)

Ju 88C-2 — 470 km/h (291 m.p.h.)

Pe-2 bis — 540 km/h (334 m.p.h.)

### ATTACK ARMAMENT

The Beaufighter had devastating armament, more powerful than its contemporaries. Although its bombload was comparatively low on paper, it rarely acted as a bomber. The single torpedo or eight rockets were more than capable of destroying a ship.

**BEAUFIGHTER TF.Mk X** 4 x 20-mm (0.79-in.) cannon; 6 x 7.7-mm (.303 cal.) MGs; 500-kg (1,100-lb.) bombload

**Ju 88C-2** 3 x 20-mm (0.79-in.) cannon; 3 x 7.92-mm (0.31-in.) MGs; 1000-kg (2,200-lb.) bombload

**Pe-2 bis** 1 x 20-mm (0.79-in.) cannon; 1 x 12.7-mm (.50 cal.) MG; 2 x 7.62-mm (.30 cal.) MGs 1000-kg (2,200-lb.) bombload

## Beaufighter variants

■ **BEAUFIGHTER Mk I:** The first Beaufighters were used as night-fighters and long-range strike fighters. They fought with distinction in North Africa and in the Mediterranean.

■ **BEAUFIGHTER Mk II:** Shortages of the Bristol Hercules radial engine meant that the Beaufighter Mk II was refitted with the Rolls-Royce Merlin. All Mk IIs served as night-fighters.

■ **TORPEDO BEAUFIGHTER Mk VI:** The first torpedo Beaufighter, known as a 'Torbeau', was the Mk VI. This used uprated Bristol Hercules VI engines and could carry bombs.

■ **TF.Mk X IN USAAF:** The TF.Mk X was one of the only British aircraft used by the USAAF in World War II. The earlier Mk VI had also been used by them in the Middle East.

■ **AUSTRALIAN Mk 21:** The Beaufighter Mk 21 was basically an Australian-built TF.Mk X, performing anti-shipping strike missions with the aid of its own nose-mounted radar.

# BRISTOL

# BLENHEIM MK IV

● Twin-engined light bomber ● European, Asian and Middle Eastern service

▲ Despite its early obsolescence in its intended role, with its slow speed and modest weapon load, Blenheim production reached 3297. Some were built by Rootes and Avro.

Its performance was startling in the early 1930s, but the Blenheim proved inadequate for the demands of World War II combat. By 1941 the bomber was clearly obsolescent, but it had been designated a 'super-priority' type and thousands more were built. The Mk IV remained in service for a further two years with Bomber Command, and survived even longer in North Africa and the Far East. More than 600 were built in Canada, mainly for training.

---

## BRISTOL BLENHEIM MK IV

▼ Groupe 'Lorraine'
Equipped with 21 Blenheim Mk IVs, this unit of Free French personnel operated in Syria and the Western Desert in 1941 and 1942. During six months in 1942, 388 day sorties were flown.

▲ RAF bomber of the early war years
An RAF Blenheim Mk IV was the first British aircraft to cross the German border, making a reconnaissance flight on 3 September 1939. The following day Blenheims made the first Bomber Command raids.

◀ Training in Canada
The bulk of Canadian-built Blenheims were engaged in training navigators and gunners for the duration of the war.

▼ Operational Training Units
Although they flew their last operations with Bomber Command in August 1942, Mk IVs continued to serve with training units.

◀ Mk IV formation
The nearest of these three Mk IVs has a Frazer-Nash remotely-controlled turret under the nose. This would normally carry two 7.7-mm (.303 cal.) Browning machine-guns to defend against attack from below.

## FACTS AND FIGURES

➤ Ten Mk IVs were built in Finland in 1944 and undertook forestry and survey work until as late as 1956.

➤ Other wartime operators of the Mk IV included Finland, Greece and Portugal.

➤ One Mk IV was experimentally fitted with a radar in a hemispherical nose radome.

➤ The only surviving airworthy Blenheim is a Bolingbroke trainer restored to flying condition and based at Duxford.

➤ The intended replacement for the Mk IV, the Mk V was slower but better armed.

➤ Blenheim IV production accounted for just over half of all Blenheims made.

# RAF light bomber veteran

*After they had outlived their usefulness in Europe, RAF Blenheims were particularly active in the Middle East. Despite their turrets, they were no match for enemy fighters.*

One of the main drawbacks of the Blenheim Mk I was its very cramped navigator's compartment. A new nose with improved accommodation was one of the principal improvements offered by the Mk IV, which replaced the Mk I in production from late 1938.

All but the first 80 Mk IVs had more powerful engines and additional fuel tanks in the wings, which improved their range. Deliveries to RAF squadrons started in March 1939, and after World War II began some were fitted with rear-firing machine-guns in a remotely-controlled turret under the nose. A fighter variant had a four-gun pack under the fuselage.

Blenheim Mk IVs carried out the RAF's first bombing raid of the war, and from late 1940 flew many missions over Germany. There was also a Mk V (briefly known as the Bisley), which was even slower than the earlier models but was used by 10 RAF squadrons in North Africa and the Far East.

Mark IVs were built under licence in Finland, and more than 600 were produced in Canada under the name Bolingbroke. Most were completed as navigation and gunnery trainers; others could be fitted with ski landing gear and used for maritime reconnaissance duties.

*Although painted to resemble a Blenheim Mk IV, the only Blenheim that is still airworthy is, in fact, a Bolingbroke Mk IV-T trainer.*

## Blenheim Mk IV

**Type:** three-seat light bomber

**Powerplant:** two 675-kW (905-hp.) Bristol Mercury XV nine-cylinder air-cooled radial piston engines

**Maximum speed:** 428 km/h (265 m.p.h.) at 3595 m (11,800 ft.)

**Range:** 2350 km (1,460 mi.)

**Service ceiling:** 8310 m (27,250 ft.)

**Weights:** empty 4441 kg (9,770 lb.); loaded 6532 kg (14,370 lb.)

**Armament:** five 7.7-mm (.303 cal.) machine-guns and 579 kg (1,274 lb.) of bombs

**Dimensions:**
| | | |
|---|---|---|
| span | 17.17 m | (58 ft. 4 in.) |
| length | 12.98 m | (42 ft. 7 in.) |
| height | 3.00 m | (9 ft. 10 in.) |
| wing area | 43.57 m² | (469 sq. ft.) |

## BOLINGBROKE MK IV

**Aircraft 9140 carries the maritime patrol markings of No. 115(BR) Squadron, Royal Canadian Air Force (RCAF), with which it operated from Patricia Bay, British Columbia, in August 1943.**

The Blenheim/Bolingbroke's three crew consisted of a pilot, navigator/observer and a gunner for the dorsal turret.

Most 'long-nosed' Blenheims were fitted with a dorsal turret, containing two 7.7-mm (.303 cal.) machine-guns, for self-defence. Late-build Mk IVs had a remotely-controlled Frazer-Nash aft-firing, two-gun turret beneath the nose.

In Canada the Fairchild Aircraft Company built 676 Blenheim IVs. Those with RCAF serials 9001 to 9201 were constructed with American instruments and equipment and were known as Bolingbroke Mk IVs.

Due to the harsh winter conditions, Bolingbroke Mk IVs were fitted with de-icing boots on their wings and tail surfaces.

The tried and tested Bristol Mercury nine-cylinder radial powered most Blenheims, although when engine supplies from England were under threat a small number were built in Canada with Pratt & Whitney Twin Wasp Juniors as the Bolingbroke Mk IV-W.

The small fuselage bomb-bay of the Mk IV bombers had a 454-kg (1,000-lb.) capacity. A further 145 kg (320 lb.) could be carried under the wings. The Bolingbrokes used for maritime patrol in Canada were equipped with dinghies.

The markings carried by home-based RCAF units were often at variance with those employed by RAF aircraft in the same role. This aircraft has an unusually small roundel on the fuselage and has its serial number painted under the port wing.

A single Bolingbroke Mk III was fitted with Edo floats for evaluation, but was later reconverted to a landplane.

## COMBAT DATA

### MAXIMUM SPEED

One of the main handicaps facing the Blenheim was its relatively slow top speed. It was at least 100 km/h slower than other light bombers of the period. Fighter speeds increased markedly within a short space of time in the early years of the war and rendered bombers like these, which appeared to be fast enough when they were designed, outdated.

| | |
|---|---|
| BLENHEIM Mk IV | 428 km/h (265 m.p.h.) |
| Pe-2FT | 534 km/h (360 m.p.h.) |
| MB.175 B.3 | 540 km/h (335 m.p.h.) |

### RANGE

The Blenheim Mk IV's range was good for its size, especially when extra wing tankage had been installed in later production examples. Both the Bloch 175 and Petlyakov Pe-2 had a shorter range. Long range was a useful attribute in the maritime reconnaissance role.

BLENHEIM Mk IV 2350 km (1,457 mi.)

Pe-2FT 1770 km (1,100 mi.)

MB.175 B.3 1600 km (995 mi.)

### ARMAMENT

In addition to its speed disadvantage, the Blenheim suffered from a shortage of defensive guns. The Pe-2 was not only fast, but was well armed. Even the Bloch 175 boasted nine guns and an equivalent bombload to the Blenheim.

| BLENHEIM Mk IV | Pe-2FT | MB.175 B.3 |
|---|---|---|
| 5 x 7.7-mm (.303 cal.) machine-guns 579-kg (1,284-lb.) bombload | 2 x 20-mm (0.79-in.) cannon 2 x 12.7-mm (.50 cal.) machine-guns 2 x 7.62-mm (.30 cal.) machine-guns 1000-kg (2,200-lb.) bombload | 2 x 20-mm (0.79-in.) cannon 7 x 17.5-mm (0.69-in.) machine-guns 600-kg (1,320-lb.) bombload |

## Blenheims at war

**FIRST BOMBER COMMAND RAIDS:** On 4 September 1939 Blenheim Mk IVs of Nos 107 and 110 Squadrons made a raid on the German fleet at Schillig Roads.

**IN THE WESTERN DESERT:** Although vulnerable to fighter attack, Blenheims were employed by Middle East Command against Axis ground forces in the early 1940s.

**ANTI-SHIPPING PATROL:** RCAF Bolingbrokes based in Canada flew patrols over the Atlantic. RAF Bomber Command's No. 2 Group sank many tons of shipping during the same period.

# BRISTOL
# BULLDOG

● 1920s design ● Export aircraft in World War II ● Biplane fighter

▲ *Finland's Bulldogs saw more combat than most. They served for longer than those operated by the RAF, which were retired in 1939.*

**B**ritain's reliance on biplane fighters during the 1920s and early 1930s caused it to lag behind other countries in fighter design. Although no successful monoplane fighters were produced, several excellent biplanes were built, including the Bristol Bulldog. Export examples of the Bulldog saw extensive combat during the Spanish Civil War of 1936-39 and the Winter War of 1939-40. A few even survived into World War II.

## BRISTOL **BULLDOG**

### ▲ Finnish deliveries
*Finland received Mk IVA aircraft in January 1935. They were the last Bulldogs built at Bristol's Filton plant and were delayed by a dispute between Bristol and Gnome-Rhône over the manufacture of their Mercury engines.*

### ▲ Denmark's Bulldogs
*Designated Type 105D, the Bulldogs supplied to Denmark were basically Mk IIAs which often operated with skis. Only four were delivered.*

### ▼ Bulldog at war
*Pictured in 1940, this Finnish Bulldog is a Mk IIA. This type was supplied to Finland by Sweden and was flown in the Winter War.*

### ▲ Swedish transfer
*Sweden took delivery of 11 Bulldogs in two batches. The second batch, of eight, was flown to Sweden from Filton by Swedish pilots in 1931.*

### ▼ Estonian line-up
*Estonia first received Bulldogs in 1930. The aircraft were popular with Baltic and Scandinavian air forces.*

## FACTS AND FIGURES

➤ A second order from Finland, together with an Austrian requirement for 45 Bulldogs, was refused in 1936.

➤ Some RAF Bulldog Mk IIAs served with fighter training schools until 1939.

➤ Only one Bulldog survives, a Finnish example serialled BU-59.

➤ A few RAF senior officers used Bulldogs as personal transports until the start of World War II.

➤ Both Finland and Sweden operated their Bulldogs on skis.

➤ Britain's last airworthy Bulldog was destroyed in a crash in 1964.

# PROFILE

# Bulldog's Winter War

Latvia received a batch of five Bulldog Mk IIs in 1929. Other export orders followed, most significantly from Sweden in 1930, Denmark in 1931 and Finland in 1933. The Finnish aircraft were the last Bulldogs built and were completed to Mk IVA standard with Mercury VIS.2 engines.

By 1936 second-hand Latvian aircraft were in Spain, flying in support of the Basque cause during the Spanish Civil War. When the Winter War with Russia began in 1939, most of Finland's 17

Bulldog Mk IVAs were still serving with fighter squadron LLv 26. They scored at least five victories. Although the type was replaced by Gloster Gladiators in 1940, one aircraft survived both the Winter War and World War II. One of three Bulldog Mk IIAs supplied to Finland from Swedish stocks served as a

trainer until 1940, together with a few Mk IVAs.

Danish plans to licence-build Bulldogs were abandoned, but the Danish Army Aviation Troop still had three of its four Type 105D Bulldogs in service as fighter trainers when Germany invaded the country in April 1940.

*Above: Swedish Bulldogs served faultlessly for several years, enduring the severe conditions of the country's harsh winter.*

*Left: All of the Bulldogs delivered to Finland direct from Bristol were Mk IVAs. This aircraft is the only surviving Bulldog in the world.*

In common with the majority of inter-war RAF fighters, the Bulldog carried two forward-firing machine-guns. One was fitted on each side of the forward fuselage, firing through the cowling.

High-tensile steel strips were used in forming the Bulldog's structure. The wings and fuselage were fabric-covered. The Mk IVA represented the pinnacle of Bulldog development, with drag reduced to a minimum.

BU-68

Bristol was unhappy with the quality of the Mercury engines being supplied under licence by Gnome-Rhône and considerable debate went on before Finland received British-manufactured powerplants.

Finnish Bulldog Mk IVAs had an uprated electrical system for operations in Arctic environments. It could be used for warming of the guns and also for the electrically-heated flying suits worn by the crew.

Unlike the more advanced I-153, against which it fought, the Bulldog had a fixed undercarriage. Here, in common with the main units, the tailwheel has been replaced by a ski.

Several Finnish aircraft, including the Bulldog, flew with skis. This alternative fixture was a common feature even before the Winter War, easing operations in the north of Finland.

## BULLDOG MK IVA

Purchased early in 1935, Finland's Bulldog Mk IVAs fought with valour and some survived into the early 1940s. This aircraft is in the colours of TLeLv 35, as worn in the opening months of 1942.

## Bulldog Mk IIA

**Type:** single-seat biplane fighter

**Powerplant:** one 328-kW (440-hp.) Bristol Jupiter VIIF air-cooled radial piston engine

**Maximum speed:** 286 km/h (177 m.p.h.) at 3050 m (10,000 ft.)

**Climb rate:** climb to 6095 m (20,000 ft.) in 14 min 30 sec

**Range:** 499 km (310 mi.)

**Service ceiling:** 8230 m (27,000 ft.)

**Weights:** empty 1008 kg (2,218 lb.); maximum take-off 1660 kg (3,652 lb.)

**Armament:** two fixed forward-firing synchronised 7.7-mm (.303 cal.) Vickers machine-guns, plus provision for four 9-kg (20-lb.) bombs

**Dimensions:**
| | | |
|---|---|---|
| span | 10.34 m | (33 ft. 11 in.) |
| length | 7.67 m | (25 ft. 2 in.) |
| height | 3.00 m | (9 ft. 10 in.) |
| wing area | 28.47 m² | (306 sq. ft.) |

## COMBAT DATA

### MAXIMUM SPEED

Compared to other types flown during the Winter War, the Bulldog was much slower, especially in its Mk IIA form as donated by Sweden. Even the Gloster Gauntlet biplane had better performance than the Bulldog.

**BULLDOG Mk IIA** 286 km/h (117 m.p.h.)

**I-16 TYPE 24** 490 km/h (288 m.p.h.)

**GAUNTLET Mk II** 370 km/h (229 m.p.h.)

### SERVICE CEILING

The Gauntlet's more powerful engine ensured that its service ceiling was superior to that of its rivals such as the I-16. In spite of its comparatively poor performance, the Bulldog achieved some success against the I-16, thanks to determined piloting.

**GAUNTLET Mk II** 10210 m (33,500 ft.)

**I-16 TYPE 24** 9470 m (31,070 ft.)

**BULLDOG Mk IIA** 8230 m (27,000 ft.)

### GUN ARMAMENT

The Bulldog Mk IIA and the Gauntlet Mk II served the Finns well, but both aircraft were handicapped by the standard inter-war RAF fighter armament of two forward-firing guns. Some I-16s carried an additional 12.7-mm (.50 cal.) weapon.

**BULLDOG Mk IIA** 2 x 7.7-mm (.303 cal.) machine-guns

**I-16 TYPE 24** 4 x 7.62-mm (.30 cal.) machine-guns

**GAUNTLET Mk II** 2 x 7.7-mm (.303 cal.) machine-guns

## At war in Finland

**FOKKER D.XXI:** Two squadrons of Fokker D.XXIs formed the backbone of Finland's Winter War air defence.

**GLOSTER GAUNTLET:** Finland flew a number of largely obsolescent biplane fighters, including the Gauntlet.

**POLIKARPOV I-153:** Several aircraft were captured by the Finns, including this I-153. The type proved very capable over Finland.

**POLIKARPOV I-16:** In the same manner as the I-153, several I-16s fell into Finnish hands. This is a two-seat I-16UTI.

# BRISTOL

# F.2B FIGHTER

● Two-seat, twin-gun fighter ● Long service career ● Army co-operation

A t a time when the RAF was reducing its forces in the peace following World War I, the Bristol F.2B Fighter became one of post-war Britain's most important and long-serving combat aircraft. Initial wartime losses with the less-developed F.2A led pilots to adopt new fighting tactics for the F.2B, making it one of the Allies' best two-seat fighters. The aircraft went on to serve into the 1930s in army co-operation and light attack roles.

▲ Serving with the RAF and many overseas air arms, the Bristol Fighter operated with distinction in countries as distant as China. It flew on into the early 1930s with No. 20 Squadron.

---

## BRISTOL F.2B FIGHTER

**Rear gun defence ▶**
Flown at its best, the F.2B used its rear gun for defensive purposes. This heavily retouched photograph shows the Lewis gun installation.

**▼ War on the Frontier**
For active service on India's North West Frontier, several F.2Bs were given larger rudders and bomb-carrying capabilities and became Bristol Fighter Mk IVs.

**▲ Civilian transport**
Substituting a Siddeley Puma engine for the Falcon of the Fighter and adding a 'coupé' cover over a modified two-seat rear cockpit produced the 206-km/h (128-m.p.h.) Bristol Tourer.

**▲ Historic start**
This preserved Bristol Fighter is being started by a Hucks starter.

**Jumping for joy ▶**
Bristol's Fighter was popular in service. The lower wing of this aircraft shows the shackles for a dozen 9-kg (20-lb.) Cooper bombs.

---

## FACTS AND FIGURES

➤ Falcon I engines were fitted to the first 150 aircraft, Falcon IIs to the next 50 and all other aircraft had the Falcon III.

➤ On 20 June 1917 the F.2B scored its first victory, against an Albatross D.III.

➤ During September and October 1917, 1,600 F.2Bs were ordered.

➤ As an alternative to the Falcon engine, Hispano-Suiza and Sunbeam Arab engines were tried, but without success.

➤ At the end of World War I the RAF had 1,583 F.2Bs in service.

➤ No. 20 Squadron was posted straight to India in 1918, without returning home.

**PROFILE**

# Revolutionary two-seat fighter

Bristol first flew its F.2A two-seat fighter on 9 September 1916. Powered by the 142-kW Rolls-Royce Falcon I, the aircraft was to have a disastrous combat debut.

Experience with the F.2A led to a number of improvements. These changes produced the F.2B Fighter, which first flew on 25 October 1916. With the introduction of the 205-kW

Falcon III engine, the F.2B became one of the greatest fighters of World War I. Pilots soon began using the forward gun for attacks, relying on their rear-seater to defend the aircraft against the enemy above and behind.

After the war many RAF squadrons were disbanded, but there was still important work to be done, especially abroad. British colonial interest

was still strong at this time and the F.2B found itself flying in a 'policing role'. These operations involved light-bombing duties and army co-operation.

Flying in the Middle East and other desert-like areas caused the F.2's engines to overheat as the radiators became clogged with sand. Fitted with new radiators, amongst other changes, the last RAF F.2B served in India until 1932.

*This is the only remaining airworthy Bristol Fighter. The Shuttleworth Collection flies the aircraft at air shows throughout the summer in the UK.*

## F.2B FIGHTER

New Zealand was one of the many countries to receive the Bristol Fighter. This aircraft served with the Royal New Zealand Air Force during 1919. Other users included Australia, Mexico and Spain.

### F.2B Fighter

**Type:** two-seat fighter and army co-operation and reconnaissance aircraft

**Powerplant:** one 205-kW (275-hp.) Rolls-Royce Falcon III 12-cylinder inline piston engine

**Maximum speed:** 198 km/h (123 m.p.h.) at 1525 m (5,000 ft.)

**Endurance:** 3 hours

**Climb rate:** climb to 3048 m (10,000 ft.) in 11 min 15 sec

**Service ceiling:** 5485 m (18,000 ft.)

**Weights:** empty 975 kg (2,145 lb.); maximum take-off 1474 kg (3,243 lb.)

**Armament:** three 7.7-mm (.303 cal.) machine-guns, plus a 108-kg (240-lb.) bombload

**Dimensions:** span 11.96 m (39 ft. 3 in.)
length 7.87 m (25 ft. 10 in.)
height 2.97 m (9 ft. 9 in.)
wing area 37.62 m² (405 sq. ft.)

### COMBAT DATA

**MAXIMUM SPEED**

In comparison with contemporaries at the time of its initial service entry, the Fighter was a fast machine. The F.2B could dive at speeds of up to 270 km/h (165 m.p.h.), without fear of structural failure. It was not as fast as the German single-seaters, however.

F.2B FIGHTER — 198 km/h (123 m.p.h.)
Br.14 A.2 — 184 km/h (114 m.p.h.)
C.II — 165 km/h (102 m.p.h.)

**MAXIMUM POWER**

The L.F.G. Roland C.II was a low-powered, slow aircraft, but the Breguet 14 A.2 featured considerably more power than the Bristol Fighter and yet, by comparison, had poor performance. The Falcon engine of the F.2B provided a reliable, constant output of power.

F.2B FIGHTER 205 kW (275 hp.) | Br.14 A.2 224 kW (300 hp.) | C.II 119.3 kW (160 hp.)

**ARMAMENT**

Many Bristol Fighters were fitted with twin Lewis guns in the rear cockpit. Attacks were carried out using the forward-firing Vickers machine-gun. A useful bombload could also be carried.

F.2B FIGHTER — 3 x 7.7-mm (.303 cal.) machine-guns, 108-kg (240-lb.) bombload
Br.14 A.2 — 2 x 7.7-mm (.303 cal.) machine-guns, 40-kg (90-lb.) bombload
C.II — 2 x 7.92-mm machine-guns

Running through a tunnel in the upper fuselage fuel tank, the forward-firing Vickers machine-gun was fitted beneath the engine cowling.

One or two 7.7-mm (.303 cal.) Lewis machine-guns were mounted on the Scarff ring in the rear cockpit. This mounting allowed the rear crewman to move the guns up or down and from side to side.

Tailplane incidence could be adjusted, allowing the aircraft to fly straight and level with the pilot's hands off the controls.

Throughout the production run of 5,329 British-built aircraft, no engine was found to be more suitable than the Rolls-Royce Falcon III. This engine powered all the service aircraft, with other powerplants quickly abandoned.

Most aircraft were fitted with very long exhaust pipes, which prevented noxious exhaust fumes entering the cockpit. Exhausts of this type covered the rear cockpit entry step, forcing the gunner to clamber over the hot exhaust when leaving the aircraft.

External cables linked the elevators to the pilot's control column. The rudder was operated by cables which disappeared into the rear fuselage just forward of the serial number.

All Bristol Fighters had a tailskid. Bomb-carrying aircraft serving in the Middle and Far East had strengthened main units with large 'desert tyres'. Special radiators were also required for desert operations.

## Bristol fighter designs of World War I

■ **SCOUT C:** A Royal Naval Air Service Scout C made the first deck take-off of the type on 3 November 1915.

■ **M.1 MONOPLANE:** Official distrust of the monoplane layout led to the few M.1s built serving away from the front line.

■ **SCOUT F:** Engine problems considerably delayed the first flight of the F until March 1918. No production aircraft were built.

■ **M.R.1:** The M.R.1 was an all-metal development of the F.2A. Only the two prototypes were built.

# BÜCKER

## BÜ 131 JUNGMANN/BÜ 133 JUNGMEISTER

● Two-seat Luftwaffe trainer ● Single-seat aerobatic aircraft

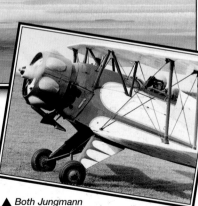

▲ Both Jungmann
and Jungmeister are docile, yet rugged,
aircraft. The Bü 133 Jungmeister has a better
performance thanks to its more powerful 119-kW
(160-hp.) Siemens radial engine.

**M**ost of Germany's World War II fighter aces had, at some time, flown Bücker's versatile light trainer, the Bü 131 Jungmann, or its sister aircraft, the single-seat Bü 133 Jungmeister advanced fighter trainer and aerobatic mount. Both of these aircraft were widely exported and production continued after the war. Large numbers of Bü 131s and Bü 133s still remain in airworthy condition.

▼ The aerobatic Jungmeister
Post-war the Bü 133 Jungmeister (Young Champion) has remained a very popular aerobatic aircraft.

▲ In the Luftwaffe
Until the arrival of the Bücker Bü 181 Bestmann, the Jungmann was the German Air Force's most important trainer.

Bü 133 stuntplane ▶
Identifiable by its larger engine cowling and single seat, this Jungmeister was used post-war as a stuntplane in the United States.

▼ Jungmann goes to war
The Jungmann was used in the war by auxiliary ground-attack squadrons, who were tasked with harassing Soviet forces at night.

▲ Bückers in Switzerland
The Swiss air force operated 75 licence-built Bü 131s. Shown here is one of 50 Swiss Dornier-Werke-built Bü 133Bs, which continued in service well into the 1950s.

## FACTS AND FIGURES

➤ Armed with light 1-kg and 2-kg bombs, Bü 131s flew night-time nuisance raids on the Eastern Front during 1941/42.

➤ The Bü 131 Jungmann was exported to a total of eight European air forces.

➤ The prototype Bü 131 first flew on 27 April 1934.

➤ The Bü 133B Jungmeister was licence-built in both Switzerland (by Dornier-Werke) and in Spain (by CASA).

➤ The entire Bü 133 series was built in a purpose-made factory at Rangsdorf.

➤ Initially flying with a Hirth inline engine, the Bü 133 later utilised a Siemens radial.

**PROFILE**

# Bücker's biplanes for the Luftwaffe

Bücker Aircraft's first ever product, the successful Bü 131 Jungmann (Youth), first flew in 1934, with the initial production Bü 131A variant serving with both the Luftwaffe and a range of civilian flying clubs. The definitive Bü 131B model, with an uprated Hirth engine, and the experimental prototype Bü 131C, with a 67-kW (90-hp.) Cirrus Minor powerplant, followed.

Bücker exported the Jungmann to various European nations, the largest customers being Hungary (100) and Romania (150). Licence production was undertaken in both Czechoslovakia and Switzerland. However, the most extensive licence construction took place in Japan, where Kyushu built 1,037 aircraft, known as the Ki-86A, for the army. The same company manufactured a further batch of K9W1s for the navy. The Bü 133 Jungmeister single-seat derivative was equally successful, both with the Luftwaffe, and when built later in Spain and Switzerland.

*Below: Switzerland was a major Bücker operator and producer. After being retired from the military, airframes were sold to civilian customers.*

*Above: The Bü 131 Jungmann makes a superb civilian light aircraft. Its military training characteristics make it relatively easy and pleasurable to fly.*

The clean lines of the Bü 131's engine cowling disappeared on the Bü 133, when a larger radial engine was introduced and overall dimensions were reduced. This resulted in a deeper, stubbier appearance.

The Jungmann had two tandem seats, for the instructor (generally behind), and the pupil (ahead). The aerobatic Jungmeister differed in having just one seat.

## BÜ 131 JUNGMANN

Both Bü 131 and the later Bü 133 served with distinction in the Luftwaffe during World War II, mainly as primary and advanced fighter trainers.

A wire-braced conventional tail was supported underneath on landing by a spring-mounted tailwheel. For winter operations, skis were fitted to all undercarriage units.

The Bü 131 was designed by the company's chief designer, Anders Andersson. German Bü 131s were built at Bücker's main Johannisthal factory.

The Jungmann was powered by a 78-kW (105-hp.) Hirth 4-cylinder inverted inline piston engine. Surprisingly, the later Jungmeister reverted to an older 119-kW (160-hp.) radial engine.

The fuselage was protected by light alloy around the engine and the crew's compartments.

The pre-war style biplane wings were of wooden construction and covered with fabric. When the aircraft was pressed into special missions operations, light bombs could be carried underwing.

The Jungmann's fuselage was built of welded steel tubing, covered, like the wings, with fabric. This machine carries Luftwaffe markings, but others were operated by civil flying clubs.

## First-generation trainers of World War II

■ **MORANE-SAULNIER 317:** France's M.S. 317, like the Bü 131, flew long before the war but remained an important part of the air arm.

■ **POLIKARPOV Po-2:** A large Russian trainer, liaison and communications aircraft of the war, the Po-2 later served as a bomber in Korea.

■ **DE HAVILLAND TIGER MOTH:** The Royal Air Force's most important biplane trainer of the war, the Tiger Moth is still widely flown.

■ **BOEING STEARMAN:** The highly successful PT-13/-17 series remained in use until the war's end; the one below still flies in the UK.

# CAPRONI

# CA.1-CA.5

● Three-engined ● Twin-boom, triple-rudder layout ● Licence production

▲ *Flown for the first time in late 1914, the ungainly looking Caproni bombers formed an important part of the Italian and French air force inventories into the mid-1920s.*

Italy led the world in establishing an army aviation section in 1884, and in 1911 the first bombing raid in history was carried out by an Italian aviator in Libya during the war with Turkey. The Italian aircraft industry was also one of the first to develop large, multi-engined aircraft. By the time Italy joined World War I in May 1915, its three-engined Caproni Ca.2s were the most advanced heavy bombers used by any national air arm.

▼ **US production**
*Two Ca.3s were built by the Standard Aircraft Corporation in the US during 1918. A third was built by Fisher Body Works.*

▲ **Italian Army Air Service**
*Having revised its bomber design through the Ca.30 and 31, Caproni went into production with the Ca.32. Known in service as the Ca.1, 164 were delivered to the Italian Army Air Service.*

▼ **Preserved Caproni**
*Now a museum piece, this Ca.3 clearly shows the type's characteristic multi-wheel undercarriage, wooden propellers and the mass of struts and bracing.*

◄ **More power**
*The Ca.3 (Ca.33) had 112-kW (150-hp.) engines in place of the 75-kW (100-hp.) Fiat units of the Ca.1.*

▼ **Triplane bomber**
*Similar in layout to the Ca.1-3, the Ca.4 was actually a new design. This is a Ca.42 variant.*

## FACTS AND FIGURES

➤ Bombs were stowed vertically on the sides of a nacelle mounted at the centre of the bottom wing of the Ca.4 triplane.

➤ Between 1917 and 1919 Caproni manufactured a total of 299 Ca.3s.

➤ A few Ca.3s were converted to six-seat airliners known as the Ca.56a.

➤ A gunner's position was provided in each of the Ca.4's tailbooms, behind the engines and wing trailing edge.

➤ Following its first flight in 1917, 659 examples of the Ca.5 were built.

➤ US manufacturers would have built 1,500 Ca.5s had World War I continued.

# World War I Italian bombers

Using a pusher propeller at the rear of the central nacelle and two tractor propellers mounted in the twin booms, driven via a complex transmission, the Ca.1 of 1914 was known by Caproni as the Ca.30. In the production Ca.2, which entered service in 1915, the tractor engines were moved to the front of the booms and drove the propellers directly.

The 164 Ca.2s which were delivered in 1915/16 were followed by 269 Ca.3s, with more powerful engines. These were used as torpedo-bombers by the Italian navy, and by the French as well as the Italian air arms.

The 38 Ca.4 series bombers delivered in 1917/18 also had three engines, but were triplanes rather than biplanes. The massive Ca.4 had a wingspan of 29.9 metres (98 ft.) and was powered by 149-kW (200-hp.) engines. Even with more powerful engines, the later Ca.4s were too slow for anything but

*Right: Ca.3s had positions for defensive gunners at the front and rear of the fuselage.*

night bombing, although they could carry 1450 kg (3,190 lb.) of bombs. Using all its bomber experience, Caproni completed the series with the improved Ca.5.

*Left: Although the Ca.4 triplane was a useful long-range bomber, it was slow and vulnerable. The Ca.5 represented an attempt to overcome these shortcomings.*

## Ca.5 (Ca.44)

**Type:** biplane heavy bomber

**Powerplant:** three 186-kW (250-hp.) Fiat A.12 in-line piston engines

**Maximum speed:** 150 km/h (93 m.p.h.) at sea level

**Endurance:** 7 hours

**Range:** 600 km (375 mi.)

**Service ceiling:** 4600 m (15,100 ft.)

**Weights:** empty 3300 kg (7,260 lb.); maximum take-off 5300 kg (11,660 lb.)

**Armament:** two 7.7-mm (.303 cal.) Revelli machine-guns and 900 kg (1,980 lb.) of bombs

**Dimensions:**
| | | |
|---|---|---|
| span | 23.40 m | (76 ft. 9 in.) |
| length | 12.60 m | (41 ft. 4 in.) |
| height | 4.48 m | (14 ft. 8 in.) |
| wing area | 150 m² | (1,614 sq. ft.) |

## CA.3

At least 83 Ca.33s were built in France by Robert Esnault-Pelterie. The aircraft were produced to the same standard as the Italian army's Ca.3s. This aircraft belonged to CEP 115 of the Aéronautique Militaire.

Two pilots sat side-by-side in separate, open cockpits just ahead of the wing leading edge. They had no windscreens or any other form of protection from the elements.

An Isotta-Fraschini V.4B engine was mounted at the forward end of each boom. A third engine was fitted in the rear part of the fuselage and drove a pusher propeller.

A substantial tailskid was mounted at the rear of each tailboom. In common with the main undercarriage units, the skid was braced by struts and wires.

Unusually, the Ca. 3 had no fixed vertical tail surfaces. A full-span tailplane connected the booms and mounted the central rudder. The abbreviation C.E.P. stands for Caproni-Esnault-Pelterie.

Although the Ca.3 was a 'tail-sitting' aircraft, it had a substantial nose undercarriage unit. The nosewheels prevented the aircraft 'nosing-over' on landing.

Construction of the aircraft was conventional, consisting of wood and fabric, but the design was unusual. As well as the twin-boom, triple-rudder layout, the Ca.3 had a multi-wheel landing gear for rough field operations.

## COMBAT DATA

### MAXIMUM SPEED

Like all World War I bombers the Ca.3 was slow. This made the aircraft vulnerable to enemy fighters, but Caproni was able to produce improved, higher performance designs based on the Ca.3 layout.

| | |
|---|---|
| Ca.3 | 140 km/h (87 m.p.h.) |
| 0/400 | 156 km/h (97 m.p.h.) |
| R.VI | 135 km/h (84 m.p.h.) |

### SERVICE CEILING

Both the Ca.3 and Handley Page 0/400 had much lower service ceilings than the huge Zeppelin-Staaken R.VI. By flying at high altitude early bombers could avoid interception by fighters, but this did little for bombing accuracy. With its advanced Ca.5 Caproni was able to exceed the service ceiling of the R.VI.

Ca.3 4100 m (13,450 ft.)
0/400 2590 m (8,500 ft.)
R.VI 4320 m (14,170 ft.)

### ARMAMENT

An early bomber design, the Ca.3 was limited in bombload and defensive armament. It was, however, available at the beginning of World War I and allowed Italy to establish a strong bomber force.

Ca.3 4 x 7.7-mm (.303 cal.) machine-guns 450-kg (1,000-lb.) bombload
0/400 5 x 7.7-mm (.303 cal.) machine-guns 907-kg (2,000-lb.) bombload
R.V1 4 x 7.92-mm machine-guns 2000-kg (8,800-lb.) bombload

## Caproni cavalcade

■ **Ca.14:** Gianni Caproni built and flew this monoplane in 1913. It later became known as the Ca.14 and was powered by a 37-kW (50-hp.) three-cylinder Gnome rotary engine.

■ **Ca.82:** Originally known as the Ca.73ter, the Ca.82 was a medium bomber powered by two 380-kW (510-hp.) Isotta-Fraschini Asso engines mounted in a push-pull configuration.

■ **Ca.90:** Powered by six 746-kW engines, this giant heavy bomber was the world's largest landplane from 1929 until the arrival of the Tupolev ANT-20 'Maxim Gorky' in 1934.

■ **Ca.97:** Used in a variety of roles, which included air ambulance, bomber and reconnaissance, the Ca.97 was available in triple-, twin- and single-engined variants.

# CAPRONI BERGAMASCHI

# CA 310 SERIES

● Developed from a transport plane ● Nearly bought by the RAF

*▲ A light bomber and reconnaissance aircraft, the Ca 310 was developed in parallel with the Ca 309, but featured a retractable undercarriage and slightly more powerful engines.*

**S**eeking to improve the military potential of the Ca 309, which had been used operationally in North Africa, Caproni Bergamaschi developed the Ca 310 Libeccio (south-west wind). The aircraft was highly impressive in the pre-war years and attracted significant foreign orders, including 300 from Great Britain and 200 from France. However, the onset of World War II meant the aircraft were diverted to the Italian air force, which had already ordered significant numbers.

## CAPRONI BERGAMASCHI CA 310 SERIES

### ▼ Order cancelled
*Count Gianni Caproni sought to export his design and for a time it looked like the RAF would purchase the type. Italy's entry into the war put an end to this potentially lucrative order.*

### ▲ Fighting for Franco
*Despite being overshadowed by more famous types, the Ca 310 nevertheless took part in the Spanish Civil War during the late 1930s.*

### Low production ▶
*The first flight of the Ca 310 took place in February 1937. A total of only 161 of this variant was built, followed by small numbers of sub-types, culminating in the Ca 316.*

### ◀ South-west winds in Africa
*Wearing Italian civil registrations, this group of Libeccios is seen being guarded by a local tribesman in Libya. Civilian Ca 310s were operated extensively in the Italian colonies in Africa during the years leading up to World War II.*

### Spanish colours ▶
*Ca 310s delivered to Nationalist Spanish units wore a distinctive mottled-green and brown camouflage. This one served with 15th Escuadrilla of Grupo 18, Spanish Nationalist air force.*

### FACTS AND FIGURES

➤ Ca 310 series aircraft were exported to Croatia, France, Germany, Norway, Sweden, Hungary and Yugoslavia.

➤ Fitted with Piaggio C.35 radial engines, the Ca 310 first flew on 20 February 1937.

➤ Hungarian aircraft were returned to Italy for service with the Regia Aeronautica.

➤ Spruce wood was used in construction of the wings, but the outbreak of war resulted in supplies being reduced.

➤ Ca 311s, 313s and 314s continued in service after Italy capitulated in 1943.

➤ A Ca 313G (for Germany) took approximately 23,000 man-hours to build.

# PROFILE

# Multi-role Italian twin

Improving on the Ca 309 by adding retractable landing gear and more powerful engines produced one of Italy's most versatile warplanes of World War II. First flying in 1937, the Ca 310 was destined to fly bombing, reconnaissance, anti-shipping, ground-attack, transport and training missions throughout the war.

In its original version the Ca 310 flew with the air forces of Norway, Peru, Yugoslavia and Italy and was tested as a civil transport with twin floats.

By the outbreak of World War II the aircraft had been developed into a number of improved variants. The Ca 311 had an extensively glazed nose for bomb aiming and reconnaissance. This was followed by the Ca 312 which had more powerful Piaggio engines and was ordered by Belgium and Norway, although these aircraft were not delivered before the German invasion.

French and British interest centred on the Ca 313, which also served with Sweden in such varied roles as transport

and torpedo bomber. The more powerfully armed Ca 314 was the final and most important variant in the Italian air force. It was built in a number of sub-variants including the Ca 314C, which carried two additional 12.7-mm (.50 cal.) machine-guns for ground-attack duties.

*Left: Despite the Ca 310's low-wing configuration, the undercarriage featured long, stalky oleo legs.*

*Right: Deliveries to the Regia Aeronautica began in 1937 and were completed some two years later. The most extensively built version of the Libeccio family was the Ca 314 convoy escort and patrol aircraft, fitted with in-line engines.*

## Ca 314A

**Type:** convoy escort and maritime patrol aircraft

**Powerplant:** two 544-kW (730-hp.) Isotta-Franschini Delta RC 35 in-line piston engines

**Maximum speed:** 365 km/h (245 m.p.h.)

**Cruising speed:** 320 km/h (198 m.p.h.)

**Range:** 1690 km (1,048 mi.)

**Service ceiling:** 6400 m (21,000 ft.)

**Weights:** empty 4560 kg (10,032 lb.); loaded 6620 kg (14,564 lb.)

**Armament:** two 12.7-mm (.50 cal.) machine-guns in the wings and one 7.7-mm (.303 cal.) gun in a dorsal turret, plus up to 320 kg (705 lb.) of bombs

**Dimensions:**
| | | |
|---|---|---|
| span | 16.65 m | (54 ft. 7 in.) |
| length | 11.80 m | (38 ft. 8 in.) |
| height | 3.70 m | (12 ft. 2 in.) |
| wing area | 39.20 m² | (422 sq. ft.) |

## CA 310 LIBECCIO

Prior to the outbreak of World War II, the Ca 310 enjoyed some export success. Norway was one nation which purchased four aircraft. These were all destroyed during the German invasion in 1940.

On top of the fuselage was a single turret, housing just one 7.7-mm (.303 cal.) machine-gun. Like many Italian aircraft, the weakness of the Libeccio lay in its poor defensive armament and slow speed. The Norwegian machines suffered severely at the hands of Luftwaffe fighters.

In service, the Libeccio series had more than its fair share of problems. Leaking hydraulics and unreliable electrics were notable among these and the aircraft was prone to catching fire. However, it was also a sturdy machine and could absorb a tremendous amount of punishment.

**603**

Depending on the variant, various engines could be specified. Ca 310s were powered by twin 350-kW (470-hp.) Piaggio P.VII C.35 radial engines driving two-bladed, variable-pitch propellers.

Tall undercarriage oleos gave the Ca 310 a dramatic raked stance on the ground. These retracted rearward into the engine nacelles with the tyres remaining exposed to facilitate 'belly' landings.

Fabric was used quite extensively in the construction of the Ca 310, particularly on the control surfaces. Many air arms which acquired the type bedecked their aircraft with large national insignia or flashes on the rudder.

## COMBAT DATA

### MAXIMUM SPEED

Italian aircraft of World War II, especially bombers, were seldom known for their high performance. Exceptions to the rule were the S.M.79 and the large four-engined Piaggio P.108B.

| | |
|---|---|
| Ca 310 LIBECCIO | 365 km/h (226 m.p.h.) |
| P.108B | 429 km/h (266 m.p.h.) |
| S.M.79-1 | 429 km/h (266 m.p.h.) |

### OPERATIONAL RANGE

Despite their other shortcomings, these three aircraft had decent endurance, a factor much needed in the Mediterranean theatre. With only a small number built, Ca 310s did not feature prominently in the air campaign, unlike the excellent SIAI-Marchetti S.M.79s.

Ca 310 LIBECCIO 1649 km (1,022 mi.)

P.108B 3519 km (2,182 mi.)

S.M.79-1 1899 km (1,177 mi.)

### BOMBLOAD

Most Italian bombers, such as the Ca 310, were limited by small bomb loads, though the P.108B could carry up to 3500 kg (7,700 lb.) if required. The S.M.79 was most often used as a torpedo bomber.

Ca 310 LIBECCIO 400 kg (880 lb.)

P.108B 3500 kg (7,700 lb.)

S.M.79-1 1250 kg (2,750 lb.)

## Italian bombers of World War II

**FIAT BR.20 CICOGNA:** Blessed with decent performance, the BR.20 Cicogna (Stork) had the distinction of being the only mass-produced, Italian twin-engined bomber of World War II.

**CANT Z.1007:** One of several three-engined designs, the Z.1007 Alcione (Kingfisher) was marred by lack of a suitable powerplant and a weak structure, which was prone to deforming.

**SIAI MARCHETTI S.M.81 PIPISTRELLO:** A forerunner of the more famous S.M.79 Sparrowhawk, this sturdy aeroplane was used extensively as a bomber/transport in the Mediterranean theatre.

# CAUDRON
# R/G/C SERIES

● Bomber and reconnaissance aircraft ● Escort fighter ● French service

▲ Caudron
continuously refined its bomber designs with the aim of improving performance. A common feature of the G and R series was unequal span wings.

C audron's R.11 was a development of the earlier R.4. Although it proved to be an outstanding design, it arrived too late to have much impact on World War I. While the R.11 was perhaps the most successful of the Caudron biplane bombers, the C and G series should not be forgotten, since they formed an important part of the French bomber force both before and after the war. The last of the Caudron biplanes in service, an R.11, was scrapped in 1922.

---

## CAUDRON R/G/C SERIES

▼ Caudron style
From the R.4 onwards, all the Caudron bombers were of similar design. The C.23 introduced wings of equal span.

▲ Late-war night-bomber
In February 1918 Caudron introduced the C.23 BN.2 night-bomber. Orders for 1,000 aircraft were received, but only 54 had been built by the time of the Armistice. Heavy and unmanoeuvrable, they were withdrawn by 1920.

▲ Design by Deville
Having flown as an observer in a G.3, Paul Deville went on to become technical designer for Caudron and was responsible for the G.6.

▲ Fighter killer
Escadrille C.46 claimed to have shot down 34 German aircraft in an eight-week period flying R.4s.

◄ British bomber
Britain's Royal Naval Air Service received 55 G.4s for bombing duties. They were involved in a number of daring raids.

### FACTS AND FIGURES

➤ Caudron produced the G.4 as an improvement on the G.3, which was unable to carry adequate armament.

➤ Two versions of the G.4 were built: the B.2 bomber and the A.2 artillery spotter.

➤ Jules Vedrines, navigating by compass, flew a G.6 more than 320 km (200 mi.).

➤ In redesigning the structure of the R.4, Paul Deville also attempted to improve its performance and created the R.11.

➤ When it first flew in 1917, the R.11 was considered a reconnaissance-bomber.

➤ C.23s were used post-war on passenger services between Paris and Brussels.

# PROFILE

# French wartime bomber family

Caudron's first bomber, the G.4 of 1915, was based on the smaller G.3 trainer and featured twin 60-kW Le Rhône engines. It was followed by the generally similar, but more powerful, G.6 bomber and reconnaissance aircraft, which had an enclosed rear fuselage and tail section.

Gaston Caudron had been largely responsible for the design of the G-series biplanes, but with the R series his brother, René, came to the fore. Breaking away from previous Caudron design trends, the new R.4 featured a completely enclosed, full-length

fuselage and a single fin and rudder. In combat during World War I the R.4 acquitted itself well, destroying several enemy fighters before structural problems began to emerge. One of the resulting accidents claimed the life of Gaston Caudron, and the R.4 was withdrawn in 1917.

Unsuccessful prototypes of the R.5 and R.10 followed, before the R.11 appeared in March 1917. Like the R.4, the R.11 was a biplane with unequal span wings. However, the wings were shorter, and more powerful engines enabled

it to carry twin Lewis guns in the upper nose and rear cockpits, plus a fifth pointing downwards in the nose. Intended for bombing and reconnaissance, the R.11 served as an escort fighter for the Breguet 14.

Below: A distinctive feature of the R.4 was the large nosewheel, which helped to prevent 'nosing-over'. The pilot was very vulnerable during such an incident.

*Above: The R.11 proved to be a highly capable escort fighter. Armed with five machine-guns and offering good performance, it was regarded as a formidable fighting machine.*

A much larger tail fin was fitted to the R.11 than the R.4. Caudron retained this distinctive tail for several of its R/G and C series aircraft and even used the design in the 1930s, when aircraft such as the C.270 touring biplane featured a tail similar to that of the R.11.

## R.11 A.3

R.11s of Escadrille C.46, Aviation Militaire (French air force), flew escort duties for 13ᵉ Escadre's bombers between February and November 1918. All surviving R.11s were scrapped in July 1922.

Three machine-guns were available to the nose-gunner. Two were fitted on a flexible mount to fire upwards, with a third firing downwards through the floor of the gunner's compartment.

A number of modifications were incorporated into the R.11 when it was developed from the R.4. They included deletion of the auxiliary nose undercarriage.

Each of the R.11's Hispano-Suiza engines was carefully faired and mounted on the lower wing. Many later aircraft had more powerful 175-kW (235-hp.) Hispano-Suiza 8Beb engines.

The R.11 had a simple, open cockpit for the pilot. Having noticed that a number of contemporary aircraft had been lost when the pilot was hit in combat, Caudron fitted a second set of flying controls in the rear gunner's cockpit for emergency recovery of the aircraft.

Although the R.11 and the R.4 which preceded it was generally of conventional construction, the R.11 introduced a one-piece upper wing. This represented a considerable achievement for the time.

## Caudron collection

**G.3:** Designed as a two-seat training and reconnaissance aircraft, the G.3 had limited potential because of its low power.

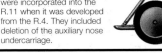

**C.449 GOELAND:** Based on the C.440 of 1934, many examples of the C.449 final production variant were built post-war.

**C.460:** Designed for the 1934 Coupe Deutsch de la Meurth air race, the C.460 went on to gain a world speed record.

**C.630 SIMOUN:** This four-seat cabin monoplane was popular both before and after the war and many were used for long-range flights.

# CONSOLIDATED

# B-24 LIBERATOR

● Heavy bomber ● Long-range maritime patrol ● Transport

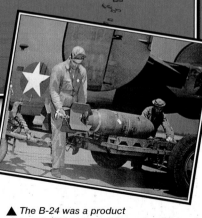

▲ The B-24 was a product of American bombing philosophy, which called for precision attacks from high altitude by well-defended aircraft using the Norden bombsight.

**C**onsolidated's B-24 Liberator is often compared unfavourably to the more famous B-17 Flying Fortress. But the B-24 was newer, more efficient and much more versatile than the Boeing design; and with nearly 20,000 aircraft completed, more Liberators were built than any other military aircraft in American history. It was a good bomber, serving on every front, but its most valuable work may have been the war against the U-boats.

◀ **Not so lucky**
After raiding southern Germany, this B-24 fought a running battle with Luftwaffe fighters all the way through Italy, crashing just after the crew bailed out.

▶ **Snarling beasts**
Garishly painted B-24s were used as 'lead ships', acting as markers on which the huge Eighth Air Force bomber formations would assemble before setting off on raids over Europe.

▲ **Blasted but alive**
Although not as strong as the B-17, the Liberator was tough enough to bring its crews home in spite of severe damage.

◀ **Nose turret**
Late-model B-24s, from the 'G' onward, were fitted with powered nose turrets after experience had shown that Luftwaffe fighter pilots often attacked head-on.

▼ **Tactical strike**
After the Allied landings in France in 1944, Liberators were used to bomb tactical targets in support of the advancing armies. Railways, bridges and troop concentrations were heavily attacked.

▼ **Work of art**
'Alley Cop' was the nickname for this B-24, which sported typically bright nose art. USAF bombers were rarely camouflaged after 1943, going into action in a natural metal finish.

## FACTS AND FIGURES

➤ Liberators were manufactured by Consolidated, Douglas, Ford and North American.

➤ The all-silver B-24 prototype made its first flight on 29 January 1940.

➤ The Luftwaffe used a captured B-24 for special covert operations.

➤ A B-24 crew crashed near Gyantse in Tibet while flying over the Himalayas on a supply mission to China.

➤ Winston Churchill used a modified B-24 as his personal transport.

➤ 19,256 Liberators and Privateers were manufactured between 1940 and 1945.

# America's long-range bomber

The B-24 Liberator was built around the Davis wing; a long, thin, large-area structure mounted high on the fuselage. Its twin bomb-bays used 'roller shutter' doors which retracted within the fuselage when opened, reducing drag. The twin tail, like the wing, was a Consolidated trademark. All this resulted in an excellent long-range bomber which had other applications; there were cargo, tanker, patrol, training and reconnaissance variants. Some were armed with even more guns as bomber escorts.

A B-24 caught on the ground at Hickam Field, Hawaii, on 7 December 1941 produced the first American casualties of the war. Liberators fought in the Pacific and China-Burma-India theatres. From the Middle East they attacked their most famous target – Romania's Ploesti oilfields. They also joined with the B-17 in the Eighth Air Force's three-year aerial campaign over Europe. The B-24 was never as popular with its crews as the B-17, as it was quicker to catch fire in battle

and sometimes suffered hydraulic problems, but it was in some ways a better aircraft, with more modern systems.

The mighty armada of B-24s went to pasture in just a few years. Soon after the war, Liberators began to disappear from the skies. Today, only a couple of surviving examples are airworthy.

Left: Although the Liberator did not carry as many bombs as some other Allied aircraft, it had exceptional performance and massive defensive armament.

Below: The need for tight formation flying was vital for daylight bombing, where mutual cover meant survival.

## B-24D Liberator

**Type:** heavy bomber with a crew of 10

**Powerplant:** four 895-kW (1,200-hp.) Pratt & Whitney R-1830-43 Twin Wasp radial piston engines

**Maximum speed:** 488 km/h (300 m.p.h.)

**Range:** 2896 km (2,850 mi.)

**Service ceiling:** 9900 m (32,500 ft.)

**Weights:** empty 15,413 kg (34,000 lb.); maximum 27,216 kg (60,000 lb.)

**Armament:** one 12.7-mm (.50 cal.) nose gun (some with additional 12.7-mm fixed nose guns), two more each in dorsal turret, tail turret, retractable ball turret, and waist positions, plus maximum internal bombload of 3629 kg (8,800 lb.)

**Dimensions:**
| | |
|---|---|
| span | 33.52 m (110 ft.) |
| length | 20.22 m (66 ft. 4 in.) |
| height | 5.46 m (17 ft. 11 in.) |
| wing area | 97.36 m² (1,048 sq. ft.) |

The very-long-span wing gave the B-24 long range and excellent performance at high altitude.

Some late-model B-24s could carry bombs on racks under the inner wing. Anti-submarine versions in RAF service carried rockets.

## B-24D LIBERATOR 'TEGGIE ANN'

'Teggie Ann' was the command ship for the 'Liberandos', the 376th Bomb Group. This unit was severely mauled following attacks on the Romanian oilfields at Ploesti in 1944.

USAF B-24s based in North Africa were painted in a desert pink camouflage.

The tricycle undercarriage was another modern feature of the B-24.

240664

The bombardier sat in the glazed nose compartment, aiming his bombs with a Norden sight.

The deep fuselage was designed to allow the 3600-kg (4-ton) bombload to be stored vertically, with a catwalk giving the crew access to the rear fuselage.

The rear gunner fired a pair of 12.7-mm (.50 cal.) machine-guns from a powered turret. This was replaced by manually controlled guns in the B-24L.

## COMBAT DATA

### MAXIMUM SPEED

The World War II generation of big four-engined bombers was reasonably fast by pre-war standards, but speed alone was never going to to get them away from marauding enemy fighters. The American solution to survival was to fly in large formations that were able to bring hundreds of guns to bear on interceptors.

| | |
|---|---|
| **B-24D LIBERATOR** | **488 km/h (300 m.p.h.)** |
| **HALIFAX** | **500 km/h (310 m.p.h.)** |
| **He 177** | **472 km/h (290 m.p.h.)** |

### BOMBLOAD

Although the B-24 had, like other American bombers, a smaller load on paper than its contemporaries, some variants could carry up to six tons of weaponry. The Heinkel, by contrast, rarely carried more than half its stated capacity, and sometimes much less. The B-24 could carry its load higher and farther.

| | |
|---|---|
| **B-24D LIBERATOR** | **3629 kg (8,800 lb.)** |
| **HALIFAX** | **5900 kg (13,000 lb.)** |
| **He 177** | **6000 kg (13,200 lb.)** |

### SERVICE CEILING

American bomber tactics called for precision strikes from high altitude. The B-24 had a long, very efficient wing, together with extremely powerful turbocharged two-row radial engines, and it customarily operated at greater heights than its European rivals. This lessened its vulnerability to fighters in the Pacific, where Japanese aircraft had to struggle to reach such high operating altitudes.

| HALIFAX | B-24D LIBERATOR | He 177 |
|---|---|---|
| 7300 m (24,000 ft.) | 9900 m (32,500 ft.) | 7000 m (23,000 ft.) |

## Closing the Atlantic Gap

**BRITAIN'S SURVIVAL LIFELINE:** Britain depended on America for war material and food to support its densely packed population, and those supplies came by convoy across the Atlantic.

**CONVOY ESCORTS:** Although most convoys were escorted by warships, the most effective weapon against the U-boat threat was continuous air cover.

B-17 FLYING FORTRESS

B-24 LIBERATOR

SUNDERLAND

**THE ATLANTIC GAP:** In the first years of conflict, aircraft lacked the range to cover the whole crossing, leaving a gap in the mid-Atlantic in which convoys were vulnerable.

**WOLF PACKS:** U-boats based in western France could be intercepted by British flying-boats in the first stage of their journeys, but once clear they were free to attack the convoys in mid-Atlantic.

**CLOSING THE GAP:** The deployment of very-long-range variants of the Liberator meant that the window of vulnerability was closed, and the U-boat menace was considerably reduced.

CONVOYS

U-BOATS

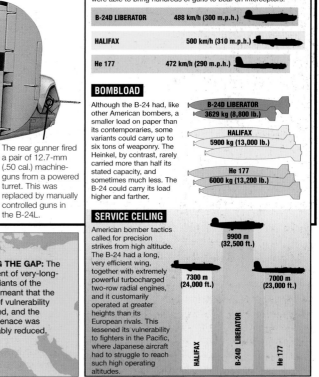

# CONSOLIDATED

# B-24 (US NAVY)

● Land-based bomber ● Anti-submarine patrols ● Surface radar

▲ *Naval Liberators*
*were instrumental in closing the area of ocean known as the 'Atlantic Gap', where German U-boats preyed on Allied convoys delivering vital supplies to Britain.*

Losses of Allied shipping in the Atlantic to German submarines hunting in 'wolf-packs' highlighted the urgent need for a long-range patrol aircraft for the US Navy. With British Coastal Command already having demonstrated the suitability of the Liberator, the US Navy received its first aircraft in August 1942. Designated PB4Ys, these Liberators – with their exceptionally long range – saw extensive service in Europe and the Pacific.

## CONSOLIDATED B-24 (US NAVY)

◀ **Great white bird**
*High over the Atlantic a PB4Y-1 Liberator flies an anti-submarine patrol. Operating far from its land base, the Liberator was one of the few forms of protection for convoys against the hunting 'wolf-packs' of German U-boats.*

**Proven design** ▶
*Early model Liberators operated by the US Navy differed very little from their Army Air Force counterparts.*

**Coastal Command** ▶
*Its radar lowered, a British-operated Liberator searches the ocean for German submarines. In addition to guns bristling from all angles, armament could include rockets mounted on either side of the nose on pylons, which were very effective against ships.*

◀ **Gear up**
*Undercarriage dangling, a Liberator takes off from Guadalcanal in 1943. The fighting around the Solomon Islands was some of the heaviest of the war.*

**Twin tails** ▶
*A distinctive feature of all Liberators was their twin tails, said to offer better handling at high altitude. Later aircraft were fitted with a single tail, and the type, renamed Privateer, had extensive post-war service.*

## FACTS AND FIGURES

➤ The B-24D served in every theatre, and in 1942–43 was the most important bomber in the Pacific.

➤ By 1942 the Liberator equipped 15 anti-submarine squadrons.

➤ More than 977 examples of the Liberator were operated by the United States Navy.

➤ Early Navy Liberators were particularly vulnerable to head-on machine-gun attacks by enemy fighters.

➤ The first operational unit of naval Liberators was based in Iceland.

➤ Reconnaissance versions remained in naval service until 1951.

# PROFILE

# Consolidated's convoy protector

Despite having already been supplying Britain with the essential materials for war by way of convoys across the Atlantic, America entered World War II still struggling to come to terms with the requirements of combat. In no area was this shortfall clearer than in the need for long-range patrol aircraft for the US Navy.

Initially denied, the request for Liberators was eventually granted after the huge losses of Allied shipping in the Atlantic.

Operated under the naval designation PB4Y, the aircraft

were equipped with air-to-surface radar and depth-charges. After only a short period of service, shipping losses were greatly reduced. With its exceptionally long range, the Liberator replaced the B-17 Flying Fortress in the Pacific. It was used for bombing and patrol duties, bringing havoc to Japanese land installations and naval vessels.

After the end of World War II, Liberators remained in service for reconnaissance duties until 1951, when they were replaced by another Consolidated product: the

Privateer. Although this variant had seen limited combat use in World War II, it went on to play a key role in the Korean War as a patrol aircraft and continued to serve into the 1960s.

*Below: After combat losses, a nose turret was installed on later variants of naval Liberators.*

*Above: Long range and the ability to carry a heavy warload let the Liberator roam the skies of the Pacific searching for enemy ships. Conventional bombing of land targets was still possible.*

## PB4Y-1 LIBERATOR

Adopted from the USAAF bomber versions, the blue coloured Liberators of the United States Navy saved countless lives by destroying enemy submarines. This example wears a late-war camouflage scheme.

### PB4Y-1 Liberator

**Type:** land-based maritime patrol aircraft

**Powerplant:** four 895-kW (667-hp) Pratt & Whitney R-1830-43 twin Wasp radial piston engines

**Maximum speed:** 488 km/h (303 mph)

**Cruising speed:** 225 km/h (140 mph)

**Operational radius:** 1730 km (1075 miles)

**Service ceiling:** 8540 m (28,000 ft)

**Weights:** empty 15,413 kg (33,980 lb); maximum take-off 27,216 kg (59,803 lb)

**Armament:** nine 12.7-mm (.50-cal.) machine guns, plus a maximum internal bomb load of 3692 kg (8139 lb)

**Dimensions:**
| | |
|---|---|
| span | 33.53 m (110 ft) |
| length | 22.73 m (74 ft 7 in) |
| height | 9.17 m (30 ft 1 in) |
| wing area | 97.36 m² (1048 sq ft) |

Following losses to head-on attacks by enemy fighters, a bulbous ERCO turret was installed on the nose of Navy Liberators. Equipped with twin Browning machine guns, it offered a formidable defence against attacking aircraft.

Crews found the aircraft much more suitable than the B-17 Flying Fortress for reconnaissance work, because of its ability to cover huge distances in a single patrol.

A three-hue blue scheme was adopted for naval Liberators, offering the best compromise for low-level and high-altitude operations over the Atlantic. Later models received an overall gloss dark blue camouflage.

The glazed position for the bombardier was retained from the land-based variants. It allowed precision bombing missions to be undertaken if required.

The large bomb-bay of the Liberator accommodated a sizeable warload, which could include depth-charges, mines and conventional bombs. The doors were electronically operated.

Positioned either side of the fuselage were two waist gun positions, which were used on low-level attacks against surface vessels and ground targets.

Rearward defence was provided by an electrically operated rear turret equipped with twin 12.7-mm (.50-cal.) machine guns. This was retained from USAAF variants and remained the standard rear defensive armament throughout the series to include the later developed Consolidated Privateer.

## COMBAT DATA

### MAXIMUM SPEED

Compared to the flying-boats operated by the US Navy in WWII, the land-based Liberator offered a vast improvement in speed. Able to cover huge areas of ocean in a single patrol, the type was instrumental in winning the war in the Atlantic.

| | |
|---|---|
| PB4Y-1 LIBERATOR | 488 km/h (303 mph) |
| PBY-5A CATALINA | 282 km/h (175 mph) |
| PB2Y-3 CORONADO | 359 km/h (223 mph) |

### SERVICE CEILING

Range was vital for aircraft assigned to convoy protection and anti-submarine warfare. Developed from the USAAF's land-based bomber, the Liberator's large size meant that a significant fuel load could be carried. Though in widespread service, the PBY-5 Catalina had poor range.

**PB4Y-1 LIBERATOR** 8540m (28,000 ft)
**PBY-5A CATALINA** 3960m (12,990 ft)
**PB2Y-3 CORONADO** 6250m (20,505 ft)

### MAXIMUM TAKE-OFF WEIGHT

Largest of the patrol aircraft in service with the US Navy was the Coronado flying-boat, which was also used as a heavy transport. Previously operated as a bomber, the Liberator easily carried a large load of mines, depth-charges and rockets.

**PB4Y-1 LIBERATOR** 27,216 kg (59,803 lb)
**PBY-5A CATALINA** 16,067 kg (35,422 lb)
**PB2Y-3 CORONADO** 30,844 kg (68,000 lb)

## Ocean patrolling in World War II

■ **PBY CATALINA:** Achieving legendary fame for its exploits in World War II, the Consolidated Catalina saw extensive combat with RAF Coastal Command and the US Navy in the Pacific.

■ **PB2Y CORONADO:** Costing five times more than a Catalina, Consolidated's Coronado gave only limited service as a transport and casualty-evacuation aircraft.

■ **PB4Y PRIVATEER:** The final development of the navalised Liberators was the single-tailed Privateer. Operational in the final stages of World War II, the aircraft remained in post-war use.

# CONSOLIDATED

# PBY CATALINA

● Amphibian and flying-boat ● Long-serving naval patrol bomber

I t was old when World War II began. It was slow and could be uncomfortable, but the Consolidated PBY Catalina was one of the classic designs; rarely has an aircraft proved so useful to so many people. A deadly adversary to an enemy submarine or warship, the PBY is better remembered as the angel of mercy which achieved thousands of rescues in all circumstances throughout the war.

▲ The Catalina operated in every theatre of the Pacific war, from the balmy southern waters to the frozen oceans of the North. This crew is seen in the Aleutians.

◀ **Slow but sure**
Although slow and cumbersome, the PBY was immensely tough and had a great range, essential for long maritime patrols.

**Flight deck ▶**
On long missions, pilots might be expected to occupy the flight deck for up to 20 hours at a time.

▼ **Shipboard operations**
Catalinas often operated from seaplane tenders, being hoisted aboard by cranes for maintenance and restocking.

▲ **Observation blisters ▶**
The large 'greenhouses' on each side of the rear fuselage could mount heavy machine-guns and were perfect for rear observation.

◀ **Assisted take-off**
The Catalina had good take-off performance, but for launching at high weights or in tight spots it could use strap-on rockets for extra boost.

## FACTS AND FIGURES

➤ In October 1935 the Catalina prototype made a non-stop flight of 5633 km (3,500 mi.) from Coco Solo to San Francisco.

➤ In the 1930s, civil PBYs were used for scientific exploration of New Guinea and later the Indian Ocean.

➤ Over 1000 Catalinas were manufactured in Russia.

➤ The 'Black Cats' squadron hunted Japanese ships at night; in addition to bombs and depth charges they unleashed empty beer bottles, which made an eerie whistling descent.

➤ The Catalina was so slow that critics joked that its navigator needed a calendar rather than a stopwatch.

# PROFILE

# 'Black Cats' over the Pacific

Here was aviation at its essence. The high-wing, twin-engine Catalina was not speedy, not flashy, not graceful, but it was more practical than anyone realised when the first ship took to the skies on 28 March 1935. With its braced parasol wing and seagoing hull, the PBY Catalina became famous and was built in larger numbers than any other flying-boat in aviation history.

The PBY revolutionised long-range patrol in the US Navy. The well-loved 'Cat' ranged outward at great distance to stalk the enemy's fleet or to attack his submarines, and British Catalinas ferreted out the elusive German warship Bismarck. A PBY spotted the periscope of a Japanese submarine at Pearl Harbor. On all the world's oceans, Catalinas fought valiantly. Some were among the first American aircraft to carry radar. They were amphibians, flying from land or sea. Also produced in Canada and Russia, the Catalina often shed its warlike duties to become a Samaritan, bringing salvation to those in peril.

*Ranging far and wide, the Catalina was instrumental in denying Axis forces the use of the sea. It was a Catalina which tracked down the Bismarck during the hunt for the battleship, which ended in its sinking.*

The large unobstructed plank-like wing gave the Catalina excellent endurance and benign handling. The outrigger stabilising floats hinged upwards to form the wingtip fairing in flight.

## PBY-5A Catalina

**Type:** seven-/nine-seat long-range maritime patrol bomber

**Powerplant:** two 895-kW (1,200-hp.) Pratt & Whitney R1830-92 Twin Wasp radial piston engines

**Maximum speed:** 288 km/h (175 m.p.h.) at 2135 m (6,500 ft.)

**Range:** 4900 km (3,045 mi.)

**Service ceiling:** 4480 m (18,100 ft.)

**Weights:** empty 9485 kg (21,000 lb.); loaded 16,066 kg (35,420 lb.)

**Armament:** two 7.62-mm (.30 cal.) machine-guns in bow, one 7.62-mm machine-gun firing aft from the hull step, and two 12.7-mm (.50 cal.) machine-guns in beam position; up to 1814 kg (4,000 lb.) of bombs or depth charges

**Dimensions:**
span 31.70 m (104 ft.)
length 19.47 m (63 ft. 10 in.)
height 6.15 m (20 ft. 2 in.)
wing area 130.06 m² (1,400 sq. ft.)

## OA-10 CATALINA

During the war the US Air Force took over a large number of Catalinas for use in the air-sea rescue role, designated OA-10. These gave valuable service long after the end of the conflict.

The basic crew of the Catalina comprised eight. In the extreme nose was an observer/bomb aimer, behind which sat the two pilots. Behind them was a compartment for the radio operator and navigator.

Catalinas were built either as pure flying-boats or, as here, as amphibians, with a retractable tricycle undercarriage. The main wheels pulled up into wells above the hull line, and were left exposed.

Most late-production PBYs had search radar, with an antenna in a teardrop fairing above the flight deck. Other aerials were carried under the wings.

Catalinas were powered by a pair of Pratt & Whitney Twin Wasp radial piston engines. Sturdy and reliable, the Twin Wasp's output was boosted from 615 kW (820 hp.) in early examples to nearly 900 kW (1,200-hp.) in the final production PBY-5s.

The flight engineer's station was in the centre of the aircraft beneath the wing, while the aft cabin usually housed two gunner/observers. Weapons were carried under the wing.

### COMBAT DATA

#### CRUISING SPEED

The Catalina was old, noisy and slow, especially when compared with its contemporaries. But it was tough and reliable, and could land and take off in anything short of a hurricane.

H6K 'MAVIS' 260 km/h (211 m.p.h.)
PBY CATALINA 188 km/h (175 m.p.h.)
BV 138 230 km/h (171 m.p.h.)

#### RANGE

The big patrol 'boats' may not have been fast, but they could cover a lot of ocean. A typical flying-boat at the beginning of World War II could stay aloft for up to 24 hours, and often crew fatigue was the limiting factor on mission length.

PBY CATALINA 4900 km (3,045 mi.)
H6K 'MAVIS' 6700 km (4,163 mi.)
BV 138 5000 km (3,107 mi.)

## World War II maritime patrollers

**KAWANISHI H6K 'MAVIS':** The H6K was Japan's main long-range flying-boat at the start of World War II. Based on a Sikorsky design, it was very tough and seaworthy.

**SHORT SUNDERLAND:** Much larger than the PBY, the Sunderland was Britain's main maritime patrol machine. It was adapted from a civil design, and first flew in 1937.

**CANT Z.506:** Italy specialised in floatplanes rather than flying-boats, and the three-engined Cant was one of the largest of its kind. It held numerous pre-war seaplane speed records.

**BLOHM UND VOSS BV 138:** Known as 'Die fliegende Holzschuh', the twin-boom three-engined BV 138, or 'Flying Clog', saw action from the Mediterranean to the Arctic.

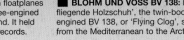

# CONSOLIDATED
# PBY CATALINA SEARCH AND RESCUE

● Flying-boat and amphibian ● Search-and-rescue aircraft ● War service

## CONSOLIDATED PBY CATALINA

**▼ Parasol wing**
The Catalina's wing lifted the engines well clear of spray from rough waters.

**▲ Navy 'non-specular sea blue'**
This matt-blue finish was typical of that applied to US Navy aircraft in 1943. The PBY-5A amphibian was developed from the PBY-5 flying-boat to give the aircraft greater flexibility.

**▼ RAF Catalina operations**
Towards the end of World War II RAF Coastal Command's No. 240 Squadron carried out air-sea rescue duties in the Far East.

**▲ RATO take-off assistance**
This OA-10A of the USAF's 10th Rescue Squadron is seen in Alaska. It carries two rocket-assisted take-off (RATO) bottles on each side.

**◄ In the Aleutians**
At the northernmost extremities of the Pacific Ocean, Catalinas were used for offensive and rescue roles in the campaigns along the Aleutian archipelago.

Near the end of WWII, an American Consolidated PBY Catalina flying-boat took off from Okinawa, flew to hostile waters within sight of the Japanese shoreline and rescued seven men from a ditched B-29 bomber. The mission involved flying over a long distance in bad weather, touching down on the water in full view of the enemy and filling the aircraft to capacity. It was a tough challenge, but the PBY Catalina was up to the demand.

**▲ The approach of a PBY Catalina** was a welcome sight for many Allied sailors or downed airmen as they bobbed on the vast ocean in a dinghy awaiting rescue.

## FACTS AND FIGURES

➤ When landing on open sea, the pilot brought the Catalina to a full stall just before touchdown.

➤ The first PBY flew in 1936 and the type stayed in production until 1945.

➤ Some PBYs carried the AR-8 airborne lifeboat, fitted under the wing.

➤ PBYs for Britain were the first military aircraft delivered by trans-Atlantic flight during the war.

➤ The US Coast Guard used PBYs for rescue duties from World War II until the 1950s.

➤ PBYs saved 161 airmen in the Solomon Islands in the first eight months of 1943.

**PROFILE**

# Search-and-rescue by 'Dumbo Cat'

No one knows how many men were rescued in combat by the courageous pilots who flew the Consolidated PBY Catalina into dangerous situations – but the number is in the thousands.

This twin-engined, parasol-wing flying-boat and amphibian was one of the slowest aircraft of the war; it was said that it was in danger of being struck by birds from behind. But, despite its unimpressive speed, the PBY was a sturdy, well-armed and versatile flying machine that could land in some of the most

difficult conditions to rescue men in peril.

More Catalinas were built than any other flying-boat in history. Designed to a US Navy requirement for a long-range patrol bomber, the PBY proved to be a highly successful anti-shipping and anti-submarine aircraft in a number of theatres, and served with several Allied air forces. PBYs also rescued more survivors from ships and aircraft than any aircraft of the war.

Perhaps the most famous of all Catalinas were the US Navy's 'Black Cats', which operated

against the Japanese in the Pacific in 1942. US Navy and USAAF 'Cats' were used for the search-and-rescue (SAR) role until the late 1940s.

*Above: The USAAF received 75 ex-US Navy PBY-6As for the SAR role. These were designated OA-10B (A-10B after 1948) and were distinguished by their taller tails.*

*Below: After 1945 USAAF OA-10As remained in the Air Rescue Service, along with converted C-47s, B-17s and B-29s.*

## PBY-5A Catalina

**Type:** long-range maritime patrol bomber and air-sea rescue aircraft

**Powerplant:** two 895-kW (1,200-hp.) Pratt & Whitney R-1830-92 Twin Wasp piston engines

**Maximum speed:** 288 km/h (179 m.p.h.) at 2135 m (7,000 ft.)

**Range:** 4096 km (2,545 mi.)

**Service ceiling:** 4480 m (14,700 ft.)

**Weights:** empty 9485 kg (20,910 lb.); loaded 16,066 kg (35,420 lb.)

**Armament:** two 7.62-mm (.30 cal.) machine-guns in bow, one 7.62-mm machine-gun firing aft from the hull step and two 12.7-mm machine-guns in beam position, plus air-sea rescue equipment including life rafts

**Dimensions:**
| | |
|---|---|
| span | 31.70 m (104 ft.) |
| length | 19.47 m (63 ft. 11 in.) |
| height | 6.15 m (20 ft. 2 in.) |
| wing area | 130 m² (1,340 sq. ft.) |

## OA-10A CATALINA

**Canadian Vickers built 230 PBY-5A amphibians for the US Navy, and all were transferred to the USAAF as OA-10A search-and-rescue craft. 44-33924 was one of this batch and is seen in post-war markings.**

The antennas on the wings are part of the Catalina's ASV (air-to-surface vessel) radar which was developed during World War II for maritime patrol aircraft hunting enemy shipping and submarines. The radar was also useful for finding downed aircraft. The radome above the cockpit contains an additional centimetric-wavelength radar.

With the Catalina's ungainly appearance and performance and in honour of the Walt Disney cartoon character of the 1940s, SAR PBY aircraft were nicknamed 'Dumbo' by USAAF and Navy personnel.

Cupolas on both sides of the fuselage, which each carried a 12.7-mm machine-gun in wartime, were introduced on the PBY-5 and were ideal for observers on the look-out for downed aircraft or personnel awaiting rescue.

Built by Canadian Vickers, the PBY-5A was known as the PBV-1A. The same company built 139 for the Royal Canadian Air Force, which called it the Canso. In RAF service the PBY-5A was known as the Catalina Mk III.

High-visibility markings distinguished USAF SAR aircraft, especially after World War II.

### ACTION DATA

**CRUISING SPEED**

USAAF Catalinas survived in the SAR role after World War II alongside the converted Douglas C-47 transports and B-17 and B-29 bombers of the Air Rescue Service. By the late 1940s, when the USAAF became the USAF and took overall responsibility for SAR, the Catalina was outmoded. The Albatross which replaced it had a higher cruising speed plus other improvements.

| | |
|---|---|
| **OA-10A CATALINA** 182 km/h (113 m.p.h.) | |
| **SA-16A ALBATROSS** 241 km/h (150 m.p.h.) | |
| **Do 24T-3** 249 km/h (155 m.p.h.) | |

**RANGE**

The SA-16A Albatross had only modest range. The Do 24 was a wartime German design which was capable of flying 1000 km (600 mi.) further than the Albatross, although not as far as the OA-10.

OA-10A CATALINA 3782 km (2,350 mi.)

Do 24T-3 2897 km (1,800 mi.)

SA-16A ALBATROSS 1850 km (1,150 mi.)

**ENGINE POWER**

The Dornier Do 24 had more power than the other two types because of its three engines. Piston engine technology advanced in the years after World War II, and the Albatross had twin engines of appreciably more power than those fitted to the Catalina. Reliability was important for maritime patrol aircraft. Engines tuned to run at less than peak power were less likely to fail in service.

| OA-10A CATALINA 1790 kW (1,200 hp.) | SA-16A ALBATROSS 2125 kW (2,850 hp.) | Do 24T-3 2238 kW (3,000 hp.) |
|---|---|---|

## Catalina rescue off Japan

**29 MAY 1945:** An OA-10A on station with a US Navy lifeguard submarine shadowing a B-29 bombing raid on Japan was called to rescue the crew of a ditched aircraft.

**CREW LOCATED:** Having located the men, the Catalina landed and picked them up. However, on take-off the aircraft slammed into three large swells and the port engine was torn from its mount and smashed into the cockpit. The pilot was badly injured and the co-pilot radioed the rescue submarine.

**SAVED BY THE SUB:** The following morning the submarine delivered the crews from the B-29 and OA-10 to Iwo Jima. Between November 1944 and 14 August 1945, the 21st Bomber Command lost 3,125 crewmen in attacks on Japan. Of these, 1,424 went down at sea. Air Force and Navy units rescued 687, nearly half of those who ditched.

# CONSOLIDATED

# PB2Y CORONADO

● Maritime reconnaissance ● Anti-shipping ● Transport

▲ This PB2Y has had its armament removed and was used in the transport role. The specialist PB2Y-5H was used as a casualty evacuation aircraft with accommodation for 25 stretchers.

**S**oon after Consolidated's famous PBY Catalina had flown, plans were drawn up to build a larger maritime patrol flying-boat with a greater weapons capacity and higher speed. The resulting XPB2Y-1 competed successfully against the Sikorsky XPBS-1 and after a number of modifications it entered production as the PB2Y Coronado. The type saw limited service in World War II with the US Navy and 10 examples were used by the RAF, mainly as transports.

▼ **Experimental squadron**
All six PB4Y-2s built were operated by VP-13 Squadron, US Navy, for experimental duties. Each could carry 5443 kg of bombs.

◄ **Principal production version**
The US Navy procured a total of 210 PBY-3s which were used in the Pacific theatre. These are early examples without radar.

**Single-fin prototype ▶**
In competition with the Sikorsky XPBS-1, the XPB2Y-1 first flew in December 1937 and was regarded as the more suitable aircraft for production. A lack of lateral stability was rectified by replacing the single fin with two endplates.

▼ **Lend-lease Coronado**
Ten PB2Y-3Bs were diverted to the RAF as Coronado GR.Mk Is. After brief service with Coastal Command they were used as transports with No. 231 Squadron.

▲ **Searching for ships**
Later-model PB2Ys were fitted with a dorsal Air to Surface Vessel (ASV) radar. This could detect targets in bad weather or at night.

### FACTS AND FIGURES

➤ Named XPB2Y-1, the Coronado prototype first flew on 17 December 1937, powered by Pratt & Whitney XR-1830-72 engines.

➤ With five defensive gun positions, a crew of nine was needed to man the PB2Y.

➤ The PB2Y-3R transport version featured faired-over turrets and R-1830-88 engines.

➤ The first squadron to operate the Coronado was VP-13, which received its first PB2Y-2 on 31 December 1940.

➤ The PB2Y-3 featured self-sealing fuel tanks and protective armour.

➤ Production PB2Ys had a much deeper hull than the prototype to improve handling.

# Patrol boat from San Diego

With heavy defensive armament, long range and a large weapons load the PB2Y had the potential to be one of the US Navy's most important patrol flying-boats of World War II. However, production preference was given to the twin-engined PBY Catalina of which thousands were built compared to a mere 226 production PB2Ys.

The prototype, designated XPB2Y-1, underwent evaluation in early 1938 and was selected over the XPBS-1, but a number of shortcomings needed to be addressed before production could begin. The most serious problem was lateral instability which was solved by modifying the tail unit. The tailplane was given significant dihedral, and endplates similar to those on the B-24 bomber were fitted. The nose profile was also changed to a more rounded appearance.

The main production version was the PB2Y-3, which saw little operational service during the War. Ten PB2Y-3Bs supplied to the RAF as Coronado GR.Mk Is were mostly used for hauling freight across the Atlantic.

Later versions were fitted with air to surface vessel (ASV) radar and other variants included the PB2Y-3R transport and the PB2Y-5H casevac aircraft. All Coronados had been withdrawn from service by VJ Day.

*Left: A number of PB2Y-3s were converted to PB2Y-5 standard. Alterations included fitting more powerful R-1830-92 engines, increased fuel capacity and provision for RATO (rocket-assisted take-off) gear.*

*Above: This photograph shows the sharp dihedral of the Coronado's tailplane and its associated endplates. The aircraft were wheeled to the water using a trolley system.*

## PB2Y-3 Coronado

**Type:** long-range flying-boat patrol bomber

**Powerplant:** four 895-kW (1,200-hp.) Pratt & Whitney R-1830-88 Twin Wasp radial piston engines

**Maximum speed:** 359 km/h (223 m.p.h.) at 6095 m (20,000 ft.)

**Range:** 3814 km (2,365 mi.)

**Service ceiling:** 6250 m (20,500 ft.)

**Weights:** empty 18,568 kg (40,850 lb.); maximum take-off 30,844 kg (67,857 lb.)

**Armament:** two 12.7-mm (.50 cal.) machine-guns in each of bow, dorsal and tail turrets, and one 12.7-mm machine-gun in each of two beam positions, plus up to 5443 kg (11,975 lb.) of bombs, depth bombs or torpedoes in bomb bays

**Dimensions:**
| | | |
|---|---|---|
| span | 35.05 m | (115 ft.) |
| length | 24.16 m | (79 ft. 3 in.) |
| height | 8.38 m | (27 ft. 6 in.) |
| wing area | 165.36 m² | (1,780 sq. ft.) |

---

## PB2Y-5 CORONADO

**Little use was made of the PB2Y Coronado in World War II. This example was used mostly for transport purposes before it was retired along with the rest of the fleet in 1944-45.**

To protect the PB2Y from enemy fighter attack the aircraft was equipped with nose, dorsal and tail turrets each with a pair of 12.7-mm (.50 cal.) machine-guns. Single 12.7-mm machine-guns were also fitted to the fuselage sides on flexible mounts.

The PB2Y-5 was fitted with more powerful R-1830-92 engines giving the aircraft much improved performance at low altitudes. The fuel capacity was also increased.

After the single fin arrangement on the XPB2Y-1 was found to be inadequate, a new tail unit with rounded endplate fins was fitted. The fins and rudders were similar to the units fitted to the B-24 Liberator.

This PB2Y-5 shows a mixture of darker non-specular sea blue merging into pale grey-blue with white undersurfaces, the camouflage scheme carried by PB2Y-5s in the later stages of World War II.

A two-step hull provided the aircraft with good handling in water. The stabilising wingtip floats retracted to form the wingtips in flight.

---

## COMBAT DATA

### MAXIMUM SPEED

Although the H6K was an earlier design than the other two types it had the edge in speed. Speed was less important than endurance and to increase fuel economy all three types generally operated at a speed of about 250 km/h (155 m.p.h.).

| | |
|---|---|
| **PB2Y-3 CORONADO** | 359 km/h (223 m.p.h.) |
| **H6K5 'MAVIS'** | 385 km/h (238 m.p.h.) |
| **SUNDERLAND Mk V** | 343 km/h (213 m.p.h.) |

### ARMAMENT

The Coronado had a massive bombload compared to the other two types, making it capable of attacking more than one target. All three types had formidable defensive armament.

| **PB2Y-3 CORONADO** | **H6K5 'MAVIS'** | **SUNDERLAND Mk V** |
|---|---|---|
| 8 x 12.7-mm (.50 cal.) machine-guns 5443-kg (11,975-lb.) bombload | 4 x 7.7-mm (.303 cal.) machine-guns 1 x 20-mm cannon 1600-kg (3,520-lb.) bombload | 8 x 7.7-mm (.303 cal.) machine-guns and 2 x 12.7-mm (.50 cal.) machine-guns 907-kg (2,000-lb.) bombload |

### RANGE

As the best flying-boat of the early years of World War II, the H6K had exceptional range, allowing it to operate deep into the Pacific Ocean on reconnaissance and anti-shipping missions. Both the Sunderland and the Coronado had modest range in comparison but could still operate 10-hour missions.

PB2Y-3 CORONADO 3814 km (2,365 mi.)

H6K5 'MAVIS' 6775 km (4,200 mi.)

SUNDERLAND Mk V 4329 km (2,684 mi.)

---

# World War II maritime patrol aircraft

■ **CONSOLIDATED LIBERATOR:** Operated by both RAF Coastal Command and the US Navy, the Liberator helped close the 'U-boat gap' in the middle of the Atlantic Ocean.

■ **FOCKE-WULF Fw 200 CONDOR:** With unprecedented range, the Fw 200 was a major threat to Allied shipping in the early years of World War II.

■ **LOCKHEED HUDSON:** As the first US-built aircraft to be used operationally by the RAF in World War II, the Hudson filled an urgent requirement for a maritime patrol bomber.

■ **SHORT SUNDERLAND:** Operating in the Atlantic and the Pacific, the Sunderland flew reconnaissance sorties as well as anti-shipping and anti-submarine missions.

# CONVAIR

# B-32 DOMINATOR

● Strategic bomber ● Late wartime service entry ● Crew trainer

**C**onsolidated built the B-32 Dominator as an 'insurance' against any possibility that Boeing's B-29 project might fail. Had events turned out differently, the big, powerful B-32 might have led the 1944/45 bombing campaign against the Japanese home islands. But the B-32 was delayed in development, and the B-29 succeeded. This meant that the Dominator became little more than a footnote in aviation history, with only a handful flying operationally.

▲ Beginning life almost as a scaled-up B-24 Liberator, progressive changes through the three prototypes of the B-32 led to the ultimate design, minus the initial round nose and twin fins.

---

## CONVAIR B-32 DOMINATOR

▼ **Cyclone power**
Wright's 1641-kW (2198 hp) R-3350-23 Cyclone engine, unrivalled at altitude, powered both the B-32 and Boeing B-29.

▲ **Long-range mission master**
In standard form, the B-32 Dominator had provision for a crew of eight, and defensive armament of five twin-gun manned turrets. Teething problems meant the B-32 Dominator would see little action.

▼ **Prototype Dominator**
Consolidated built just three XB-32 prototypes before receiving a joint order with Boeing, who also built three XB-29 prototype aircraft.

▲ **Service entry**
Only 15 B-32s were to become operational before VJ-Day, all equipping the USAAF's 386th Heavy Bombardment Squadron. A total of 40 TB-32 crew trainers was also built, but withdrawn post-war.

**Heavy bombload ▶**
Each of the B-32's bomb-bays could carry 4536 kg (10,000 lb) of iron bombs. Had it not been beaten by the B-29, the Dominator might have made the nuclear strikes on Japan.

### FACTS AND FIGURES

➤ The 386th Bomb Group moved from the Philippines to Okinawa, bombing Japan during the last week of the war.

➤ Convair's B-32 beat the B-29 into the air by 14 days, flying on 7 September 1942.

➤ A double tail in the style of the B-24 was featured on the first two Dominators.

➤ The first mission was flown from Clark Field on 29 May 1945 against a Japanese Army depot deep in the Cagayan Valley.

➤ Some 118 Dominators were built before further development was cancelled.

➤ Consolidated's chief test pilot was killed when a prototype crashed on 10 May 1943.

# PROFILE

# Superfortress understudy

When it first flew in 1942, the B-32 was one of the biggest and most capable bombers ever built. This high-winged, four-engined giant had many of the innovative features of its competitor, the B-29, including pressurisation and remote-controlled gun turrets.

Consolidated (which became Convair in the mid 1940s) had many problems developing the B-32 and was not able to begin delivery of production bombers until November 1944, almost eight months after B-29s had been deployed to begin their campaign against Japan. Even

then, production B-32s had the intended pressurisation and armament deleted.

Although this was an impressive aircraft, only 15 became operational before the war's end, equipping the 386th Bombardment Squadron on Okinawa. Forty TB-32s were also used for training, out of a total B-32 production run of 118.

While the B-32 saw very little combat, one B-32 flew the final US bombing mission of World War II. Between 15 and 18 August 1945, Dominators flew 'reconnaissance' missions over Tokyo, encountered hostile

ground fire and attacks by Japanese pilots who rebelled against the 15 August surrender. On 18 August, an engagement with fighters caused the death of a crewman, a significant event in history since he was the last American to be killed in World War II.

*Below: The second XB-32 was an 'in-between' stage, with the twin fins of the first and glazed nose of the third.*

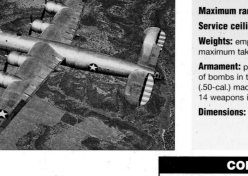

*Above: By the time the first production B-32 had taken to the air, it was a different machine altogether, incorporating the stepped glazed nose and conventional tail unit of the second and third XB-32 prototypes, respectively.*

## B-32 Dominator

**Type:** long-range strategic bomber

**Powerplant:** four 1641-kW Wright R-3350-23 Cyclone radial piston engines

**Maximum speed:** 575 km/h (357 mph) at 7620 m (25,000 ft)

**Range:** 1287 km (800 miles) with maximum bombload

**Maximum range:** 6115 km (3800 miles)

**Service ceiling:** 10,670 m (35,000 ft)

**Weights:** empty 27,339 kg (60,272 lb); maximum take-off 50,576 kg (111,500 lb)

**Armament:** provision for 9072 kg (20,000 lb) of bombs in two bomb-bays; 10 12.7-mm (.50-cal.) machine guns in five barbettes, but 14 weapons in seven barbettes were planned

**Dimensions:**
| | | |
|---|---|---|
| span | 41.15 m | (135 ft) |
| length | 25.32 m | (83 ft 1 in) |
| height | 10.06 m | (33 ft) |
| wing area | 132.10 m² | (1422 sq ft) |

Dimensions: span 41.15 m (135 ft); length 25.32 m (83 ft 1 in); height 10.06 m (33 ft); wing area 132.10 m$^2$ (1422 sq ft)

## B-32 DOMINATOR

Seeing only limited service in the Pacific theatre, the B-32's life as a US Army Air Force heavy bomber was brief. A few flew as navigation trainers, but the aircraft were soon surplus to requirements.

One of five gun turrets, each with two 12.7-mm (.50-cal.) machine guns, was located in the nose. Originally, the B-32 was intended to carry advanced, remote-controlled gun turrets, like those of the B-29.

Like the B-29, the Dominator utilised four powerful Wright Cyclone radial piston engines, driving large-diameter, four-bladed propellers.

The B-32 usually carried its bombload in vertical stacks within the two capacious bomb-bays. Only the 386th Bombardment Squadron became operational on the type, and this machine carries 11 mission symbols.

The Dominator's enormous tail was a necessity in order to replicate the surface area of the two separate tails of the prototype aircraft. Because of hurried manufacture, the fuselage pressurisation system was deleted.

2108532

Like most heavy bombers of the period, the B-32 had a manned tail turret. In later machines, the tail and nose twin machine guns were replaced with single 20-mm cannon.

### COMBAT DATA

#### ARMAMENT
Designed and built to the same specification as the B-29, the B-32 had a very similar weapons load. The German He 277 had a greater emphasis on defensive guns, and like many German bomber types had only a limited bombload.

**B-32 DOMINATOR** — 10 x 12.7-mm (.50-cal.) machine guns 9072-kg (20,000-lb) bombload

**B-29 SUPERFORTRESS** — 11 x 12.7-mm (.50-cal.) machine guns 9072-kg (20,000-lb) bombload

**He 277B-5/R2** — 6 x 20-mm cannon, 4 x 13-mm cannon 3000-kg (6614-lb) bombload

#### SERVICE CEILING
Although unpressurised, the B-32 had a greater ceiling than the riva l Superfortress. From the outset, the He 277 was also designed for high-altitude missions in order to escape fighters.

**B-32 DOMINATOR** 10,670 m (35,000 ft)
**He 277B-5/R2** 15,000 m (49,213 ft)
**B-29 SUPERFORTRESS** 9710 m (31,857 ft)

#### RANGE
Although smaller than the B-29, the B-32 had a considerably greater range. It also had a slightly longer range than the Heinkel He 277. Had its development been smoother, it may well have been the Dominator, not the Boeing B-29, that went on to be remembered as one of the most successful heavy bombers of all time.

**B-32 DOMINATOR** 6115 km (3800 miles)
**B-29 SUPERFORTRESS** 5230 km (3250 miles)
**He 277B-5/R2** 6000 km (3728 miles)

## Late-war bomber projects

**AVRO LINCOLN:** Initially known as the Lancaster Mk IV, the Lincoln was too late to fly operationally in World War II but became an important RAF heavy bomber after the war.

**HEINKEL He 277:** A four-engined development of the He 177 Grief, eight production machines had been completed when maufacturing priority turned to fighters in 1944.

**NAKAJIMA G8N1 RENZAN:** Coming too late too enter service as the Japanese navy's first four-engined heavy bomber, the Renzan ('Rita') was tested in America after the war.

**VICKERS WINDSOR:** This experimental bomber was notable for its main undercarriage, which consisted of four separate units. Its skin was an unusual woven steel wire/fabric composite.

# CURTISS

# C-46 COMMANDO

● Biggest wartime twin ● Vital transport ● Long serving

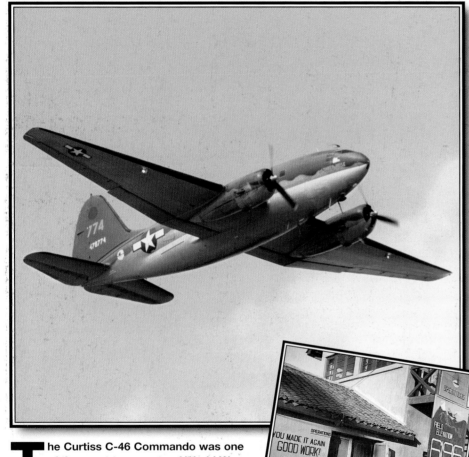

The Curtiss C-46 Commando was one of the great transports of World War II and has proved to be a rugged and reliable workhorse in both military and civil service ever since. The twin-engine, double-bubble C-46 is best remembered, however, for hauling war supplies over the 'Hump'. This was the transport route from India to China that traversed the Himalayan range and contained some of the most difficult flying conditions anywhere in the world.

▲ First flown on 26 March 1940 the C-46 was ordered by the USAAF in September as a troop and cargo transport. Its cavernous fuselage was well used in the Far East and Pacific theatres.

▲ Flight deck
Unlike the contemporary bombers the C-46's cockpit was roomy and relatively uncomplicated for the pilots.

▲ Air ambulance
The majority of C-46s built for the USAAF served in Asia. This Commando served in the role of air ambulance at Saipan in the Marianas in June 1944. It could carry up to 33 stretchers and additional medical staff.

▲ Para-dropper
In service with Troop Carrier Command, the C-46D dedicated troop carrier was adapted to, but saw little use as, a parachute aircraft.

◄ Production line
The main production line was established at Curtiss' plant in Buffalo, New York.

CW-20 prototype ►
The first prototype was briefly used by the USAAF before being sold to British Overseas Airways Corporation and used for flights between Gibraltar and Malta in 1942.

## FACTS AND FIGURES

➤ The prototype CW-20 with twin fin and rudder first flew on 26 March 1940; the fuselage sides were also rounded.

➤ C-46s had carried 2.5 million kgs (2756 tons) of cargo over the 'Hump' by December 1943.

➤ Total production of the C-46 Commando numbered 3181 aircraft.

➤ US Air Force C-46 Commandos ended their service career at Howard Air Force Base, Panama, in 1968.

➤ C-46s fought a 'secret war' in Laos, flown by airlines that worked for the CIA.

➤ The Commando was built in 23 variants for the US Army, Navy and Marine Corps.

## PROFILE

# Heavylift hero of the Far East

To carry fuel, food, supplies and ammunition to Allied troops in China, C-46 Commando pilots braved the horrendous weather, terrible cold and dizzy altitude of the Himalayan mountain range, flying from bases in India.

The aircraft were loaded and flown under the most primitive conditions, their fuel pumped by hand from drums. On the Assam-Chunking route, which was typical, Commando pilots had to vault peaks of about 4000 m (13,100 ft), even though ice began to form on the aircraft's wings at 3050 m (10,000 ft).

The bulky, swollen-looking C-46 Commando never quite achieved the elegance of its near-contemporary the Douglas DC-3, but it had a greater capacity to carry people and freight. The Commando dropped in and out of airfields all over the world and they were used in action in the Korean War and for training for Vietnam. Hundreds of

*Above: C-46s were used after the war in glider towing experiments, using a solid towing link between the two aircraft. This C-46F is towing a WACO CG-15A.*

Commandos later became civil servants operating with airlines in dozens of countries.

*Above: More than half a century after it was first flown by the USAAF, this C-46A, built by Curtiss-Wright, is still flying regularly with the Confederate Air Force in Texas.*

### C-46 Commando

**Type:** medium-range passenger/cargo transport

**Powerplant:** two 1566-kW (2100-hp) Pratt & Whitney R-2800-34 Double Wasp 18-cylinder radial engines

**Maximum speed:** 435 km/h (270 mph) at 3048 m (10,000 ft)

**Cruising speed:** 378 km/h (235 mph) at 2745 m (9006 ft)

**Range:** 2897 km (1800 miles)

**Service ceiling:** 6705 m (21,998 ft)

**Weights:** empty 13,290 kg (29,299 lb); maximum take-off 22,680 kg (50,000 lb)

**Dimensions:**
| | | |
|---|---|---|
| span | 32.93 m (108 ft) |
| length | 23.27 m (76 ft 4 in) |
| height | 6.63 m (21 ft 9 in) |
| wing area | 126.16 m² (1358 sq ft) |

### C-46 COMMANDO

**The Commando was the biggest and heaviest twin-engined US cargo transport aircraft of World War II which became famous for flying supply missions over the Himalayan mountains.**

Power was provided by two 1566-kW (2100-hp) Pratt & Whitney Double Wasp 18-cylinder radial piston engines driving Hamilton Standard propellers.

The fuselage was formed from two partial rings, one above the other, which met at a tension diaphragm – the cabin floor. This gave the C-46 its double-bubble appearance.

Similar in structure to the wings, the all-metal single fin, rudder and tailplane are of the cantilever monoplane type. Trim tabs are fitted on the elevators and rudder.

This C-46 is in the colours of the Japan Self-Defence Force in about 1973. It was being used for general transport and utility duties.

51-1114

The crew of four comprised the pilot, co-pilot, navigator and radio operator. The flush windscreen was replaced by a stepped version in the C-46D.

The cantilever low wing was built in three main sections. The centre-section was built into the fuselage. Hydraulically-operated slotted flaps extended from the ailerons to the fuselage.

### COMBAT DATA

#### MAXIMUM SPEED

With its powerful Pratt & Whitney R-2800-34 Double Wasp engines, the C-46 had a top speed nearly 20 per cent faster than its main rival the Douglas C-47 and 40 per cent faster than the three-engined Ju-52 operated by the Luftwaffe.

| | |
|---|---|
| **C-46 COMMANDO** | 435 km/h (270 mph) |
| **C-47** | 370 km/h (230 mph) |
| **Ju-52** | 270 km/h (168 mph) |

#### RANGE

Greater fuel capacity and a high all-up weight gave the C-46 an exceptional range which enabled it to fly over the 'Hump'. It could fly further than the C-47 and over three times as far as the Ju-52 which was designed for the European theatre.

C-47 2575 km (1600 miles)

Ju-52 917 km (570 miles)

C-46 COMMANDO 2897 km (1800 miles)

#### PAYLOAD

Although the C-47 could lift the same weight as the C-46 it only had the fuselage space to take 28 fully armed troops while the C-46 could take 50 troops. The smaller Ju-52 had less than half of the payload and could carry only 18 troops. All three flew vital supply missions to their troops.

| | |
|---|---|
| **C-46 COMMANDO** | 4536 kg (10,000 lb)/50 troops |
| **C-47** | 4536 kg (10,000 lb)/28 troops |
| **Ju-52** | 1202 kg (2650 lb)/18 troops |

## Over the 'Hump'

To supply the Allied war against the Japanese a constant flow of food, ammunition and other vital supplies were lifted over the Himalayas by hardworking C-46s.

Chunking

Assam

**C-46 MAINSTAY:** A massive air transport supply effort was undertaken from the Assam region of India to supply friendly forces fighting the Japanese in the south-west of China.

**OVER THE HIMALAYAS:** For the 805-km (500-mile) flight from Assam to Chunking the C-46s had to climb fully laden to 4265 m (13,993 ft), through the icing layer at 3050 m (10,000 ft), then land in appalling weather conditions.

**PRIMITIVE FACILITIES:** The Assam airfields were largely unpaved and were transformed into boggy conditions by the monsoon rains for nearly half of the year. The aircraft were refuelled by hand from drums.

# CURTISS
# P-1 & P-6 HAWK

● Interwar biplane fighter ● Classic US design ● Air racing heritage

▲ *Over a 10-year period, Curtiss developed a series of increasingly capable Hawk biplanes. Together with the Boeing P-12 they formed the backbone of the US Army's fighter force until the mid-1930s.*

**F**lying Curtiss biplane fighters was one of the great adventures in aviation. Powerful and nimble, the Curtiss P-1 and P-6 were the flagships of a family of great warplanes that equipped the US Army in the 1920s. The decade was called the 'Roaring Twenties' by Americans who celebrated the end of the Great War and the dawn of a new age of progress. Advances in aviation were happening quickly, with Hawk fighters at the forefront.

▼ **Six-gun fighter**
*One P-6E had two additional 7.62-mm (.30 cal.) machine-guns installed in each wing by the manufactuer; it was designated the XP-6H.*

▲ **Ice-bound Hawk**
*Aircraft belonging to the 1st Pursuit Group, home-based in Michigan, often used a ski undercarriage for Arctic operations.*

▼ **Aerobatics over Washington**
*With higher weights, larger landing wheels, an improved radiator and V-1150-3 engine, the P-1B was an improved, although slightly slower, development of the P-1A. Twenty-three P-1B Hawks were delivered from October 1926 and served alongside earlier aircraft.*

▲ **Skis on P-1Cs**
*Curtiss received its first large Hawk order for the P-1C model. The aircraft was heavier and slower than earlier variants, but 33 were delivered. Some flew with this optional ski undercarriage.*

**Prestone-cooled Conqueror** ▶
*Some of the original water-cooled YP-6 Hawks were re-engined with a Prestone cooling system and were designated P-6As. The system used much smaller radiators.*

## FACTS AND FIGURES

➤ A P-6 prototype, actually a converted P-1, won the 1927 National Air Races trophy at a speed of 320 km/h (198 m.p.h.).

➤ A US Army air pioneer, Lt Frank Tyndall, died in a P-1 crash on 15 July 1930.

➤ Curtiss manufactured a total of 239 Hawk biplane fighters.

➤ Curtiss Hawk biplanes served for exactly 10 years before giving way to the Boeing P-26 monoplane.

➤ Some Hawks had turbo superchargers for high-altitude performance.

➤ A single export Hawk was sold to Japan in the late 1920s.

## PROFILE

# End of the biplane era

Arriving at McCook Field, Dayton, Ohio, in August 1925, the Curtiss P-1 Hawk was the first aircraft in the US Army's 'P' for 'Pursuit' category, which later included immortals like the P-47 and P-51. A standard, single-seater biplane of the type which was popular in the 1920s, the P-1 was widely used. It was joined in 1928 by the P-6 Hawk, which had the same basic airframe but many improvements. These included better all-round performance, spats on the wheels and machine-guns mounted on the fuselage sides, rather than on top, to provide better visibility.

The P-1 and P-6 were the greatest fighters of their brief moment in history, between the Great War and the Depression. Army pilots used them in aerobatic displays and entered them in races, but the Curtiss Hawk never went to war.

The best-known fighter in this series, the P-6E, began to reach the 17th Pursuit Squadron in 1932. But, by then, an era had ended: the first monoplane fighters were beginning to appear, and the biplane fighter soon disappeared for ever.

*Eight P-6Es, in the flamboyant markings of the 17th Pursuit Squadron, demonstrate their highly polished formation flying skills. These formations were of no practical use in combat.*

### P-6E Hawk

**Type:** single-seat pursuit biplane

**Powerplant:** one 522-kW (700-hp.) Curtiss V-1750C Conqueror inline piston engine

**Maximum speed:** 317 km/h (198 m.p.h.)

**Service ceiling:** 7285 m (24,700 ft.)

**Range:** 459 km (285 mi.)

**Weights:** empty equipped 1224 kg (2,693 lb.); maximum take-off 1559 kg (3,430 lb.)

**Armament:** two synchronised fuselage-mounted 7.62-mm (.30 cal.) machine-guns

**Dimensions:**
| | | |
|---|---|---|
| span | 9.60 m | (31 ft. 6 in.) |
| length | 7.06 m | (23 ft. 2 in.) |
| height | 2.72 m | (8 ft. 11 in.) |
| wing area | 23.41 m² | (252 sq. ft.) |

Most P-6Es were fitted with three-bladed, variable-pitch propellers. The two machine-guns fired through the propeller arc.

Curtiss studied the effects of wing flutter after one of its racers lost its wings. This research allowed them to use only two sets of main wing struts.

Moving the radiator back from its former chin position to a location just forward of the undercarriage legs, improved the aerodynamics of the P-6E. In addition, single-strut main landing gear units, with spatted wheels, were installed. The machine-guns were moved from high on the nose to low on the fuselage sides.

### P-6E HAWK

**Wearing the distinctive black and white markings of the 17th Pursuit Squadron of the 1st Pursuit Group, this aircraft was delivered in 1932.**

The most colourful of all Hawk markings were applied by the 17th Pursuit Squadron. The overall paint scheme was based on the Arctic snow owl which was the unit insignia.

On the P-6E the tailskid was replaced with a fixed tailwheel. This, together with other improvements, produced a 13 km/h (8 m.p.h.) speed increase over the P-6A.

### COMBAT DATA

#### MAXIMUM SPEED

With its racing heritage and refined design, the P-6E was better than both of its contemporaries in terms of speed. British fighters had advanced little since World War I, hence the poor speed of the Siskin.

| | |
|---|---|
| P-6E HAWK | 317 km/h (198 m.p.h.) |
| P-12 | 272 km/h (169 m.p.h.) |
| SISKIN IIIA | 251 km/h (156 m.p.h.) |

#### ARMAMENT

Boeing's P-12 was the US Army Air Corps' second fighter. It was more heavily armed than the P-6E but could not match its performance. The Siskin retained World War I standard armament.

| P-6E HAWK | P-12 | SISKIN IIIA |
|---|---|---|
| 2 x 7.62-mm (.30 cal.) machine-guns | 1 x 12.7-mm (.50 cal.) machine-gun 1 x 7.62-mm (.30 cal.) machine-gun 1 x 227-kg (500-lb.) bomb | 2 x 7.7-mm (.303 cal.) machine-guns 4 x 9-kg (20-lb.) bombs |

#### SERVICE CEILING

While the Armstrong Whitworth Siskin lagged behind in other areas, it did offer a good service ceiling. Without engine superchargers, however, none of these aircraft was capable of exceptional performance at high altitudes. The open cockpits of these machines also made flying at altitude very uncomfortable.

| P-6E HAWK | P-12 | SISKIN IIIA |
|---|---|---|
| 7285 m (24,700 ft.) | 8199 m (26,900 ft.) | 8230 m (27,000 ft.) |

## Curtiss Hawk evolution

**R-6:** This specialist air racing machine set a new world speed record in 1922, and inspired the Hawk fighter designs.

**P-2 HAWK:** Curtiss' own V-1400 engine powered the P-2, but it proved disappointing. The aircraft were therefore converted back to P-1As.

**EXPORT HAWK:** Powered by Pratt & Whitney R-1340 radials, 16 of these aircraft were delivered.

**HAWK P-3:** Only five production P-3A Hawks were built. This experimental aircraft has a retractable undercarriage.

# CURTISS

# P-36/HAWK 75

● Monoplane fighter ● Exported widely ● Asian and European combat

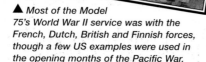

▲ *Most of the Model
75's World War II service was with the
French, Dutch, British and Finnish forces,
though a few US examples were used in
the opening months of the Pacific War.*

Initial attempts by Curtiss to sell the US
Army Air Corps its Model 75 monoplane
fighter were unsuccessful. Curtiss was
beaten by Seversky and its IXP design,
known as the P-35. Undaunted, Curtiss
produced the re-engined Model 75B for
the USAAC and the simplified Hawk 75 for
export. Sales drives during the late 1930s
were a great success, especially once the
USAAC ordered 210 Hawk 75s (P-35As) – the
biggest US fighter order placed since 1918.

## CURTISS P-36/HAWK 75

▲ **Fighting the Japanese**
*Twenty H75-A7s served in the Dutch
East Indies from May 1940 and saw
intensive fighting against the Japanese.*

▲ **RAF Mohawk**
*The RAF's Model 75s were
known as Mohawks. All
those delivered had been
originally ordered by France.*

**US Army P-36C** ▶
*The USAAC's few P-36Cs
featured extra wing-mounted
7.62-mm (.30-cal) guns.*

◀ **Large French orders**
*France's Armée de l'Air ordered
a total of 1130 Model H75s
before World War II; only about
600 were completed and of
these about 200 reached France.
Some were diverted to Morocco;
others escaped to Britain.*

**Preserved Hawk** ▶
*In the colours of a P-36C serving with the
27th Pursuit Squadron, USAAC in
September 1939, this aircraft is preserved
by the USAF Museum in Ohio. The
colourful paint scheme was applied for
participation in the National Air Races.*

## FACTS AND FIGURES

➤ China and Argentina were granted
licences to build a simplified Model 75
with fixed landing gear.

➤ A few captured Hawks were impressed
into service by the Luftwaffe.

➤ Most USAAC P-36As had been replaced
by Curtiss P-40s by December 1941.

➤ In its infancy, Hindustan Aircraft Ltd
(HAL) of India built at least five Hawk
75s. French Hawks diverted to Britain
were fitted with British equipment and
sent to Portugal, South Africa and India.

➤ The original USAAC contract for 210
aircraft was valued at US$4,113,550.

## PROFILE

# Exported Hawks go to war

It was the Hawk 75 export model that saw the most service and combat during World War II, and was destined to serve on both sides.

Though it was the main US Army fighter at the time of the Japanese attack on Pearl Harbor, US combat use was to be virtually confined to the few that managed to get airborne over Hawaii on 7 December 1941.

Sales to France, Norway and the Netherlands had followed the original US order; the 200 that entered French service were their most effective fighters before the German invasion in 1940. However, though it was a sound aircraft with excellent manoeuvrability, the Hawk was outclassed in speed and firepower by more modern European designs such as the Messerschmitt Bf 109, often its main adversary.

Aircraft en route to France were delivered to the UK. A few later served with the RAF in the Burma campaign, while Dutch machines in the East Indies saw limited action against the

Japanese, as did a small number of H75Ns in Siam.

Apart from Finland's use of Hawks against the Russians, other Axis Hawks included Vichy French aircraft that briefly fought US forces in North Africa.

*Above: Registered NR1277, this is the second Hawk 75 demonstrator featuring fixed gear and bomb racks.*

*Below: Hawk 75s captured by the Nazis in 1940 were assembled in Germany and passed on to Finland for use against the Russians after the German invasion of the USSR in June 1941. Some remained in service as late as 1948.*

### Hawk 75A-8 (P-36G)

**Type:** single-seat monoplane fighter

**Powerplant:** one 895-kW (1200-hp) Wright R-1820-G205A Cyclone radial piston engine

**Maximum speed:** 518 km/h (322 mph) at 4633 m (15,200 ft)

**Cruising speed:** 420 km/h (261 mph)

**Initial climb rate:** 6 min to 4572 m (15,000 ft)

**Range:** 1046 km (650 miles)

**Service ceiling:** 9860 m (32,350 ft)

**Weights:** empty 2121 kg (4676 lb); maximum take-off 2667 kg (5880 lb)

**Armament:** four wing-mounted 7.62-mm (.30-cal.) and two fuselage-mounted 12.7-mm (.50-cal.) machine guns

**Dimensions:**
| | |
|---|---|
| span | 11.27 m (37 ft) |
| length | 8.68 m (28 ft 6 in) |
| height | 2.81 m (9 ft 3 in) |
| wing area | 21.92 m² (236 sq ft) |

## HAWK 75A-8

**Norway ordered 36 of these aircraft just prior to the German occupation. Six were delivered to Free Norwegian forces in Canada in February 1941 (including this aircraft based in Toronto), but the rest were requisitioned by the US Army as P-36Gs.**

Among the improvements introduced with the Model 75B was the scalloped rear fuselage behind the cockpit to provide a rear view for the pilot.

When Curtiss engineers realised that the service life of the radial-engined P-36 would be limited, a P-36 was re-engined with a new 12-cylinder, liquid-cooled Allison V-1710. This became the XP-37 and led directly to the P-40 Warhawk fighter family.

443

Though the Model 75 prototype was powered by a 671-kW (900-hp) Wright XR-1720 radial, the export models employed a large diameter R-1820 Cyclone 9. The Army's P-36s, on the other hand, had a Pratt & Whitney R-1830 Twin Wasp installed.

By the time the H75A-8 appeared, the Hawks were fitted with much improved armament totalling six machine guns; four in the wings and two above the engine, firing through the propeller arc.

Curtiss's Hawk 75 was a stressed-skin, cantilever low-wing monoplane with hydraulically-operated split flaps and main landing gear. Even the tail wheel retracted. However, at time of the aircraft's design in 1934, other manufacturers were also building advanced monoplane fighter aircraft, including Seversky.

### COMBAT DATA

**MAXIMUM SPEED**

Though it was a manoeuvrable aircraft, the P-36 lacked the speed of its European contemporaries. Some Japanese designs also had a superior top speed.

| | |
|---|---|
| **P-36C HAWK** | 501 km/h (311 mph) |
| **HURRICANE Mk IIC** | 541 km/h (366 mph) |
| **Ki-43-IIb 'OSCAR'** | 530 km/h (329 mph) |

**RANGE**

While lacking in range compared to the Nakajima 'Oscar', the Hawk compared favourably with the Hawker Hurricane which was limited to 740 km in cannon-armed Mk IIC form. The four Hispano cannon imposed a weight penalty.

| | |
|---|---|
| **P-36C HAWK** 1320 km (820 miles) | **HURRICANE Mk IIC** 740 km (460 miles) |
| | **Ki-43-IIb 'OSCAR'** 3200 km 1988 miles) |

**ARMAMENT**

The first Hawk 75/P-36 variants were fairly lightly armed, though the P-36C fared better than the 'Oscar'. Cannon armament featured prominently on British and other countries' aircraft later in the war; the Hurricane was a prime example, with four 20-mm Hispanos.

| | |
|---|---|
| **P-36C HAWK** | 1 x 12.7-mm (.50-cal.) machine gun 3 x 7.62-mm (.30-cal.) machine guns |
| **HURRICANE Mk IIC** | 4 x 20-mm cannon |
| **Ki-43-IIb 'OSCAR'** | 2 x 12.7-mm (.50-cal.) machine guns |

## Model 75 Hawk colours

■ **FINLAND:** This Hawk 75A-3 was attached to LeLv 32 at Suulajärvi in September 1941. It was among a number assembled in Germany from captured French and Norwegian examples.

■ **NETHERLANDS EAST INDIES:** The 1st Squadron of the Royal Netherlands East Indies Army Air Corps operated Hawk 75A-7s against the Japanese until February 1942.

■ **UNITED STATES:** The US Army's P-36s were never officially named. The only operational finish carried by these aircraft was olive drab/neutral grey as applied to this P-36C.

■ **VICHY FRANCE:** Among the 200 examples delivered to the Armée de l'Air, this Hawk 75A-3 ultimately served in 'Vichy' French markings with the 2nd Escadrille of GC1/4 at Dakar in Senegal.

# CURTISS

# P-40 WARHAWK (EARLY VERSIONS)

● US Army fighter ● Widely used ● Fighter-bomber

▲ Not one of the best American fighters of World War II, the early P-40 was nevertheless an effective aircraft and achieved everlasting fame with the American Volunteer Group.

**P**erhaps the best-known Curtiss aircraft of World War II, the P-40 was developed from the radial-engined P-36 fighter of 1936. Although considered by many to be obsolete when it first appeared, the P-40 went on to be built in very large numbers, as the US had no better fighter at the time. Despite poor performance at altitude, the P-40 distinguished itself in the North African theatre and became famous as the mount of the 'Flying Tigers' in China.

## CURTISS P-40 (EARLY VERSIONS)

**Desert Tomahawk ▶**
In RAF service, the early P-40 was known as the Tomahawk. Operating primarily as ground attack aircraft in the North African theatre, they were often seen with sharkmouth insignia, as here.

**◀ Evolutionary design**
The fitting of an in-line engine gave much improved performance, but manoeuvrability remained mediocre.

**▼ Armament removed**
In RAF service, the two 12.7-mm (.50-cal.) machine guns mounted on top of the engine were often removed. This aircraft is an exception.

**▼ Army fighter**
Although outclassed even at the start of World War II, the P-40B acquitted itself well in US service.

**Early colour scheme ▶**
When first delivered to US Army pursuit squadrons in 1940, P-40s originally wore this green paint scheme and had striped rudders. This aircraft is seen next to a huge Boeing XB-15.

### FACTS AND FIGURES

➤ The first prototype P-40 was actually a production Curtiss P-36 fitted with a liquid-cooled Allison V12 engine.

➤ Early P-40s were built in three versions, known as the P-40, P-40B and P-40C.

➤ Based at Langley Field in Virginia, the 8th Pursuit Group was the first P-40 unit.

➤ During 1942 the P-40B-equipped 'Flying Tigers' shot down 286 Japanese army aircraft in just six months.

➤ Tomahawks were widely used by the RAF in North Africa.

➤ RAF P-40Cs were the slowest of all production Warhawks.

## PROFILE

# Slow but tough US fighter

Behind the times when it first appeared, the Curtiss P-40 never did catch up. Factors such as its modestly powered engine and its light armament were compounded by very poor performance at altitude and mediocre manoeuvrability.

These shortcomings were not because of poor design, but were a reflection of the outmoded US Army specification which called for low-level ground-support fighters.

In 1940 the P-40 was placed into large-scale production for

the US Army and found export customers in France and Britain, who were desperately seeking fighters in their struggle with Germany. Britain took over the French order after France fell to Germany. These aircraft, named Tomahawks by the RAF, were heavily committed to the fighting in North Africa. They performed bravely in this theatre and achieved good results at low level, but at high altitude suffered heavy losses to German Bf 109E fighters.

By 1941 the improved P-40B had entered service, and it was

this model which was transferred to the famous American Volunteer Group, or 'Flying Tigers', in China. Under the skilful leadership of Claire Chennault, these aircraft achieved a remarkable kill-to-loss ratio against the Japanese.

*Above: An early USAAF P-40 in flight. This was among the last aircraft delivered to the US before late 1941.*

*Below: In RAF service, Tomahawk IIBs proved too slow as fighters to tackle Luftwaffe Bf 109s and were thus relegated to the ground attack role.*

### P-40B Warhawk

**Type:** single-seat fighter-bomber and pursuit aircraft

**Powerplant:** one 776-kW (1040-hp) Allison V-1710-33 in-line piston engine

**Maximum speed:** 552 km/h (343 mph)

**Initial climb rate:** 6 min to 4500 m (14,764 ft)

**Range:** 386 km (240 miles)

**Service ceiling:** approx 10,000 m (32,800 ft)

**Weights:** empty 2724 kg (6005 lb); loaded 4010 kg (8841 lb)

**Armament:** two 12.7-mm (.50-cal.) machine guns mounted in the nose and four 7.62-mm (.30-cal.) machine guns in the wings

**Dimensions:**
| | | |
|---|---|---|
| span | 11.42 m | (37 ft 6 in) |
| length | 10.00 m | (32 ft 10 in) |
| height | 3.77 m | (12 ft 4 in) |
| wing area | 21.95 m² | (236 sq ft) |

Fabric was used to cover the control surfaces in an attempt to save weight and enhance manoeuvrability, but the Curtiss P-40 was no dogfighter.

### P-40B WARHAWK

Although flown by American pilots, aircraft of the American Volunteer Group (AVG) wore Chinese markings. This particular P-40B was the mount of Charles Olders, based at Kunming, China in 1942.

It may have been slow and performed inadequately at altitude, but the P-40 had considerable pilot protection in the form of an armoured cockpit and windscreen.

In terms of construction, the P-40 was fairly advanced for its time, incorporating an all-alloy frame and alclad skin. This allowed the aircraft to absorb tremendous battle damage.

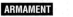

## COMBAT DATA

### ARMAMENT

Both the P-40 and unusual Bell P-39 Airacobra were average fighters and not very effective or hard-hitting. The Messerschmitt Bf 109E was one of the best fighters of the early war years.

**P-40B TOMAHAWK** — 2 x 12.7-mm (.50-cal.) machine guns / 4 x 7.62-mm (.30-cal) machine guns

**P-39N AIRACOBRA** — 2 x 12.7-mm (.50-cal.) machine guns / 4 x 7.62-mm (.30-cal.) machine guns, 1 x 20-mm cannon

**Bf 109E-7** — 4 x 7.92-mm machine guns / 1 x 20-mm cannon

Early P-40s were powered by a liquid-cooled Allison V-12 V1710 engine, which provided adequate performance, though the type was no real threat against Japanese fighters.

Original armament consisted of just four machine guns. On the P-40B this was increased to six, with an additional pair of 7.62-mm (.30-cal.) guns mounted in the wings.

Although dressed in a rather drab green and brown camouflage scheme, aircraft of the three AVG squadrons were adorned with large, vicious-looking sharkmouths on the nose, complete with eyes. A tiger motif was located on each side of the fuselage, just behind the cockpit.

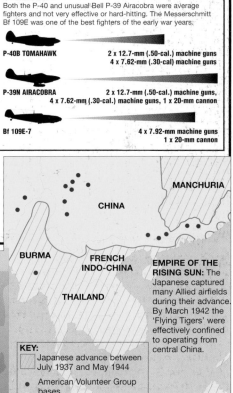

## 'Flying Tigers' combat tactics

**TIGERS' TACTICS:** In order to mount the most effective attack against enemy fighters, AVG pilots would work in pairs, flying their lumbering P-40Bs in from the sun and diving through the Japanese formations.

**MINIMAL INVOLVEMENT:** In order to destroy the maximum number of enemy aircraft for the fewest losses, pilots were instructed to avoid dogfighting at all costs. Once in a 'furball' with an A6M2 'Zero', an early P-40 was a sitting duck.

**ATTACKING BOMBERS:** Long-range Japanese bombers had little armour and huge unprotected fuel tanks. A few bursts from the P-40s' guns was usually enough to turn a 'Betty' or 'Nell' into flames.

**EMPIRE OF THE RISING SUN:** The Japanese captured many Allied airfields during their advance. By March 1942 the 'Flying Tigers' were effectively confined to operating from central China.

**KEY:**
Japanese advance between July 1937 and May 1944
• American Volunteer Group bases

# CURTISS
# P-40 WARHAWK

● Single-seat fighter ● Desert fighter-bomber ● 'Flying Tiger' in China

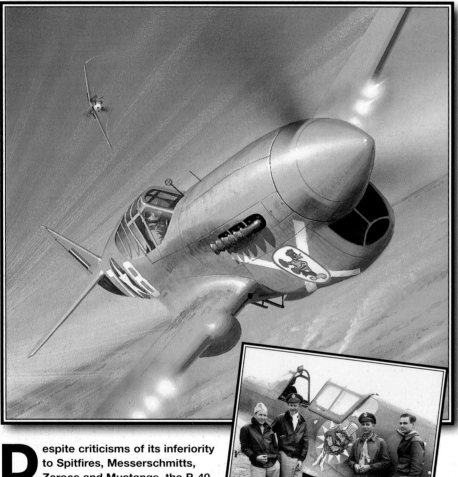

D espite criticisms of its inferiority to Spitfires, Messerschmitts, Zeroes and Mustangs, the P-40 was important – if not critical – to victory in World War II. As the most numerous US Army fighter at the time of Pearl Harbor, the P-40 bred a generation of fighter pilots and won fame with General Chennault's 'Flying Tigers', who took it to the limit against superior Japanese forces.

▲ The P-40 was immortalised by the 'Flying Tigers' of the American Volunteer Group in China, who used the type with great success against the previously all-conquering Japanese.

## CURTISS P-40 WARHAWK

**▲ Still flying**
This P-40 has been restored, and flew at a British air show in 1984. The shark mouth marking was used by No. 112 Squadron RAF, which flew ground-attack missions in Egypt in 1942.

**▲ Lucky escape**
A Zero fighter almost claimed this P-40, flown by John Wood of the USAAC, over Guadalcanal. The P-40 was better able to withstand a hit than a Zero, but was inferior to it in most other respects.

**◀ Kittyhawk**
The first Tomahawks lacked performance, but the improved Kittyhawk Mk III had a more powerful Allison engine and enlarged tailfin.

**▲ Desert airstrip**
Tactical air support meant using rough strips just behind the front line. The rugged P-40 did well in the severe conditions of the desert, where sand was a constant problem as engines wore out.

**Scramble ▶**
Pilots race for take-off as enemy aircraft approach. The P-40 was an excellent attack aircraft, but never really did well as an interceptor fighter.

**◀ Loading up**
The Warhawk family carried six powerful 12.7-mm (.50 cal.) machine-guns, which were excellent weapons for the ground-attack role as well as for air combat.

## FACTS AND FIGURES

➤ The prototype for the P-40 series was flown in October 1938.

➤ At Pearl Harbor on 7 December 1941, 73 P-40s were among 152 US Army aircraft destroyed by the Japanese attack.

➤ Production of all P-40s totalled 16,802, including 13,738 for US forces.

➤ The 'Flying Tigers' in China were credited with 286 aerial victories while losing 23 American P-40 pilots.

➤ P-40s served with Australia, Britain, China, the USSR and South Africa.

➤ When World War II ended, the US had only one P-40 group still in service.

# PROFILE

# Close air support in the Warhawk

Known by many names, including Hawk, Kittyhawk, Tomahawk and Warhawk, 31 variants of the P-40 battled on every continent. The definitive P-40N entered production in 1943, and reached US Army Air Force squadrons in March 1944.

By then, the P-40 was not a world-class pursuit ship. To some extent it was purposely assigned to secondary theatres so that more advanced warplanes (P-38, P-47, P-51)

could fly where the US perceived its first priorities. But none of this meant much to American pilots slogging in the Aleutians, Australians in New Guinea, or South Africans in Libya; they took this solid, rugged fighter and made the most of what they had.

It was plenty. The P-40 excelled when primitive maintenance, terrible weather and heavy odds were the order of the day. It was not in the category of a Bf 109 or Zero

*Like many imperfect or obsolete fighters, the P-40 came in very useful as a ground-attack machine. The Desert Air Force used the type extensively, often working alongside the equally rugged Hawker Hurricane.*

as a dogfighter, but was superb at providing close support to ground troops. When production ended in September 1944 the P-40 had served almost everywhere and had been used for just about everything.

Early P-40s had a pair of 12.7-mm (.50 cal.) machine-guns on top of the fuselage, but these were often deleted in RAF aircraft.

RAF Desert Air Force P-40s all wore a two-tone brown camouflage scheme.

The only parts of the P-40 which were fabric-covered were the control surfaces. This was to save weight and to make flying easier.

## P-40N Warhawk

**Type:** single-seat interceptor and fighter-bomber

**Powerplant:** one 1015-kW (1,360-hp.) Allison V-1710-81 inline piston engine

**Maximum speed:** 609 km/h (378 m.p.h.) at 3210 m (10,530 ft.)

**Range:** 386 km (240 mi.)

**Service ceiling:** 11,630 m (38,160 ft.)

**Weights:** empty 2724 kg (6,045 lb.); loaded 4018 kg (8,858 lb.)

**Armament:** six 12.7-mm (.50 cal.) machine-guns in wing; provision for 227-kg (500-lb.) bomb or 197-litre drop-tank under fuselage

**Dimensions:**
| | | |
|---|---|---|
| span | 11.42 m | (37 ft. 6 in.) |
| length | 10.20 m | (33 ft. 6 in.) |
| height | 3.77 m | (12 ft. 4 in.) |
| wing area | 21.95 m² | (236 sq. ft.) |

## TOMAHAWK MK IIB

This Curtiss Tomahawk Mk IIB served with No. 112 Squadron RAF, based at Sidi Haneish, North Africa, in the autumn of 1941. The squadron later received Kittyhawks and took part in the Italian campaign.

The 'shark mouth' was one of the most characteristic of all Warhawk markings. No. 112 Squadron aircraft was the first to wear it.

The canopy was later improved to give better visibility. The front windscreen was bulletproof and the cockpit was armoured.

For an average performer, the P-40 had a good level of equipment fit, with effective cockpit heating, heat ducting to the guns, armour and self-sealing fuel tanks.

The Allison V-1710 engine was fitted with a supercharger. The cowling was later changed, with an enlarged air scoop.

Wing armament was four Browning 7.7-mm (.303 cal.) guns. This was later changed to six 12.7-mm (.50 cal.) machine-guns, with 235 rounds per gun.

The fuselage hardpoint could carry a single 227-kg (500-lb.) bomb or a 197-litre (43-gal.) fuel tank.

The fuselage was of modern construction, with all-alloy framework covered by an 'Alclad' skin. Additional fuel was contained in a fuselage tank.

The Kittyhawk Mk II (P-40F) had a lengthened fuselage. With the rudder hinge behind the elevator hinge, the pilot had increased manoeuvrability and better control.

## COMBAT DATA

### MAXIMUM SPEED

The original P-40 was as fast as its contemporaries, but it lacked the agility and acceleration of the Zero. It could dive very fast, however, and the American Volunteer Group in China used it to make quick slashing attacks on the Japanese, accelerating away to avoid a dogfight.

| | |
|---|---|
| **HURRICANE Mk II** | 540 km/h (336 m.p.h.) |
| **TOMAHAWK Mk IIB** | 555 km/h (345 m.p.h.) |
| **A6M5 ZERO** | 540 km/h (336 m.p.h.) |

### SERVICE CEILING

Allison-engined aircraft often had very good performance at low level, but unless boosted by a powerful supercharger they tended to be somewhat sluggish at high altitude. The early P-40s were no exception, and high-level performance was far from ideal.

HURRICANE Mk II 10,000 m (33,000 ft.)
A6M5 ZERO 11,000 m (36,000 ft.)
TOMAHAWK Mk IIB 9200 m (30,200 ft.)

### ARMAMENT

Originally fitted with 12.7-mm (.50 cal.) machine-guns, the Tomahawks in British service usually carried 7.7-mm (.303 cal.) Brownings like other RAF fighters to ease logistic problems. Later aircraft switched back to 12.7-mm weapons, and although the aircraft could carry cannon these were never fitted.

TOMAHAWK Mk IIB 6 x 7.7-mm (.303 cal.) machine-guns
A6M5 ZERO 2 x 20-mm (0.79-in.) cannon 2 x 7.7-mm (.303 cal.) machine-guns
HURRICANE Mk II 8 x 7.7-mm (.303 cal.) machine-guns

# Warhawk development

■ **CURTISS P-36 HAWK:** First flown in 1935, the radial-engined Hawk was an intermediate step between the great Hawk biplanes and the P-40.

■ **P-40B:** Fitting an Allison inline engine to the P-36 produced a better fighter, which was used by the Flying Tigers in China.

■ **TOMAHAWK:** Early P-40s were known as Tomahawks in RAF service, and flew with distinction in the desert campaigns of 1941 and 1942.

■ **KITTYHAWK:** Later P-40s with bigger engines were known as Kittyhawks. This example is a P-40F with a Rolls-Royce Merlin engine.

■ **WARHAWK:** The final P-40s were known as Warhawks, a name which the US Air Force applied to the whole Hawk series. This is a P-40N of 1943.

# CURTISS

# SBC HELLDIVER

● Dive bomber ● Combat trainer ● Complex development

▲ Although the SBC was a strong aircraft with very good handling characteristics, it was totally outclassed by new monoplanes by the time World War II started in Europe.

As the second of three aircraft named Helldiver by the Curtiss company, the SBC was probably the least successful. Originally a parasol-winged fighter, the SBC went through major changes in design and role before becoming a carrier-based scout-bomber. The outbreak of World War II saw the Helldiver exported to France and Great Britain, but its only combat service was with the US Navy aboard the aircraft carrier USS *Hornet*.

## CURTISS SBC HELLDIVER

### Staggered wings ▶
After the failure of the initial parasol design, it was realised that a much stronger wing unit was needed to withstand the stresses of dive-bombing. The solution was a strong biplane arrangement with the upper wing further forward than the lower wing and a single sturdy interplane strut.

### ▼ Improved version
The last SBC-3 on the production line became the XSBC-4, with a more powerful Wright R-1820 engine and the ability to carry a 454-kg (1,000-lb.) bomb.

### ▲ Capable trainer
Although intended as a front-line aircraft, the SBC made a vital contribution to the US war effort as a combat trainer.

### ▼ French deliveries
In 1940 the US diverted 50 SBC-4s to beleaguered France although they arrived too late to be used in combat. This example is seen at the factory prior to delivery.

### Diverted to Britain ▶
After the fall of France in 1940, five SBC-4s were acquired by the RAF as instructional airframes and were named Clevelands.

## FACTS AND FIGURES

➤ The prototype XSBC-1 crashed in September 1934 when the wing folding mechanism failed in flight.

➤ British Clevelands differed from standard SBC-4s in having self-sealing fuel tanks.

➤ The SBC-4 was the last biplane combat aircraft ever ordered by the USA.

➤ In 1940, SBC-4s aboard a French aircraft carrier were diverted to Martinique where they were eventually scrapped.

➤ The SBC was the second of three Curtiss bomber types named Helldiver.

➤ US Marine Corps SBC-4s remained in service until June 1943.

## PROFILE

# Last American combat biplane

In 1932 the US Navy ordered a new two-seat fighter prototype from Curtiss. Designated XF12C-1 and fitted with a parasol wing, the aircraft proved to be unsuitable in this role. However, it was decided to use the design as a scout aircraft and the XSBC-1 prototype was constructed. More problems followed as the aircraft suffered a structural wing failure during tests, and the parasol wing layout was abandoned.

The resulting XSBC-2 biplane was a far better aircraft and went into production for the US Navy with an uprated Pratt & Whitney Twin Wasp Junior engine as the SBC-3 Helldiver.

Entering service in 1936, 83 SBC-3s were delivered before production switched to the SBC-4 fitted with a more powerful engine. The US Navy ordered 174 of this new model, but 50 were diverted to France as the situation in Europe worsened.

The type saw brief wartime service with the US Navy and Marines before being withdrawn to second-line duties.

*Below: During the early years of World War II many SBC-4s served with US Naval Reserve Units. This example was based in Chicago.*

*Above: SBC-4s of VS-8 and VB-8 from USS Hornet are seen engaged in manoeuvres days before the Japanese attack at Pearl Harbor.*

### SBC-4 Helldiver

**Type:** two-seat carrier-based scout-bomber

**Powerplant:** one 708-kW (950-hp.) Wright R-1820-34 Cyclone 9 radial piston engine

**Maximum speed:** 381 km/h (236 m.p.h.) at 4635 m (15,000 ft.)

**Initial climb rate:** 497 m/min (1,630 f.p.m.)

**Range:** 950 km (590 mi.) with 227-kg (500-lb.) bombload

**Service ceiling:** 8320 m (27,900 ft.)

**Weights:** empty 2196 kg (4,831 lb.); maximum take-off 3462 kg (7,616 lb.)

**Armament:** two 7.62-mm (.30 cal.) machine-guns plus up to 454 kg (1,000 lb.) of bombs

**Dimensions:**
| | |
|---|---|
| span | 10.36 m (34 ft.) |
| length | 8.64 m (28 ft. 4 in.) |
| height | 3.84 m (12 ft. 7 in.) |
| wing area | 29.45 m² (317 sq. ft.) |

## SBC-3 HELLDIVER

The brightly painted red tail is the marking carried by aircraft from USS *Yorktown* in 1937. The black 'Man O'War Bird' emblem denotes that this aircraft is from VS-5.

After the failure of the parasol wing design a biplane unit was introduced. The wings were of metal frame covered with metal skin on the upper wing and fabric on the lower wing.

A forward-firing 7.62-mm machine-gun was aimed by the pilot using a sight attached to the windshield. A second 7.62-mm (.30 cal.) machine-gun could be fitted on a flexible mounting in the rear cockpit.

A large 'greenhouse'-type cockpit covered both crew members. It was situated behind the top wing and so gave the pilot poor vision above and forward.

The SBC-3 was fitted with a 615-kW (825-hp.) Pratt & Whitney R-1535-82 Twin Wasp Junior piston engine.

The landing gear retracted into the all-metal monocoque fuselage in a similar fashion to the Grumman F2F and F3F. An arrester hook was fitted for aircraft carrier operations.

### COMBAT DATA

#### MAXIMUM SPEED

Although the Skua was a more modern monoplane design, it was slower than the biplane SBC-4. A lack of speed with all early war scout bombers resulted in heavy losses to enemy fighters.

| | |
|---|---|
| SBC-4 HELLDIVER | 381 km/h (236 m.p.h.) |
| SKUA Mk II | 362 km/h (224 m.p.h.) |
| SB2U-3 VINDICATOR | 391 km/h (242 m.p.h.) |

#### BOMBLOAD

Although the SB2U-3 Vindicator was a significantly more powerful aircraft, it could only match the earlier SBC-4 in bomb-carrying capacity. The Skua was less capable than either American design.

| | |
|---|---|
| SBC-4 HELLDIVER | 454-kg (1,000-lb.) bombload |
| SKUA Mk II | 227-kg (500-lb.) bombload |
| SB2U-3 VINDICATOR | 454-kg (1,000-lb.) bombload |

#### RANGE

With the large areas covered by a carrier group, long range is essential for naval aircraft. Again the Vindicator was far superior, allowing it to strike at targets beyond the range of most carrier-based bombers. The Skua had the shortest range but generally operated in the smaller North and Mediterranean Seas.

SBC-4 HELLDIVER 950 km (590 mi.)
SKUA Mk II 760 km (471 mi.)
SB2U-3 VINDICATOR 1802 km (1,117 mi.)

## US Navy carrier aircraft of 1939

**■ DOUGLAS TBD DEVASTATOR:** Entering service in 1937, the TBD remained the US Navy's primary torpedo aircraft until 1942.

**■ GRUMMAN F3F:** Following on from the successful FF and F2F biplane fighters, the F3F served with both the US Navy and US Marines.

**■ GRUMMAN JF/J2F DUCK:** Being of amphibious design, the Duck was very versatile and was used in patrol, survey and rescue roles.

**■ VOUGHT SB2U VINDICATOR:** Operated as a scout and a bomber, the SB2U served with front-line units for six years from 1936.

# CURTISS

# SB2C HELLDIVER

● Dive-bomber ● Carrier strike ● US Navy

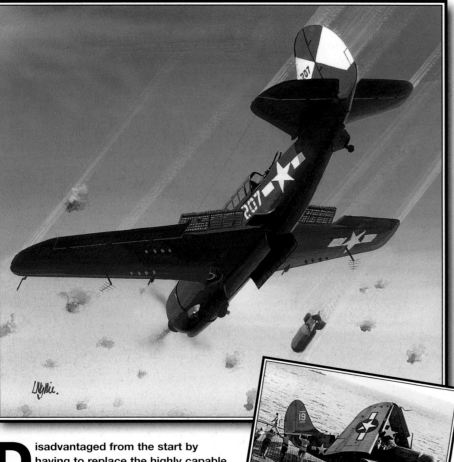

**D**isadvantaged from the start by having to replace the highly capable SBD Dauntless, the Helldiver never quite won a similar place in the hearts of US naval aviators. It took time to prove itself in action and eventually became an effective carrier-launched dive- and torpedo-bomber in the war against the Japanese. But the SB2C did not win the reliability battle soon enough for some commanders and picked up the derogatory nickname 'Beast'.

▲ The Helldiver was a hard-hitting aircraft which gained many combat successes, but pilots hated it. The designation SB2C was said to stand for 'son of a bitch, second class' by aircrews.

### ▼ Hook down to land
Ready to land, this SB2C pilot has lowered the tail hook of his aircraft. When landing, Helldivers often revealed their poor handling to careless pilots.

### ▲ Weapons away
Helldivers were built to carry a large 907-kg (2,000-lb.) bomb internally, or two 725-kg (1,600-lb.) bombs.

### Rear gunner ▶
In combat, the Helldiver's rear gunner slid back the hood to fire a pair of 7.62-mm (.30 cal.) Browning machine-guns.

### ▼ Big bird
Even with its wings folded, the Helldiver was a big aircraft. This was due to the requirement for an internal bomb-bay.

### ▲ Fleet strike force
By 1944 hundreds of SB2Cs were in service with the carrier battle groups of the US Pacific Fleet.

## FACTS AND FIGURES

➤ From an order for 450 Helldivers for the Royal Navy, only 26 reached Britain. None of them were used operationally.

➤ In total, 5516 Helldivers were delivered to the US Navy during World War II.

➤ One of the prototype SB2Cs fell to pieces in a dive-bombing trial.

➤ The Helldiver specification was influenced by the Luftwaffe's success with the Ju 87 Stuka dive-bomber.

➤ SB2Cs first went to war with carrier squadron VB-17 on USS Bunker Hill.

➤ The USAAF used the SB2C as a trainer and target-towing aircraft.

**PROFILE**

# Dive-bomber from hell

Taking its name from an earlier Curtiss type, the Helldiver was a powerful, modern dive-bomber designed to undertake a variety of combat missions. It was also tentatively required by the US Marines and the Army Air Forces which compromised the SB2C, giving the manufacturers the demanding task of creating a 'multi-role' aircraft in the middle of a war. There was no time to perfect the requirement and when the Army did not order the aircraft in quantity, it was left to the Navy

to sort out the teething troubles. A long list of 'fixes' was required, which delayed the Helldiver's deployment for some months.

But the job was done, and from November 1943 when Helldivers pounded the Japanese island garrison of Rabaul until the end of the war the Navy used the Helldiver in every major surface action as an integral part of its carrier air groups. Cannon armament, a relative rarity on World War II American aircraft, was fitted to the SB2C-1C, the

*Below: The Royal Navy tested the Helldiver, but rejected it immediately because of its appalling handling, which was said to be even worse than the Fleet Air Arm's Barracuda.*

*Above: The SB2C was not a good marketing tool for Curtiss. The company boss, Guy Vaughan, called it 'one of the biggest crosses we had to bear'.*

last suffix indicating the heavier, more powerful guns. One of the most effective models was the SB2C-4 which introduced the distinctive 'cheese grater' split flaps to aid stability during a dive.

### SB2C Helldiver

**Type:** three-seat dive-/torpedo-bomber

**Powerplant:** one 1268-kW (1,900-hp.) Wright R-2600-8 Cyclone air-cooled engine

**Maximum speed:** 452 km/h (294 m.p.h.)

**Range:** 1786 km (1,200 mi.)

**Service ceiling:** 7530 m (29,100 ft.)

**Weights:** empty 4990 kg (10,978 lb.); loaded 7550 kg (16,610 lb.)

**Armament:** two 20-mm (0.79-in.) cannon or four 12.7-mm (.50 cal.) machine-guns in wings and two 7.62-mm (.30 cal.) machine-guns in rear cockpit; up to 907 kg (2,000 lb.) of bombs in internal bay

**Dimensions:** span 15.20 m (49 ft. 6 in.)
length 11.20 m (36 ft. 8 in.)
height 5.10 m (13 ft. 2 in.)
wing area 39.20 m² (422 sq. ft.)

## SB2C HELLDIVER

In June 1944, the US Navy changed the colour scheme of all its aircraft to overall gloss dark blue. The Helldiver served from 1943 to 1949 with the USN.

Tail buffeting was a constant problem, and despite a redesign it never entirely disappeared.

The gunner was protected by a large sheet of armour. Between him and the pilot was the radio bay, the life raft, the autopilot controls and a large fuel tank.

One early source of trouble was the Wright Cyclone engine and its Curtiss Electric four-bladed propeller. Many of the propellers, like this one, had the spinner removed in service. The carburettor intake was in the top of the cowling.

Engine oil and hydraulic fluid tanks were fitted behind the engine, with an oil cooler at the bottom of the engine bay.

Upper surface divebrakes were fitted to the wing, and the the trailing-edge flaps were split. The leading-edge slat opened simultaneously with undercarriage operation.

Unlike earlier dive-bombers, the SB2C had a large internal bomb-bay with displacement gear for the bombs and hydraulic doors over the bay. The wingroot contained additional fuel tanks.

The arrester hook was connected to a large hydraulic damper to reduce the impact of catching the deck wire.

### The Battle of Leyte Gulf

**3 DECOY FORCE:** A third decoy force was sent in from the north to distract the Americans. Task Force 38 eventually gave chase. The decoy was not noticed for some time.

**PHILIPPINE ISLANDS**

Japanese aircraft sink US carrier *Princeton*

Force 'A'

SB2Cs attacked from here

**2 AMERICAN AIR RAIDS:** Japanese efforts to thwart American landings failed after SB2Cs attacked and sank a battleship and damaged a cruiser.

Japanese Naval Forces

US Pacific Fleet

Force 'C'

**1 JAPANESE STRIKE FORCES:** The Japanese Plan Sho-1 operation was intended to stop American landings at Leyte. The First Striking Force ('A' and 'C') sailed from Brunei; a second fleet came from the north.

BRUNEI

## ACTION DATA

**RANGE**

An important feature of a carrier-based aircraft was its range performance due to the fact that it operated over water. The D4Y3 traded range for a higher top speed, while the Barracuda had a superior range but a comparatively low top speed.

SB2C HELLDIVER 1786 km (1,107 mi.)

D4Y3 'JUDY' 1520 km (942 mi.)

BARRACUDA Mk II 1850 km (1,147 mi.)

**MAXIMUM SPEED**

Dive-bombers were vulnerable to attack from enemy fighters due to their low speeds. The D4Y3 had fairly good speed and was a streamlined design compared to the SB2C, with its bulbous radial engine.

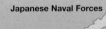

SB2C HELLDIVER 452 km/h (280 m.p.h.)

D4Y3 'JUDY' 575 km/h (357 m.p.h.)

BARRACUDA Mk II 367 km/h (228 m.p.h.)

# CURTISS
# SOC SEAGULL

● Scout aircraft ● Operated from battleships ● Seaplane

▲ One of the last biplanes to serve with the US Navy, the SOC Seagull flew extensively from battleships and cruisers during World War II. It actually outlasted its replacement.

The Curtiss SOC Seagull was the US Navy's top observation aircraft in the years just before World War II. The battleship was still thought to be the most important 'war wagon' on the high seas, and the Seagull was the 'eyes' of the fleet's battleships and cruisers. The pilot and observer aboard were expected to spot targets and direct the big guns of the huge ships. Obsolete by the time war arrived, the SOC was still in service in 1945.

## CURTISS SOC SEAGULL

◄ On dry land
When operating from shore bases, Seagulls were fitted with a wheeled undercarriage.

▼ Boss bird
Painted overall dark blue, this aircraft was assigned to the Commander of the Fleet.

◄ Use over North Africa
Although famous for their involvement in the Pacific war, these aircraft also gave valiant service in other theatres, flying in support of the Allied landings in North Africa in 1942 during Operation Torch, for example.

▲ Recovery
Seaplanes landed alongside their parent ships and were hoisted aboard by cranes.

Start of a patrol ►
Catapulted from a US Navy cruiser, an SOC sets out on a mission during the Pacific war.

## FACTS AND FIGURES

➤ In original configuration, the prototype SOC was an amphibian that had wheels incorporated into the floats.

➤ The 64 aircraft built by the Naval Aircraft Factory were designated SON-1.

➤ Production of the SOC Seagull began in 1935 and ended in 1938.

➤ A proposed successor, the SO3C Seamew, was unsatisfactory and was replaced in service by Seagulls!

➤ SOCs featured prominently in most of the major battles of the Pacific war.

➤ When the SOCs were finally withdrawn, the era of the combat seaplane ended.

# PROFILE

# Long-serving naval scout

*In the late 1930s, few aviation experts would have envisaged that this biplane scout would outlast several monoplanes in service.*

The last of the Curtiss biplanes to be used operationally by the US Navy, the SOC Seagull originated in 1933. It was out of date by the time America entered World War II in 1941, but remained on duty until the war was over.

The SOC Seagull had folding wings and tail structure made of fabric-covered light metal alloy, and a welded, steel-tube fuselage. The pilot and observer/gunner were accommodated in tandem cockpits, enclosed by a continuous transparent canopy with sliding panels for access.

Very much a product of 1930s' technology, the Seagull appeared outmoded by rapid changes occurring in aviation as the war loomed; nevertheless, it performed admirably during World War II and was well loved by those who flew it.

Production Seagull floatplanes began to reach the fleet in 1935. In due course, about three dozen naval scouting squadrons were equipped with the type. A decade later, in 1945, when American Marines were landing on Iwo Jima in one of the final actions of the war, SOCs were still in front-line service.

Being a biplane, the SOC was blessed with remarkable agility, and in wheeled configuration could out-turn many faster monoplanes. To facilitate stowage in tight spaces on board battleships or aircraft carriers, the wings could be folded back.

## SOC-3 SEAGULL

US aircraft operating in support of Operation Torch in North Africa had a distinctive yellow circle added outboard of their national insignia. This SOC-3 Seagull is quite unusual in that it carries no unit markings.

Powering the SOC-3 was a Pratt & Whitney R-1340 engine, which churned out 447 kW. It provided more than adequate performance for a seaplane, though the Seagull remained vulnerable to fighter attack.

In the SOC, the standard crew consisted of a pilot and observer. A 7.62-mm (.30 cal.) MG was fitted in each cockpit and provided some defence. For take-off and landing, the canopies were often left in the open position.

In seaplane configuration, the SOC-3 was fitted with a single large centreline float. When the parent ship was in port, the aircraft were assigned to land bases and the floats were exchanged for a spatted wheeled undercarriage.

Construction of this aeronautical anachronism consisted of a welded tubular steel fuselage with aluminum framed wings and tail surfaces, all covered in fabric.

A pair of small outrigger floats was fitted to the lower wings. Their purpose was only to provide stability for the aircraft while on the water.

## SOC-3 Seagull

**Type:** two-seat scout/observation aircraft

**Powerplant:** one 447-kW (600-hp.) Pratt & Whitney R-1340-18 Wasp radial engine

**Maximum speed:** 266 km/h (165 m.p.h.)

**Cruising speed:** 214 km/h (133 m.p.h.)

**Initial climb rate:** 321 m/min (1,050 f.p.m.)

**Range:** 1086 km (673 mi.)

**Service ceiling:** 4540 m (14,900 ft.)

**Weights:** empty 1648 kg (3,626 lb.); loaded 2492 kg (5,482 lb.)

**Armament:** two 7.62-mm (.30 cal.) machine-guns, plus external racks for two 147-kg (325-lb.) bombs

**Dimensions:**

| | |
|---|---|
| span | 10.97 m (36 ft.) |
| length | 9.47 m (31 ft. 1 in.) |
| height | 4.44 m (14 ft. 7 in.) |
| wing area | 31.77 m² (328 sq. ft.) |

## COMBAT DATA

### MAXIMUM SPEED

Dismissed as an anachronism at the start of the war, the SOC was slower than the two main rival enemy types, although, as a biplane, it had much greater agility and was a more flexible aircraft. The 'Jake' was its primary opponent in the Pacific war.

| | |
|---|---|
| **SOC-1 SEAGULL** | 266 km/h (165 m.p.h.) |
| **ARADO AR 196** | 310 km/h (192 m.p.h.) |
| **AICHI E13A 'JAKE'** | 375 km/h (233 m.p.h.) |

### RANGE

An important criterion for naval seaplanes was an ability to range far from the parent ship to observe enemy activity. In the Pacific, the Seagull could roam extensively. The Japanese E13A could range even further and was one of the best scouts of World War II.

SOC-1 SEAGULL 1086 km (673 mi.)

ARADO AR 196 1070 km (663 mi.)

AICHI E13A 'JAKE' 2090 km (1,296 mi.)

### BOMBLOAD

Scout aircraft were sometimes called upon to drop bombs, and here the Seagull received top marks, being able to carry a greater load than either of its main rivals. Bombs were mainly used to attack smaller warships, while leaving more specialised aircraft to attack larger capital ships.

SOC-1 SEAGULL 295 kg (650 lb.)

ARADO AR 196 100 kg (220 lb.)

AICHI E13A 'JAKE' 250 kg (550 lb.)

## Curtiss naval aircraft in World War II

■ **SBC HELLDIVER:** This early dive-bomber was obsolete at the start of the war, though some remained in service until late 1942.

■ **SB2C HELLDIVER:** Also named Helldiver, this monoplane dive-bomber replaced the Douglas Dauntless from 1943 onwards.

■ **SC SEAHAWK:** Designed in 1942, the Seahawk was really too late to see service; only 66 examples were delivered before VJ-Day.

■ **SO3C SEAMEW:** Intended as a successor to the SOC, these aircraft proved unsuccessful and had short careers in the Navy.

# DE HAVILLAND

# DH.98 MOSQUITO

● Unarmed high-speed bomber ● Versatile 'Wooden Wonder'

W e think of Mosquitoes fighting the Luftwaffe or pressing relentlessly to bomb their targets, but it was probably the most useful Allied aircraft of World War II. Fighter, bomber, night-fighter, attack aircraft, torpedo-bomber, transport – these are just a few of the roles that de Havilland's design performed with miraculous success. The Mosquito was all the more impressive as it was mostly made of wood. The RAF virtually ignored the aircraft at first, but it became one of its most valuable planes.

▲ The key to the Mosquito's success was its light wooden construction and the power of its twin Merlin engines, which gave it the speed to outfly almost every other bomber and fighter of the war.

---

## DE HAVILLAND DH.98 MOSQUITO

▼ Reconnaissance Mosquito
This brightly-painted PR.Mk 16 was an unarmed photographic aircraft. These Mosquitoes performed the hazardous task of gathering intelligence from enemy territory, relying on speed for safety.

▲ Loading up
The usual load for a tactical strike was 113-kg (250 lb.) or 227-kg (500-lb.) bombs, but the Mosquitoes of Bomber Command later carried a modified 1814-kg (3,690-lb.) 'Cookie'.

◀ Bomber crews
The Mosquito B.Mk IV became a very important part of the bomber offensive, target-marking for the larger Lancaster and Halifax force.

▼ Desert mission
These FB.Mk VI bombers patrolled the Suez Canal while based in the Middle East. The hot, dry desert climate presented little problem, but the aircraft had structural weaknesses when based in the Far East, due to the humidity affecting the wood glue.

▲ Speedster
Mosquito bombers carried their bombs internally; nothing was allowed to break the aircraft's smooth aerodynamic lines. Later variants had a bulged bay for larger weapons.

### FACTS AND FIGURES

➤ The prototype 'plywood' Mosquito made its first flight on 25 November 1940.

➤ 7781 Mosquitoes in 43 versions were manufactured in England (6439), Canada (1134) and Australia (208).

➤ Mosquitoes were flown by air forces of 12 Allied nations during World War II.

➤ A Mosquito became the first twin-engined aircraft to land on a ship on 25 March 1944 aboard the carrier HMS Indefatigable.

➤ The last Mosquito built was a night-fighter, delivered on 28 November 1950.

➤ Mosquitoes were among the first aircraft to carry bombing radar.

# Mosquito – the wooden wonder

The Mosquito came from obscurity and rose to glory. Official interest was lukewarm when de Havilland made a private proposal for a fast, twin-engined, two-man bomber. But its performance was so outstanding that it went into production.

The Mosquito was fast and nimble, and performed well in an attack on Gestapo headquarters in Oslo which

was thwarted by dud bombs. High-speed, precision air strikes became the stock-in-trade for the Mosquito, which also adapted quickly to other roles and missions.

Almost four dozen versions of the Mosquito carried out every wartime duty, from whisking spies behind the lines to photo-mapping enemy territory. Precision-bombing of special targets persisted throughout the war – Amiens prison, Gestapo headquarters

in the Hague, V-1 'buzz bomb' launching sites. Each time, the Mosquito demonstrated its unique ability to strike fast, hit hard, and get away clean.

More than a dozen overseas air forces used Mosquitoes in the years after the war.

*The Mosquito could fly almost unchallenged over occupied Europe, day or night, and deliver devastating attacks from rooftop height. The bomber versions were as fast and agile as fighters, and could generally escape from an enemy attacker.*

## Mosquito B.Mk IV

**Type:** high-speed light bomber

**Powerplant:** two 918-kW (1,230-hp.) Rolls-Royce Merlin 21 inline piston engines

**Maximum speed:** 612 km/h (379 m.p.h.) at 6400 m (21,000 ft.)

**Range:** 3000 km (1,860 mi.)

**Service ceiling:** 10,500 m (34,450 ft.)

**Weights:** empty 6400 kg (14,080 lb.); loaded 10,200 kg (22,440 lb.)

**Armament:** maximum internal bombload four 227-kg (500-lb.) bombs;

**Dimensions:**
| | |
|---|---|
| span | 16.51 m (54 ft.) |
| length | 12.43 m (41 ft.) |
| height | 4.65 m (15 ft.) |
| wing area | 42.18 m² (454 sq. ft.) |

Like the fuselage, the wing was of wooden construction. The main parts were screwed, glued and pinned together, with a fabric covering. This had the unexpected advantage that enemy gunfire often passed through without doing much damage.

## MOSQUITO B.MK IV

No. 105 Squadron was the first unit to operate the Mosquito B.Mk IV. The squadron carried out many daytime attack missions, but later received 'Oboe' equipment and flew at night instead.

Although pilots liked the Mosquito, it was a very tricky machine to escape from. The pilot had a small door to get out of, and the navigator exited through a small hatch.

Mosquitoes had a huge number of different noses. The B.Mk IV had a glazed nose for a bomb-aimer to lie in.

The beautiful curved tail profile of the Mosquito was a classic de Havilland feature, present in pre-war aircraft like the DH.88 as well as the post-war Chipmunk trainer.

The outer fuselage consisted of two plywood skins separated by spruce blocks.

Weapons were carried internally in a small bomb-bay. Rockets could be carried externally beneath the wings.

The Mosquito's Merlin engines were constantly uprated to keep the aircraft out in front. The propellers both turned the same way, which gave the Mosquito a pronounced 'swing' on take-off that occasionally surprised unwary pilots.

The glazed nose was common to both bomber and reconnaissance versions of the Mosquito.

### COMBAT DATA

#### MAXIMUM SPEED

Several aircraft flying during World War II proved to be extremely versatile. The well-known Ju 88 was larger than the Mosquito, but was considerably slower and was much more vulnerable to enemy fighters. The less-well-known Soviet Pe-2 was more of a match for the Mosquito, and like the other two aircraft was also developed into a potent fighter and fighter-bomber.

| | |
|---|---|
| MOSQUITO B.Mk IV | 612 km/h (379 m.p.h.) |
| Ju 88A-4 | 435 km/h (270 m.p.h.) |
| Pe-2 | 580 km/h (359 m.p.h.) |

#### RANGE

The Mosquito's sleek aerodynamic shape translated into excellent range, even at the high speeds and altitudes adopted on many of its missions. It could fly much further than both of its contemporaries, and led to the type's employment as a long-range reconnaissance machine.

Pe-2 1150 km (713 mi.)

MOSQUITO B.Mk IV 3000 km (1,860 mi.)

Ju 88A-4 1800 km (1,115 mi.)

#### DEFENSIVE ARMAMENT

The Mosquito bomber's relative invulnerability to interception meant that it needed no defensive armament, nor extra crew to man the guns. Although the Russian Pe-2 was almost as fast, it carried machine-guns. The slower German Ju 88 was vulnerable to fighters and carried a heavy defensive armament.

| | |
|---|---|
| MOSQUITO B.Mk IV | no guns |
| Ju 88A-4 | up to 8 x 7.92-mm (0.31-in) MGs |
| Pe-2 | 4 x 7.62-mm (.30 cal.) MGs |

## Arming the Mosquito bomber

The Mosquito was designed primarily as a light bomber. Early variants did not have a heavy warload, but the aircraft's speed meant that it could attack targets that would have been suicide for heavier, more conventional aircraft. It also proved to be extremely good at pinpoint low-level attacks, where accuracy of delivery was more important than sheer tonnage of high explosive dropped.

**EARLY WARLOAD:** For pinpoint raids the Mosquito was generally armed with four 227-kg (500-lb.) high-explosive bombs.

**BULGED BOMB-BAY:** The bulged bomb-bays of later bomber variants of the Mosquito meant that they could carry the brutally simple 1814-kg (4,000-lb.) demolition bomb.

**FIGHTER-BOMBER:** Although fitted with a heavy gun armament, many fighter Mosquitoes were still capable of carrying bombs. A typical warload was two 227-kg (500-lb.) and two 112-kg (240-lb.) weapons.

# DEWOITINE

# D.520

● Interceptor ● Fought in Tunisia ● Flown by ace pilot Pierre Le Gloan

▲ **Many D.520s**
were taken by the Germans with the fall of France in 1940, and were used as fighter trainers. Others flew on with Vichy forces, fighting against the RAF.

**D**ewoitine's D.520 was an inspired design, into which its builders hoped to install an engine of around 1000 kW (1,500 hp.). Although there was no suitable powerplant available, this elegant fighter performed well, and was one of the few modern craft available when France was invaded in 1940. Even with inadequate power, pilots took great delight in its agility and fine handling qualities. The D.520's short career ended after the liberation campaign in 1944.

## DEWOITINE D.520

▲ **First test**
This D.520 was restored to working order and taken over by the Musée de l'Air in Paris. The cowling panels were removed to allow access to the engine.

▲ **Squadron memorial**
After the war around 30 D.520s survived to form an instructor's squadron, No. 704. This was finally disbanded in 1947.

**Moroccan warrior** ▶
This D.520 was flown by Sergeant Hardouin at Casablanca, Morocco. The mask badge on the tail was the unit emblem of 5ᵉ Group III/6.

▼ **Last in action**
This D.520 was one of the last surviving examples seized by the Germans. It was restored to action and then used by GCB 1/18 in April 1945.

▲ **Light fighter**
With its mixed cannon and machine-gun armament, small size and fine agility, the D.520's design philosophy was similar to that of Russian fighters, and proved a match for the Bf 109E.

## FACTS AND FIGURES

➤ The open cockpit prototype of the Dewoitine D.520 took to the air for the first time on 2 October 1938.

➤ World War II users of the D.520 included France, Bulgaria, Italy and Romania.

➤ French ace Pierre Le Gloan gained 18 of his 22 kills while flying the D.520.

➤ Famed test pilot Marcel Doret forgot to lower the undercarriage and wrecked the D.520 prototype in 1938.

➤ In 1940, French industry produced 300 D.520 fighters in a single month.

➤ French fighter groups flying the D.520 were credited with 147 aerial victories.

## PROFILE

# Dogfighting for France

Dewoitine had considerable experience with advanced stressed-skin monoplane construction in the 1930s. The Dewoitine D.520 which appeared on the eve of World War II was a rakish, low-wing monoplane, resembling its predecessor, the D.513. Forward of the cockpit, however, was a wing with a new shape and a cleaner-looking engine installation.

By May 1939, the French air arm had ordered 200 D.520s. Later, the purchase was increased to 710 and again (under Vichy rule) to 740.

With major improvements, the production D.520 of 1939 became the most capable fighter of French design used in the early days of the war. French pilots fought valiantly and the D.520 acquitted itself well against the Luftwaffe. In 1942, the Luftwaffe seized 411 D.520s and passed many to allied countries. After serving with the Vichy air arm (in some cases in locations as distant as Syria), these attractive fighters were

again in the hands of free French pilots in late 1944 when they flew their final combat sorties against the last German pockets in southern France.

*Flying examples of the D.520 are very rare, as few were made and even fewer survived the war. Many were used as fighter trainers by the Luftwaffe in 1944.*

The wing armament consisted of two 7.5-mm (0.3-in.) machine-guns, with 675 rounds of ammunition for each. The middle section of the wing also contained a small fuel tank.

A small baggage compartment was located aft of the cockpit, with an access door on the port side.

### D.520

**Type:** single-seat fighter

**Powerplant:** one 697-kW (935-hp.) Hispano-Suiza 12Y 45 inline piston engine with Szydlowski supercharger

**Maximum speed:** 535 km/h (332 m.p.h.)

**Initial climb rate:** to 4000 m (13,120 ft.) in 5 minutes 48 seconds

**Range:** 890 km (950 mi.)

**Service ceiling:** 10,500 m (39,440 ft.)

**Weights:** empty 2036 kg (4,479 lb.); maximum take-off 2677 kg (5,889 lb.)

**Armament:** one 20-mm (0.79-in.) HS 404 rapid-fire cannon and four wing-mounted 7.5-mm (0.3-in.) MAC 34 M39 machine-guns

**Dimensions:** span 10.20 m (34 ft.)
length 8.60 m (28 ft.)
height 2.57 m (8 ft.)
wing area 15.97 m² (172 sq. ft.)

### D.520

**Displaying the red and orange 'Vichy stripes' adopted at Gabes, Tunisia, by D.520 Escadrilles, this aircraft fought against the Allied invasion of North Africa.**

The D.520's engine was reliable if slightly underpowered. The rival French M.S.406 was powered by a similar engine.

The Hispano-Suiza cannon fired through the airscrew, with the engine acting as a recoil buffer. This powerful weapon was superior to the Bf 109's MG FF.

The main undercarriage retracted inwards, with the wheels fitting into wells in the fuselage.

The forward fuselage contained the main fuel tank, which gave the D.520 its long nose shape. The 60-round cannon magazine was located between the tank and the engine in the upper nose section.

The cockpit was a long way aft of the long engine cowling, making landing and taxiing a tricky business for the inexperienced pilot.

The black panther badge belonged to 40 Escadrille, Group de Chasse II/7.

### COMBAT DATA

**ARMAMENT**

Experiments in 1938 showed that two cannon were better than eight machine-guns. The cannon in the Bf 109 was a modified anti-aircraft gun, and it suffered poor muzzle velocity and had a low rate of fire. The Hispano-Suiza cannon was a much better weapon and was well respected.

D.520 1 x 20-mm (0.79-in.) cannon 4 x 7.5-mm (0.3-in.) MGs
HURRICANE Mk I 8 x 7.7-mm (.303 cal.) MGs
Bf 109E 2 x 20-mm (0.79-in.) cannon 2 x 7.9-mm (0.31-in.) MGs

**MAXIMUM SPEED**

The sleek Bf 109 with its powerful fuel-injected DB 601 engine could outrun a Hurricane or D.520 with ease, especially in a dive. The Dewoitine was slightly underpowered in comparison. Although the Hurricane had a superb engine, the powerful Rolls-Royce Merlin, it was a larger and less streamlined machine than its rivals.

HURRICANE Mk I 550 km/h (342 m.p.h.)
Bf 109E 575 km/h (357 m.p.h.)
D.520 534 km/h (332 m.p.h.)

**RANGE**

Another advantage of the Bf 109's fuel-injected engine was increased efficiency, especially at altitude, giving greater range. Luckily for the British and French air forces in 1940, they were generally on the defensive, and were often taking on Bf 109 pilots who were flying at the limit of their range.

HURRICANE Mk I 740 km (477 mi.)
Bf 109E 1000 km (620 mi.)
D.520 890 km (552 mi.)

# Fighters of the 1940 campaign

■ **HAWKER HURRICANE:** Despite lacking cannon armament, the Hurricane was manoeuvrable and rugged, and was the RAF's most numerous fighter during the battles in France in 1940.

■ **MESSERSCHMITT Bf 109E:** Arguably the best fighter in the world in 1940, the Bf 109E was popular with German pilots, some of whom retained the 'Emil' even after the Bf 109F appeared.

■ **MORANE-SAULNIER M.S.406:** The main fighter of the French air force in 1940, the M.S.406 was an inferior design to the D.520 and Bf 109, but played an important part in resisting the Luftwaffe.

# DORNIER

# Do 18

● Wal successor ● Maritime patrol flying-boat ● Search and rescue

▲ For its transatlantic mail-carrying role, the Do 18 carried two pilots, a radio operator and a flight engineer. Four fuel tanks holding 3920 litres (862 gal.) and a mail compartment were amidships.

**W**ith its origins in the Wal series of flying-boats which Dornier had been developing since 1922 and which had culminated in the military Do 15, the Do 18 was developed to provide both a replacement for the Do 15 and a transatlantic mail carrier for the German airline Lufthansa. Using the new, fuel-efficient Junkers Jumo 205 diesel engine, the Do 18 proved to have outstanding range, but its main military use was for air-sea rescue.

## DORNIER Do 18

▼ **Junkers-type flaps**
The large 'double-wing' flaps, of Junkers design, can clearly be seen here.

**▲ Over the Baltic**
D-ABYM was the V3 third prototype of the Do 18. Redesignated Do 18E, it flew a 30-hour 21-minute test flight over the Baltic before been delivered to Lufthansa.

**▲ Launching trolley**
After being removed from the water, the Do 18 was craned onto a launching trolley and pushed down a slipway for relaunch.

**▲ Catapult launch**
Lufthansa extensively used seaplane tenders, equipped with Heinkel catapults, before World War II.

**Military developments ▶**
Here, the first prototype (V4) of the military Do 18D is seen operating from rough seas. The lower fuselage sponsons aided stability.

## FACTS AND FIGURES

➤ Unarmed rescue Do 18N-1s in Red Cross markings were allegedly used by the Luftwaffe for clandestine operations.

➤ Just over 100 Do 18s, including 70 Do 18Gs, were built, the last in 1939.

➤ In transatlantic service Do 18Es made a number of record-breaking flights.

➤ The first German aircraft shot down by the British in World War II was a Do 18 attacked by an Royal Navy Skua.

➤ The Do 18's compartmentalised Stümmel sponsons were a Dornier trademark.

➤ In the training role the Do 18H-1 was fitted with dual controls.

## PROFILE

# Early wartime search and rescue

First flown in March 1935 with two Jumo 5 diesel engines, the Do 18 was one of the most refined flying boats of its era. Its wide hull and sponsons made it extremely stable on the water, while internal watertight compartments meant that it was difficult to sink.

As well as operating its four Do 18Es on the southern Atlantic mail route, Lufthansa used the single Do 18F to set a new distance record for seaplanes in March 1938. The aircraft flew 8390 km (5,213 mi.) after being catapult-launched from the tender Westfalen.

The Luftwaffe's Do 18D entered service in 1936 and served with maritime reconnaissance units during the Polish and Norwegian campaigns before being used as an air-sea rescue aircraft during the Battle of Britain in 1940. With just two 7.9-mm (0.31-in.) machine-guns, however, it proved to be too poorly armed for military service. New engines and heavier armament were installed to produce the Do 18G. The Do 18H was a training version.

During 1941 many Do 18Gs were converted to Do 18Ns for the air-sea rescue role. This was the Do 18's main task for the remainder of its career.

*Above: Although this aircraft carries a civilian registration, it is actually the pre-production Do 18D-01. The position of the bow 7.9-mm (0.31-in.) machine-gun is clearly visible.*

*Left: As a maritime patrol aircraft the Do 18 was very vulnerable to enemy fighters and its front-line career came to an end in August 1941.*

### Do 18G-1

**Type:** four-seat maritime patrol and reconnaissance flying-boat

**Powerplant:** two 656-kW (880-hp.) Junkers Jumo 205D six-cylinder in-line diesel engines

**Maximum speed:** 267 km/h (166 m.p.h.) at 2000 m (6,562 ft.)

**Climb rate:** 1000 m (3,280 f.p.m.) in 7 min 48 sec

**Range:** 3500 km (2,175 mi.)

**Service ceiling:** 4200 m (13,780 ft.)

**Weights:** empty 5980 kg (13,184 lb.); maximum take-off 10,795 kg (23,800 lb.)

**Armament:** one 13-mm (0.51-in.) machine-gun, one 20-mm (0.79-in.) cannon and two 50-kg (110-lb.) bombs

**Dimensions:**
| | |
|---|---|
| span | 23.70 m (77 ft. 9 in.) |
| length | 19.38 m (63 ft. 7 in.) |
| height | 5.32 m (17 ft. 5 in.) |
| wing area | 98 m² (1.055 sq. ft.) |

---

### Do 18G-1

**This aircraft flew in the search and rescue role during 1941/42, after the type had been retired from combat duties. It was on the strength of 6. Seenotstaffel, based in the central Mediterranean area.**

Placing the engines in this fore and aft arrangement, back to back on the centreline of the wing, allowed both propellers to be kept clear of the water.

The Junkers Jumo 205D six-cylinder in-line engines of the Do 18G ran on diesel.

A large rudder allowed the pilot to keep the aircraft steady, especially when operating on rough seas.

The Do 18G was introduced as a stop-gap between the obsolescent Do 18D and the delayed BV 138. Improvements included a 13-mm (0.51-in.) MG 131 machine-gun in the open bow position.

A turret containing a single 20-mm (0.79-in.) MG 151/20 cannon replaced the open position and single MG 15 of the Do 18D.

For operations over water, accurate navigation is vital. This loop aerial served the radio direction-finding equipment.

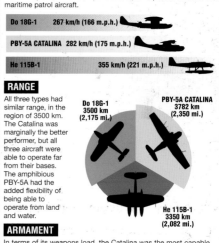

Large sponsons, known as Stümmel, were mounted on the fuselage sides and were typical of Dornier flying-boats.

Dornier retained its traditional two-step hull for the Do 18.

For additional directional control while taxiing, a water rudder was added at the rear of the second hull step.

Long struts braced the high-set tailplane. To avoid salt spray the entire tail section was mounted in an elevated position on the extreme rear fuselage.

---

## COMBAT DATA

### MAXIMUM SPEED

The Do 18 had a top speed which was comparable to that of the Allies' Catalina, but almost 100 km/h less than that of the Heinkel He 115. Speed, however, was not the most important attribute of a maritime patrol aircraft.

| | |
|---|---|
| **Do 18G-1** | 267 km/h (166 m.p.h.) |
| **PBY-5A CATALINA** | 282 km/h (175 m.p.h.) |
| **He 115B-1** | 355 km/h (221 m.p.h.) |

### RANGE

All three types had similar range, in the region of 3500 km. The Catalina was marginally the better performer, but all three aircraft were able to operate far from their bases. The amphibious PBY-5A had the added flexibility of being able to operate from land and water.

Do 18G-1 3500 km (2,175 mi.)

PBY-5A CATALINA 3782 km (2,350 mi.)

He 115B-1 3350 km (2,082 mi.)

### ARMAMENT

In terms of its weapons load, the Catalina was the most capable patrol flying-boat of World War II. In its PBY-5A version it carried four defensive guns and could lift more than 1.5 tons of bombs and/or depth charges. The He 115 was also a well-armed aircraft.

| Do 18G-1 | PBY-5A CATALINA | He 115B-1 |
|---|---|---|
| 1 x 13-mm machine-gun 1 x 20-mm (0.79-in.) cannon 100-kg (220-lb.) bombload | 1 x 12.7-mm machine-gun 3 x 7.62-mm machine-guns 1816-kg (4,004-lb.) bombload | 1 x 12.7-mm (.50 cal.) machine-gun 3 x 7.62-mm (.30 cal.) machine-gun 1250-kg (2,756-lb.) bombload |

---

## World War II search and rescue

■ **DORNIER Do 24:** Having been designed to satisfy a pre-war Dutch civilian requirement, the exceptional Do 24 went on to replace the Do 18 in the search and rescue (SAR) role.

■ **GRUMMAN JF DUCK:** Operating mainly around the US coast, the Duck served as a utility and SAR amphibian with the US Navy and Coast Guard.

■ **SUPERMARINE WALRUS:** Despite its antiquated appearance, the Walrus was one of the UK's primary SAR aircraft and flew with distinction during the Battle of Britain.

# DORNIER
# Do 24

● Search and rescue ● Transport missions ● Mine-sweeping

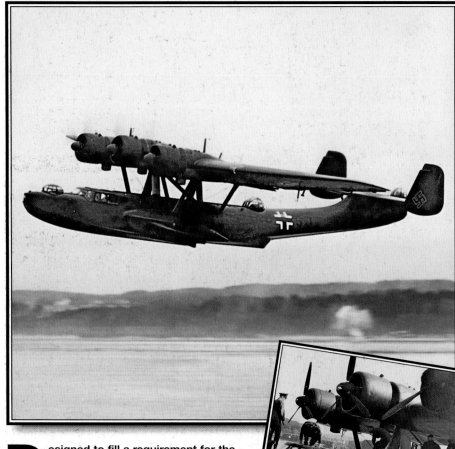

**D**esigned to fill a requirement for the Royal Netherlands Naval Air Service, the Do 24 was a three-engined all-metal flying-boat which came to excel in the air-sea rescue role. Exported to the Dutch before the start of World War II, the aircraft was to serve both sides during the conflict. Although very few modifications were introduced during the production run, such was the enduring nature of the design that it continued to serve until the late 1970s.

▲ A German pilot and his crew prepare to board their Dornier Do 24 at the start of a long-range patrol that may see them rescue pilots, search for submarines and observe enemy activity.

## DORNIER Do 24

▼ **Post-war service**
Twelve Do 24T-3s were supplied to Spain in June 1944. Remarkably these aircraft remained in service into the 1970s in the search and rescue role.

▲ **Mine-sweeper**
The Do 24MS was a special variant fitted with a degaussing loop and on-board generators for mine-sweeping duties.

**Dependable Dornier ▶**
Crews soon came to marvel at the capabilities of their aircraft. This early Do 24 is being put through its paces during rough water tests. The aircraft proved to be extremely reliable.

▼ **Safe and sound**
Here a Do 24 retrieves a downed bomber crew from the Atlantic Ocean. Search and rescue was one of the main roles of the Do 24.

▲ **Royal Dutch Navy**
Designed to meet a requirement for the Royal Dutch Navy, many of the Do 24s were quickly armed and pressed into Luftwaffe service after the outbreak of World War II, and were used for patrol flights.

### FACTS AND FIGURES

➤ In the rescue role Dornier Do 24s served in the Arctic, Mediterranean, English Channel and the Pacific.

➤ Five aircraft were operated by the RAAF for operations against the Japanese.

➤ During the evacuation of Crete, aircraft flew with more than 24 passengers.

➤ One Do 24 lost its entire tail unit during a rescue attempt. The crew sealed the aircraft and simply taxied back to base.

➤ Twelve aircraft were supplied to Spain in 1944 for search and rescue duties.

➤ A Do 24 was used as a testbed for an advanced wing design in 1983.

## PROFILE

# Slender-wing saviour

The Do 24 was an excellent search-and-rescue aircraft which first flew in July 1937. It was soon delivered to the Dutch navy for service evaluation, and after acceptance of the type the Dutch acquired 11 factory-built examples and also licence-built another 25 aircraft powered by three Wright R-1820 engines and designated Do 24Ks.

At the outbreak of World War II Germany had only one airworthy prototype. However, with the defeat of Holland all semi-completed Do 24Ks were shipped to Germany and were fitted out for air-sea rescue duties. Under the supervision of the German company, Weser-Flugzeugbau, production also continued in Holland. During the next four years about 170 BMW-Bramo-powered Do 24Ts were produced. These served with Luftwaffe rescue units in the Atlantic and Mediterranean.

Before being overrun by the Japanese the Dutch used a number of Do 24s successfully in the East Indies. The aircraft

*Above: An early Jumo-powered example awaits its next call to rescue. Crews found the Dutch design more capable than their own aircraft.*

were later passed to the Royal Australian Air Force. Spain also acquired Do 24s and used these after World War II. A number of these remained in service for almost 30 years.

*Above: Despite the large size of the Do 24 the aircraft was surprisingly agile.*

Early Do 24 variants were not fitted with a nose turret but, after combat losses, an enclosed turret with a 7.9-mm (0.31-in) machine gun was installed. Cockpit visibility was reasonable but was improved by the addition of large side windows.

Mounted high above the fuselage the wing provided the Do 24 with excellent lift, particularly when taking-off.

Rear defensive firepower was provided by a fully enclosed turret. The high-set tail of the Do 24 allowed the aircraft to be towed up onto the beach for repairs. One Do 24 had its entire tail blown off but survived.

Protruding from the lower fuselage on either-side were large winglets which helped stabilise the aircraft in rough seas. On two particular variants a large loop was attached around the fuselage of the aircraft for the mine-sweeping role.

Despite its slim profile the Do 24 was able to accommodate huge loads within its fuselage. During the evacuation of the Greek islands the aircraft airlifted more than 24 troops each with 30 kg (66 lb.) of equipment, before the advancing Allied army could capture them.

### Do 24T-2

The skull emblem identifies this Do 24 as belonging to 8. Seenotstaffel, which operated in the Black Sea under Seenotbereichskommando XI during 1942. These aircraft were transferred from Mamaia, Romania, to Varna in Bulgaria.

### COMBAT DATA

#### MAXIMUM TAKE OFF WEIGHT

With one of the largest take-off weights of any World War II flying-boat, the Do 24 proved itself capable of airlifting huge loads consisting of both troops and cargo. Earlier Dornier designs like the Do 18 simply could not match the Do 24's ability.

Do 24T-1 18,400 kg (40,480 lb.) — Do 18G-1 10,795 kg (23,749 lb.) — He 115B-1 10,400 kg (22,880 lb.)

#### MAXIMUM RANGE

Because of its long-range the Do 24 was ideal for search and rescue and reconnaissance duties. The Do 18 and He 115 also had respectable endurance. Like the Do 24, the He 115 served on both sides during World War II, the RAF operating a few captured He 115s on covert missions in the Mediterranean theatre.

Do 24T-1 4700 km (2,915 mi.) — Do 18G-1 3500 km (2,170 mi.) — He 115B-1 3350 km (2,077 mi.)

#### MAXIMUM SPEED

Equipped with three BMW engines, the Do 24 was capable of reaching a relatively high speed. However, Heinkel's He 115 was able to out-perform the Do 24 because of its lightweight fuselage and streamlined design.

Do 24T-1 331 km/h (205 m.p.h.)
Do 18G-1 267 km/h (166 m.p.h.)
He 115B-1 355 km/h (220 m.p.h.)

## Flying boats of World War II

■ **CATALINA:** Operated by the US Navy and the Royal Navy Consolidated's Catalina was the Allies' main flying-boat for rescue work, serving both in the European and Pacific wars.

■ **SUNDERLAND:** Developed from the Shorts Empire flying-boat, the Sunderland allowed the RAF to search the whole of the Mediterranean for German submarines.

■ **WALRUS:** First flown in June 1933, the Supermarine Walrus was used for rescue duties and mine-spotting. The aircraft was small enough to be operated from battleships.

# DOUGLAS

# A-20 BOSTON/HAVOC

● Multi-role light bomber ● Low-level strike attack

▲ The A-20 was greatly feared by the enemy as it combined speed, agility and a hard-hitting weapon load. It successfully fulfilled many roles that it was never designed to undertake.

**D**uring World War II the Douglas A-20 Havoc, called Boston by the RAF, fought on every continent and in every theatre of the war. It was not the fastest plane in its class, but it was extremely tough, handled well and was a popular and effective fighting machine, especially in the low-level attack role. Pilots knew they could fly the A-20 much like a fighter, inflicting considerable damage on their adversaries in the process.

## DOUGLAS A-20 BOSTON/HAVOC

**Slim profile ▶**
The narrow fuselage of the A-20 is apparent when seen from ahead. The shape gave speed and agility, but restricted the movement of the navigator and gunner.

**▼ Boston bomber**
The RAF was one of many satisfied foreign users. The Boston Mk III was used as a light bomber, but other Bostons served as radar night-fighters.

**▲ Formation flying**
Swarms of A-20s ranged at will over north-west Europe both before and after the invasion of Normandy.

**Precision ▶ bomber**
Bombing with deadly accuracy, Bostons and Havocs were used to attack communications targets in France and Belgium.

**▲ Rocket-launcher**
The hard-hitting Boston Mk III could be armed with 27-kg (60-lb.) rockets. The great strength of all the A-20 variants was their versatility in accepting almost any armament.

### FACTS AND FIGURES

➤ The prototype for the A-20 Havoc series, the DB-7, first flew on 23 January 1939.

➤ One A-20 was evaluated by the US Navy as the BD-1, and eight reached the Marine Corps, designated BD-2.

➤ The first American A-20s used in combat flew from England in 1942.

➤ Russia received 3,125 A-20s, Britain 1,800 and the United States 1,962.

➤ The final A-20 was rolled out at Santa Monica on 20 September 1944.

➤ An F-3A Havoc photo ship was the first Allied aircraft to land at Itazuke, Japan, after the August 1945 surrender.

**PROFILE**

# The all-purpose attack bomber

When designers Jack Northrop and Edward Heinemann designed the Douglas DB-7 in 1938, the idea of a twin-engined attack bomber with tricycle gear seemed futuristic. Although considered very advanced when it was purchased by Britain in 1940, it was no match for top fighters like the Spitfire and Bf 109. Known as the Boston in

RAF service, it was used as a bomber and as a carrier for Turbinlite, a searchlight used to illuminate Luftwaffe warplanes by night for RAF Hurricanes to stalk.

As the A-20 Havoc the aircraft entered service with US Forces as a heavily-armed attack bomber. Havocs saw a lot of service. They ranged far and wide over the Pacific, strafing

and bombing in the war against Japan, and supplied devastating fire support for the Normandy landings of June 1944. They were also popular with the Soviet air force, which was the largest user of the type. The P-70 night-fighter version and the F-3 Havoc reconnaissance craft were used mostly for training and saw limited combat.

*Havocs flew some extremely dangerous missions. This raid on a Japanese anchorage in New Guinea resulted in the loss of one of the attacking A-20s.*

## A-20G Havoc

**Type:** two-/three-seat light-attack bomber

**Powerplant:** two 1193-kW (2,625-hp.) Wright R-2800-23 Double Cyclone radial piston engines

**Maximum speed:** 546 km/h (340 m.p.h.) at 3780 m (12,400 ft.)

**Range:** 1754 km (1,087 mi.)

**Service ceiling:** 7865 m (25,800 ft.)

**Weights:** empty 7250 kg (14,950 lb.); loaded 12,338 kg (27,144 lb.)

**Armament:** six forward-firing 12.7-mm (.50 cal.) machine-guns in nose; two 12.7-mm machine-guns in power-operated dorsal turret; one manual 12.7-mm machine-gun in the ventral position; up to 1814 kg (3,990 lb.) of bombs

**Dimensions:**
| | | |
|---|---|---|
| span | 18.69 m | (61 ft.) |
| length | 14.63 m | (48 ft.) |
| height | 5.36 m | (18 ft.) |
| wing area | 43.11 m² | (464 sq. ft.) |

Early DB-7 had sometimes shown a lack of directional stability, therefore the fin and rudder were enlarged to cope with increased engine power.

Additional underwing bomb racks increased the A-20G's warload by 1000 kg (2,200 lb.).

Emergency flight controls were fitted to the rear crew compartment of early A-20s.

The Wright Cyclone was a powerful and dependable radial engine, fitted with superchargers.

The A-20G carried a pair of 12.7-mm (.50 cal.) guns in a power-operated rear turret. The Soviets put their own turrets onto A-20s.

The pilot enjoyed a good view ahead from the small cockpit.

A-20s had a variety of different noses. Attack variants had a heavy gun armament in place of the original glazed bomb-aimer's position.

## A-20G HAVOC 'QUEEN JULIA'

The A-20G was an attack variant, with improved armour, navigation equipment and bomb-aiming controls. It saw action in the Pacific and with Soviet forces on the Eastern Front.

The A-20's tricycle landing gear was an extremely unusual feature in a pre-war aircraft design.

The Havoc's long, slim bomb-bay usually carried small bombs suitable for attacking tactical targets.

## COMBAT DATA

### MAXIMUM SPEED

The Douglas DB-7 from which the A-20 was developed was one of the fastest bombers in service at the beginning of World War II. The Bristol Blenheim was, like the Douglas design, intended to be a light, fast bomber, but proved far more fragile. The Dornier Do 17 was classed as a medium bomber, but had similar performance to the smaller American machine.

| | |
|---|---|
| **A-20B HAVOC** | 475 km/h (295 m.p.h.) |
| **Do 17Z** | 425 km/h (264 m.p.h.) |
| **BLENHEIM Mk IV** | 470 km/h (291 m.p.h.) |

### RANGE

The A-20's range was sufficient for most tactical purposes, although the advanced Douglas design had less of a reach than its British equivalent. But the Blenheim had been developed from a record-breaking light transport, and had exceptional long-distance performance.

**A-20B HAVOC** 1600 km (992 mi.)
**Do 17Z** 1100 km (682 mi.)
**BLENHEIM Mk IV** 2500 km (1,550 mi.)

## Havocs around the world

■ **FRANCE:** The first user of what was to become the Boston and then the Havoc was the French air force. Some were operated by the Vichy air force and others diverted to the RAF after the defeat of France in 1940.

■ **ON THE EASTERN FRONT:** The Soviets flew more A-20s than anybody else, receiving more than 3000 under Lend Lease. This Soviet navy A-20B served with the Northern Fleet in the Arctic late in 1943.

■ **DEFENDER OF THE EMPIRE:** British and Commonwealth air forces operated large numbers of Douglas bombers. This Boston Mk III was in action in March 1943 in New Guinea with No. 22 Squadron, Royal Australian Air Force.

### BOMBLOAD

Early versions of the Havoc had a relatively small weapons load, although the Dornier, classified as a medium bomber, could carry very little more. By the end of the war A-20s were routinely carrying nearly two tons of bombs.

| A-20B HAVOC | Do 17Z | BLENHEIM Mk IV |
|---|---|---|
| 907 kg (2,000 lb.) | 1000 kg (2,200 lb.) | 454 kg (1,000 lb.) |

# DOUGLAS

# A-26 INVADER

● Twin-engined bomber ● European and Pacific service

P erhaps better known for its post-war exploits, the Douglas A-26 Invader first served in the European and Pacific theatres of World War II from September 1944. Designed by Ed Heinemann to replace the A-20 Havoc, the A-26 was very similar to the Havoc in configuration. The roles of bomber, night-fighter and ground-attack aircraft were envisaged for the type, but it was for air-to-ground roles that production aircraft were ordered.

▲ Almost too late for combat during World War II, the Invader was destined for service during the Korean War and even flew, in refurbished form, during the Vietnam conflict.

## DOUGLAS A-26 INVADER

◀ XA-26 prototype
In an olive drab finish and fitted with large propeller spinners, the XA-26 prototype 41-19504 runs its engines. The serial '219504' was erroneously painted on its fin.

Wheels up on Okinawa ▶
This eight-gun Invader of the 89th Bomb Squadron, 3rd Bomb Wing, made a belly landing on Okinawa after one of the last strikes of the war on 11 August 1945.

Early gun nose ▶
This 'gun nose' B-model has four 12.7-mm (.50 cal.) machine-guns on the starboard side and two to port.

▼ Flak damage
A direct hit by German flak took off the port wing of this A-26B over Europe.

▼ First Invaders in Europe
In heavily overcast conditions at Beaumont-sur-Oise, A-26Bs of the 552nd Bomb Squadron, 386th Bombardment Group, share the apron with B-26 Marauders in May 1945.

### FACTS AND FIGURES

➤ In all, 67 A-26s were lost in operations in the European theatre. Seven air-to-air victories by A-26s were confirmed.

➤ Douglas 'mocked-up' a 14-gun version of the A-26B; it failed to enter production.

➤ A-26s were known as B-26s in 1948, after the last Martin Marauders were retired.

➤ Unlike other bomber types, most A-26s were retained after 1945, and many became staff transports and target tugs.

➤ As well as A-20s, the A-26 was also used to replace B-25 Mitchells in some units.

➤ Of 2452 Invaders built, 2446 were A-26Bs and A-26Cs.

# Just in time for the war

XA-26 41-19504, the Invader prototype, first took to the air on 10 July 1942. This aircraft had the glazed nose of the projected A-26C bomber variant. The A-26A night-fighter would have had a radar set in the nose, with four 20-mm cannon in a ventral pack.

For attack missions, the A-26B had six 12.7-mm (.50 cal.) machine-guns in its nose, remotely-controlled dorsal and ventral turrets, each with two 12.7-mm machine-guns, and up to 10 more in underwing and under-fuselage packs.

The night-fighter was cancelled, but the A-26B and A-26C models were rushed into production. The first Invaders in combat were four A-26Bs used in New Guinea, where the aircraft proved unpopular on low-level sorties. Clearly, all the type's 'bugs' had yet to be ironed out.

In September 1944 the 553rd Bomb Squadron at Great Dunmow, England received 18 machines. Their results were more promising. Eventually, 11,567 missions were flown, delivering 18,344 tonnes (18,054 tons) of bombs. One aircraft was even

*Left: With eight extra machine-guns guns in four underwing two-gun packs, the two A-26s nearest the camera are a glazed-nose A-26C (in the foreground) and an A-26B.*

credited with a probable 'kill' of an Me 262 jet fighter.

In the Pacific, air-to-ground and anti-shipping strikes were typical. Three USAAF bomb groups used A-26s against targets in Okinawa, Formosa and mainland Japan; A-26s were active near Nagasaki when the second A-bomb was dropped on 9 August 1945.

*Above: A mixed complement of A-26s within the squadrons of a bomb group was not unusual. The 386th Bombardment Group operated both A-26Bs and Cs.*

## A-26C Invader

**Type:** three-seat light attack bomber

**Powerplant:** two 1419-kW (2,000-hp.) Pratt & Whitney R-2800-79 Double Wasp radial piston engines

**Maximum speed:** 600 km/h (372 m.p.h.)

**Initial climb rate:** 619 m/min (2,030 f.p.m.)

**Range:** 2253 km (1,400 mi.)

**Service ceiling:** 6735 m (22,100 ft.)

**Weights:** empty 10,365 kg (22,803 lb.); maximum take-off 15,876 kg (34,927 lb.)

**Armament:** six 12.7-mm (.50 cal.) machine-guns (two each in nose, dorsal and ventral positions), plus 1814 kg (4,000 lb.) of bombs internally

**Dimensions:**
| | |
|---|---|
| span | 21.34 m (70 ft.) |
| length | 15.62 m (51 ft. 3 in.) |
| height | 5.56 m (18 ft. 3 in.) |
| wing area | 50.17 m² (540 sq. ft.) |

## A-26B INVADER

*Stinky* was an A-26B built at Douglas's Tulsa, Oklahoma plant. Attached to the 552nd Bomb Squadron, 386th Bombardment Group, it was based at Beaumont-sur-Oise in April 1945.

As well as a pilot, A-26s were crewed by a bombardier/navigator, who normally sat next to the pilot but also had a work station in the nose, and a gunner.

Poor visibility was a problem on early-build Invaders. The original heavily-framed canopy was hinged at the front and was difficult to open into the airstream during an in-flight emergency. Later aircraft had a two-section 'clam shell' canopy, hinged at the sides and meeting in the middle. These greatly improved visibility and made emergency exits easier.

Pratt & Whitney's R-2800 Double Wasp 18-cylinder radial engine powered the A-26 Invaders. During the production life of the B model, the oil cooler air intakes were redesigned, which accounted for 80 per cent of the later improvement in the aircraft's performance. The inside of the engine cowlings were painted in an olive drab anti-dazzle finish to reduce glare problems encountered by pilots.

Nose gun armament fitted to the B-model Invader varied from batch to batch. Six or eight 12.7-mm (.50 cal.) machine-guns were typical. Some carried cannon.

A bomb bay with capacity for up to 1814 kg (4,000 lb.) of bombs filled the space between the cockpit and the gunner's position. Large two-piece bomb bay doors were even longer, stretching from the cockpit almost as far as the ventral turret.

The Invader's gunner reached his position via a bomb bay entry hatch and remotely controlled the dorsal and ventral turrets, each of which held two 12.7-mm (.50 cal.) machine-guns. In the 'gun-nose' C-model, the navigator also served as a gun loader for the nose armament.

## COMBAT DATA

### MAXIMUM SPEED

Among the improvements introduced with the A-26 was an increased top speed. The A-26C had a speed advantage of close to 100 km/h (62 m.p.h.) over its predecessor, the A-20 Havoc. The Havoc's contemporary, the B-26 Marauder, was slower still.

| | |
|---|---|
| A-26 INVADER | 600 km/h (372 m.p.h.) |
| A-20G HAVOC | 510 km/h (316 m.p.h.) |
| B-26 | 454 km/h (281 m.p.h.) |

### CEILING

The Invader had a lower service ceiling than the A-20, of about 6700 m (22,000 ft.), just 300 m (1,000 ft.) more than that of the B-26. The Invader's initial operations in the Pacific theatre were at low level. Bomb-release altitudes were higher in Europe.

A-26C INVADER 6735 m (22,100 ft.)
A-20G HAVOC 7865 m (25,800 ft.)
B-26 MARAUDER 6400 m (21,000 ft.)

### RANGE

One of the greatest improvements to come with the Invader was range. The A-26C had a 400–500 km (250–350 mi.) advantage over the types it was to replace. This added to the versatility of the type, and was especially useful in the 'over-water' operations carried out in the Pacific.

A-26C INVADER 2253 km (1,400 mi.)
A-20G HAVOC 1754 km (1,087 mi.)
B-26 MARAUDER 1851 km (1,148 mi.)

## Douglas's famous wartime designs

**A-20/P-70 HAVOC:** Immediate predecessor of the Invader, the A-20 was built in bomber and attack versions; the P-70 was a night-fighter.

**C-47 SKYTRAIN:** Known by the RAF and Commonwealth as the Dakota, the C-47 was the Allies' standard wartime transport aircraft.

**DB.7 BOSTON:** The RAF employed a bomber variant of the A-20 known as the Boston and a night-fighter version called the Havoc.

**SBD DAUNTLESS:** This carrier-borne scout bomber served the US Navy in large numbers in the Pacific theatre.

# DOUGLAS

# B-18 BOLO

● Twin-engined bomber ● DC-2 airliner development ● Foreign service

▲ Intended to replace the Martin B-10 as the USAAC's standard bomber, the DB-1 (Douglas Bomber 1) beat competition for orders from the Martin 164 and Boeing 299.

Incredible as it seems now, the Douglas B-18 was the US Army's standard bomber in 1940. At a time when Spitfires and Messerschmitts were duelling in the Battle of Britain, American bomber crews were training and preparing for war in this slow machine, with inadequate range, that was little more than a military adaptation of a transport aircraft. The B-18 (dubbed 'Bolo' officially, although the name was rarely used) was inadequate for modern warfare.

## DOUGLAS B-18 BOLO

▼ **Comparatively sluggish**
With a top speed of just 346 km/h (215 mph), the B-18 soon found itself outclassed when the US entered World War II in 1941.

▲ **RCAF Digby**
Twenty general reconnaissance Digby Mk Is (as they were known in Canadian service) were delivered to the air force during 1939 and 1940.

▼ **Wartime camouflage**
Camouflage was soon applied to USAAC Bolos once war had broken out. This one crashed at Hickam Field, Hawaii, in 1943.

▲ **Round nose B-18**
The first production Bolos were designated B-18 and featured this round, turretless, but more aerodynamic, nose design.

**Ready for action at March Field ▶**
The 7th Bombardment Group's fleet of Bolos is seen at March Field, California, in 1940. The 7th BG was the first unit to receive production B-18s. By 1940 most USAAC bomber squadrons were equipped with B-18/B-18As, but a number were destroyed in Hawaii on 7 December 1941.

## FACTS AND FIGURES

➤ The RAF investigated the purchase of B-18s in the maritime reconnaissance-bomber role as the Digby Mk I.

➤ Post-war, some surplus B-18s were used for crop-spraying and as freighters.

➤ Three air forces operated B-18s; Brazil received two B-18s in 1942.

➤ The USAAF's 7th Bombardment Group commander, Major Austin Straubel, was killed in a B-18 crash in Java in 1942.

➤ The first B-18s were evaluated by test pilots at Wright Field, Ohio, in 1935.

➤ The B-18 bomber's span was 1.37 m (4 ft 6 in) greater than that of the Douglas DC-2.

## PROFILE

# Bomber cousin of the DC-2

Douglas developed the B-18 in 1934 to provide the US Army Air Corps with an aircraft which had twice the bomb-carrying capacity of the Martin B-10. Douglas drew upon engineering work on the DC-2 airliner, the predecessor of the famous DC-3. The result was the utilitarian B-18 bomber, which was ready for examination by Army experts in 1935.

The Army ordered the B-18 into production in January 1936, even though fighters that were far faster than this low-wing, somewhat underpowered,

medium bomber were already appearing on the scene.

With its deep fuselage, the B-18 had space for two pilots and a crew totalling six men, including three gunners and a bombardier. B-18s participated in many realistic military exercises in the late 1930s.

Pilots were satisfied with the aircraft, but knew that it did not measure up to world standards.

By the time America entered the war, the B-18 was being used only to train bombardiers, but as many as 122 were fitted with special equipment to hunt for

*Above: The 7th Bombardment Group fly from their California base in the late-1930s.*

*Right: This Bolo has spray booms fitted under its wings. A number were converted as 'ag' aircraft post-war.*

submarines. Few, if any, B-18s saw actual combat and by the end of the war none remained in service.

B-18As had a small globular turret mounting for a flexible 7.62-mm (.30-cal.) machine gun. Above this was the bomb aimer's position in an extended glazed nose.

The Bolo's crew consisted of a pilot and co-pilot, a bomb aimer/navigator and nose, dorsal and ventral gunners.

The B-18 was designed around the wings and engines of the DC-2 and proved adaptable to other roles, including maritime reconnaissance as the B-18B. For this role it was fitted with a nose-mounted search radar and a magnetic anomaly detector (MAD) in a tail 'stinger' and carried depth charges in its bomb-bay. Two B-18s were converted as unarmed transports, designated C-58.

The retractable dorsal turret housed a 7.62-mm (.30-cal.) machine gun. When manned, it was extended upwards to allow the gunner to see the enemy. A ventral gun fired through a tunnel in the fuselage floor.

In common with the DC-2 airliner, the Bolo was fitted with two Pratt & Whitney R-1820 Cyclone 9 radial piston engines. In their -53 form they produced 746 kW.

An internal bomb-bay below the B-18A's wing centre-section carried up to 2948 kg (6500 lb) of bombs. Its relatively spacious fuselage made the Bolo adaptable for other roles, such as transport.

### B-18A Bolo

**Type:** medium bomber, maritime patrol and training aircraft

**Powerplant:** two 746-kW (1000-hp) Wright R-1820-53 Cyclone 9 radial piston engines

**Maximum speed:** 346 km/h (215 mph) at 3050 m (10,000 ft)

**Range:** 1931 km (1200 miles)

**Service ceiling:** 7285 m (23,900 ft)

**Weights:** empty 7403 kg (16,321 lb); maximum take-off 12,552 kg (27,672 lb)

**Armament:** three hand-operated, flexible 7.62-mm (.30-cal.) machine guns (in nose, ventral and dorsal positions), plus up to 2948 kg (6500 lb) of bombs carried in an internal bay

**Dimensions:**
| | | |
|---|---|---|
| span | 27.28 m | (89 ft 6 in) |
| length | 17.63 m | (57 ft 10 in) |
| height | 4.62 m | (15 ft 2 in) |
| wing area | 89.65 m² | (965 sq ft) |

### B-18A BOLO

The 18th Reconnaissance Squadron was one of three reconnaissance units equipped with the B-18A Bolo. This example operated from Mitchell Field, New York, in 1940.

### COMBAT DATA

#### MAXIMUM SPEED

Designed to fulfil an airliner role for Lufthansa, as well as a bomber role for the Luftwaffe, the He 111 possessed a respectable turn of speed, a healthy 75 km/h faster than the B-18. The RAF's Wellington was not far behind.

| | |
|---|---|
| B-18A BOLO | 346 km/h (215 mph) |
| WELLINGTON Mk I | 394 km/h (245 mph) |
| He 111E-3 | 420 km/h (261 mph) |

#### ARMAMENT

The B-18 had an excellent bombload for a medium bomber of the period – almost one tonne more than the He 111 and Wellington. Light defensive armament was typical of the late 1930s.

| B-18A BOLO | WELLINGTON Mk I | He 111E-3 |
|---|---|---|
| 3 x 7.7-mm (.303-cal.) machine guns 2948 kg (6500 lb) of bombs | 4 x 7.7-mm (.303-cal.) machine guns 2041 kg (4500 lb) of bombs | 3 x 7.9-mm (.303-cal.) machine guns 2000 kg (4409 lb) of bombs |

#### SERVICE CEILING

The early variants of the Wellington had an inferior ceiling to other medium bombers. This deteriorated further in the wartime Mk IC variant, although the problem was addressed in the Merlin-engined versions.

| B-18A BOLO | WELLINGTON Mk I | He 111E-3 |
|---|---|---|
| 7285 m (23,900 ft) | 6584 m (21,600 ft) | 7200 m (23,622 ft) |

## Douglas bombers for the USAAC

■ **B-7:** This monoplane, equipped with retractable undercarriage, was developed from the XO-35 reconnaissance aircraft of 1930.

■ **A-17/A-33:** In 1942 the USAAC took over 31 Douglas 8As (export derivatives of Northrop's A-17 attack-bomber) bound for Norway.

■ **B-23 DRAGON:** To address the B-18's shortcomings, Douglas developed the larger B-23. It first flew in 1939, but few were built.

■ **XB-19:** Douglas' response to a 1934 USAAC requirement for a large bomber, the B-19 was defeated by a lack of funding.

# DOUGLAS
# C-47 SKYTRAIN

● Worldwide service ● Transport and glider tug ● Still flying

**B**ased on the DC-3, the Douglas C-47 Skytrain became the most widely used transport of the war. This familiar and versatile military transport hauled cargoes, dropped paratroops and towed gliders. No airfield was too close to the front or too rough for the versatile Skytrain. Eisenhower called the C-47 one of the four most important weapons of the war, along with the bazooka, the Jeep and the atomic bomb.

▲ Many crewmembers owed their lives to the strength of the C-47, when the aircraft were caught by enemy fighters or anti-aircraft fire. Equally, many troops were saved by supplies and reinforcements delivered by the Skytrain.

---

## PHOTO FILE

## DOUGLAS C-47 SKYTRAIN

▲ **Skytrain gathering**
Many hundreds of aircraft were involved in operations from the UK. Here, closely parked C-47s prepare for a mission in support of the D-Day invasion forces.

▲ **Floating transport**
A single XC-47C was built with floats and a few aircraft were converted to this configuration in the field.

▲ **'Gooney Bird'**
US Army Air Force personnel nicknamed the C-47 'The Gooney Bird'.

▼ **Last of the line**
Douglas built 10,691 C-47s, this aircraft being the last manufactured at the Long Beach factory. Some aircraft were built in Japan and the USSR.

▲ **Supply drop**
Troops in every theatre, from Europe through Africa to the Pacific, regarded the C-47 as a lifeline. All types of equipment, food and medical supplies were dropped by parachute to the front line.

---

## FACTS AND FIGURES

➤ On 10 July 1943 Skytrains dropped 4381 Allied paratroopers during the invasion of Sicily.

➤ The prototype for the DC-3/C-47 made its maiden flight on 17 December 1935.

➤ More than 1000 C-47s participated in the D-Day invasion.

➤ Skytrains were fine glider tugs and were used to haul glider-borne troops into battle in France and Burma.

➤ Some C-47s were flown with floats, instead of their wheeled undercarriage.

➤ Skytrains were built in Japan by Nakajima and in the USSR by Lisunov.

# PROFILE

# Unsurpassed military transport

The qualities which made the DC-3 a fine airliner made the C-47 a superb military transport, which served in every theatre of the war. The twin-engined C-47 was rugged and reliable, and could fly from primitive airfields in the midst of the war zone, carrying cargo, troops or towing gliders.

The Skytrain was in many respects the most versatile military aircraft ever built and

flew in a number of very important operations. The most memorable C-47 mission was the dropping of paratroopers in Normandy in the hours before the 6 June 1944 invasion of Europe by Allied armies.

But the C-47 was everywhere: in Burma, an enterprising Skytrain pilot poked a Browning automatic rifle out of his cockpit and shot down a Japanese Zero fighter. In the Aleutian Islands C-47s equipped with

skis brought supplies to American soldiers by landing on and taking off from ice-covered surfaces.

Many Skytrains survived being hit by gunfire and being attacked by fighters, and were deemed the 'most survivable' of all Allied transport aircraft.

*Left: Gliders were too valuable to be used only once and therefore a system of retrieval was devised. The glider's towline was held above the ground between two poles and snatched by a long hook trailing from a low-flying C-47 Skytrain.*

*Above: Although it was an exceptional airlifter, the C-47 was not very easy to load. All cargo had to be hauled through the left-hand side cargo doors.*

## C-47A SKYTRAIN

**During the D-Day landings 'Buzz Buggy' flew from a British base with the 81st Troop Carrier Squadron of the 436th Troop Carrier Group.**

A three-man crew of pilot, co-pilot and radio operator flew the C-47. The radio operator sat in a separate compartment behind the cockpit and the aircrew entered by the small forward door.

Folding wooden seats along the cabin sides could accommodate up to 28 fully equipped paratroops. As well as cargo, standard internal fittings allowed 18 stretchers to be carried.

Two large cargo doors allowed cabin access, one opening forwards and the other backwards. A small door inset into the forward freight door was used for in-flight paratroop dropping.

Two Pratt & Whitney R-1830 14-cylinder air-cooled radial piston engines, each of 30-litre (6.5-gal.) capacity, drove the Hamilton Standard propellers of all the standard production Skytrains.

Douglas designed the C-47 with a structure of metal stressed-skin and multiple spars, which produced a wing which was very resistant to fatigue.

All Allied aircraft taking part in the D-Day operations were painted with these black and white 'invasion stripes' as a recognition aid.

## Skytrain versatility

This highly versatile aircraft flew many types of mission, but its primary role was as a transport and glider tug.

**DROPPING PARATROOPS:** Several daring airborne raids would not have been possible without large numbers of C-47s; 28 troops could be dropped in quick succession.

**GLIDER TUG:** Several hundred gliders were used in the D-Day assault on Normandy. Packed with troops and equipment, the glider was released near the landing zone.

**WACO CG-4A HADRIAN:** Using gliders, the Allies were able to increase the capacity of their transport fleet quickly and cheaply.

**FREIGHTER:** Loading freight, especially heavy wheeled equipment into the C-47 was difficult because of the aircraft's tailwheel undercarriage.

# DOUGLAS

# SBD DAUNTLESS

● Carrier-borne dive-bomber ● Hero of the Pacific war

▲ Deck and air crew prepare for a mission. No aircraft did more to win the Pacific war than the SBD Dauntless: it sank more Japanese ships than any other type.

I f it had done nothing else but fight at Midway – where a handful of carrier pilots turned the tide of the Pacific war – the Douglas SBD Dauntless would be counted among important aircraft of the 20th century. But the SBD did more than wreck the Japanese fleet in that battle on 4 June 1942. From its conception in 1938 until late 1944 the SBD showed itself to be the most important American dive-bomber ever built.

## DOUGLAS SBD DAUNTLESS

Dive attack ▶
The leader of a section of SBDs rolls into the attack. Dive strikes were usually made from an altitude between 4500 and 6000 m (15,000 and 20,000 ft.), with the dive angle reaching about 70°. This gave great accuracy.

▲ Dauntless 'Leathernecks'
Although best known as a US Navy warplane, the Dauntless also served in large numbers with the US Marine Corps, operating from land bases.

▲ In North Africa
Atlantic Fleet SBDs got their first taste of major action in November 1942, during the Allied landings in North Africa, known as Operation 'Torch'.

▲ Difficult Dauntless
Despite its successes, the SBD Dauntless was underpowered, vulnerable and, above all, exhausting to fly for any length of time.

Carrier launch ▶
An SBD gets the signal to take off from its carrier. The air wing was carefully arranged on the deck in the order in which the aircraft were due to fly.

### FACTS AND FIGURES

➤ Pilot Lieutenant Robert Dixon signalled 'Scratch one flat-top' after his attack on the Japanese carrier Shoho.

➤ The first Dauntless, a modified XBT-2, was test-flown on 22 April 1938.

➤ At the battle of Midway, Dauntlesses sank Japan's four main aircraft-carriers.

➤ One US Navy Dauntless gunner was credited with shooting down seven Mitsubishi Zero fighters in two days.

➤ SBDs sank more Japanese shipping than any other US aircraft in the Pacific.

➤ The last Dauntless, an SBD-6, was rolled out on 22 July 1944.

# Douglas' deadly dive-bomber

The Douglas SBD Dauntless pounded the Japanese at Coral Sea, Midway and in the Solomons, and supported US Navy and Marine Corps actions until late 1944. This was a fair achievement for an aircraft that was underpowered, vulnerable, short on range and exhausting to fly. For all its flaws, the Dauntless, designed by Jack Northrop and Ed Heinemann, was a dramatic success.

Pilots of the SBD Dauntless sat high in a relatively 'clean' aircraft optimised to hurl bombs at targets while flying straight down into the enemy's midst. The pilot aimed the aircraft, and a crutch-like trapeze threw forth a centreline bomb that narrowly cleared the propeller arc before boring downwards. The SBD roared, rattled and required constant attention on stick, throttle and rudder, but pilots took pride in mastering it and praised its achievements as a dive-bomber.

The US Army Dauntless, the A-24, was outfought on Java in 1942 and was later used mostly for training. By the end of the war, Navy Dauntlesses were replaced by the Curtiss SB2C Helldiver, but this aircraft never won the affection routinely bestowed on its predecessor.

Above: Three SBD-5s return from a mission. The furthest aircraft has its aft defensive guns deployed from the rear cockpit.

Above: Until mid-1942, US aircraft wore highly visible red and white rudder stripes.

Left: In the dive the Dauntless used 'Swiss cheese' divebrakes to keep the speed down.

## SBD-5 Dauntless

**Type:** two-seat carrier-based scout and dive-bomber

**Powerplant:** one 895-kW (1,200-hp.) Wright R-1820-60 Cyclone air-cooled radial piston engine

**Maximum speed:** 410 km/h (254 m.p.h.) at 3050 m (10,000 ft.)

**Initial climb rate:** 518 m/min (1,700 f.p.m.)

**Range:** 730 km (453 mi.) on a bombing mission; 1244 km (771 mi.) on a scouting mission

**Service ceiling:** 7400 m (24,275 ft.)

**Armament:** two 12.7-mm (.50 cal.) fixed machine-guns in the nose and two 7.62-mm (.30 cal.) manually aimed machine-guns in the rear crewman's position, plus up to 725 kg (1,600 lb.) of bombs under the fuselage and 295 kg (650 lb.) of bombs under the wings

**Dimensions:**
| | |
|---|---|
| span | 12.66 m (42 ft.) |
| length | 10.09 m (33 ft.) |
| height | 4.14 m (14 ft.) |
| wing area | 30.19 m² (325 sq. ft.) |

## SBD-4 DAUNTLESS

Clutching a bomb to its belly, this Dauntless served with the US Marine Corps in July 1943, flying in New Guinea. The US Navy and USMC SBDs exacted a huge toll on the Japanese shipping fleet.

Power for the Dauntless came from the trusty Wright R-1820 Cyclone engine. Even at 746 kW (1,000 hp.) in the SBD-3/4 this was not really enough, so the SBD-5 introduced an uprated Cyclone offering 895 kW (1,200 hp.).

The pilot had a telescopic bombsight projecting through the windshield. This tended to fog over because of the change in temperature during the dive.

In the rear cockpit sat the radio operator. It was also his task to operate the rear defensive armament, which consisted of a pair of 7.62-mm (.30 cal.) Browning machine-guns. In transit these weapons were stowed in the fuselage behind hinged doors. On entering the combat zone, the rear canopy was stowed in the fuselage and the guns deployed from their bay, giving the gunner a wide field of fire.

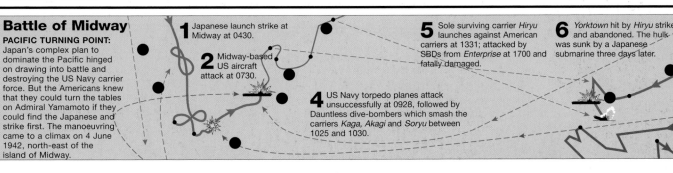

The bomb armament consisted of a single weapon of up to 726 kg on the centreline, with 295 kg of bombs under the wings.

The centreline bomb was carried on a special double-armed cradle. When the bomb was released by the pilot, the cradle swung forwards so that the bomb would clear the propeller arc.

The wings had a strange brake assembly which extended on both the upper and lower surfaces. On the undersides the brake surfaces were located right the way across the fuselage. All the surfaces had large holes in them, hence the name 'Swiss cheese' divebrakes, to avoid buffeting problems.

## COMBAT DATA

### MAXIMUM SPEED

The Dauntless was a neat design, but the lack of power did not give it a blistering turn of speed. However, compared to its early-war rivals it was well placed. Its intended replacement in the US Navy, the Curtiss SB2C Helldiver, was not much faster at about 470 km/h (291 m.p.h.).

| | |
|---|---|
| SKUA Mk II | 362 km/h (224 m.p.h.) |
| SBD-5 DAUNTLESS | 410 km/h (254 m.p.h.) |
| D3A1 'VAL' | 385 km/h (239 m.p.h.) |

### BOMBLOAD

Compared to its rivals the Dauntless carried an exceptional load, due largely to the high stressing of the centreline cradle. This in turn allowed it to carry bombs of true ship-killing size. The small wing bombs gave added firepower, notably in attacks against land targets.

SBD-5 DAUNTLESS 1020 kg (2,245 lb.)
D3A1 'VAL' 370 kg (814 lb.)
SKUA Mk II 330 kg (725 lb.)

### RANGE

One area where the Dauntless did not perform well was range, certainly compared to its main rival in the Pacific, the D3A. This gave Japanese carrier commanders a slight advantage: they could position their ships so that the D3As could just reach the Americans, but were themselves out of range of the Dauntless force.

SBD-5 DAUNTLESS 1244 km (771 mi.)
D3A1 'VAL' 1470 km (911 mi.)
SKUA Mk II 1223 km (758 mi.)

## Battle of Midway

**PACIFIC TURNING POINT:** Japan's complex plan to dominate the Pacific hinged on drawing into battle and destroying the US Navy carrier force. But the Americans knew that they could turn the tables on Admiral Yamamoto if they could find the Japanese and strike first. The manoeuvring came to a climax on 4 June 1942, north-east of the island of Midway.

**1** Japanese launch strike at Midway at 0430.

**2** Midway-based US aircraft attack at 0730.

**4** US Navy torpedo planes attack unsuccessfully at 0928, followed by Dauntless dive-bombers which smash the carriers Kaga, Akagi and Soryu between 1025 and 1030.

**5** Sole surviving carrier Hiryu launches against American carriers at 1331; attacked by SBDs from Enterprise at 1700 and fatally damaged.

**6** Yorktown hit by Hiryu strike and abandoned. The hulk was sunk by a Japanese submarine three days later.

**3** Main US Navy carrier strikes launched between 0800 and 0900.

# DOUGLAS

# TBD DEVASTATOR

● Carrier-based torpedo-bomber ● All metal ● World War II service

▲ Although the Devastator represented the state of the art in the mid-1930s, it was to be tragically outclassed during the battles in the Pacific in the early 1940s.

This American torpedo-bomber is mainly remembered for a tragic reason – at Midway an entire squadron of Douglas TBD Devastators was lost in a matter of minutes. The Devastator was a perfectly acceptable aircraft by pre-war standards, but it came on the scene when change was occurring rapidly. By the time men and machines were pitted in combat in the Pacific, the TBD was no longer an effective warplane.

## DOUGLAS TBD DEVASTATOR

◀ First squadron equipped
VT-3 was the first unit to receive the Devastator, in October 1937. Three more squadrons received the aircraft in 1938, and in 1942 all four saw action against the Japanese.

▲ First Devastator – the XTBD-1
Flown in April 1935, the first TBD had a lower cockpit canopy. This was raised on production aircraft to improve visibility on take-off and landing.

▲ Devastator floatplane
The first production TBD was fitted with Edo floats, as the TBD-1A, and was test flown from Newport, Rhode Island, in 1939.

Hydraulic wing folding ▶
TBDs were the first US naval aircraft with hydraulically-powered wing folding. The upward fold of the wings was also unusual.

California ▶ factory
These TBDs are seen under construction at Douglas' Santa Monica factory. The left-hand aircraft carries the markings of the US Navy's VT-2 unit.

▲ Aboard *Enterprise* before Midway
Only four of these TBDs from torpedo-bomber squadron VT-6 returned from their next mission.

### FACTS AND FIGURES

➤ One of the first Technicolour films about US naval aviation was *Dive Bomber* of 1941, which featured VT-3 TBDs.

➤ TBD carrier trials began in December 1935 aboard USS *Lexington*.

➤ Devastators ended their careers as communications and training aircraft.

➤ The Devastator was the US Navy's first all-metal, low-wing aircraft and its first carrier-based monoplane.

➤ The first TBD was delivered to the Navy just nine days after its maiden flight.

➤ Douglas built 129 production TBD-1s while also developing the SBD Dauntless.

## PROFILE

# First Navy all-metal monoplane

Donald Douglas' fine aircraft company developed the TBD Devastator in 1934 to give the US Navy a much-needed torpedo-bomber which was able to fly from aircraft-carrier decks. The low-wing, tailwheel-equipped Devastator was able to carry a torpedo or bomb beneath its fuselage, or smaller bombs under its fuselage and wings.

The crew of three, consisting of pilot, gunner and navigator/torpedo officer operator, faced a great deal of danger. From the very beginning of World

War II, it was obvious that the Devastator was outclassed.

On 4 June 1942 at Midway, no fewer than 35 Devastators were shot down. They included all of the US Navy's Torpedo Squadron Eight (VT-8). Sole survivor Ensign George Gay, having succumbed to Japanese fire and bobbing in a life raft, had a horrific view as Japanese guns blasted his colleagues out of the sky. Many were victims of withering fire from the ships' guns; others were shot down by fighters.

Soon afterwards, the Devastator was withdrawn from

combat units – left behind by a war that was moving faster than it did – and relegated to training duties.

*Above: Seen over Wake Island in February 1942, this TBD from the* Enterprise *carries a fresh coat of sea green and pale grey paint. In May a US Navy dispatch ordered the red national insignia and tail markings to be removed.*

*Below: This pre-war view shows Devastators of VT-5. By early 1942 TBDs from this unit, stationed aboard USS* Yorktown, *were raiding Japanese targets in the Gilbert Islands.*

### TBD-1 Devastator

**Type:** three-seat torpedo-bomber

**Powerplant:** one 671-kW (900-hp.) Pratt & Whitney R-1830-64 Twin Wasp radial piston engine

**Maximum speed:** 332 km/h (205 m.p.h.) at 2440 m (8,000 ft.)

**Cruising speed:** 206 km/h (128 m.p.h.)

**Range:** 670 km (415 mi.)

**Service ceiling:** 6005 m (19,700 ft.)

**Weights:** empty 2804 kg (6,169 lb.); maximum take-off 4624 kg (10,173 lb.)

**Armament:** one 7.62-mm (.30 cal.) forward-firing machine-gun and one 7.62-mm gun on flexible mount, plus one 454-kg (1,000-lb.) torpedo or up to 680 kg (1,500 lb.) of bombs

**Dimensions:**
| | |
|---|---|
| span | 15.24 m (50 ft.) |
| length | 10.67 m (35 ft.) |
| height | 4.60 m (15 ft.) |
| wing area | 39.20 m² (422 sq. ft.) |

## TBD-1 DEVASTATOR

**TBD-1 0322 carries the pre-war markings of Torpedo Squadron 6 (VT-6), one of four units equipped with the Devastator from 1937.**

The R-1830 variant of Pratt & Whitney's well-known Twin Wasp powered the TBD. This powerplant was also widely used in other types, such as the C-47 Skytrain.

Devastators were manned by three crew: a pilot, a navigator/torpedo officer and a gunner. The latter sat at the rear of the cockpit 'glasshouse' and fired a 7.62-mm (.30 cal.) machine-gun. A forward-firing machine-gun was also fitted in the inner port wing.

Although the TBD was built with wing flotation bags to allow the crew time to escape the aircraft if it ditched, these were removed in wartime. This ensured that the TBD would sink, taking its advanced Norden bombsight with it.

Although the TBD boasted a powered wing-folding mechanism, it lacked sufficient power to move the wings in a strong cross wind. This required assistance from the ground handlers.

The TBD's usual load was a 454-kg (1,000-lb.) torpedo carried under the fuselage. An alternative often used in 1942 against Japanese targets in the Gilbert and Marshall Islands was up to three 227-kg (500-lb.) bombs or a dozen 45-kg (100-lb.) bombs, six under each wing.

At the beginning of their service TBDs suffered a number of crashes after pilots, who were not used to folding wings, failed to check that their wings were locked in position.

### COMBAT DATA

#### MAXIMUM SPEED

The Avenger, which also suffered losses during the Battle of Midway, had a top speed some 100 km/h (60 m.p.h.) higher than the TBD. This, combined with its better defensive armament, made it less vulnerable to Japanese fighters.

| | |
|---|---|
| **TBD-1 DEVASTATOR** | 332 km/h (205 m.p.h.) |
| **TG-2** | 204 km/h (126 m.p.h.) |
| **TBF-1 AVENGER** | 436 km/h (270 m.p.h.) |

#### RANGE

Range was very important for a torpedo-bomber, allowing it to fly missions over longer distances from the carrier, and therefore reducing the risk to the ship. The TBD's range was more than twice that of the TG-2.

TBD-1 DEVASTATOR 1152 km (714 mi.)
TG-2 531 km (329 mi.)
TBF-1 AVENGER 1955 km (1,212 mi.)

#### ARMAMENT

In a similar way that the Devastator was a huge improvement over the TG-2, so the Grumman Avenger was a much better armed aircraft, both defensively and offensively. It carried more machine-guns and had a high-capacity weapons bay.

TBD-1 DEVASTATOR 2 x 7.62-mm (.30 cal.) machine-guns 1 torpedo or 680 kg (1,500 lb.) of bombs
TG-2 1 x 7.62-mm (.30 cal.) machine-gun 1 torpedo
TBF-1 AVENGER 2 x 7.62-mm (.30 cal.) machine-guns 1 x 12.7-mm (.50 cal.) machine-guns 1 torpedo or 726 kg (1,600 lb.) of bombs

## US Navy aircraft at Midway

■ **CONSOLIDATED PBY CATALINA:** Catalina patrol bombers based at Midway and with a 4500-km (2,790-mi.) range gave the Navy prior warning of the approaching Japanese fleet.

■ **DOUGLAS SBD DAUNTLESS:** Carrier-based Dauntless dive-bombers inflicted the bulk of the damage on the Japanese fleet, helping to sink four of its carriers.

■ **GRUMMAN F4F WILDCAT:** Fighter escort for the bombers was provided by carrier-based Wildcats. In all, 79 were deployed aboard three carriers: Enterprise, Hornet and Yorktown.

■ **GRUMMAN TBF AVENGER:** Some of the Navy's first Avengers were deployed in Midway and flew missions against the Japanese in which they suffered huge losses.

# FAIREY

# III

● Inter-war general-purpose aircraft ● RAF, FAA and foreign use

▲ One of the best known British military aircraft of the 1920s and 1930s, the Fairey III was developed over several years as a landplane and seaplane for both the RAF and FAA. Most of the type's operational service was spent overseas, in the Middle East, Far East and Africa. The IIIF variant served for some 14 years in a number of roles.

**W**ith its origins in a floatplane prototype known as the N10 by the Royal Naval Air Service, the Fairey Series III family comprised three major variants – the IIIC, IIID and IIIF – that between them were used for over 23 years by the services that became the Fleet Air Arm and the RAF. Starting life as a bomber and mine spotter, the Fairey III developed into a general-purpose type in shore-based and ship-board use with the Royal Navy.

## FAIREY III

**▲ From Cairo to the Cape**
In 1926 the RAF's Cape Flight made a long-distance formation flight to South Africa to 'show the flag'. S1105 was among the four IIIDs involved.

**▲ No. 481 Flight, FAA**
Fairey IIID seaplanes of No. 481 Flight, Fleet Air Arm, were based in Malta for sea search operations around the island. In 1929 the flight was renumbered No. 202 Squadron, RAF, and re-equipped with float-equipped IIIFs.

**▲ Portuguese floatplane**
Eleven Fairey IIIDs ordered for the Portuguese navy had either Rolls-Royce Eagle or Napier Lion engines.

**▲ Fairey IIIFs of 202 Sqdn**
Malta-based No. 202 Squadron, RAF was equipped with longer-range IIIFs until 1935.

**Napier Lion engine ▶**
In the IIIF, the Lion engine was enclosed in a redesigned cowling of more streamlined appearance.

## FACTS AND FIGURES

➤ The last RAF and FAA IIIFs in service are believed to have been several used as target tugs until 1941.

➤ Fairey IIIFs were the Fleet Air Arm's most widely-used inter-war type.

➤ Fairey IIIAs and Bs were built in small numbers toward the end of World War I.

➤ A radio-controlled gunnery training version of the IIIF was called the Fairey Queen; three were built.

➤ Fairey's Gordon and Seal were both developments of the IIIF.

➤ Two RAF IIIFs were configured as VIP communications aircraft.

# PROFILE

# Long-serving inter-war biplane

Combining the bombing capability of the IIIB floatplane with the IIIA's ship-board reconnaissance role, the IIIC was just too late to see service in World War I, though a small number took part in bombing operations with the North Russian Expeditionary Force based at Archangel. Including aircraft converted from IIIB production, 36 were built.

In 1920 the first flight of a IIID took place. Another bomber/reconnaissance type, this IIIC development served widely overseas, both as a landplane and as a seaplane catapulted from warships. By 1926, 207 had been built for the RAF, FAA and various foreign customers, including Portugal and Australia.

Perhaps the best known of the Fairey IIIs was the IIIF. Built in greater numbers than any other inter-war British military aircraft (other than Hawker Hart variants), the IIIF first entered service as a two-seat general-purpose aircraft with the RAF in Egypt in 1927. As the largest user of the type, the FAA employed more than 330 IIIF three-seat reconnaissance aircraft. They operated from every aircraft carrier, land bases and as catapult floatplanes.

*Above: A Fairey IIID leaves its launching trolley and the deck of HMS Argus in August 1922.*

*Below: Among a number of civil-registered IIIs was this Jaguar radial-engined IIIF used for survey work in Sudan from 1930 until it crashed in 1934.*

Australian IIIDs were equipped with Rolls-Royce Eagle VIII 12-cylinder liquid-cooled engines rated at 280 kW (375 hp.). This drove a two-bladed, fixed-pitch wooden propeller.

A10-3 was among six Fairey IIID seaplanes ordered by the Australian government, the first of which was delivered in August 1921. The first, then serialled ANA.1, was 'launched' by the wife of the Australian Prime Minister, W.M. Hughes.

The all-wooden fuselage structure was fabric-covered. The forward fuselage, the engine and its steel bearers, could be removed as a single unit.

Though standard IIIDs, the Australian examples were finished in a special aluminium dope and had white-painted floats to keep internal temperatures down in the Australian heat.

In naval service, the IIID was operated as a three-seater, with an observer and gunner positioned behind the pilot.

By far the most common powerplant fitted to Fairey IIIs was the unusual Napier Lion 'broad arrow', liquid-cooled, 12-cylinder engine.

Armament for general-purpose aircraft consisted of a forward-firing 7.7-mm (.303 cal.) Vickers machine-gun, a Scarff ring-mounted 7.7-mm Lewis in the gunner's position and a small bomb load on external racks.

For stowage aboard naval vessels the IIID had folding wings, hinged either side of the centre-section. One IIID was built with a metal wing structure and metal floats.

Fairey IIIFs introduced major improvements over the IIID. An all-metal fuselage, and later an all-metal wing, were used, as well as a metal propeller and a simplified undercarriage design.

## IIID

Originally serialled ANA.3 (Australian Naval Aircraft No. 3), this aircraft was flown on the Britannia Trophy-winning flight round the entire Australian coastline in 1924.

## BRITANNIA TROPHY WINNERS

Australian Navy Fairey IIID A10-3, crewed by Wing Commander S.J. Goble and Flying Officer I.E. McIntyre, was flown around Australia's 13,789-km (8,550-mi.) coastline over a period of 44 days between 6 April and 19 May 1924. Flying time was 90 hours. For this achievement they were awarded the 1924 Britannia Trophy. Setting out from the RAAF base at Point Cook, near Melbourne, the aircraft headed north. Bad weather and equipment failure dogged the trip; a new engine and floats were fitted at different points en route. The leg between Thursday Island and Elcho Island, across the open sea of the Gulf of Carpentaria, was one of the most difficult.

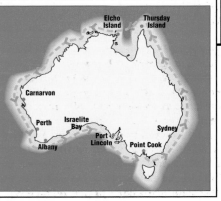

## Wartime and inter-war Fairey types

■ **CAMPANIA:** The first aircraft intended from the outset to operate from a carrier vessel, this was Fairey's second design. The first example flew from a converted liner, Campania, in 1917.

■ **FAWN:** A landplane derivative of the Pintail amphibian, the Fawn was the RAF's first post-war light bomber to enter service. Replacing DH.9As, 70 production examples were built.

■ **FLYCATCHER:** Though clumsy looking, the Flycatcher fighter handled well and was thus popular with FAA pilots. Between 1922 and 1930, 195 were built, including amphibians.

■ **HENDON:** With an all-metal structure and a cantilever wing, the Hendon night bomber was advanced for its day. First flown in 1931, the type was built in small numbers (14) for the RAF.

# FAIREY

# ALBACORE

● Biplane torpedo-bomber ● Designed to replace the Swordfish

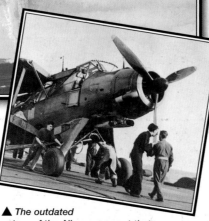

▲ The outdated
nature of the Albacore meant that
it did not replace the Swordfish as
planned. The last Albacores served with
an RAF squadron until January 1945.

**B**y 1945 there were still nine FAA
squadrons equipped with the Fairey
Swordfish. The Albacore, 800 of
which had been built to replace the old
'Stringbag', was serving with just one unit –
and this was an air force squadron.
As a development of an already out-dated
design, the Albacore represented an
insufficient improvement over the old, but
reliable, Swordfish. However, the type was
useful, often flying from land bases.

## FAIREY ALBACORE

▲ **Final days with the RAF**
The last operational Albacores served with No. 415 Squadron, Royal
Canadian Air Force, later No.119 Squadron of the RAF, flying night
anti-shipping sorties over the English Channel and the North Sea.

▲ **Over Malta**
Albacores in the Mediterranean
flew bombing operations in the
Western Desert and marked
targets for RAF bombers.

▲ **Departing HMS Illustrious**
The Albacores of No. 829 Squadron were stationed aboard HMS
Illustrious between June 1940 and June 1941.

▲ **Convoy escorts**
The first carrierborne
operations for the
'Applecore' came at
the end of 1940, with a
convoy escort to Cape
Town aboard HMS
Formidable.

◀ **Torpedo
away!**
The Albacore's
principal anti-
ship weapon
was a 730-kg
(1.600-lb.)
torpedo. Bombs
and depth
charges were
also used.

### FACTS AND FIGURES

➤ No. 826 Squadron, the first unit to equip
with the type in March 1940, attacked
E-boats off Zeebrugge later in the year.

➤ During the D-Day landings of June 1944,
Albacores patrolled the English Channel.

➤ The last carrier-borne Albacores flew
during the invasion of Sicily.

➤ Last operations involving Albacores were
carried out by the RAF's No. 119 Squadron
against Dutch-based E-boats in 1945.

➤ All 800 Albacores were built at Fairey's
factory in Hayes, Middlesex.

➤ Aircraft from Victorious sank German
submarine U-517 on 21 November 1942.

# Torpedo-bombing 'Applecore'

Due to the improvements over its predecessor, the Albacore was described as the 'gentleman's Swordfish'. However, it was a development of an already obsolete idea.

Produced to a 1937 specification for a Swordfish replacement, this was one of a number of Fairey designs submitted. The Fleet Air Arm saw the monoplane as an 'unknown quantity' for the maritime role and so opted for an aircraft that, in the event, represented little advance over the 'Stringbag', as the Swordfish was known.

Inevitably known as the 'Applecore' by its crews, 800 Albacores were built between 1938 and 1943. The type's first carrier operations were convoy escorts aboard HMS Formidable, and one of its notable actions was a fruitless attack on the battleship Tirpitz in 1942.

As Barracudas re-equipped FAA units from 1942, British-based Albacores defended the Channel, with the last examples flying with a Belgium-based RAF unit in this role. Others, based in North Africa, patrolled the Mediterranean and flew bombing and target-marking sorties for the RAF.

*Above: During tests the Albacore did not receive good marks for its handling, although it was steady in a dive and recovered well from a torpedo run.*

*Right: The pilot's view was excellent, but the cockpit was hot in summer; the rear was cold and draughty.*

## Albacore

**Type:** carrier- or shore-based torpedo-bomber

**Powerplant:** one 794-kW (1,065-hp.) Bristol Taurus II or 843-kW (1,130-hp.) Taurus XII radial piston engine

**Maximum speed:** 259 km/h (160 m.p.h.) at 2135 m (7,000 ft.)

**Initial climb rate:** 8 minutes to 1829 m (6,000 ft.)

**Range:** 1319 km (820 mi.)

**Service ceiling:** 6310 m (20,700 ft.)

**Weights:** empty 3266 kg (7,185 lb.); maximum take-off 5715 kg (12,757 lb.)

**Armament:** two 7.7-mm (.303 cal.) Vickers machine-guns

**Dimensions:**
| | | |
|---|---|---|
| span | 15.24 m | (50 ft.) |
| length | 12.13 m | (39 ft. 9 in.) |
| height | 4.65 m | (15 ft. 3 in.) |
| wing area | 57.9 m² | (623 sq. ft.) |

The aircraft had a variable-pitch propeller and hydraulically operated flaps.

For self-defence the Albacore carried two Vickers 'K' machine-guns: one in the starboard wing firing forward and the other in the rear cockpit.

### ALBACORE

N4159 was delivered to No. 827 Squadron, based at Yeovilton, in September 1940. By March 1942 it was with No. 826 Squadron, in whose markings it is seen here. No. 826 was the first unit to be equipped with the type.

The Albacore was described as the 'gentleman's Swordfish' with its enclosed cockpits with central heating and a windscreen wiper for the pilot. A lavatory was fitted as well as a dinghy-launching system in case of ditching.

Albacores were fitted with either a 794-kW (1,065-hp.) Bristol Taurus II or 843-kW (1,130-hp.) Taurus XII 14-cylinder two-row radial engine. This was the only change made to the aircraft during the production run.

As an alternative to a Mk XIIA torpedo, the aircraft could carry six 113-kg (250-lb.) or four 227-kg (500-lb.) bombs beneath the wings. Other stores included mines and flares. In late 1940 land-based Albacores flew mine-laying missions along the north coast of France.

### COMBAT DATA

#### MAXIMUM SPEED

The Albacore's top speed was an improvement over that of the Swordfish, but it was still more than 100 km/h (60 m.p.h.) slower than the Barracuda torpedo- and dive-bomber.

| | |
|---|---|
| ALBACORE | 259 km/h (160 m.p.h.) |
| SWORDFISH Mk II | 222 km/h (138 m.p.h.) |
| BARRACUDA Mk II | 367 km/h (228 m.p.h.) |

#### ARMAMENT

The gun- and bomb-carrying capabilities of these three Fleet Air Arm aircraft did not vary greatly. However, the biplanes were considerably deficient in speed and range.

| | |
|---|---|
| ALBACORE | 2 x 7.7-mm (.303 cal.) machine-guns 907 kg (2,000 lb.) of bombs or torpedoes |
| SWORDFISH Mk II | 2 x 7.7-mm (.303 cal.) machine-guns 731 kg (1,600 lb.) of bombs or torpedoes |
| BARRACUDA Mk II | 2 x 7.7-mm (.303 cal.) machine-guns 816 kg (1,800 lb.) of bombs or torpedoes |

#### RANGE

The Albacore and Barracuda both had much longer ranges than earlier types. The Barracuda combined this with improved speed and little reduction in load-carrying capacity, whereas the Albacore's design was merely a development of the outmoded Swordfish and its inherent weaknesses.

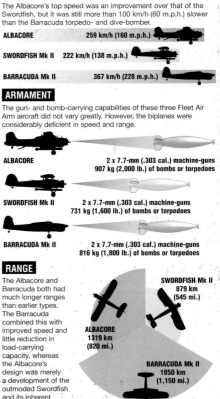

SWORDFISH Mk II 879 km (545 mi.)

ALBACORE 1319 km (820 mi.)

BARRACUDA Mk II 1850 km (1,150 mi.)

## Fairey's carrier-borne warplanes

■ **SWORDFISH:** Known as the 'Stringbag', the Swordfish torpedo-bomber first flew in 1934. Despite its inferior performance it was preferred to its intended replacement, the Albacore.

■ **FULMAR:** As the first Fairey-built FAA fighter since the Flycatcher, the Fulmar entered service in 1940. Its lack of speed compared to single-seaters was a handicap, however.

■ **BARRACUDA:** These aircraft were given a range of duties from torpedo reconnaissance to dive-bombing. Operational from 1943, the type made attacks on the battleship *Tirpitz* in 1944.

■ **FIREFLY:** A fighter reconnaissance aircraft that was later adapted for a strike role, the Rolls-Royce Griffon-powered and cannon-armed Firefly entered FAA service in 1943.

# FAIREY

# FIREFLY

● Carrier-based ● Night-fighter ● Attack and reconnaissance

## FAIREY FIREFLY

**◀ In the Pacific**
*Displaying the large white and blue Pacific theatre markings of the period, a Firefly sets off in search of Japanese surface vessels during the closing stages of World War II.*

**Aboard HMS *Pretoria Castle* ▶**
*As the pilot walks away, deck hands prepare to remove a crashed Firefly, the victim of a failed arrester hook.*

**Radar-equipped ▶**
*Carrying American ASH radar in a pod under its nose, the Firefly F.Mk I became the FR.Mk I. Firefly night-fighters used a modified version of the same radar and were designated NF.Mk I. The NF.Mk I was a conversion, unlike the purpose-built NF.Mk II.*

**▼ Night fighter**
*Equipped with a bulky AI.Mk X radar, the NF.Mk II Firefly featured an extended forward fuselage to retain the same centre of gravity for the aircraft.*

**▲ Trials flying**
*With the brightly painted yellow under-surfaces of a trials machine, this early Firefly Mk I is seen on a test flight. Minor differences compared to later machines include the unfaired cannons and low profile cockpit canopy.*

Fighter-reconnaissance aircraft had been part of the Royal Navy's inventory since the mid-1920s, when machines like the Fleetwing and Osprey were conceived. The first monoplane in this class was the Fairey Fulmar of 1940 and it was to replace this aircraft that another Fairey product, the Firefly, was designed. Perhaps better known for its post-war service, the Firefly served from 1943 and was active on raids against the *Tirpitz* and in the Pacific.

**▲** *Like other carrier-borne aircraft the Firefly had folding wings to facilitate storage aboard ship. These were heavy and had to be manhandled into position by deck crews before each flight.*

### FACTS AND FIGURES

➤ Fireflies were the first FAA aircraft to fly over, and the first British aircraft to land on, the Japanese mainland in 1945.

➤ The Firefly was the second Fairey naval design to bear the name.

➤ FAA NF.Mk Is were used to intercept He 111s carrying V-1 flying bombs in 1944.

➤ The Firefly's first air-to-air victory was on 2 January 1945 when a No. 1770 Squadron pilot downed a Japanese Nakajima Ki-43.

➤ Post-war, a number of Firefly Mk Is were converted to pilot and observer trainers.

➤ FAA Fireflies raided Japan prior to the planned invasion of the mainland.

# PROFILE

# Fairey's fearsome Firefly

Among the Firefly's features that made it such an advance over the Fulmar were its more powerful Rolls-Royce Griffon engine, 20-mm (0.79-in.) cannon armament, a higher top speed and a set of Fairey-Youngman flaps. The latter greatly improved low-speed handling and all-round manoeuvrability.

The Firefly prototype flew on 22 December 1941 and the following year 200 Firefly F.Mk Is were ordered for the Fleet Air Arm (FAA). Between 1943 and 1946 850 Mk Is were built, including a batch by General Aircraft.

Following the F.Mk I into service was the FR.Mk I fighter-reconnaissance version, with American ASH air-to-surface vessel radar fitted. (F.Mk Is converted to FR standard were known as F.Mk IAs.) The only Firefly Mk IIs built were 37 NF.Mk II night-fighters, with AI.Mk X radar. When it was decided to convert FR.Mk Is for the role (as NF.Mk Is with modified ASH radar), further Mk II production was cancelled.

The Mk I was operational for the first time in July 1944, when aircraft from No.1770 Squadron aboard HMS *Indefatigable* attacked gun positions and

*Above: Despite its size, the Firefly was a fairly nimble aircraft. This example has a radar pod bracket fitted.*

auxiliary vessels during raids on the German battleship *Tirpitz*. In the Far East, FAA Fireflies attacked Japanese oil refineries on Sumatra in January 1945. After joining the British Pacific Fleet, three Firefly squadrons took part in raids on the Caroline Islands during June.

*Below: Deck crews hurriedly fold the wings of rocket-firing FAA Fireflies after a strike against Japanese oil refineries on Sumatra. These attacks disrupted enemy fuel supplies.*

## Firefly F.Mk I

**Type:** two-seat reconnaissance fighter and fighter/bomber

**Powerplant:** one 1290-kW (1,730-hp.) Rolls-Royce Griffon IIB piston engine

**Maximum speed:** 509 km/h (316 m.p.h.) at 4265 m (14,000 ft.)

**Range:** 2092 km (1,300 mi.)

**Service ceiling:** 8535 m (28,000 ft.)

**Weights:** empty 4423 kg (9,731 lb.); maximum take-off 6359 kg (13,990 lb.)

**Armament:** four 20-mm (0.79-in.) Hispano cannon in wings, plus provision for up to eight 27-kg (60-lb.) rockets or two 454-kg (1,000-lb.) bombs on wing racks

**Dimensions:**
| | | |
|---|---|---|
| span | 13.56 m | (44 ft. 6 in.) |
| length | 11.46 m | (37 ft. 7 in.) |
| height | 4.14 m | (13 ft. 7 in.) |
| wing area | 30.47 m² | (326 sq. ft.) |

The Firefly prototype and the early production aircraft were distinguished by their shallower windscreen and more confining cockpit canopy. Later machines, like this one, had larger canopies to improve the pilot's view.

The aircraft's observer was accommodated in the rear cockpit. When ASH radar was fitted, as on the FR.Mk I and NF.Mk I, the radar screen was situated here for operation by the observer. The NF.Mk II, of which only 37 were built, had such a heavy radar set that the aircraft's centre of gravity was upset, necessitating the fitting of a longer nose.

ROYAL NAVY
Z2035

## FIREFLY F.MK I

Firefly Mk I Z2035 was delivered in May 1944 and employed as a Fleet Air Arm torpedo training aircraft before being assigned to No. 730 Squadron, a communications unit, at Ayr, Scotland.

Rolls-Royce's then new Griffon engine was installed in the Firefly, greatly improving performance over that of the Fulmar. This drove a three-bladed propeller on early production aircraft.

In common with other British fighters of the second half of World War II, the Firefly had an armament fit consisting of four 20-mm (0.79-in.) Underwing racks were used to carry rockets.

Fairey-Youngman flaps fitted to the Firefly greatly improved the aircraft's handling at the slow flight speeds associated with aircraft carrier approaches.

## ACTION DATA

### MAXIMUM SPEED

Of the various Fairey types employed by the FAA in the air-to-surface role during World War II, the Firefly Mk I was by far the fastest. Intended to fill a fighter role, the Griffon-powered Firefly needed a good turn of speed.

| | |
|---|---|
| **FIREFLY F.Mk I** | 509 km/h (316 m.p.h.) |
| **BARRACUDA Mk II** | 367 km/h (228 m.p.h.) |
| **SWORDFISH Mk II** | 222 km/h (138 m.p.h.) |

### SERVICE CEILING

Service ceiling was also an area in which the Firefly had a definite edge. It had a 3000 m advantage over the Fairey Barracuda and an even larger margin over the Fairey Swordfish. Height was an important advantage for an interceptor like the Firefly.

| FIREFLY F.Mk I | BARRACUDA Mk II | SWORDFISH Mk II |
|---|---|---|
| 8535 m (28,000 ft.) | 5060 m (16,700 ft.) | 3260 m (10,700 ft.) |

### RANGE

In terms of range the differences between the types were less pronounced. A slow, torpedo-carrying aircraft, the old Swordfish biplane had a good range, about 50 per cent more than that of the more modern Barracuda, another anti-shipping aircraft.

FIREFLY F.Mk I 2092 km (1,300 mi.)

BARRACUDA Mk II 1104 km (685 mi.)

SWORDFISH Mk II 1658 km (1,030 mi.)

## FAA fighter-reconnaissance types

**FAIREY FLEETWING:** In 1926 the FAA saw the need for a spotter-reconnaissance aircraft with a limited ability as a fighter. The sole Fleetwing (N235) was among several prototypes built to meet the FAA requirement, but failed to achieve an order; losing out to the Osprey.

**HAWKER OSPREY:** A deck-landing variant of the RAF's Hart bomber, the Osprey entered service in 1932. A number were completed with floats and were joined by the single-seat Nimrod (derived from the Fury) in 1933. The last examples were retired in 1939.

**FAIREY FULMAR:** The Firefly's immediate predecessor, the Fulmar entered service in 1940 as the FAA's first eight-gun fighter. Active for almost the entire war, this carrier-based type was also used as a night-fighter from shore bases. A drawback was its lack of speed.

# FAIREY
# FLYCATCHER

● 1920s carrier-borne fighter ● Popular with pilots ● Floatplane

▲ Flight from
aircraft carriers has always been
hazardous, especially at night. A Fairey
Flycatcher performed the first night-time
carrier landing by a UK fighter in 1929.

**A** distinctive aircraft with a curious
name; this is one way of describing
the Fairey Flycatcher of the 1920s. It
was an aircraft of odd appearance, and with
a long roster of good and bad points. With
the fuselage looking as though it was sag-
ging in the middle, it was not good looking
from any angle. The Flycatcher was not
particularly fast either, but it was a valuable
warplane with great maneuverability and the
flexibility afforded by both floats and wheels.

## FAIREY FLYCATCHER

**◄ Fleet fighter**
The Flycatcher was the Royal
Navy's standard fighter for over
10 years; in fact it was their only
Fleet fighter for the period 1924 to
1932. Here an example flies over
one of the Royal Navy's carriers.

**Worldwide bases ►**
The Royal Navy's deployments
around the globe during the 1920s
meant that Flycatchers could be
seen from Malta to Hong Kong.

**◄ Ship protection**
As well as flying from aircraft carriers, Flycatchers
were deployed from turret platforms aboard
selected battleships.

**Carrier-borne ►**
No. 403 Flight flew
the Flycatcher
Mk I from 1924
until 1934. No. 403
was based at
Leuchars and
served aboard the
aircraft carrier
HMS Hermes.

**▲ Flycatcher amphibian**
N9678 was the first production amphibian
and flew for the first time in October 1925.

## FACTS AND FIGURES

➤ The Flycatcher Mk II was an advanced
carrier-fighter, first flown in October 1926.
It bore little resemblance to the Mk I.

➤ Production of Flycatchers added up to
196 aircraft, including four test aircraft.

➤ The prototype Fairey Flycatcher made its
initial flight in November 1922.

➤ Flycatchers operated with the British
Fleet until 1934 when the last floatplane
versions were retired.

➤ The Flycatcher replaced the Nieuport
Nightjar just after World War I.

➤ The second prototype Flycatcher, flown
in May 1923, was the first to use floats.

## PROFILE

# Fly in the Queen's fleet

This remarkable specimen from the vintage years of aviation went into action with Britain's Fleet Air Arm in 1923. It was ugly, unusual, but much-loved by the pilots who flew it. With its short span, the Flycatcher could be raised or lowered on the elevator of an aircraft carrier without the need for wing folding. Apart from its

ability to be equipped with floats or wheels, another unusual feature of the Flycatcher's construction was that the airframe was designed to be dismantled easily with no section more than 4 m (13 ft.) long.

Although not exactly a spectacular performer, the Flycatcher was comparable to most other

fighters of its era and would have acquitted itself well in battle. Its popularity with its pilots was due to its responsiveness and strength in spite of its mixed wood and metal construction with fabric covering. It could be dived vertically at full throttle. As a floatplane, it was even capable of the full range of aerobatic manoeuvers.

*Left: On some carriers, Flycatchers took off directly over the bows from a forward hangar below the main deck.*

*Below: A Flycatcher was the first FAA aircraft fitted with hydraulic wheel-brakes, a standard feature from 1933.*

### Flycatcher Mk I

**Type:** Single-seat Fleet fighter

**Powerplant:** One 298-kW (400-hp.) Armstrong Siddeley Jaguar III or IV 14-cylinder radial piston engine

**Maximum speed:** 214 km/h (133 m.p.h.)

**Initial climb rate:** 372 m/min (1,222 f.p.m.)

**Range:** 500 km (310 mi.)

**Service ceiling:** 5,790 m (19,000 ft.)

**Weapons:** Twin fixed, forward-firing 7.7-mm (.303 cal.) Vickers machine guns on fuselage; plus up to four 9-kg (20-lb.) bombs carried beneath the wings

**Weights:** Empty 2,032 lb.; max takeoff 3,018 lb.

**Dimensions:**
| | | |
|---|---|---|
| span | 8.84 m | (29 ft.) |
| length | 7.01 m | (23 ft.) |
| height | 3.66 m | (12 ft.) |
| wing area | 26.76 m² | (288 sq. ft.) |

### FLYCATCHER MK I

S1061 was one of 14 Flycatchers (S1060-1073) ordered in August 1925. A total of 192 was delivered to the Fleet Air Arm.

The pilot had two machine guns at his disposal; a pair of 7.7-mm (.303 cal.) Vickers guns mounted on the forward fuselage and firing through the propeller arc.

Among the type's distinctive features were the dihedral (upward bend) of the top wing and the apparent kink in the rear fuselage, which combined to give an ungainly overall appearance.

A distinctive fin shape was a feature of the Flycatcher. Float-equipped aircraft generally had a taller fin and rudder to maintain directional stability.

Flycatchers were powered by an Armstrong Siddeley Jaguar engine like those equipping the RAF's Armstrong Whitworth Siskin of the same period. This engine drove a two-blade propeller.

Wheeled landing gear was readily interchangeable with floats, as fitted to Flycatchers deployed aboard battleships. Amphibious landing gear could also be fitted, though this did not perform well on water.

Though principally a fighter, the Flycatcher had a limited bombing capability, with wing racks for four 9-kg (20-lb.) bombs. This allowed them to attack surface ships, but only at close range and considerable risk.

Bright and distinctive markings were a feature of inter-war warplanes. FAA Flycatchers were no exception.

### ACTION DATA

#### SPEED

Compared to the Vought FU fighter and the later Boeing FB of the mid 1920s, the Flycatcher compared fairly well in terms of its speed. The FB differed from the other two types in having an inline engine. A version of the FU was equipped with floats.

| | |
|---|---|
| FLYCATCHER Mk I | 214 km/h (133 m.p.h.) |
| FB-1 | 256 km/h (159 m.p.h.) |
| FU-1 | 196 km/h (122 m.p.h.) |

#### RANGE

Both the American types boasted a better range performance than the Flycatcher, by more than 60 miles. Range translated to endurance when operating from a carrier deck, which governed how long an aircraft could remain on patrol. US types operated in the Pacific and Atlantic Oceans and required extra range.

FU-1 660 km (410 mi.)
FB-1 628 km (390 mi.)
FLYCATCHER Mk I 500 km (310 mi.)

#### POWER

As engine manufacturers began to produce reliable, more powerful engines, these engines were fitted to new aircraft. This increase is mirrored in the dates that these three aircraft entered service, the Flycatcher being the second of the three.

FU-1 164 kW (220 hp.)    FLYCATCHER Mk I 298 kW (400 hp.)    FB-1 324 kW (435 hp.)

## Fairey aircraft between the wars

■ **FIREFLY:** Built as a private venture, the Firefly fighter competed with and lost to the Hawker Fury in the competition for RAF orders.

■ **SEAL:** The equivalent of the RAF's Fairey Gordon, the Navy's Seal was an armed carrier-borne spotter-reconnaissance aircraft.

■ **FOX:** When this day-bomber entered RAF service in the mid 1920s, it was faster than the fighters of the period. Only 28 were delivered.

■ **FERRET:** Fairey's first aircraft with an all-metal structure, it was intended for FAA use. Despite good performance, none were ordered.

# FAIREY
# Fox

● Day bomber designs ● RAF and foreign forces ● High speed

▲ Clean lines,
an especially small frontal area
and a powerful Curtiss D-12 engine were the
keys to the Fox's speed. Despite its performance,
the type was destined to equip just one RAF unit.

**A**ny account of the development and career of the Fairey Fox needs to consider two different aircraft designed to fill the same role. The RAF's Fox Mk I of 1925 was faster than any other day bomber of the period, thanks in no small part to its powerful American engine. It was also faster than most fighters! Fairey's later design proposal for a Mk I replacement, the Fox Mk II, was rejected by the RAF, but it found favour overseas, especially in Belgium.

## PHOTO FILE

# FAIREY Fox

**Clean lines of the Mk I ▶**
Compared with its contemporaries, the Fox Mk I, with its single-bay wing and small frontal area, was an exceptionally aerodynamic machine.

**▼ Fox Mk VI at Evère, 1936**
Fox Mk VIs were built at the Avions Fairey factory as late as 1939. Most were either Mk VIR reconnaissance or Mk VIC combat machines. Two were sold in Switzerland.

**▲ Fox Mk IV on floats**
For Peru, Fairey produced the Fox Mk IV with floats. The aircraft were shipped from London Docks in 1933.

**▼ Enclosed cockpit**
This Belgian-built aircraft was the first Fox VI, powered by a 641-kW (860-hp.) Hispano-Suiza 12Ybrs engine. This was the most-produced Fox Mk II variant, with about 85 built.

**▲ First Mk IIs**
Belgium's first 12 Fox Mk IIs were built in Britain. One of these took first prize in the 1932 International Circuit of the Alps race, averaging 258 km/h (160 m.p.h.).

## FACTS AND FIGURES

➤ An RAF Fox Mk IA was landed aboard and flown from HMS *Furious* in April 1926.

➤ Though just over 200 kg (440 lb.) heavier than the Fox Mk I, the Mk IA was 6 km/h (4 m.p.h.) faster.

➤ The first RAF crews to be saved by parachutes bailed out from two Foxes after a collision in 1925.

➤ Two single-seat fighter variants of the Mk VI (the Mk VII Mono-Fox) were built.

➤ Dual-control versions of both the Fox Mk I and Mk II family were built.

# PROFILE

# Faster than the fighters of the day

Built as a private venture by Fairey, the Fox changed the RAF's thinking about performance levels and specification requirements. With a top speed some 80 km/h (50 m.p.h.) faster than that of the then-current Fairey Fawn, the Fox was able to carry the same bomb load and was faster than most fighters.

First flown on 3 January 1925, the prototype was described by its test pilot as one of the easiest and most viceless aircraft he had ever flown.

Financial constraints limited the size of the RAF's Fox fleet to just 23 service examples. That the Fox Mk I was powered by an American engine was controversial; the final four examples were fitted with Rolls-Royce F.XIIAs, as Fox Mk IAs, and the D-12's reliability problems led to others being re-engined.

Fairey was unsuccessful with its entry in the competition to find a replacement for the Fox. The Fox Mk II, a new, Kestrel-engined design with an all-metal structure employing the

*Below: The last four Mk Is were built with Rolls-Royce F.XIIA engines (later known as Kestrel IIAs) and designated Mk IAs. Other Curtiss-engined Mk Is were also re-engined.*

*Above: Though it retained the Fox Mk I's basic layout, the Mk II was an entirely new design with an all-metal fuselage structure.*

Mk I's layout, was instead offered to foreign operators. Belgium became the largest user, and Fairey established an assembly line for the type at Gosselies.

## Fox Mk IA

**Type:** two-seat day bomber

**Powerplant:** one 358-kW (480-hp.) Curtiss D-12 liquid-cooled piston engine

**Maximum speed:** 251 km/h (156 m.p.h.) at sea level; 246 km/h (152 m.p.h.) at 3048 m (10,000 ft.)

**Initial climb rate:** 1.8 min to 610 m (2,000 ft.)

**Range:** 805 km (500 mi.) at 209 km/h (130 m.p.h.)

**Service ceiling:** 5182 m (17,000 ft.)

**Weights:** empty 1183 kg (2,609 lb.); loaded 1892 kg (4,117 lb.)

**Armament:** one forward-firing Vickers 7.7-mm (.303 cal.) machine-gun, one Lewis 7.7-mm machine-gun in rear cockpit, plus up to 209 kg (460 lb.) of bombs

**Dimensions:**
| | |
|---|---|
| span | 11.48 m (38 ft.) |
| length | 8.61 m (31 ft. 2 in.) |
| height | 3.25 m (10 ft. 8 in.) |
| wing area | 30.1 m² (324 sq. ft.) |

The Fox's American engine powered a Curtiss-Reed all-metal propeller which was licence-built.

For self-protection, the Fox Mk I carried a 7.7-mm (.303 cal.) Lewis machine-gun on a high-speed mounting in the rear cockpit and a forward-firing 7.7-mm Vickers on the port side of the forward fuselage. Offensive stores totalled 209 kg of bombs.

## Fox Mk I

No. 12 (Bomber) Squadron, RAF was the only unit to receive production Foxes. J7943 was the third aircraft in the first order for 18 aircraft. Only 23 were built; by 1931 they had been replaced by Hawker Harts.

In recognition of its association with the Fairey Fox, No. 12 Squadron incorporated a fox's mask into its unit crest with the motto 'Leads the Field', both of which the unit retains to this day.

Though relatively untried, the Curtiss D-12 was chosen to power the Fox because there was no equivalent British design of sufficient power. The D-12 had powered a Curtiss CR-3 racing floatplane to victory in the 1923 Schneider Trophy Race. Plagued by unreliability, the D-12s were later replaced by Rolls-Royce Kestrels.

Wood was used in the construction of the Fox's wings, rear fuselage and empennage, while the load-bearing forward fuselage was of steel tube.

## COMBAT DATA

### POWER

While the power produced by the Curtiss D-12 engine was only slightly more than that of the Napier Lion in the Fairey Fawn III, the Fox's design allowed higher top speeds. The Rolls-Royce Kestrel in the Hawker Hart offered an extra 41 kW (45 hp.) over the Lion engine.

| FOX Mk I 358 kW (480 hp.) | FAWN Mk III 350 kW (470 hp.) | HART SEDB 391 kW (525 hp.) |
|---|---|---|

### MAXIMUM SPEED

Fairey designed the Fox to make better use of its engine's power and produced an aircraft that was faster than some fighters of the day. Hawker's Hart was faster still, at almost 300 km/h (170 m.p.h.), having been designed with a view to producing a fast bomber like the Fox that it was intended to replace.

| | |
|---|---|
| FOX Mk I | 252 km/h (156 m.p.h.) |
| FAWN Mk III | 183 km/h (113 m.p.h.) |
| HART SEDB | 296 km/h (167 m.p.h.) |

### RANGE

Hawker's Hart SEDB (Single-Engined Day Bomber) was fast, but lacked the range of both the Fox and the Fawn. Both of these aircraft were supported by wings designed not so much for speed as long range at lower speed. While the Hart and the Fawn were able to carry comparable bombloads, the Fox was limited to about 200 kg (400 lb.).

FOX Mk I 805 km (500 mi.)

FAWN Mk III 1046 km (650 mi.)

HART SEDB 692 km (430 mi.)

# RAF inter-war day bombers

**DE HAVILLAND DH.9A:** Entering service in 1918, the DH.9A was the RAF's standard home-based bomber until the Fawn was introduced.

**FAIREY FAWN:** The RAF's first new bomber type, the Fawn Mk II was produced from 1924 and had a top speed of 183 km/h (114 m.p.h.).

**HAWKER HART:** Replacing the Fox Mk I, the 296-km/h (184-m.p.h.) Hart joined RAF units in 1930. Small numbers served as late as 1939.

**HAWKER HIND:** A development of the Hart, the Hind was an interim type before Battles and Blenheims entered service in the late 1930s.

# FAIREY

# FULMAR

● Carrier-based fighter ● Fleet reconnaissance ● Night-fighter

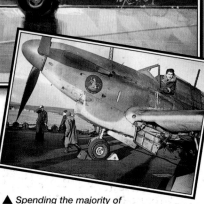

▲ *Spending the majority of its operational service life flying from Royal Navy aircraft-carriers in the Mediterranean, the Fulmar gained notable victories against both Italian and German opposition.*

**D**esigned in the 1930s, when Britain's Fleet Air Arm desperately needed new warplanes, the Fulmar was handicapped by Royal Navy demands for twin-seat fighters. Underpowered, and with modest manoeuvrability and rate of climb, the Fulmar could be easy prey for a seasoned enemy fighter pilot. Yet, with heavy armament and a robust structure, the Fulmar did achieve notable success, particularly in the Mediterranean theatre.

## FAIREY FULMAR

▼ **Reconnaissance work**
*With its excellent endurance, the Fulmar was used as a carrier-borne spotter. In 1941, Fulmars successfully located and trailed the Bismarck.*

▲ **Bomber origins**
*The Fulmar was developed from the P.4/34 day bomber project which was abandoned in 1936.*

▲ **Catching a wire**
*Rudder and elevator control was poor at low speeds, making carrier landings difficult. Fulmars also had a tendency to crab bodily to the left during take-off.*

▲ **Ubiquitous Merlin**
*Powered by the popular Merlin engine, the Fulmar had spritely performance for a two-seater. This example is serviced during the defence of Ceylon.*

**Saving Malta ▶**
*In August 1942, Fulmars on HMS* Victorious *protected 14 merchant ships carrying vital supplies to Malta.*

## FACTS AND FIGURES

➤ The first of two Fulmar prototypes completed its maiden flight on 13 January 1937.

➤ About 100 Fulmars were converted to night-fighters, but with limited success.

➤ Fulmars were involved in catapult launch tests from merchant ships.

➤ Altogether, Fulmars served with 20 squadrons and with eight fleet aircraft-carriers and five escort carriers.

➤ The first prototype Fulmar is preserved at the Fleet Air Arm Museum in England.

➤ The last of 600 Fulmars to be built was delivered to the FAA in February 1943.

# Defender of the Malta convoys

*Below: By mid-1941, the Fulmar equipped eight operational FAA squadrons. This example is leaving HMS* Victorious *on a dawn patrol.*

Developed from the P.4/34 light bomber project, which was eventually abandoned, the Fulmar filled the Royal Navy's desperate need in the late 1930s for a modern monoplane fighter.

Because of a lack of precision navigational instruments, the FAA deemed it necessary for their new fighter to have a second seat to accommodate a navigator, and thus ensure a return to an aircraft-carrier in any weather. Although slower and more cumbersome than its single-seat land-based counterparts, the Fulmar was an excellent aircraft considering the design constraints.

Entering service in 1940, the Fulmar Mk I was soon in action protecting the vital supply convoys to the beleaguered island of Malta. During autumn 1940, Fulmars from No. 806 Squadron were especially busy, managing to shoot down 10 Italian bombers as well as downing six enemy fighters, while giving cover to the famous Swordfish raid on Taranto.

*Above: As the best FAA fighter of 1940–42, the Fulmar had good range and firepower, but lacked the speed and agility of single-seat fighters.*

In addition to fighter duties, Fulmars were also engaged in the fleet reconnaissance role, most notably against the Bismarck, and a number of the later, more powerful Mk IIs were modified to become night-fighters.

### Fulmar Mk I

**Type:** two-seat carrier-based fighter

**Powerplant:** one 805-kW (1,080-hp.) Rolls-Royce Merlin VIII 12-cylinder Vee piston engine

**Maximum speed:** 398 km/h (247 m.p.h.) at 2745 m (9,000 ft.)

**Patrol endurance:** 4 hours, with reserve

**Initial climb rate:** 366 m/min (1,200 f.p.m.)

**Service ceiling:** 6555 m (21,500 ft.)

**Weights:** empty 3955 kg (8,700 lb.); maximum take-off 4853 kg (10,677 lb.)

**Armament:** eight 7.7-mm (.303 cal.) machine-guns in wings

**Dimensions:**
| | | |
|---|---|---|
| span | 14.14 m | (46 ft. 5 in.) |
| length | 12.24 m | (40 ft. 2 in.) |
| height | 4.27 m | (14 ft.) |
| wing area | 31.77 m² | (342 sq. ft.) |

## FULMAR MK I

**From the first production batch, this example is a Fulmar Mk I fitted with the Merlin VIII engine. These aircraft were employed on the Malta convoys and first saw action in September 1940.**

Like the successful Spitfire and Hurricane fighters, the Fulmar was powered by the Rolls-Royce Merlin engine. The Mk II was upgraded with the more powerful Merlin 30.

Unlike the P.4/34, the Fulmar had a non-continuous cockpit canopy. A dinghy was added, as with all naval aircraft, for use in the event of the aircraft ditching.

The rear cockpit housed the navigator/wireless operator who was given the task of finding the Fulmar's floating home in even the worst weather. The second pair of eyes was also very useful during reconnaissance sorties.

The tailplane was raised by 20.3 cm (8 in.) from the prototype, but elevator and rudder control was still fairly heavy. Engine power had to be high during landing so that the slipstream could increase elevator and rudder effectiveness.

ROYAL NAVY  N1860

As with all British fighters of the period, the Fulmar was equipped with a tailwheel-type undercarriage arrangement. The main gear retracted inwards and the tailwheel was fixed.

Modifications from the P.4/34 included reducing the wingspan by 40.6 cm (16 in.) and fitting folding wings for stowing in the confined space aboard aircraft-carriers.

Fairly aerodynamically clean, the Fulmar was structurally strong thanks to its origins as a conventional bomber or dive-bomber. The Fulmar was noted for its ability to take significant punishment and still return home.

### COMBAT DATA

#### MAXIMUM SPEED

Although all three types were powered by the Rolls-Royce Merlin engine, the Fulmar's extra weight and size, incurred by its two-seat design, gave the aircraft mediocre performance. This enabled it to tackle bombers but it was noticeably outclassed by other fighters.

**FULMAR Mk I** — 398 km/h (247 m.p.h.)

**SEA HURRICANE Mk IIC** 550 km/h (341 m.p.h.)

**SEAFIRE Mk III** — 581 km/h (360 m.p.h.)

#### ARMAMENT

Entering service earlier than these other two naval fighters, the Fulmar had only machine-guns to fight with. The Sea Hurricane and Seafire benefited from cannon armament which had greater destructive power, making a 'kill' more likely.

**FULMAR Mk I** — 8 x 7.7-mm (.303 cal.) machine-guns

**SEA HURRICANE Mk IIC** — 4 x 20-mm (0.79-in.) cannon

**SEAFIRE Mk III** — 4 x 7.7-mm (.303 cal.) machine-guns 2 x 20-mm (0.79-in.) cannon, 227-kg (500-lb.) bombload

#### RANGE

Designed from the outset as a naval aircraft, the Fulmar had excellent range and endurance, making it ideal for reconnaissance as well as fighter duties. The Seafire and Sea Hurricane were both developed from land-based fighters, and could not cover such a wide area of ocean.

**FULMAR Mk I** 1136 km (704 mi.)

**SEA HURRICANE Mk IIC** 740 km (459 mi.)

**SEAFIRE Mk III** 748 km (464 mi.)

## Royal Navy Merlin-powered aircraft

■ **HAWKER SEA HURRICANE:** Originally used aboard CAM (Catapult Aircraft Merchantmen) ships, the Sea Hurricane went on to serve successfully on conventional aircraft-carriers.

■ **SUPERMARINE SEAFIRE:** Entering service in 1942, the Seafire was a capable naval fighter, but it was notoriously difficult to land because of its narrow-track undercarriage.

■ **DE HAVILLAND SEA MOSQUITO:** Again a modified land-based aircraft, the Sea Mosquito TR.Mk 33 was used as a carrier- or shore-based long-range strike aircraft.

■ **DE HAVILLAND SEA HORNET:** As the only two-seat version of the Hornet to be produced, the Sea Hornet was the FAA's standard carrier-borne fighter from 1949 to 1954.

# FAIREY

# SWORDFISH

● Carrier-based torpedo-bomber ● Anti-submarine ● Taranto attacker

I t was a most unlikely warplane. A fabric and wire biplane in an age of high-speed monoplanes, the Fairey Swordfish was obsolete before it even entered service. But although it was lumbering and slow, this classic warplane was no anachronism. As a carrier-based torpedo-bomber it amassed a combat record second to none, from the historic attack on the Italian fleet at Taranto to its final years as a radar- and rocket-equipped anti-submarine patroller.

▲ Swordfish crews carried out some of the most devastating attacks of the war and achieved many firsts, including the first torpedo attack on a fleet in home port at Taranto in 1940.

## FAIREY SWORDFISH

▲ **Floatplane Swordfish**
The floatplane version of the Swordfish was an effective aircraft, but the drag from the floats and weight of a torpedo limited its speed quite drastically.

▲ **Strike mission**
Swordfish from HMS Courageous begin an anti-shipping strike. Torpedo attacks required enormous nerve, as the weapon had to be released at close range in the face of heavy gunfire.

▲ **Memorial flight**
Swordfish still fly with the Royal Navy's Historic Flight, and are star attractions at air shows.

▲ **Sub-chaser**
Equipped with radar and rockets, the Swordfish was a lethal foe to U-boats, especially when flying from small escort carriers.

**Slow mover** ▶
A loaded Swordfish could barely make 180 km/h (112 m.p.h.). But it was very stable and could deliver a torpedo accurately.

▲ **Open cockpit**
With little weather protection Swordfish crews were prone to the elements.

### FACTS AND FIGURES

➤ The prototype Swordfish flew on 17 April 1934, when it was known as the T.S.R.II.

➤ At the outbreak of World War II, the Royal Navy's Fleet Air Arm had 13 Swordfish squadrons.

➤ On 13 April 1940 a Swordfish made the Fleet Air Arm's first U-boat kill.

➤ The Swordfish Mk III carried an airborne radar scanner between its mainwheels.

➤ 2391 Swordfishes were built between 1934 and 1944, 1699 by Blackburn.

➤ The last front-line Swordfish squadron disbanded on 21 May 1945.

# PROFILE

# The victor of Taranto

On 11 November 1940, 21 Swordfish torpedo-bombers from the carrier HMS *Illustrious* ripped the heart out of the Italian fleet at Taranto, sending two battleships, a cruiser and a destroyer to the harbour bottom and effectively taking Italy's navy out of the war.

The Swordfish entered service with Britain's Fleet Air Arm (FAA) in 1936, where it became known as the 'Stringbag'. It was originally used with great success as a torpedo-bomber, making the crucial hit on the *Bismarck*, among other feats; but by 1942 it was simply too slow for the job. In an heroic but futile attack on the battlecruisers *Gneisenau* and *Scharnhorst*, five out of six Swordfishes were downed and the flight leader posthumously awarded the Victoria Cross.

But the big biplane still had plenty to offer, and remained in production until 1944. Assigned instead to anti-submarine, mine-laying, bombing and reconnaissance duties, the Swordfish also tested, and used, the FAA's first air-to-ground rocket projectiles.

## SWORDFISH MK II

**The Fairey Swordfish was the most successful British torpedo-bomber of the war, sinking more ships than all the Royal Navy's battleships put together.**

A large notch was cut out of the upper wing to increase crew visibility upwards.

Most Swordfish wore a grey-green sea camouflage scheme, but some were painted white for Arctic operations.

The radio operator/air gunner was not always carried. He enjoyed an excellent field of fire, but the single Vickers 'K' 7.7-mm (.303 cal.) machine-gun would have deterred very few enemy fighter pilots.

A single forward-firing 7.7-mm (.303 cal.) Vickers gun was fitted in the upper fuselage, synchronised to fire through the propeller disc.

The pilot communicated with his crew by a very primitive but effective system of voice pipes, known as 'Gosport tubes'.

The structure of the Swordfish was from an earlier age, with fabric covering and wire bracing. But it was surprisingly strong, and could tolerate a rocket-assisted take-off.

The Pegasus radial engine proved extremely reliable, and was known to keep running even when one cylinder head was blown away by gunfire.

The Swordfish carried standard 457-cm (18-in.) torpedoes. A hit by one of these weapons was enough to fatally damage the steering gear of the *Bismarck*.

A large arrester hook was standard fit in all Swordfish.

## Swordfish Mk II

**Type:** two-/three-seat torpedo-bomber/reconnaissance biplane

**Powerplant:** one 559-kW (750-hp.) Bristol Pegasus XXX nine-cylinder radial piston engine

**Maximum speed:** 222 km/h (138 m.p.h.)

**Range:** 1658 km (1,028 mi.)

**Service ceiling:** 3260 m (10,690 ft.)

**Weights:** empty 2132 kg (4,690 lb.); loaded 3406 kg (7,493 lb.)

**Armament:** one forward-firing 7.7-mm (.303 cal.) Vickers machine-gun in fuselage and one 7.7-mm Lewis or Vickers 'K' gun mounted in rear cockpit; one 730-kg (1,600-lb.) torpedo, or depth charges, mines or bombs up to 680 kg (1,500 lb.), or eight rocket projectiles

**Dimensions:**
| | |
|---|---|
| span | 13.87 m (45 ft.) |
| length | 10.87 m (36 ft.) |
| height | 3.76 m (12 ft.) |
| wing area | 56.39 m² (607 sq. ft.) |

## COMBAT DATA

### MAXIMUM SPEED

Roughly contemporary with the Swordfish, the US Navy's Devastator was a modern low-wing monoplane, as was the Imperial Japanese Navy's 'Kate', which flew some two years after the British 'Stringbag'. Both the other bombers were very much faster than the Swordfish.

SWORDFISH 222 km/h (138 m.p.h.)

TBD DEVASTATOR 330 km/h (205 m.p.h.)

B5N 'KATE' 378 km/h (234 m.p.h.)

### RANGE

In spite of its size, the Swordfish's slow speed and light weight did not place much demand on the engine, and the archaic biplane had a very good range. This was to stand in its favour late in its career, when aircraft based on light carriers could mount anti-submarine patrols over convoys for hours at a time.

B5N 'KATE' 1990 km (1,234 mi.)

SWORDFISH 1658 km (1,028 mi.)

TBD DEVASTATOR 700 km (434 mi.)

### WARLOAD

SWORDFISH one torpedo or 680 kg (1,600 lb.) of bombs

TBD DEVASTATOR one torpedo or 454-kg (1,000-lb.) bomb

B5N 'KATE' one torpedo or 800 kg (1,760 lb.) of bombs

High lift from its biplane wings and sturdy construction meant that the Swordfish could carry almost 30 per cent of its empty weight in weapons. It could hold its own with the much more advanced Japanese 'Kate', and could carry a heavier load than the USA's surprisingly ineffective Devastator.

## Torpedo attackers of World War II

■ **DOUGLAS TBD DEVASTATOR:** The Devastator was a much more advanced aircraft than the Swordfish but was much less successful.

■ **NAKAJIMA B5N 'KATE':** The best torpedo bomber of the early years of World War II, the B5N ripped the heart out of the US Navy at Pearl Harbor.

■ **FAIREY ALBACORE:** Designed to replace the Swordfish, the Albacore was a more modern aircraft built on the same general principles.

■ **GRUMMAN TBF AVENGER:** Tough and very versatile, the highly successful Avenger's combat debut took place at Midway in June 1942.

■ **FAIREY BARRACUDA:** Never performing as well as expected, the ugly Barracuda was nevertheless an effective torpedo- and dive-bomber.

# FIAT

# CR.1

● Italian fighter design ● Inverted sesquiplane ● Exported to Latvia

▲ With its distinctive engine installation and unusual wing layout, the CR.1 was a highly successful inter-war fighter which inspired a generation of Fiat designs.

**D**esigned in 1922 by Ing Celestino Rosatelli to take part in a Regia Aeronautica competition for a new single-seat fighter, the CR.1 was the first of a successful line of biplane fighters built by the Fiat company. Although never seeing combat, the CR.1 was undoubtedly a capable aircraft and was the Italian air force's primary fighter of the late 1920s. The CR.1 was so enduring and popular that the final examples were not retired until 1937.

▲ **Frontal radiator**
A radiator mounted above the propeller hub cooled the eight-cylinder Hispano-Suiza engine. A number of engines were tested.

▲ **Fiat fighter, Fiat engine**
Equipping the CR.1 with a Fiat A.20 engine transformed it into the CR.10. The distinctive radiator installation was lost in this form. Instead, two Lamblin radiators were used, mounted on the undercarriage struts.

▲ **Balanced ailerons**
Small aerofoil surfaces, mounted on the ailerons of the CR.1 and CR.10, acted as aerodynamic balances.

◀ **Minimum bracing**
With its Warren-truss rigid wing-bracing struts, the CR.1 required the minimum of wire rigging.

**Sesquiplane layout** ▶
Fiat remained faithful to the sesquiplane layout for its biplane fighters, although it abandoned the inverted configuration employed on the CR.1.

## FACTS AND FIGURES

➤ The CR.1 prototypes, MM.1 and MM.2, were the first aircraft designated under the current Italian numbering system.

➤ Belgium and Poland tested the CR.1, but did not place production orders.

➤ Modified from the CR.1, the CR.10 was capable of 300 km/h (185 m.p.h.).

➤ The CR.1 was the first of a famous line of successful Fiat biplane fighters that culminated in the CR.42.

➤ The first production CR.1s were delivered to the Regia Aeronautica in 1925.

➤ A single CR.2 was built, fitted with a British Armstrong Siddeley Lynx engine.

## PROFILE

# Fiat's faithful inter-war fighter

Eclipsing its rival the SIAI S.52 biplane, in the competition for a new Italian fighter, the CR.1 was a fast and highly manoeuvrable biplane which entered squadron service in 1925.

Featuring an unusual inverted sesquiplane layout, the CR.1 was meticulously developed at prototype stage. Minor handling problems were ironed out and the design was adapted to fit the requirements. Initial trials were followed by a production order for 109, built by Fiat. Licence-production was subsequently carried out by OFM (later IMAM-Meridionali) with 40 examples, and by SIAI with another 100.

After serving with up to eight Italian front-line squadrons, a number of CR.1s were modified in the early 1930s to take a more powerful Isotta Fraschini engine, which improved performance.

The only export order received was that for nine

*Below: Various refinements were incorporated into the CR.1 in regular service. Several aircraft had their spoked wheels faired over.*

*Above: Fiat tested a single example of the CR.1 with an Armstrong Siddeley Lynx radial, as the CR.2. Belgium, Poland and Latvia tested the CR.1, but only the Baltic state placed an order.*

examples for the Latvian navy. Other variants included the CR.2, CR.5 and CR.10 with various powerplants, but none of them proceeded past prototype stage.

---

## CR.1

**Type:** single-seat fighter biplane

**Powerplant:** one 224-kW (300-hp.) Hispano-Suiza 42 eight-cylinder vee piston engine

**Maximum speed:** 272 km/h (169 m.p.h.)

**Climb rate:** climb to 5000 m (16,000 ft.) in 16 min 27 sec

**Service ceiling:** 7450 m (24,400 ft.)

**Weights:** empty equipped 839 kg (1,845 lb.); maximum take-off 1154 kg (2,540 lb.)

**Armament:** two fixed forward-firing, synchronised 7.7-mm (.303 cal.) Vickers machine-guns

**Dimensions:**
| | |
|---|---|
| span | 8.95 m (29 ft. 4 in.) |
| length | 6.16 m (20 ft. 3 in.) |
| height | 2.40 m (7 ft. 10 in.) |
| wing area | 23 m² (247 sq. ft.) |

---

Built mostly of wood, the CR.1 gained a reputation in service for strength and reliability. The aircraft beat off a challenge from the rival SIAI S.52 to win its initial production orders.

For the CR.1, Fiat produced one of the cleanest engine installations of any 1920s fighter. Some aircraft were re-engined later in their lives, with the 328-kW Isotta Fraschini Asso Caccia engine giving a considerable performance improvement.

Taken literally, the sesquiplane arrangement requires the lower biplane wing to have half the area of the upper wing. This comparatively rare layout was made all the more unusual by Fiat's use of it in an inverted form.

Another unusual feature of the CR.1 was its Warren-truss struts. From the front, they formed a 'W' shape and appeared to be in two sections which ran in parallel along the forward and aft edges of the wing.

With the canvas skinning of the rudder pulled tight over the ribs beneath, the trailing edge appeared to be scalloped. This feature was retained on the CR.20, but discarded thereafter.

### CR.1

**Wearing the typical colours and markings of the 1920s, this CR.1 is depicted in the service of the Regia Aeronautica (Italian air force).**

---

## ACTION DATA

### MAXIMUM SPEED

A comparison of mid- to late 1920s biplane fighters shows the Fiat CR.1 to be considerably faster than either the British Gloster Grebe Mk II or the American Boeing PW-9D. None of these types was to see combat, but all served their countries well.

| | |
|---|---|
| CR.1 | 272 km/h (169 m.p.h.) |
| GREBE Mk II | 245 km/h (152 m.p.h.) |
| PW-9D | 249 km/h (154 m.p.h.) |

### ENDURANCE

Although both the Grebe Mk II and PW-9D were at least 75 kW (100 hp.) more powerful than the CR.1, all had similar endurance. The British and American machines were heavier aircraft with a larger fuel load, but their more powerful, heavier engines consumed fuel at a higher rate and gave them little advantage over the CR.1.

| CR.1 | GREBE Mk II | PW-9D |
|---|---|---|
| 2 hours 35 minutes | 2 hours 45 minutes | 2 hours 50 minutes |

### SERVICE CEILING

Altitude performance was another of the CR.1's qualities. It easily outperformed the Gloster and Boeing aircraft, and was one of the finest fighters of its day.

| CR.1 | GREBE Mk II | PW-9D |
|---|---|---|
| 7450 m (24,400 ft.) | 7010 m (23,000 ft.) | 5557 m (18,000 ft.) |

---

## Fiat's fighter family

■ **CR.20:** Retaining a considerable resemblance to the CR.1, the CR.20 served until 1936 as a fighter trainer. This CR.20bis belonged to the Paraguayan national army air force.

■ **CR.32:** First flown in 1932, the CR.32 was exported widely and served successfully with the Regia Aeronautica. It is best remembered for its service in the Spanish Civil War.

■ **CR.42:** Perhaps the greatest biplane fighter ever, the CR.42 served in great numbers at home and abroad. It saw service in both the Spanish Civil War and World War II.

# FIAT
# CR.32

● Thoroughbred fighter ● Highly aerobatic ● Multi-role aircraft

▲ In August
1936 Italian CR.32s were flown to Spain to fight for the Spanish Nationalists. It became the chief fighter aircraft of the Aviacion Legionaria and was built by Hispano.

One of the most agile biplanes, the Fiat CR.32 fought many air battles over Spain during the civil war but it actually made its combat debut over China against the invading Japanese. Highly regarded by Italian fighter pilots, who loved its superb aerobatic qualities, the little Fiat was strongly built and did well in combat. It was equipped with two 12.7-mm (.50 cal.) guns, which had a better range than the smaller calibre weapons of its opponents.

---

## FIAT CR.32

▲ Spanish squadron
Spanish Nationalists received a full squadron of CR.32s from Italy.

▲ Sturdy fighter
Smaller than the CR.30, the fighter was much stronger and able to withstand the most violent manoeuvres.

Braced biplane ▶
The CR.32 had 'W'-type Warren strut bracing between the unequal span wings, giving it considerable strength.

▼ Built in Spain
The Spanish Nationalists were extremely impressed with the Fiat CR.32 and they decided to build their own version, the Chirri, in Spain. At least 380 took part in air battles against Republican Polikarpov I-15s and I-16s.

▲ Chinese combat
The first 24 CR.32s were ordered by China, but in the event just nine were delivered in 1935 and were used to fly against the invading Japanese.

### FACTS AND FIGURES

➤ Export models of the CR.32 served with the air arms of Austria, Chile, China, Hungary, Paraguay and Spain.

➤ Fiat built over 1,000 CR.32s for the Regia Aeronautica before production ended.

➤ The biplane fighter had outstanding manoeuvrability and was very strong.

➤ During World War II, Spain built its own CR.32s under a licence agreement covering 100 examples made by Hispano.

➤ The CR.32 was obsolete by 1939, but some saw service in World War II.

➤ The final CR.32 was fitted with exhaust shrouds for night flying.

# Fiat's sturdy dogfighter

Flying for the first time on 28 April 1933, the Fiat CR.32 represented a peak of aeronautical design evolution which had begun in the 1920s with the CR.1. Fiat's fabric-covered, light alloy and steel construction resulted in a strong structure and an excellent power-to-weight ratio making the CR.32 an outstanding aerobatic aircraft and a very able dogfighter.

Armed with four machine-guns, the Fiat CR.32 made its combat debut in China. Further action was achieved by Italian pilots in the Spanish civil war, who fought for Franco's Nationalist cause. This 'force within a force' operated in every campaign of the war.

The Fiat's 12.7-mm guns outranged the weapons carried by its opponents, and in dogfights this became a

*Above: With its 12.7-mm (.50 cal.) Breda-SAFAT machine-guns, the CR.32 was a formidable fighter with Franco's forces.*

considerable advantage. The CR.32 was also able to absorb a considerable degree of battle damage and gained a legendary reputation for bringing its pilots home safely.

*Above: When Italy entered the war some 400 CR.32s out of a total of over 1200 single-seat biplane fighters on strength were still in front-line service with the Regia Aeronautica.*

## CR.32

**Type:** single-seat interceptor fighter

**Powerplant:** one 447-kW (560-hp.) Fiat R.A.30 R.A.bis liquid-cooled piston engine

**Maximum speed:** 330 km/h (204 m.p.h.) at sea level; 354 km/h (219 m.p.h.) at 3000 m (10,000 ft.)

**Range:** 780 km (484 mi.) at 315 km/h (195 m.p.h.)

**Service ceiling:** 8800 m (28,865 ft.)

**Weights:** empty 1454 kg (3,205 lb.); loaded 1914 kg (4,220 lb.)

**Armament:** two 12.7-mm and two 7.7-mm (.303 cal.) Breda-SAFAT machine-guns; rack under fuselage for one 100-kg (220-lb.) or two 50-kg (110-lb.) bombs

**Dimensions:**
| | | |
|---|---|---|
| span | 9.50 m (31 ft.) | |
| length | 7.45 m (24 ft.) | |
| height | 2.63 m (9 ft.) | |
| wing area | 22.1 m² (238 sq. ft.) | |

---

Armament normally comprised two 12.7-mm (.50 cal.) Breda-SAFAT machine-guns housed in the upper cowling and firing through the propeller. Two 7.7-mm Breda machine-guns could be carried in the lower wings.

The CR.32 was very much a pilot's aircraft, with a pleasant cockpit and excellent controls. The similar CR.40 had the top wing attached to the top of the fuselage.

The aircraft had all-metal tail construction with fabric-covered rudder and elevators. The tailplane was braced to the base of the rear fuselage and the tailwheel was spatted to reduce drag.

**V.137**

## CR.32

First flown on 28 April 1933, the CR.32 was one of the top single-seat fighters of the early 1930s. A total of 1,312 aircraft were built in Italy and Spain up until 1943. Most were flown by the Regia Aeronautica (Italian air force), although the Spanish air force was the last to fly them.

The fuselage and wings were of conventional steel framing with light-alloy formers and, in the main, covered by fabric. The unequal span wings were substantially braced in 'W' form with additional wire bracing in between for added strength.

This CR.32 is in the Hungarian air force colours of 1939. A total of 90 CR.32s were flown by the Hungarians, including 38 originally delivered to Austria.

The CR.32's engine was a 447-kW (560-hp.) Fiat R.A.30 R.A.bis inverted, in-line piston engine, driving a two-blade propeller.

## ACTION DATA

### MAXIMUM SPEED

The CR.32's Fiat RA.30 engine gave it a top speed of 354 km/h (219 m.p.h.) at 3000 metres (10,000 ft.), which was good for the early 1930s. It was not as fast as the cleaner-designed Gladiator, but had comparable performance to the bulky Polikarpov I-15.

| | |
|---|---|
| CR.32 | 354 km/h (219 m.p.h.) |
| GLADIATOR | 414 km/h (257 m.p.h.) |
| I-15 | 367 km/h (228 m.p.h.) |

### SERVICE CEILING

Although the CR.32 had good manoeuvrability it did not have the Gladiator's power to climb to high altitude, its ceiling being some 2770 metres (9,000 ft.) less than the RAF fighter. The Wright-Cyclone-powered I-15 also had a better service ceiling than the CR.32.

| CR.32 8800 m (28,865 ft.) | GLADIATOR 11,570 m (37,950 ft.) | I-15 9800 m (32,144 ft.) |
|---|---|---|

### RANGE

With its large fuel tanks, the CR.32 had a maximum range of 780 km (484 mi.) at a constant speed of 315 km/h (195 m.p.h.). This was 10 per cent better than the Gladiator's range and appreciably more than the short-range Polikarpov I-15.

| | |
|---|---|
| CR.32 | 780 km (484 mi.) |
| GLADIATOR | 706 km (438 mi.) |
| I-15 | 510 km (316 mi.) |

---

## Fiat biplane fighter aircraft

■ **CR.1:** Equipping the newly reformed Regia Aeronautica in the 1920s, 240 CR.1s were built. The type was modified with more powerful Isotta-Fraschini engines in the 1930s, and the type soldiered on until 1937 before being retired.

■ **CR.20:** Used extensively in the campaigns in Abyssinia and Libya, the Fiat-engine-powered CR.20 was also exported to Lithuania and Hungary. In the early 1930s the type was the mainstay of the Regia Aeronautica fighter strength.

■ **CR.42 'FALCO':** Used widely in Libya in World War II, the CR.42 was a very good biplane fighter but was totally outclassed by the RAF's Hurricanes and Gladiators. The Luftwaffe also used the CR.42 during the war for night-attack duties.

# FIAT

# CR.42

● Italian fighter ● Manoeuvrable biplane ● Unequal-span wings

▲ An ignominious end for a CR.42 of 95ª Squadriglia of the Corpo Aereo Italiani. Poor training and a lack of support equipment had contributed to low CR.42 availability.

**B**y the late 1930s most of the leading warplane producers were abandoning open-cockpit, fabric-covered biplane designs in favour of stressed-skin monoplanes with a retractable landing gear. But in Italy, Celestino Rosatelli of Fiat believed there was still a role for a highly manoeuvrable biplane fighter. Fiat thus produced the CR.42 Falco, the best fighter available to either side in North Africa from the start of the war until the arrival of the RAF's Hawker Hurricane.

---

## PHOTO FILE

# FIAT CR.42

### Effective camouflage ▶
*The Italian air force adopted a new dappled, two-tone brown camouflage for its Fiat CR.42s operating in North Africa.*

### ▼ Foreign sales
Sixty-eight CR.42s were ordered by the Hungarian air force in 1941. Falcos took part in the campaign against Yugoslavia.

### With the Swedish air force ▶
*One of Sweden's 72 CR.42s of J 11/3 Division, operating from Save in 1942.*

### ▼ Aegean theatre
*Italian CR.42s operated in 1941 from the Isle of Scarpanto.*

### Hungarian Fast Corps ▶
*Flying in the Soviet Union during late 1941, this CR.42 was flown by 1/3 Sqn, 1/II Group of the Hungarian Fast Corps.*

---

## FACTS AND FIGURES

➤ Although the prototype CR.42 did not fly until January 1939, it entered service with the Italian air force the following November.

➤ A robust, clean and fast design, it was already obsolete when it entered service.

➤ The CR.42 was the last biplane fighter produced by Fiat.

➤ Fifty CR.42s provided the Italian fighter element operating from Belgium against England during 1940/41.

➤ Overall production of all CR.42 versions totalled 1784.

➤ One CR.42 was built in 1940 as a twin-float seaplane.

# Last of the Fiat biplane fighters

After World War I, the Fiat company commenced production of a series of biplane fighters. These aircraft became the mainstay of the Italian air force's fighter squadrons. By the early 1930s, the CR.32 was in service. This was to be the main fighter in Franco's forces during the Spanish Civil War in 1936.

By the late 1930s, most of the world's major air forces were gradually re-equipping with low-wing monoplane fighters. Fiat still believed that there was a place for the biplane and designed the CR.42, with the prototype making its maiden flight in January 1939. It was instantly ordered into production for the Italian air force. With a number of export orders following, some 1784 had been built by 1943.

In service with the Regia Aeronautica, CR.42s were used as day fighters and escort fighters in the Mediterranean theatre and as night-fighters for home defence.

By 1942, Fiat had managed to raise the top speed to 518 km/h (322 m.p.h.) but the design still fell short in other respects. Biplane fighter production was at an end.

*Above: A converted two-seat trainer version of the CR.42, painted overall silver with the markings of the post-war Sezione Autonoma Collegiamenti.*

*Below: A standard Italian air force fighter in the markings of 95ª Squadriglia, 18º Gruppo. It had a bright yellow engine cowling and spinner on the three-bladed propeller.*

## CR.42 Falco

**Type:** single-seat biplane fighter

**Powerplant:** one 626-kW (840-hp.) Fiat A.74 R1C.38 14-cylinder, two-row radial piston engine

**Maximum speed:** 420 km/h (261 m.p.h.)

**Initial climb rate:** 732 m/min (2,402 f.p.m.)

**Combat range:** 775 km (482 mi.)

**Service ceiling:** 10,500 m (34,450 ft.)

**Weights:** empty 1782 kg (3,929 ft.); maximum take-off 2295 kg (5,060 lb.)

**Armament:** two fixed forward-firing Breda-SAFAT 12.7-mm (.50 cal.) machine-guns, plus up to 198 kg (437 lb.) of bombs

**Dimensions:**
| | |
|---|---|
| span | 9.70 m (31 ft. 10 in.) |
| length | 8.27 m (27 ft. 2 in.) |
| height | 3.59 m (11 ft. 9 in.) |
| wing area | 22.40 m² (241 sq. ft.) |

### CR.42 FALCO

This CR.42 carries the markings of the 97ª Squadriglia, 9º Gruppo 'Caccia Terrestre', of the Regia Aeronautica's 4º Stormo based at Benina in Libya during 1940.

The wing was manufactured from light alloy and steel, with a fabric covering. Ailerons were fitted only to the top wings.

The pilot's open cockpit was situated aft of the cut-out in the trailing edge of the upper wing to give better all-round vision.

CR.42s were powered by a Fiat A.74R1C.38 radial air-cooled, geared and supercharged engine.

CR.42s featured a sesquiplane with rigidly-braced wings constructed in two sections, joined at the centreline and supported above the fuselage.

The steel-tube fuselage structure was welded and faired to an oval section and covered with metal panels from the cockpit forwards. The rear section was fabric-covered.

A faired, non-retractable tailwheel was situated at the end of the lower fuselage. A fuel tank was situated in the rear fuselage behind a fireproof bulkhead.

The fixed main landing gear had two oleo-pneumatic legs.

### COMBAT DATA

#### MAXIMUM SPEED

Clearly, in terms of its speed performance the biplane had had its day by 1940. Hawker's Hurricane, which equipped RAF fighter squadrons in large numbers, was a full 100 km/h (62 m.p.h.) faster. The Luftwaffe's Messerschmitt Bf 109 was faster still.

| | |
|---|---|
| CR.42 | 420 km/h (261 m.p.h.) |
| HURRICANE Mk I | 520 km/h (323 m.p.h.) |
| Bf 109E-7 | 578 km/h (359 m.p.h.) |

#### ARMAMENT

With only two machine-guns, the CR.42 was also out-gunned by the monoplane fighters of the day. However, as a biplane the Fiat was a comparatively manoeuvrable machine.

| | |
|---|---|
| CR.42 FALCO | 2 x 12.7-mm (.50 cal.) machine-guns |
| HURRICANE Mk I | 8 x 7.7-mm (.50 cal.) machine-guns |
| Bf 109E-7 | 1 x 20-mm (0.79-in.) cannon, 4 x 7.9-mm (0.31-in.) MGs |

#### RANGE

The range advantage enjoyed by the German Messerschmitt Bf 109 was useful in the type's escort role during the Battle of Britain. The Fiat's range was much less but actually slightly superior to that of early models of the RAF's Hurricane.

CR.42 FALCO 775 km (482 mi.)

Bf 109E-7 1094 km (680 mi.)

HURRICANE Mk I 740 km (460 mi.)

## CR.42s in three liveries

**BELGIUM:** Serving with the Belgian air force in May 1940, this CR.42, one of 15 in service, had Italian-style camouflage markings but a Belgian roundel and white cocette.

**NORTH AFRICA:** This Italian air force CR.42 carries the colours of the 20ª Squadriglia, 46º Gruppo Assolto, 15º Stormo that served in North Africa in the summer of 1942.

**BATTLE OF BRITAIN:** An Italian air force CR.42 from the 18º Gruppo 'Caccia Terrestre', based in Belgium and operating over southern England during the Battle of Britain in 1940.

# FIAT

# G.55 CENTAURO

● Fastest Italian fighter ● Daimler-Benz powered ● Post-war service

▲ Similar in appearance to the Macchi 202 and 205, the Fiat G.55 Centauro was an excellent Italian fighter which was unique in being adopted for the torpedo-bombing role.

**J**ust as a powerful in-line engine transformed the Macchi MC.202 into the MC.205, the same powerplant resulted in the Fiat G.55 – a speedy derivative of the sluggish G.50 Freccia. The G.55 Centauro (Centaur) was produced in limited numbers before the armistice in September 1943, but production continued in German-held parts of Italy. Most Centauros served with the Italian forces that fought alongside the Luftwaffe until 1945.

▼ **German powerplant**
Originally intended to be powered by a Fiat A38, the G.55 was fitted with a licence-built Daimler-Benz DB 605 V12 engine.

▲ **Maximum velocity**
Two G.56s, with DB.603 engines, were built. This would have been the fastest Italian fighter of the war, but production was cancelled.

**Postwar service** ▶
Production was resumed after the end of the war and the G.55 served with the Aeronautica Militare Italiana (AMI) until the early 1950s.

◀ **Two-seat Centaur**
A two-seat derivative, known as the G.55B, was also built but did not fly until 1946. Ten were supplied to the AMI, and a further 15 were purchased by Argentina.

**Allied to the Luftwaffe** ▶
After the Armistice a small number of G.55s continued to fly with the Aviazione Nazionale Repubblicana (Fascist Republic Air Arm) alongside the Germans.

## FACTS AND FIGURES

➤ Built in direct competition with the Macchi MC.205 and Reggiane 2005, the G.55 was the best aircraft.

➤ Centauros first saw action during the defence of Rome in 1943.

➤ One of the two Fiat G.56s survived the war and was used as a testbed.

➤ Heavy bombardment by the Allies in 1944 meant that Fiat was not able to supply enough G.55s to the front line.

➤ A Fiat test pilot, Serafino Agostini, flew a British prisoner of war to safety in a G.55.

➤ Torpedo bombing saved the Centauro and enabled post-war production.

# PROFILE

# Fiat's flying Centaur

Left: An elegant design, the G.55 was also sturdy and its airframe could withstand very high g manoeuvres during dogfights.

Despite their pre-war success with powerful in-line engines installed in Schneider Trophy racing seaplanes, Italian fighter manufacturers concentrated on radial engines for their fighters of the 1930s. Consequently, when war began in 1939 the Regia Aeronautica's fighter units were ill-equipped. Aircraft like the Fiat G.50 were underpowered and suffered at the hands of more modern Allied types. In addressing this problem,

manufacturers developed new variants of these machines, fitted with more powerful German engines. The Daimler-Benz DB.605, which powered the Luftwaffe's Messerschmitt Bf 109G and late-model Bf 110s, was put into production by Fiat as the RA.1050 Tifone (Typhoon). This engine was installed in both the Macchi MC.205 and a reworked Fiat G.50, the G.55.

The resulting aircraft vie for the title of the best Italian fighter of the period. First flown in

April 1942, the G.55 was an all-metal aircraft armed with three 20-mm (0.79-in.) cannon and two machine-guns and carried a modest bombload. Very few were delivered before the Italian surrender in 1943, but continued production allowed a small number to see service with the fascist Aeronautica Nazionale Repubblicana, fighting alongside the Luftwaffe.

Above: Surviving G.55s were pressed into service with the fledgling air arm of the Fascist Republic in 1944. Many of them were destroyed or damaged during Allied air attacks.

## G.55/I Centauro

**Type:** single-seat fighter and torpedo-bomber

**Powerplant:** one 1100-kW (1,475-hp.) Fiat RA 1050 Tifone (Daimler-Benz DB 605A) inverted V12 liquid-cooled piston engine

**Maximum speed:** 630 km/h (391 m.p.h.)

**Range:** 1200 km (744 mi.)

**Service ceiling:** 12,700 m (41,700 ft.)

**Weights:** empty 2630 kg (5,786 lb.); loaded 3520 kg (8,180 lb.)

**Armament:** three 20-mm (0.79-in.) Mauser MG 151/20e cannon and two fuselage-mounted Breda SAFAT 12.7-mm (.50 cal.) machine-guns, plus two 160-kg (352-lb.) bombs on underwing racks

**Dimensions:**
| | |
|---|---|
| span | 11.85 m (38 ft. 10 in.) |
| length | 9.37 m (30 ft. 9 in.) |
| height | 3.13 m (10 ft. 3 in.) |
| wing area | 21.11 m² (227 sq. ft.) |

## G.55S CENTAURO

Powering this sleek fighter was a Fiat RA 1050 Tifone inverted V12 engine. A licence-built version of the Daimler-Benz DB.605, this gave the G.55 superb performance.

A high mounted cockpit offered superb visibility for the Centauro pilot and was similar to that found on the rival MC.205 Veltro. The heavily framed canopy hinged to starboard for entry and exit.

**Designed to replaced the tri-motored SM. 79s in the torpedo bombing role, the G.55S saved the design from extinction, though this variant had failed to enter service in wartime.**

Common characteristics of many Italian World War II fighters were fragile tail surfaces. The Centauro did not suffer from such problems and in the air possessed viceless handling.

Centauros were to be seen in a variety of colour schemes. This example wears a distinctive two-tone mottled camouflage.

A wide-track undercarriage gave the G.55 excellent ground handling. Both main oleos were immensely strong and hydraulically actuated, retracting inward for flight.

When the aircraft was fully laden with a 930-kg (2,046 lb.) torpedo, pilots felt the G.55S to be slow and lumbering, though it was by no means an easy target for enemy fighters.

To provide adequate ground clearance for the massive torpedo, the tail wheel oleo had to be extended and strengthened.

## COMBAT DATA

### MAXIMUM SPEED

Sleek and fast, the Fiat G.55 and Reggiane Re.2005 were arguably two of the best fighters of World War II. The Reggiane Re.2001 Falco was slightly slower because of the drag induced by the its larger powerplant.

| | |
|---|---|
| G.55 CENTAURO | 630 km/h (391 m.p.h.) |
| Re.2005 SAGITTARIO | 630 km/h (391 m.p.h.) |
| Re.2000 FALCO I | 529 km/h (328 m.p.h.) |

### OPERATIONAL RANGE

The range of Italian late-war fighters was adequate, with the G.55 having one of the greatest endurances. It was, however, poorer than that of the US Fifteenth Air Force's North American P-51 Mustangs, which began arriving in the Mediterranean theatre of operations in large numbers during the spring of 1944.

G.55 CENTAURO 1200 km (744 mi.)

Re.2000 FALCO I 1400 km (868 mi.)

Re.2005 SAGITTARIO 1250 km (775 mi.)

### NORMAL TAKE-OFF WEIGHT

Lighter than the Re.2005, the Centauro also had slightly better handling, in the air and on the ground. Both were heavier still than the radial-engined Falco which owed much to American fighter design, particularly that of the Republic P-43 Lancer.

| G.55 CENTAURO | Re.2005 SAGITTARIO | Re.2000 FALCO I |
|---|---|---|
| 3520 kg (8,180 lb.) | 3610 kg (7,942 lb.) | 2595 kg (5,709 lb.) |

## Daimler-Benz powered late-war fighters

**KAWASAKI Ki-61 HIEN 'TONY':** This superb fighter was unique in Japanese service in being powered by a liquid-cooled in-line engine.

**MACCHI MC.205 VELTRO:** Based on the MC. 202 Folgolore, the Veltro (Greyhound) was capable of meeting the P-51 on even terms.

**REGGIANE Re.2005 SAGITTARIO:** Only 48 examples of Reggiane's most capable fighter ever saw operational service, with Gruppo 22°.

**MESSERSCHMITT Bf 109K:** Among the last variants of this famous aircraft, the K was more powerful but less agile than earlier Bf 109s.

# FIESELER

# FI 156 STORCH

● Observation aircraft ● Short take-off and landing

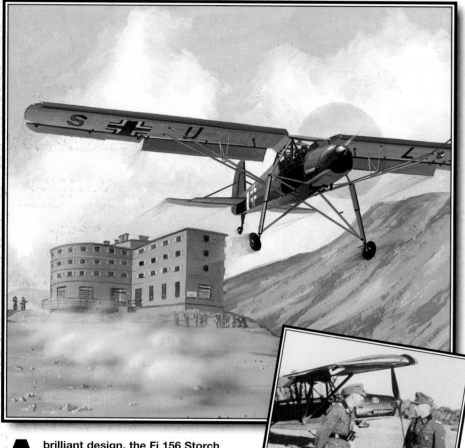

**A** brilliant design, the Fi 156 Storch was so perfect at what it did that even if it was designed today, 60 years after its first flight, it could not be improved. The best observation and army co-operation aircraft of World War II, it had an almost unbelievable short take-off and landing capability, reflected in an uncanny ability to operate out of restricted spaces and to perform a wide variety of liaison tasks.

▲ *Storch missions*
*varied from the humdrum air-taxi job of ferrying Wehrmacht officers to the front line to the dramatic rescue of Benito Mussolini from mountain-top captivity.*

## FIESELER FI 156 STORCH

**▲ Crash landing**
*The light construction of the Storch meant that battle damage usually brought it down. The best defence of the Storch was to fly as low and as slow as possible to avoid fighters.*

**▲ Alpine Storch**
*The Storch was especially useful to the Swiss, because the mountainous terrain was often only accessible to short take-off planes.*

**Ski Storch ▶**
*Croatian forces found the Storch a useful machine when fitted with skis. It was also easy to manhandle when on the ground.*

**▲ Czech made**
*The Storch was so good that after the end of World War II large numbers were produced in both Czechoslovakia and France.*

**Light weight ▶**
*This view shows just how tiny a Storch was. The aircraft weighed less than a modern family car.*

**▲ Multi-role**
*The Fi 156C-5 was able to carry an underfuselage drop-tank or an optional camera, and had an improved Argus 10P engine.*

## FACTS AND FIGURES

➤ The prototype Fi 156 Storch flew on or around 24 May 1936.

➤ In 1943, an Fi 156 rescued Italy's Benito Mussolini by landing and taking off in less than 100 metres (330 ft.) at high altitude.

➤ The last plane to take off before the fall of Berlin in May 1945 was a Storch.

➤ The Fi 256 was a concept similar to the Storch which would have served as a four-place civil aircraft.

➤ Between 1937–45, the Luftwaffe accepted just short of 2900 Storchs.

➤ Numerous Storchs are still flying today, appearing as warbirds at air shows.

# PROFILE

# The plane that flew everywhere

Gerhard Fieseler, an ace of the Great War with 22 victories, combined with designers Reinhold Mewes and Erich Bachem to create a most remarkable aircraft with the high wing, flaps and stalky landing gear needed to land and take off almost anywhere.

No Allied warplane measured up to the Storch, which in a stiff breeze could land in a matter of metres. But apart from its obvious qualities as a liaison

and spotter craft, the Fi 156 was incredibly versatile. It was so manoeuvrable at speeds of less than 55 km/h (35 m.p.h.) that it could elude much faster fighters; it could be rigged to drop small bombs, and one was even tested against a U-boat with 135-kg (300-lb.) depth charges. There was seemingly nothing the Storch could not do.

In the end, the Fi 156 even landed and took off in a Berlin under siege from advancing

*Morane-Saulnier of France had produced the Fi 156 during World War II. After the end of the war, it built the MS.500, 501 and 502. A projected five-seat version was not produced.*

Russian armies. The Storch outlived the Third Reich, and remained in production in Czechoslovakia and France long after the war.

*Although the Storch looked flimsy with its braced construction and fabric covering, it was in fact a very sturdy aircraft.*

*The long, straight wing, with its flaps and slats, could keep the Storch airborne at almost any airspeed, and it could 'hover' when flying into a breeze.*

## Fi 156C Storch

**Type:** three-seat liaison, observation and rescue aircraft

**Powerplant:** one 179-kW (240-hp.) Argus As 10C-3 inverted Vee-8 air-cooled piston engine

**Maximum speed:** 175 km/h (108 m.p.h.)

**Range:** 385 km (239 mi.)

**Service ceiling:** about 6800 m (22,300 ft.)

**Weights:** empty 930 kg (2,046 lb.); loaded 1325 kg (2,915 lb.)

**Armament:** provision for one 7.92-mm (0.3-in.) MG 15 machine-gun with four spare 75-round magazines

**Dimensions:** 
| | |
|---|---|
| span | 14.25 m (47 ft.) |
| length | 9.90 m (32 ft.) |
| height | 3.00 m (10 ft.) |
| wing area | 26.00 m² (280 sq. ft.) |

## FI 156C-3 STORCH

**This Storch served with a Kurierstaffel of the Luftwaffe in the communications role.**

*The secret of the Storch's remarkable performance was its wing. The slotted ailerons and flaps were advanced features when the Storch was designed in the 1930s.*

*The Storch carried a 7.92-mm machine-gun for defence, but very few crews ever managed to shoot their way out of trouble.*

*The Fi 156E-0 had a tandem wheeled undercarriage with a pneumatic rubber track linking each wheel.*

*Most Storchs had a tailskid, as the landing and take-off were so short that a tailwheel was not really a necessity.*

*The Storch featured 'long travel' undercarriage legs, rather like a modern trail bike, that could cope with the bumpy landing on rough strips.*

*With a high-mounted wing and a canopy that protruded outside the airframe, the Storch was an excellent spotter plane. But it was very vulnerable to enemy small-arms fire.*

### COMBAT DATA

#### CRUISING SPEED

High speed is not a prerequisite for army co-operation aircraft. Aircraft like the Storch are at their most effective when flying slowly: in a light breeze the Storch could take off in less than 70 m (230 ft.), and could land in about one-third of that distance.

| | |
|---|---|
| Fi 156C STORCH | 130 km/h (80 m.p.h.) |
| L-4 GRASSHOPPER | 121 km/h (75 m.p.h.) |
| AUSTER Mk V | 180 km/h (112 m.p.h.) |

#### LOADED WEIGHT

**Fi 156C STORCH** 1325 kg (2,915 lb.)
**L-4 GRASSHOPPER** 533 kg (1,173 lb.)
**AUSTER Mk V** 840 kg (1,848 lb.)

Observation craft do not need to carry weapons or heavy cargo, and are generally of very light construction. In spite of its frail appearance, the Storch was more solidly-built than its British or American equivalents.

#### RANGE

Endurance is more important than range in an observation aircraft. Although its range was negligible, the Storch was usually based very close to the front line, and flew so slowly that it could stay in the air for two or three hours at a time.

FI 156C STORCH 385 km (239 mi.)
L-4 GRASSHOPPER 300 km (286 mi.)
AUSTER Mk V 400 km (248 mi.)

## World War II Army co-operation

**HENSCHEL Hs 126:** Larger than the Storch, the Henschel served as a spotter and reconnaissance aircraft in the first years of World War II.

**FOCKE-WULF Fw 189:** Replacing the Hs 126, the Fw 189 'Uhu' became the Luftwaffe's most important 'eye in the sky' on the Eastern Front.

**WESTLAND LYSANDER:** Closer to the Henschel than the Storch, the Lysander won fame landing British agents in occupied Europe.

**POLIKARPOV U-2:** This archaic Russian biplane served with distinction in roles as varied as air ambulance and harassment bomber.

**PIPER L-4 GRASSHOPPER:** America built thousands of light liaison aircraft. By far the most successful was the long-serving L-4.

# FIESELER
# FI 167

● Ship-based design ● Torpedo bomber ● Reconnaissance aircraft

▲ *Erprobungsstaffel 167*
*received 12 Fi 167s for service trials. Some aircraft went on to perform undercarriage tests, while the remainder were sold to Rumania.*

**V**ery few prototypes equal their target specification without further modification and development. Even fewer exceed all expectations, but the Fi 167 can rightfully claim a place in this elite group. Designed as a torpedo bomber and general reconnaissance aircraft for Germany's aircraft carrier, the *Graf Zeppelin*, Fiesler's Fi 167 was to play only a minor role in World War II after construction of the carrier ceased.

## FIESELER FI 167

▲**Folding for the** *Graf*
*Folding wings allowed the Fi 167 to take up minimum deck space.*

▲ **Naval features**
*Jettisonable main undercarriage units increased the Fi 167A-0's chances of a successful ditching.*

▼ **Purposeful design**
*Large flaps and slats gave the Fi 167 exceptional flying qualities. None ever flew from a ship.*

▲ **Pre-production batch**
*Fi 167s entered service in the second half of 1940 and flew a range of service evaluations and trials, until their withdrawal from the Netherlands in 1943.*

**Tall and angular** ▶
*The unusually stalky and awkward appearance of the Fi 167 resulted in an aircraft that was exceptionally well suited to its design role.*

## FACTS AND FIGURES

➤ Fiesler was so pleased with initial trials that it completed only the Fi 167V1 and V2 prototypes, abandoning V3.

➤ Reinhold Mewes designed the Fi 167 for maximum maintainability.

➤ Fi 167s carried out tests to find the best camouflage for maritime operations.

➤ Erprobungsstaffel 167 returned to Germany to disband. Three of its aircraft then went on to undercarriage trials.

➤ Trials were flown with the Fi 167 as a heavily loaded sesqui (wing-and-a-half) plane.

➤ Daimler-Benz used the 11th Fi 167A-0 as an engine testbed.

# PROFILE

# Striking from the *Graf Zeppelin*

Launched in December 1938, the Graf Zeppelin was to be the pride of the German navy's fleet.

A considerable force of aircraft would be required to arm the new ship and in 1937 a specification was issued for a two-seat general-purpose machine, capable of flying in the torpedo-bombing role.

Two companies submitted prototypes, but Arado's Ar 195 was little more than a redesigned Ar 95 and it failed to meet the requirements of the specification.

Conversely, the Fi 167 was a superb aircraft that exceeded all requirements and exhibited stunning slow-speed performance. With the engine throttled right back and the elevators deflected fully upward, the aircraft would sink almost vertically. Gerhard Fiesler once climbed the aircraft 3050 m (10,000 ft.) over the same spot on the ground!

With the cancellation of the Graf Zeppelin, 12 Fi 167A-0 aircraft briefly entered service, flying from Dutch land bases.

*Below: If Graf Zeppelin had been completed, the Fi 167 might never have flown from it. In 1942, it was decided that the Ju 87E could adequately fulfill the torpedo bomber and reconnaissance role.*

*Above: By removing a number of light-weight metal panels, access was gained to the whole powerplant unit.*

## Fi 167A-0

**Type:** Two-seat ship-based general-purpose reconnaissance/torpedo bomber biplane.

**Powerplant:** One 820-kW (1,100-hp.) Daimler-Benz DB601B 12-cylinder inverted-Vee

**Maximum speed:** 325 km/h (202 m.p.h.) in the recon role

**Climb rate:** 2.7 min. to 1000 m (3,280 ft.)

**Range:** 1545 km (930 mi.) on a recon mission with a 364-litre (80-gal.) drop tank.

**Service ceiling:** 8200 m (26,900 ft.)

**Weights:** Empty 2974 kg (6,160 lb.); max take-off 4840 kg (10,670 lb.)

**Weapons:** One 7.92-mm MG 15 machine gun in the rear cockpit; one fixed forward-firing 7.92-mm MG 17 machine gun; and 1000 kg (2,200 lb.) of bombs or one 765-kg (1,686-lb.) torpedo.

**Dimensions:**
| | | |
|---|---|---|
| span | 13.51 m | (44 ft. 4 in.) |
| length | 11.41 m | (37 ft. 5 in.) |
| height | 4.76 m | (15 ft. 8 in.) |
| wing area | 48.50 m² | (522 sq. ft.) |

## Fi 167A-0

**The aircraft shown was based in the Netherlands with Erprobungsstaffel 167 during 1942. Several camouflage schemes were worn.**

Automatic leading-edge slats were fitted to both upper and lower wings, helping to give the Fi 167 its incredible handling qualities. The aircraft was also faster than required by the original specification.

Designed not only for ease of manufacture as well as maintenance, the center fuselage was covered with light alloy sheet and the rear fuselage was a stressed-skin monocoque.

Mounted on a pivot-mount, the rear machine gun could defend the rear upper area of the airplane. Remarkably, the Fi 167 carried twice the required bomb load.

Compared to the prototypes, the Fi 167A-0 pre-production aircraft had modified flame-damping exhausts and improved inlets and outlets for the DB601B's supercharger.

Large fairings covered the long undercarriage legs. Strong shock-absorbers were fitted to withstand the force of a heavy carrier landing. Larger low-pressure tires were also included on the Fi 167A-0s.

Large trailing-edge flaps were mounted on the lower wing only. The wings were designed to fold at a point just outboard of the main undercarriage attachment points.

As a specialized naval aircraft, the Fi 167 was fitted with an arrester hook from the outset. A combination of the Graf Zeppelin's cancellation and Ju 87 developments denied the Fi 167 any opportunity to fly from a carrier.

## Warplanes of the German fleet

■ **ARADO Ar 195:** Unsuccessful in competition with the Fi 167, the Ar 195 suffered from excessive drag.

■ **ARADO Ar 197:** In 1936, Germany had no experience with carrier aircraft, hence Arado's decision to build a simple biplane fighter.

■ **JUNKERS Ju 87:** Although represented here by the Ju 87B, two naval variants of the Ju 87 were proposed: the Ju 87C and Ju 87E.

■ **MESSERSCHMITT Bf 109T:** Based on the Bf 109E, the Bf 109T-1 had a larger wing area, arrester hook and other modifications.

## ACTION DATA

### SPEED

For maximum effectiveness, especially in the reconnaissance role, a reasonably high cruising speed with economical fuel burn is essential. The Fi 167A-0 greatly outperforms the Swordfish in this respect, but falls short of the navalized Ju 87C-0.

| | |
|---|---|
| Fi 167A-0 | 269 km/h (167 m.p.h.) |
| SWORDFISH Mk II | 208 km/h (129 m.p.h.) |
| Ju 87C-0 | 335 km/h (208 m.p.h.) |

### WEAPONS

Using its rear, pivot-mounted machine gun for defence while attacking with its forward gun and 1000 kg) (2,200-lb.) ordnance load, the Fi 167 would have packed a much harder punch than either the Fairey Swordfish Mk III or Junkers Ju 87C-0.

**Fi 167A-0** — 2 x 7.92-mm machine guns 1000-kg (2,200-lb.) bomb load

**SWORDFISH Mk II** — 2 x 7.7-mm machine guns, 1000-kg (2,200-lb.) bomb load

**Ju 87C-0** — 3 x 7.92-mm machine guns 500-kg (1,100-lb.) bomb load

### RANGE

Junkers proposed the Ju 87C-0 as a naval aircraft capable of reconnaissance, dive bombing, and general duties. As such, it took over much of the Fi 167's role. In reconnaissance configuration, however, it could not match the Fi 167 in range.

**Fi 167A-0** 1297 km (806 mi.)
**SWORDFISH Mk II** 1654 km (1,028 mi.)
**Ju 87C-0** 789 km (490 mi.)

# FLETTNER

# FL 282 KOLIBRI

● Operational helicopter ● Highly manoeuvrable ● All weather

▲ Kolibris quickly proved their worth flying a variety of missions with the German navy. The aircraft were very stable and performed well.

**F**lettner, together with Sikorsky, pioneered the design and production of the military helicopter. The Fl 282 Kolibri was the result of Flettner's experience with rotorcraft and was fitted with intermeshing rotors mounted side-by-side. The aircraft was operated successfully as a reconnaissance platform for the German navy, from both shore bases and ships. The Luftwaffe also used the Kolibri for rescue and resupply missions in the later stages of the war.

▼ **Post-war testing**
Three aircraft were claimed by the Allies. Two, including the V15 prototype shown here, went to the US, and one went to the USSR.

▲ **Kolibri prototypes**
To speed up development, 30 prototypes were ordered in 1940. Here V23 is seen in the US.

◄ **Enclosed single-seater**
Only the first three prototypes were completed with enclosed cockpits, as seen on V3. These were the only single-seat Fl 282s.

◄ **Into service**
With 20 aircraft completed by 1943, some, including V6, were assigned to convoy protection in the Aegean and Mediterranean.

**Shipborne ►
operations**
V5 paved the way for naval operations in harsh conditions by flying from a platform above a gun turret on the cruiser Köln in the Baltic. Here V6 is recovered by a ship in the Aegean.

## FACTS AND FIGURES

➤ Only 24 of the 30 prototypes and 15 pre-production aircraft were completed before the end of the war.

➤ One Fl 282 accumulated 95 flying hours without any repairs.

➤ Pulling back violently on the controls could cause the rotors to strike the fin.

➤ One aircraft is retained at the Midland Air Museum in Coventry and another at the US Air Force Museum, Ohio.

➤ Using his Fl 282 experience, Flettner began designing the 20-passenger Fl 339.

➤ Hans E. Fuisting performed most of the Fl 282 test-flying.

## PROFILE

# Hummingbird goes to war

Anton Flettner had tried several schemes for helicopters before hitting on the 'egg-beater' system. The two twin-bladed rotors cancelled out each other's torque, so there was no need for additional rotors. In 1938 Flettner's Fl 265 won a small order from the German navy.

In addition to flying trials from surface ships and submarines, one of the six Fl 265s was tested in simulated combat against Bf 109 and Fw 190 fighters. It was able to evade their gunsights for a full 20 minutes and led to

increased military confidence in the improved Fl 282.

The Kolibri had an additional seat for an observer behind the engine. Two dozen were delivered for service trials with the Luftwaffe and navy. Operating from escort ships in the Aegean, they were used to hunt for hostile submarines.

The Kolibri's success led to an order for 1,000 aircraft. These were to be built by BMW at Munich and Fisenach, but Allied bombing raids in 1944/45 disrupted production, and none had been completed by the end of the war.

*Once the Kolibri had landed and been secured to the deck, its rotor blades were carefully tied down to prevent damage.*

The two rotor blades were mounted so that they were parallel at the 45° position.

Each rotor blade was made of wooden ribs on tubular steel spars, with a fabric-over-plywood covering.

## FL 282 V21 KOLIBRI

**Shown while flying evaluation tests in 1943, this aircraft was the 21st of 24 prototypes built. Most Kolibris were destroyed to avoid their capture just before the German capitulation.**

Although of considerable size, the horizontal stabiliser was fitted only for trimming purposes. The inter-meshing rotor system allows designers to dispense with a tail rotor.

An experienced pilot could fly the Kolibri from a ship in almost any weather. Conditions for the pilot must have been severe, however, especially during trials in the Baltic, since the forward cockpit was completely open.

An observer's cockpit was provided in the rear fuselage. It was open and provided excellent visibility. An observer was carried at the expense of fuel, and range was therefore limited.

For maximum ground manoeuvrability, the nosewheel could be steered via the rudder pedals. A crude instrument panel was mounted forwards of the controls.

Mounting the engine in this central position gave both crewmembers an excellent view. Air was drawn into the engine from below the fuselage by a wooden fan.

An abnormally large rudder was fitted to the vertical fin. The shape of the rear fuselage was not ideal and caused a great deal of turbulence, which meant that much of the rudder area was ineffective.

## Fl 282B Kolibri

**Type:** single- or two-seat reconnaissance and transport helicopter

**Powerplant:** one 119-kW (160-hp.) Bramo Sh 14 seven-cylinder radial piston engine

**Maximum speed:** 150 km/h (93 m.p.h.) at sea level

**Vertical climb rate:** 91.5 m/min (300 f.p.m.) at loaded weight

**Range:** 300 km (185 mi.) with pilot only

**Service ceiling:** 3292 m (10,800 ft.)

**Weights:** empty 760 kg (1,672 lb.); maximum take-off 1000 kg (2,200 lb.)

**Dimensions:**
| | |
|---|---|
| main rotor diameter | 11.96 m (39 ft. 3 in.) |
| fuselage length | 6.56 m (21 ft. 6 in.) |
| height | 2.20 m (7 ft. 3 in.) |
| total rotor disc area | 224.69 m² (2,148 sq. ft.) |

## ACTION DATA

### MAXIMUM SPEED

The Fl 282 was not only a practical helicopter design, it also offered good performance. Sikorsky's YR-4B had similar capabilities and looked more advanced, but it could not match the Kolibri's speed.

| | |
|---|---|
| Fl 282 V21 KOLIBRI | 150 km/h (93 m.p.h.) |
| YR-4B HOVERFLY | 121 km/h (75 m.p.h.) |
| R-5B DRAGONFLY | 171 km/h (106 m.p.h.) |

### MAXIMUM TAKE-OFF WEIGHT

Early helicopters had limited payloads, with an empty Fl 282 weighing only 240 kg (528 lb.) less than its maximum take-off weight. Sikorsky, unhindered by the enemy bombing which troubled Flettner, was able to develop the larger R-5B.

| Fl 282 V21 KOLIBRI | YR-4B HOVERFLY | R-5B DRAGONFLY |
|---|---|---|
| 1000 kg (2,200 lb.) | 1150 kg (2,530 lb.) | 2189 kg (4,816 lb.) |

### RANGE

In full operational configuration with pilot and observer, the Fl 282 V21 had less range than the American machines. The majority of its operational missions were flown around a convoy, however, and refuelling was not a problem.

Fl 282 V21 KOLIBRI 170 km (105 mi.)
YR-4B HOVERFLY 209 km (130 mi.)
R-5B DRAGONFLY 579 km (359 mi.)

## Rotorcraft in World War II

■ **FLETTNER Fl 265:** Having proved Flettner's ideas for a practical military helicopter, only six examples of the Fl 265 were built before it gave way to the more promising Fl 282.

■ **FOCKE ACHGELIS Fa 223 DRACHE:** Designed to satisfy a Lufthansa requirement, only a few military Fa 223s were completed due to continuous Allied bombing.

■ **SIKORSKY R-4:** An R-4 achieved the first helicopter landing aboard a ship in May 1943 and later went on to perform a number of combat rescue missions.

■ **SIKORSKY R-5:** A completely new design, the R-5 first flew on 18 August 1943. The all-metal aircraft was later built in large numbers in the US and the UK.

169

# FOCKE-ACHGELIS

# FA 223 DRACHE

● Transport helicopter ● Twin-rotor layout ● Post-war service

▲ Using experience gained with the smaller Fa 266 Hornisse, Focke-Achgelis sought to develop a larger aircraft capable of undertaking transport and rescue missions.

In the years immediately preceding World War II Germany had become one of the world's leading helicopter nations. In 1932 Prof. Heinrich Karl Focke began a series of experiments commencing with licence-built autogyros and culminating in the Fa 266 Hornisse. This outrigger-mounted twin-rotor design was the world's first genuine transport helicopter, and when war arrived it was developed for military use as the Focke-Achgelis Fa 223 Drache.

◀ Mountain operations
The Drache proved suitable for use in a variety of environments and was often employed by high-ranking German military officers to attend important meetings at Hitler's secluded mountain-top command post in Bavaria.

Rotor position ▶
To provide a stable lifting platform the rotors were positioned on outriggers on either side of the fuselage. This allowed larger blades to be used.

Indoor flight ▶
Prior to the outbreak of World War II the helicopter was seen as a tool for propaganda use, with flight demonstrations even taking place at indoor conferences.

▲ Post-war service
After World War II, two Fa 223s were constructed in Czechoslovakia from German-manufactured aircraft components. They saw limited service.

Early birds ▶
Numerous configurations were tested before a practical design was adopted for operational use with the Luftwaffe during the war.

## FACTS AND FIGURES

➤ The first flight of the Fa 223 Drache occurred in August 1940. The project was under military control.

➤ After the first successful flight, 39 pre-production examples were ordered.

➤ The roles envisaged for the Drache were rescue and anti-submarine patrols.

➤ One variant was to be fitted with machine guns and two 250-kg (550-lb.) bombs for armed reconnaissance missions.

➤ An Fa 223 became the first helicopter to cross the English Channel.

➤ After the war both France and Czechoslovakia developed the design.

# Pioneering transport helicopter

Left: Unconventional in layout, the Fa 223 Drache proved itself a highly capable helicopter during the war.

Designed for the German national airline Lufthansa, the Fa 266 was developed from the earlier twin-rotor Fa 61. When war broke out, the military potential of the aircraft was realised and 39 pre-production examples of the newly designated Fa 223 were ordered. Intended roles were to include anti-submarine patrol, reconnaissance, rescue, transport and training.

When production commenced at Bremen, problems were immediately encountered because the factory was bombed. Production was switched to Laupheim, near Stuttgart, and, by early 1942, 17 Fa 223s had been completed and operational trials had commenced.

Despite more delays caused by bombing the trials were generally successful and 100 production examples were ordered. Allied bombing again hampered production and, although strenuous efforts were made, only 10 aircraft had flown by 1944. The Fa 223 did, however, demonstrate many of the roles that the helicopter has made its own in the postwar years. Successful rescue missions using a winch were carried out and deployments of troops to confined areas were also achieved by Luft-Transportstaffel 40. Only three machines were serviceable by the end of the war and one of these became the first helicopter to cross the English Channel.

Above: The prototype Drache was initially flown tethered to the ground to allow the pilot to explore its handling safely.

## Fa 223 Drache

**Type:** transport/rescue/reconnaissance helicopter

**Powerplant:** one 746-kW (1,000-hp.) BMW 301 R nine-cylinder radial engine

**Maximum speed:** 175 km/h (109 m.p.h.)

**Cruising speed:** 120 km/h (74 m.p.h.)

**Range:** 700 km (434 mi.), with auxiliary fuel tank

**Service ceiling:** 2010 m (6,600 ft.)

**Weights:** empty 3175 kg (6,985 lb.); maximum take-off 4310 kg (9,480 lb.)

**Armament:** one 7.92-mm MG 15 machine-gun and two 250-kg (550-lb.) bombs

**Dimensions:**
| | |
|---|---|
| span | 24.5 m (80 ft. 4 in.) |
| length | 12.25 m (40 ft. 2 in.) |
| height | 4.35 m (14 ft. 3 in.) |
| rotor disc area | 226.19 m² (2,434 sq. ft.) |

A heavily glazed cockpit afforded the pilot excellent visibility, particularly when coming in to land when a downward view was required. Pilots found the Drache relatively easy to master and this was demonstrated by two German pilots flying one across the Channel to Britain for evaluation at the conclusion of World War II.

Positioned on outriggers the twin rotors were powered by a single nine-cylinder radial engine. Providing enough power for the helicopter was a particular problem that the makers had to overcome in order to achieve military backing.

After numerous trials the tail configuration that offered the best handling qualities during the hovering phase was a high-set design. This allowed the Drache to make precise landings at mountain heli-pads even when fully loaded with troops.

## FA 223 DRACHE

Revolutionary for its time, the Focke-Achgelis Fa 223 Drache achieved only limited service because of Allied bombing of the production line. Despite this, those that saw service use were a complete success.

Roles envisaged for the Drache were battlefield transport, observation and rescue work. For the last of these an extra fuel tank and rescue winch were provided.

Substantial tyres were fitted to the Fa 223 Drache to allow the helicopter to land on unprepared airfields. These were adapted from other German transport aircraft. Steering on the ground was accomplished through the large nose wheel.

### ACTION DATA

#### MAXIMUM SPEED

Despite its relatively large size, the Fa 223 had good performance and was faster than the American Sikorsky Hoverfly and the light-weight observation Fl 282 Kolibri. Such fine performance also meant that the Fa 223 could operate in many difficult locations.

| | |
|---|---|
| Fa 223 DRACHE | 175 km/h (109 m.p.h.) |
| Fl 282 V21 KOLIBRI | 150 km/h (93 m.p.h.) |
| YR-4B HOVERFLY | 121 km/h (75 m.p.h.) |

#### POWER

With the need to undertake both transport duties and rescue operations the power available to the Drache was of vital importance. A single radial engine powered a dual set of rotors allowing the Drache to airlift sizeable loads. America's YR-4B had limited power.

| | |
|---|---|
| Fa 223 DRACHE | 746 kW (1,000 hp.) |
| Fl 282 V21 KOLIBRI | 119 kW (160 hp.) |
| YR-4B HOVERFLY | 134 kW (180 hp.) |

#### MAXIMUM TAKE-OFF WEIGHT

In the transport role the Fa 223 Drache was unsurpassed by other WWII helicopters. Quick to see the potential of the design, the Luftwaffe hoped to operate the helicopter as a battlefield transport but Allied bombing of the factories halted its wider use.

| Fa 223 DRACHE | Fl 282 V21 KOLIBRI | YR-4B HOVERFLY |
|---|---|---|
| 4310 kg (9,480 lb.) | 1000 kg (2,200 lb.) | 1150 kg (2,540 lb.) |

## Pioneering rotors

**FLETTNER Fl 282 KOLIBRI:** Used as an observation helicopter, the Fl 282 was operated by the German navy allowing ship captains to view Allied shipping over the horizon.

**HAFNER R-11:** Utilising a standard army Willys jeep, the English company Hafner adapted the vehicle to be used as a battlefield air observation platform. The project met with limited success and was soon cancelled.

**SIKORSKY R-4:** The most successful helicopter of World War II, the R-4 was used in the rescue and scout roles and saw extensive service in the Pacific theatre.

# FOCKE-WULF

# FW 189 UHU

● Tactical reconnaissance ● Army co-operation ● Observation post

▲ The Uhu (Eagle Owl) served with distinction on the Eastern Front, its superb agility and reliable engines making it a far from easy quarry even for agile fighters.

**B**uilt in France and Czechoslovakia as well as at Focke-Wulf's Bremen factory during World War II, the Fw 189 was one of the Luftwaffe's most useful multi-role aircraft. Originally designed for tactical reconnaissance as a successor to the Hs 126, it was also used for casualty evacuation, ground support and night-fighting. In the process it earned an outstanding reputation for reliability and became popular with its pilots.

## FOCKE-WULF FW 189 UHU

▼ Prototype Fw 189
The Focke-Wulf Fw 189, piloted by its chief designer Kurt Tank, first flew in 1938, and was dubbed 'The Flying Eye' by the media.

▲ Uhu trainer
The Fw 189B was a five-seat dedicated training platform for reconnaissance pilots.

▼ Cockpit glazing
The Uhu had unsurpassed all-round vision from the rear, with no tail to obscure the view.

▼ Battleproof platform
A very stable and rugged platform, the Uhu could absorb a certain amount of heavy-calibre gunfire with little adverse effect on flight.

◄ Assault variant
The Fw 189C, which was never adopted for service, was an experimental assault aircraft with a tiny, heavily armoured cabin for the pilot and gunner.

◄ Low-level reconnaissance
The Uhu was essentially a low-altitude tactical reconnaissance aircraft and was particularly at home on the front-line fighting in support of the army.

## FACTS AND FIGURES

➤ The Fw 189 first flew in June 1938, competing with the BV 141 and unsuccessful Ar 198 for orders.

➤ It was first known as the Eule (Owl) before becoming the Uhu.

➤ The Uhu was exported to the Slovakian and Hungarian air forces.

➤ The Fw 189C assault version was never ordered into production; the Luftwaffe preferred the all-new Henschel Hs 129.

➤ The Fw 189 V4 prototype carried equipment to spray mustard gas.

➤ The Fw 189D was a floatplane trainer version, but it never flew.

## PROFILE

# The Luftwaffe's eye in the sky

Designer Kurt Tank selected the twin-boom configuration for the Fw 189, which had the advantage of allowing different fuselage nacelles to be used in the same basic airframe.

For its basic role of tactical reconnaissance, the Fw 189A's three-man nacelle was extensively glazed and carried machine-guns in the top and rear. There was a further machine-gun in each wing, in addition to racks for a total of eight 50-kg (110-lb.) bombs. The aircraft entered service in late 1940, and went on to equip nine long-range and 15 short-range reconnaissance Gruppen, most of which served on the Eastern Front. Among its qualities were the agility to evade fighter interception and the strength and firepower to survive if it did come under attack. Some even survived being rammed, managing to return to base with large sections of their tailfins missing.

*Late in the war a number of Fw 189s were refitted as stop-gap night-fighters flying in Scandinavia.*

The Fw 189B, a five-seater with an enclosed nacelle, was intended for training but only a few were built. And the two-seat 189C, which had a reduced-sized, heavily armoured nacelle and was intended for assault and close support, was rejected in favour of the cheaper Hs 129.

The Fw 189A-2 was produced in large numbers in three different countries until it was replaced in production by the Fw 189A-4 which had heavier armour and new 20-mm (0.79-in.) wingroot cannon.

The large tailplane between the twin-booms allowed a full-length elevator which made the Fw 189 surprisingly agile.

The long wings were of strong, three-spar stressed-skin construction with tapering outer panels and electronically operated, fabric-covered trailing-edge flaps. Rudders, elevator and ailerons were manually controlled.

## Fw 189A-2 Uhu

**Type:** three-seat tactical reconnaissance and army co-operation aircraft

**Powerplant:** two 343.8-kW (460-hp.) Argus As410A-1 12-cylinder piston engines

**Maximum speed:** 350 km/h (217 m.p.h.)

**Economical cruising speed:** 305 km/h (189 m.p.h.)

**Endurance:** 2 hours 10 min

**Range:** 670 km (415 mi.)

**Service ceiling:** 7300 m (23,950 ft.)

**Weights:** maximum take-off 4170 kg (9,174 lb.)

**Armament:** six 7.9-mm (0.31-in.) machine-guns, plus 400 kg (880 lb.) of bombs

**Dimensions:**
| | | |
|---|---|---|
| span | 18.40 m | (60 ft. 4 in.) |
| length | 12.03 m | (39 ft. 5 in.) |
| height | 3.10 m | (16 ft. 2 in.) |
| wing area | 38.0 m² | (409 sq. ft.) |

## Fw 189A-2 Uhu

**This A-2 Uhu served with Aufklarungsgruppe (H)/14 flying from Salzburg during 1945. The aircraft was eventually captured by US forces in the area.**

The heavily glazed nacelle accommodated the pilot, navigator/observer and, in the rear, a gunner with a revolving Ikaria-powered cone turret fitted with two MG 81 7.9-mm (0.31-in.) machine-guns.

Further gun armament was provided by two fixed MG 17 7.9-mm (0.31-in.) machine-guns in the wingroots and two MG 81 7.9-mm machine-guns on flexible dorsal mounts directly above the navigator's position.

The twin-boom layout was ideal for reconnaissance and observation missions. It also made the aircraft supremely stable, as well as agile enough to avoid enemy aircraft and anti-aircraft guns.

The powerful Argus 12-cylinder inverted-Vee engines were renowned for their reliability, and their speed enabled the Fw 189 to escape from fighters.

The tailwheel-type undercarriage was exceptionally tough and when retracted it was protected by armoured undercarriage doors. The Uhu was at home on rough airstrips.

Four ETC 50 racks, each capable of carrying two SC50 50-kg (110-lb.) anti-personnel or anti-armour bombs for the support of the ground forces fighting below, were fitted underwing. These carriers were often empty.

The tailwheel neatly retracted to port to lie within the tailplane.

## COMBAT DATA

### MAXIMUM SPEED

The Fw 189 was never designed for all-out speed. Like the British Lysander, however, its speed plus the unquestioned agility of the airframe were quite adequate to outmanoeuvre, if not out-run, the opposition's faster fighters.

| | |
|---|---|
| **Fw 189A-1** | 335 km/h (208 m.p.h.) |
| **LYSANDER** | 341 km/h (2121 m.p.h.) |
| **Ki-15** | 480 km/h (298 m.p.h.) |

### RANGE

Unlike the Lysander and Japanese Ki-15, the Uhu was designed for spotting and support of land forces over the battlefield. Therefore the Uhu could have a shorter range and heavier warload than the other aircraft, as it could easily land nearby to refuel.

LYSANDER 966 km (600 mi.)

Fw 189A-1 670 km (415 mi.)

Ki-15 2400 km (1,488 mi.)

### ARMAMENT

The Fw 189 was a well-armed machine. In addition to a heavy non-disposable armament, the Uhu could also carry up to 400 kg of bombs. In comparison, in terms of armament, the smaller, longer-ranged Ki-15 and Lysander were relative lightweights.

| | |
|---|---|
| Fw 189A-1 | 4 x 7.9-mm (0.31-in.) MGs |
| Ki-15 | 1 x 7.7-mm (.303 cal.) MG |
| LYSANDER | 4 x 7.7-mm (.303 cal.) MGs |

## The Luftwaffe over the battlefield

■ **BLOHM UND VOSS BV 141:** Designed to the same specification as the Fw 189, the unique BV 141 featured twin fuselages – one contained the tail and engine and the other a glazed cabin.

■ **FIESELER Fi 156:** The Storch was undoubtedly the finest air observation post of the war. Serving on all fronts, its short take-off and landing capability was a major asset.

■ **HENSCHEL Hs 126:** The Hs 126 was the aircraft that the Fw 189 was destined to replace. It first flew in 1935, but survived in service throughout World War II as a light reconnaissance aircraft/trainer.

# FOCKE-WULF
# Fw 190A

● Interceptor ● Ground-attack aircraft ● Bomber destroyer

▲ Luftwaffe ace Josef 'Pips' Priller climbs from his Fw 190. Allied pilots had a healthy respect for the aircraft in the hands of such experienced combat fliers.

**K**urt Tank's superb Focke-Wulf Fw 190 first saw combat over the English Channel in September 1941. The new fighter was a shock to the RAF, being faster and more agile than the Spitfire. Known as the 'Butcher Bird', the Fw 190 went on to become a dominant force in aerial combat in Europe, performing with equal distinction as a fighter and as the Luftwaffe's most important ground-attack machine.

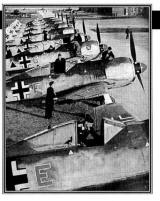

## PHOTO FILE
# FOCKE-WULF Fw 190A

◀ **Conversion trainer**
This two-seat trainer was developed to help former Stuka pilots convert from the lumbering Ju 87 to the vastly more powerful Fw 190.

▲ **Squadron line-up**
A squadron prepares to take on the RAF from its French base. The Fw 190 came as a very unwelcome surprise to the RAF, and gave German pilots the edge over Mk V Spitfires in 1941 and early 1942.

▲ **Dogfighter**
The Fw 190 was a hard opponent in a dogfight, with heavy armament, excellent manoeuvrability and high speed.

**Stripdown time** ▶
The Fw 190's compact and complex BMW radial engine could often be troublesome to service in the field.

▼ **Pairs formation**
Pilots needed to give each other support in battle. The Fw 190 cockpit allowed good visibility for crews to check behind, and they always flew as a tactical combat pair.

◀ **Broken nose**
In spite of its wide-track undercarriage, the Fw 190 could be difficult for an inexperienced pilot to land. By the end of the war, such accidents had become common.

## FACTS AND FIGURES

➤ On 14 October 1943, Fw 190s decimated US bombers attacking Schweinfurt and Regensburg, shooting down 79.

➤ The prototype Fw 190 made its first flight on 1 June 1939.

➤ Fw 190s could carry a huge range of weapons, from bombs and rockets to aerial torpedoes.

➤ The long-nosed Fw 190D, or 'Dora', series performed superbly after being introduced in mid-1944.

➤ Later models of the Fw 190 carried 30-mm (1.18-in.) cannon and air-to-air rockets.

➤ The Fw 190A-8/R8 was a heavily armoured variant designed to destroy American bombers by ramming them.

## PROFILE

# The 'Butcher Bird'

Conceived in 1937 as a complement to the Bf 109, Focke-Wulf's Fw 190 became a potent threat to Allied air power in every region where the Luftwaffe fought. Fw 190s inflicted cruel punishment on Flying Fortress and Liberator crews, and were almost impossible to defeat until the long-range P-51 Mustang finally became available in 1944 to escort bombers to their targets.

As a fighter-bomber and anti-tank aircraft, the Fw 190 was Germany's best air-to-ground fighter.

The Fw 190A-8 was used extensively in Defence of the Riech operations during 1944. Heavily armed with four cannon and two machine-guns it wreaked havoc upon US daylight bombers. The long-nosed Tank Ta 152 versions of the Fw 190 reached air speeds as high as 760 km/h (472 m.p.h.), and might have altered the outcome of the war if more than 93 had been built before hostilities ended.

No one who fought in the hotly contested skies of Europe will forget the feats of Fw 190 pilots such as Oberleutnant Otto Kittel, the Luftwaffe's fourth-ranking ace, who scored most of his 267 victories in the type. It is truly one of the great fighters of all time.

The Fw 190 carried out many combat tasks. It even replaced the Ju 87 Stuka as the Luftwaffe's tank-busting machine.

The flaps of the Fw 190 were electrically-operated, which was a first for a fighter aircraft of the 1940s.

The Fw 190-A1 was armed with two 20-mm (0.79-in.) MG FF cannon and two MG 17 machine-guns in the wings, with two more MG 17s above the engine.

## Fw 190A-1

The first operational Fw 190 unit was 6 Staffel, JG 26 'Schlageter'. Flying out of the Pas de Calais, the squadron took the new fighter into action for the first time early in September 1941.

The first Fw 190s were powered by the BMW 801C-1 engine, rated at 1200 kW (1,600 hp.). Early examples of the compact 18-cylinder radial were prone to overheating.

The 190's cockpit was a major improvement over the Bf 109. It had all-electric-powered systems, excellent visibility and good armour plating. The light controls made it easy to fly.

The cut-down fuselage made it easy for the pilot to see to the rear.

The wide-track undercarriage was much more stable than that of either the Spitfire or the Bf 109.

The small size of the Fw 190 was a big advantage in a dogfight, where being seen first was a problem. This aircraft carries a standard Luftwaffe grey/green camouflage scheme.

The aircraft depicted was flown by Oberleutnant Walter Schneider, Staffelkapitän of 6./JG 26. Schneider was killed in December 1941.

### Fw 190A-8

**Type:** single-seat fighter and fighter-bomber

**Powerplant:** one 1567-kW (2,100-hp.) BMW 801D-2 14-cylinder radial piston engine

**Maximum speed:** 654 km/h (406 m.p.h.)

**Combat radius:** 800 km (497 mi.) on internal fuel

**Service ceiling:** 11,400 m (37,400 ft.)

**Weights:** empty 3170 kg (6,989 lb.); loaded 4900 kg (10,803 lb.)

**Armament:** two 7.92-mm (0.31-in) MG 17 machine-guns; four 20-mm (0.79-in.) MG 151/20 cannon; one 500-kg (1,100-lb.) and two 250-kg (550-lb.) bombs or one 300-litre (67-gal.) drop-tank

**Dimensions:**
| | | |
|---|---|---|
| span | 10.50 m | (34 ft. 5 in.) |
| length | 8.84 m | (29 ft.) |
| height | 3.96 m | (13 ft.) |
| wing area | 18.30 m² | (197 sq. ft.) |

## COMBAT DATA

### ARMAMENT

The Fw 190's armament was characteristically much heavier than that of British or American aircraft. Goaded by the bitter experience of being on the receiving end of German gun power, the British were now fitting cannon to most of their fighters, while the otherwise superb Mustang was woefully undergunned.

**Fw 190A-8** 4 x 20-mm (0.79-in.) cannon 2 x 7.92-mm (0.31-in) machine-guns

**SPITFIRE Mk IX** 2 x 20-mm (0.79-in.) cannon 4 x 7.7-mm (.303 cal.) machine-guns

**P-51B MUSTANG** 4 x 12.7-mm (.50 cal.) machine-guns

### MAXIMUM SPEED

| | |
|---|---|
| Fw 190A-8 | 654 km/h (406 m.p.h.) |
| SPITFIRE Mk IX | 657 km/h (408 m.p.h.) |
| P-51B MUSTANG | 700 km/h (435 m.p.h.) |

The speed of the Fw 190 spurred Britain to fit a more powerful engine into the Spitfire, the resulting Spitfire Mk IX bringing performance up to the German fighter's levels. Both were soon to be outclassed by the American P-51 Mustang, which turned out to be the most outstanding fighter of the European theatre.

### SERVICE CEILING

The Fw 190 was almost unbeatable at medium altitudes, between 4000 and 8000 m (13,000 and 26,000 ft.). However, at high altitudes its performance fell off considerably, and at 10,000 m (33,000 ft.) it was vulnerable to Spitfires and Mustangs. US bombers operated as high as possible to avoid the Fw 190 threat.

Fw 190A-8 11,400 m (37,400 ft.)
SPITFIRE Mk IX 12,750 m (42,000 ft.)
P-51B MUSTANG 12,750 m (42,000 ft.)

# Weapons variations

**GROUND ATTACK:** One 250-kg (550-lb.) and four 50-kg (110-lb.) bombs was a standard attack mission load.

**HEAVY BOMBER :** The SC1000 bomb, weighing 1800 kg (3,968 lb.), was the largest and most powerful carried by any fighter of the war.

**BOMBER DESTROYER:** Four 20-mm (0.79-in.) MG 151s increased drag and reduced range. An auxiliary tank was fitted to compensate.

**FORMATION DESTROYER:** WfrGr 21 mortars were designed to launch high-explosive shells into a bomber formation from beyond the range of the bomber box's defensive fire.

**TANK-BUSTER:** Two 30-mm (1.18-in) Mk 103 cannon were capable of destroying enemy tanks as well as bombers.

# FOCKE-WULF

# FW 200 CONDOR

● Long-range reconnaissance bomber ● Anti-shipping strike

▲ A crew undergo a final briefing and map check in front of their Condor. The aircraft ranged far over the Atlantic to attack Allied convoys in an attempt to starve Britain into submission.

**C**hurchill called it 'the scourge of the Atlantic'. The Focke-Wulf Fw 200 Condor prowled the seaways and sank an enormous number of Allied ships, disrupting maritime operations so severely that it almost changed the course of World War II. This was an incredible achievement for an aircraft which, although gifted with rare beauty and remarkable endurance, had never been designed as a long-range bomber at all.

## FOCKE-WULF FW 200 CONDOR

▲ **Flying the Condor**
The Fw 200's cockpit was fairly standard for a large aircraft. The type was slow and cumbersome, but did fight some slow-motion dogfights against RAF Sunderlands.

▲ **French base**
For much of the war the Condors operated from Bordeaux-Mérignac, flying out over the Atlantic to hunt convoys.

▼ **Bomb carriage**
Bombs were carried under the wings and engine nacelles.

▲ **Ventral gondola**
Scabbed under the belly of most Condors was this gondola. In the front was a Lofte 7D bombsight (in the strange protuberance) and an MG 131 machine-gun.

**Ex-airliner ▶**
The Condor was originally developed as an airliner, although it was swiftly turned into a makeshift patroller. Unfortunately, it was structurally weak, and many of the early ones broke their backs.

▲ **Fighter fodder**
After the early days of success, Fw 200s increasingly fell foul of shipborne fighters.

### FACTS AND FIGURES

➤ The first flight of the Condor occurred after only 12 months of development.

➤ In 1938 an Fw 200 flew from Berlin to Tokyo in 42 hours 18 minutes' flying time.

➤ Two Condors each were exported to Finland and Brazil. A Japanese order for five aircraft was never filled.

➤ With fuel connections for the engines on its underside, the Condor was extremely vulnerable to anti-aircraft fire.

➤ Though Lufthansa never had more than a handful of Fw 200s, one of these flew the last wartime airline flight on 14 April 1945 from Barcelona to Berlin.

## PROFILE

# 'The scourge of the Atlantic'

The Fw 200 Condor was intended for peaceful air commerce. It was an attractive, greyhound-like airliner, one example of which was used by Adolf Hitler as his personal transport.

But the Condor was to become famous as a warplane. Britain depended on a transatlantic lifeline for survival, and the Luftwaffe knew that everything possible had to be done to prevent convoys from crossing the ocean with the weapons and equipment being churned out by American factories. The Condor was hastily pressed into action as a long-range maritime reconnaissance bomber. Under very difficult circumstances of extremely bad weather and near impossible navigation challenges, Condor crews fought a dramatic campaign over the Atlantic.

Co-operating with U-boat packs, the Condor overcame the handicaps of its inherently frail design and inflicted enough damage to threaten Britain's survival. But the deployment of fighters aboard escort carriers was to signal the end of the Condor's career.

*When the Wehrmacht's needs were pressing, military Condors were rushed into service as makeshift transports. They took part in the Stallingrad airlift.*

## Fw 200C-3 Condor

**Type:** seven-seat long-range maritime reconnaissance bomber

**Powerplant:** four 895-kW (1,200-hp.) BMW-Bramo 323 R-2 Fafnir radial engines

**Maximum speed:** 360 km/h (220 m.p.h.)

**Range:** 4400 km (2,700 mi.)

**Service ceiling:** 6000 m (19,000 ft.)

**Weights:** empty 13,000 kg (28,000 lb.); loaded 23,000 kg (51,000 lb.)

**Armament:** four 13-mm (0.51-in.) MG 131 machine-guns in dorsal and beam positions and one MG 131 or 20-mm (0.79-in.) MG 151 in a ventral gondola; up to 2100 kg (4,600 lb.) of bombs carried in the ventral gondola and under the wings

**Dimensions:**
| | | |
|---|---|---|
| span | 32.85 m | (107 ft. 9 in.) |
| length | 23.45 m | (77 ft.) |
| height | 3.30 m | (20 ft. 8 in.) |
| wing area | 119.85 m² | (1,290 sq. ft.) |

## Fw 200C-8 Condor

The Fw 200 grew from being little more than an airliner in camouflage to a fully equipped ship-killer. The Fw 200C-8/U10 was the ultimate Condor, carrying a heavy load of radar, missiles and full defensive armament.

Most Condor variants were fitted with radar to aid sea searches. Antennas were mounted in the nose and on the wings. The standard equipment was the FuG 200 Hohentwiel.

In addition to the fore and aft guns in the gondola, the Fw 200 had two dorsal positions for guns, and two firing laterally through the beam hatches.

The Condor's chief weakness was a tendency to structural failure in the rear fuselage.

The ventral gondola of the Fw 200C-8 was longer than that of the earlier variants, and had a very neat installation of the accurate bombsight. The gun at the front was the MG 131.

The Henschel Hs 293 was one of the first successful air-to-surface guided missiles. It was command guided by the bomb aimer.

Flares mounted at the back of the missile allowed the bomb aimer to follow its progress after launch. He had a joystick which transmitted control signals to the missile, which he 'flew' to the target like a model plane.

## ACTION DATA

### RANGE

The key to successful maritime reconnaissance is the ability to stay aloft over the ocean for a long time. With maximum fuel the Condor had a range of more than 4000 km (2,400 mi.). It could intercept an Allied convoy 1000 km (620 mi.) out into the Atlantic, and shadow it for up to 10 hours at a time. Operating in relays, the Condors would then vector U-boat wolfpacks in for the kill.

| B-24 LIBERATOR 4000 km (2,485 mi.) | Fw 200 CONDOR 4400 km (2,700 mi.) | SUNDERLAND 4600 km (2,900 mi.) |
|---|---|---|

## Shadowing the convoys

**3 ATTACK:** Condor patrol sectors were generally flown at very low level, with periodic pop-ups to about 300 m (1,000 ft.) for an orbiting radar search. If a target was detected, the Condors climbed to about 3000 m (10,000 ft.) for the bombing attack.

**2 SHADOWING:** The normal operating procedure for Condor units was to take off in fours, which then fanned out into parallel search paths, or sectors, covering several hundred kilometres of ocean. Once a convoy was detected, the crew could choose either to attack or to shadow.

**1 REPORTING:** When shadowing, the big bombers flew in circles around the convoy, all the while transmitting reports to naval headquarters and guiding U-boat wolfpacks to their quarry.

# FOCKE-WULF

# TA 152

● Fw 190 development ● Interceptor/fighter-bomber ● High altitude

▲ A truly exceptional aircraft, the Ta 152 might have been a highly effective weapon, but the desperate war situation led to it being used outside its intended role.

**B**rilliant German designer Kurt Tank was credited with dramatic improvements to his Focke-Wulf Fw 190 fighter, producing the Ta 152 high-altitude interceptor. Tank's Ta 152 and the related Ta 153 were similar to 'long-nosed' versions of the Fw 190 but were meant to have even greater performance. It was not an easy task for a new aircraft to measure up to a predecessor that was immortal in aviation, but the Ta 152/153 were exceptional designs.

## FOCKE-WULF TA 152

▼ Post-war US testing
The third production Ta 152H-0 was taken by the British after the war and passed on to the Americans. British markings have been replaced with inaccurate Luftwaffe equivalents.

▲ British evaluation
This Ta 152 underwent limited flight testing in the UK and is seen at a display of 'captured' German aircraft in October 1945.

▼ Supercharged engine
A large air inlet on the right-hand side of the nose fed the supercharger of the powerful Jumo 213EB engine. The propeller blades required very broad chord to handle the enormous power.

▲ All-weather fighter
Full bad-weather flying equipment equipped the three Ta 152C-0/R11 test aircraft.

◀ Mixed ancestry
Flying as a Ta 152H-03 in August 1944, this aircraft was rebuilt from the Fw 190 V30/U1 and was powered by a Jumo 213A-1; engine accessories were taken from an Fw 190D-9.

## FACTS AND FIGURES

➤ Although the Ta 152 was a high-altitude interceptor, attack and reconnaissance versions were also designed.

➤ The Ta 152C developmental prototype first flew on 19 November 1944.

➤ The first of 20 pre-production Ta 152 fighters flew at Cottbus in October 1944.

➤ Most Ta 152s differed from the 'long-nosed' Fw 190D in having a pressurised cockpit.

➤ Trials of the Ta 152 were carried out by Erprobungskommando 152 at Rechlin.

➤ A photo-reconnaissance Ta 152 variant was never employed operationally.

## PROFILE

# High-altitude Reich defender

Two of many projects being pursued by Germany near the end of the war, the Ta 152 and Ta 153 were high-altitude versions of the Fw 190. Intended to intercept high-flying US Army Air Force bombers, they were used to safeguard bases where the newly developed jets would be stationed. The Luftwaffe rushed ahead with several versions of the Ta 152, the variants having short- and long-span wings and various sets of armament. However, all had the ability to take off quickly, climb

at a phenomenal rate and intercept Allied bombers at their operating height.

This thoroughbred aircraft was difficult to master, but in the right hands it was a fantastic performer. However, the Ta 152 was not used for the role for which it had been intended. Pilots found themselves fighting at medium and even low altitude, where other fighters, including the traditional Fw 190, would have performed better. They were rarely given a chance to fight at altitude, where the Ta 152 was superior.

*Below: A Ta 152H-0 is prepared for delivery. Calibration of the aircraft's compass is performed on this compass-swinging platform.*

*Above: Considered to be a heavy fighter, the Ta 152C was to have been delivered from April 1945, but the Allies overran the factories before production started.*

Like so many of the Luftwaffe's advanced projects, the Ta 152 entered service too late and in too few numbers to alter the course of the war.

### Ta 152H-1

**Type:** single-seat high-altitude fighter

**Powerplant:** one 1305-kW (1,750-hp.) Junkers Jumo 213E 12-cylinder inverted-Vee piston engine

**Maximum speed:** 760 km/h (471 m.p.h.) at 12,500 m (41,000 ft.)

**Initial climb rate:** 1050 m/min (3,445 f.p.m.)

**Range:** 1200 km (745 mi.)

**Service ceiling:** 14,800 m (48,550 ft.)

**Weights:** empty 3920 kg (8,624 lb.); maximum take-off 4750 kg (10,450 lb.)

**Armament:** one 30-mm (1.18-in.) Mk 108 cannon with 90 rounds firing through the spinner and two wing-mounted 20-mm (0.79-in.) MG 151/20 cannon with 175 rounds per gun

**Dimensions:**
| | | |
|---|---|---|
| span | 14.50 m | (48 ft. 6 in.) |
| length | 10.80 m | (35 ft. 5 in.) |
| height | 4.00 m | (13 ft. 2 in.) |
| wing area | 23.50 m² | (253 sq. ft.) |

---

Water-methanol (MW 50) injection on take-off boosted power from 1305 kW (1,750 hp.) to 1529 kW (2,050 hp.). At 8000 m (26,250 ft.) the power from the 12-cylinder inverted-Vee inline engine was 1342 kW (1,800 hp.). With a large fuel capacity the Ta 152H-1 was a heavy aircraft and required a great deal of power, especially during take-off and at low level.

Ta 152H-1 pilots sat in a pressurised cockpit. World War II fighter designers did not often use this type of cockpit, since it added weight and complexity to the design. Flying the Ta 152H-1 for long periods at high altitude was stressful and the aircraft was equipped with autopilot.

### TA 152H-1

'Black 14' flew with JG 301 on Defence of the Reich duties during the last few months of the war. The unit mainly flew top cover for Me 262 jet fighters during their landing and take-off cycles.

In order to counter the huge power and torque of the Jumo 213E engine and to provide adequate directional stability at high altitudes, the Ta 152 series were fitted with fins of far greater chord than the Fw 190D. This and the long-span wings caused some loss of roll rate.

As an aircraft assigned to Defence of the Reich, this machine carries brightly coloured bands. The small, inclined black bar indicates that this was the personal aircraft of a Geschwader adjutant.

At 8000 m (26,250 ft.) the exhausts produced 2.17 kN (485 lb.) of residual thrust. This thrust was in addition to the pull of the three-bladed VS 111 propeller. The inboard tank of the left wing carried 70 litres (18.5 gal.)of MW 50.

A long, high-aspect ratio wing gave the Ta 152H-1 outstanding climb and altitude performance. Unfortunately, necessity forced the aircraft to be used at low level where Fw 190D-9s would have performed better.

Although many Fw 190 variants left their retracted main undercarriage partly exposed, that of the Ta 152H-1e was entirely enclosed by two sets of doors. The tailwheel of all models was stowed partially retracted.

---

### COMBAT DATA

#### CEILING

Both the Spitfire PR.Mk 19 and Ta 152H-1 used a complicated engine super-charging system to provide additional power in the thin air encountered at high altitudes. They also had pressurised cockpits.

- Ta 152 H-1 14,800 m (48,550 ft.)
- SPITFIRE PR.Mk 19 13,106 m (43,165 ft.)
- P-51H MUSTANG 12,680 m (41,600 ft.)

#### MAXIMUM SPEED

Except for the Messerschmitt Me 262 and Heinkel He 162 jets, the P-51H was the fastest production fighter of World War II. Nitrous oxide (GM 1) injection at high altitudes gave the Ta 152H an additional performance boost, while water-methanol (MW 50) injection boosted take-off performance.

| | |
|---|---|
| Ta 152 H-1 | 760 km/h (471 m.p.h.) |
| SPITFIRE PR.Mk 19 | 740 km/h (459 m.p.h.) |
| P-51H MUSTANG | 784 km/h (486 m.p.h.) |

#### ARMAMENT

Although it carried only three guns, the Ta 152H-1 was armed with powerful cannon: the 30-mm (1.18-in.) MK 108 fired through the spinner and the MK 151s from the wings. The Spitfire relied on speed and altitude for safety in its photo-reconnaissance role.

| | |
|---|---|
| Ta 152 H-1 | 1 x 30-mm (1.18-in.) cannon<br>2 x 20-mm (0.79-in.) cannon |
| SPITFIRE PR.Mk 19 | none |
| P-51H MUSTANG | 6 x 12.7-mm (.50 cal.) machine-guns |

---

## Kurt Tank's warplane dynasty

■ **Fw 189 UHU:** Designed as an army co-operation and reconnaissance aircraft, the Fw 189 also flew as a night-fighter.

■ **Fw 200 CONDOR:** Developed from an outstanding airliner, the Condor became infamous in the anti-shipping role.

■ **Fw 190:** Built as a contemporary of the Hawker Typhoon, the Fw 190 developed into a series of fighters and attack aircraft.

■ **Ta 154 MOSKITO:** Tank's design genius was recognised by the adoption of the Ta prefix for later Focke-Wulf aircraft.

# FOKKER
# C.V

● Inter-war design ● Light reconnaissance bomber ● Licence built

One of the most successful aircraft of its era in terms of numbers built, the C.V originated in the mid-1920s. Its performance was not very distinguished, but most of the 1000-plus examples assembled subsequently in seven other countries were still in service at the start of World War II. It was offered with a series of wings and a wide range of engines, which helped the type to meet the requirements of a dozen different countries in various roles.

▲ Built in sizeable numbers in a number of factories throughout Western Europe, the C.V was a very important inter-war design. Engine interchangeability was an important feature.

## FOKKER C.V

▲ Easily distinguished
Inter-plane 'V' struts distinguished the C.V-D from the later C.V-E, which had 'N' struts.

▲ Kestrel-powered C.VI
Not a new type as its designation suggests, the C.VI was a version of the C.V-D for the Dutch Air Division. To prolong their service life they were re-engined with Rolls-Royce Kestrel engines in 1936.

Inter-war export success ▶
First flying in May 1924 the C.V was, in its different variants, a versatile and popular multi-role machine.

◀ Swedish S.6A
Sweden's State Aircraft Factory built Jupiter-engined C.V-Es under licence, designating them J.3s and then S.6s.

Finnish Fives ▶
Finland purchased an unknown number of C.Vs, some of which were licence-built. The first was a Jupiter-powered C.V-E, like this one; later examples had Pegasus radials. Skis were fitted in winter.

### FACTS AND FIGURES

➤ Fokker complained that the C.V was so reliable that none needed overhaul, causing work shortages at the factory.

➤ A C.V-E has been restored to airworthy condition at Malmen, Sweden.

➤ Norwegian C.V-Ds saw action against German forces during the 1940 invasion.

➤ As well as in the Netherlands, C.Vs were built in Denmark, Finland, Hungary, Italy, Norway, Sweden and Switzerland.

➤ Record-breaking flights by Italian C.Vs included a Naples – Tripoli flight in 1927.

➤ C.Vs are believed to have been built with engines from eight different builders.

**PROFILE**

# Fokker's versatile sesquiplane

Fokker's first C.V flew for the first time in May 1924, and around 90 A, B and C models with different wing areas and liquid-cooled in-line engines were built in the following two years. Some were built under licence in Denmark, and the total included C.V-W floatplanes.

In 1926 production switched to the D and E models, which could use either in-line or radial engines, the C.V-E having an increased wing area over the D-model. The latter, with their much smaller lower wings, were generally used as two-seat fighters, while the C.V-Es were bombers; both were used for other missions including battlefield reconnaissance.

Over 1000 Ds and Es were built in Hungary, Italy, Norway, Sweden and Switzerland, and by Fokker in the Netherlands. Versatile and easy to maintain, they followed traditional Fokker construction practice with their fabric-covered steel-tube fuselages and wooden wings. Later aircraft had more powerful engines; 544-kW (730-hp.) Bristol Pegasus were used by Dutch, Danish and Swedish forces, while aircraft built in Switzerland by EKW and Dornier until 1936 used Hispano powerplants.

*Above: As well as float-equipped C.V-Cs, the Dutch Naval Air Service flew C.V-Es with wheeled landing gear.*

*Below: Of the 10 C.V-Es that survived in Danish service until 1940, two were taken over by the Luftwaffe, including 3W+OD, formerly R-42. After the war this aircraft was returned to Denmark, having survived hostilities.*

## C.V-D

**Type:** two-seat light fighter and reconnaissance aircraft

**Powerplant:** one 455-kW (610-hp.) Bristol Jupiter VI nine-cylinder, air-cooled radial engine

**Maximum speed:** 245 km/h (152 m.p.h.)

**Climb rate:** 1 min 54 sec to 1000 m (3,300 ft.)

**Range:** 770 km (480 mi.)

**Service ceiling:** 7300 m (24,000 ft.)

**Weights:** empty 1125 kg (2,475 lb.); loaded 1725 kg (3,795 lb.)

**Armament:** one or two fixed forward-firing machine-guns and one or two machine-guns in a flexible mounting in the rear cockpit

**Dimensions:**

| | | |
|---|---|---|
| span | 12.50 m | (41 ft.) |
| length | 9.46 m | (31 ft. 1 in.) |
| height | 3.30 m | (10 ft. 10 in.) |
| wing area | 28.8 m² | (310 sq. ft.) |

---

Denmark's C.V-Es were powered by various engines. This example has a Bristol Pegasus radial; others had Lorraine-Dietrich and Jupiter engines.

Depending on the role this versatile aircraft was performing, the C.V had up to four machine-guns installed, including two flexibly mounted in the rear cockpit.

Having a welded steel tube and fabric fuselage, with wooden wings, the C.V followed traditional Fokker design rules of the period.

The ability of the C.V to be fitted with different liquid-cooled in-line and air-cooled radial engines was a strength of the design. Often operators used mixed fleets; the Dutch, for example, ordered C.V-Ds with both Hispano-Suiza and Jaguar engines.

Designed to fill several different roles, from bombing to reconnaissance, the C.V also sported wings that could be changed in less than one hour if necessary. The C.V was a sesquiplane, i.e. the lower wing had less than half the area of the upper.

**C.V-E**

A sample C.V-E, serialled R-21, arrived in Denmark from the Netherlands in July 1933. Thirty were then licence-built for the Danish Air Troops, including R-31. By 1940 only 10 were still in service.

Danish air force Captain Botved flew a C.V from Copenhagen to Tokyo and back via the British East Indies and Siberia between March and June 1926. In 72 flying hours he covered 10,395 km (6,445 mi.).

---

## COMBAT DATA

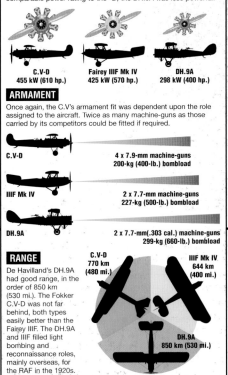

**POWER**

The C.V's power rating depended on its engine and could vary between 186 kW (250 hp.) and 544 kW (730 hp.). The Fairey had a comparable power rating to the -D; the DH.9A was less powerful.

| C.V-D | Fairey IIIF Mk IV | DH.9A |
|---|---|---|
| 455 kW (610 hp.) | 425 kW (570 hp.) | 298 kW (400 hp.) |

**ARMAMENT**

Once again, the C.V's armament fit was dependent upon the role assigned to the aircraft. Twice as many machine-guns as those carried by its competitors could be fitted if required.

C.V-D — 4 x 7.9-mm machine-guns 200-kg (400-lb.) bombload

IIIF Mk IV — 2 x 7.7-mm machine-guns 227-kg (500-lb.) bombload

DH.9A — 2 x 7.7-mm (.303 cal.) machine-guns 299-kg (660-lb.) bombload

**RANGE**

De Havilland's DH.9A had good range, in the order of 850 km (530 mi.). The Fokker C.V-D was not far behind, both types easily better than the Fairey IIIF. The DH.9A and IIIF filled light bombing and reconnaissance roles, mainly overseas, for the RAF in the 1920s.

C.V-D 770 km (480 mi.)
IIIF Mk IV 644 km (400 mi.)
DH.9A 850 km (530 mi.)

---

# Fokker's inter-war combat designs

■ **D.XI:** This fighter design of 1923 had a 225-km/h top speed, but was unable to generate orders from the Dutch air force.

■ **D.XIII:** First flown in September 1924, the D.XIII was a single-seat fighter derived from the D.VII. Power came from a Napier Lion.

■ **D.XVII:** Able to achieve 376 km/h in level flight, the sleek D.XVII fighter was an enlarged development of the D.XVI with twin machine-guns.

■ **C.X:** Designed to replace the C.V, this Pegasus-powered light bomber and fighter-reconnaissance type served from the late 1930s.

# FOKKER

# D.VII

● Scout fighter ● Flown by fighter ace Ernst Udet ● Best of its time

▲ The combination
of skilled pilots and the superb D.VII
gave the Imperial German air service a new
breath of life in 1918, with the capability of
matching any other fighter in the world.

**F**okker's D.VII was the greatest
single-seat scout used by Germany in
World War I, and possibly the best
flown by any nation. It took a courageous
pilot to do battle with the West's greatest
planes and pilots. The D.VII gave German
airmen the chance to fight on more than
equal terms with the Sopwith Camel,
Spad XIII and other fine fighters which had
swung the balance of the air war to the
Allies after the disasters of April 1917.

## PHOTO FILE

## FOKKER D.VII

▲ **Fokker heritage**
The D.VII was not a totally new design, inheriting
features from previous Fokkers. But the
Fokker D.VII's performance was unprecedented.

▲ **Powerful engine**
Much of the D.VII's success was
due to its efficient engines, which
were far more powerful and
reliable than those used by
fighters in the early years.
The additional power also
compensated for the extra weight
of the twin machine-guns.

◀ **Survivors**
Few D.VIIs survived
the war and only a
handful of the original
aircraft remain in
museums; one is
owned by the RAF
Museum. Many more
replica aircraft exist
than real examples.

▼ **Fokker fragments**
The remnants of this D.VII show just how
strong the aircraft's tubular steel structure
was, with the main fuselage still intact after
being shot down.

▲ **Dutch service post-war**
The Armistice at the end of World War I specifically
mentioned the D.VII among items to be handed over
to the Allies. Anthony Fokker took some dismantled
aircraft to Holland and more were built there, some
serving with the Dutch air force until the late 1920s.

## FACTS AND FIGURES

➤ By November 1918, 700 D.VIIs had been
delivered to the German air arm.

➤ The cost of one of today's European
Fighter Aircraft (EFA) would pay for
30,000 Fokker D.VIIs.

➤ The D.VII strongly influenced the Fokker
C.I, which appeared in the post-war era.

➤ Almost 43 groups of D.VIIs were in
service when the war ended.

➤ The D.VII was specifically singled out
for confiscation in the terms of the
Versailles Peace Treaty.

➤ Three replicas of the D.VII fly at air
shows in the United States.

## PROFILE

# Fokker's finest biplane fighter

First flown in January 1918, designer Reinhold Platz's Fokker D.VII was an immensely strong yet simple aircraft. Built around a steel tube frame, it performed superbly yet was easy to build and maintain.

It was immediately evident that this was a top-performing warplane. The D.VII was so much better than the Albatros D.V. series that Albatros Werke

GmbH was ordered to build the fighter under sub-contract at both of its factories. The Fokker D.VII was termed a 'major threat' by an Allied pilot who flew against it.

It combined speed, agility and firepower with a strong prospect of surviving any fight. So strong was the combat capability of this famous aircraft that the Versailles Treaty which

brought the war to an end specified that all planes of this type must be handed over to the Allies. The D.VII and the Zeppelin airships were the only German aircraft singled out for confiscation.

*Left: Among the D.VII's many virtues was its power, which allowed the aircraft to maintain a climbing attitude when other fighters would have stalled.*

*Right: In the late- and post-war periods pilots applied personal markings to the sides of their aircraft. This Swiss machine was one of many export D.VIIs.*

### D.VII

**Type:** single-seat fighter/scout

**Powerplant:** one 138-kW (185-hp.) BMW 6-cylinder in-line piston engine

**Maximum speed:** 200 km/h (124 m.p.h.) at 1000 m (3,300 ft.)

**Climb rate:** 1000 m (3,300 ft.) in 2½ min

**Service ceiling:** 7000 m (22,965 ft.)

**Weights:** empty 735 kg (1,620 lb.); max take-off 880 kg (1,940 lb.)

**Armament:** two fixed forward-firing 7.92-mm LMG 08/15 machine-guns

**Dimensions:** span 8.90 m (29 ft.); length 6.95 m (23 ft.); height 2.75 m (9 ft.); wing area 20.5 m² (221 sq. ft.)

The armament consisted of a pair of air-cooled LMG 7.92-mm machine-guns.

The pilot sat in an open cockpit, typical of aircraft of the day. He was close enough to his gun breeches to clear any jams by hand, and many pilots carried hammers or chisels for the job.

The main part of the airframe was a metal tube frame with a doped fabric covering.

Later D.VIIs had a small fuel tank in the fairing between the undercarriage wheels, giving much needed endurance.

The first D.VIIs used Mercedes engines, but later versions used BMW engines, all of the inline type.

The strange 'lozenge' pattern on German aircraft was the result of using pre-printed fabric. Many pilots added their own artwork.

A round tailfin was another distinctive feature of many Fokker aircraft. A simple tail skid protected the fin on the ground.

### D.VII
The Fokker D.VII served on the Western Front with distinction, and became the most feared German fighter scout of World War I.

### COMBAT DATA

#### MAXIMUM SPEED
The fastest fighters in World War I could reach around 200 km/h (125 m.p.h.), with the heavy and powerful French Spads being among the fastest. But pilots valued other features just as highly. Rate of climb was considered vital, and agility was especially desirable. The D.VII combined all of these qualities in one aircraft.

| | |
|---|---|
| D.VII | 200 km/h (124 m.p.h.) |
| CAMEL | 185 km/h (115 m.p.h.) |
| SPAD XIII | 220 km/h (136 m.p.h.) |

#### ENDURANCE
Scout fighters were required to make standing patrols over the battlefield to prevent opposing aircraft crossing their territory. The heavier Spad and Camel carried more fuel than the D.VII, and could stay on patrol for a longer period.

D.VII 1½ hours    CAMEL 2 hours    SPAD XIII 2 hours

#### SERVICE CEILING
The D.VII had a high power-to-weight ratio, giving excellent climb performance and a high service ceiling. In practice, flying at such altitudes without oxygen equipment in open cockpits was extremely tough on the pilots, many of whom suffered from anoxia or frostbite. Patrols were usually carried out at about 5000 metres (16,500 ft.).

7000 m (22,960 ft.)    5790 m (19,000 ft.)    6650 m (21,810 ft.)
D.VII    CAMEL    SPAD XIII

## Finest fighters of the Great War

**SOPWITH CAMEL:** Sopwith's finest scout fighter, the Camel featured superb manoeuvrability and speed, but was not an easy aircraft to fly, being prone to flick into spins when mishandled.

**SPAD XIII:** The French Spad XIII was a fast and rugged fighter used by several Allied fighter aces such as Rickenbacker and Fonck. It was also used by the fledgling US Army Air Corps.

**FOKKER DR.1:** The legendary Fokker Triplane was flown by many German air aces, including Baron Manfred von Richthofen. It was highly agile and possessed an excellent rate of climb.

# FOKKER

# D.VII STUNT FLYER

● Ace maker ● Film star fighter ● World War I veteran

S pinning and spiralling, twisting and diving biplanes fill the sky at an assortment of angles and altitudes. A pilot hastily looks over his shoulder to search for the enemy fighter looming up on his tail. A flash of guns, and smoke billows from the engine cowling as the enemy dives away. Time and again Hollywood war movies featured such performing aircraft and valiant heroes, and prominent amongst the melées was the Fokker D.VII.

▲ Once left
derelict, the few remaining
Fokker D.VIIs are now highly prized possessions.
This example was restored to flying condition for
exhibition at airshows in Europe.

## FOKKER D.VII

▼ **Air pirate**
Restored to former wartime markings, this Fokker D.VII is painted with a skull and crossbones on its fuselage. During the war Fokkers wore some of the most elaborate colour schemes.

▲ **Everlasting design**
By using steel tubes for the fuselage and tailplane structure the Fokker designers produced a fighter that was strong and able to withstand extraordinary stunts, qualities that were not wasted in front of the movie cameras.

**Elite units, elite fighter ▶**
The exceptional capabilities of the Fokker design allowed the aircraft to be the chosen mount for Germany's fighter aces in 1918.

▼ **Revered past**
These Fokkers of World War I are displayed here next to a former enemy.

**Superior scout ▶**
If the Fokker D.VII was not battling with British fighters it was being used as a fast scout. Prominent on most machines were large German crosses on the wheels.

## FACTS AND FIGURES

➤ The Fokker D.VII was ordered into production having won Germany's January 1918 fighter competition.

➤ Its performance was matched in combat only by that of the British Sopwith Snipe.

➤ By the end of World War I, some 700 examples had been built.

➤ A number of Fokker D.VIIs were lost when the phosphorous ammunition carried in the aircraft ignited.

➤ During manoeuvres the centre-section fuselage often became over stressed.

➤ Hollywood stunt pilots praised the aircraft for its superb handling.

**PROFILE**

# Silver screen fighter

Hollywood developed as the world centre for the film industry during the Roaring Twenties, with film stars and directors flocking to propose and produce numerous action films.

Having already captured the public's imagination in war, pilots and their aircraft were soon appearing in front of the cameras to thrill the film-going population.

One of the most ambitious movies involving massive aerial dogfights was Hell's Angels, directed by Howard Hughes. The success of this film led studios to produce a host of thrilling aerial productions.

With huge numbers of surplus fighter aircraft from World War I being sold for just a few dollars, highly elaborate and complex aerial battles could be staged. The participating aircraft were often destroyed to add to the overall dramatic effect.

A leading star among these ex-military aircraft was the Fokker D.VII.

*Below: A pilot looks over his shoulder to the chase aircraft in anticipation of beginning another dogfight for the cameras.*

*Above: Though lacking the graceful lines of the Albatros and Pfalz scouts, the Fokker D.VII proved to be a startling surprise to RFC pilots.*

## D.VII

Fokker D.VII aces wore a succession of elaborate colour schemes during World War I. After the war these were often faithfully reproduced by Hollywood producers to add realism to their war movies. This particular example wears a black and white colour scheme along its fuselage.

An important feature of the the Fokker fighter was its ability to 'hang' on its propeller at high altitude. This allowed pilots to fire upwards when other fighters would spin away.

Because of the immense strength of the fuselage and wing construction, the Fokker fighter could be manoeuvred vigorously in aerial combat. This sparkling performance allowed Hollywood producers to direct enormous and elaborate dogfights to thrill and excite movie audiences.

As with most fighters of the period a tail-skid was positioned at the rear of the fuselage. Handling of the aircraft was praised by both German and British pilots. With such performance capabilities the Fokker D.VII became a star aircraft in Hollywood.

Early series Fokker D.VIIs were equipped with a Mercedes D.III powerplant. This low-powered engine limited the type's performance. Later models were fitted with a much improved and more powerful BMW engine.

The reputation of the Fokker fighter allowed the aircraft to become the chosen mount of a host of Germany's World War I aces. After the war civilian pilots were equally as keen to obtain an example.

### D.VII

**Type:** single-seat fighter/scout

**Powerplant:** one 138-kW (185-hp.) BMW III six-cylinder in-line piston engine

**Maximum speed:** 200 km/h (124 m.p.h.)

**Endurance:** 1 hr 30 min

**Initial climb rate:** 321 m/min (1053 f.p.m.)

**Service ceiling:** 7000 m (22,970 ft.)

**Weights:** empty 735 kg (1,620 lb.); maximum take-off 880 kg (1,940 lb.)

**Armament:** two fixed forward-firing 7.92-mm LMG 08/15 machine guns

**Dimensions:**
| | |
|---|---|
| span | 8.90 m (29 ft. 2 in.) |
| length | 6.95 m (22 ft. 10 in.) |
| height | 2.75 m (9 ft.) |
| wing area | 20.50 m² (221 sq. ft.) |

## ACTION DATA

### POWER

A steady increase in engine performance allowed the Fokker company to develop a highly powerful fighter in the Fokker D.VII. With the power available the fighter was able to perform the complex manoeuvres which were vital during aerial combat.

| D.VII | E.III | D.V |
|---|---|---|
| 138 kW (185 hp.) | 75 kW (100 hp.) | 149 kW (197 hp.) |

### ENDURANCE

Because of the practice of mounting standing aerial patrols, long endurance was a particularly important quality in World War I fighters. Despite the advantages that the Fokker D.VII offered in many areas, its endurance was no more than comparable to that of other fighters of the period.

| D.VII | E.III | D.V |
|---|---|---|
| 1 hr 30 min | 1 hr 30 min | 2 hr |

### MAXIMUM SPEED

Speed and manoeuvrability were the key design requirements for fighters of World War I. Light in weight and equipped with a high-powered engine, the Fokker D.VII proved to have exceptional speed, a capability not lost on Hollywood's movie makers.

| | |
|---|---|
| D.VII | 200 km/h (124 m.p.h.) |
| E.III | 140 km/h (87 m.p.h.) |
| D.V | 186 km/h (116 m.p.h.) |

## Fantastic Fokkers

■ **A DOPED 'D MODEL':** Serving as a two-seat trainer this particular example wore an overall fabric-dope colour scheme. The forward-firing guns were removed from this aircraft.

■ **'BLUEBIRD':** Using a mixture of pre-printed fabric on its fuselage and 'lozenge' pattern for both wings, this particular D.VII was flown by Lieutenant Piel of Jasta 13.

■ **CLOUD COLOURS:** An overall light grey colour was adopted late in the service life of the Fokker D.VII in order to conceal the aircraft at high altitude during scouting missions.

# FOKKER

# DR.1

● Agile hunter of the skies ● Von Richthofen's fighter

**S**upremely agile, the Fokker Dr.1 was a powerful tool in the hands of Baron von Richthofen's Flying Circus in the last two years of World War I. The Dr.1 overcame serious manufacturing flaws to become the scourge of Allied aces on the Western Front, weaving a pattern of destruction with its twin machine-guns. A ferocious adversary, this potent fighter was for a brief period the monarch of the skies.

▲ A Fokker Triplane gets a push across muddy ground on the Western Front. The middle wing and steep fuselage angle made it a bit of a handful on the ground.

---

# FOKKER DR.1

**▲ Horned wings**
Ailerons were on the upper wing only. They were fitted with large 'horns', making the aircraft roll at an unbelievable rate. The large tailplane allowed the pilot to hold the turn better than Allied fighters.

**▲ Lightweight fighter**
Like other World War I fighters, the Dr.1 was so light that the best way to move it was to pick it up and carry it!

**Ace machine ▲**
The Dr.1 had plenty of vices and was not for the novice airman. Only the best pilots could handle this tricky little fighter.

**▲ Modern triplane**
Few aviation stories have achieved the notoriety of that of Baron von Richthofen, making the Fokker Dr.1 a popular subject for replica-builders.

**Movie star ▶**
Many of the replicas of Dr.1s have been spurred by the requirements of Hollywood; the Red Baron legend is an enduring one.

## FACTS AND FIGURES

➤ The Dr.1 was the fastest-climbing and most manoeuvrable fighter of its day.

➤ Triplanes had weak wings, which often collapsed in combat.

➤ Despite its sensational performance, the Fokker was grounded in 1917 while its wings were redesigned.

➤ A Luftwaffe F-4 Phantom today weighs 98 times as much as a Dr.1.

➤ More than 300 Fokker Dr.1s were built and the type remained in service until the end of World War I.

➤ Triplanes were flown by many aces, the most notable being von Richthofen.

# Triplanes over the Western Front

Anthony Fokker, the Dutch planemaker working in Germany, joined the triplane craze started by Britain's Sopwith and created the splendid three-winged Dr.1 in 1917. Air ace Baron Manfred von Richthofen told pilots that Fokker Dr.1s 'are manoeuvrable as the Devil and climb like monkeys'. Richthofen was killed flying a blood-red Dr.1 after scoring many of his 80 aerial conquests in the triplane.

The Fokker Dr.1 moved aviation design forward with wings that needed no bracing struts. At first the design was unreliable; two aces were killed when their wings tore apart in mid-air. Fokker solved construction problems and the Dr.1 became a superb aircraft to fly, and by 1918 it was a terror to British airmen who faced it in combat.

The Fokker Dr.1 won glory and wreaked havoc amongst its opponents until newer biplane fighters matched its spectacular performance, closing the short but brilliant career of this truly great fighting machine.

*The Dr.1 earned a reputation that far outweighed the numbers produced. At no time did the number in service exceed 171 (in May 1918), and by the summer it had virtually disappeared from the front line.*

### Dr.1 Triplane

**Type:** single-seat fighter/scout

**Powerplant:** one 108-kW Thulin-built Le Rhône or Oberursel Ur.II nine-cylinder rotary piston engine

**Maximum speed:** 185 km/h (115 m.p.h.) at 4000 m (13,100 ft.)

**Endurance:** 1 hr 30 min

**Rate of climb:** 1000 m (3,300 ft.) in 2 min 54 sec; time to 3000 m (10,000 ft.) 7 min 6 sec

**Service ceiling:** 6100 m (20,000 ft.)

**Weights:** empty 430 kg (948 lb.); loaded 610 kg (1345 lb.)

**Armament:** two 7.92-mm LMG 08/15 air-cooled machine-guns

**Dimensions:**
| | |
|---|---|
| span | 7.20 m (23 ft. 8 in.) |
| length | 5.77 m (18 ft. 11 in.) |
| height | 2.95 m (9 ft. 8 in.) |
| wing area | 18.7 m² (201 sq. ft.) |

## DR.1 TRIPLANE

**Arguably the most famous fighter of all time, the Fokker Dr.1 achieved this position through the achievements of just one man, Rittmeister Manfred, Freiherr von Richthofen, better known as the Red Baron. He was flying this type when he was finally brought down.**

Armament of the Dr.1 was the standard German fit of two LMG 08/15 guns mounted on top of the fuselage.

There is much controversy surrounding the death of Manfred von Richthofen on 21 April 1918. The official RAF version is that he was shot down by Canadian Camel pilot Captain A.R. Brown. But examination of his wounds when he was found slumped in the cockpit of his crashed Dreidecker would suggest that he was actually killed by Australian troops firing from the ground.

The triplane layout gave the pilot a much better view than with conventional biplane fighters.

By using three wings, the Dr.1 was very compact, enabling its pilots to perform astonishing aerial manoeuvres.

Early triplanes were fitted with poorly manufactured upper wings, which tended to collapse under hard manoeuvring.

As with all aircraft of the period, the triplane was fitted with a simple tail skid rather than the heavier and more complex castoring wheel which was to appear on later machines.

The origins of the Fokker Dr.1 lay in the Sopwith Triplane, which greatly impressed the Germans. When one crashed behind enemy lines Anthony Fokker managed to steal it away from the authorities to his own factory, and rapidly set to work copying many of its features.

### COMBAT DATA

#### MAXIMUM SPEED

Extremely agile machines such as the Dr.1 or the Camel were not known for their great speed, but their light construction meant that they had good acceleration, and could out-turn and outfight faster machines.

| | |
|---|---|
| **DR.1 TRIPLANE** | 185 km/h (115 m.p.h.) |
| **CAMEL** | 187 km/h (116 m.p.h.) |
| **SPAD VII** | 192 km/h (119 m.p.h.) |

#### ENDURANCE

German scouts generally fought over their own lines. Allied fighters, on the other hand, needed longer endurance since they often patrolled aggressively over German-occupied territory.

| DR.1 TRIPLANE 1 hour 30 minutes | CAMEL 2 hours 30 minutes | SPAD VII 2 hours 15 minutes |
|---|---|---|

## 'The Fokker Scourge'

**FOKKER E.III**
The 'Eindecker' was the first scoutplane with a machine-gun which fired between the propeller blades. It created havoc over the skies of France in 1915 and 1916, downing hundreds of Allied aircraft and helped create the Fokker legend.

**FOKKER DR.1**
Its three wings gave the Triplane phenomenal lift, and for a time in 1917 it was as dominant as its monoplane ancestor had been two years before. However, it was tricky to fly and the three wings severely restricted ground visibility.

**FOKKER D.VII**
The D.VII was the pinnacle of Imperial German fighter design. Fast, tough, and with all the agility of the triplane, it was perhaps the first fighter of World War I, although it appeared too late to influence the air war.

# FOKKER

# DR.1: JG 1

● JG 1's most famous fighter ● von Richthofen's final aircraft

▲ Jasta 11's pilots included Manfred von Richthofen's brother Lothar (seated, cross-legged), who joined the unit in March 1917. He was to amass 40 victories and was credited with the SE.5 of Captain Albert Ball, No. 56 Squadron, RFC – Britain's most famous fighter pilot of the time.

**F**or brave pilots who flew with Baron Manfred von Richthofen, the 'Flying Circus' meant high risks and no safety net. Richthofen was Germany's top ace and the Dr.I was one of its best fighters. But climbing into a fragile, fabric-covered Fokker and going aloft often meant an appointment with peril. Meeting Allied pilots in battle was the greatest challenge of all. This was the cutting edge of fighter aviation during the Great War.

## FOKKER **DR.I**

▲ First 'Dreideckers' arrive
von Richthofen (right) looks on as a pilot is introduced to the new Fokker. Aircraft 102/17, later flown by von Richthofen himself, carries the early F.I designation.

▲ Highly manoeuvrable
While von Richthofen appreciated the Dr.I's handling, he was not the fan of the type that the press portrayed. The greatest exponent of the Dr.I was Werner Voss, who gained 48 victories in the Dr.I.

▲ Albatros D.III
Richthofen's Jagdgeschwader 1 used a number of types, including the Albatros D.III.

▼ Jasta 11 aces
von Richthofen is seen here with two other aces: Scholz (seven victories) and Mohnicke (nine victories).

▲ von Richthofen's first Dr.I
This aircraft was the second production Fokker F.I (later Dr.I) and was the first machine assigned to von Richthofen. While flying it he scored his 60th kill, and Kurt Wolff of Jasta 11 later met his end in it.

### FACTS AND FIGURES

➤ JG 1's third and final commander was Oberleutnant Hermann Göring, World War II Luftwaffe commander-in-chief.

➤ The exact cause of Richthofen's death is unclear, although ground fire seems likely.

➤ Jasta 10's aircraft were yellow; Jastas 4 and 6 wore black and white spirals.

➤ One of JG 1's greatest rivals was the Royal Flying Corps' No. 56 Squadron, led by British ace Captain James McCudden.

➤ von Richthofen's Albatros D.III was known to RFC pilots as 'le petit rouge'.

➤ 'Jagdgeschwader Richthofen' was reborn twice – in 1936 (JG 2) and 1959 (JG 71).

# JG 1: the world's first fighter wing

A pril 1917 – 'Bloody April' – saw Imperial Germany's Army Air Service, the Luftstreikräfte, in virtual control of the skies over the Western Front. To maintain this hard-won position, a decision was taken in June to formally amalgamate four Jagdstaffeln (Jastas) that had been flying together experimentally against enemy fighter patrols. Jagdgeschwader Nr.1 was the result. Jasta 11's commander, the 25-year-old Rittmeister Manfred von Richthofen, the 'Red Baron', was to be its first leader. Each Jasta had its own distinctive colour scheme (Jasta 11's was red) and pilots often had their

own personal markings; JG 1 soon became known as 'von Richthofen's Flying Circus'. Their aircraft included the Albatros D.III and D.V and, later, the Fokker D.VII, although they are perhaps best known for their exploits in Fokker's Dr.I. Among the pilots were the most accomplished Air Service aces of the day, including Werner Voss and Ernst Udet.

In its 17-month lifespan the wing amassed 644 aerial victories, but 56 of its pilots were killed and 52 were wounded.

*Often discounted as a copy of the Sopwith Triplane (at least one early example of which fell into German hands), the Dr.I obviously owed its conception to the British scout. However, when originally produced the design featured three cantilever wings without interplane struts.*

## Dr.I

**Type:** single-seat fighting scout

**Powerplant:** one 82-kW (110-hp.) Oberursel UR II rotary piston engine

**Maximum speed:** 165 km/h (103 m.p.h.) at 4000 m (13,120 ft.)

**Initial climb rate:** 7.1 min to 3000 m (9840 ft.)

**Endurance:** 1 hr 30 min

**Service ceiling:** 6100 m (20,000 ft.)

**Weights:** empty 430 kg (948 lb.); maximum take-off 626 kg (1,380 lb.)

**Armament:** two fixed 7.92-mm LMG 08/15 on nose firing through propeller arc

**Dimensions:**
| | | |
|---|---|---|
| span | 7.19 m | (23 ft. 7 in.) |
| length | 5.77 m | (18 ft. 11 in.) |
| height | 2.95 m | (9 ft. 8 in.) |
| wing area | 18.66 m² | (201 sq. ft.) |

Two fixed Spandau machine-guns were synchronised to fire through the propeller arc. They could be fired independently.

von Richthofen flew four triplanes in total, one of which (152/17) was displayed after the war in a Berlin museum. It was destroyed by Allied bombs in 1944.

## Dr.I

**Arguably one of the best-known aircraft, this Dr.I (425/17) was the aircraft flown by von Richthofen when he was killed on 21 April 1918.**

Contrary to many reports, this aircraft was not all-red. It featured blue undersides, metal cowling and white wheels and vertical tail.

The Fokker Dr.I (or F.I as it was originally known) was powered by either an Oberursel UR II or Thulin-built Le Rhône nine-cylinder rotary engine, rated at 82 kW (115 hp.), driving a two-bladed 2.6-m (8-ft. 6-in.) diameter wooden propeller.

On this aircraft the straight-sided national marking, known as the 'Balkenkreuz', had been recently applied, and traces of the original 'Iron Cross' were still visible.

During late 1917 a number of pilots were killed after the main wing structure failed; this caused the Dr.I to be temporarily grounded.

## ACTION DATA

### MAXIMUM SPEED

The Albatros D.III was followed in JG 1 service by the Fokker Dr.I. This, in turn, was replaced by the Fokker D.VII towards the end of the war. The Dr.I introduced better manoeuvrability over the D.III.

| | |
|---|---|
| Dr.I | 165 km/h (103 m.p.h.) |
| D.III | 165 km/h (103 m.p.h.) |
| D.VII | 186 km/h (116 m.p.h.) |

### ENDURANCE

The rotary-engined Dr.I actually had less endurance than the D.III which it replaced. Greater power and handling improvements were viewed as more important to counter new British fighters like the Sopwith Triplane.

| Dr.I | D.III | D.VII |
|---|---|---|
| 1½ hours | 2 hours | 1½ hours |

### ENGINE POWER

While it is true that engine power increased steadily as the war progressed, resulting in improved performance, the later Fokker Dr.I actually had a smaller engine than the Albatros D.III as it was a much lighter aircraft.

| Dr.I | D.III | D.VII |
|---|---|---|
| 82 kW (110 hp.) | 119 kW (160 hp.) | 138 kW (185 hp.) |

## Dogfight manoeuvres

**TACTICAL EVOLUTION:** As aircraft improved, so air combat manoeuvring developed.

**SNAP TURN:** Using engine torque to increase turn rate allowed the target to get behind his opponent.

**IMMELMANN:** Named after its inventor Max Immelmann, this climbing turn was used mainly as a means of escape.

**SPLIT-S:** The split-S was used by more experienced pilots as a variation of the snap turn and was intended to force the opponent to overshoot the target.

**LUFBERY:** This was a variation of the split-S and introduced climbing and diving turns.

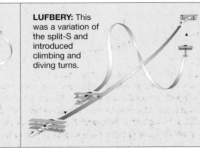

# FOKKER

# G.1

● Heavy fighter/ground attack ● Early war service ● Luftwaffe use

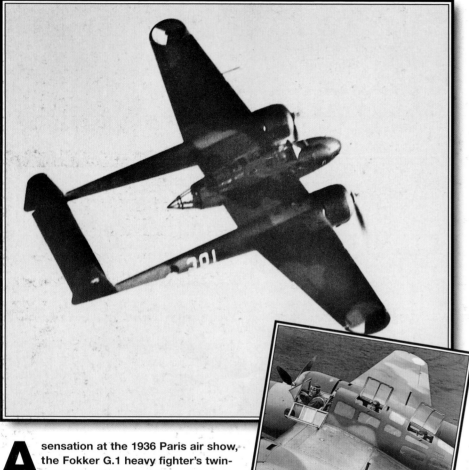

▲ A radical design departure for Fokker, the G.1 was poised to sell well in export markets when the outbreak of war in 1939 saw the Dutch air force commandeer production in order to bolster its own G.1 units.

**A** sensation at the 1936 Paris air show, the Fokker G.1 heavy fighter's twin-engined, twin-boom shape was new and innovative. The aircraft appeared to set a new standard of speed and performance. In fact, the Fokker G.1 was a transitional design, merging ageing technology of the 1930s with improved features that were to characterise World War II aircraft. Outperformed by single-seaters, the G.1 had a modest and short career.

# FOKKER **G.1**

▼ **Undelivered Finnish G.1B**
Upon arrival in Finland the G.1Bs were to be fitted with two Oerlikon 20-mm (0.79-in.) cannon and two 7.92-mm (0.31-in.) machine-guns. In 1939 all completed aircraft were kept by the Dutch.

▲ **On test over Schipol Airport**
Only part of the aircraft's serial number has been applied to this production G.1A.

◄ **In Luftwaffe service**
After four days of fighting, the Netherlands capitulated on 14 May 1940. At the Fokker factory the German invaders found two serviceable G.1As and a number of G.1Bs, originally destined for Finland. They were completed and transferred to Germany.

▲ **Captured G.1**
G.1B no. 348 was one of a number captured by the Luftwaffe and employed as trainers. It retains its Dutch serial number and wing markings but has gained a set of Luftwaffe insignia.

◄ **Decimated**
Outclassed by the Luftwaffe, the small force of Dutch G.1s sustained heavy casualties during the German invasion. By 14 May, the last day of operations, only five G.1s were left in service.

## FACTS AND FIGURES

➤ When the Netherlands entered the war in May 1940, just 23 machine-gun-armed G.1As were in service with three units.

➤ After its Paris show appearance, the G.1 made its maiden flight on 16 March 1937.

➤ The Dutch navy was on the point of ordering G.1s when World War II began.

➤ Fokker's G.1 made use of advanced wooden construction and was a leader in this field for years after its first flight.

➤ Among planned G.1 developments was the G.2 with Mercedes DB600 engines.

➤ Sweden tested a G.1 at a speed of 644 km/h (400 m.p.h.) in the dive-bomber role.

# PROFILE

# Holland's heavy fighter

Originally flown with Hispano-Suiza radials, the G.1 was initially slow in development, after a mishap in which the prototype suffered brake failure and rammed a hangar at Schipol Airport on 4 July 1937.

A private venture by Fokker, the G.1 proved to be a sound design and attracted the attention of the Dutch Army Air Service. Changes were made to meet their requirements, which caused further delay, and the G.1 finally began to reach

squadrons in mid-1939. As the aircraft went into Dutch service, export orders were placed by several European countries, though deliveries were not possible – war had broken out in 1939 and the Netherlands would need all the aircraft it could get.

When Germany occupied the Netherlands in May 1940, G.1s (armed with eight machine-guns or mixed cannon/machine-gun armament) made little impact against the advancing forces. The G.1s made a few bomb

attacks on the invaders and shot down some German aircraft, but their own losses were high.

Germany later made use of captured aircraft as trainers. Of 62 G.1s built, none has survived.

Below: The Fokker G.1 prototype, X-2, was equipped with the 559-kW (750-hp.) Hispano-Suiza 80-02 radial engines, which failed during testing.

Above: On 5 May 1941 two Dutch workers at the German-controlled Fokker works fled to England in a G.1 while on a test flight. The aircraft was examined at the Royal Aircraft Establishment.

## G.1A

**Type:** twin-engined heavy fighter and ground attack aircraft

**Powerplant:** two 619-kW (830-hp.) Bristol Mercury VIII radial piston engines

**Maximum speed:** 432 km/h (268 m.p.h.)

**Range:** 1400 km (870 mi.)

**Service ceiling:** 9100 m (30,000 ft.)

**Weights:** empty 3150 kg (6,930 lb.); gross 4400 kg (9,680 lb.)

**Armament:** eight 7.92-mm (0.31-in.) FN-Browning machine-guns in the nose, one flexible 7.92-mm FN-Browning machine-gun in the rear fuselage, plus up to 300 kg (660 lb.) of bombs

**Dimensions:** span 16.50 m (54 ft. 2 in.); length 11.50 m (37 ft. 9 in.); height 3.40 m (11 ft. 2 in.); wing area 35.70 m² (381 sq. ft.)

## G.1B

No. 343 was one of a batch of 26 G.1Bs (nos 337 to 362) ordered by Finland and taken over by the Luchtvaartafdeling (Dutch air force) in April 1940. Only 12 were delivered before the German invasion.

Originally envisaged as having a mixed cannon/machine-gun armament (as planned for the smaller G.1B), production G.1As were armed with a battery of eight 7.92-mm (0.31-in.) FN-Browning machine-guns in the nose of the aircraft.

The standard G.1 cabin layout allowed a crew of two to be carried: a pilot and radio operator/rear gunner. Production aircraft allowed for a third crewman, an observer, to be accommodated.

In the glazed tailcone at the rear of the cabin, the upper panels folded inward to allow operation of the defensive machine-gun mounted on an internal horizontal bar.

Intended for export, the G.1B (originally known as 'G.1 Wasp') was 1.2 m shorter than the G.1A. Its wingspan was similarly narrowed by 0.65 m (2 ft.). Consequently, less powerful engines were used.

After the Hispano-Suiza radials fitted to the original G.1 prototype proved unsuitable, 619-kW (830-hp.) Bristol Mercury VIIIs were substituted on the G.1A. G.1Bs for export were powered by 559-kW (750-hp.) Pratt & Whitney Twin Wasp Juniors.

Principally a heavy fighter, the G.1 had only a modest bomb load. Bomb stowage and release equipment was fitted under the fuselage, with a capacity of 300 kg (660 lb.) on the G.1A and 400 kg (880 lb.) on the G.1B.

Had the outbreak of war not intervened, Fokker would have been able to fulfill export orders for the G.1 from Finland, Estonia and Sweden. Denmark planned to build a number under licence.

The Netherlands changed its national markings to the orange and black insignia depicted on this aircraft in October 1939, shortly after the beginning of World War II. Some captured G.1s kept these markings while flying with the Luftwaffe.

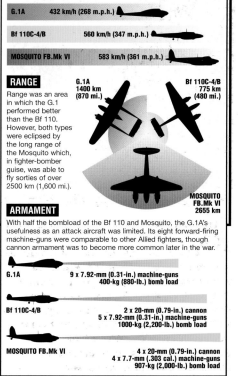

## COMBAT DATA

### MAXIMUM SPEED

By the time World War II had begun, the Fokker G.1A was outclassed in terms of its top speed. Even the Messerschmitt Bf 110 was considerably faster. Both aircraft were outpaced by the later de Havilland Mosquito.

G.1A 432 km/h (268 m.p.h.)
Bf 110C-4/B 560 km/h (347 m.p.h.)
MOSQUITO FB.Mk VI 583 km/h (361 m.p.h.)

### RANGE

Range was an area in which the G.1 performed better than the Bf 110. However, both types were eclipsed by the long range of the Mosquito which, in fighter-bomber guise, was able to fly sorties of over 2500 km (1,600 mi.).

G.1A 1400 km (870 mi.)
Bf 110C-4/B 775 km (480 mi.)
MOSQUITO FB.Mk VI 2655 km

### ARMAMENT

With half the bombload of the Bf 110 and Mosquito, the G.1A's usefulness as an attack aircraft was limited. Its eight forward-firing machine-guns were comparable to other Allied fighters, though cannon armament was to become more common later in the war.

G.1A 9 x 7.92-mm (0.31-in.) machine-guns 400-kg (880-lb.) bomb load

Bf 110C-4/B 2 x 20-mm (0.79-in.) cannon 5 x 7.92-mm (0.31-in.) machine-guns 1000-kg (2,200-lb.) bomb load

MOSQUITO FB.Mk VI 4 x 20-mm (0.79-in.) cannon 4 x 7.7-mm (.303 cal.) machine-guns 907-kg (2,000-lb.) bomb load

# Fokker G.1 markings

**PROTOTYPE G.1** In this view, prototype X-2 is seen after being re-engined with two Pratt & Whitney Twin Wasp Juniors. X-2 was later rebuilt to G.1B standard and became aircraft no. 341 of the undelivered Finnish order.

**PRE-OCTOBER 1939 MARKINGS:** Aircraft no. 314, a 619-kW Bristol Mercury VIII-engined G.1A (also known as the 'G.1 Mercury'), is seen in pre-October 1939 Dutch national markings. This machine flew with either the Third or Fourth Fighter Group.

**LUFTWAFFE SERVICE:** As well as taking delivery of the 12 ex-Finnish G.1Bs, the Luftwaffe ordered the completion of the other 14 machines still at the Fokker factory and shipped them to Germany for use as fighter trainers.

# GLOSTER

# GAMECOCK

● Biplane fighter ● Wooden construction ● Aerobatic star

▲ The Gamecock's nine-cylinder Bristol Jupiter IV engine produced 317 kW (425 hp.) and turned a wooden propeller to give the aircraft a top speed of 248 km/h (154 m.p.h.). All RAF examples used this powerplant.

**G**loster's Gamecock fighter burst onto the scene in the mid 1920s and, while far from beautiful, it astounded pilots with its performance. The Gamecock was the last wooden biplane fighter in Britain's Royal Air Force and typified the end of an era. Because of this, it embodied all that was known about air combat maneuverability. The Gamecock was meant for battle, but it also was extremely popular for its aerobatic qualities.

## GLOSTER GAMECOCK

**▼ Built under licence**
Gloster supplied three aircraft to Finland and these were followed by another 15 built under licence. The last aircraft was retired in 1941.

**▲ A pilot's dream**
The aerobatic capabilities of the Gamecock were loved by its pilots. Wearing the spectacular markings of the era and being flown to the limit, these fighters were great air show performers.

**◀ In RAF service**
The Royal Air Force received almost 100 Gamecocks, which served with five squadrons. J7900 was one of the first production batch of 30 Gamecock Mk Is.

**Aerodynamic problems ▼**
Early test flights revealed wing problems at high speeds. To solve these and to make the aircraft safer, a V-shaped strut was fitted between the wings.

**▲ Fighter development**
The main difference between the Gamecock and World War I fighters was its increased power.

## FACTS AND FIGURES

➤ The Gamecock was designed by H.P. Folland to meet British Air Ministry Specification 37/23.

➤ Developed from the Grebe, the Gamecock had a more powerful engine.

➤ The Gamecock first flew in 1925 and served in Finland as a trainer until 1941.

➤ The first squadron to be equipped with the Gamecock, No. 23, received its aircraft in May 1926.

➤ Many of the RAF's 100 Gamecock fighters were operational up to 1931.

➤ Before its first flight, progress in fighter design was overtaking the Gamecock.

**PROFILE**

# The last wooden fighter

The most potent fighter in the RAF in the mid 1920s was the Gloster Gamecock, a pilot's airplane and responsible for many fine aerobatic displays. Although it had an ungainly, swollen shape and was sometimes prone to wing flutter problems (making it necessary to add strengthening struts on the outer wing), the Gamecock was universally admired by the pilots who flew it and was deemed to be almost the perfect fighter. Much like the biplane fighters of the Great War, but with far greater power, the Gamecock was able to fly circles around most comparable aircraft then in service.

The Gamecock was constantly improved throughout its service life (changes to the design of the tail had proven necessary in early testing) and naturally drew the attention of foreign observers who were watching the RAF.

Gloster supplied three Gamecocks to Finland which then built 15 more in 1929–30. Named Kukko in Finnish service, these were in frontline service from 1929 to 1935 and were then used as trainers until the last was retired in 1941.

*An early Gamecock Mk I in service with No. 23 Squadron of the Royal Air Force. Aircraft such as this thrilled audiences at air shows during the late 1920s.*

### Gamecock Mk I

**Type:** Single-seat fighter.

**Powerplant:** One 317-kW (425-hp.) Bristol Jupiter VI nine-cylinder radial piston engine

**Maximum speed:** 248 km/h (154 m.p.h.)

**Range:** 1160 km (720 mi.)

**Service ceiling:** 6095 m (20,000 ft.)

**Weapons:** 2 fixed forward-firing 7.7-mm (.303 cal.) Vickers Mk I machine guns

**Weights:** Empty 873 kg (1,925 lb.); loaded 1103 kg (2,431 lb.)

**Dimensions:**
| | | |
|---|---|---|
| span | 9.07 m | (29 ft. 9 in.) |
| length | 5.99 m | (19 ft. 8 in.) |
| height | 2.95 m | (9 ft. 8 in.) |
| wing area | 24.53 m² | (264 sq. ft.) |

## GAMECOCK MK II

Known in Finnish service as the Kukko, the Gamecock Mk II had strengthened wings and other improvements.

The cylinder heads of the Bristol Jupiter VI engine protruded through the forward fuselage. A blast trough ahead of the machine gun protected the area from damage.

Unlike the Grebe, the open cockpit of the Gamecock was fitted with a windscreen, but Kukko pilots would have suffered in the cold of a Finnish winter.

The wooden construction of the Gamecock made it light and strong. During flight tests one aircraft reached 446 km/h (277 m.p.h.) in a dive and completed a 22-turn spin.

The prototype was fitted with a tail similar to that of the SE.5a. On production aircraft the tail was re-designed as shown.

The fixed main undercarriage featured suspension. The wheels were faired, but no other aerodynamic streamlining was attempted.

Ailerons were fitted to both sets of wings. These gave the Gamecock its outstanding agility and aerobatic performance. The Mk II no longer required the V-shaped strut.

This Mk II wears the national markings of Finland. Only three Mk IIs entered RAF service, but all of them were colorfully decorated with squadron markings.

A spring tailskid protected the rear fuselage on the ground. Tailwheels were quite uncommon on aircraft of this period.

### ACTION DATA

**POWER**

The less powerful Jupiter IV of the Woodcock gave it inferior performance to the Gamecock. American fighter designs were more advanced at this time and used far more powerful engines. British engine designers rapidly improved their technology.

| GAMECOCK Mk I | WOODCOCK Mk II | F4B-4 |
|---|---|---|
| 317 kW (425 hp.) | 283 kW (380 hp.) | 694 kW (930 hp.) |

**SPEED**

The higher speed of the Boeing F4B-4 results from its more advanced design and extra power. The British fighters, though slower than the F4B-4, are evenly matched. The RAF was soon to receive aircraft of much higher performance such as the Fury.

GAMECOCK Mk I    248 km/h (154 m.p.h.)
WOODCOCK Mk II   225 km/h (140 m.p.h.)
F4B-4            303 km/h (188 m.p.h.)

**CEILING**

Altitude can be a significant advantage in a dogfight. Here the Gamecock falls behind, but any lack of altitude performance could be compensated for by its stunning maneuverability.

F4B-4 8200 m (26,900 ft.)
WOODCOCK Mk II 6858 m (22,500 ft.)
GAMECOCK Mk I 6095 m (20,000 ft.)

## Gloster-built biplanes for the RAF

■ **GREBE:** This was the first radial-engine fighter to enter quantity production for the RAF and the predecessor of the Gamecock.

■ **GORCOCK:** Three Gorcocks were delivered in 1927. They were used for trials work and aided future fighter development.

■ **GAUNTLET:** The Gauntlet served successfully with the RAF in considerable numbers and was also widely exported.

■ **GLADIATOR:** Developed from the Gauntlet, this was the ultimate RAF biplane fighter with a 619-kW (830-hp.) engine and enclosed cockpit.

# GLOSTER

# GLADIATOR

● Single-seat fighter ● Last RAF and Royal Navy biplane fighter

**B**iplane fighters were already on the way out when the Gladiator development of the Gloster Gauntlet was proposed in 1933, but Britain's urgent need for combat aircraft led to orders for an eventual total of 581. These included 350 Gladiator Mk IIs, which had improved equipment and three-blade metal propellers in place of the Gladiator Mk I's two-bladed wooden airscrew. All had been delivered by April 1940 and a number went into combat.

▲ The Gladiator prototype flew for the first time in September 1934 as a private venture. The Air Ministry ordered the type the following year, with 480 being delivered. The Royal Navy took 60.

---

**PHOTO FILE**

## GLOSTER **GLADIATOR**

**▲ Last flyer**
The last surviving airworthy Gladiator is this Mk I, which belongs to the Shuttleworth Collection in Bedfordshire. Here it wears the colours of No. 247 Squadron, RAF, while they were flying defensive patrols over Plymouth.

**▲ Twenty RAF squadrons**
No fewer than 20 home-based RAF squadrons were equipped with the Gladiator from 1937 to 1940.

**▼ Air display practice**
Representing the RAF's fighter force of 1938, these tethered Gladiators practise for the 1938 Hendon air display.

**Scandinavian ▶ Gladiators**
The Swedish and Finnish air forces bought Gladiators in the late 1930s. These saw action early in World War II.

**◀ Battle of Britain**
One of the last home-based Gladiator units was No. 247 Squadron, which flew the type until late 1940 over Plymouth.

### FACTS AND FIGURES

➤ One Swedish squadron fighting with the Finns claimed 12 Soviet aircraft for only three losses.

➤ Gladiators entered RAF service in 1937, the year of the first Hurricane deliveries.

➤ The last RAF Gladiators, meteorological and liaison aircraft, were retired in 1944.

➤ The Sea Gladiators that defended Malta in early June 1940 were dubbed 'Faith', 'Hope' and 'Charity' by the Maltese.

➤ Sea Gladiators had catapult points, an arrester hook and a dinghy fairing fitted.

➤ Early Mk Is had two Vickers and two Lewis 7.7-mm (.303 cal.) machine-guns.

## PROFILE

# The last British biplane fighter

Despite being a biplane the Gladiator saw widespread action during the early stages of World War II. However, the results only underlined the type's obsolescence. The single squadron of Gladiators in Norway and the two squadrons based in France were all but wiped out during the German invasions in May and June 1940.

Other Gladiator squadrons fought in North Africa, Greece and Palestine in 1939 and 1940. Many were flown by Australian and South African units and a few were transferred to Egypt and Iraq. Another 36, which were supplied to China, joined the war against Japan in 1938.

The Sea Gladiator variant served aboard the aircraft-carriers *Courageous*, *Eagle* and *Glorious* and a handful were based in Malta when Italy joined the war in June 1940. For the next month, just four aircraft were the island's only defence against the Italians.

*K5200 was the Gladiator prototype. The enclosed cockpit had yet to appear, although the gun armament was fitted at an early stage.*

*A major improvement on the Gladiator in terms of pilot comfort was the fully enclosed cockpit, which had a rear-sliding Perspex canopy.*

*The forward and rear spars of the mainplanes were made of high-tensile steel of 'dumb-bell' cross-section. The wing leading edge was made of duralumin.*

### Gladiator Mk I

**Type:** single-seat interceptor

**Powerplant:** one 627-kW (840-hp.) Bristol Mercury Mk IX air-cooled radial engine

**Maximum speed:** 407 km/h (253 m.p.h.) at 4420 m (14,500 ft.)

**Climb rate:** 9.5 min to 6095 m (20,000 ft.)

**Range:** 547 km (340 mi.)

**Service ceiling:** 10,060 m (33,000 ft.)

**Weights:** empty 1565 kg (3,450 lb.); maximum take-off 2155 kg (4,751 lb.)

**Armament:** four 7.7-mm (.303 cal.) Browning machine-guns; two nose-mounted and two wing-mounted

**Dimensions:**
| | | |
|---|---|---|
| span | 9.83 m | (32 ft. 3 in.) |
| length | 8.36 m | (27 ft. 5 in.) |
| height | 3.15 m | (10 ft. 4 in.) |
| wing area | 30.01 m² | (323 sq. ft.) |

*The two-bladed wooden airscrew was a feature of the early Mk I Gladiators; Mk IIs were fitted with a three-bladed metal propeller.*

*Four fuselage- and wing-mounted 7.7-mm (.303 cal.) Browning machine-guns were fitted.*

*A silver dope finish was standard on RAF fighters between the wars. Often squadrons would add their individual markings to aircraft.*

*Behind the pilot's seat was the radio compartment, the aerials for the radio being strung between the wings and the tailfin.*

*Bristol's Mercury Mk IX radial engine also powered the earlier Gauntlet and other types like the twin-engined Blenheim bomber.*

### GLADIATOR MK I

K7985 was a Gladiator Mk I, one of a batch of 180 ordered in September 1935. Here it carries the well-known markings of No. 73 (Fighter) Squadron.

*Like most fighters of the 1930s, the Gladiator was of basically metal construction with a fabric skin.*

### COMBAT DATA

**MAXIMUM SPEED**

Arriving on the scene at the end of the biplane era, the Gladiator was fast for an aircraft of this type. It had an advantage over the He 51, but a lower top speed than the CR.42 which saw considerable wartime service.

| | |
|---|---|
| **GLADIATOR Mk I** | 407 km/h (253 m.p.h.) |
| **He 51** | 330 km/h (205 m.p.h.) |
| **CR.42 FALCO** | 420 km/h (261 m.p.h.) |

**SERVICE CEILING**

Again, the Gladiator and Falco had the edge over the earlier He 51. The monoplane was soon to make an impact, however. The first monoplane bombers were able to operate at higher altitudes.

GLADIATOR Mk I 10,060 m (33,000 ft.)
CR.42 FALCO 10,200 m (33,465 ft.)
He 51 7700 m (25,260 ft.)

**ARMAMENT**

Four machine-guns was about the limit for the last of the biplane fighters. These had to be fuselage-mounted or fitted under the wings. On monoplanes, guns were carried inside the wing assembly; monoplane wings were thicker and had more space.

GLADIATOR Mk I 4 x 7.7-mm (.303 cal.) machine-guns
CR.42 FALCO 2 x 12.7-mm (.50 cal.) machine-guns
He 51 2 x 7.92-mm (0.31-in.) machine-guns

## Gladiators around Europe

■ **FINLAND:** This Gladiator Mk II of the Suomen Ilmavoimat saw service in late 1939 and early 1940. Unlike the other Gladiator users, Finland flew its machines on the Axis side.

■ **NORWAY:** This Gladiator Mk II of the Norwegian Haerens Flyvevaben was based at Fornebeu, near Oslo, during April 1940. Ski landing gear was regularly fitted.

■ **PORTUGAL:** An important part of Portugal's airpower during World War II, this Gladiator II is shown in the markings of Esquadrilha de Caca de Base Aerea 2, flying from Ota in 1940.

# GLOSTER

# METEOR

● RAF's first jet fighter ● Flying bomb interceptor ● Single squadron

Even before Britain's first jet aircraft, the E.28/39, proved the practicality of this radical power source, Gloster was planning a new fighter to use the jet engine. After convincing the Air Ministry to draw up a specification (F.9/40) around their design, Gloster built a number of prototypes and by mid-1944 had equipped the first RAF jet unit, No. 616 Squadron. The intention was that the new jet would be pitted against Germany's jet fighter, the Me 262.

▲ Entering service
in 1944, the Meteor scored most of its victories against the high-speed V-1 flying bombs that plagued the British Isles towards the end of the war.

## GLOSTER METEOR

▲ Meteor F.Mk 1s in colour
Contemporary colour images of wartime Meteors are rare. This photograph was taken in June 1944, at Farnborough, prior to a flight to Manston.

▲ No. 616 re-equips
No. 616 Squadron, RAF, was flying Spitfire Mk VIIs when it was announced that the unit was to become the RAF's first jet squadron. Here, Mk 1s and Mk 3s can be seen at RAF Manston.

▲ Short service life
Issued to No. 616 Squadron in July 1944, this Meteor F.Mk 1 was written off one month later after suffering a forced landing.

▼ Clear-view canopy
Unlike the F.9/40, the Meteor had a clear-view canopy to allow the pilot to see the rear of his aircraft.

▲ Three different engines
Of the three engine types fitted to F.9/40s, the Rover W.2B and Halford H.1 were centrifugal flow designs, while the Metropolitan-Vickers F.2 had an axial-flow compressor. One aircraft flew with the Metro-Vickers engines installed, but soon crashed.

## FACTS AND FIGURES

➤ Among the other names suggested for the Meteor were Ace, Reaper, Scourge, Terrific, Thunderbolt and Wildfire.

➤ F.Mk 1s took part in trials to give USAAF crews experience of jet fighter tactics.

➤ When first deployed in Europe, Meteors were forbidden from flying over Germany.

➤ F.9/40 prototype, DG202/G, was later used for deck handling trials aboard HMS Pretoria Castle.

➤ The Halford H.1 engine was developed as the Goblin for the Vampire jet fighter.

➤ DG202, the first F.9/40, is displayed at the Aerospace Museum, Cosford.

# RAF jet pioneer at war

As the first jet engines produced little thrust, Gloster was forced to design a twin-engined aircraft. As this allowed the installation of different engine types with relative ease, it was decided to test three different engines in the F.9/40 prototypes, eight of which were built.

Delays with the Rover W.2B engine (based on Frank Whittle's engine for the E.28/39 aircraft) resulted in prototype DG206/G, powered by two Halford H.1s, taking to the air first on 5 March 1943. As the other prototypes

were flown, testing revealed a lack of directional stability, though these teething problems were corrected by modifications to the aircraft's tail.

On 12 January 1944, the Meteor F.Mk 1 made its first flight. This was effectively an F.9/40 powered by Rolls-Royce W.2B/23C Welland engines (Rolls having taken over development of the W.2B from Rover) and fitted with four 20-mm (0.79-in.) nose-mounted cannon.

Twelve F.Mk 1s were handed to No. 616 Squadron in July 1944 and the following month

Flying Officer Dean scored the RAF's first jet 'kill', when he downed a V-1 flying bomb.

In December, No. 616 re-equipped with the improved F.Mk 3. In 1945 the unit moved to Holland to make armed reconnaissance flights over Germany, but no Messerschmitt Me 262s were ever encountered.

*Below: A Meteor F.Mk 3 is seen here just prior to touch-down. The Meteor Mk 3 benefitted from improved Rolls-Royce Derwent engines.*

*Above: EE214/G was the fifth F.Mk 1 and was used to test a ventral fuel tank. It was scrapped in 1949.*

## Meteor F.Mk 1

**Type:** single-seat day fighter

**Powerplant:** two 7.56-kN (17,000-lb.-thrust) Rolls-Royce W.2B/23C Welland Series 1 turbojets

**Maximum speed:** 675 km/h (419 m.p.h.) at 3048 m (10,000 ft.)

**Service ceiling:** 12,192 m (40,000 ft.)

**Weights:** empty 3737 kg (8,221 lb.); loaded 6258 kg (13,768 lb.)

**Fuel capacity:** 1363 litres (360 gal.)

**Armament:** four Hispano 20-mm (0.79-in.) cannon in the nose

**Dimensions:** span 13.10 m (42 ft. 11 in.)
length 12.50 m (41 ft.)
height 3.90 m (12 ft. 9 in.)
wing area 34.70 m² (373 sq. ft.)

## F.9/40

**DG205/G was the fourth F.9/40 prototype and the second to fly, on 12 June 1943. It was therefore the first example to fly with W.2 engines fitted, but had only a short life, being written off in April 1944.**

Among the improvements introduced in the Meteor F.Mk 3 were a sliding cockpit canopy, increased fuel capacity, new Derwent I engines, slotted air brakes and a strengthened airframe.

Like many of the Meteor variants that followed it, the F.9/40 was an all-metal, stressed-skin design. The fuselage was constructed in three sections: the front fuselage with cockpit and armament; the centre-section with the fuel tank, main landing gear, engines and air brakes; and the rear fuselage and lower fin.

To correct the directional stability problems exhibited by the F.9/40, an enlarged fin and rudder, test flown on DG 208/G, were fitted, along with flat-sided rudders and an 'acorn' fairing at the intersection of the fin and tailplane.

Though not fitted to the F.9/40 prototypes, four Hispano 20-mm (0.79-in.) cannon were installed in the F.Mk 1 and F.Mk 3 service variants. These were prone to jamming in early production aircraft.

DG205/G was powered by W.2 engines derived from Frank Whittle's original design for the E.28/39 pioneer jet. Five of the eight F.9/40s were so-equipped; two others had Halford H.1s, the eighth having Metro-Vickers F.2s.

Standard Fighter Command day-fighter camouflage was applied to the upper surfaces of the F.9/40s, with prototype yellow on the undersides to aid recognition. The 'P' marking in a yellow circle indicated a prototype aircraft.

The aircraft had a 'G' suffix added to its serial number to indicate that it was to have an armed guard at all times when on the ground. This was a reflection of the secret nature of jet-powered aircraft at the time of their appearance.

## Early Meteor variations

■ **METEOR F.Mk 3:** For service in Europe in the final weeks before VE-Day, No. 616 Squadron's Meteor F.Mk 3s wore this overall white paint scheme during a harsh winter.

■ **'TRENT METEOR':** EE227, the eighth Meteor F.Mk 1 completed 80 hours of trials fitted with two Rolls-Royce Trents – the world's first turboprop engines.

■ **'CAMERA NOSE' Mk 3:** During planning for the still-born photo-reconnaissance version of the post-war Meteor Mk 4, Gloster fitted Mk 3 EE338 with a nose-mounted camera.

■ **'HOOKED' F.Mk 3:** With EE387, EE337 was fitted with an arrester hook for deck-landing trials aboard HMS *Implacable*. Thirty-two highly successful landings were made in all.

### MAXIMUM SPEED

With its Derwent engines, the Meteor F.Mk 3 was able to exceed the top speed of the RAF's fastest piston-engined fighter, the Hawker Tempest Mk V (and tropicalised Mk VI). The Luftwaffe's Messerschmitt Me 262 was faster than both aircraft, but suffered serious engine reliability problems.

METEOR F.Mk 3 — 793 km/h (492 m.p.h.)
TEMPEST Mk V — 685 km/h (425 m.p.h.)
Me 262A-1a SCHWALBE — 869 km/h (539 m.p.h.)

### OPERATIONAL RANGE

An area in which the Meteor very comfortably outperformed the Me 262 was its range. It was able to fly almost as far as the Tempest Mk V, nearly three times the German jet's range. Later Meteors carried ventral fuel tanks to increase range even further.

TEMPEST Mk V 2462 km (1,526 mi.)
METEOR F.Mk 3 2156 km (1,337 mi.)
Me 262A-1a SCHWALBE 844 km (523 mi.)

### MAXIMUM TAKE-OFF WEIGHT

Though heavier than the Hawker Tempest, the Gloster Meteor had a lower maximum take-off weight than the Messerschmitt Me 262. Unlike the other two types, the Meteor was also limited to gun armament and carried no air-to-surface weapons. The Luftwaffe was forced to use its Me 262s in the ground-attack role.

METEOR F.Mk III 6033 kg (13,272 lb.)
TEMPEST Mk V 5897 kg (12,973 lb.)
Me 262A-1a SCHWALBE 6400 kg (14,080 lb.)

# GLOSTER

# METEOR

● RAF's first jet fighter ● Worldwide exports ● Long career

**F**irst flown in March 1943, the Meteor was the only Allied jet fighter to see action during World War II. Later versions included trainers, two-seat night fighters and both high- and low-level photo-reconnaissance types. It was also the RAF's standard interceptor of the early 1950s. More than 3500 were built for the air forces of a dozen countries, and the last night fighters were not retired from RAF service until 1961.

▲ As Britain's premier immediate post-war jet fighter, the Meteor served with many regular and reserve squadrons. The aircraft also had great success on the export market and was combat tested, in Australian hands, over Korea.

## GLOSTER METEOR

**Ground-attack Meteor ▶**
As a private venture Gloster developed a specialized variant of the Meteor, with wingtip fuel tanks and wings strengthened to carry up to 1814 kg (4,000 lb) of bombs or rockets. Only one machine was built.

**▲ Meteor T.Mk 7**
With the Meteor flying at speeds of up to 966 km/h (600 mph), the RAF urgently required a fighter trainer.

**Target drone ▶**
Meteor U.Mk 16s were converted to radio-controlled targets by modifying F.Mk 8 airframes.

**▲ Topping up the tanks**
Several Meteor F.Mk 4s were fitted with refuelling probes for trials with No. 245 Squadron.

**Meteors for cotton ▶**
Ten Meteor T.Mk 7s and 60 F.Mk 8s were delivered to Brazil in exchange for raw cotton.

### FACTS AND FIGURES

➤ The Rover W.2B engine was to have powered the Meteor, but delays with this engine led to others being developed.

➤ On 5 March 1943 the first Meteor, fitted with de Havilland engines, lifted off.

➤ Rolls-Royce took over the W.2B engine and developed it into the Welland.

➤ A Meteor was sent to the USA for tests in 1944; in exchange the UK received a Bell XP-59A Airacomet.

➤ Meteor F.Mk Is were slower than both the Tempest Mk V and Spitfire Mk XIV.

➤ A total of 1090 Meteor F.Mk 8s were built for the RAF.

**PROFILE**

# Fifty years of service

Early Meteors were powered by a number of jet engines. The 20 Mk Is had Rolls-Royce Wellands, the single Mk II used de Havilland Goblins, and most of the 280 Mk IIIs had Rolls-Royce Derwents. The Mk I's first operational task was intercepting FZG-76 flying bombs, while ground-attack Mk IIIs took part in the final Allied advance into Germany.

In 1945 and 1946 clipped-wing Mk IIIs set new world speed records of 975 and 991 km/h (606 and 616 mph). The F.Mk 4 retained the clipped wing, but faster fighters were already starting to appear and a major redesign was carried out to produce the F.Mk 8.

Royal Australian Air Force F.Mk 8s were used on both fighter and ground-attack missions during the Korean War. This model was also built in Belgium and the Netherlands.

There were photo-reconnaissance and trainer versions of the F.Mk 4 and night-fighter variants were built by Armstrong Whitworth.

Experimental versions included an F.Mk 4 modified to serve as the world's first turboprop-powered aircraft.

*This modified Meteor T.Mk 7 is still used by Martin-Baker for live ejection seat tests from the rear cockpit.*

The high-set, conventional tailplane was typical of the 'low-risk', conservative approach to the Meteor's design.

Two 20-mm (0.79-in) Hispano cannon were installed on either side of the nose. A total of 780 rounds supplied the four weapons.

An interesting feature of all Meteors was the continuation of the wing leading edge through the nacelle.

### Meteor F.Mk 8

**Type:** single-seat day-fighter

**Powerplant:** two 15.6-kN (3,509-lb-thrust) Rolls-Royce Derwent Series 8 turbojets

**Maximum speed:** 956 km/h (594 mph) at sea level

**Range:** 1110 km (690 miles)

**Service ceiling:** 13,106 m (43,000 ft)

**Weights:** empty 4846 kg (10,684 lb); maximum take-off 7122 kg (15,701 lb)

**Armament:** four 20-mm (0.79-in) cannon plus up to 16 rockets or one 454-kg (1,000-lb) bomb

**Dimensions:** span 11.28 m (37 ft)
length 13.41 m (44 ft)
height 3.96 m (13 ft)
wing area 32.85 m² (354 sq ft)

## METEOR F.MK 8

Squadron Leader Des de Villiers had his aircraft brightly painted in the colours of No. 500 (County of Kent) Squadron, Royal Auxiliary Air Force, in September 1952.

Meteor pilots had an excellent view through the raised canopy. Australian F.Mk 8s in Korea had the rear metal section of the canopy glazed.

A two-compartment main fuel tank was located in the centre section of the fuselage. The tank was self-sealing and had a capacity of 1500 litres (396 US gal). An auxiliary tank could be installed beneath the mid-fuselage.

With the extra fuel tank of the F.Mk 8 and the ammunition drums empty, this mark was almost impossible to fly with the F.Mk 4-style fin. Hence this modified fin was fitted to all F.Mk 8s.

The fuselage of the F.Mk 8 was extended and an extra fuel tank was added between the main fuel tank and the ammunition bay.

None of the regular service Meteors was fitted with afterburners. One experimental F.Mk 4 was fitted with augmented Derwent 5 engines for tests.

On this aircraft the squadron markings were painted on the fin, with the blue area extending over the tailplanes. Blue symbolized the English Channel, white the cliffs at Dover and green the fields of Kent.

### COMBAT DATA

**MAXIMUM SPEED**

In order to speed up service entry, the Meteor was designed conservatively with straight wings. This limited its potential speed, even when compared to very early post-war rivals. Britain was forced to rapidly develop new, swept-wing fighters.

METEOR F.Mk 8 — 956 km/h (549 mph)
F-86E SABRE — 1072 km/h (666 mph)
MD452 MYSTÈRE II — 1060 km/h (659 mph)

**ARMAMENT**

Six cannon were specified for the Meteor, but engine power was limited and only four were fitted as a weight-saving measure. The Sabre carried lighter machine guns, but was rarely seen with bombs. Later Meteors with more power could carry bombs or rockets.

METEOR F.Mk 8 — 4 x 20-mm (0.79-in) cannon, 16 x 76.2-mm (3-in) rockets
F-86E SABRE — 6 x 12.7-mm (0.5-in) machine guns, 1814-kg (4,000-lb) bombload
MD452 MYSTÈRE II — 2 x 30-mm (1.18-in) cannon

**THRUST**

The twin engines fitted to the Meteor gave it comparatively high power, especially when more powerful engines were fitted after the war. It could never match swept-wing types for performance, however, even in its later F.Mk 8 variant.

METEOR F.Mk 8 — 31.2 kN (7,017 lb thrust)
F-86E SABRE — 23.1 kN (5,196 lb thrust)
MD452 MYSTÈRE II — 29.45 kN (6,624 lb thrust)

## Worldwide Meteor operators

■ **AUSTRALIA:** No. 77 Squadron of the Royal Australian Air Force flew the F.Mk 8 over Korea between 1951 and 1953. The aircraft accounted for three MiG-15s destroyed and served with distinction in the attack role.

■ **DENMARK:** Denmark placed the first overseas order for factory-fresh F.Mk 8s. The Danish air force received 20 aircraft, all equipped to RAF standard and delivered between January and June 1951.

■ **UNITED KINGDOM:** Using the long-span wings and tail surfaces of the F.Mk 4, with the nose-mounted cameras of the FR.Mk 9, the PR.Mk 10 was an unarmed, high-altitude reconnaissance aircraft; 59 were built and many served in Germany.

# GOTHA

# G.IV AND G.V

● Long-range bomber ● Raids on Britain ● Pusher engines

▲ *Easily identifiable by their pusher engines and twin main wheels, the Gotha force became a common sight over southern England during 1917–18.*

**S**o notorious did the Gotha bombers of World War I become that their name came to be applied generally to all large German bombers. It was the series of highly public daylight raids on Great Britain in 1917 that gained the Gotha name its notoriety. Developed from the earlier G.II and G.III, the G.IV and G.V variants were built in greater numbers and carried out the majority of the attacks, replacing the limited Zeppelin airship raids.

## GOTHA **G.IV** AND **G.V**

### ▲ Sting in the tail
The G.V's rear gunner could fire not only upwards and backwards, but downward through a specially designed 'tunnel' in the base of the fuselage.

### ▼ Reconnaissance Gotha
Although famed for their bomber designs, Gotha also built a wide range of land- and sea-planes during World War I. This example is a photo-reconnaissance G.VII.

### ▼ Safety at height
One of the primary reasons for the Gotha's success was the performance of its Mercedes engines, allowing it to operate at heights above 4600 m (15,000 ft.).

### ▲ Bomber developments
As the war progressed Gotha sought to develop its bomber designs including the modified G.Vb, the G.VI and the G.VIII. This example is a G.IX, of which only two were built by LVG.

### Massive wings ▶
The Gotha bomber types were characterised by their wide-span biplane wings. The ailerons on the top wing extend beyond the main wing structure, giving the wingtips a distinctive shape. The twin pusher engines are visible between the wings.

## FACTS AND FIGURES

➤ The first G.IV raids on England were made by the 'Ostend Carrier-Pigeon' squadron in November 1916.

➤ Of 61 Gothas destroyed, 24 were lost to Allied defences and 37 in accidents.

➤ The G.IV and G.V were developed from the G.II and G.III designs of early 1916.

➤ With extra landing wheels fitted to the undercarriage chassis, the G.Vb was the last production 'Gotha twin'.

➤ Gotha also produced a wide variety of combat floatplanes during World War I.

➤ A number of G.Vs built by LVG were handed over to the Austrian government.

## PROFILE

# Gotha's giant bombers

Entering service in the autumn of 1916, the Gotha G.IV was not committed to major bombing raids on Britain until the spring of 1917. Yet in the period from May to November that year the Gotha force had remarkable success, and a low loss rate.

G.IV defensive armament consisted of two machine-guns whose fields of fire were co-ordinated with those of other bombers to defend against enemy fighters. A considerable toll was taken of British fighters

until effective evasive tactics had been evolved.

Although very little material damage was achieved by the Gotha raids, the effect on the British public was such that the government withdrew a number of front-line fighter squadrons from France to combat the threat. By September 1917 the British defences had improved enough to force the Gothas to revert to night raids, which continued until May 1918.

Gothas were also used to bomb positions on the Western

*Left: As well as the effect the Gotha raids had on their targets on the ground and on the morale of the British people, they also kept many British fighter aircraft away from the Western Front on home defence duties.*

*Below: Among the Gotha's assets was an ability to withstand a large amount of punishment from enemy fighters. More Gothas were lost in accidents than to enemy action.*

Front but it was the raids by Bombengeschwader 3 on southern England which made the Gothas famous. Altogether, 84,745 kg (186,440 lb.) of bombs were dropped in 22 raids.

### G.V

**Type:** twin-engined long-range day or night bomber

**Powerplant:** two 194-kW (260-hp.) Mercedes D !Va 6-cylinder in-line piston engines

**Maximum speed:** 140 km/h (87 m.p.h.) at 3660 m (12,000 ft.)

**Initial climb rate:** 28 min to 3000 m (9,800 ft.)

**Range:** 491 km (300 mi.)

**Service ceiling:** 6500 m (21,300 ft.)

**Weights:** empty 2740 kg (6,028 lb.); loaded 3975 kg (8,745 lb.)

**Armament:** single manually operated 7.92-mm Parabellum machine-guns in nose and rear cockpits plus up to 500 kg (1,100 lb.) of bombs

**Dimensions:**
| | | |
|---|---|---|
| span | 23.70 m | (77 ft. 9 in.) |
| length | 11.86 m | (38 ft. 11 in.) |
| height | 4.30 m | (14 ft. 1 in.) |
| wing area | 89.5 m² | (963 sq. ft.) |

### G.IV

Operated by Kampfgeschwader 3 based at Ghent, this G.IV participated in daylight bombing raids on London during the spring and summer of 1917.

Sitting on the port side of the fuselage, the pilot looked over the front gunner's cockpit which was situated in the extreme nose. The main fuel tanks were situated immediately aft of the pilot's position.

The upper wings were composed of two panels joined at the centre. The two spruce main spars supported plywood ribs and the whole structure was covered with fabric.

Of fairly conventional construction, the fuselage was a one piece wooden structure of spruce longerons and spacers. The skin was plywood, and the whole structure was braced with stranded steel cables.

Constructed from light-gauge steel tubing, the tail unit was fabric-covered. The rudder was very large in comparison to the fin and was balanced to reduce the weight on the controls. Steel tube struts braced both the rudder and the tailplane. Beneath the rear fuselage was a steel-reinforced wooden tailskid.

Despite the aircraft's relatively large size, the bombs were mounted externally on removable racks. A maximum of 500 kg (1,100 lb.) could be carried.

Each undercarriage leg was fitted with two wheels which were sprung with long tension springs mounted inside the undercarriage leg.

### COMBAT DATA

#### MAXIMUM SPEED
All large bombers of World War I were very slow, even by the standards of the day. Flying into a strong wind could double the time taken to reach a target.

| | |
|---|---|
| G.V | 140 km/h (87 m.p.h.) |
| G.III | 135 km/h (84 m.p.h.) |
| R.VI | 135 km/h (84 m.p.h.) |

#### ARMAMENT
A well co-ordinated defensive strategy was a feature of the German bombing raids, forcing the British to re-evaluate their interception tactics.

| | |
|---|---|
| G.V | 2 x 7.92-mm machine-guns<br>500-kg (1,100-lb.) bombload |
| G.III | 3 x 7.92 -mm machine-guns<br>1500-kg (3,300-lb.) bombload |
| R.VI | 4 x 7.92-mm machine-guns<br>2000-kg (4,400-lb.) bombload |

#### POWER
The R.VI was powered by four of the same engines which powered the twin-engined Gotha designs. This extra power allowed the Zeppelin design to carry a much bigger bombload, although it did not provide superior flight performance.

| G.V | G.III | R.VI |
|---|---|---|
| 388 kW (520 hp.) | 388 kW (520 hp.) | 776 kW (1,040 hp.) |

## Great War German bombers

**AEG G.IV:** Without the range or the lifting power of the Gotha designs, the AEG G.IV was used for tactical bombing on the Western Front.

**FRIEDRICHSHAFEN G.III:** Along with the Gotha designs, this aircraft formed the backbone of Germany's long-range bomber force.

**ZEPPELIN-STAAKEN V.G.O III:** One of the true German giants of World War I, this type was powered by six engines driving three airscrews.

**ZEPPELIN-STAAKEN TYPE 8301:** Although intended as a seaplane, the Type 8301 was fitted with wheels for trials as a bomber.

# GOTHA

# Go 229 (HORTEN HO IX)

● Jet-powered, flying-wing fighter-bomber ● Flown in 1945

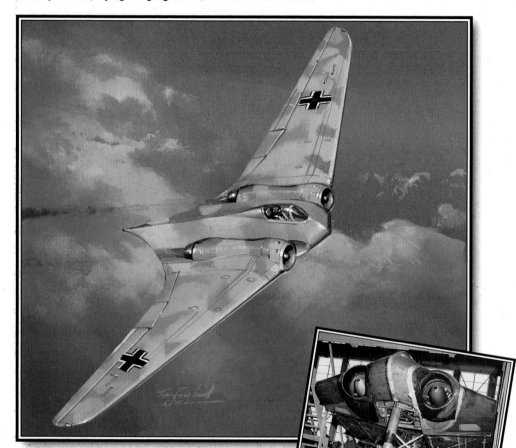

One of the most remarkable of Germany's many advanced aircraft designs of the late 1930s and '40s, the Gotha Go 229 was the culmination of more than 10 years of research by Reimar and Walter Horten. Their Ho I sailplane of 1931 was the first of a dozen designs exploring the flying-wing concept; some were powered aircraft. Their jet-powered Ho IX, which Gotha was to mass produce as the Go 229, was intended for combat.

▲ Ho IX V2 was the world's first jet-powered, flying-wing aircraft. Parallel research by Northrop in the U.S. produced a rocket-powered flying wing, which flew in 1944.

## GOTHA Go 229 (HORTEN HO IX)

▲ Captured by the Allies
Ho IX V3 was nearly complete when U.S. troops arrived at Gotha's Friedrichsroda plant. Notice the sturdy construction of the undercarriage.

▲ Junkers turbojets
Ho IX V2's Junkers engines exhausted over the wing. Metal skins protected the wing's surface.

▲ Ho IX V1 glider
There was no official recognition of the Ho IX programme until after Ho IX V1 had flown. The RLM soon ordered powered trials to begin.

◄ Ho IIIB, classic flying wing
The Horten brothers designed a number of flying wing gliders during the 1930s. The Ho IIIB was a classic example.

Ho IX V1 plan view ▶
This view from above shows the 32° leading edge sweep of the Ho IX V1.

## FACTS AND FIGURES

➤ Among other Horten flying-wing proposals was the Ho VIII, a transport with a 262-foot span and six engines.

➤ The elimination of parasitic drag was the primary aim of flying-wing research.

➤ Gothaer Waggonfabrik was founded in 1898 as a builder of railway locomotives.

➤ The Horten brothers were attached to the Luftwaffe's Sonderkommando (Special Detachment) 9 during World War II.

➤ Gotha was one of the few manufacturers that built aircraft for World War I and II.

➤ Postwar, Reimar Horten designed an aircraft for production in Argentina.

**PROFILE**

# Luftwaffe's fighting flying wing

Despite intelligence reports that Northrop was conducting similar research in the U.S., official interest in the Horten flying wings was fading in 1943. An order for 20 Ho VIIs, officially two-seat research and communications aircraft (which were in fact trainers for the Hortens' projected Ho IX fighter) had been cancelled after just two had been completed.

Undaunted, the Hortens continued unauthorized work on their fighter, constructing Ho IX V1 as a glider to test the aircraft's

flight characteristics. When the RLM (Air Ministry) became aware of the Hortens' work in early 1944, the brothers' reputation was enough to gain official sanction from the Luftwaffe commander Reichmarschall Göring. Successful gliding trials with Ho IX V1 led to the construction of a second aircraft, V2, with two Junkers turbojets installed. The RLM ordered seven more prototypes and 20 preproduction aircraft in the summer of 1944.

V2 flew in January 1945 and in March reached 798 km/h (496

m.p.h.) in level flight. It suffered engine failure and crashed shortly afterward. Meanwhile, Gotha had begun construction of the first Go 229, V3. This aircraft was nearing completion at Gotha's Friedrichsroda plant when, in May, it was overrun by troops from the U.S. Third Army.

*Above: It is not known whether the Ho IX V1 was ever intended to carry engines; it was completed as a glider and flew in 1944.*

*Above: Horten Ho IX V2, the second example and the first with engines, is seen at Oranienburg near Berlin for test flying. It was destroyed in a landing accident in March 1944, after reaching a speed of 798 km/h (496 m.p.h.).*

---

### Go 229A-0

**Type:** Single-seat, jet-powered, flying-wing fighter-bomber

**Powerplant:** Two 8.73 kN (1,965-lb.-thrust) Junkers 004B-1, -2 or -3 axial-flow turbojet engines

**Maximum speed:** 962 km/h (598 m.p.h.) at normal loaded weight; 974 km/h (605 m.p.h.) at 11887 m (39,000 ft.)

**Range:** 1896 km (1,178 mi.) with max internal fuel at 631 km/h (392 m.p.h.) average speed

**Maximum ceiling:** 16,000 m (52,500 ft)

**Weights:** Empty equipped 4590 kg (10,120 lb.); normal loaded 7484 kg (16,500 lb.); max takeoff 8981 kg (19,800 lb.)

**Weapons:** Four 30-mm MK103 or MK108 cannon; plus two 1000-kg (2,200-lb.) bombs

**Dimensions:**
| | |
|---|---|
| Span | 16,76m (54 ft. 11in.) |
| Length | 7,5 m (24 ft. 6 in.) |
| Height | 2,7 m (9 ft. 2 in.) |
| Wing area | 52,49 m² (565 sq. ft.) |

---

The pilot of the Ho IX/Go 229 sat in a conventional cockpit with a spring-operated ejection seat. The control column could be raised vertically to increase leverage at high speeds.

Originally intended to have BMW 003 turbojets, Ho IX V2 had two of the more reliable Junkers 004s installed. They were fed by intakes in the leading edge of the wing and exhausted over the top side of the wing.

## Go 229 V1 (Ho IX V3)

**Had the first Go 229 (Ho IX V3) been completed and flown, it would have looked, finished in standard camouflage and national markings.**

Four 30-mm cannon were mounted in the leading edge of the wing, outboard of the engine intakes. Hardpoints along the center section carried two 1000 kg (2,200-lb) bombs or two long-range fuel tanks. A night-fighter version, the Go 229B, was planned. It would have been a two-seater with radar antenna in front of the cockpit.

The Go 229 had a tricycle undercarriage. The large nose leg retracted rearward while the main gears retracted inward. A braking parachute was installed to assist deceleration on landing. Elevons and plain flaps on the trailing edge of the outer wing panels, and glide control spoiler flaps on the undersurface of the wing, provided lateral and logitudinal control.

Coventional welded steel tube construction was used in the center section of the aircraft. Apart from metal tips, the rest of the wing was wooden. The Go 229's outer wing sections each held five fuel tanks. The surface coating is said to be radar-absorbent.

---

### ACTION DATA

**SPEED**

Had it entered service, the Go 229A-0 would have had a greater top speed than the rocket-powered Messerschmitt Me 163 Komet and the Heinkel He 162. The latter was a more basic aircraft than the Gotha.

| | |
|---|---|
| Go 229A-0 | 977 km/h (598 m.p.h.) |
| Me 163B KOMET | 965 km/h (595 m.p.h.) |
| He 162 SALAMANDER | 890 km/h (553 m.p.h.) |

**RANGE**

To be a viable fighter-bomber, the Go 229 would have required good range performance. The Gotha's range was much better than that of the Salamander and the short-ranged Komet interceptor. Long range is easily accomplished with flying-wing designs.

Go 229A-0 1900 km (1,178 mi.)
Me 163B KOMET 100 km (60 mi.)
He 162 SALAMANDER 620 km (384 mi.)

---

## Horten flying-wing family

**1 Ho I:** Development of the Ho I glider began in 1931. The aircraft had a 24° wing leading-edge sweep. The pilot flew the Ho I from a prone position.

**2 Ho II:** Dissatisfied, the Hortens burned the Ho I in 1934, and built the Ho II later that year. Again they used wood and fabric construction. Four gliders were built, followed by a powered version with a 60 kW (80-hp.) engine.

**3 Ho III:** In 1938, the Hortens built the Ho III, with official backing. Essentially an enlarged Ho II, the Ho III was built in four different versions, the last of which had an engine. During gliding flight, its propeller blades were folded away.

**4 Ho V:** The first of the Horten flying wings designed from the outset as a powered aircraft, the Ho V of the late 1930s used bonded plastics in its construction and had two engines.

**5 Ho IX:** With everything they had learned during the 1930s, the Hortens designed the Ho IX using a mixture of steel and wooden construction. It had jet engines and the top speed of nearly 800 km/h (500 m.p.h.).

# GRUMMAN

# F2F/F3F

● Single-seater ● Carrier based ● Last USN biplane fighter

▲ *The famous 'Fighting Two' squadron based on the USS Lexington flew F2F and F3Fs continuously from 1935 until 1940.*

**A** natural development of the FF1 two-seat naval fighter of 1931, Grumman proposed a single-seat fighter, the F2F, in 1932. The larger F3F followed in 1934 and was destined to be the last biplane fighter ordered by the US Navy for delivery in 1937/38. These tubby biplanes, with their characteristic retractable landing gear (a Grumman patented design), were to keep the biplane era alive in the American fleet until late in 1940.

---

## GRUMMAN **F2F/F3F**

### ▼ Fleet fighter
*When the last F3F-2 was accepted in May 1938, all seven US Navy and Marine Corps fighter squadrons operated Grumman single-seaters. This situation lasted until December 1939.*

### ▲ New factory
*When 27 FF-1s were ordered, Grumman rented a new factory at Farmingdale to build them.*

### ▼ Red Rippers
*Production of 55 F2F-1s ended in October 1935, with nine aircraft going to VF-5B 'Red Rippers'.*

### ▼ Top guns
*The Mk III Mod 4 telescopic gunsight was mounted on top of the cowling, projecting forward from the small windscreen, for the two fixed, forward-firing (through the propeller) 7.62-mm (.30 cal.) Browning machine-guns that were fitted in the upper fuselage.*

### ▼ Last US Navy biplane fighter
*The bigger and more powerful F3F was the US Navy's basic carrier-borne fighter until the early-1940s. This F3F-2 served with VMF-2 Squadron.*

### FACTS AND FIGURES

➤ The F2F and F3F were stressed to 9*g*, similar to that of the F-16 and F/A-18.

➤ Grumman's unique undercarriage design on the F2F/F3F became a distinctive feature of the F4F Wildcat carrier fighter.

➤ The first aircraft-carrier to have the F2F on board was the USS *Lexington* in 1935.

➤ Grumman delivered the last F2F in August 1935 and F3F in May 1939.

➤ The first two XF3Fs were destroyed in high-speed dives, the airframe being strengthened for production aircraft.

➤ A total of 140 F2Fs and F3Fs remained in service as station hacks in 1942.

**PROFILE**

# The US Navy's 'Flying Barrels'

Taking the nickname 'Flying Barrel' on account of its deep forward fuselage and engine cowling, the Grumman biplane fighter was a legend in its time. The mainstay of the US carrier force immediately before World War II, it provided many young aviators, who would later hold command positions, with a sound training in shipboard fighter operations.

Starting life as the Grumman G-8 (later XF2F), the F2F-1 first entered service in 1935. One of the Navy's most illustrious fighter squadrons, VF-2B

'Fighting Two', helped prove the aircraft, which had a production run of 54.

Before the F2F entered service, Grumman anticipated future Navy requirements and secured orders for its G-11 (F3F). Similar to its predecessor, it had a longer fuselage and increased wingspan to enhance handling qualities. The first two XF3Fs crashed during flight tests, but an order for 35 F3F-1s was confirmed.

A larger diameter Cyclone

engine powered the F3F-2 and this was the subject of an order for 81 aircraft for 1937/38 delivery. More engine power and other improvements produced the F3F-3, 27 of which were built. Few better tributes could be made to these biplanes than the longevity of service and late phase-out date of November 1943.

Left: This F3F carries the 'M' prefix to the squadron letter ('F') denoting a Marine Corps aircraft. In this case the aircraft belongs to Marine Fighter Squadron Two (VMF-2), indicated by the '2' prefix.

After front-line service the F3F-1s were used for pilot training at NAS Norfolk and Miami until February 1941.

## F3F

**Type:** single-seat carrier fighter/bomber

**Powerplant:** one 708-kW (950-hp.) Wright R1820-2Z Cyclone air-cooled engine

**Maximum speed:** 425 km/h (264 m.p.h.)

**Initial climb rate:** 701 m/min (2,300 f.p.m.)

**Range:** 1328 km (824 mi.)

**Service ceiling:** 9205 m (30,200 ft.)

**Weights:** empty 1478 kg (3,252 lb.); loaded 2042 kg (4,492 lb.)

**Armament:** two 7.62-mm (.30 cal.) Browning machine-guns, plus two 52.6-kg (115-lb.) bombs

**Dimensions:**
| | |
|---|---|
| span | 9.75 m (32 ft.) |
| length | 7.07 m (23 ft. 3 in.) |
| height | 2.84 m (9 ft. 4 in.) |
| wing area | 24.15 m² (260 sq. ft.) |

---

## F3F-2

With a more powerful Wright engine, the F3F-2 was the ultimate 'Flying Barrel'. This version had an improved speed, climb rate and performance range.

The tube ahead of the pilot's windscreen is a Mk III Mod 4 telescopic gunsight.

Two 7.62-mm (.30 cal.) Browning machine-guns were mounted forward of the cockpit and fired through the propeller arc.

F3F-2 '1009' was one of a relatively small number of F3Fs to serve with the US Marine Corps units, in this case VMF-1.

Compared to the F2F, the F3F's fuselage was nearly 0.5 m (1 ft. 7 in.) longer, the wingspan was increased by 1.07 m (3 ft. 6 in.) and it had a slightly bigger tail unit; improved handling was the goal.

F3F-2s used the 708-kW Wright R1820-22 Cyclone nine-cylinder single-row radial air-cooled engine.

Grumman's patent undercarriage had the mainwheels retracting into the fuselage behind the engine.

Watertight compartments in the lower fuselage provided flotation during an emergency water landing.

---

## Grumman's naval fighters

■ **SF-1:** The US Navy ordered 33 SF-1 (G-6) scouts in 1932, the first being delivered to Squadron VS-3B 'Scouting Three' based on USS *Lexington* on 30 March 1934.

■ **F2F-1:** The first single-seat fighter from Grumman, the all-metal F2F-1 entered service with VF-2 aboard USS *Lexington* in January 1935, serving until 1940.

■ **F4F WILDCAT:** One of the great naval fighters of World War II and the first monoplanes produced by Grumman, the XF4F was initially flown in February 1939 and was soon ordered.

---

**COMBAT DATA**

### MAXIMUM SPEED

Grumman's reputation as a builder of fighters for the US Navy was just developing during the 1930s, the F3F going some way towards its enhancement. The F3F was a relatively quick aircraft, though the days of the biplane were numbered.

| | |
|---|---|
| **F3F** | 425 km/h (264 m.p.h.) |
| **GLADIATOR** | 414 km/h (257 m.p.h.) |
| **P-26 PEASHOOTER** | 377 km/h (234 m.p.h.) |

### RANGE

Naval aircraft must possess good range performance because of the nature of their operation, often some distance from an aircraft-carrier. Long range allows a good radius of operation and an increased time spent patrolling the skies on the lookout for enemy aircraft that may threaten the fleet. Both the P-26 and Gladiator were land-based machines.

P-26 PEASHOOTER 579 km (358 mi.)
GLADIATOR 710 km (440 mi.)
F3F 1328 km (530 mi.)

### ARMAMENT

By American standards the F3F was typically armed with two machine-guns, while the British Gladiator demonstrates that fighter types of the period were generally better armed. This trend continued into the early years of World War II. Higher calibre machine-guns then became the norm.

F3F 2 x 7.62-mm (.30 cal.) MGs
GLADIATOR 4 x 7.7-mm (.303 cal.) MGs
P-26 PEASHOOTER 2 x 7.62-mm (.30 cal.) MGs

# GRUMMAN
# F4F WILDCAT

● Carrier-based fighter bomber ● Pacific War hero ● Royal Navy service

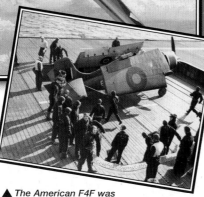

▲ The American F4F was exported to the Royal Navy for operation aboard its carriers, and was for a while designated the Grumman Martlet until the service returned to the name Wildcat.

**W**ildcat squadrons used by the American Marines and Navy made their stand against Japan's superior Mitsubishi A6M Zero. While the Zero held the advantage in performance, the Wildcat achieved its greatness in part due to the exceptional men who flew it. As Foster Hailey of the *New York Times* said in 1943: 'The Grumman Wildcat, it is no exaggeration to say, did more than any single instrument of war to save the day in the Pacific.'

---

## GRUMMAN F4F WILDCAT

**◄ Carrier operations**
*With its folding wings and catapult gear the Wildcat was a dedicated carrier fighter both with the US Navy and the Royal Navy. However, the F4F also saw action from land bases.*

**▲ Grumman heritage**
*The Wildcat was one of a long line of Grumman-built naval fighters, from the F3F to today's F-14 Tomcat.*

**▲ Carrier battlegroup protector**
*The Wildcat shared the decks of the US Navy's Pacific carriers in the early battles of the war with other classic types such as the Douglas Dauntless, Grumman Avenger and later the Vought Corsair.*

**Fleet Air Arm fighter ▶**
*The Royal Navy's first American fighter, the Wildcat was greatly respected.*

**◄ Pacific warrior**
*Until it started being replaced by the Hellcat from 1943, the Wildcat was the US Navy's most important fighter. This example carries the markings of fighter squadron VF-41. The red centre of the national marking was deleted from late 1942.*

### FACTS AND FIGURES

➤ Total production was 7825 Wildcats, including 1988 Grumman F4Fs and 5837 General Motors FMs.

➤ The Wildcat was first flown by Robert L. Hall on 2 September 1937.

➤ Fleet Air Arm Wildcats were the remnant of orders by France and Greece.

➤ A long-range reconnaissance version of the Wildcat was effective but was quickly replaced by a photo-reconnaissance F6F.

➤ Top Wildcat ace was Major John L. Smith who shot down 19 Japanese warplanes.

➤ Wildcats were also used by the Royal Canadian Air Force and US Marines.

# PROFILE

# Grumman's fleet defender

In the 1930s the US Navy mistakenly chose the Brewster Buffalo over the Grumman F4F Wildcat. By the 1941 Pearl Harbor attack, however, the decision was reversed: the Wildcat replaced Navy biplane fighters and battled Japanese Zeros in the Pacific. A far better fighter than the Brewster, the Wildcat did not meet the standards of the Japanese Zero but it contributed mightily to the American war effort. Lieutenant Edward 'Butch' O'Hare, flying an F4F, shot down five Japanese

bombers in five minutes to become the first US Navy ace.

The Wildcat was sturdy and very manoeuvrable. It was not the easiest aircraft to fly but, once mastered, was incredibly responsive. Most Wildcats were manufactured by General Motors as the FM-2. Some went to Britain's Royal Navy, which called it the Martlet.

This portly, mid-winged fighter made a vital contribution: outnumbered and outgunned, it held the line until the most

successful naval fighter in history, the Grumman F6F Hellcat, became available to turn the tide of the Pacific War.

*A US Navy Wildcat drops its tailhook in order to catch the wire aboard the deck of a carrier in the Pacific.*

The pilot was protected by thick armour behind the cockpit, bulletproof glass ahead and the massive engine in front of him.

All-metal vacuum operated split trailing-edge flaps were fitted.

Wing tanks contained 606 litres (158 gal.) of aviation gasoline, and were self sealing.

## F4F-4 Wildcat

**Type:** single-seat carrier-based fighter

**Powerplant:** one 895-kW (1,200-hp.) Wright R-1830-36 Cyclone radial piston engine

**Maximum speed:** 512 km/h (317 m.p.h.)

**Cruising speed:** 249 km/h (154 m.p.h.)

**Range:** 1239 km (768 mi.)

**Service ceiling:** 12,010 m (39,400 ft.)

**Weights:** empty 2612 kg (5,746 lb.); maximum take-off 3607 kg (7,935 lb.)

**Armament:** six fixed 12.7-mm (.50 cal.) Browning air-cooled machine-guns with 240 rounds per gun plus two 45-kg (100-lb.) bombs

**Dimensions:**

| | | |
|---|---|---|
| span | 11.60 m | (38 ft.) |
| length | 8.50 m | (28 ft.) |
| height | 3.60 m | (12 ft.) |
| wing area | 24.15 m² | (260 sq. ft.) |

A rugged and powerful Wright Cyclone engine gave the F4F a good power-to-weight ratio. The two-stage blower sometimes caused problems and was replaced by a single-stage model.

The cockpit was rather cramped and visibility was not great, but the problems were resolved on Grumman's F4F replacement, the F6F Hellcat. Immediately behind the pilot was a Mk 1A liferaft.

## F4F-4 WILDCAT

**The F4F was heavily involved in Operation Torch in November 1942, the codename for the important Allied invasion of French North Africa.**

This F4F carries early intermediate markings. The red spot has been removed from the centre of the star, but the yellow recognition circle around the roundel has yet to be applied.

The F4F was heavily armed with no less than six wing machine-guns. Although not as powerful as cannon, they were quite adequate against most Japanese opposition.

The undercarriage design was little changed from that on inter-war Grumman biplanes, with the mainwheels only half retracting to lie flat against the lower fuselage in a shallow well.

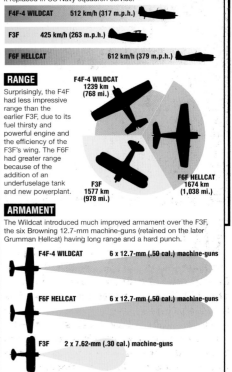

## COMBAT DATA

### MAXIMUM SPEED

The power of engines and improved aerodynamics during the 1940s led to a consistently higher maximum speed of the F4F over its predecessor the F3F, and the F6F over the Wildcat which it replaced in US Navy squadron service.

| | |
|---|---|
| F4F-4 WILDCAT | 512 km/h (317 m.p.h.) |
| F3F | 425 km/h (263 m.p.h.) |
| F6F HELLCAT | 612 km/h (379 m.p.h.) |

### RANGE

Surprisingly, the F4F had less impressive range than the earlier F3F, due to its fuel thirsty and powerful engine and the efficiency of the F3F's wing. The F6F had greater range because of the addition of an underfuselage tank and new powerplant.

F4F-4 WILDCAT 1239 km (768 mi.)

F3F 1577 km (978 mi.)

F6F HELLCAT 1674 km (1,038 mi.)

### ARMAMENT

The Wildcat introduced much improved armament over the F3F, the six Browning 12.7-mm machine-guns (retained on the later Grumman Hellcat) having long range and a hard punch.

| | |
|---|---|
| F4F-4 WILDCAT | 6 x 12.7-mm (.50 cal.) machine-guns |
| F6F HELLCAT | 6 x 12.7-mm (.50 cal.) machine-guns |
| F3F | 2 x 7.62-mm (.30 cal.) machine-guns |

## Wildcats over Wake Island

**AERIAL PATROL:** Flying in close formation on interception duties above the clouds, the Wake Island Wildcats did not catch sight of the attacking Japanese aircraft because of the bad weather.

**AIRBASE ASSAULT:** After evading the attentions of the defending F4Fs, the Japanese aircraft were free to bomb Wake's air base and destroy most of the island's 12 Wildcats before they had time to react.

**REVENGE:** The four Wildcats which had not been on the ground during the raid were able to attack the invading Japanese fleet, and managed to sink two destroyers.

# GRUMMAN

# F6F HELLCAT

● Fleet carrier aircraft ● Naval strike-fighter ● Used by US Navy aces

▲ *Most of the*
US Navy's wartime aces notched
up their kills using the tough and manoeuvrable F6F.
Lieutenant Hanks was a Hellcat ace, shooting down
five Japanese aircraft in just one month.

**P**owerful and pugnacious, the Hellcat is one of the few aircraft in history which was right from the start. Designed after Pearl Harbor, the Hellcat required almost no testing or development work before being rushed into production. Swarms of these beefy, gloss-blue fighters wrested control of Pacific skies from the vaunted Japanese Zero and chalked up a record of success in air combat that has rarely been matched.

## GRUMMAN F6F HELLCAT

▲ **Radar goes to sea**
Later Hellcats had advanced instruments such as radio altimeters and radar.

▲ **Strike Hellcat**
Hellcats served on with France after the war and saw extensive action in Indochina.

▼ **Take-off flag**
Lieutenant John Clarke gives the take-off signal flag to an F6F pilot. Taking off with the canopy open meant that it was easy to escape if the aircraft ditched after leaving the ship.

▲ **Spreading wings**
Like most naval fighters, the Hellcat had folding wings. They used the typical Grumman feature of swivelling back to lie each side of the fuselage.

▼ **Crowded decks**
The US Navy's carriers carried more aircraft than could be hangared, and many Hellcats were parked on deck alongside Avengers and SBDs.

## FACTS AND FIGURES

➤ The XF6F-1 prototype made its first flight on 26 June 1942.

➤ Of 6477 aerial victories claimed by US Navy pilots during World War II, 4947 were credited to F6F Hellcat pilots.

➤ On 3 April 1944, Royal Navy Hellcats attacked the *Tirpitz* at Kaafjord, Norway.

➤ Grumman made 12,275 Hellcats at its New York plant between June 1942 and November 1945, the largest number of fighters ever produced at a single factory.

➤ F6F-3K drones gathered particles from atomic clouds during the 1946 nuclear tests at Bikini atoll.

## PROFILE

# King of the carrier fighters

The sturdy, powerful F6F Hellcat is one of the few fighters developed after the outbreak of World War II to succeed in that conflict. A big, heavy machine in an age when experts lauded small, light fighters, the Hellcat was fast enough and agile enough to become the outstanding dogfighter of the Pacific war.

Pilots also praised the strength of the F6F, which they jokingly called a product of the 'Grumman Iron Works' because they knew that sustaining damage in combat no longer meant certain death. The Hellcat could and did bring its pilot home.

This remarkable aircraft also proved its merit as a night-fighter (using early air-intercept radar)

and a reconnaissance aircraft. Britain employed the Hellcat throughout the East Indies, Malaya, Burma and in the final assault on Japan. Half a decade later, the Hellcat was all but gone from American service when the final examples were used as unmanned flying bombs – the Korean War's equivalent of today's cruise missile.

*Two of the elements which won the Pacific War: the F6F Hellcat aboard an 'Essex'-class carrier.*

### F6F-5 Hellcat

**Type:** single-seat carrier-based fighter

**Powerplant:** one 1492-kW (2,000-hp.) Pratt & Whitney R-2800-10W Double Wasp 18-cylinder radial piston engine

**Maximum speed:** 620 km/h (380 m.p.h.) at medium altitude

**Range:** 1675 km (1,040 mi.)

**Service ceiling:** 11,500 m (37,500 ft.)

**Weights:** empty 4191 kg (9,200 lb.); loaded 6991 kg (15,400 lb.)

**Armament:** six 12.7-mm (.50 cal.) Browning M2 machine-guns; up to 907 kg (2,000 lb.) of bombs; six 127-mm (5-in.) rockets

**Dimensions:**
| | | |
|---|---|---|
| span | 13.08 m | (42 ft. 10 in.) |
| length | 10.23 m | (33 ft. 7 in.) |
| height | 3.99 m | (13 ft. 1 in.) |
| wing area | 31.03 m² | (334 sq. ft.) |

### F6F-5 HELLCAT

**This Hellcat was flown by fighter squadron VF-27 from the light carrier USS *Princeton*, sunk during the Battle of Leyte Gulf in October 1944.**

The F6F was strongly built. For added protection, it was equipped with a self-sealing fuel tank and a tough sheet of armour to protect the pilot.

The F6F was powered by the 18-cylinder Pratt & Whitney Double Wasp engine, one of the largest piston powerplants available during World War II.

This VF-27 fighter is armed for a ground-attack mission, with bombs and 127-mm high-explosive rockets.

The fin and tailplanes were built around very strong central spars. The aircraft itself was extremely strong, and could survive substantial battle damage.

Like the rest of the fighter, the undercarriage was extremely tough to withstand repeated carrier landings.

On internal fuel the F6F had a combat radius of 800 km (500 mi.), but this could be extended by the use of external tanks.

## COMBAT DATA

### MAXIMUM SPEED

| | |
|---|---|
| **F6F-5 HELLCAT** | 620 km/h (380 m.p.h.) |
| **A6M5 ZERO** | 570 km/h (355 m.p.h.) |
| **P-38J LIGHTNING** | 666 km/h (415 m.p.h.) |

The Hellcat was not particularly fast by European standards, and it was outperformed by US land-based fighters like the P-38. But it had a significant advantage over its main rival in the Pacific, the previously all-conquering Mitsubishi Zero.

### ARMAMENT

American fighters were always fairly lightly armed, especially compared to their opponents. But the USA more than made up for any inferiority by the ruggedness of its aircraft, the superior training of its pilots, and the accuracy of their shooting. The A6M5 Zero was equipped with cannon giving more deadly firepower but it lacked defensive armour.

**F6F-5 HELLCAT** 6 x 12.7-mm (.50 cal.) machine-guns

**A6M5 ZERO** 2 x 20-mm (0.79-in.) cannon 2 x 13-mm (0.51-in.) machine-guns

**P-38J LIGHTNING** 1 x 20-mm (0.79-in.) cannon 4 x 12.7-mm (.50 cal.) machine-guns

## Battle of the Philippine Sea

Fought on 19 and 20 June 1944, the Battle of the Philippine Sea saw the final elimination of Japanese carrier air power as a factor in the Pacific war. An American invasion fleet was approaching the Mariana Islands; capture of the islands would give the USA air bases from which its bombers could strike direct at the Japanese homeland. It was the task of the Imperial Navy to stop the landings and defeat the US Pacific fleet.

**FIRST MOBILE FLEET:** On 15 June three fleet carriers and six light carriers sail from Japanese bases in the Philippines 800 km (500 mi.) west.

**INVASION FORCE:** On 11 June the American amphibious fleet approaches from the east, guarded by the massive Task Force 58 – seven battleships and no less than 15 carriers. After destroying the Japanese fighters on the islands, TF 58 moves to guard the landings from the Japanese fleet approaching from the Philippines.

**HEAVY LOSSES:** Japanese aircraft are shot out of the sky by F6F Hellcats. 253 Japanese fighters lost for 30 American.

SAIPAN
TINIAN
GUAM

1. **19 JUNE** Japanese fleet divides to launch air attack
2. **19 JUNE** Carriers *Taiho* and *Shokaku* sunk by US submarines
3. **19 JUNE** Japanese air power annihilated, fleet withdraws
4. **20 JUNE** Pursuing US fleet launches air strike
5. **20 JUNE** US aircraft sink one carrier and damage three

# GRUMMAN

# J2F DUCK

- Early Grumman amphibian ● Pacific rescue missions ● USCG service

▲ Grumman's G-20 Duck design
paved the way for a number of monoplane amphibian designs, beginning with the twin-engined G-21 Goose of 1937. Examples of each are still flying today.

**T**his new family of single-engined biplane amphibians was among Grumman's first designs. The US Navy of the mid-1930s immediately found them ideally suited to utility duties aboard aircraft-carriers. Grumman Ducks were somewhat awkward-looking, but highly functional flying machines. Built by Grumman and Columbia, JF and J2F Ducks served with distinction in the Pacific island-fighting campaign during World War II, and around the world.

## PHOTO FILE

# GRUMMAN J2F DUCK

▼ Coast Guard JF-2
Grumman's first amphibious design, the JF, made its maiden flight in 1933. From 1936, the type equipped US Navy utility squadrons aboard aircraft-carriers. The JF-2 rescue variant was built for the USCG.

▲ Preserved J2F-6
This preserved airworthy example of the J2F-6, built by Columbia Aircraft, wears the pre-war markings of Navy utility squadron VJ-4.

US Navy photo-ship ▲
Seen in 1942 colours, this J2F-5 also carries the markings of an Atlantic Fleet air photographic unit.

▲ First US Navy deliveries
BuNo. 0162 was the first J2F-1 delivered to the US Navy, arriving at Naval Air Station, Anacostia, in April 1936.

◀ Duck!
J2F tasks included target-towing, for which this Duck is equipped.

## FACTS AND FIGURES

➤ The Duck was the first aircraft built after Leroy Grumman left Loening Aircraft to form his own company.

➤ Columbia Aircraft was still building these amphibians when World War II ended.

➤ Argentina, Colombia and Mexico received Ducks in the 1930s and 1940s.

➤ Between 1942 and 1945, US Navy and Marines Ducks rescued downed aircrew from the battle for Guadalcanal.

➤ A J2F-5 and five J2F-6s were operated by the USAF as OA-12s for air-sea rescue.

➤ As the Japanese invaded the Philippines, US Navy J2F-5s rescued VIPs.

210

## PROFILE

# First of the Grumman amphibians

After the attack on Pearl Harbor on 7 December 1941, a lone Grumman Duck set forth to search for the Japanese fleet, its radio operator armed with a bolt-action Springfield rifle. The single-engined Grumman Duck biplane was neither a fighter nor a bomber, but it found itself in action more than once in the Pacific. And, at the time of the US entry into World War II in 1941, the Duck was unique as the only biplane still in production for a US Navy operational role.

When originally ordered into production in 1932, these amphibians (JF-1 to JF-3 and J2F-1 to J2F-6) were deemed quite advanced, with their all-metal construction and relatively clean lines. The US Navy, Marines and Coast Guard employed them for a variety of utility missions. Under pressure to deliver naval fighters and attack aircraft, Grumman transferred production to the nearby plant of the Columbia Aircraft Corporation.

Post-war, Ducks saw limited use and some were assigned to US Army Air Forces. A few have been preserved.

*Below: At the US Navy's request, J2F-6 production was transferred to Columbia Aircraft on Long Island.*

*Above: USCG JFs and J2Fs served until the early 1950s, when they were phased out after some 17 years of service.*

Two or three crewmembers were carried aboard the US Navy's Ducks – apart from the pilot, there was an observer and, if required, a radio operator. The rear cockpit had provision for a 7.62-mm (.30 cal.) machine-gun, but this was seldom fitted. Two wing bomb racks were installed; in the J2F-5 and J2F-6, they were each able to carry a 147-kg (325-lb.) depth charge or bomb.

Ducks shared airframe design features, such as a semi-monocoque fuselage, with Grumman's first fighter design, the XFF-1.

As the US Navy's Ducks were intended for utility transport duties aboard aircraft-carriers, providing a ship-to-shore link, they were fitted with arrester hooks for deck recovery.

The first JF-1 Ducks were powered by a Pratt & Whitney R-1830 Twin Wasp 14-cylinder radial engine driving a three-bladed propeller. However, JF-2s for the Coast Guard were fitted with Wright R-1820 Cyclone 9s. This engine became the standard Duck powerplant, the J2F-6 having a 783-kW (1,050-hp.) R-1820-54.

The large central amphibian float was faired into the J2F's fuselage. The fuselage had sufficient room for two passenger seats. The seats could be replaced with a stretcher in the casualty evacuation role.

### J2F-6 DUCK

Columbia Aircraft built 330 J2F-6s, production ending in August 1945. In World War II, Pacific-based US Navy and Marine Corps J2Fs flew air-sea rescue missions.

---

### J2F-6 Duck

**Type:** two/three-seat utility amphibian

**Powerplant:** one 783-kW (1,050-hp.) Wright R-1820-54 Cyclone 9 nine-cylinder radial piston engine

**Maximum speed:** 306 km/h (190 m.p.h.)

**Cruising speed:** 249 km/h (154 m.p.h.)

**Initial climb rate:** 405 m/min (1,328 f.p.m.)

**Maximum range:** 1370 km (850 mi.)

**Normal range:** 1085 km (673 mi.)

**Service ceiling:** 8140 m (26,700 ft.)

**Weights:** empty 2470 kg (5,430 lb.); maximum take-off 3307 kg (7,290 lb.)

**Armament:** usually unarmed, although provision was made for one 7.62-mm (.30 cal.) machine-gun in rear cockpit and up to 294 kg (647 lb.) of bombs or depth charges

**Dimensions:**
| | | |
|---|---|---|
| span | 11.89 m | (40 ft.) |
| length | 10.36 m | (34 ft.) |
| height | 3.76 m | (12 ft. 4 in.) |
| wing area | 38 m² | (409 sq. ft.) |

---

### ACTION DATA

#### CRUISING SPEED

Grumman's Duck had a good turn of speed, although this was marginally less than that of the Arado Ar 196. Aichi's 'Jake' was a significantly slower machine.

| | |
|---|---|
| **J2F-6 DUCK** | 249 km/h (165 m.p.h.) |
| **Ar 196A-3** | 267 km/h (166 m.p.h.) |
| **E13A1a 'JAKE'** | 222 km/h (138 m.p.h.) |

#### POWER

Duck amphibians and 'Jake' floatplanes had a similar power rating. The Arado had a smaller engine, but was a smaller, lighter machine without the need for a powerful engine.

| J2F-6 DUCK | Ar 196A-3 | E13A1a 'JAKE' |
|---|---|---|
| 783 kW (1,050 hp.) | 716 kW (960 hp.) | 790 kW (1,060 hp.) |

#### RANGE

The Japanese Aichi E13A design had a 2000-km (1,300-mi.) range, useful for its naval reconnaissance role. Like the Duck and Ar 196, the E13A was employed from both ships and shore bases. Both the Arado and Aichi were floatplane designs; the J2F was a more versatile amphibian, able to operate from aircraft-carrier decks and land bases.

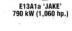

Ar 196A-3 800 km (496 mi.)

J2F-6 DUCK 1207 km (748 mi.)

E13A1a 'JAKE' 2090 km (1,296 mi.)

---

## Grumman's amphibian family

■ **G-21 GOOSE:** Grumman's first twin-engined design, the G-21, flew in May 1937. In all, 345 were built for military and civil users. Wartime aircraft served with the USN, USCG and RAF.

■ **G-44 WIDGEON:** Grumman flew the Widgeon, which was cheaper than the Goose, in June 1940. Early examples saw military service; some civil G-44s remain airworthy today.

■ **G-73 MALLARD:** An enlarged variation of the G-21 design, the Mallard, first took to the air in 1946. All 59 built went to civil users, except for two received by the Egyptian air force in 1949.

■ **G-64/G-111 ALBATROSS:** Large numbers of this air-sea rescue amphibian, first flown in 1947, were delivered to the USN and USAF. Anti-submarine warfare versions were exported.

# GRUMMAN
# TBF/TBM AVENGER

● Three-seat torpedo-bomber ● Battle of Midway veteran

▲ Avengers saw their
first combat in the Battle of Midway in June 1942.
Although their losses were high, production was
stepped up, with nearly 10,000 being built in
several variants before the war ended.

**G**rumman's portly TBF Avenger
(built by Eastern Aircraft as the TBM)
was the most important American
torpedo-bomber of World War II. Big, noisy
and powerful, the Avenger flew from carrier
decks and spanned vast Pacific distances
to attack the Japanese Navy with its torpedo
or bombs. The Avenger had staying power,
with many Allied nations using the type long
after the war. US Navy Avengers were still on
hand for transport duty in the Korean War.

## GRUMMAN TBF/TBM AVENGER

▲ Royal Navy Avengers
This TBF-1 (Avenger Mk I) flew
with the Fleet Air Arm's
No. 846 Squadron. FAA aircraft
were carrier and land based.

▲ Flying on into the 21st century
A number of Avengers have survived to be restored
by enthusiasts. In service until the 1950s, some
surplus aircraft were converted into water bombers
and were used to fight forest fires for many years.
Some of the restored aircraft are ex-fire bombers.

▲ Barrel shaped
For a single-engined aircraft the TBM
was fairly big. The same engine was
fitted to the B-25 Mitchell bomber.

▼ Airborne early warning
To provide early warning protection for
USN carriers the TBM-3W, with its large
radome, entered service after the war.

▲ Carrier-borne
A US Navy Avenger lumbers off the deck of a
carrier. The bulk of Avengers were built by General
Motors (Eastern Division) as Grumman was fully
committed to building fighters for the Navy.

### FACTS AND FIGURES
➤ US President George Bush was the youngest naval aviator when he flew Avengers in combat in the Pacific.
➤ Avenger production totalled 9839; 7546 by General Motors, the rest by Grumman.
➤ The TBF was initially called the 'Tarpon' in the Royal Navy and later the 'Avenger'.
➤ When used against submarines, Avengers destroyed or shared in the destruction of 42 U-boats.
➤ Avengers used the first high-velocity aircraft rockets (HVARs) in January 1944.
➤ Six TBFs saw action in the Battle of Midway on 4 June 1942; only one returned.

# General Motors torpedo truck

Grumman Iron Works was a nickname for the company that designed the Avenger. Grumman created shipboard aircraft that were sturdy, heavy and tough. When it replaced the inadequate Douglas TBD Devastator as the US Navy's torpedo-bomber in the Pacific, the Grumman Avenger had the strength and power to do the job.

However, as Grumman was busy fulfilling large orders for fighters, the job of constructing the bulk of the Avenger order

was subcontracted to the Eastern Aircraft Division of the General Motors Corporation.

Despite a poor start at the 1942 Battle of Midway, the Avenger performed superbly through to the end of the war and, in addition to torpedo bombing, took on other roles including close air support of ground troops.

The Avenger was pleasant to fly, although spinning was prohibited. When flown with determination by a strong pilot, it could almost turn like a fighter,

hence its single, and later twin, forward-firing gun armament.

Britain (921 aircraft) and New Zealand (63) also used Avengers during the war. Canada, France, Japan and the Netherlands employed it after 1945.

*Above: The Avenger's weapons bay was big enough for a torpedo or 907-kg (2.000-lb.) bomb. The prototype first flew on 1 August 1941.*

*Above: A Royal Navy Avenger aboard HMS* Illustrious. *Thirty-three first- and second-line FAA squadrons were equipped with the Avenger, which served from numerous carriers and shore bases from Canada to the Far East.*

### TBF-1 Avenger

**Type:** three-seat carrier-based torpedo-bomber

**Powerplant:** one 1268-kW (1,700-hp.) Wright R-2600-8 Cyclone 14-cylinder radial piston engine

**Maximum speed:** 436 km/h (270 m.p.h.) at 5030 m (15,000 ft.)

**Climb rate:** 435 m/min (1,425 f.p.m.)

**Range:** 1778 km (1,100 mi.)

**Service ceiling:** 6830 m (22,400 ft.)

**Weights:** empty 4788 kg (10,534 lb.); maximum take-off 7876 kg (17,327 lb.)

**Armament:** (TBF-1C) two fixed forward-firing 12.7-mm (.50 cal.) machine-guns; one 12.7-mm machine-gun in rear turret, one 7.62-mm (.30 cal.) machine-gun in ventral position; 907 kg (2,000 lb.) of bombs or one torpedo in internal bomb-bay

**Dimensions:**
| | |
|---|---|
| span | 16.51 m (54 ft. 2 in.) |
| length | 12.20 m (40 ft.) |
| height | 5.00 m (16 ft. 5 in.) |
| wing area | 45.52 m² (490 sq. ft.) |

## TBM-1 (AVENGER MK II)

**As well as the US Navy, Britain's Fleet Air Arm and the Royal New Zealand Air Force operated Avengers during World War II.**

Power for the Avenger was supplied by Wright's big R-2600 Cyclone 14 radial engine. Three main fuel tanks were fitted with a total capacity of 1248 litres (330 gal.).

Two crewmembers sat in the long cockpit 'glasshouse': the pilot, who also fired the wing guns and released the torpedo, and the radio operator, who also manned the rear gun turret.

To ease stowage aboard aircraft-carriers the Avenger had hydraulically folding wings. The main undercarriage retracted into the wings; the rear wheel also retracted. The arrester hook was electrically operated.

Avenger Mk II serial number JZ490 was based in Britain in mid-1944 and carried the black and white identification stripes worn by Allied aircraft during the invasion of Europe.

NAVY 490

The ventral machine-gun position was occupied by the bomb-aimer. The hydraulically operated bomb-bay doors could be controlled by the bomb-aimer or the pilot.

### COMBAT DATA

#### ARMAMENT

The Avenger was in every way an improvement over the TBD. Its gun armament was significantly greater and it could deliver twice the weight of bombs or a larger torpedo. The B6N was lightly armed.

**TBD-1 DEVASTATOR**
2 x 7.62-mm (.30 cal.) machine-guns
454 kg (1,000 lb.) of bombs/torpedoes

**TBF-1 AVENGER**
3 x 12.7-mm (.50 cal.) machine-guns
1 x 7.62-mm (.30 cal.) machine-gun
907 kg (2,000 lb.) of bombs/torpedoes

**B6N TENZAN**
2 x 7.7-mm (.303 cal.) machine-guns
800 kg (1,760 lb.) bombs/torpedo

#### MAXIMUM SPEED

The TBF had a 100 km/h (60 m.p.h.) speed advantage over the TBD. The more streamlined B6N was faster still, due to its more powerful engine and lighter weight. The B6N was intensively used in the last two years of the war, latterly as kamikaze aircraft.

**TBD-1** 332 km/h (206 m.p.h.)

**TBF-1 AVENGER** 436 km/h (270 m.p.h.)

**B6N TENZAN** 480 km/h (298 m.p.h.)

#### RANGE

With well over twice the range of the TBD, the TBF still lagged far behind the equivalent Japanese design. Range is a very important attribute for a carrier-based aircraft. The B6N's long range allowed it to strike first in a carrier battle.

**TBD-1 DEVASTATOR** 669 km (415 mi.)

**TBF-1 AVENGER** 1778 km (1,100 mi.)

**B6N TENZAN** 3045 km (1,890 mi.)

## Post-war Avengers

■ **CANADIAN NAVY TBM-3E:** The Canadian navy was one of several to receive Avengers under the Mutual Assistance Program after World War II. Another was the former enemy, Japan.

■ **FIRE BOMBER:** As the TBF/TBM was retired by the US Navy in the 1950s, surplus aircraft found other uses. This example is one of a number used as water bombers in Canada and the US.

■ **CROP SPRAYER:** Another role for the civilian Avenger in Canada was that of forest or agricultural crop sprayer. In New Zealand experimental crop dusting was tried with Avengers.

# HALBERSTADT

# D.I-D.V

● Single-seat ● Fighting scout ● Exported to Turkey

▲ The major production versions of the Halberstadt series were the D.II and D.III. The D.III was basically an improved D.II with more agile handling and with the Mercedes engine replaced by an Argus.

From the end of 1915 until the conclusion of World War I, the Halberstadt series of fighting scouts were a common sight, participating in dogfights above the trenches on the Western Front. Although outclassed in 1916–17 by the Albatros D.I and Allied aircraft such as the Sopwith Pup and SPAD VII, the Halberstadts gave a good account of themselves and were certainly treated with respect by their Allied adversaries.

## HALBERSTADT D.I-D.V

◀ First in the line
The D.I first flew in late 1915 and entered operations soon after. It was powered by a 74.5-kW (100-hp.) Mercedes engine.

▼ Advanced design
The D.Va featured a new tail design but did not enter large-scale production.

▼ High-lift wings
The wings on the D.III provided tremendous lift allowing a good rate-of-climb. To help prevent engine fumes entering the cockpit, the exhaust extended down the starboard side of the fuselage.

▼ Family lines
The Halberstadt series of fighters carried distinctive family traits including the triangular rudder which was attached by two steel struts and was believed to be prone to failure.

◀ Turkish scout
With modified centre-section struts and ailerons, the D.V was virtually identical to the D.III. This damaged example is one of a number which were supplied to Turkey.

## FACTS AND FIGURES

➤ The unsuccessful D.I became a much better aircraft when fitted with the Mercedes engine and designated D.II.

➤ Only 100 D.IIs and D.IIIs were in front-line service by January 1915.

➤ The D.IV was the first in the series to be fitted with two machine-guns.

➤ Halberstadt also produced B series reconnaissance and CL series ground-attack aircraft during World War I.

➤ The D.V had the best handling of the series and was reputedly a delight to fly.

➤ D.IIs and D.IIIs were contract-built by the Aviatik and Hannover companies.

# PROFILE

# Halberstadt's fighting family

Although produced in only small numbers compared to Germany's illustrious Fokker and Albatros designs, the fighters of the Halberstadt series were well designed and performed admirably in combat during the mid-war years.

The single-gun D.I was the first Halberstadt fighting scout to appear but was quickly replaced in production by the improved D.II. To help solve the problem of fumes in the cockpit a number of different exhausts were fitted to this model including a long exhaust down the starboard side of the fuselage and later a chimney-type manifold exhausting over the top wing. The D.II was extremely strong and could take significant punishment for which pilots were extremely grateful, since they had no parachutes.

The D.III featured larger ailerons which improved the aircraft's manoeuvrability. It was these aircraft, along with Fokker D.IIIs and and D.IVs, which formed the basis of the first Jastas in the summer of 1916 and revolutionised air combat.

By the end of 1916 the D.II and D.III were obsolescent and production switched to the D.IV, which although capable did not receive large orders. The final version, the D.V, was basically a slightly modified D.III.

*Left: This D.II was flown by the famous German ace Oswald Boelcke. He was killed in combat on 28 October 1916.*

*Below: The D.IV of 1917 owed many of its features, such as its neatly spinnered nose, to the firm's CL.II two-seater.*

## D.II

**Type:** single-seat fighting scout

**Powerplant:** one 89.5-kW (120-hp.) Mercedes D.II six-cylinder in-line engine

**Maximum speed:** 150 km/h (93 m.p.h.)

**Initial climb rate:** 4 min to 1000 m (3,300 ft.); 15 min to 3000 m (9,850 ft.)

**Range:** 250 km (155 mi.)

**Service ceiling:** 5975 m (19,600 ft.)

**Weights:** empty 520 kg (1,144 lb.); maximum take-off 730 kg (1,606 lb.)

**Armament:** one fixed forward-firing 7.92-mm LMG 08/15 machine-gun

**Dimensions:**
| | |
|---|---|
| span | 8.80 m (28 ft. 10 in.) |
| length | 7.30 m (23 ft. 11 in.) |
| height | 2.67 m (8 ft. 9 in.) |
| wing area | 23.60 m² (254 sq. ft.) |

## D.V

Virtually a D.III airframe with a number of minor modifications, the D.V was used as a scout. A small number, such as this example, were supplied to the Turkish Government in late 1917 and early 1918.

The two-bay wing structure fitted to the D Series of scouts was extremely strong. Like the D.III, the D.V had larger ailerons for increased agility.

Delivered in late 1917 this example carries the Turkish insignia of the period and was used against Allied opposition during the last year of the war.

The aircraft's rudder was of approximately triangular profile and was braced by two steel struts. The elevators were of similar trapezoidal shape to those of its Fokker contemporaries.

The steel vee-type undercarriage chassis had two spreader bars welded from streamlined steel tube. The wheels were fitted with elastic-cord shock absorbers.

The fuselage was of a conventional wooden structure with hollow square-section longerons. Curved metal panels held the engine in place at the nose. The rear fuselage tapered in a wedge shape to a horizontal knife-edge and was fabric-covered; the front fuselage was plywood covered.

## COMBAT DATA

### MAXIMUM SPEED

The D.II had excellent climb performance and good manoeuvrability but this was at the expense of speed with the aircraft having a large amount of drag. Contemporary Allied fighters like the Nieuport 17 and Sopwith Pup were able to outrun the Halberstadt design if they got into difficulties during a dogfight.

| | |
|---|---|
| **HALBERSTADT D.II** | 150 km/h (93 m.p.h.) |
| **SOPWITH PUP** | 180 km/h (112 m.p.h.) |
| **NIEUPORT 17** | 170 km/h (105 m.p.h.) |

### CLIMB RATE

The Halberstadt D.II's wings had excellent lift qualities which allowed a good rate-of-climb although the corresponding increase in drag reduced the aircraft's speed performance. The Pup had the poorest rate of climb but the highest speed.

| | |
|---|---|
| **HALBERSTADT D.II** | 250 m/min (820 f.p.m.) |
| **NIEUPORT 17** | 211 m/min (690 f.p.m.) |
| **SOPWITH PUP** | 140 m/min (460 f.p.m.) |

### SERVICE CEILING

The Halberstadt's excellent wing design gave the aircraft a superior service ceiling over its contemporaries. The good rate-of-climb was also a big asset in a dogfight allowing the aircraft to climb above and make diving attacks.

| HALBERSTADT DII 5975 m (19,600 ft.) | SOPWITH PUP 5355 m (17,600 ft.) | NIEUPORT 17 5350 m (17,550 ft.) |
|---|---|---|

## Other Great War Halberstadts

■ **CL.II:** Designed to a light-escort and ground-attack specification, the CL.II first flew in 1917 and was built in considerable numbers.

■ **CL.IV:** In 1918 the German ground-attack aircraft fleet was undergoing rapid expansion and the capable CL.IV was built to fill this need.

■ **CL.IV (ROLAND-BUILT):** To satisfy the German demand for more of the excellent C.IV a sub-contract was undertaken by Roland.

■ **CLS.I:** Designed to succeed both the CL.II and CL.IV, the CLS.I was smaller, lighter and faster than its predecessors.

# HANDLEY PAGE

# O/100 AND O/400

- Long-range heavy bomber ● Built in large numbers ● Pioneer 'airliner'

▲ *Warplanes began the war armed with a rifle and tiny bombs. By 1918 they were dropping monster 748-kg (1,650-lb.) weapons such as this. In Britain, the name Handley Page was virtually synonymous with large aircraft.*

A t the beginning of World War I, aircraft looked as if someone could tie a piece of string to them and fly them in a light breeze. In four short years the fighting plane had evolved into a potent military weapon, in such diverse forms as high-speed fighters and multi-engined long-range heavy bombers. Among the most powerful of them all were the Handley Page O/100 and the improved O/400.

## HANDLEY PAGE O/100 AND O/400

▲ **Stuck in the mud**
The O/400 series had a wide undercarriage, with fat tyres to take its weight. This aircraft was used by No. 207 Sqn at Ligescourt in 1918.

▲ **Roaring Eagle**
In place of Rolls-Royce Eagle engines, the O/400 could use the Sunbeam Maori or Liberty 12-N.

▼ **Daring mission**
Navy O/100 crews attacked the German battlecruiser Goeben in Stenia Bay, Turkey, in 1917.

◄ **Lift-off**
The O/400 took off at about 80 km/h (50 m.p.h.). Its top speed was not much higher, due to high drag.

**Canal bomber** ►
This O/400 is seen on a practice flight over the Thames. Operational flights were made to attack the Zeebrugge canal, to stop it being used by U-boats.

◄ **Civil service**
The O/400 was used to carry passengers after World War I. G-EAKG was an ex-service aircraft bought by Handley Page Transport and used for flights to Paris.

## FACTS AND FIGURES

- ➤ The first O/100 left the ground at 1.51 p.m. on 18 December 1915.

- ➤ In July 1916 an O/100 took 20 passengers to an altitude of 2000 m (6,500 ft.).

- ➤ In 1917 an O/100 was flown to the Middle East via Paris, Rome and the Balkans, and was used to bomb Constantinople.

- ➤ On the night of 14/15 September 1918, 40 Handley Page O/400s attacked military targets in the Saar.

- ➤ The O/400 could drop a 748-kg (1,650-lb.) bomb, then the heaviest British bomb.

- ➤ An O/400 was used in December 1918 to survey the route from Egypt to India.

## PROFILE

# Britain's first heavy bomber

Designed to an Admiralty specification, the big Handley Page bomber was Britain's largest aeroplane when it first entered service late in 1916. The first recorded mission took place on the night of 16/17 March 1917, when the 'Handley Page Squadron', as it was then known, made an attack on a German-held railway junction and marshalling yard.

The O/100 was powered by two 198-kW (265-hp.) Rolls-Royce Eagle engines. It originally had an enclosed cockpit and armour plate to protect engines and crew, but performance was sluggish and production aircraft had an open cockpit and no armour.

Production deliveries of the O/400 began in 1918. This was a much improved aircraft, having more powerful engines

and a revised fuel system, and could carry around a ton of bombs. Although only 46 O/100s had been built, more than 400 of its replacement were in service as the Armistice was signed. The US Army Air Service selected the O/400 as its standard heavy bomber and ordered 1,500, but only 107 were completed before the end of the war brought about the cancellation of the contract.

*The O/400 was a massive aircraft by the standards of the time, and it was not until the Fairey Hendon of 1936 that the RAF again had a bomber of this size in service in numbers.*

### O/400
The O/400 served with the Royal Naval Air Service and later the RAF with great success. It saw combat in Europe and Turkey and went on to support the British Army in Egypt and India.

Drag from the engine nacelles was a problem for the Handley Page designers. Moving the large radiators helped to alleviate this, but the O/400 was never a fast machine.

The wing was made of two large spruce spars, with hollow compression pieces between the front and rear spars.

Rolls-Royce Eagles were in short supply, so Sunbeam Cossack engines were sometimes installed.

A Lewis gun provided some protection for the observer in the rear cockpit. Crew members had armour protection, known as the 'bath'.

The fuselage was assembled from four main sections, with reinforced metal plates at the joints and internal wire bracing.

The nose gunner sat in an exposed forward cockpit, armed with a single Lewis gun. Trials of a Davis recoilless gun for attacking U-boats were not successful, as the gun often did more damage to the aircraft than to its target.

Unlike the upper wing, the lower wing had no ailerons.

The rear fuselage of the early O/100 prototypes experienced severe vibration problems when the aircraft reached 130 km/h (80 m.p.h.), but strengthening the structure provided a cure.

The elevators were fitted with large aerodynamic 'horn balances' to reduce the effort of controlling the aircraft.

## O/400
**Type:** long-range heavy bomber

**Powerplant:** two 268-kW (360-hp.) Rolls-Royce Eagle VIII V-12 piston engines

**Maximum speed:** 156 km/h (96 m.p.h.)

**Ferry range:** 1200 km (745 mi.)

**Service ceiling:** 2600 m (8,900 ft.)

**Weights:** empty 3719 kg (8,182 lb.); loaded 6350 kg (13,970 lb.)

**Armament:** up to five flexibly-mounted 7.7-mm (.303 cal.) Lewis guns, plus up to 907 kg (2,000 lb.) of bombs or one 748-kg (1,650-lb.) bomb

**Dimensions:** span 30.48 m (100 ft.)
length 19.16 m (63 ft.)
height 6.71 m (22 ft.)
wing area 153.1 m² (164 sq. ft.)

### COMBAT DATA

#### MAXIMUM SPEED
None of the early heavy bombers were fast. The O/400 was faster than the comparable but slightly smaller German Gotha, and both were much faster than the pioneering Russian Ilya Mouramets, designed by Igor Sikorsky before the war. The high drag produced by the biplane wings and bracing wires reduced speed.

O/400 156 km/h (96 m.p.h.)
GOTHA G.V 140 km/h (87 m.p.h.)
MOURAMETS 100 km/h (62 m.p.h.)

#### SERVICE CEILING
The O/400 was a little underpowered, and it was never able to climb very high when carrying a bombload. It did not have the advantage of the Gotha's exceptionally high ceiling, which meant that it was very difficult for British and French fighters to intercept. However, since the O/400 generally flew at night, its low ceiling was not a great handicap.

GOTHA G.V 6500 m (21,320 ft.)
O/400 2600 m (8,900 ft.)
MOURAMETS 2500 m (8,200 ft.)

#### WEAPONS LOAD
The O/400 was one of the first aircraft able to deliver around one ton of high explosive over appreciable distances. German 'R' class giants could carry more, but could not fly as far when carrying a heavy load. The big Russian bombers had good lifting ability, but rarely carried more than 10 small bombs.

O/400 907 kg (2,000 lb.) of bombs
GOTHA G.V 500 kg (1,100 lb.) of bombs
MOURAMETS 160 kg (350 lb.) of bombs

## Heavy bombers of World War I
**CAPRONI Ca 3:** Italy was a pioneering force in multi-engine aviation, and the highly successful Caproni series of biplane and triplane heavy bombers were used by France and Britain as well as by the Italian air force.

**GOTHA G.IV:** The G-type could carry up to 500 kg (1,100 lb.) of bombs, and bore the brunt of Germany's campaign against England in 1917 and 1918. Although several manufacturers produced such aircraft, they all became known to their enemies as 'Gothas'.

**ZEPPELIN-STAAKEN R:** The 32 R-type giant bombers built in Germany in the last two years of the war evolved into seven-man aircraft able to carry a significant bombload. They were used on the Eastern Front and in bombing raids on London.

# HANDLEY PAGE

# HALIFAX

● Heavy bomber ● Long-range maritime patroller ● Transport

**A**s one of the four-engined bomber types which provided the backbone of the Royal Air Force's night bombing offensive against Germany the Halifax was a vital cog in the Allied war effort. Although the Avro Lancaster grabbed the glory, its pilots and crews found the Halifax to be a superb heavy bomber with formidable striking power. It also flew a wide variety of missions, ranging from anti-submarine patrols to para-dropping agents into occupied Europe.

▲ Halifaxes served in every part of the European and Atlantic theatres. In the maritime role crews like this ranged far over the ocean, protecting convoys from the U-boat threat.

## HANDLEY PAGE HALIFAX

▲ **Cargo master**
The Halifax Mk VIII transport variant, distinguished by its lack of gun turrets and its bulging belly, could carry 3600 kg (7,920 lb.) of freight.

▲ **Merlin cargo**
Although designed to carry bombs of up to 1800 kg (3,690 lb.), the bomb-bay could hold more unusual loads, like this engine.

▲ **Night bird**
The black undersides were designed to hide the aircraft from searchlights when night-bombing. Although overshadowed by the Lancaster, the Halifax was an effective combat aircraft.

▲ **Caught in the glare**
Silhouetted against the glare of target indicator flares, a Halifax drops its bombs on a V-weapon site. The bomb-run was the most dangerous part of the mission.

◄ **Defensive formation**
Even when it kept to a tight defensive formation, the Halifax's gun turrets could not defend it effectively enough by day. Most bombing missions by the aircraft were at night.

## FACTS AND FIGURES

➤ First flight of a Halifax prototype was on 25 October 1939.

➤ In addition to Bomber Command, the Halifax was flown by RAF Coastal Command for anti-submarine and other maritime duties.

➤ 6178 Halifaxes were built, but not one survives fully intact today.

➤ Because of its great hauling capacity, the Halifax was used as a freighter and transport by the RAF and civil users.

➤ The almost-complete wreckage of a Halifax bomber was retrieved from Lake Hoklingen, Norway, in 1973.

➤ The Halifax was the first aircraft to carry H2S radar-bombing equipment.

## PROFILE

# Handley Page's great all-rounder

Its reputation has been overshadowed to some extent by its great contemporary, the Lancaster. But at its peak the Handley Page Halifax equipped 34 squadrons of RAF Bomber Command, and in 75,532 sorties over Europe between 1941 and 1945 the type dropped 231,263 tonnes (227,609 tons) of bombs.

It was in some respects the best aircraft in its class, gifted with great bomb-carrying capacity, toughness and the strength to survive when hit.

The Halifax was also the most versatile RAF heavy bomber. Remembered for nocturnal raids over Europe, the Halifax took on many duties, including pathfinder, ambulance, freighter, glider-tug, personal transport and maritime reconnaissance aircraft.

The Halifax offered as much protection as feasible, but flying this bomber was a dangerous business, especially during the bloody campaign over Berlin (November 1943–March 1944), which cost the RAF 1,000 aircraft to the barrage of anti-aircraft artillery and swarms of Luftwaffe night-fighters encountered on every sortie. Every man in a Halifax crew shared a bond. Some of the most courageous pilots were those who brought the Halifax home burning and crippled from battle damage – to a safe landing.

*The Halifax Mk III introduced the Bristol Hercules radial engine, an extended-span wing, new tailfins and a long glazed nose without a gun turret. The enhanced performance endeared it to crews.*

### Halifax B.Mk III

**Type:** seven-seat long-range heavy bomber; also troop transport and long-range anti-submarine aircraft

**Powerplant:** four 1204-kW (1,613-hp.) Bristol Hercules XVI 14-cylinder radial piston engines

**Maximum speed:** 500 km/h (281 m.p.h.)

**Service ceiling:** 7315 m (24,000 ft.)

**Range:** 2000 km (1,240 mi.) with maximum bombload

**Weights:** empty 17,345 kg (38,159 lb.); loaded 29,484 kg (64,865 lb.)

**Armament:** nine 7.7-mm (.303 cal.) machine-guns in nose and quad dorsal and tail turrets, plus up to 5897 kg (13,200 lb.) of bombs

**Dimensions:** span 31.75 m (104 ft.)
length 21.82 m (72 ft.)
height 6.32 m (21 ft.)
wing area 118.45 m² (1,275 sq. ft.)

## HALIFAX B.MK I

**Halifax L9530 was one of the very first production aircraft, which was delivered to the RAF's No. 76 Squadron in the winter of 1940–41.**

The 'acorn' on top of the fuselage housed a rotating radio-direction-finding antenna.

The B.Mk I had gun positions in the beam windows. Later versions were equipped with two- or four-gun dorsal turrets.

The twin-fin tail was a desirable feature, as more than one Halifax crew was forced to fly home with half the tail unit shot away.

Although a co-pilot's seat was fitted, Halifaxes were, like Lancasters, flown by a single pilot.

The original small tailfins seen here were later replaced by larger square surfaces.

Early Halifaxes were fitted with a two-gun nose turret. This was replaced in later variants by a streamlined Perspex moulding which created much less drag.

Although intended to be a twin-engined bomber, early examples were powered by four Rolls-Royce Merlins.

The capacious bomb-bay could carry almost 6000 kg (13,200 lb.) of bombs of up to 1800 kg (4,000 lb.) in size, and was later adapted to carry cargo.

All Halifax bombers carried a four-gun tail turret to counter German night-fighters, which generally attacked from astern.

### COMBAT DATA

#### MAXIMUM SPEED

The original Halifax was underpowered with four Merlins, and could be fairly sluggish with a heavy load. Mk IIIs were equipped with powerful Bristol Hercules radial engines, which transformed the bomber into one of the fastest aircraft in its class.

**HALIFAX B.Mk III** 500 km/h (310 m.p.h.)
**B-17D** 462 km/h (286 m.p.h.)
**LANCASTER B.Mk I** 460 km/h (285 m.p.h.)

#### MAXIMUM BOMBLOAD

British bombers generally carried near-capacity bombloads on operations. American bombers rarely used their full lifting capacity, and a typical load for the B-17 was usually about 2500 kg (5,500 lb.).

**HALIFAX B.Mk III** 5897 kg (12,973 lb.)
**B-17D** 5800 kg (12,760 lb.)
**LANCASTER B.Mk I** 6350 kg (13,970 lb.)

#### RANGE

Most Western four-engined bombers had the range to carry a heavy weapons load from bases in England to attack targets as far away as east Prussia or the oilfields in Romania. Losses to unescorted bombers could be great, however, as they braved the heavily defended skies over the Reich. The RAF bombers' main defence was operating in darkness.

**HALIFAX B.Mk III** 2000 km (1,240 mi.)
**B-17D** 1750 km (1,085 mi.)
**LANCASTER B.Mk I** 2675 km (1,658 mi.)

## Night bombers raid the Reich

**MISSION LAUNCHED:** RAF bomber raids were extremely complex operations. Up to 1000 heavy aircraft would take off from fields all over eastern England, crossing the coast of Europe in several streams. Late in the war they were accompanied by aircraft equipped with electronic countermeasures equipment, as well as heavily armed Mosquito night-fighters, to counter the fierce German defences.

HAMBURG
THE RUHR
MUNICH

**SPOOF RAIDS:** Bombers would appear to be heading for any one of a number of widely dispersed cities, forcing the Luftwaffe's defences to be divided.

**THE REAL TARGET:** At a pre-determined point the bomber streams converged, aiming to be over the primary target almost simultaneously, overwhelming the defences and giving a greater chance of survival.

**MULTIPLE THREAT:** Defenders were faced with an overwhelming threat coming from differing directions at differing heights. Precision planning was essential to prevent collision. By the end of the war a 1000-bomber raid took only minutes to unload its deadly cargo, compared to the hours it had taken three years earlier.

# HANDLEY PAGE

# HEYFORD

● Biplane bomber ● Last of its kind ● Bomber trainer

L ast of the RAF's biplane bombers, the Heyford had the unusual distinction of having the fuselage attached to the upper wing. Another oddity was the rear gunner's retractable 'dustbin' turret. After questions about whether bombing might be outlawed by the League of Nations, the Heyford entered service and flew as the RAF's premier night-bomber. But it had a short life, being introduced in 1933 and progressively withdrawn by 1939.

▲ Heyfords were very much in the public eye in the 1930s, appearing at Hendon air pageants in impressive formations. This aircraft was reviewed by His Majesty King George VI and Air-Marshal Trenchard at the 1935 Jubilee Review at RAF Mildenhall.

## HANDLEY PAGE HEYFORD

**▼ Improved Heyford**
Handley Page were only too aware of the Heyford's failings, and the company improved the aircraft throughout its life. Problems with engine cooling were cured by fitting new nacelles.

**▲ Flying monstrosity**
With its top wing-mounted fuselage the Heyford was one of the RAF's most unconventional designs. However, this arrangement gave the aircraft excellent take-off performance.

**Dustbin turret ▶**
The retractable gun turret was produced in response to the opinions of RAF aircrew. The mock-up of the turret was built in just four hours.

**▼ Nose high**
The curious design resulted in a large 'ground angle' (high nose attitude), which in turn gave the Heyford a short landing roll and low touchdown speed.

**◀ Fun to fly**
For such a big aircraft, the Heyford was unusually agile and also had surprising structural strength, which is important for a bomber.

**▼ Open cockpits**
Heyford crews were exposed to the elements, making operating at its ceiling rather unpleasant.

### FACTS AND FIGURES

➤ One Heyford pilot flew for an hour with his starboard propeller smashed by empty rounds from the nose gun.

➤ Early in 1940 at least seven Heyfords were still in use as bomber trainers.

➤ Heyfords took part in the first secret trials of the Hotspur assault glider.

➤ Heyfords were also used in trials of a 'frictionless take-off trolley and track' and new de-icing equipment.

➤ Six Heyfords crashed in one day in 1936 after encountering severe icing.

➤ Eleven RAF squadrons used Heyfords between 1933 and 1939.

# Britain's last biplane bomber

Having made do with a variety of lamentable designs in the 1920s, the RAF required a big bomber to equip the bombing force that it considered so important. The Heyford's designers faced the challenge of having to use a biplane configuration and indifferent engines, knowing that monoplanes with much better powerplants would soon be produced. Variable-pitch airscrews were another feature

that was newly available but ruled out because they presented technical difficulties.

Despite looking very awkward, the Heyford was described by a test pilot as being 'devoid of vice' and 'possessing all the essential features required by a night-bomber'. It was an unusual aircraft, having the fuselage attached to the upper wing, and the bombs stored in a bulged compartment in the lower wing. The production

aircraft received Rolls-Royce Kestrel or Armstrong Siddeley Tiger engines, and various features to reduce drag, but the result was still a rather slow aircraft. Surprisingly, the Heyford had commendable agility and could even be looped. It was also easy to maintain and was quite strong. However, the monoplane spelled the end for the Heyford, and the last few were used as trainers in 1940.

*One aviator managed to ground-loop a Heyford no less than two-and-a-half times on landing, and another survived a misadvertant high-speed dive caused by icing.*

*While crews generally liked the Heyford, the nose gunner was very exposed. Stieger and Hubbard nose turrets were tested but never adopted for service.*

## HP.50 HEYFORD

**Wearing the 'Nivo' dark-green night-bomber scheme, this Heyford was operated by No. 10 Squadron, RAF.**

The wings had a metal structure with fabric covering. The fuselage was half fabric and half metal covered.

The first Heyfords (B.19/27) were powered by Bristol Jupiter VIII or Napier Lion engines (as used by the Dornier Wal), but the HP.50 used the Rolls-Royce Kestrel III or VI.

The two rear gunners each had a Lewis 7.7-mm (.303 cal.) machine-gun. The gunners had excellent fields of fire, but the Heyford's dire lack of speed meant that the gunners would have had a difficult task in a combat situation.

The twin-fin tail was retained in later Handley Page designs, notably the Hampden monoplane bomber. The horn balance was extended on the rudders to make the controls feel lighter on production Heyfords.

The nose gunner was armed with a 7.7-mm (.303 cal.) machine-gun on a Scarff ring mounting. The pilot's cockpit was revised after test pilots complained about its poor layout and the seats being too low. The bomb-aimer was seated in the nose.

Bombs were stored in the lower wing and thus could only be of rather small size. Normal bombload was four 227-kg (500-lb.) or ten 90-kg (200-lb.) weapons. There was very little ground clearance for the trailing edge of the wing.

The famous 'dustbin' turret was a very confined space, and the smaller gunners in a squadron were often 'volunteered' to fly in this position. Handley Page modified the turret to make more room for the gunner's knees.

## RAF bombers of the 1930s

**ARMSTRONG WHITWORTH WHITLEY:** Whitleys formed the backbone of the night-bomber force at the outbreak of war.

**BRISTOL BOMBAY:** The Bombay flew in 1935 and remained in service long enough to see action in North Africa in the 1940s.

**FAIREY HENDON:** The first monoplane to enter service with the RAF, in 1936 the Hendon was soon replaced by the Wellington from 1938.

**HANDLEY PAGE HARROW:** A stop-gap between the Heyford and the Whitley, the Harrow entered service in 1937.

## COMBAT DATA

### RANGE

Designed as a strategic night-bomber, the Heyford had enough range to bomb targets in Europe from the UK. The Do 17 was designed for tactical support missions.

HEYFORD Mk 1 1480 km (918 mi.)
B.10 1996 km (1,238 mi.)
Do 17E-1 667 km (414 mi.)

### MAXIMUM SPEED

No amount of power could make up for the enormous drag of the Heyford's biplane design. The sleek Do 17 was actually much faster than the fighters of its day, but by 1940 even this excellent aircraft could never outrun a pursuing fighter aircraft.

HEYFORD 228 km/h (141 m.p.h.)
B.10 343 km/h (213 m.p.h.)
Do 17E-1 347 km/h (215 m.p.h.)

### BOMBLOAD

British bombers had high bombloads, gained at the expense of speed or equipment fit. The Heyford's bomb capacity was as large as any other aircraft in service in the mid-1930s outside the USSR.

HEYFORD Mk 1 1200 kg (2,640 lb.)
B.10 1025 kg (2,250 lb.)
Do 17E-1 750 kg (1,650 lb.)

# HANRIOT

# HD.1

● French biplane fighter ● Highly successful ● Maneuverable

▲ Having been eclipsed by the more powerful SPAD S.VII in France, the HD.1 achieved favor with the wartime forces of Belgium and Italy. The Belgians received 125 and the Italians more than 1000. Late in World War I, an HD.1 was modified with a float undercarriage to become the HD.2 floatplane fighter.

This highly maneuverable biplane fighter was the first military aircraft designed and built by the company of René Hanriot, who started his French manufacturing enterprise on the eve of the Great War. The Hanriot HD.1 was a workman-like little aircraft built largely of wood with fabric covering. Although lightweight and lightly armed, it captured the enthusiasm of Belgian and Italian pilots and remained in Italian service until 1925.

## HANRIOT HD.1

▲ Streamlined design
The 89-kW (120-hp.) Le Rhône 9Jb rotary engine was neatly faired. Forward sections were covered in sheet metal.

▲ Staggered wings
Considerable stagger was adopted for the wings and a faired headrest for the pilot.

Battleship take off ▶
From a gun-turret platform on the USS Mississippi, the U.S. Navy flew HD.2 variants of the HD.1.

▲ Postwar developments
Hanriot continued to design and build aircraft into the 1930s. The HD.14 was a brilliant trainer.

Vickers armed ▶
A single machine gun armed the HD.1, and the cockpit boasted a luxuriously padded headrest.

### FACTS AND FIGURES

➤ French records indicate that total production of the HD.1 was 1145 aircraft.

➤ The prototype HD.1 fighter completed its maiden flight in June 1916.

➤ The Hanriot HD.1 replaced the Nieuport Scout in several Belgian units.

➤ Belgian pilots began flying the Hanriot fighter in August 1917 and had considerable success with it.

➤ Macchi manufactured 901 of these fighters under license in Italy.

➤ An HD.1 was flown by the French navy from a battleship gun turret.

## PROFILE

# Original French fighter design

Designed by Emile Dupont, the HD.1 was its builder's first original product. Previously, the Hanriot firm, founded in 1916, had manufactured the Sopwith 1-1/2-Strutter reconnaissance biplane under license. The HD.1 had wings closely resembling those of the British aircraft and was characterized by its compact appearance and staggered wings of unequal span.

The HD.1 might have achieved greater success had it not been a competitor of the better-known SPAD S.VII, which performed extremely well. The HD.1 did not have enough power, despite its otherwise fine qualities, so Hanriot had to watch France order the SPAD instead. The Belgians and Italians, both desperately needed new fighters and settled on the HD.1. Macchi undertook production in Italy under licence.

The Belgian and Italian air arms flew the HD.1 with considerable success and it won the praise of Belgium's top ace Lieutenant Willy Coppens, who was among the first to fly it. After the First World War, a small number of these fighters turned up in other countries, such as Switzerland and Latin America, and the aircraft went on to form an important part of Italy's defences, six front-line squadrons facing Austria until at least the mid 1920s.

Above: Shown is a ghoulishly marked HD.1; probably after World War I. In addition to Swiss service, postwar HD.1s also found their way to South America and the U.S.

Above: Willy Coppens was largely responsible for the successful introduction of the HD.1 into Belgian service. His aircraft is preserved in a Belgian museum.

### HD.1

Greatly impressed by tests carried out on a force-landed Italian HD.1, the Swiss purchased 16 war-surplus aircraft from Italy.

Pilots enjoyed the well-balanced controls and rugged construction.

Ailerons were fitted to the larger, forward staggered upper wing. They were large and powerful and gave outstanding agility.

An unusual feature among its contemporaries was the HD.1's lack of rigging wires or control cables around the tail surfaces.

Originally powered by an 82-kW (110-hp.) Le Rhône 9J, the HD.1 was delivered with the more powerful 9Jb. Engines up to 127 kW (170 hp.) were tried with little success.

Conventional construction techniques using wooden frames with fabric covering accounted for most of the fuselage and wings. Dural, a metal alloy, was used for covering the forward fuselage.

A framework of steel tubing, covered with fabric, was selected for the tailplane. The strength of the resulting structure may explain the lack of any support other than the single tail strut on either side of the fuselage.

### HD.1

**Type:** Single-seat fighter scout

**Powerplant:** One 89-kW (120-hp.) Le Rhône 9Jb nine-cylinder rotary piston engine

**Maximum speed:** 183 km/h (114 m.p.h.)

**Cruising speed:** 156 km/h (97 m.p.h.)

**Service ceiling:** 6000 m (19,700 ft.)

**Endurance:** 2 hr 30 min

**Weapons:** 1 fixed forward-firing 7.7-mm (.303 cal.) Vickers machine gun with 110 rounds

**Weights:** Empty 399 kg (880 lb.); max take-off 649 kg (1,430 lb.)

**Dimensions:** Span 8.69 m (28 ft. 6 in.)
Length 5.84 m (19 ft. 2 in.)
Height 2.85 m (9 ft. 8 in.)
Wing area 18.21 m² (196 sq. ft.)

### ACTION DATA

#### ENDURANCE

World War I fighter tactics were either to act as escorts for reconnaissance and bomber types or to remain airborne in the hope of enemy contact. Long endurance was therefore desirable.

HD.1 2¹/₂ hr | ALBATROS D.I 2¹/₂ hr | SPAD S.VII 1¹/₂ hr

#### WEAPONS

A single Vickers machine gun was usually the preferred armament of Allied fighters; a second gun decreased performance. The Albatros was the slowest of these three.

HD.1 1 x 7.7-mm (.303 cal.) machine gun
ALBATROS D.I 2 x 7.92-mm machine guns
SPAD S.VII 1 x 7.7-mm (.303 cal.) machine gun

#### POWER

Extra power allowed the SPAD a stronger, heavier structure, which was more able to withstand the stresses of combat. Its strength and speed allowed it to become one of the War's most successful fighters, even though it could not match the agility of types like the HD.1. The Albatros D.1 led to a series of exceptional fighters.

HD.1 89 kW (120 hp.)
ALBATROS D.I 119 kW (160 hp.)
SPAD S.VII 134 kW (180 hp.)

## Early 1920s contemporaries

**SOPWITH PUP:** Excellent maneuverability and altitude performance made the low-powered Pup a formidable fighter.

**SPAD S.VII:** Higher power allowed the SPAD to be fast and strong. It was less agile than other designs but nevertheless very successful.

**NIEUPORT 17:** Nieuport pilots used the excellent rate of climb and overwing gun of the 17 to attack enemy aircraft from below.

**SOPWITH TRIPLANE:** The Triplane had all the qualities of the Pup, combined with higher speed and greater climb rate.

# HANSA-BRANDENBURG
# W.12 AND W.29

● Seaplane ● Imperial German Navy ● Fighter scout

▲ Inhibited by their floats, seaplanes were not usually the most capable fighters of the war, but the Hansa-Brandenburgs were among the most effective. They were dangerous to attack from any angle.

**H**ansa-Brandenburg gave Germany two highly effective seaplane fighters during the Great War. Designed by the brilliant Ernst Heinkel, the W.12 of 1917 was a two-seat fighter seaplane with an observer-gunner in the back seat. The W.29, which was introduced a year later, improved on this concept. Both Hansas were among the most successful seaplanes used by German naval flyers, destroying submarines and aircraft.

▲ **British model**
This replica of a W.29 was based at Thorpe Park in Surrey. It was complete with replica LMG 7.92-mm machine-guns.

▲ **Replica fighter**
Finland built the W.29 under licence at a factory near Helsinki. Based at Viipuri in the late 1920s, a number were fitted with skis.

**Final version ▶**
The W.33 was basically a scaled-up version of the W.29, which used a more powerful 183-kW (245-hp.) engine. Twenty-six of these aircraft were built in the autumn of 1918.

▼ **Ready to roll**
For taxiing on land the W.12 was mounted on a trolley. The exhaust pipes fed into a collector box, routed over the upper wing.

▲ **Prototype**
The first W.12 was built in 1917, with flying trials limited by harsh weather. The early models were powered by Mercedes D.III engines.

## FACTS AND FIGURES

➤ At an airfield north of the Arctic Circle, Finland was flying its version of the W.29 on skis as late as 1930.

➤ Seaplane fighters were being developed by Britain as recently as the 1960s.

➤ During the war years 146 W.12 and 78 W.29 seaplane fighters were built.

➤ A W.12 based at Zeebrugge destroyed the British non-rigid airship C.27 during December 1917.

➤ Improvements to the W.12 design increased endurance by adding fuel capacity.

➤ Hansa-Brandenburg designed more than 20 flying-boat types between 1914 and 1918.

## PROFILE

# Seaplane fighter goes to war

Seaplane fighters have fallen out of fashion, even though the idea has considerable merit. But in both world wars, these fighters carried out important duties.

The W.12 biplane and W.29 monoplane were both of wood and fabric construction, with the vertical tail behind and below the fuselage. When they went into combat, they provided their users with enormous firepower and speed, although range was limited. Almost any

landplane was better looking, but Ernst Heinkel's seaplanes were both trailblazers and successful warriors.

The W.12 was assigned to seaplane bases, where it enjoyed modest success combating Allied airships. Searching for improved performance, Heinkel decided on a single wing for the W.29, which began to enter service in 1918. The latter aircraft was even more successful, prompting the government of Finland to

manufacture its own version. The W.12 and W.29 contributed enormously to increasing the knowledge of the engineering community on how to build small, operational seaplanes for combat, and both had a fine fighting record.

*Below: By late 1917 the W.12 was making an appearance at German seaplane bases in an attempt to fight off the increasing attentions of the Royal Navy. It soon proved successful in combat.*

*Above: The unusual downward curved tail was designed to allow the gunner an unrestricted field of fire for his machine-gun.*

Forward-firing armament consisted of one or two fixed LMG 08 machine-guns which were semi-recessed in the fuselage above the engine.

Defence was provided by a gunner in a rear cockpit equipped with a Parabellum machine-gun on a flexible mount.

The upswept rear fuselage and curved tailfin and rudder were distinct features of the W.12 and W.29. The red and white squares were a unit marking and not national identification.

Power was provided by a Mercedes D.III in the early versions of the W.12 and a Benz Bz.III in just over half of the production run.

The biplane wings were of equal length. The W.29 had a monoplane configuration that permitted higher speed and better manoeuvrability.

**1414**

### W.12

**Flown from Zeebrugge by Leutnant Becht of the Imperial German Navy Air Service, this W.12 flew defensive missions against British naval aircraft during 1918.**

W.12s were fitted exclusively with floats, but some W.29s (especially those in Finland) had skis for ice operation; the bracing on the floats was very strong. Camouflage was painted on the upper surface.

### COMBAT DATA

#### MAXIMUM SPEED

The single-seat Sopwith Pup is the fastest of the trio, however, it was lightly armed. The W.12 and the F.2A both had average performance for flying-boats of the period but the W.12 was more manoeuvrable.

| | |
|---|---|
| W.12 | 160 km/h (99 m.p.h.) |
| F.2A | 153 km/h (95 m.p.h.) |
| PUP | 180 km/h (112 m.p.h.) |

#### ENDURANCE

For naval aircraft of World War I endurance was vitally important as it allowed far ranging patrols over water. The F.2A had exceptional endurance and often destroyed airships or U-boats during patrols.

| | |
|---|---|
| W.12 | 3½ hours |
| F.2A | 6 hours |
| PUP | 3 hours |

#### ARMAMENT

Most land-based scouts of World War I were lightly armed with one or two machine-guns. The excellent W.12 had slightly heavier armament, but the larger F.2A could carry up to six guns.

| W.12 | F.2A | PUP |
|---|---|---|
| 3 x 7.92-mm MGs | 6 x 7.7-mm (.303 cal.) MGs | 1 x 7.92-mm MGs |

## Attack on submarine C.25

■ **ON THE SURFACE:** A Royal Navy submarine, C.25, was caught off Harwich. A flight of Hansa-Brandenburg W.29s attacked and killed the captain, Lieutenant Bell, within minutes.

■ **NO ESCAPE:** Machine-gun fire riddled the hull, killing four more sailors. The hull was punctured, so the submarine could not dive. The crew replied with fire from a Lewis gun.

■ **UNDER TOW:** Submarine E.51 took the stricken C.25 under tow, but Oberleutnant Christiansen's W.29s kept up a fierce attack. Some of the aircraft dropped small bombs.

■ **WOUNDED:** The second coxswain was mortally wounded. He shouted 'never mind me sir, dive' as he fell, unaware that the captain was dead and the boat could not dive.

# HAWKER

# HART SERIES

● Basic pilot trainer ● Army co-operation ● Target tug

◀ **Demon target tug**
*The Demon was replaced in front-line combat service by the Blenheim from 1938, but a few remained in service during World War II as target tugs. High-visibility markings were carried along with a target winch.*

▼ **Hart T trainer**
*Hart bombers remained in service in the Middle East during the war and soldiered on at home as trainers.*

▲ **Audax wartime trainer**
*This Audax of No. 11 Flying Training School flew from Little Rissington.*

▼ **Hart day bomber**
*The Hart saw action as day bomber and general-purpose biplane with the South Africans, and as an RAF communications aircraft until 1943.*

▲ **Audax decoys**
*These unserviceable Audax aircraft at Habbaniyah airfield in Iraq had their upper mainplanes removed in order to appear like serviceable Hurricanes to enemy aircraft above.*

**F**aster than most fighters when it entered service in 1930, the Hart light bomber spawned a host of diverse derivatives. They included the Hart (Special) for the Middle East, the Hart (India) and the Hart (C) for communications work. The Hartbees was developed for South Africa, where 65 were built from 1935. Most Harts were replaced by modern types by September 1939, but some were still operational with front-line squadrons.

▲ *The Audax saw the most wartime action. No. 237 Squadron flew against the Italians in East Africa in 1940. Others based at Habbaniyah saw use in the 1941 Iraqi revolt.*

## FACTS AND FIGURES

➤ So fast was the Hart bomber when it entered service, it was used as a development aircraft in fighter trials.

➤ A fighter variant of the Hart, the Demon carried three machine-guns.

➤ The Audax was widely exported, to Iraq, Persia and the Straits Settlements.

➤ The Hartbees was developed from the Hart specifically for the South African Air Force, where it was flown until 1946.

➤ In 1938 all Hind trainers had blind-flying hoods fitted for instrument training.

➤ The Osprey was essentially a navalised Hart for fleet reconnaissance/spotting.

**PROFILE**

# War service in their twilight years

No. 5 Squadron, based at Lahore in India (now Pakistan), replaced its Wapitis with Harts in June 1940. In February 1941, after the Japanese had joined the war, the squadron was redeployed to Calcutta, where it operated another Hart derivative, the Audax, until September 1942.

A second India-based squadron, No. 27, became a training unit and swapped its Wapitis for Harts and Tiger Moths at Risalpur in October

1939. It operated the biplanes for a year before switching to operations with the Blenheim.

Four South African Air Force squadrons operated the Hartbees from Kenya and East Africa against the Italian forces in Ethiopia during 1940. Between June and September they were supported by the RAF's No. 237 Squadron, which deployed its Hart, Audax and Hardy ground-support aircraft from their bases at Nairobi as far as the Ethiopian border.

At home in England, a few single Harts were used by communications squadrons based at Northolt and then at Hendon. The type was also used for training by the Glider Exercise Unit, which became No. 296 Squadron in January 1942. Based at Netheravon, No. 296 used its Harts and Hectors to tow Hotspur gliders on training flights.

*Above: Neutral Sweden's 42 licence-built, Perseus-engined Harts saw service throughout the war years.*

*Below: A development of the Hart, the Hind remained in wartime RAF service as a Volunteer Reserve Flying Training School light bomber trainer.*

## HIND

A number of Hind light bombers saw service during World War II, those based in the UK, like this one, being assigned such tasks as communications and glider towing. This aircraft was equipped as a blind-flying trainer.

A two-bladed, fixed-pitch propeller was the standard fitting to aircraft of the Hart family.

Rolls-Royce's tried and tested Kestrel 12-cylinder engine powered most members of the Hart family. Ratings between 400 kW (536 hp.) and 500 kW (670 hp.) were typical.

Hind bombers included a synchronised, forward-firing 7.7-mm (.303 cal.) Vickers machine-gun mounted on the left of the engine cowling and firing through the propeller arc.

Given its new role as a bomber trainer, the Hind retained its underwing bomb racks.

In the light day-bomber role for which it was designed the Hind had a crew of two, the rear cockpit usually being equipped with a Lewis 7.7-mm (.303 cal.) machine-gun for self defence.

During the early months of the war, RAF aircraft were fitted with gas detection patches, often on the upper surface of the wings, or in this case, the rear fuselage. In the event they were not needed.

Modifications made to the Hind bomber for the bomber trainer role included removal of all armament and the fitting of dual controls for an instructor.

### Hart

**Type:** two-seat light bomber, close-support aircraft and trainer

**Powerplant:** one 391-kW (525-hp.) Rolls-Royce Kestrel IB, or 380-kW (510-hp.) Kestrel X (DR) liquid-cooled piston engine

**Maximum speed:** 296 km/h (184 m.p.h.) at 1525 m (5,000 ft.)

**Range:** 756 km (470 mi.)

**Service ceiling:** 6510 m (21,360 ft.)

**Weights:** empty 1148 kg (2,531 lb.); maximum take-off 2066 kg (4,555 lb.)

**Armament:** one or two forward-firing 7.7-mm (.303 cal.) machine-guns, one 7.7-mm machine-gun in rear cockpit; 236 kg (520 lb.) of bombs

**Dimensions:**
| | | |
|---|---|---|
| span | 11.35 m | (37 ft. 3 in.) |
| length | 8.94 m | (29 ft. 4 in.) |
| height | 3.17 m | (10 ft. 5 in.) |
| wing area | 32.33 m² | (348 sq. ft.) |

### ACTION DATA

**MAXIMUM SPEED**

The Hart was a very fast aircraft for its day, particularly bearing in mind its bomber status. When it first reached No. 33 Squadron, it was as much as 80 km/h faster than any contemporary bomber. The powerful Helldiver appeared at the beginning of the war.

| | |
|---|---|
| **HART** | 296 km/h (184 m.p.h.) |
| **S.328** | 280 km/h (174 m.p.h.) |
| **SBC-4 HELLDIVER** | 381 km/h (237 m.p.h.) |

**SERVICE CEILING**

The Hart was not capable of such extreme altitudes as the Helldiver or S 328. However, during the war most of its army co-operation and training missions were flown at low level. The Curtiss SBC's ceiling was useful for its dive-bombing role.

| HART | S.328 | SBC-4 HELLDIVER |
|---|---|---|
| 6510 m (21,360 ft.) | 7200 m (23,620 ft.) | 8320 m (27,300 ft.) |

**BOMBLOAD**

For its day, the Hawker Hart carried a very useful bombload. By 1939, however, its offensive capabilities were less often called upon. Typical wartime roles were army observation, communications, liaison and aircrew training.

| | |
|---|---|
| **HART** | 236 kg (520 lb.) |
| **S.328** | 500 kg (1,100 lb.) |
| **SBC-4 HELLDIVER** | 454 kg (1,000 lb.) |

## Hart series aircraft colours

■ **AUDAX:** Production of the Audax ended in 1937 with 624 built. It served as an army co-operation aircraft and an advanced trainer.

■ **DEMON:** Operational in 1940, this example is one of 64 built for the Royal Australian Air Force. The Demon II was a trainer version of the fighter.

■ **HART:** First entering service in 1930, this Hart light bomber is seen with No. 57 Squadron, based at RAF Upper Heyford, 1932–36.

■ **HART TRAINER:** Unarmed, this RAF Hart Trainer Series 2A is currently preserved at the RAF's Museum at Hendon, London.

# HAWKER

# HART/DEMON

● Inter-war two-seat light bomber ● Interceptor ● Foreign service

**P**olicing British colonies in the Middle East and protecting the borders of India were two of the RAF's main tasks in the years between World Wars I and II. The Hart bomber proved ideal for this, being deployed rapidly to deal with emergencies and attack ground targets with guns and bombs. It was also fast enough to serve as the basis for the Demon fighter, and a whole generation of other combat and support aircraft.

▲ The Hart was used for a variety of tasks, from bombing and interception to training and army co-operation. In the latter role, the RAF used the Audax in the Middle East until 1941.

## HAWKER **HART/DEMON**

◄ **Hinds in formation**
These Hind Mk Is equipped No. 40 Squadron based at Abingdon in Oxfordshire for just over two years, until they were replaced by Fairey Battles in 1938.

**Bombers ▶**
In February 1930, the RAF's No. 33 (B) Squadron was equipped with Hart bombers. In 1938, however, No. 33 became a fighter squadron.

▲ **Hart (India)**
The Hart (India) was built for action on the North West Frontier, the first examples arriving there in 1932.

▼ **Pegasus Hart with skis**
A Bristol Pegasus radial engine and enclosed cockpit were fitted to K3012 in 1934, to test a ski undercarriage in Canada.

▲ **Auxiliary Air Force on exercise**
No. 603 (City of Edinburgh) Squadron was one of eight Auxiliary Air Force units equipped with the Hart.

### FACTS AND FIGURES

➤ Many RAF pilots who flew in World War II gained their 'wings' on Hart trainers between 1935 and 1939.

➤ Armstrong Whitworth, Gloster and Vickers also built Harts for the RAF.

➤ Audax army co-operation aircraft had an underfuselage message-collecting hook.

➤ One inter-war Hawker biplane remains airworthy today – a Hind belonging to the Shuttleworth Collection in Bedfordshire.

➤ No. 237 (Rhodesian) Squadron, RAF, flew the Audax during the 1941 Iraqi rebellion.

➤ Royal Navy Ospreys had folding wings for use aboard aircraft-carriers.

# PROFILE

# The versatile Hart family

First flown in 1928, the Hart entered service in 1930. Powerful and streamlined, it carried a two-man crew and could deliver up to 227 kg (500 lb.) of bombs. Gun armament consisted of a single forward-firing Vickers gun and a hand-aimed Lewis gun in the rear cockpit.

As well as the 452 standard bombers delivered by four companies in the early 1930s, specialised versions were developed for use in India and the Middle East. Another 500

aircraft were built as trainers.

The Hart's ability to outperform contemporary fighters also resulted in the development of the Demon two-seat interceptor, which was equipped for night flying. To enable the rear crewman to aim the gun against the force of the slipstream, later models of the Demon introduced a powered 'lobster-back' turret.

Other derivatives of the Hart included the Audax army co-operation aircraft and the

*Above: In its heyday during the early months of the RAF's mid-1930s expansion, the Hind bomber was developed from the Hart but was powered by a more powerful Kestrel engine.*

Osprey carrier-based fighter. Many remained in RAF service until the eve of World War II, and Harts also served with the air forces of several other countries, including India.

*Above: Hawker's inter-war biplanes were widely exported. This Estonian Hart was one of eight delivered in 1932, and had interchangeable wheel and float undercarriages.*

## Hart

**Type:** two-seat light day-bomber

**Powerplant:** one 392-kW (525-hp.) Rolls-Royce Kestrel IB or 380-kW Kestrel X (DR) inline engine

**Maximum speed:** 277 km/h (172 m.p.h.) at 3048 m (10,000 ft.)

**Climb rate:** 8 minutes to 3048 m (10,000 ft.)

**Range:** 756 km (470 mi.)

**Service ceiling:** 6498 m (21,300 ft.)

**Weights:** empty 1148 kg (2,526 lb.); loaded 2066 kg (4,545 lb.)

**Armament:** one 7.7-mm (.303 cal.) machine-gun forward and one 7.7-mm machine-gun aft, plus up to 227 kg (500 lb.) of bombs

**Dimensions:**
| | | |
|---|---|---|
| span | 11.35 m | (37 ft. 3 in.) |
| length | 8.94 m | (29 ft. 4 in.) |
| height | 3.17 m | (10 ft. 5 in.) |
| wing area | 32.33 m² | (348 sq. ft.) |

Twin Vickers 7.7-mm (.303 cal.) guns mounted ahead of the cockpit fired through the propeller arc.

The Rolls-Royce Kestrel VDR 12-cylinder vee engine powered the 'Australian Demon'. Producing 447 kW, it was more powerful than that fitted to RAF Demons.

The Demon's undercarriage was of the straight axle type with Vickers Oleo shock absorbers. Dunlop made the wheels and Palmer supplied the hydraulic brakes.

## 'AUSTRALIAN DEMON'

Australia ordered 64 'Australian Demons', as they were known by Hawker. They were employed as army co-operation fighter-bombers and target tugs.

The Demon was a two-seater, with an observer/gunner occupying the rear seat. A 7.7-mm (.303 cal.) Lewis machine-gun could be fitted.

The Hart family were of all-metal construction with fabric covering.

'Australian Demons' had provision for up to six electromagnetic bomb carriers under the wings.

A1-59 was one of the last 10 'Australian Demons' delivered and was equipped to perform target-towing duties. 'A1' was the serial prefix used by Demons.

## COMBAT DATA

### MAXIMUM SPEED

Although it was an interceptor, the Demon was a two-seater with a gunner behind the pilot. This extra weight and drag contributed to a slightly lower top speed than that of single-seaters.

| | |
|---|---|
| **DEMON** | 249 km/h (154 m.p.h.) |
| **P-1A HAWK** | 258 km/h (159 m.p.h.) |
| **I-3** | 278 km/h (172 m.p.h.) |

### ARMAMENT

With three machine-guns the Demon was well-armed. Two machine-guns of around 7.7-mm (.303) calibre were the norm on single-seat fighters during the early 1930s.

**DEMON** 3 x 7.7-mm (.303 cal.) machine-guns

**P-1A HAWK** 2 x 7.7-mm (.303 cal.) machine-guns

**I-3** 2 x 7.62-mm (.30 cal.) machine-guns

### RANGE

The Demon's range was average for the interceptors of the day. Range was largely dependent on the space available for fuel aboard the aircraft.

**DEMON** 756 km (470 mi.)

**P-1A HAWK** 966 km (600 mi.)

**I-3** 585 km (363 mi.)

## Hart derivatives

**AUDAX:** Introduced in 1932, the Audax army co-operation aircraft served until 1941.

**HARDY:** The Hardy was a general-purpose model of the Audax. It served with the RAF in Iraq.

**OSPREY:** The Royal Navy's Osprey fighter-reconnaissance aircraft had folding wings.

**HIND:** A day-bomber derived from the Hart, the Hind was the last RAF biplane light bomber.

# HAWKER
# FURY

● Single-seat fighter ● Cutting edge of RAF air defence

**S**erving the Royal Air Force in the defence of the homeland, the Hawker Fury symbolised the excitement of flying fighters in the 1930s. It was a clean, appealing biplane with speed, agility and an open cockpit. The pilot lived in a world of engine fumes and wind rushing through the wing braces. Incredibly, long after its streamlined shape had become dated, the Fury fought in World War II with South African pilots.

▲ *The Fury was renowned for its speed. This aircraft was dubbed the High-Speed Fury and was a company testbed for various engines and wing configurations, all of which were intended to increase the maximum performance of the type. Trials with this led to the Kestrel VI-powered Fury Mk II for the RAF.*

## HAWKER FURY

**Undercarriage developments ▶**
*In the interests of ever greater speed, the High-Speed Fury introduced these close-fitting wheel spats. Later aircraft had a single-strut landing gear offering less drag.*

**◀ Aerobatic mount**
*The Fury was a joy to fly, with beautifully harmonised controls. It was regularly displayed in aerobatic performances at the Hendon Air Pageant and other prestigious air shows.*

**◀ Massive propeller**
*Propeller technology lagged behind that of engines in the 1930s, so the Fury had to rely on a huge two-bladed airscrew.*

**▼ Civil testbed**
*Preceding the High-Speed Fury was this aircraft, known to Hawker as the Intermediate Fury. Unusually wearing a civilian registration, it was powered by a supercharged Goshawk engine.*

**▲ Export success**
*Large numbers of Furies were sold overseas, this being one of three built for Portugal.*

## FACTS AND FIGURES

➤ Three prototype Furies and 18 production aircraft all made initial flights in 1931.

➤ The improved Fury Mk II entered service with RAF No. 25 Squadron in 1936.

➤ Persia acquired Fury fighters and used some of these against the RAF during the Raschid Ali revolt of 1941.

➤ Three Furies were delivered to Spain with more powerful Hispano-Suiza engines.

➤ As late as 1940 a Fury pilot shot down a Messerschmitt Bf 109 in a dogfight.

➤ The closely-related Nimrod naval fighter appeared in Buenos Aires at the British Empire Trade Exhibition in 1931.

## PROFILE

# Hawker's famous fighting biplane

Graced with superbly clean and simple lines, the beautiful Fury biplane designed by the great Sydney Camm was the first RAF fighter able to fly over 200 m.p.h. (320 km/h). In the early 1930s, the daring men who flew the Fury were envied as the fortunate elite in 'the best flying club ever'.

The Fury went into RAF service in 1931 and was a superstar from the beginning. Its dramatic flying displays, including memorable tied-together aerobatics at Hendon, inspired several other countries to purchase this much-admired British fighter.

Dramatic advances were made to improve the Fury design and improved engine, wing design and armament were introduced in new versions.

A close relative, the Nimrod, joined the Fleet Air Arm in the late 1930s. The few pilots who flew this remarkable craft in World War II fought courageously against great odds.

Owing to the steep angle of the fuselage, the Fury was notoriously difficult to taxi as the pilot could not see over the nose. In order to avoid obstacles he had to zigzag the aircraft on the ground.

---

## FURY MK I

Arguably the finest-looking biplane fighter, the Fury was also one of the fastest. It was very expensive to produce, so only three RAF squadrons flew the Mk I.

The front of the propeller spinner had a fitting for attachment to an external Hucks starter.

Between the undercarriage struts was the large bath for the radiator. The Kestrel engine was liquid-cooled, and such a radiator was necessary to dissipate the heat generated by the engine.

The key to the Fury's performance lay in its streamlined shape and the enormous power generated by the Rolls-Royce Kestrel II. Gun armament was no different to that of a World War I fighter: two Vickers 7.7-mm (.303 cal.) guns in the top decking of the fuselage, firing through the propeller arc.

In the late 1920s/early 1930s, RAF squadrons wore colourful unit markings, these being presented on the fuselage sides and on the wing panels. The black/white checkerboard signified No. 43 Squadron, the famous 'Fighting Cocks'.

K 3731

K 3731

---

### Fury Mk II

**Type:** single-seat biplane fighter

**Powerplant:** one 477-kW (640-hp.) Rolls-Royce Kestrel VI 12-cylinder Vee piston engine

**Maximum speed:** 359 km/h (223 m.p.h.) at 5030 m (16,500 ft.)

**Range:** 435 km (270 mi.)

**Service ceiling:** 8990 m (29,500 ft.)

**Weights:** empty 1240 kg (2,728 lb.); maximum take-off 1637 kg (3,600 lb.)

**Armament:** two forward-firing synchronised 7.7-mm (.303 cal.) machine-guns

**Dimensions:**
| | |
|---|---|
| span | 9.14 m (30 ft.) |
| length | 8.15 m (26 ft. 8 in.) |
| height | 3.10 m (10 ft. 2 in.) |
| wing area | 23.41 m² (262 sq. ft.) |

Fitting a radial engine (in this case a Panther on a Norwegian aircraft) greatly altered the look of the Fury.

---

## ACTION DATA

### MAXIMUM SPEED

For a short while the Fury was the world's fastest fighter, but the Fiat CR.32, arguably the best biplane fighter ever built, easily outperformed it. The P-26, first of the monoplane fighters, was just a shade quicker than the Fiat, and pointed the way forward for fighter development.

| | |
|---|---|
| P-26 | 377 km/h (234 m.p.h.) |
| CR.32 | 375 km/h (232 m.p.h.) |
| FURY Mk II | 359 km/h (223 m.p.h.) |

### SERVICE CEILING

The pre-war fighters were all still equipped with open cockpits, making flight at high altitude almost unbearable due to the cold. The thin atmosphere at these heights also led to the development of oxygen breathing apparatus, which began to appear in the mid-1930s.

| P-26 | CR.32 | FURY Mk II |
|---|---|---|
| 8350 m (27,500 ft.) | 8800 m (28,850 ft.) | 8990 m (29,500 ft.) |

---

## Inter-war biplane fighters of the RAF

■ **GLOSTER GREBE:** The Grebe entered service in 1923, replacing World War I–vintage Sopwith Snipes.

■ **HAWKER WOODCOCK:** The first aircraft to bear the Hawker name, the Woodcock served from 1925.

■ **ARMSTRONG WHITWORTH SISKIN IIIA:** Large numbers were delivered between 1926 and 1931.

■ **BRISTOL BULLDOG:** The main replacement for the Siskin, the Bulldog entered service in 1929.

■ **GLOSTER GAUNTLET:** Last of the open-cockpit biplanes, the Gauntlet reached the squadrons in 1935.

# HAWKER

# HURRICANE MK II/IV

● Fighter-bomber ● Cannon and rocket armament ● Anti-tank role

▲ Fighter-bomber
*Hurricane Mk IIs and IVs remained in production in Britain and Canada for the duration of World War II, serving with home-based and overseas RAF squadrons.*

**B**ritish fighter development during World War II, like that of the other combatants, centred on improvements in engine power output and armament firepower. Hawker's Hurricane was typical in this respect. Although outclassed as an interceptor by 1941, the Rolls-Royce Merlin-powered Hurricane, armed with cannon and rockets, went on to serve as a valuable fighter-bomber in Europe, the Far East and North Africa.

**Mk IIC night intruder ▶**
*No. 247 'China-British' Squadron was one of five RAF squadrons equipped with cannon-armed Mk IICs for raids over France and the Low Countries.*

**▼ Twelve-gun 'Hurribomber'**
*Armed with twelve 7.7-mm (.303 cal.) Browning machine-guns and able to be fitted with racks for two 227-kg (500-lb.) bombs, the Mk IIB was the first dedicated attack Hurricane.*

**▼ Rocket projectiles**
*Although more often associated with the Hawker Typhoon, the 76.2-mm, 27-kg (60-in.) rocket projectile was pioneered on the Mk IV.*

**◀ Anti-tank Mk II**
*With two 40-mm (1.57-in.) 'S' cannon, the Mk IID was a formidable anti-armour aircraft. The first unit equipped, No. 6 Squadron, RAF, was appropriately known as the 'Flying Can Openers'.*

**3rd TAF, India 1944 ▶**
*Seen in a muddy Assam, India during the monsoon season of 1944, this Mk IIC attached to the Third Tactical Air Force has a Vokes tropical air filter fitted under its nose and twin 200-litre (53-gal.) drop tanks under its wings.*

## FACTS AND FIGURES

➤ Early 20-mm (0.79-in.) cannon-equipped Mk IICs were tested operationally during the Battle of Britain by No. 151 Squadron.

➤ No. 6 Squadron was the RAF's last Hurricane unit, retaining Mk IVs until 1946.

➤ The last Hurricane built, PZ865, is a Mk IIC and remains airworthy with the RAF.

➤ Canadian Hurricane production included the Mk XII – a Mk II with varied armament and a Packard Merlin engine.

➤ The stillborn Mk III was a proposal for a Packard Merlin-engined Hurricane.

➤ Russia, Turkey, Ireland, Egypt and India used Hurricane Mk IIs during World War II.

# PROFILE

# 'Hurribombers' and tank-busters

Persia ordered Hurricanes in 1939, but their delivery was delayed until after World War II. This two-seat Mk IIC trainer was among them.

Merlin XXs were first fitted to a Hurricane Mk I in 1940. The re-engined fighter immediately demonstrated a 32 km/h (20 m.p.h.) speed improvement over the Mk I and entered production as the Mk IIA. It was soon joined by the Mk IIB with 12 7.7-mm (.303 cal.) machine-guns. During 1941 Mk IIs began fighter and later fighter-bomber sweeps over France, the latter armed with up to 454 kg (1,000 lb.) of bombs. Other units performed

'Channel Stop' anti-shipping patrols. In autumn 1941, Mk IIAs and IIBs were sent to the Eastern Front. With the emphasis moving toward the Hurricane as a ground attacker, new armament (four 20-mm/0.79-in. cannon) was introduced. From April, the Mk IIC entered day-fighter service; from August, night-fighter units were also equipped. From late 1941, the Mk IID was available, primarily as an anti-tank aircraft armed with two Vickers 40-mm (1.57-in.) cannon. They proved

effective both in Burma and the Western Desert.

In 1943, on the Mk IV, a 'universal' wing was introduced for adaptation in the field. Mk IVs carried 40-mm (1.57-in.) cannon, drop tanks, or two 113-kg (250-lb.) or 227-kg (500-lb.) bombs. Extra armour was also fitted. It was the Mk IVs, entering service in 1943, that pioneered the use of 27-kg (60-lb.) rocket armament in the RAF.

Four 20-mm (0.79-in.) Hispano or Oerlikon cannon were the most common armament fitted to Mk IIs. The 'universal' wing of the Mk IV was not able to carry four cannon.

## Hurricane Mk IIC

**Type:** fighter and fighter-bomber

**Powerplant:** one 954-kW (1,280-hp.) Rolls-Royce Merlin XX liquid-cooled piston engine

**Maximum speed:** 541 km/h (335 m.p.h.) 'clean'

**Initial climb rate:** 6100 m (20,000 ft.) in 9.1 min

**Range:** 740 km (460 mi.) 'clean'; 1480 km (920 mi.) with two 200-litre (53-gal.) drop tanks

**Service ceiling:** 10,850 m (35,600 ft.)

**Weights:** empty 2631 kg (5,788 lb.); loaded 3674 kg (8,083 lb.)

**Armament:** four Hispano or Oerlikon 20-mm (0.79-in.) cannon and underwing racks for two 113-kg (250-lb.) or 227-kg (500-lb.) bombs

**Dimensions:** span 12.19 m (40 ft.)
length 9.75 m (32 ft.)
height 3.99 m (13 ft. 1 in.)
wing area 23.92 m² (257 sq. ft.)

Late production Mk IIAs and all Mk IIs built subsequently were 17.8 cm (7 in.) longer than the Mk I, to accommodate an extra fuselage bay for an enlarged engine coolant tank.

KZ352 is finished in the RAF's so-called 'SEAC' (Southeast Asia Air Command) camouflage scheme of grey and olive drab with two-tone blue roundels, as used in the Far East.

In May 1942 the first Mk IICs arrived in India and Ceylon. By June the following year, 16 squadrons in India, northern Burma and Ceylon were equipped. By 1944, this number had reached 29, seven of which were IAF units. No. 1 Squadron, IAF, had a secondary tactical reconnaissance role, its Mk IICs carrying a wing-mounted camera.

The addition of a two-stage supercharger boosted the power of the Rolls-Royce Merlin XX initially to 884 kW (1,185 hp.) and later 954 kW (1,620 hp.). Hurricane Mk IVs were fitted with a 1208-kW Merlin 23 or 27. Unusually, this aircraft did not have a Vokes air filter fitted.

## HURRICANE MK IIC

The Indian Air Force used about 300 Hurricane Mk IIBs, IICs, IIDs and IVs during World War II. KZ352 was with No. 1 Squadron, IAF, in 1944.

Unlike contemporaries such as the Spitfire, the Hurricane had a fabric-covered rear fuselage, which it retained throughout its production history.

### COMBAT DATA

**POWER**

The relatively modest power of the Hurricane is illustrated by this comparison with the Hawker Typhoon and a ground-attack variant of the Focke-Wulf Fw 190. All three types were originally conceived as fighters.

HURRICANE Mk IIB 954 kW (1,280 hp.) | TYPHOON Mk IB 1626 kW (2,180 hp.) | Fw 190F-3/R1 1268 kW (1,700 hp.)

**RANGE**

Hurricanes were able to undertake missions over reasonable distances with their 772-km (480-mi.) range. The Typhoon was marginally more capable in this respect, and the Fw 190 was quite 'short-legged' by comparison.

HURRICANE Mk IIB 772 km (480 mi.) | TYPHOON Mk IB 821 km (510 mi.) | Fw 190F-3/R1 531 km (330 mi.)

## Ground-attack armament

**40-mm (1.57-in.) CANNON:** Mk IIDs sported twin 40-mm (1.57-in.) Vickers 'S' cannon, each with 15 rounds of ammunition, as well as two 7.7-mm (.303 cal.) machine-guns for sighting purposes. The cannon, and extra armour, added a performance penalty.

**ROCKET PROJECTILES:** 'Universal' wings fitted to the Mk IV (originally designated Mk IIE) allowed the carriage of eight 27-kg (60-lb.), 76.2-mm (3-in.) rocket projectiles. Extra armour was also fitted to protect the aircraft's Merlin 27 engine, which was optimised for low-level operations in high temperatures.

**UNDERWING STORES:** The most-produced Hurricane, the Mk IIC, featured four 20-mm (0.79-in.) cannon and a variety of underwing stores.

**BOMBS AND FUEL TANKS:** Mk IIC stores included two 200-litre (53-gal.) drop tanks or two 113-kg (240-lb.) or 227-kg (500-lb.) bombs. Ground-attack Hurricanes sometimes carried asymmetric loads, mixing, for example, four rockets and a fuel tank.

# HAWKER

# TEMPEST

● Strong and powerful ● Flying bomb destroyer ● Last piston fighter

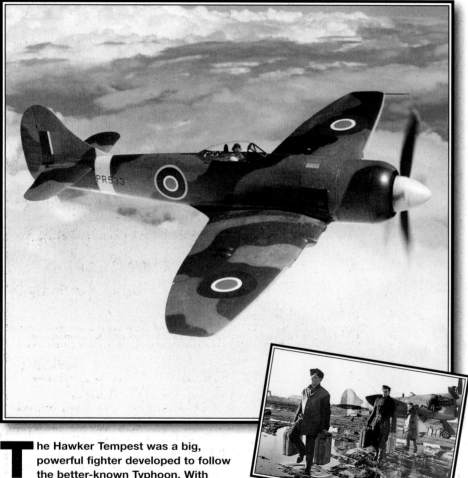

## HAWKER TEMPEST

### ▼ Tempest Mk II
The Bristol Centaurus-powered Tempest Mk II never saw service in World War II, but served in the Far East after the war.

### ▲ Powerful fighter
The Tempest's Centaurus engine made it the most powerful single-engined fighter of the time. It served principally with the Far East Air Force.

### ▲ Tropicalised Tempest
This Mk VI was a tropicalised version of the Mk V with the Sabre V engine and a bigger radiator.

### Thin wing ▶
A new, thin, elliptical, laminar flow wing was produced for the Tempest. Sydney Camm, the designer, said he only designed this wing shape because of the RAF's fixation with the success of the Spitfire.

### ▲ Tempest production
The first version of the Tempest, the Mk V, was equipped with four 20-mm (0.79-in.) Hispano guns and had provision for rockets or bombs under its wings.

The Hawker Tempest was a big, powerful fighter developed to follow the better-known Typhoon. With a huge engine, 'bubble' canopy and high performance, the Tempest proved to be a tremendous weapon for the Allies in the war in Europe. This fine fighter took on many challenges, but is best remembered for intercepting and shooting down V-1 'flying bombs' that were launched against England in 1944 and 1945.

▲ The Hawker Tempest Mk V (above) was the last RAF fighter aircraft to enter service before the end of World War II. The Centaurus-powered Tempest Mk II (main picture) was intended for operations in the Far East against the Japanese, but the war ended before the aircraft were ready.

## FACTS AND FIGURES

➤ Top-scoring Tempest pilot was D. C. Fairbanks, an American in the RAF, credited with 11 air-to-air victories.

➤ The first Tempest to fly, a Mk V, was converted from a Typhoon.

➤ Tempests remained in service with the RAF as target tugs until July 1955.

➤ Tempests destroyed 240 Luftwaffe planes, including 80 Messerschmitt Bf 109s and 115 Focke-Wulf Fw 190s.

➤ One Tempest pilot is credited with shooting down over 60 V-1 buzz-bombs.

➤ Total production of the Tempest fighter was more than 1400 aircraft.

## PROFILE

# RAF's flying bomb destroyer

The Hawker Tempest began on engineers' drawing boards as an improvement of the famous Typhoon with a different wing design and more power. An early flight test report by Royal Air Force pilots called the Tempest 'a manoeuvrable and pleasant aircraft to fly, with no major handling faults'. It was a robust and powerful fighter and at low altitudes it was up to 70 km/h (45 m.p.h.) faster than the Luftwaffe's Messerschmitt Bf 109 or Focke-Wulf Fw 190. In combat, pilots found that the Tempest was

able to take devastating hits from gunfire and still remain in the air.

Tempests began service in April 1944 and were active during the build-up to the Normandy invasion two months later. Pitted against the V-1 flying bomb, Tempest pilots were credited with shooting down 638 of the RAF's total of 1771 destroyed. Tempests supported the Allied advance across Europe and fought the Messerschmitt Me 262 jet fighter successfully, shooting down at least 11.

After the war Tempest Vs continued in service with

British Air Force of Occupation (BAFO) squadrons until they were replaced by Tempest Mk IIs and Vampires. The tropicalised, more powerful Tempest Mk VI was also operated by the RAF in the Middle East. Centaurus-powered Tempest Mk IIs entered service in 1946 and were flown by squadrons based in Germany, Hong Kong, India and Malaya until they were replaced by Hornets in 1951. The Indian and Pakistan air forces also flew Tempest Mk IIs.

*Above: During 1944-45 RAF Tempest Mk Vs were successfully engaged in ground attack, train busting, destroying V-1s and supporting the Allied assault through Belgium and Holland.*

*Left: These Tempest Mk V Series 2s flew in trials with the RAF's Central Fighter Establishment at West Raynham in 1945. The nearest Tempest has eight lengthened rocket rails fitted under the wings.*

## TEMPEST MK VI

The RAF's last and most powerful wartime piston-engined fighter and effective ground-attack aircraft, the Tempest Mk VI was also used against the V-1 flying bombs.

The forward fuselage housed the powerplant. The fuel tank had detachable metal panels.

Protection was good, with a bulletproof windscreen and single-piece bubble canopy that could be jettisoned. Armour plating was fitted forward and aft of the pilot.

The forward fuselage was formed from a rectangular rigid-braced tubular structure. The rear fuselage was a monocoque structure with oval shaped frames, longitudinal stringers and stressed skin.

This Tempest Mk VI was flown by No. 213 Squadron, based at Shallufa near to the Suez Canal. It carried the squadron's hornet emblem on its fin.

The four-bladed de Havilland Hydromatic constant speed propeller was fixed to a large spinner.

Four 20-mm (0.79-in.) Hispano Mk V cannon were carried in the wings, firing outside of the propeller arc. Provision was made for two 227-kg (500-lb.) or two 454-kg (1,000-lb.) bombs or eight rocket projectiles under the wings.

The Tempest's tail was a cantilever all-metal tail unit with a dorsal fin extension. Tailplane and fin were stress skin covered, but the rudder was fabric-covered. All control surfaces had trim tabs.

### COMBAT DATA

#### MAXIMUM SPEED

Tempests were very fast. They were capable of catching V-1 flying bombs in a dive, and some shot down Me 262s. Many pilots flew the Tempest close to the sound barrier in long dives.

| | |
|---|---|
| **TEMPEST Mk V** | 686 km/h (425 m.p.h.) |
| **Fw 190D-9** | 627 km/h (389 m.p.h.) |
| **P-47 THUNDERBOLT** | 689 km/h (450 m.p.h.) |

#### ARMAMENT

Four cannon armament was standard on British fighters by 1944. The large 20-mm (0.79-in.) shells were far more effective than bullets. A pair of bombs or eight rockets could also be carried.

**TEMPEST Mk V** 4 x 20-mm (0.79-in) cannon plus 2 x 454-kg (1,000-lb.) bombs

**Fw 190D-9** 2 x 20-mm (0.79-in) cannon plus 2 x 13-mm (0.51-in.) MGs, 1 x 500-kg (1,100-lb.) bomb

**P-47 THUNDERBOLT** 8 x 12.7-mm (.50 cal.) MGs plus 1 x 1134-kg (3,600-lb.) bomb

#### CLIMB RATE

With its powerful engine and superb wing design, the Tempest was a superb climber. The heavy Thunderbolt was inferior to the Fw 190 in climb, but could easily outdive its German rival.

| | |
|---|---|
| **TEMPEST Mk V** | 1060 m/min (3,475 f.p.m.) |
| **Fw 190D-9** | 1000 m/min (3,280 f.p.m.) |
| **P-47 THUNDERBOLT** | 976 m/min (3,200 f.p.m.) |

## Doodle-bug defender

**1 FLYING-BOMB LAUNCHED:** Blasting off from the occupied Channel coast the V-1 is detected by the RAF's radar chain and the defending Tempest fighters are alerted.

**2 RACE TO DESTRUCTION:** Making use of altitude, the Tempest dives in to attack the flying bomb before it reaches its city target.

**3 KNOCK OUT BLOW TO V-1:** An effective method of bringing down a V-1 was for the Tempest to fly alongside the bomb and destabilise it using its wingtip.

# HAWKER

# TYPHOON

● Lethal low-level ground attacker ● Rocket-armed train-buster

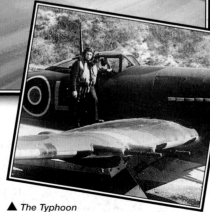

▲ The Typhoon
was designed as an interceptor,
but made its name as a high-speed, low-
level strike aircraft. It was one of the Allies'
most important anti-tank weapons.

**A**n interceptor that failed, the
Hawker Typhoon was nearly
cancelled before it blossomed into
the finest close-support aircraft of World
War II. With its pugnacious snub nose, four
long-barrelled cannon and whining Sabre
engine, the big fighter-bomber wreaked
havoc on its foes. Ranging far and wide
over the battlefields of north-west Europe,
swarms of Typhoons made an indelible
mark on the history of warfare.

▼ **Brute power**
The massive radiator for
the Napier Sabre engine
gave the Typhoon a very
brutal appearance.

▲ **Tornado prototype**
The Typhoon was designed in parallel with the
Rolls-Royce Vulture-powered Tornado.

▼ **Chunky**
The compact, strong
design of the Typhoon
resembled the Fw 190
from certain angles,
which caused more
than one 'friendly fire'
incident with Spitfires.

▲ **Tail problem**
The Typhoon was almost cancelled because
at first it suffered tail flutter problems that
caused several crashes.

**'Bomb-** ▶
**phoon'**
Bomb-armed
Typhoons were
known as
'Bombphoons',
and were very
effective ground-
attackers.

## FACTS AND FIGURES

➤ The Typhoon prototype made its maiden
flight on 24 February 1940.

➤ The Typhoon, nicknamed the 'Tiffy', did
not reach reach its first operational
squadron until September 1941.

➤ The Tornado was a similar aircraft with a
different, endlessly troublesome engine.

➤ The only surviving Typhoon, retrieved from
the USA, is on display in the RAF Museum
at Hendon, north London.

➤ The Typhoon shot down 246 Luftwaffe
aircraft during European fighting.

➤ The top-scoring Typhoon 'ace' was
J. R. Baldwin, with 15 aerial victories.

## PROFILE

# Hawker's tank-buster supreme

Although it first flew in 1940, the Hawker Typhoon did not come into its own until much later in the war. Rushed into service in 1941 as an Fw 190 destroyer, the Typhoon was fast enough to do the job but was not as agile as its foe, and its engine was plagued by reliability problems.

But as a low-level close-support machine, the Typhoon was supreme. It was a superb gun platform, and could carry

and deliver with precision a heavy load of bombs or air-to-surface rockets.

The climax of the Typhoon's career came in the third week of August 1944 when all of the surviving German forces in northern France – 5th Panzer Army, 7th Army and Panzer Group 'Eberbach' – were caught in a trap near Falaise. Typhoons, mainly from the RAF's No. 83 Group, unleashed rockets, cannon shells and bombs until

hardly one German vehicle was capable of movement.

Once the war was over, the Typhoon's lack of reliability meant that the type was rapidly taken out of service. Only one Typhoon survives intact today.

*Rocket-armed Typhoons were one of the most powerful weapons in the Allied inventory after D-Day, making life very difficult for German armoured forces fighting in France.*

*Originally carrying 12 Browning 7.7-mm (.303 cal.) machine-guns, the Typhoon was soon equipped as standard with a harder-hitting fit of four 20-mm (0.79-in.) Hispano cannon and eight 27-kg (60-lb.) rockets.*

### Typhoon Mk IB

**Type:** single-seat fighter-bomber

**Powerplant:** one 1626-kW (2,180-hp.) Napier Sabre IIA inline piston engine

**Maximum speed:** 664 km/h (413 m.p.h.) at 6000 m (19,685 ft.)

**Range:** 975 km (606 mi.); 1500 km (932 mi.) with drop-tanks

**Service ceiling:** 10,700 m (35,100 ft.)

**Weights:** empty 3992 kg (8,800 lb.); loaded 6010 kg (13,250 lb.)

**Armament:** four 20-mm (0.79-in.) Hispano cannon each with 140 rounds; two bombs of up to 454 kg (1,000 lb.) each; numerous other combinations including eight or 12 27-kg (60-lb.) rockets or two 205-litre (45-gal.) drop-tanks

**Dimensions:**
| | | |
|---|---|---|
| span | 12.67 m | (41 ft. 7 in.) |
| length | 9.73 m | (31 ft. 11 in.) |
| height | 4.52 m | (14 ft. 10 in.) |
| wing area | 25.90 m² | (279 sq. ft.) |

## TYPHOON MK IB

**Typhoons were crucial to the Allied advance through France in 1944. The squadrons deployed there were part of the 2nd Allied Tactical Air Force.**

The Typhoon was much improved as a combat aircraft when a sliding bubble canopy was installed.

*All Allied aircraft were painted with large 'invasion stripes' just before the invasion of France in June 1944.*

Typhoon pilots were well protected, with a bulletproof canopy, a huge engine in front of them and superb armour plate behind.

The Napier Sabre was a hugely powerful engine, but suffered from chronic problems at first, with engine life as low as 20 hours.

The Typhoon had a wide-track undercarriage, which made it a safe aircraft to use on rough tactical airstrips.

The Typhoon wing was a very solid structure, allowing the aircraft to carry large bombs and to make power dives at almost 800 km/h (500 m.p.h.).

The early tail problems of the Typhoon were cured by the fitting of 'fish plates' to strengthen the structure.

## COMBAT DATA

### MAXIMUM SPEED

The Typhoon had a good turn of speed and could just outrun the Fw 190, especially at low level. Early P-47s were of similar power and speed to the Typhoon, but continuous development was to see the massive American fighter leap ahead.

| | |
|---|---|
| **TYPHOON Mk IB** | 664 km/h (413 m.p.h.) |
| **P-47D THUNDERBOLT** | 690 km/h (429 m.p.h.) |
| **Fw 190A** | 654 km/h (406 m.p.h.) |

### RANGE

Both the Typhoon and the Fw 190 were designed as interceptors and were used tactically. The P-47 was specifically designed to escort bombers, and had much greater range.

| | |
|---|---|
| **TYPHOON Mk IB** | 975 km (606 mi.) |
| **P-47D THUNDERBOLT** | 2030 km (1,261 mi.) |
| **Fw 190A** | 805 km (500 mi.) |

### ARMAMENT

The Typhoon's four-cannon armament was far more powerful than the P-47's machine-guns, and almost as potent as the standard fit on the Fw 190. However, the German fighter was often modified to carry a pair of hard-hitting 30-mm (1.18-in.) cannon.

**TYPHOON Mk IB** 4 x 20-mm (0.79-in.) cannon

**P-47 THUNDERBOLT** 8 x 12.7-mm (.303 cal.) MG

**Fw 190** 2 x 13-mm (0.51-in.) MG 4 x 20-mm (0.79-in.) cannon

## Typhoons on call

**CLOSE SUPPORT:** Blockhouses were capable of delaying an advance, and the Typhoon was often called upon to demolish them with 454-kg (1,000-lb.) high-explosive bombs.

**'CAB RANK':** Developed by the British Desert Air Force in North Africa, the 'cab ranks' were patrols of fully-armed Typhoons orbiting over the battlefield, on call to give immediate assistance to ground units in need of air support.

**TANK-BUSTER:** A single Pzkpfw VI 'Tiger' tank could, and often did, hold up an entire Allied armoured advance in Normandy. A single salvo of eight 27-kg (60-lb.) rockets from a Typhoon had the explosive power of a destroyer broadside, and was enough to remove the problem.

# HEINKEL

# HE 51

● Single-seat biplane ● Luftwaffe's first fighter ● Légion Condor

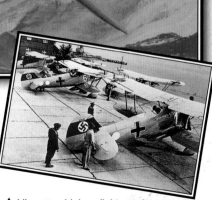

▲ Like many biplane fighters of the 1930s, the He 51 was a fine machine when it was delivered in 1934, but was soon made obsolete by the appearance of much faster aircraft.

**W**hen the new Luftwaffe was rebuilt in the early 1930s, it required a fighter aircraft above all else. The Heinkel company had already designed biplane fighters for export, and it refined the HD 37 design to produce the He 51. This aircraft demonstrated the resurgence of air power in the Third Reich, especially when it was used during the civil war in Spain fighting against the Republican forces.

## HEINKEL HE 51

▲ Légion Condor service
A total of 79 He 51s were delivered to Spain: 51 for the Nationalists and the remainder for the Légion Condor.

▲ Diving pair
Although far from ideal for the role, the He 51 equipped the first Stukagruppe dive-bombing units before the arrival of more suitable types like the Hs 123.

▼ Prototype Heinkel
Wearing the code D-IQEE, this He 51 was one of nine pre-production machines used for evaluation.

▼ He 51B-2 floatplane
After a He 51A-1 was fitted with floats, 38 He 51B-2 floatplanes were built. This one was used by I/JG 136.

▲ Lively handling
The Heinkel had higher wing loading than earlier machines and was therefore less manoeuvrable. This caused a number of accidents.

## FACTS AND FIGURES

➤ To speed up production of the first 75 He 51A-1s, many were built under licence by AGO, Erla, Arado and Fieseler.

➤ The He 51's first victims in Spain were a Breguet XIX and two Hispano Nieuports.

➤ In April 1937 the Légion Condor replaced its He 51s with Bf 109Bs.

➤ Fighter chief Ernst Udet fought against an Ar 68 in a trial dogfight; the He 51 he flew was judged to have lost.

➤ The proposed high-altitude He 52E was never put into production.

➤ The He 49 and He 51 were the first Heinkel designs by the Günter brothers.

# PROFILE

# The Luftwaffe's first fighter

When the He 49a single-seat biplane first flew in November 1932, it was supposedly a civilian advanced trainer. However, its top speed of almost 320 km/h (200 m.p.h.) suggested leisurely intentions.

Its true role as the forerunner of the Luftwaffe's first fighter became clear when examples of the longer He 51 were delivered in mid-1934. The following year the new Luftwaffe was formed, with He 51As equipping its first fighter unit, Jagdgeschwader 'Richthofen'.

In 1936 the strengthened He 51B (some of which were equipped with floats) followed, plus 79 export He 51Cs which were delivered to Spain. The civil war there saw the He 51 in action for the first time, with the Légion Condor operating 28 of the Spanish machines fighting Soviet-built Polikarpovs. Later,

*This early He 51 has a civil registration and swastika marking, the former was to suggest a civil role for the aircraft.*

the Luftwaffe took delivery of a number of He 51Cs with an improved radio and some flew close-support sorties in Poland in 1939. As a trainer the He 51 lasted until 1943.

## HE 51B

This aircraft was flown by the Gruppe commandant of II/JG 132 'Richtofen' based at Döberitz.

The markings on this aircraft are typical of the late 1930s, the civil registration having been deleted once the establishment of the Luftwaffe had taken place. Note that the commandant's chevron marking is repeated on the wing.

The wings were two-spar units with fabric covering, the upper surfaces carrying the ailerons and the lower surfaces carrying the trailing-edge flaps.

Two 7.92-mm Rheinmetall MG 17 machine-guns were fitted above the engine to fire through the propeller arc.

Chevron markings on the fuselage and centre section indicated that it was flown by the unit's commandant.

One important improvement over the early He 49s was the extension of the rear fuselage and a broader tailfin in an effort to improve directional stability.

A powerful BMW VI inverted-Vee 12-cylinder piston engine rated at 559 kW propelled the He 51 to a top speed of 330 km/h (205 m.p.h.).

He 51B s and Cs were often fitted with an auxiliary fuel tank to increase their range, especially in the ground attack role.

The superstructure of the He 51 was metal, but the bulk of the skin was fabric as was common on fighters of the day.

## He 51B-1

**Type:** single-seat biplane fighter

**Powerplant:** one 559-kW (750-hp.) BMW VI 7,3Z 12-cylinder liquid-cooled inverted-Vee piston engine

**Maximum speed:** 330 km/h (205 m.p.h.) at sea level

**Cruising speed:** 280 km/h (174 m.p.h.) at sea level

**Range:** 570 km (353 mi.)

**Service ceiling:** 7700 m (25,250 ft.)

**Weights:** empty 1460 kg (3,212 lb.); maximum take-off 1895 kg (4,169 lb.)

**Armament:** two 7.92-mm MG 17 machine-guns

**Dimensions:**
| | | |
|---|---|---|
| span | 11.00 m | (36 ft. 1 in.) |
| length | 8.40 m | (27 ft. 6 in.) |
| height | 3.20 m | (10 ft. 6 in.) |
| wing area | 27.2 m$^2$ | (293 sq. ft.) |

## COMBAT DATA

### MAXIMUM SPEED

Speeds in the region of 350 km/h (220 m.p.h.) were fairly common for fighters of the day. It was not until the application of the monoplane to fighter aircraft in the late 1930s that speeds increased greatly. At a stroke the biplane became obsolete.

| | |
|---|---|
| He 51B-1 | 330 km/h (205 m.p.h.) |
| CR.32 | 375 km/h (233 m.p.h.) |
| GAUNTLET | 370 km/h (229 m.p.h.) |

### RANGE

Being a larger aircraft with a less powerful engine, the Fiat CR.32 had a greater fuel capacity and lower fuel consumption. This translated as greater range. One of the last British biplane designs, the Gauntlet was better still. A few were still in service in 1939.

He 51B-1 570 km (353 mi.)
CR.32 680 km (422 mi.)
GAUNTLET 740 km (459 mi.)

### SERVICE CEILING

A combination of wing design, engine power and the relatively light weight of the airframe combined to give the Gloster Gauntlet the edge in ceiling capability. Service ceiling, the ability to maintain altitude and manoeuvrability at altitude, were important attributes, especially for a dogfighting aircraft.

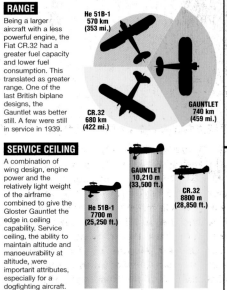

He 51B-1 7700 m (25,250 ft.)
GAUNTLET 10,210 m (33,500 ft.)
CR.32 8800 m (28,850 ft.)

## European fighters of the 1930s

■ **FIAT CR.32:** Another type to see service with the Légion Condor, the CR.32 was designed by Celestion Rosatelli for the Italian air force and saw service in World War II.

■ **GLOSTER GLADIATOR:** Entering service in 1937, the Gladiator was to be the RAF's last biplane fighter. Despite its inferior performance a few remained in frontline use as late as 1942.

■ **POLIKARPOV I-15:** The last and best Polikarpov biplane fighter, a total of 550 were supplied to Republican Spain and flew against aircraft like the Fiat CR.32. Finland was also an operator.

# HEINKEL

# HE 59

● Air–sea rescue ● Torpedo bomber ● Maritime reconnaissance

▲ When it first appeared in the early 1930s, the He 59 exceeded in size by a substantial margin any aircraft previously produced by the Heinkel company. It normally held a crew of four.

I n the early 1930s Germany possessed a small but industrious aircraft industry, and by far the most prolific of these companies was the Heinkel works at Warnemünde. When the expansion of the clandestine German air arm was launched in 1934, the He 59 was one of the first aircraft developed. After employment during the Spanish Civil War, flying night-bombing and reconnaissance sorties, the He 59 served in a wide variety of duties during World War II.

## HEINKEL HE 59

### ▼ Legion Condor
Ten He 59B-2s were assigned to naval reconnaissance squadron AS/88 during the Spanish Civil War.

### ▲ Anti-ship sorties
The He 59 carried a single 700-kg (1.540-lb.) or 1000-kg (2,200-lb.) torpedo. Alternatively, 1000 kg (2,200 lb.) of bombs could be carried in the weapons bay.

### ▼ Open cockpit position
The He 59 was certainly not designed with crew comfort in mind. The bow and dorsal gunners as well as the pilot sat in an open position at the mercy of the elements.

### ▲ Rescue response
During the fierce fighting of the Battle of Britain, white-painted He 59C-2s were regularly called into action to rescue downed Luftwaffe pilots.

### Land-based prototype ▶
Posing as a civilian freight aircraft, the first He 59 to fly was actually the second prototype. It was the only example to feature a wheeled undercarriage.

### FACTS AND FIGURES

➤ The first flight was made by the He 59A in September 1931; the first float-equipped prototype did not fly until January 1932.

➤ Twelve He 59s were used to transport troops for a surprise attack on Rotterdam.

➤ The He 59E-1 was a photographic training variant with three camera positions.

➤ Some Spanish Civil War He 59s were fitted with 20-mm cannon for attacking road and rail communications.

➤ After the Spanish Civil War, three He 59s were handed over to the Spanish navy.

➤ Several He 59s were transferred to the Finnish air force for rescue duties.

## PROFILE

# Battle of Britain rescue craft

Conceived by Reinhold Mewes in 1930, the He 59 was developed as a general-purpose floatplane suitable for roles such as naval co-operation, maritime patrol and torpedo bombing. First flying in 1931, the He 59 masqueraded as a civilian freight transport to avoid the ban on the development of military aircraft in Germany.

Successful trials with the two prototypes (one wheeled, the other float-equipped) led to an order for the fully militarised He 59B-1 production version, featuring a bomb-aimer's position and defensive machine-guns.

Deliveries began in the summer of 1934, and during the next two years of intensive training the He 59B-1 was replaced in production by the improved B-2 and B-3 versions built under licence by Arado. In 1936 the He 59 became part of the Condor Legion force committed to the Spanish conflict, flying night-bombing attacks on important harbours.

In 1938 the He 59 was replaced in production by newer types but by the outbreak of World War II more than 100 were still in service. After brief front-line use many were modified to He 59C, D and E standard and flew air-sea rescue, training and transport tasks. By 1943 the type had all but disappeared from service.

*Left: In service with 3./Kü.Fl.Gr.106 of the coastal aviation group, this He 59B-2 operated in the North Sea area during 1939. It was used for controlling shipping in the North and Baltic Seas.*

*Above: Sporting large red crosses and civil identities, He 59s were believed by Britain to be transporting agents onto the British mainland. After a number were shot down they returned to a military identity.*

### He 59B-2

**Type:** four-seat, twin-engined torpedo bomber, reconnaissance and air-sea rescue floatplane

**Powerplant:** two 492-kW (660-hp.) BMW VI 6,0 ZU 12-cylinder piston engines

**Maximum speed:** 220 km/h (137 m.p.h.) at sea level

**Range:** 1750 km (1,090 mi.)

**Service ceiling:** 3500 m (11,500 ft.)

**Weights:** empty 6215 kg (13,700 lb.); maximum take-off 9000 kg (19,840 lb.)

**Armament:** three 7.92-mm MG 15 machine-guns in nose, dorsal and ventral positions plus one torpedo or up to 1000 kg (2,200 lb.) of bombs

**Dimensions:**
| | |
|---|---|
| span | 23.70 m (77 ft. 9 in.) |
| length | 17.40 m (57 ft. 1 in.) |
| height | 7.10 m (23 ft. 4 in.) |
| wing area | 153.3 m² (1,650 sq. ft.) |

The front of the aircraft was stepped to provide the pilot with a good view over the navigator in the front cockpit. A solid metal nose section replaced the nose section of the He 59B-2, which contained a nose gunner in that version.

On the He 59D-1 defensive armament was normally removed, making room for inflatable dinghies and emergency medical equipment. On the B-2 version the dorsal gunner's position featured a 7.92-mm machine-gun.

Two BMW 12-cylinder engines were mounted between the wings and drove four-bladed fixed-pitch wooden propellers.

Of two-bay biplane design, the He 59 was of mixed construction. The two-spar wooden wings were braced with light-metal interplane struts. The welded steel-tube fuselage was fabric-covered, as were the control surfaces.

### He 59D-1

This aircraft of the Seenotzentrale Agaisches Meer was fitted with emergency equipment for air-sea rescue duties in the Aegean Sea during 1941, saving downed Luftwaffe pilots.

Divided into eight watertight compartments, the single-step wooden floats had a hydronalium skin and were braced to the fuselage at the wingroots.

## COMBAT DATA

### POWER

The Do 18 which replaced the He 59 was a more powerful and faster design. The Walrus was a single-engined, smaller, lighter design and was considerably slower.

| He 59B-2 | Do 18G-1 | WALRUS Mk II |
|---|---|---|
| 984 kW (1,320 hp.) | 1312 kW (1,760 hp.) | 578 kW (775 hp.) |

### RANGE

The Walrus was designed for operations close to its mother ship or in coastal waters and did not require a long range. The Do 18 had a much longer range and was able to patrol far out into the Atlantic Ocean. The He 59 operated close to the shore.

He 59B-2 1750 km (1,090 mi.)

Do 18G-1 3500 km (2,175 mi.)

WALRUS Mk II 966 km (600 mi.)

### ARMAMENT

Designed originally for anti-shipping and reconnaissance duties, the He 59 had the best bombload of the three types. All three carried defensive machine-guns for protection against fighters.

| | |
|---|---|
| He 59B-2 | 3 x 7.92-mm machine-guns 1000-kg (2,200-lb.) bombload |
| Do 18G-1 | 1 x 13-mm machine-gun 1 x 20-mm cannon 100-kg (220-lb.) bombload |
| WALRUS Mk II | 3 x 7.7-mm (.303 cal.) machine-guns 345-kg (760-lb.) bombload |

## World War II rescue seaplanes

■ **CONSOLIDATED CATALINA:** Used for anti-shipping attacks and spotting as well as air-sea rescue, the PBY saved hundreds of airmen.

■ **DORNIER Do 18:** Replacing the He 59 in service, the Do 18N rescue version served in Denmark, France, Holland and Norway.

■ **DORNIER Do 24:** Being first delivered in the autumn of 1941, the Do 24 excelled in the air-sea rescue role thanks to its rugged design.

■ **SUPERMARINE WALRUS:** Obsolete before World War II, the 'Shagbat' became famous for daring rescues of downed Allied pilots.

# HEINKEL

# HE 111

● Medium bomber ● Torpedo-bomber ● Transport

▲ *The Heinkel He 111 flew on every front in World War II, from the Arctic to the desert. It first saw combat in the Spanish Civil War, and was still in action as the Third Reich crumbled into ruin.*

**L**ike the Luftwaffe, the military purpose of the He 111 was at first a secret: it was a high-speed airliner that could be converted into a bomber. This twin-engine, low-wing aircraft with its glazed nose and elliptical wing was the muscle of Germany's bomber force during the hard-fought Battle of Britain, and even though obsolete it kept on bombing until the war's final days.

## HEINKEL HE 111

**▲ First of many**
*Although the He 111 entered service with Lufthansa in 1936, this ostensible high-speed airliner was actually designed to be a bomber.*

**▲ Glazed nose**
*The transparent nose area gave excellent visibility to both the gunner and bomb-aimer, but was very vulnerable to gunfire.*

**◀ Balloon buster**
*This huge framework was an attempt to deflect barrage balloon cables, but it was too cumbersome and reduced speed.*

**Survivor ▶**
*Ability to survive huge battle damage was one of the He 111's greatest assets.*

**▼ Rocket assist**
*For operations from rough fields or at very heavy take-off weights, He 111s could be, and often were, equipped with disposable rockets.*

**▲ Over the Thames**
*He 111s attacked London in large numbers in 1940. After being beaten off by day, they were switched to night raids.*

## FACTS AND FIGURES

➤ The prototype for the He 111 series first flew at Marienehe on 24 February 1934.

➤ He 111s served with the Condor Legion during the Spanish Civil War in 1937.

➤ He 111s made very successful attacks on the Bristol and Supermarine factories during the Battle of Britain.

➤ Heinkel He 111s destroyed 43 American B-17s and 15 P-51s at Poltava airfield, Russia, on 21 June 1944.

➤ More than 7300 Heinkel He 111s were built before and during the war.

➤ Spanish He 111s with British Merlin engines were built by CASA after the war.

## PROFILE

# Mainstay of the Luftwaffe's bomber force

Obsolescent at the start of World War II, and testimony to Germany's mistake in not developing four-engine bombers, the He 111 was nevertheless an effective strike machine. From the Spanish Civil War via the London Blitz and on through every Luftwaffe campaign until the end of 1944, this reliable machine provided the backbone of Germany's air power.

Although considered quite advanced when introduced as a pseudo-airliner, the 'Spaten' – so called because of the spade-like shape of the characteristic Heinkel elliptical wing – quickly became outmoded. But it was tough and serviceable, and the Luftwaffe never really managed to find a replacement.

But the spectacle of He 111 bomber formations pressing through swarms of Allied fighters is just part of the story: the He 111 attacked ships with torpedoes and the first guided missiles, towed gliders, dropped secret agents, transported VIPs, and hauled high-value cargoes.

Many special versions were produced for experimental purposes. One in particular was noteworthy, carrying and launching the Fieseler Fi 103 (V-1) flying bomb from beneath the starboard wing.

*The crew could all see each other in the He 111, which in spite of increased vulnerability was considered a good morale feature by German designers. The He 111 was able to accommodate extra armour and defensive weaponry, unlike the Dornier Do 17.*

The bomb-aimer lay on a horizontal pad, looking down at the target. The excellent forward view was especially useful when making torpedo attacks.

A large fuel tank with a capacity of 700 litres (182 gal.) was contained in the inner section of the wing.

### He 111H-16

**Type:** four-/five-seat medium bomber

**Powerplant:** two 1006-kW (1,350-hp.) Junkers Jumo 211F-2 inline piston engines

**Maximum speed:** 435 km/h (270 m.p.h.) at 6000 m (20,000 ft.) (light load)

**Range:** 1950 km (1,200 mi.)

**Service ceiling:** 8500 m (28,000 ft.)

**Weights:** empty 8680 kg (19,096 lb.); loaded 14,000 kg (30,800 lb.)

**Armament:** one 20-mm (0.79-in.) cannon, one 13-mm (0.51-in.) and up to nine 7.92-mm (0.31-in.) machine-guns, plus provision for up to 3307 kg (7,275 lb.) of bombs carried internally and externally

**Dimensions:**
| | | |
|---|---|---|
| span | 22.60 m | (74 ft. 1 in.) |
| length | 16.40 m | (53 ft. 9 in.) |
| height | 4.00 m | (13 ft. 1 in.) |
| wing area | 86.50 m² | (931 sq. ft.) |

---

### He 111H-16

The He 111H was the major production variant of the bomber, being produced in at least 23 official variants and in innumerable field modified forms. It served in many different roles, including bombing, torpedo-carrying, transport and glider towing.

The pilot sat on the left of the cabin, with a folding seat for the bombardier to his right. A gangway between the bomb racks led to the rear compartment, which housed the gunners and radio operator.

The long, broad dihedral wing was lightly loaded, and gave the He 111 pleasant, stable flying characteristics allied to the ability to carry large loads.

The He 111's rugged undercarriage left plenty of clearance to carry large weapons externally, even over rough forward airfields.

The entire fuselage and tail section was of metal construction, with metal skinning. The He 111 could just about fly with one elevator entirely shot away.

Despite the presence of a nose gun, Allied fighter pilots soon found that the way to attack the He 111 was from the front, where there was no cockpit armour.

The ventral gondola mounted a single machine-gun and was horribly vulnerable to attack from below. It was known as the 'Sterbebett' (Deathbed) to its occupants.

### COMBAT DATA

#### MAXIMUM SPEED

Designed as an airliner, with a streamlined shape, the He 111 was as fast as most service fighters when introduced. With its contemporaries, however, it was quickly outclassed by the new generation of monoplane fighters.

| | |
|---|---|
| He 111H-16 | 435 km/h (270 m.p.h.) |
| B-25 MITCHELL | 438 km/h (272 m.p.h.) |
| WELLINGTON | 411 km/h (255 m.p.h.) |

#### RANGE

The Luftwaffe's primary mission was to support the Wehrmacht, so the He 111 was designed for tactical rather than strategic missions. It had a fairly good range nevertheless, although it could not match a long-range bomber like the Wellington.

| He 111H-16 | WELLINGTON |
|---|---|
| 1950 km (1,200 mi.) | 2480 km (1,488 mi.) |
| **B-25 MITCHELL** | |
| 2170 km (1,345 mi.) | |

#### INTERNAL BOMBLOAD

Both the Heinkel and the Wellington put bombload in front of defensive armament. The B-25, however, had a light bombload, as it relied on its defensive armament and high speed to survive.

| WELLINGTON | B-25 MITCHELL |
|---|---|
| 2040 kg (4,488 lb.) | 1360 kg (2,992 lb.) |
| **He 111H-16** | |
| 2500 kg (5,500 lb.) | |

---

## History of a classic warplane

■ **PROTOTYPE:** Used by Lufthansa for mail flights and to carry four passengers, the He 111 was never a commercial proposition as an airliner in the pre-war years.

■ **COMBAT DEBUT:** In 1937, Kampfgruppe 88 of the Legion Condor took the He 111 into action with great success during the Spanish Civil War.

■ **LUFTWAFFE WORKHORSE:** The He 111P and the later He 111H series were the backbone of Germany's bomber force in World War II, taking part in all theatres of the war.

■ **SPECIAL PURPOSE:** He 111s were modified for many roles. The double-fuselage 'Zwilling' was developed as a tug for the Luftwaffe's giant gliders.

■ **SURVIVORS:** Some 236 Rolls-Royce Merlin-powered He 111s were built in Spain after the war, serving into the 1960s as transports and trainers.

# HEINKEL
# HE 177 GREIF

● Maritime strike aircraft ● Heavy bomber ● Guided-missile launcher

▲ As a heavy bomber the Greif was used only to a limited extent and it is best remembered as an anti-shipping aircraft equipped with guided air-to-surface missiles, torpedoes and bombs.

**G**ermany's only wartime heavy bomber, the He 177 was also one of its most troublesome aircraft. It was designed to use two pairs of engines, each driving a single propeller, to have three remotely controlled gun positions. Predicted performance figures included a top speed of 550 km/h (341 m.p.h.) and a range of 6700 km (4,150 mi.) with a 1000-kg (2,200-lb.) bombload, but the He 177 was never completely successful in service.

---

## PHOTO FILE
## HEINKEL HE 177 GREIF

▼ **Tricky take-off**
Engine fires were the most serious threat faced by He 177 crews, but take-off could also be difficult. Any slight imbalance in power output between left and right engines resulted in a vicious tail swing.

▲ **Came to grief**
Of 35 He 177A-0 aircraft built, 25 were destroyed in accidents or fires. At least seven crashed while taking off.

**Greif bomber ▶**
This He 177A-5/R2 belonged to 6. Staffel, Kampfgeschwader 100, and was used on bombing missions during May 1944. It was based at Toulouse-Blagnac and is seen fitted with Hs 293 and Fritz X launching racks.

◀ **Atlantic reconnaissance**
During the spring of 1944 He 177A-5/R6s began flying attack and reconnaissance missions over the Atlantic. This aircraft belonged to II./KG 40.

**Special variants ▶**
Several special versions of the He 177 were built, including this aircraft with an unusual bulged and glazed nose. A further variant, the V38, based on the A-5, was possibly intended as a delivery platform for a German nuclear bomb.

### FACTS AND FIGURES

➤ On its first flight the V1 prototype proved to be slow with insufficient range, but it showed no other problems.

➤ V2, the second prototype, broke-up in flight; V4 and V5 were also lost.

➤ Arado built five of the He 177A-0 pre-production aircraft.

➤ Production of the improved He 177A-3 was planned at 70 aircraft per month but only five per month were completed.

➤ A-3/R7 and A-5 aircraft could launch the LT 50 glider torpedo.

➤ I./KG 50 flew some He 177A-1s, with MK 101 cannon, for flak suppression duties.

## PROFILE

# Heinkel's fiery Greif

Things started to go wrong at an early stage in the He 177's development. First the advanced cooling system for the twin engine installations was abandoned in favour of bigger radiators. This increased drag, however, and so more fuel was needed and the fuselage had to be strengthened, which made the aircraft heavier and reduced performance.

Then the remotely-controlled defensive armament was replaced by manned gun positions, adding more weight. And to meet the requirement for 60° diving attacks, further strengthening was required, which increased the weight still further.

Many prototypes were lost during test flights as a result of structural failure or engine fires. In service, take-offs proved tricky and led to several more accidents. More operational aircraft were lost to engine fires than to combat.

Attempts to cure the aircraft's faults were never successful. Even so, more than 1000 of the various models were built. In 1943/44 three were converted to prototypes of the He 277, with four separate engines each driving its own propeller, and

a single prototype of the improved four-propeller He 274 was completed by Farman in France and flown in December 1945.

*Above: Early production aircraft had full-span flaps which extended below the ailerons. From the A-3 onwards, these aileron flaps were abandoned.*

*Right: Combining two DB 601 engines to produce the DB 606 unit produced a high degree of complexity in the He 177. This was magnified by the way the engine was installed, which made it prone to fire.*

## HE 177A-5/R2 GREIF

Tasked with anti-ship duties this aircraft was based at Bordeaux-Mérignac with 4. Staffel, II Gruppe, Kampfgeschwader 100, during 1944.

### He 177A-5/R2 Greif

**Type:** heavy bomber, reconnaissance and anti-shipping aircraft

**Powerplant:** two 2200-kW (2,950-hp.) Daimler-Benz DB 610 24-cylinder liquid-cooled engines

**Maximum speed:** 488 km/h (303 m.p.h.) at 6100 m (20,000 ft.)

**Initial climb rate:** 190 m/min (623 f.p.m.) at sea level

**Range:** 5500 km (3,400 mi.) with two Hs 293 missiles

**Service ceiling:** 8000 m (26,250 ft.)

**Weights:** empty 16,800 kg (39,960 lb.); maximum take-off 31,000 kg (68,200 lb.)

**Armament:** two 20-mm (0.79-in.) cannon, three 7.9-mm (0.31-in.) and three 13-mm (0.51-in.) machine-guns, up to 1000 kg (2,200 lb.) in the bomb bay plus two missiles under the wings

**Dimensions:**
| | | |
|---|---|---|
| span | 31.44 m | (103 ft. 2 in.) |
| length | 22.00 m | (72 ft. 2 in.) |
| height | 6.39 m | (20 ft. 11 in.) |
| wing area | 102.00 m² | (1,098 sq. ft.) |

---

Extensive nose glazing gave the flight crew good forward visibility, while retaining the clean, aerodynamic lines of the fuselage. An MG 81 7.9-mm (0.31-in.) machine-gun with 2000 rounds could be fired from the front glazing, completing the He 177's all-round defence.

With two MG 131 machine-guns and a total of 1500 rounds, this forward dorsal barbette was remotely controlled. The gunner sat beneath the glazed dome above the flightdeck. Originally, only the tail turret was intended to be manned, but problems led to this plan being scrapped.

The risk of engine fire was one of the many problems of the He 177. The engine installation was extremely poor, with exhausts, fuel and oil lines crammed together so tightly that a fire was almost inevitable.

A spacious position was provided for the tail gunner, who sat beneath the rudder to operate an MG 151.

An FuG 203 transmitter relayed control inputs from the bombardier's joystick in the under-nose gondola to either the Hs 293 or FX 1400 missile. The missile was tracked by visually following flares on its tail.

This aircraft carries underwing racks for the Hs 293 and FX 1400 missiles. In addition, the cover of the blanked-off forward bomb-bay also carries a missile launch rack.

Pilots attempted to keep the tailwheel on the ground as long as possible on take-off to minimise the risk of swinging.

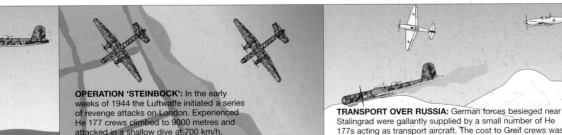

## Greif in action

**ANTI-SHIP ATTACKS:** Attacking from a distance of 10 to 15 km, the He 177 was able to use radio-controlled Hs 293 and FX 1400 missiles, in addition to Fritz X glide-bombs and torpedoes.

**OPERATION 'STEINBOCK':** In the early weeks of 1944 the Luftwaffe initiated a series of revenge attacks on London. Experienced He 177 crews climbed to 9000 metres and attacked in a shallow dive at 700 km/h, avoiding interception by fighters.

**TRANSPORT OVER RUSSIA:** German forces besieged near Stalingrad were gallantly supplied by a small number of He 177s acting as transport aircraft. The cost to Greif crews was high, however, with many falling to Soviet fighters.

## COMBAT DATA

### MAXIMUM SPEED

From the outset the He 177, with its streamlined airframe, was designed to be very fast. Although it never achieved its design speed, it was still faster than contemporary heavy bombers.

| | |
|---|---|
| He 177A-5/R2 GREIF | 488 km/h (303 m.p.h.) |
| LIBERATOR GR.Mk VI | 467 km/h (290 m.p.h.) |
| Fw 200C-3/U4 CONDOR | 360 km/h (223 m.p.h.) |

### RANGE

Offering significantly greater range than other similar designs, the He 177 would have made an exceptional bomber and maritime aircraft had it proved reliable. Official requirements called for even greater range, but modifications and problems made the aircraft heavier and less efficient than intended.

He 177A-5/R2 GREIF 5500 km (3,400 mi.)

LIBERATOR GR.Mk VI 3380 km (3,100 mi.)

Fw 200C-3/U4 CONDOR 3560 km (2,200 mi.)

### ARMAMENT

As a legacy of its heavy bomber design, the He 177A-5/R2 was able to carry a large anti-ship warload, including guided missiles and advanced torpedoes. Defensive armament was also heavy.

| | |
|---|---|
| He 177A-5/R2 GREIF | 3 x 7.9-mm machine-guns<br>3 x 13-mm (0.51-in.) machine-guns<br>2 x 20-mm (0.79-in.) cannon<br>2 x Hs 293 missiles<br>1000-kg (2,200-lb.) bombload |
| LIBERATOR GR.Mk VI | 10 x 11.7-mm machine-guns<br>2268-kg (5,000-lb.) bombload |
| Fw 200C-3/U4 CONDOR | 4 x 13-mm (0.51-in.) machine-guns<br>1 x 20-mm (0.79-in.) cannon<br>2100-kg (4,600-lb.) bombload |

# HEINKEL

# HE 162 SALAMANDER

● Wooden construction ● Single-seat 'Volksjäger'

▲ Novice pilots, with training only on gliders, were to have flown the He 162, and would have completed their training in combat. The Salamander was an interesting concept, but it was doomed to fail.

**H**einkel rushed the design of the He 162 Salamander in an attempt to develop a mass-produced fighter that would stem the tide of Allied bombers over the Reich. One of the first operational jet aircraft, the He 162 was a sound concept but suffered from structural and aerodynamic problems as a result of its hasty introduction. This was a tricky and difficult aircraft to fly, and few saw any combat action before the end of hostilities.

## HEINKEL HE 162 SALAMANDER

▲ **Underground production**
US units advancing on Magdeburg found a massive production facility for the He 162 in abandoned salt mines. Several of the jets were near completion.

▲ **Post-war testing**
Large numbers of former Luftwaffe aircraft, including He 162s, were captured by the Allies and tested in Britain and the United States.

▼ **Narrow track**
A very narrow undercarriage, combined with the heavy, dorsally mounted engine, would have made ground handling tricky.

▲ **Perfectly preserved**
Several He 162s survive in museums. This aircraft is finished in the colours of II/Jagdgeschwader 1, which became part of Einsatz-Gruppe I/JG 1.

**Tail prop** ▶
Parked aircraft, especially those with their guns removed, tended to fall back onto their tails, and therefore a tail prop was used to prevent damage.

## FACTS AND FIGURES

➤ The prototype He 162 made its first flight on 6 December 1944 but was lost in a mishap four days later.

➤ A Gruppe equipped with 50 He 162 fighters was formed at Leck on 4 May 1945.

➤ More than 270 He 162s were completed and 800 unfinished aircraft were captured.

➤ Heinkel's jet was one of the first aircraft to use an ejection seat for emergency escape by the pilot.

➤ Plans were in existence to build 5000 He 162s per month.

➤ Loss of the prototype in December 1944 was due to the break-up of the right wing.

**PROFILE**

# Luftwaffe's last line of defence

Designed, developed and built in an extraordinarily short time, the Heinkel He 162 was first flown as the pressures of war closed in on Germany. The prototype was in the air just 38 days after detail drawings were issued to the factory.

An attractive and potentially useful fighter, the He 162 was plagued by problems resulting from its over-hasty development. This single-seat, single-engined warplane was supposed to be a 'people's fighter', devoid of frills, inexpensive to manufacture and easy to use. In fact it proved to be extremely difficult to fly. Wartime leaders had hoped that pilots with little or no experience could be recruited and trained quickly to fly the aircraft, but the He 162 could be fatally difficult, even in the hands of experienced fighter aces with hundreds of hours in the Messerschmitt Bf 109 or Focke-Wulf Fw 190. One pilot called the He 162 'totally unforgiving', but spoke of the jet as a pleasure to fly in favourable circumstances.

The programme, and not the aircraft, was called the Salamander and designer Ernst Heinkel called the jet the 'Swallow'. The He 162 became operational but no reports of actual combat were ever confirmed.

*Photographed during a high-speed pass, this He 162 underwent tests in Britain. One aircraft was destroyed in a fatal crash.*

Mounting the BMW 003 engine above the fuselage made the aircraft unstable in pitch, which made it very difficult to fly.

A cartridge-actuated ejection seat provided an escape route for the pilot. Leaving the aircraft by the conventional means of bailing out with a parachute would have been impossible with the jet intake behind and above the cockpit.

## He 162A-2

**Type:** single-seat jet fighter

**Powerplant:** one BMW 003E-1 axial-flow turbojet engine rated at 7.80 kN (1,755 lb. thrust) for take-off and 9.02 kN (2,030 lb. thrust) for maximum bursts of up to 30 seconds

**Maximum speed:** 890 km/h (490 m.p.h.) at sea level

**Range:** 620 km (384 mi.)

**Service ceiling:** 12,010 m (39,400 ft.)

**Weights:** empty 1663 kg (3,659 lb.); empty equipped 1758 kg (3,868 lb.); loaded 2805 kg (6,171 lb.)

**Armament:** two 20-mm (0.79-in.) MG 151 cannon in forward fuselage

**Dimensions:**
| | | |
|---|---|---|
| span | 7.20 m | (23 ft. 7 in.) |
| length | 9.05 m | (29 ft. 8 in.) |
| height | 2.60 m | (8 ft. 6 in.) |
| wing area | 11.20 m² | (121 sq. ft.) |

## He 162A-2

**This aircraft was captured by the British at Leck. It had previously served with 3. Staffel, Einsatz-Gruppe I/JG 1 and was the personal aircraft of the Staffelkapitän.**

A one-piece canopy and windscreen glazing gave the pilot an exceptional view. The raised position of the cockpit glazing was similar to that of modern fighters.

An unusually narrow main undercarriage was fitted to the He 162. This resulted from there being no room for the structure in the wings, and therefore all systems had to be accommodated in the narrow, cramped fuselage.

Oberleutnant Erich Demuth had 16 kill markings on the tail of his He 162, all gained in other types.

A single MG 151 cannon was mounted in a recess on either side of the lower forward fuselage. By good fortune, Heinkel had chosen a configuration which avoided engine gun-gas ingestion problems.

Aerodynamic problems led to the adoption of turned down wingtips. The small wings were mostly of wood, with light alloy flaps. Much of the wooden wing, tail and undercarriage door structure was of adhesively bonded wood and after an undercarriage door had broken away in flight, it was discovered that acid in the adhesive was corroding the wood.

---

## COMBAT DATA

### THRUST

Both the Meteor and Me 262 employed twin engines to overcome the low thrust available from early turbojets. Fitted with only one engine the He 162 was a much simpler, lighter design.

| He 162A-2 | METEOR F.Mk 1 | Me 262A-1A |
|---|---|---|
| 9.02 kN (2,030 lb. thrust) | 15.1 kN (3,397 lb. thrust) | 17.66 kN (3,973 lb. thrust) |

### MAXIMUM SPEED

Due to its streamlined fuselage and small size the He 162 was a fast aircraft, especially compared to Britain's first operational jet fighter, the Gloster Meteor. The speed shown is for maximum engine power.

| | |
|---|---|
| He 162A-2 | 890 km/h (521 m.p.h.) |
| METEOR F.Mk 1 | 668 km/h (414 m.p.h.) |
| Me 262-1A | 869 km/h (540 m.p.h.) |

### ARMAMENT

Early jets relied on their speed for surprise attacks, with armament limited by the need to save weight to maintain performance. The Me 262 was the most successful design and had powerful weapons.

| He 162A-2 | METEOR F.Mk 1 | Me 262A-1A |
|---|---|---|
| 2 x 20-mm (0.79-in.) cannon | 4 x 20-mm (0.79-in.) cannon | 4 x 30-mm (1.18-in.) cannon 12 x rockets |

---

## German jet developments

**■ ARADO Ar 234 BLITZ:** Ar 234s saw some operational service, mostly in the reconnaissance role, and proved to be immune to interception by Allied fighters. However, they suffered from short engine life and servicibility problems.

**■ GOTHA Go 229 (HORTEN Ho IX):** Gotha developed the radical Ho IX tailless glider as the Go 229 jet-powered fighter. Tests showed the aircraft had exceptional handling, but the war ended before production aircraft were completed.

**■ HEINKEL He 280:** Having lost out in the competition with the exceptional Me 262, examples of this single-seat, twin-jet interceptor were used as research aircraft and included a version with a V-tail.

**■ MESSERSCHMITT P.1101:** Although failing to fly before the end of the war, the P.1101 was a highly advanced aircraft which indicated Germany's lead in jet aircraft design. It was used by the US as the basis of the Bell X-5.

# HEINKEL

# HE 219 UHU

● Radar-equipped night-fighter ● Mosquito hunter

It could have been the best combat aircraft of World War II, but the Heinkel He 219 Uhu suffered from misjudgements by the German high command which never used it to its best effect. Conceived as a multi-purpose warplane, it saw service only as a heavily armed night-fighter. It was one of the few Luftwaffe aircraft which stood any chance of intercepting the fast-flying British Mosquito.

▲ Had it been available in numbers to replace slower aircraft like the Ju 88, the He 219 might have made a difference to the Luftwaffe's fierce night-time struggle with the bombers of the Royal Air Force.

## HEINKEL HE 219 UHU

### ▲ Captured test plane
The RAF evaluated the He 219 after many were captured in 1945. The aircraft was received enthusiastically by Allied pilots, who were very impressed with its high performance and the novel ejection seat.

### ▲ Radar nose
The prominent aerials in the nose were part of the Lichtenstein FuG 220 radar, which was far more effective than previous sets. The secret of the FuG 220 was revealed after one was captured when a straying Ju 88 landed by accident in Britain.

### ▲ Heinkel graveyard
Heinkel produced 296 He 219s, far too few to make a difference to the eventual outcome of the war.

### ▼ Touching down
The He 219 was easy to land; ace pilot Major Werner Streib managed a landing without flaps.

### ▲ From prototype to night warrior ▼
The He 219 VI prototype demonstrated excellent performance from the start. Only radar and guns were needed to turn a test aircraft into one of the finest night-fighters of the war.

## FACTS AND FIGURES

➤ The He 219 was one of the few aircraft which could catch the fast and agile de Havilland Mosquito.

➤ The Heinkel He 219 prototype first took to the air on 15 November 1942.

➤ The He 219 won a fly-off against the Dornier Do 217N and Junkers Ju 88S.

➤ Due to the priority assigned to jets and single-engine fighters, the Luftwaffe halted He 219 production in May 1944.

➤ Some He 219 variants had a knockout armament of eight heavy cannon.

➤ Final production of the He 219 was 296 aircraft, with some built from spares.

## PROFILE

# Heinkel's night stalker

Many features of the He 219 were at the outer edge of technology. It was the Luftwaffe's first operational aircraft with tricycle landing gear – criticised by some staff officers as 'this unnecessary American innovation'. It was also one of the first warplanes to be equipped with ejection seats, and the first to use them in combat.

Derived from Heinkel's P.1060 fighter-bomber proposal, which attracted only lukewarm support in Berlin, the all-metal, shoulder-wing He 219 seated its pilot and navigator back-to-back. It was a practical, sensible design and performed well, but bitter opposition, led by Generalfeldmarschall Erhard Milch who favoured the Junkers Ju 188, delayed production.

As a result of squabbling, the He 219 was late reaching service. But this fighter showed its capabilities on 11/12 June 1943 when a mission led by

*The combination of a slim fuselage and two very powerful engines was a recipe for a good fighter. The He 219 had the advantage over its rivals by being a dedicated design rather than a conversion from another role.*

Major Werner Streib shot down five RAF Lancasters. The He 219 had some limited success in combat, but built in larger numbers it might have had a dramatic impact on the war.

The DB 603 engines were fitted with superchargers, located on the outboard side of the engine cowling.

Variants with wing guns fitted had a very large 300-round magazine contained in the inboard wing section.

The Schräge Musik upward-firing cannon installation allowed the He 219 to attack from below, which was a blind spot for most night bombers.

### He 219A-7/R1 Uhu

**Type:** two-seat night-fighter

**Powerplant:** two 1417-kW (1,900-hp.) Daimler-Benz DB 603G piston engines

**Maximum speed:** 670 km/h (415 m.p.h.)

**Cruising speed:** 630 km/h (390 m.p.h.)

**Range:** 2000 km (1,240 mi.)

**Service ceiling:** 12,200 m (40,000 ft.)

**Weights:** empty 11,200 kg (24,640 lb.); loaded 15,300 kg (33,660 lb.)

**Armament:** two upward firing 30-mm (1.18-in.) MK 108, two 30-mm (1.18-in.) MK 108 in wingroots, two 20-mm (0.79-in.) MG 151/20 and two 30-mm (1.18-in.) MK 103 cannon in ventral tray

**Dimensions:**
| | | |
|---|---|---|
| span | 18.50 m | (60 ft. 8 in.) |
| length | 15.54 m | (51 ft.) |
| height | 4.10 m | (13 ft. 6 in.) |
| wing area | 44.50 m² | (479 sq. ft.) |

## HE 219A-7/R2 UHU

**This aircraft was flown by Hauptmann Paul Forster, a member of Stab I/NJG 1 based at Münster in the summer of 1944.**

The bulletproof front windscreen had hot-air demisting and screen wipers.

Most He 219s carried the bulk of their armament in a ventral tray, but other locations included Schräge Musik cannon in the rear fuselage and wingroot-mounted guns.

The He 217A-7/R4 had a tail warning radar system to inform the crew of impending attacks by the much-feared Mosquito night-fighter.

With the cockpit far forward of the engines and guns, the noise and flash of exhausts and gun muzzle blast were not a problem for the crew.

A tricycle undercarriage was not just the gimmick some senior officers said it was. Landing a damaged aircraft at night was much easier than with a more conventional tail dragger.

The He 219's three fuel tanks were located in the fuselage. The tanks were self-sealing and well protected.

The He 219R3 had a single machine-gun in the tail, but this was abandoned in subsequent versions. Experiments with guns in the engine nacelles were also tried, without much success.

### COMBAT DATA

#### MAXIMUM SPEED

The He 219 was very fast – it could even outpace the Mosquito, which very few German aircraft had been able to do. But it was probably less agile than the British fighter, although it could easily outfight the very large and somewhat clumsy American Black Widow, which had appeared over Europe late in 1944.

**P-61 BLACK WIDOW** 600 km/h (372 m.p.h.)

**He 219A-7/R1 UHU** 670 km/h (415 m.p.h.)

**MOSQUITO NF.Mk XII** 660 km/h (409 m.p.h.)

#### RANGE

The Heinkel He 219 had one great advantage over its opponents. It was operating over home territory, and did not need the range of the Allied aircraft. However, it could fly far enough to follow the British bomber streams all the way home, acting as intruders over airfields in Britain.

**P-61 BLACK WIDOW** 4500 km (2,790 mi.)

**MOSQUITO NF.Mk 12** 2000 km (1,240 mi.)

**He 219A-7/R1 UHU** 2000 km (1,240 mi.)

#### ARMAMENT

The Heinkel carried a phenomenally heavy cannon fit, with four cannon in a belly tray, two in the wing roots, and two upwards-firing in the rear fuselage. The Mosquito and P-61 had much lighter armament, although their four cannon still made them formidable opponents.

**P-61 BLACK WIDOW** 4 x 20-mm (0.79-in.) cannon 4 x 12.7-mm (.303 cal.) MGs

**MOSQUITO NF.Mk XII** 4 x 20-mm (0.79-in.) cannon

**He 219A-7/R1 UHU** 2 x upward firing 30-mm (1.18-in.) cannon, 4 x 30-mm (1.18-in.) cannon, 2 x 20-mm (0.79-in.) forward firing cannon

## Interception at night

**1 DETECTION:** Incoming British bomber raids were detected by the extensive network of Würzburg and Freya radars.

**2 ALARM:** Raid data was fed to night-fighter units, who took off and were vectored onto target by ground controllers.

**3 AIRBORNE INTERCEPT:** The fighter's own radar was effective from about three km (two miles) and the radar operator controlled the last stage of the intercept.

**4 SURPRISE ATTACK:** Most British bombers had a blind spot beneath the belly, so the ideal night-fighter attack meant flying in formation and shooting with upward-pointing cannon.

# HENSCHEL

# Hs 123

● Dive-bomber ● Close support ● High combat survivability

D ive-bombers were an essential element of the German Blitzkrieg concept of warfare. Therefore, in 1933, Henschel was asked to design an interim machine for use until the Ju 87 was ready for service. Although regarded as obsolete by the late-1930s, the Hs 123 proved to be a rugged and reliable close-support aircraft. After being scheduled for retirement in mid-1940, it fought on for another four years until the last examples were lost in action.

▲ Pilots appreciated the Hs 123's ability to absorb combat damage when operating just above the heads of enemy troops. The aircraft excelled in the dive-bombing and ground-attack roles.

## PHOTO FILE

## HENSCHEL Hs 123

▲ Building for war
A partially assembled Hs 123A demonstrates the nine-cylinder BMW engine, before the cowling has been fitted.

▲ Close-support units
Wearing the badge of the Infanterie-Sturmabzeichen, this Hs 123A has the standard weapon load of four 50-kg (110-lb.) bombs.

▲ Further developments
In 1938 Henschel flew the Hs 123 V5 prototype. Powered by a 716-kW (960-hp.) BMW 123K radial, the aircraft was the prototype for the cancelled Hs 123B.

▲ Spanish Civil War
Five Hs 123A-1s were evaluated with great success in combat over Spain from early 1937.

Upper wing failures ▶
After two prototypes shed their upper wings in flight, stronger centre-section struts were fitted.

## FACTS AND FIGURES

➤ The Luftwaffe high command intended to use the Hs 123 to establish the dive-bomber units ready for the Ju 87.

➤ Fieseler submitted its Fi 98 design but lost out to the superior Hs 123.

➤ Almost no bracing was used between the wing and the fuselage on the prototypes.

➤ Over Spain the Hs 123 was so impressive that the Spanish bought all five aircraft and ordered a further 11.

➤ During flight tests the Hs 123 demonstrated its ability to pull out of near-vertical dives.

➤ Many military people wanted the Hs 123 put back into production during 1943.

## PROFILE

# Attacking across Europe

*Above: An extremely broad chord and smooth cowling distinguished the first prototype Hs 123 V1.*

This exceptional dive-bomber and close-support machine was a sesquiplane, or 'one-and-a-half-wing' aircraft, rather than a true biplane. With its strut-braced wings, fixed undercarriage and two-bladed propeller, the Hs 123 proved itself in the Spanish Civil War. It demonstrated that it could be extremely effective in the close-support role, operating in the thick of the fighting and surviving multiple direct hits.

Nevertheless, production ended in 1938 and there

was only one Hs 123 Gruppe in service by the time of the invasion of Poland in September 1939. This unit achieved such remarkable results, both in Poland and again during the invasion of France in May 1940, that it was still flying its old biplanes during the May 1941 invasion of Russia.

On the Eastern Front the

Hs 123 again proved its worth as a close-support aircraft and, as a result, additional units were formed using retired aircraft. There was even a move to resume production in 1943, but the tooling had been destroyed.

*Above: Demonstrating a three-colour splinter camouflage scheme, this Hs 123A-1 flies without the armoured headrest.*

### Hs 123A-1

**Type:** dive-bomber and close-support aircraft

**Powerplant:** one 649-kW (870-hp.) BMW 132Dc nine-cylinder air-cooled radial engine

**Maximum speed:** 341 km/h (211 m.p.h.) at 1200 m (3,900 ft.)

**Initial climb rate:** 900 m/min (2,950 f.p.m.) at sea level

**Range:** 860 km (533 mi.)

**Service ceiling:** 9000 m (29,500 ft.)

**Weights:** empty 1505 kg (3,311 lb.); normal loaded 2217 kg (4,877 lb.)

**Armament:** two 7.9-mm (0.31-in.) MG 17 machine-guns in forward fuselage plus two 20-mm (0.79-in.) MG FF cannon or up to four 50-kg (110-lb.) bombs under wings

**Dimensions:** span 10.50 m (34 ft. 5 in.)
length 8.33 m (27 ft. 4 in.)
height 3.22 m (10 ft. 6 in.)
wing area 24.85 m² (267 sq. ft.)

### Hs 123A-1

This early machine was based at Fürstenfeldbruck, with 7./Stukageschwader 165 'Immelmann', during October 1937. Later aircraft adopted the armoured headrest tested on the Hs 123 V6 prototype.

Most in-service Hs 123s flew with the headrest and fairing in place. Some may have used a sliding cockpit hood, as trialled on the Hs 123 V6. The first aircraft were also delivered with a crutch beneath the fuselage for launching an SC250 bomb, but in service this was usually replaced by an auxiliary fuel tank.

In the immediate pre-war period, German military aircraft had their tail swastikas painted on a red band. This was similar to the markings used on civilian aircraft and was an attempt at making the Luftwaffe's new military machines look like civilian aircraft to foreign observers.

Only the Hs 123 V1 flew with the smooth cowling. All production Hs 123s had a cowling with 18 fairings covering the engine valves. Twin exhaust pipes protruded from the rear of the cowling on both sides.

During wet weather, especially on the Eastern Front, the Hs 123 was kept operational by removing the spats, preventing mud from clogging the wheels.

Although the tailwheel was fixed, it was very neatly faired with a spat and partial trouser fairing. Many of the features of the Hs 123 appeared to be outdated, but several aircraft were returned to the front line once their abilities had been realised.

## COMBAT DATA

### MAXIMUM SPEED

Heinkel's He 50A was the Luftwaffe's first operational dive-bomber and served on into World War II, gradually being replaced by the Hs 123. The Hs 123 was only marginally slower than the Skua.

| Hs 123A-1 | 341 km/h (211 m.p.h.) |
| SKUA Mk II | 362 km/h (224 m.p.h.) |
| He 50A | 235 km/h (146 m.p.h.) |

### RANGE

Blackburn's Skua monoplane offered greater range than the Hs 123A-1, but was larger and of similar vintage. The Skua was carrier-based, however, while the Hs 123 flew from forward strips. This gave the Hs 123 a quick turnaround time which allowed more missions to be flown per day.

Hs 123A-1
860 km (533 mi.)

He 50A
600 km (372 mi.)

SKUA Mk II
1223 km (758 mi.)

### ARMAMENT

With its secondary fighter role, the Skua carried more offensive machine-guns. It also carried a greater bombload but could not offer the versatility of the Hs 123 in combat.

| Hs 123A-1 | 2 x 7.9-mm machine-guns 200-kg (440-lb.) bombload |
| SKUA Mk II | 5 x 7.7-mm (.303 cal.) machine-guns 227-kg (500-lb.) bombload |
| He 50A | 1 x 7.9-mm (0.31-in.) machine-gun 250-kg (550-lb.) bombload |

## World War II biplanes

■ **FIAT CR.42:** Italy flew a large number of these biplane fighters at the beginning of the war. Some early missions were flown over the UK.

■ **GLOSTER GLADIATOR:** Representing the last and ultimate development of the Gloster biplane fighter, the Gladiator fought gallantly.

■ **HEINKEL He 60:** By early-1940 this shipboard reconnaissance floatplane had been largely withdrawn, but reappeared in 1941.

■ **POLIKARPOV I-153:** When the USSR was attacked in June 1941, most of its fighter strength consisted of I-153s.

# HENSCHEL

# Hs 126

● Battlefield reconnaissance ● Short takeoff ● Glider tug

**H**enschel's 126 was based on an earlier company design for an army co-operation and short-range reconnaissance aircraft. The Hs 122 had proved its ability to operate from short strips and at low airspeeds, but was too slow. With a more powerful engine and refined wings to improve performance, the resulting Hs 126 became the Luftwaffe's standard tactical reconnaissance aircraft in the early years of World War II.

▲ Design of the Hs 126 included a high-lift parasol wing, which gave the aircraft excellent short- and rough-field performance. Access to the cockpit was via a ladder on the fuselage side.

# HENSCHEL Hs 126

**▼ Photo reconnaissance**
Over the battlefield, the Hs 126 was the aerial eyes of the Wehrmacht. Leaning over the side of the fuselage a gunner photographs enemy positions.

**▲ Desert campaign**
The Hs 126 participated in all German theaters of operation up until 1942. In North Africa, they were used extensively for spotting Allied positions.

**Pre-war production ▶**
Production Hs 126A-1s line up at Henschel's Schönefeld factory field in 1938 prior to delivery to the Luftwaffe. Later in the year six were sent to Spain for service with the Légion Condor.

**▼ High-lift wing**
The Hs 126's parasol wing provided excellent lift, allowing the aircraft to operate from short strips close to the front line. Large flaps allowed the Hs 126 to land and take off at low speeds.

**▲ Open cockpit**
Unusual for German aircraft of the period, the Hs 126 featured an open rear cockpit. Although this was not a problem in North Africa, it was unpleasant during the harsh Russian winter.

## FACTS AND FIGURES

➤ The Hs 126 was developed from the Hs 122, which was powered by a Rolls-Royce Kestrel engine.

➤ The prototype Hs 126 first flew in the autumn of 1936.

➤ As well as reconnaissance, the Hs 126 also strafed and bombed enemy positions.

➤ During the invasion of Russia in June 1941, no fewer than 48 Staffeln were equipped with Hs 126B-1s.

➤ From 1942, many Hs 126s were relegated to glider-towing duties.

➤ Late in the war, Hs 126s were employed as night harassment aircraft.

# Eyes of the Wehrmacht

As well as providing the right combination of performance and handling characteristics, the Hs 126 was well equipped for its role. The sliding canopy over the cockpit incorporated deflector panels to shield the observer's gun from slipstream, while a bay in the rear fuselage could carry cameras or ten 10-kg (22-lb.) bombs. Deliveries to the Luftwaffe started in the

spring of 1938, and in September 1939 a total of 13 tactical reconnaissance squadrons operating the Hs 126 took part in the invasion of Poland. They were used for ground attack, as well as reconnaissance missions, and with little opposition their losses were light.

By mid 1940 over the Western Front, life was growing harder for the Hs 126. Production ended in January 1941 as

deliveries of its replacement, the Fw 189, got under way. Most of the operational units had been transferred to the Eastern Front by June 1942, though one squadron operated the Hs 126 in North Africa.

Although it was used mainly as a glider tug after mid 1942, the Hs 126 was also used to equip several units specializing in night-time, close-support operations.

*Above: Armed with a single 50-kg (110-lb.) bomb fitted to an optional fuselage side rack, an Hs 126 prepares for takeoff. This example flew highly successful combat evaluation sorties in Spain.*

*Left: At low level over the battlefield, the Hs 126 was in a dangerous environment. It could, however, take considerable battle damage and survive.*

## Hs 126B-1

**Type:** two-seat tactical reconnaissance aircraft

**Powerplant:** one 671-kW (900-hp.) BMW Bramo Fafnir 323 nine-cylinder air-cooled radial engine

**Maximum speed:** 354 km/h (220 m.p.h.) at 3050 m (10,000 ft.)

**Climb rate:** 3.5 minutes to 600 m (1,968 ft.)

**Endurance:** 2 hours 15 minutes

**Service ceiling:** 8200 m (26,900 ft.)

**Weapons:** Two 7.92-mm (0.31-in.) machine guns, one in forward fuselage and one in rear cockpit; 10 x 10-kg (22-lb.) and one 50-kg (110-lb.) bombs.

**Weights:** empty 4,470 lb.); loaded 3270 kg (7,209 lb.)

**Dimensions:**
| | | |
|---|---|---|
| Span | 14.50 m | (47 ft. 7 in.) |
| Length | 10.85 m | (35 ft. 7 in.) |
| Height | 3.73 m | (12 ft. 3 in.) |
| Wing area | 31.59 m² | (340 sq. ft.) |

## Hs 126A-1

As well as serving on the Eastern and Western Fronts and in the Mediterranean, the Hs 126 also saw extensive service in North Africa. This example flew with the Fliegerführer Afrika Unit during July 1941.

The Hs 126 owed its responsive, yet docile handling to its parasol wing, developed by Henschel's chief designer Friedrich Nicolaus.

Developed from the Hs 122, the Hs 126 incorporated several improvements, including a canopy over the pilot to give protection from the elements.

The camouflage scheme and the white band around the fuselage were typical markings for Hs 126s operating in the North African theater.

Armament comprised one forward-firing 7.92-mm (0.31-in.) MG 17 machine gun, plus one similar weapon on a trainable mounting in the rear cockpit.

Power for the first production version, the Hs 126A-1, was provided by a BMW 132Dc radial engine. The later Hs 126B-1 was fitted with the more powerful Bramo 323 engine.

The cantilever main undercarriage featured long struts, giving the aircraft a pronounced 'nose high' appearance on the ground. Wheel spats could be fitted to reduce drag.

The back-seat crewmember operated a topographic camera, a hand-held camera and a 7.92-mm (0.31-in.) machine gun from his open-cockpit position.

A Zeiss Rb topographic camera is situated in a bay behind the gunner/observer, which he operated from his position.

## ACTION DATA

### SPEED

The Hs 126 was the slowest of the types, although all three relied more on escort fighters or camouflage to escape enemy fighters rather than speed. The more powerful Ki-51 was a later design, but was still easy prey for fighter aircraft.

| | |
|---|---|
| Hs 126B-1 | 354 km/h (220 m.p.h.) |
| LYSANDER Mk I | 367 km/h (228 m.p.h.) |
| Ki-51 "SONIA" | 425 km/h (264 m.p.h.) |

### WEAPONS

All three types carried armament for self-defense and for attacking targets of opportunity on the ground. The observer in each aircraft would use a trainable machine gun to ward off enemy fighters.

Hs 126B-1    2 x 7.9-mm (0.31-in.) machine guns

LYSANDER Mk I    4 x 7.7-mm (.303 cal.) machine guns

Ki-51 'SONIA'    3 x 7.7-mm (.303 cal.) machine guns

### POWER

All three aircraft have a similar amount of horse power at their disposal. The slightly larger engine in the Ki-51 allowed it to climb quicker and possess a higher top speed. The power in the engines gave the Lysander and Hs 126 a very short take-off run.

| Hs 126B-1 | LYSANDER Mk I | Ki-51 'SONIA' |
|---|---|---|
| 671 KW (900 hp.) | 664 kW (890 hp.) | 700 kW (940 hp.) |

## Battlefield spotters of World War II

**POLIKARPOV U-2:** The U-2 was used in a number of roles by Soviet forces, including battlefield reconnaissance and ground attack.

**WESTLAND LYSANDER:** More than 1600 Lysanders were built and flew many roles during World War II, including army co-operation.

**MITSUBISHI Ki-51 'SONIA':** This Japanese tactical reconnaissance aircraft also flew ground-attack missions during World War II.

**FOCKE-WULF Fw 189 UHU:** Designed to replace the Hs 126, the Fw 189 was a success, especially over the Eastern Front.

# Henschel

# Hs 129

● Anti-tank aircraft ● Poor serviceability ● Heavily armoured

▲ To keep the risk of damage by small arms fire to a minimum, the Hs 129 was designed to have a small cross-sectional area. This resulted in a small and very cramped cockpit.

**D**esigned in 1938, the Hs 129 was the only aircraft of World War II to be designed from the outset explicitly for destroying hostile armour. Its angular shape and small cross-section made the aircraft look aggressive, and its powerful cannon could penetrate any tank's armour. However, the type suffered from a protracted development and the problems of lack of power and unreliability from its twin engines were never fully solved.

## HENSCHEL **Hs 129**

▼ **Tank buster**
To provide a hard-hitting weapon for use against Soviet tanks, the Hs 129B-3/Wa was developed with a 75-mm Pak 40 gun.

▲ **Allied evaluation**
Captured in North Africa, this Hs 129B was flown to the United States for evaluation. It carries the 'Foreign Equipment' registration FE-4600.

◀ **Final sorties**
As the Allies advanced, a lack of spares and fuel resulted in many Hs 129s being abandoned. By the spring of 1945, very few remained in service.

▼ **Desert service**
Arriving in North Africa at the end of 1942, the Hs 129B encountered serious reliability problems. Its twin Gnome-Rhône engines were prone to seizure and the aircraft were rapidly withdrawn to Tripoli for overhaul.

▲ **Early engines**
The pre-production Hs 129A-0s were fitted with Argus engines. They were found to be underpowered and were assigned to a training unit.

## FACTS AND FIGURES

➤ In mid-1938 Henschel received orders to build three Hs 129 prototypes, the first of which flew in March 1939.

➤ The Hs 129 cockpit was so cramped that many pilots could not fit in it.

➤ When production ended in September 1944, 871 Hs 129s had been built.

➤ An Hs 129 was tested with the SG 113A weapon which fired tubes containing explosive triggered by light-sensitive cells.

➤ The Hs 129B-3/Wa's 75-mm (2.95-in.) Pak 40 gun could destroy a tank with one shell.

➤ After a *coup* in 1944, Romanian Air Corps Hs 129s were used against Germany.

## PROFILE

# Eastern Front tank destroyer

In 1937 the Technische Amt issued a specification for a cannon-armed close-support aircraft, small in size but heavily armoured. The final competing aircraft were the Focke-Wulf Fw 189 and the Hs 129. Both aircraft performed particularly badly in tests, showing sluggish performance, and the Hs 129's cramped cockpit was unpopular.

The Hs 129 eventually won, not because it was superior but because it cost about two-thirds as much as the other type, and was smaller. Eight pre-production

Hs 129A-0s with Argus As 410A-1 engines were tested, but it soon became obvious that the aircraft was under-powered. Henschel's chief engineer set about designing a new larger version with Gnome-Rhône engines.

The resulting Hs 129B was a great improvement. The cockpit was modified with larger areas of armoured glass, giving better vision and superior protection.

After the invasion of the Soviet Union in June 1941, it became obvious that the Hs 129B would be an essential weapon, but poor

engine reliability and production problems lowered confidence in the aircraft. When introduced to North Africa in 1942 the first Hs 129 unit suffered engine problems caused by sand ingestion, and was evacuated with no serviceable aircraft.

Various improvements incorporated into the Hs 129B-2 finally resulted in some success against Soviet armour, but by the spring of 1945 few remained in service.

Early production Hs 129B-2s featured a central nose aperture for an Rb 24 automatic camera.

Two small diagonal white stripes on each wing were used by the pilot as guides for adjusting the ailerons and flaps.

### Hs 129B-2/R2

Seen in Eastern Front markings, this Hs 129 served with 8./Schlachtgeschwader (Assault Group) in June 1943. Red was not used in the markings to avoid confusion with the enemy.

The blue code markings denote that this aircraft was from II. Gruppe. All German combat aircraft on the Eastern Front carried yellow theatre bands.

The Hs 129's cockpit was very cramped owing to the triangular shape of the forward fuselage. The gunsight was mounted outside the cockpit and the engine instruments were located on the engine nacelles.

Hs 129s possessed an impressive internal gun armament of two 20-mm (0.79-in.) cannon in the upper fuselage sides and two 7.9-mm (0.31-in.) machine-guns mounted in the wingroots.

The main undercarriage assemblies retracted hydraulically into the rear of the engine nacelles. A portion of the wheel was left exposed to help minimise damage in the event of a wheels-up landing.

Two SC 50 50-kg bombs or 24 SD 2 2-kg (4-lb.) bomblets could be carried on underwing racks as standard. The R4 field modification allowed centreline bombs to be carried, increasing the Hs 129's ability to attack 'soft' targets.

The light metal stressed-skin fuselage was married to an armoured shell forming the fuselage nose. The floor and front of this shell were built from 12-mm (½-in.) armour plating with 6-mm (¼-in.) plating on the sides. The engines also had armour protection.

### Hs 129B-2

**Type:** single-seat close support and anti-tank aircraft

**Powerplant:** two 522-kW (700-hp.) Gnome-Rhône 14M 4/5 14-cylinder radial air-cooled piston engines

**Maximum speed:** 407 km/h (252 m.p.h.)

**Cruising speed:** 315 km/h (195 m.p.h.)

**Initial climb rate:** 486 m/min (1,594 f.p.m.)

**Range:** 688 km (425 mi.)

**Service ceiling:** 9000 m (29,500 ft.)

**Weights:** empty 3810 kg (8,382 lb.); maximum take-off 5250 kg (11,550 lb.)

**Armament:** two 7.9-mm (0.31-in.) MG 17 machine-guns and two 20-mm (0.79-in.) MG 151 cannon in nose plus either one 30-mm cannon, four 50-kg (110-lb.) bombs, 92 2-kg (4-lb.) anti-personnel bombs or one 250-kg (550-lb.) bomb beneath the fuselage; two 50-kg (110-lb.) bombs or 48 2-kg (4-lb.) anti-personnel bombs on wing racks

**Dimensions:**
| | | |
|---|---|---|
| span | 14.20 m | (46 ft. 7 in.) |
| length | 9.75 m | (13 ft. 1 in.) |
| height | 3.25 m | (10 ft. 8 in.) |
| wing area | 29.00 m² | (312 sq. ft.) |

### COMBAT DATA

#### MAXIMUM SPEED
The Hs 129 was regarded as being underpowered, and this is reflected in its top speed, which was actually inferior to the earlier Ju 87 design. The Hurricane Mk IID, which the RAF used as a tank buster in North Africa, was basically a fighter design and possessed superior performance.

**Hs 129B-2** 407 km/h (252 m.p.h.)
**Ju 87D-1** 410 km/h (254 m.p.h.)
**HURRICANE Mk IID** 518 km/h (321 m.p.h.)

#### ARMAMENT
Both the Hs 129B-2 and the Hurricane Mk IID were designed as tank busters and their primary weapon was a powerful cannon whose shells could penetrate a tank's armour. The Hs 129 could also carry bombs for use against 'soft' targets. The Ju 87 was designed as a dive bomber and its machine-guns would not destroy a tank.

**Hs 129B-2** 2 x 7.9-mm machine-guns / 2 x 20-mm (0.79-in.) cannon / 350-kg (770-lb.) bombload
**Ju 87D-1** 5 x 7.9-mm machine-guns / 1800-kg (3,960-lb.) bombload
**HURRICANE Mk IID** 2 x 40-mm cannon / 2 x 7.7-mm (.303 cal.) machine-guns

## Hs 129 colours and variants

■ **Hs 129B-1:** This aircraft belonging to 4./Sch.G.2 was delivered in September 1942 and served in Poland before adopting this colour scheme for operations in North Africa.

■ **Hs 129B-2/R2:** Incorporating many improvements over the B-1, this B-2 wears temporary winter camouflage for operations against Soviet tanks on the Eastern Front.

■ **Hs 129B-3/Wa:** This version was factory-fitted with the very powerful 75-mm cannon. Two Eastern Front units operated the B-3/Wa in the winter of 1944/45.

# Ilyushin
# IL-2/10 Shturmovik

- Eastern Front 'flying tank'   ● Anti-armour ground-attack specialist

T he Shturmovik – an armoured attack warplane – is a uniquely Russian concept. The Ilyushin Il-2 entered service in 1941, only months before the German invasion of the Soviet Union. Ilyushin began designing the aircraft by fitting armour around a pilot and engine, and then thinking about the aerodynamics. The Il-2 and the developed Il-10 were used on a vast scale and proved to be devastating ground-attack weapons. The Shturmovik became a legend to the Soviet public, who saw it as an instrument of salvation and cheered its successes in battle.

▲ The Soviet Il-2 was an effective weapon in World War II. Like most Soviet equipment, it was unsophisticated, but extremely rugged. Heavily-armed and armoured, it was built in greater numbers than any other warplane.

▲ Mass produced
Production of Il-2s was made a top priority. Demand was so high that major modifications were deliberately discouraged.

**Shturmovik ▶ expert**
Ilyushin Il-2s were used by Allied units fighting on the Eastern Front. Lieutenant Cheben of the 3rd Air Regiment flew an Il-2 with the Czech division, fighting through the Ukraine in 1944.

▲ Strike formation
Il-2s flew in huge formations, forming a large 'circle of death' to attack. This allowed them to keep a target area under constant fire.

**Korean warrior ▶**
The Shturmovik's career did not end in 1945. It was used against UN troops in Korea, but often fell victim to more modern Western fighters.

▲Lethal harvest
Casualties among Il-2 squadrons were always high. The aircraft had good protection, but their low-level role was extremely perilous.

## FACTS AND FIGURES

➤ In 1941/42 an experimental Il-2 powered by an M-82 radial engine was tested, but it was not manufactured.

➤ At one stage, production of Il-2s reached more than 1000 aircraft per month.

➤ German soldiers in the Soviet Union called the Il-2 the 'Black Death'.

➤ A dual-control Il-2 capable of carrying torpedoes was built in small numbers for the Soviet navy.

➤ Il-2s were sometimes flown by women pilots in the Soviet air force.

➤ A few Il-2s were converted to two-seat tandem trainers for flight instruction.

# PROFILE

# Stalin's flying battle tank

An incredible 36,000 Il-2 Shturmoviks were manufactured, making this the most numerous military aircraft in history. The Il-2 was called a 'flying tank', because it was heavily armoured and had great firepower from its cannon and rockets.

A low-wing metal craft with wood in the aft fuselage, the Il-2 began as a single-seater. At first production difficulties plagued its builders. Premier Josef Stalin cabled factory workers saying, 'The Red Army needs the Il-2 as it needs air and bread.' Though handicapped by the war, Soviet industry rose to the occasion.

In February 1942 a two-seat Il-2 was introduced. This had a rear gunner under an extended canopy. Production versions appeared at the Front, while single-seaters were converted in the field.

The Il-2 could carry 1200 kg (2,640 lb.) of bombs over a distance of 400 km (250 mi.), and was agile enough to give attacking fighters a good run for their money.

Even more potent was the Il-10 Shturmovik, which arrived just as the war was ending. The aircraft saw extensive action in Korea with the Communist forces.

*Czechoslovakia built large numbers of Il-10 aircraft, under the name Avia B.33. They served into the late 1950s, as did the Soviet-built machines supplied to Poland. Both countries used the Il-2 in the last year of the war.*

## Il-2M3 Shturmovik

**Type:** one-/two-seat armoured close-support aircraft

**Powerplant:** one 1282-kW (1,720-hp.) Mikulin AM-38F piston engine

**Maximum speed:** 430 km/h (267 m.p.h.) at 6700 m (22,000 ft.)

**Range:** 600 km (375 mi.)

**Service ceiling:** 9700 m (31,825 ft.); 6500 m (21,320 ft.) with bombload

**Weights:** empty 3250 kg (7,150 lb.); loaded 5872 kg (12,920 lb.)

**Armament:** two 20-mm (0.79-in.) and/or two 37-mm (1.47-in.) cannon in wings and one manually-aimed 12.7-mm (.50 cal.) machine-gun in rear cockpit, plus 600 kg (1,320 lb.) of bombs, or eight RS-82 or four RS-132 rockets under outer wing

**Dimensions:**
| | | |
|---|---|---|
| span | 14.60 m | (48 ft.) |
| length | 11.65 m | (38 ft.) |
| height | 3.40 m | (11 ft.) |
| wing area | 38.50 m² | (414 sq. ft.) |

## IL-10 SHTURMOVIK

The Ilyushin Il-10 served with the Soviet Tactical Air Force on the Eastern Front in Poland in 1945. A development of the Il-2, the Il-10 had an uprated engine and an enclosed rear gunner's cockpit.

Both the Il-2 and Il-10 used a three-bladed variable-pitch propeller.

The 20-mm (0.79-in.) VYa cannon were later replaced by more powerful NS 23-mm (0.9-in.) weapons.

The Il-10 had a new wing, capable of mounting a four-cannon armament with a reduced bombload. Aerodynamic refinement also gave it improved manoeuvrability.

A rear gunner fired a 12.7-mm (.50 cal.) machine-gun from his position. He also acted as the radio operator.

The wood and fabric rear fuselage and tail of the Il-2, designed to preserve scarce resources, were replaced by all-metal structures in the Il-10.

The Il-10 had a Mikulin inline liquid-cooled engine like the Il-2, but the AM-42 was rated at 1491 kW (2,000 hp.), compared to the 1282-kW (1,720-hp.) AM-38 in the earlier aircraft.

A large sheet of armour plate under the fuselage protected the engine from ground fire.

The crew were protected by all-round armour plate, and the thick canopy glass was proof against most small-arms fire.

The tailwheel semi-retracted into the fuselage.

## COMBAT DATA

### MAXIMUM SPEED

Ground-attack fighters required protection more than ultimate performance, and the heavy weapons and armour plate carried by aircraft like the Ilyushin Il-2 and Henschel Hs 129 meant that they were not very fast. The Shturmovik was nevertheless quite an agile machine.

| | |
|---|---|
| **Il-2M3 SHTURMOVIK** | 430 km/h (267 m.p.h.) |
| **Ju 87D STUKA** | 400 km/h (250 m.p.h.) |
| **Hs 129** | 410 km/h (255 m.p.h.) |

### BOMBLOAD

The famous Stuka was originally designed as a bomber rather than a ground-attacker, and so could carry a heavier weapons load then either of the two armour-plated aircraft. These generally carried large numbers of small armour-piercing or anti-personnel weapons.

| Il-2M3 SHTURMOVIK | Ju 87D STUKA | Hs 129 |
|---|---|---|
| 600 kg (1,300 lb.) | 1800 kg (3,960 lb.) | 250 kg (550 lb.) |

### ARMAMENT

Destroying a tank calls for a powerful gun, and the standard 37-mm (1.47-in.) calibre weapons on the Eastern Front could penetrate the thin top or rear armour of most tanks. However, the Shturmovik needed bombs or rockets to deal with the immensely well-protected Panthers and Tigers which Germany fielded after the battle of Kursk in 1943.

**Il-2M3 SHTURMOVIK**
2 x 37-mm (1.47-in.) cannon
2 x 20-mm (0.79-in.) cannon

**Ju 87D STUKA**
2 x 37-mm (1.47-in.) cannon

**Hs 129**
1 x 37-mm (1.47-in.) cannon
up to 4 x 20-mm (0.79-in.) cannon, 2 x 7.92-mm (0.31-in.) machine-guns

## Shturmovik on the Eastern Front

**GERMANY INVADES:** Many of the German tanks in Operation Barbarossa, the great invasion of Russia in 1941, were surprisingly light. The Shturmovik could deal with the thin armour of a Pzkpfw II or III with cannon fire or small bombs and rockets.

**HARDER TARGETS:** As German tanks got bigger and vehicles such as the Pzkpfw IV were given extra armour, the Shturmovik needed larger and more sophisticated bombs and rockets to deal with them.

**THE ULTIMATE CHALLENGE:** To destroy the Pzkpfw V Panther which equipped the Wehrmacht at the end of the war, Shturmoviks needed to attack with large RS-132 rockets or PTAB armour-piercing bombs.

# ILYUSHIN

# IL-4

● Medium bomber ● Major redesign ● Torpedo-bomber

▲ By 1943 Soviet forces were much better organised. These Il-4s have been prepared for another mission by the groundcrew and the chief engineer confirms that the aircraft are ready to fly.

Ilyushin's Il-4 was a redesigned version of the DB-3. Instead of the earlier model's nose turret, the Il-4 had a glazed nose with a simple machine-gun mounting. Two more guns, one in a turret and one firing through lower hatches, were carried in the aft fuselage and an internal bay could hold 1000 kg (2,200 lb.) of bombs. First flown in January 1940 and redesignated from DB-3F to Il-4 in March 1942, the aircraft had a new streamlined shape and simplified structure.

## ILYUSHIN IL-4

▼ Rapid production
By 1944 Soviet industry was producing aircraft at a rapid rate. Eventually, 5256 Il-4s were built.

▲ Bombing Berlin
When the Soviet Union entered World War II DB-3Bs of the ADD (Long-Range Aviation) made some of the earliest attacks on Berlin. This DB-3B was captured and then operated by the Finnish air force against the Soviet Red Army.

▲ Record attempt
The prototype DB-3 crash-landed on Miscou Island after covering 8000 km (4,960 mi.) in an attempt to fly from Moscow to New York non-stop. Here one of the crew rests on a life raft.

◀ Forward firepower
The Il-4 had a completely revised nose which housed the navigator/bombardier. The nose-mounted ShKAS machine-gun was mounted on a universal joint.

▲ Salvaging aircraft
As the Germans invaded western Russia, materials became scarce. Vital equipment was salvaged from damaged aircraft.

## FACTS AND FIGURES

➤ The Il-4 was developed from the DB-3, which set several world altitude records during the late 1930s.

➤ Improved production meant that the Il-4 took half the time to build of the DB-3.

➤ Captured DB-3s and Il-4s were used by Finland against Soviet forces.

➤ The DB-3F (Il-4) showed very impressive performance in State Acceptance Trials which were completed in June 1939.

➤ Most Il-4s were fitted with a cleat for towing A-7 or G-11 gliders.

➤ Many Il-4s were converted post-war for cargo or geophysical survey work.

# Russia's superb wartime bomber

*Left: With good range and speed, a respectable bombload and effective armament, the Il-4 was one of the best Soviet bombers.*

The Il-4 became the workhorse of the Soviet long-range and naval aviation units. With a full load of fuel it could carry an internal load of ten 100-kg (220-lb.) bombs more than 3500 km (2,450 mi.) at 270 km/h (167 m.p.h.). Three 500-kg (1,100-lb.) bombs could be carried under the wings and fuselage over shorter ranges, and a maximum 2500-kg (5,500-lb.) bombload could be loaded for short-range tactical missions.

In its naval version it could be loaded with at least one torpedo.

Improvements during production run included replacing the M-87A engines with M-88s. Wood was used instead of light metal alloys wherever possible, and 12.7-mm (.50 cal.) machine-guns became standard. More than 5000 Il-4s had been built by the time production ended in 1944.

In August 1941, 15 Il-4s mounted the first Soviet raid

on Berlin, which caused minor damage. The type also saw extensive service on the German Eastern Front attacking supply lines and strategic targets.

As well as for their primary missions, Il-4s were also used for transport, glider towing and strategic reconnaissance (with a camera in the bomb-bay). Some naval aircraft remained in service until 1949, and NATO designated the type 'Bob'.

*Above: As a result of a shortage of metal after the German invasion, the outer wing panels, cockpit floor and tailcone had to be made from wood.*

## Il-4

**Type:** long-range bomber and torpedo-bomber

**Powerplant:** two 820-kW (1,100-hp.) Tumanskii M-88B 14-cylinder air-cooled radial engines

**Maximum speed:** 420 km/h (230 m.p.h.) at 6000 m (19,700 ft.)

**Climb rate:** 5000 m (16,400 ft.) in 12 min

**Combat radius:** 1510 km (936 mi.)

**Range:** 3585 km (2,220 mi.) with maximum fuel

**Service ceiling:** 9400 m (30,850 ft.)

**Weights:** empty 5800 kg (12,760 lb.); maximum take-off 10,300 kg (22,660 lb.)

**Armament:** three machine-guns plus up to 2500 kg (5,512 lb.) of bombs or one torpedo

**Dimensions:** span 21.44 m (70 ft. 4 in.)
length 14.80 m (48 ft. 6 in.)
height 4.20 m (13 ft. 9 in.)
wing area 66.70 m² (718 sq. ft.)

The most noticeable design change from the DB-3B was the more streamlined, fully-glazed nose. The gunner, firing a 7.62-mm (.30 cal.) or 12.7-mm (.50 cal.) machine-gun or a 20-mm (0.79-in.) cannon, sat in front of the navigator/bombardier.

A shortage of metal meant the cockpit floor was made of wood. Equipment included a radio compass, automatic pilot and a de-icing system. All crewmembers were protected by 6-mm or 9-mm (¼ or ⅓ in.) thick armour plating.

The Ilyushin dorsal power turret could be fitted with either a UBT 12.7-mm (0.5 cal.) machine-gun or the ShVAK 20-mm (0.79-in.) cannon. These gave good protection from attack from above or behind.

The fixed ventral machine-gun ring fitted to the DB-3B was replaced by a much more complex semi-retractable mount on the Il-4. This gave greater protection against attack from below.

### COMBAT DATA

#### MAXIMUM SPEED

For an aircraft of its type the Il-4 had a good top speed of around 430 km/h (267 m.p.h.), marginally more than that of the He 111. With its better range and load-carrying ability, the Il-4 was perhaps the better suited of the three types to the tactical bombing role.

| | |
|---|---|
| Il-4 | 430 km/h (267 m.p.h.) |
| He 111H-13 | 370 km/h (230 m.p.h.) |
| A-20G HAVOC | 510 km/h (317 m.p.h.) |

#### RANGE

Range was a particular strength of the Il-4, and it was able to reach Berlin from well inside the Soviet Union. The shorter-ranged A-20 was used for tactical missions. Heinkel He 111s were always hampered by their short range.

Il-4 3585 km (2,220 mi.)
He 111H-13 1950 km (1,209 mi.)
A-20G HAVOC 1754 km (1,087 mi.)

Power for the Il-4 came from two Tumanskii M-88B radial engines with direct fuel injection. In 1942 the propellers were changed to a fully-feathering type.

The Il-4 had all-metal wings. However, most aircraft built in 1942 had wooden wing spars because of a shortage of light alloy metals.

Compared to the earlier DB-3, the fuselage was simplified to make production easier. The bomb-bay could hold up to 2700 kg (5,940 lb.) of bombs or mines. Alternatively, low-level or high-level torpedoes could be carried.

## IL-4

This Red Air Force Il-4 belonged to an unidentified bombardirovoshchnaya aviatsionnyi polk (bomber regiment) operating over the Eastern Front in 1944.

#### ARMAMENT

The USAAF's A-20G had a formidable set of nose-mounted guns, which were ideal for ground strafing. Both the He 111 and Il-4 had better bomb-carrying ability, being able to carry about 2.5 tons.

Il-4 1 x 12.7-mm (.50 cal.) machine-gun, 2 x 7.62-mm (.30 cal.) machine-guns, 2500-kg (5,940-lb.) bombload

He 111H-13 1 x 20-mm (0.79-in.) cannon, 1 x 13-mm (0.51-in.) cannon 7 x 7.9-mm (0.31-in.) machine-guns, 2500-kg (5,500-lb.) bombload

A-20G 9 x 12.7-mm (.50 cal.) machine-guns, 1364-kg (3,000-lb.) bombload

## Ilyushin twin-engined bombers

■ **DB-3B:** The forerunner of the Il-4, the DB-3B proved to be vulnerable to enemy fighters as it was not as well armed or as fast as its successor. This is a captured Finnish example.

■ **Il-28 'BEAGLE':** As the primary Soviet bomber during the first few years of the Cold War, the Il-28 was an important aircraft. Built in large numbers, the 'Beagle' is still in limited service in China.

■ **Il-54 'BLOWLAMP':** Only one example of this supersonic bomber was constructed. Aerodynamic difficulties on take-off caused major problems and the project was cancelled in 1957.

# JUNKERS

# JU 52/3M

● Tri-motor transport ● World War II fame ● Nicknamed 'Tante Ju'

▲ Troop-carrying and parachuting were major roles for the Ju 52/3m. It made possible some of the earliest and most daring paratroop raids of the war and served postwar in several countries.

**L**uftwaffe personnel bestowed the name 'Tante Ju' ('Aunt Ju') upon Hugo Junkers' three-engine transport design as a gesture of faith in the slow, but strong and reliable aircraft. Ju 52/3ms formed the backbone of German airlift capability throughout World War II, delivering thousands of troops and tons of supplies to European theatres. Suffering heavy losses, it was often the strength of the aircraft that carried it through a mission.

---

## JUNKERS JU 52/3M

◀ **Flying to Crete**
Float-equipped Ju 52/3ms were active in Norway and the Mediterranean. Access to the aircraft was gained via a ladder.

**Under attack ▶**
A Ju 52/3m under Allied attack in North Africa. Losses on the ground and to Allied fighters were high.

▼ **Parachuting from 'Tante Ju'**
Paratroops leap from a Luftwaffe Ju 52/3m. Note the static line attached to the soldier's parachute and the low altitude.

▲ **Float-equipped**
The floats fitted to some Ju 52s would have decreased its slow top speed even more. This aircraft taxies on one engine.

▲ **North Africa 1941**
Luftwaffe Ju 52/3ms prepare for a supply dropping sortie in support of the Afrika Korps.

### FACTS AND FIGURES

➤ In all, 4835 Ju 52/3ms are said to have been built in Germany; on VE-Day fewer than 50 were airworthy.

➤ As an airliner the Ju 52/3m flew in 28 countries from the UK to Uruguay.

➤ Postwar, 400 aircraft were built in France and 170 in Spain.

➤ In just three months, 22,399 tonnes (22,045 tons) of supplies were airlifted to six divisions of troops trapped at Demyansk.

➤ Three Ju 52/3ms were flown by the Swiss Fliegertruppe until the early 1980s.

➤ At 10,476 kg (23,100 lb.) a Ju 52/3m lifted off at 109 km/h (68 m.p.h.) in just 350 m (1,150 ft.).

# 'Tante Ju': the Luftwaffe's 'Aunt'

First flown in April 1932, the Junkers Ju 52/3m was the culmination of Junkers' vast experience in building single-engine civil transports of all-metal construction with their characteristic load-bearing, corrugated skin.

Originally a single-engine design, the Ju 52/3m was intended primarily as a freighter. Deutsche Lufthansa took delivery of 230, equipped as airliners; many were exported.

From 1932 the covert establishment of the Luftwaffe was

beginning and in 1934 the first military version, the Ju 52/3mg3e bomber appeared. Ju 52s seldom, if ever, performed in this role during World War II (though a number had in the Spanish Civil War). The type will be remembered as a transport.

Active from the first days of the Blitzkrieg on Poland, the aircraft flew in every European theater in a number of versions, though, with two exceptions, these differed only in detail.

The float-equipped Ju 52/3m Wasser alighted on fjords during

the Norwegian campaign to disembark troops and equipment, while the Ju 52/3m(MS) was fitted with energized dural hoops, which were used to explode Allied mines.

Tactical transport remained its primary role, however, a role in which the lumbering 'Tante Ju' suffered huge losses, but served widely and with distinction.

Left: Ju 52/3ms were the Luftwaffe's primary means of deploying paratroops, in the same way the Douglas C-47 was the Allies' main transport aircraft.

Above: Minesweeping sorties had to be flown at low level and were therefore extremely hazardous.

## Ju 52/3mg7e

**Type:** 18-seat military transport

**Powerplant:** three 619-kW (830-hp.) BMW 132T-2 nine-cylinder air-cooled radial engines

**Maximum speed:** 295 km/h (183 m.p.h.) at sea level

**Initial climb rate:** 208m/min (682 f.p.m.)

**Service ceiling:** 5500 m (18,050 ft.)

**Weapons:** typically three 7.92-mm (0.31-in.) machine gun, one in dorsal position and two mounted to fire abeam through the side windows

**Weights:** empty 6546 kg (14,432 lb.); max 10,493 kg (23,133 lb.)

**Dimensions:**
| | | |
|---|---|---|
| span | 29.24 m | (95 ft. 11 in.) |
| length | 18.80 m | (61 ft. 8 in.) |
| height | 4.50 m | (14 ft. 9 in.) |
| wing area | 110.46 m² | (1,189 sq. ft.) |

## JU 52/3MG7E

1Z+LK served with 2.Staffel, KGzbV 1, based at Milos in Greece, in May 1941 immediately prior to the invasion of Crete. A fleet of 493 Ju 52/3ms was assembled for these landings.

A three-member crew sat in a cockpit that was elevated above cabin level. In the cabin 18 passengers could be seated, or with seats removed a large amount of cargo could be carried.

A small glass windshield protected the gunner from the slipstream while he operated the dorsally mounted 7.92-mm (0.31-in.) MG 15 machine gun.

Mechanical controls on the Ju 52/3m worked by chain links and pulleys. The control lines for the tail surfaces ran beneath the cabin floor.

Three BMW 132T-2 engines powered the Ju 52/3m. Those on the wings were angled outward slightly, to make control easier in the event of a single wing engine failure. Wings and fuselage became characteristically exhaust stained.

Many Junkers designs of the period featured flaps and ailerons that hung behind the main wing. The ailerons could drop at low speed, complimenting the flaps for STOL.

The corrugated duralumin skin of the Ju 52 was load-bearing and therefore immensely strong, without a weight penalty. This type of construction was a feature of many early airliners.

## ACTION DATA

### SPEED

The slow maximum speed of the Ju 52/3m left it vulnerable, with crews relying on its rugged construction for their safety. The Li-2, a Russian-built C-47, was slower than the American-built version.

| | |
|---|---|
| Ju 52/3mg7e | 295 km/h (183 m.p.h.) |
| Li-2 | 299 km/h (186 m.p.h.) |
| C-47A SKYTRAIN | 481 km/h (299 m.p.h.) |

### RANGE

While range is an important quality for any transport, these aircraft were more often involved in tactical operations where cargo or troop capacity over shorter distances was most important.

| | |
|---|---|
| Ju 52/3mg7e | 1287 km (800 mi.) |
| Li-2 | 2492 km (1,550 mi.) |
| C-47A SKYTRAIN | 2414 km (1,500 mi.) |

### POWER

Three engines gave the Ju 52/3m a significant safety advantage in the event of a single engine failure. The additional power also allowed excellent load carrying abilities and combined with the wing design to give exceptional STOL performance.

| Ju 52/3mg7e | Li-2 | C-47A SKYTRAIN |
|---|---|---|
| 3 x 619 kW (830 hp.) | 2 x 746 kW (1,000 hp.) | 2 x 895 kW (1,200 hp.) |

## Ju 52/3m in many theaters

**MINESWEEPING IN FINLAND:** This Ju 52/3mg6e flew from Malmi with the Minensuchgruppe, minesweeping over the Gulf of Finland during the winter of 1943–44.

**IN THE MEDITERRANEAN:** This Ju 52/3mg6e, with an unusual gun turret fitted above the flight deck, was based in Italy in 1942. White markings indicate the Mediterranean theatre.

**ON THE RUSSIAN FRONT:** Wearing a water-soluble temporary white camouflage, this Ju 52/3m was active on the Russian front in the winter of 1942/43, supplying ground troops.

# JUNKERS
# Ju 86

● Spanish Civil War ● Poor visibility ● High-altitude bomber

▲ *Criticism from*
*pilots resulted in Junkers modifying the cockpit area of the Ju 86, but accidents still occurred during ground operations. Swedish examples served until 1956.*

As the Luftwaffe secretly expanded during the 1930s, the German air ministry (RLM) and the national airline, Deutsche Lufthansa (DLH), collaborated in preparing a specification for a dual-purpose medium bomber for the Luftwaffe and a 10-seat transport for Lufthansa's high-speed routes. Heinkel and Junkers were asked to prepare designs to meet this demanding specification. They were, respectively, the He 111 and Ju 86.

## JUNKERS Ju 86

**English raider ▶**
*One of the specialised variants was the high altitude Ju 86P-1, used to raid Britain. They achieved little success, although were a nuisance to RAF fighters.*

**▲ Pilot vision**
*One unimpressive aspect of the Ju 86 was the extremely poor visibility from the cockpit. It led to numerous accidents while aircraft were taxiing or landing.*

**▲ Airline service**
*Although designed for combat operations, a limited number of Ju 86s saw service as airliners. After World War II some Ju 86s remained in service as cargo haulers with the Swedish air force until the 1950s.*

**▲ Lufthansa operations**
*Prior to the outbreak of World War II, Ju 86s were flown as high-speed airliners by the German airline. Later, the aircraft were operated by the Luftwaffe.*

**Nose over ▶**
*This Ju 86 crashed while attempting to land on a snow-covered Eastern Front airfield.*

### FACTS AND FIGURES

➤ During the siege of Stalingrad, Ju 86 trainers airlifted supplies to the trapped German soldiers; 40 Ju 86s were lost.

➤ A few Ju 86 bombers served on the Eastern Front in September 1943.

➤ The Hungarian air force employed Ju 86s against Soviet targets until mid-1944.

➤ Ju 86 airliners delivered to South African Airways were impressed by the South African air force for training duties.

➤ Sweden operated Ju 86 transports, built by Saab, into the 1950s.

➤ Junkers developed the Ju 86P into the Ju 86R, but it was too late to see service.

**PROFILE**

# Junkers goes to war

Heinkel's He 111 was produced to the same specification as the Ju 86 and served throughout World War II. The Ju 86, on the other hand, was obsolete by 1939. The Ju 86 was a twin-engined, low-wing monoplane of stressed-skin construction, powered by two Junkers Jumo diesel engines.

On 4 November 1934, the first Ju 86 (V1) bomber took to the air. Early flights revealed stability problems which were cured by a new wing and in 1936 Ju 86A-1 bombers entered

Luftwaffe service. DLH took delivery of Ju 86B-0s about the same time.

Five Ju 86D-1s (with modified tail cones to cure persistent control problems) were evaluated by the Condor Legion. Weaknesses of the Jumo diesel were confirmed and the Ju 86E-1 entered service in 1937 with BMW 132 radials.

Meanwhile, Junkers was developing the Ju 86 as a high-altitude reconnaissance/bomber. The Ju 86P prototype, with supercharged Jumo 207s and a

pressurised cabin, first flew in February 1940.

Prototypes flew unchallenged on high altitude sorties over Britain in the summer of 1940. Ju 86Ps (converted from Ju 86Ds) were later active over the Soviet Union also.

*Above: Though an advanced bomber for its day, the Ju 86 in Luftwaffe service was found to be unreliable.*

*Below: Early operations by the Luftwaffe utilised massed formations of bombers working in concert with ground forces.*

## Ju 86D-1

**Type:** four-seat medium bomber

**Powerplant:** two 447-kW (600-hp.) Jumo 205C-4 six-cylinder diesel engines

**Maximum speed:** 325 km/h (202 m.p.h.) at 3000 m (9,850 ft.)

**Cruising speed:** 285 km/h (177 m.p.h.) at 3500 m (11,485 ft.)

**Range:** 1500 km (932 mi.)

**Service ceiling:** 5900 m (19,360 ft.)

**Weights:** empty 5150 kg (11,354 lb.); maximum take-off 8200 kg (18,078 lb.)

**Armament:** three 7.92-mm (0.31-in.) machine-guns in the nose, dorsal and ventral positions, plus a bomb load of 800 kg (1,764 lb.)

**Dimensions:** span 22.50 m (73 ft. 10 in.)
length 17.87 m (58 ft. 8 in.)
height 5.06 m (16 ft. 7 in.)
wing area 82.00 m² (883 sq. ft.)

Pilots complained about the lack of visibility from the cockpit of the Ju 86, and many examples were damaged in landing accidents when pilots lost sight of the ground on approach.

Though featuring a number of design innovations, the Ju 86 was hindered by the poor performance of its engines. When war broke out the aircraft was quickly replaced in front-line service, although high-altitude examples remained in reconnaissance roles.

## Ju 86D

The Ju 86 was originally developed as an airliner for Lufthansa, in an effort to hide its military potential. Though eventually outclassed, the Ju 86 paved the way for the He 111 and Ju 88.

Displaying a large swastika on its tail surfaces, this Ju 86 is shown in early World War II colours. The need to camouflage the aircraft against attack from enemy fighters led to the adoption of a much more sombre colour scheme.

Junkers received some export orders for military models with alternative powerplants. Sweden acquired three aircraft fitted with Pratt & Whitney Hornet radial engines. Other variants were powered by Polish-built Bristol Pegasus engines.

A retractable gondola was positioned on the underside of the fuselage. Mounted on this was a single machine-gun, operated by a member of the bomber's crew. Speed was reduced while the gun was deployed.

## COMBAT DATA

### MAXIMUM SPEED

Junkers was one of the main suppliers of bombers for the Luftwaffe. Constant advances in aviation technology meant that their aircraft improved in performance.

Ju 86D-1   325 km/h (202 m.p.h.)
Ju 88A   440 km/h (273 m.p.h.)
Ju 188D-2   539 km/h (335 m.p.h.)

### MAXIMUM RANGE

Recognising that it would need to attack targets at a greater distance, the Luftwaffe requested a more modern design than the Ju 86. The Ju 88 became one of the principal bombers of the wartime Luftwaffe.

Ju 86D-1 1500 km (932 mi.)
Ju 88A 1800 km (1,118 mi.)
Ju 188D-2 3395 km (2,110 mi.)

### SERVICE CEILING

More powerful engines gave aircraft the ability to operate from a higher altitude and elude enemy fighters. One variant of the Ju 86 was specially adapted for the high-flying reconnaissance role. The later Ju 188 could reach double the altitude of the standard Ju 86.

Ju 86D-1 5900 m (19,360 ft.)
Ju 88A 8200 m (26,900 ft.)
Ju 188D-2 10,000 m (32,800 ft.)

## Junkers wartime designs

■ **Ju 52:** The 'Tante Ju' was the Luftwaffe's primary transport aircraft in 1939. A host of variants were later produced. This view shows a specialised mine counter-measures version that saw limited service.

■ **Ju 87:** Developed as a ground attack aircraft, the 'Stuka' was used extensively during the early stages of the war. Later, the design proved extremely vulnerable to enemy fighters.

■ **Ju 88:** Developed to replace the Ju 86, the Ju 88 was used extensively by the Luftwaffe. A number of specialised variants were produced, including night-fighters.

# JUNKERS

# JU 87 'STUKA'

● Dive-bomber ● Anti-tank aircraft ● Ship attack

▲ The 'Stuka' acted as a long-ranged artillery piece for the advancing Wehrmacht. Able to operate from fields just behind the front line, it could decimate a target holding up the advance in minutes.

**F**ew memories of war have endured more than the high-pitched scream of the Junkers Ju 87 'Stuka' swooping to strike its prey with claws of gunfire and bomb blast. This dive-bomber made its reputation during the Polish campaign, where it excelled at close support of ground troops. The Ju 87 fought on every front between 1939 and 1945. Adaptable and cheap, the 'Stuka' became a potent anti-tank machine on the Eastern Front.

## JUNKERS JU 87 'STUKA'

▲ Carrier strike
Ju 87Rs operating in the Mediterranean caused the Royal Navy many casualties, severely damaging the aircraft carrier HMS Illustrious.

Gunfighter ▶
In the hands of experts like Hans-Ulrich Rudel, the Ju 87G was lethal to tanks, but it was also very vulnerable to fighters.

▲ Lucky escape
This rear gunner was lucky to have survived this damage, the result of a close battle with Russian fighters.

▼ Death in the desert
'Stukas' performed well in support of the Afrika Korps, particularly in bombing Tobruk. When the RAF regained air superiority, however, the 'Stuka' was very vulnerable.

▲ Winter skier
Skis were more use than wheels when the 'Stuka' fought in Russia. By 1943 the type was being replaced by the Fw 190 in the close-support role.

## FACTS AND FIGURES

➤ The prototype 'Stuka' flew in the spring of 1935, powered by a 477-kW (640-hp.) Rolls-Royce Kestrel engine.

➤ The last of more than 5700 Ju 87s was delivered in September 1944.

➤ Hans-Ulrich Rudel destroyed over 500 Soviet tanks while flying the Ju 87G.

➤ The Ju 87 was fitted with a device to pull the aircraft out of a steep dive even if the pilot blacked out and lost control.

➤ A batch of naval Ju 87s was built for use aboard the aircraft-carrier Graf Zeppelin.

➤ The 'Stuka' was used by Bulgaria, Hungary, Italy, Romania and Slovakia.

# PROFILE

# Blitzkrieg dive-bomber

Designed to work closely with the Wehrmacht, the Ju 87 could attack with deadly accuracy, acting as a kind of highly mobile artillery. Swarming down on Poland, Norway, France and the Low Countries, the 'Stuka' (from the word Sturzkampfflugzeug, or dive-bomber) left a trail of devastation and struck terror even in the hearts of seasoned combat troops.

The Ju 87's invincible reputation took a hammering, however, when it came up against Hurricanes and Spitfires in the Battle of Britain. The distinctive aircraft with its gull wings and fixed landing gear proved slow and highly vulnerable to modern fighter opposition.

Even so, it remained a rugged and reliable machine, and was used extensively on the Eastern Front. The Ju 87 destroyed more tanks than any aircraft except for Russia's Ilyushin Il-2 Sturmovik.

From 1939, every Ju 87 was made by Weser at Tempelhof. Improvements to the 'Stuka'

saw it gaining more power and better protection, but it was never to overcome its vulnerability to fighters.

*Below: The 'Stuka' was a good ground-attack aircraft, but its success was totally dependent on having air cover. Enemy fighters found the Ju 87 very easy prey as it lacked armament and speed.*

*Above: The Ju 87's gun packs were a powerful weapon, but the drag further reduced the aircraft's speed.*

## Ju 87D-1 'Stuka'

**Type:** two-seat dive-bomber/attack aircraft

**Powerplant:** one 1051-kW (1,410-hp.) Junkers Jumo 211J-1 12-cylinder inverted Vee piston engine

**Maximum speed:** 410 km/h (254 m.p.h.) at 3840 m (12,600 ft.)

**Range:** 1535 km (950 mi.)

**Service ceiling:** 7290 m (23,910 ft.)

**Weights:** empty equipped 3900 kg (8,580 lb.); maximum take-off 6600 kg (14,520 lb.)

**Armament:** 7.92-mm (0.31-in.) MG 17 machine-guns in wings and two 7.92-mm MG 81Z guns in rear cockpit, plus up to 1800 kg (3,960 lb.) of bombs beneath fuselage, or alternate underfuselage/underwing loads

**Dimensions:**
| | |
|---|---|
| span | 13.80 m (45 ft.) |
| length | 11.50 m (38 ft.) |
| height | 3.90 m (13 ft.) |
| wing area | 31.90 m² (343 sq. ft.) |

The Ju 87 was also armed with two forward-firing cannon or machine-guns, which were useful in suppressing return fire from the ground.

The 'Stuka' featured a cranked-wing design so that the undercarriage could be short and strong while having enough room to carry a large bomb under the fuselage.

## Ju 87G 'Stuka'

This 'Stuka' was flown by SG.3 in the USSR during spring 1944, commanded by Major Theo Nordmann. He flew over 1200 combat missions in Ju 87s.

Defensive armament was one or two machine-guns, usually insufficient to ward off fighters.

The original tail was a twin-fin arrangement, but this was replaced by a single fin after the early prototypes.

The Ju 87G was powered by the Junkers Jumo 211 engine. The marking on the cowling is a 'kill' badge. The Jumo also powered the Ju 88 and Heinkel 111.

The cannon were modified 37-mm (1.47-in.) Flak 18 guns. In the hands of an expert like Theo Nordmann the Ju 87's fire was lethal.

The 'Stuka' was designed for mass production, with the fuselage being made in two halves joined along the aircraft's centreline by a metal frame.

**1 OVERHEAD:** The 'Stuka' began its attack by flying straight and level until it was nearly over the target.

**2 ROLL AND PULL:** Just short of the target the pilot performed a half roll and then pulled back on the stick, putting the aircraft in a near vertical dive.

**3 STEEP AND PULL:** During the dive the pilot used his ailerons to keep the aircraft aligned on the target. The divebrakes automatically set up the dive at the correct angle.

**4 SIREN SCREAM:** A wind-driven siren was mounted on the undercarriage leg, releasing a terrifying wail during the dive to heighten the psychological effect of the attack.

## Dive-bombing attack

**PRECISION STRIKE:** Dive-bombing is lethally accurate. The pilots would begin a dive from about 2000 m (6,000 ft.) or less, releasing their bombs from as low as 300 m (900 ft.). Diving at an angle of between 60° and vertical, the pilot looked down at exactly where the bomb would hit. Because of this, 'Stuka' crews often dropped a bomb within a few metres of their target, or even scored direct hits. The final pull-out from the dive was a vulnerable moment.

**5 AUTOMATIC PULL-OUT:** With the bombs released, an automatic recovery system pulled the 'Stuka' out of its near-vertical dive. The system used a contact altimeter and was activated by the pilot by means of a stick-mounted knob. Pull-out was usually accomplished at 6g.

# JUNKERS
# Ju 88

● Fast bomber ● Night-fighter ● Multi-role aircraft

**T**he Junkers Ju 88A was one of the most versatile warplanes in history. No match for a fighter in a dogfight, it could nevertheless perform just about every other military mission. Ju 88s were employed as bombers, escort fighters, night-fighters, tank busters, torpedo-bombers, transports and reconnaissance platforms, and in many other roles. Fast, tough and reliable, by the middle of World War II it had become the Luftwaffe's most important tactical bomber.

▲ *Luftwaffe crews liked the Ju 88A because of its toughness and speed. As enemy fighters became faster, the aircraft mounted more guns and armour. As a heavy fighter, it also carried large cannon.*

## JUNKERS Ju 88

**▲Shipping attack**
*Formations of Ju 88 bombers wreaked havoc among Allied convoys, from the Mediterranean to the Arctic.*

**◄ Field maintenance**
*Although complex, field maintenance still had to be carried out on the Ju 88. Ground crews were expected to be able to change engines anywhere, from the Steppes to the desert.*

**▼ Close quarters**
*The crew were tightly grouped in the Ju 88: good for morale, but it made them more vulnerable when the aircraft was shot at. Even so, Ju 88s were tough and often survived fighter attacks.*

**▲ Flying bomb**
*War-weary Ju 88s were used as Mistel flying bombs. The pilot sat in the fighter, flying both aircraft. He aimed the explosive-packed bomber at the target before separating and escaping.*

**▼ 'Schnell' bomber**
*Unlike their night-fighter colleagues, bomber crews did not have enough firepower. The high speed of the Ju 88A was its main defence.*

**Taxiing out ▶**
*The glazed nose of the Ju 88A gave the crew an excellent view, essential for accurate bombing. However, as with all bombers with this feature, it proved very vulnerable to head-on fighter attacks.*

## FACTS AND FIGURES

➤ The Ju 88A prototype first flew on 21 December 1936.

➤ The fifth Ju 88A set a 1000-km (620-mi.) closed-circuit record in March 1939, carrying a 2000-kg (4,100-lb.) payload at a speed of 517 km/h (320 m.p.h.).

➤ A Ju 88A was used as a flying testbed for one of the first jet engines.

➤ The ultimate Ju 88S bombers had a top speed of more than 600 km/h (370 m.p.h.).

➤ Total production of bomber and reconnaissance versions of the Ju 88 is estimated at 10,774.

# PROFILE

# Mainstay of the Luftwaffe

Brought into service after the invasion of Poland, the Ju 88 was one of the few bombers used in Germany's attack on Britain which stood much chance of getting away from a fighter. But the Ju 88 was more than a survivor. Fighting in all conditions from the desert to the Arctic, it proved itself in combat roles as diverse as reconnaissance and night-fighting.

Even when Germany had all but lost the war, Ju 88 bombers were still flying lone-wolf raids against English cities. Endurance, performance and a wealth of new electronic gadgetry made fighter and bomber variants of the Ju 88 tremendously successful.

In its ability to fly and fight, the Ju 88 was the best ship in its class. Most Ju 88s had a four-man crew in a cramped flight compartment, more men than needed in a craft of this size. Even three-man versions were far from comfortable, but the Ju 88 had plenty of power and was responsive enough in almost any situation.

*The Ju 88A-V7 was yet another special version. The prototype of the Ju 88 fighter, it was later converted as a high-speed communications aircraft.*

### Ju 88A-4

**Type:** four-seat medium- and dive-bomber

**Powerplant:** two 1000-kW (1,200-hp.) Junkers Jumo 211J 12-cylinder liquid-cooled engines

**Maximum speed:** 440 km/h (280 m.p.h.)

**Range:** 1800 km (1,200 mi.)

**Service ceiling:** 8200 m (27,000 ft.)

**Weight:** empty 8000 kg (17,600 lb.); loaded 14,000 kg (31,000 lb.)

**Armament:** two 13-mm (0.51-in.) machine-guns, four 7.92-mm (0.31-in.) machine-guns and 3000 kg (6,600 lb.) of bombs

**Dimensions:**
| | | |
|---|---|---|
| span | 20.13 m | (60 ft. 3 in.) |
| length | 14.40 m | (47 ft. 1 in.) |
| height | 4.85 m | (17 ft. 6 in.) |
| wing area | 54.50 m² | (587 sq. ft.) |

## Ju 88A-1

The bomber versions of the Ju 88A served in all theatres of the war, scoring many successes, including hitting the British carrier HMS *Ark Royal* in the Mediterranean.

Ju 88 bombers generally had a crew of four: pilot, bombardier, flight engineer and radio operator.

Early Ju 88As were powered by Jumo 211 radial engines, although some variants had more powerful BMW 801s.

The Ju 88A used stressed-skin manufacturing techniques new to Junkers, which had specialised in ugly but functional corrugated-skin machines.

The wing had two main spars and, like the fuselage, was covered in flush-riveted stressed aluminium.

The Ju 88A was originally designed to be capable of dive-bombing attacks, and the wing carried slatted divebrakes as well as bomb racks.

The fuselage was all metal, the aluminium stressed skin being riveted directly onto the oval-section fuselage structure.

The ventral gondola carried a machine-gun and was fired by the radio operator when needed.

The landing gear retracted backwards. The main wheels swivelled through 90° on retraction so that they lay flat and fitted easily into the thin wing.

The small weapons bay could only hold 500 kg (1,100 lb.) of bombs, but external racks increased the possible load to 3000 kg (6,600 lb.).

---

## COMBAT DATA

### MAXIMUM SPEED

| | |
|---|---|
| Ju 88A-4 | 440 km/h (280 m.p.h.) |
| B-25C MITCHELL | 460 km/h (286 m.p.h.) |
| G4M1 'BETTY' | 428 km/h (264 m.p.h.) |

Although considered very fast when first flown, the twin-engined bombers in development at the start of World War II were soon outclassed by new generations of fighters. They still managed a fair turn of speed, however.

### RANGE

Ju 88A-4 1800 km (1,200 mi.)

B-25C MITCHELL 2400 km (1,500 mi.)

G4M1 'BETTY' 5000 km (3,100 mi.)

Japanese bombers were designed for operations across the vast reaches of the Pacific, while German machines were designed to support the army, never being too far from a forward operating base.

### DEFENSIVE ARMAMENT

| Ju 88A-4 | B-25C MITCHELL | G4M1 'BETTY' |
|---|---|---|
| 2 x 13-mm (0.51-in.) MGs | 4 x 12.7-mm (.50 cal.) MGs | 1 x 20-mm (0.79-in.) cannon |
| 4 x 7.92-mm (0.31-in.) MGs | 3 x 7.62-mm (.30 cal.) MGs | 3 x 7.7-mm (.303 cal.) MGs |

All the bombers which relied on speed as a defence were found wanting when this proved not to be enough. With its crew in close proximity in a very small cabin, it was particularly difficult to up-gun the Ju 88.

---

## Arctic attack

The Allied convoys taking badly-needed supplies to Russia ran a gauntlet of attacks. One of the most effective weapons in the Luftwaffe's armoury was the torpedo-armed Ju 88. Based at airfields in northern Norway, Ju 88s sank thousands of tons of British shipping in icy-cold Arctic waters.

■ **TORPEDO BOMBING:** (Right) The Ju 88s of Kampfgeschwader 30 mounted mass attacks on convoys, with as many as 12 aircraft flying in line abreast releasing torpedoes.

■ **NORTHERN CONVOYS:** (Left) The convoy route to Russia took Allied merchant ships into the high Arctic. In summer, the midnight sun north of the Arctic Circle meant that they were vulnerable to air attack 24 hours a day.

# JUNKERS
# Ju 90/290

● Airliner derivative ● Long-range maritime patrol ● Transport

**A**fter its Ju 89 bomber was cancelled, Junkers was keen to gain something from the effort expended on the aircraft. By mating a new fuselage with the Ju 89's wings, a new transport aircraft, known as the Ju 90, was produced. Further development of this design led to the Ju 290 maritime reconnaissance aircraft and, ultimately, to the giant, six-engined Ju 390 which flew to within 20 km (12 mi.) of the US coast.

▲ Both the Ju 290 and Ju 90 gave good service with the Luftwaffe, at a time when the force was stretched to its limits and suitable aircraft were in desperately short supply.

## JUNKERS Ju 90/290

**▲ Germany's largest**
The Ju 390 V2 was the second of only two aircraft completed, and remains the largest conventional aircraft to be built in Germany.

**▲ US missile launcher**
This rare Ju 290A-7 was evaluated in America after the war. The variant introduced a glazed nose and the ability to launch guided anti-ship missiles.

**▲ Henschel 293 and Fritz X**
If more Ju 290A-7s, with their Henschel Hs 293, 294 and Fritz X missiles and Hohentwiel radar, had been delivered, they would have made a powerful anti-shipping force.

**▲ Airliner origins – Ju 90 V1**
With World War II imminent, Junkers was not allowed to use the strategically important Jumo 211 or DB 600 engines that had been tested on the prototypes.

**Transport to maritime reconnaissance ▶**
Defensive armament was introduced on the Ju 90 V8, which led to development of the Ju 90 V11. This was redesignated the Ju 290 V1.

## FACTS AND FIGURES

➤ D-AALU, the first Ju 90 V1 prototype, was lost in an accident during February 1938; V3 was lost later that year.

➤ Two Ju 290A-0s and five Ju 290A-1s were used in the relief of Stalingrad.

➤ Operations over the Atlantic began with 1./FAGr 5 on 15 October 1943.

➤ South African Airways aircraft would have been powered by Pratt & Whitney Twin Wasp engines.

➤ Three Ju 290A-5s, stripped of equipment, were used on transport missions to Japan.

➤ The Ju 290A-6 may have carried escaping Nazi leaders to Spain in April 1945.

## PROFILE

# Junkers giant on patrol

Lufthansa ordered eight Ju 90s and South African Airways a further two aircraft, but all were impressed into Luftwaffe squadrons. In 1940 work started on a new version, designated Ju 290, which was bigger than the original. It was to be built in both transport and maritime reconnaissance versions.

The Ju 290A-0 and A-1 transport aircraft were immediately put into service since the Luftwaffe was desperately short of transport capacity. The A-2 to A-5 variants were maritime reconnaissance models, and the A-6 was intended as a transport for the personal use of Adolf Hitler. The A-7 and A-8 were to be missile-armed anti-ship aircraft.

About 40 Ju 290s were built, nearly half of them by Letov in Czechoslovakia. Maritime versions were based in southwest France and used to locate Atlantic convoys for the German U-boats. The Ju 290A-6 was completed as a 50-seat VIP transport. It flew to Barcelona in April 1945 and later served with the Spanish air force until the mid-1950s. Ju 290B, D and E bomber variants, the C transport/reconnaissance aircraft and the MS mine-clearer were all abandoned during the final years of the war.

Restricted to low-powered engines, Junkers set about redesigning the Ju 90 to give improved performance using the available power. New features were incorporated into the Ju 90 V4, an aircraft which also introduced the twin-wheel undercarriage and Trapoklappe ramp of the Ju 290.

*Eleven Ju 290A-5s were built, making this the most common sub-type. The antennas of the Hohentwiel system can be clearly seen on the nose of this aircraft.*

### Ju 290A-5

**Type:** long-range maritime reconnaissance aircraft

**Powerplant:** four 1268-kW (1,700-hp.) BMW 801D 14-cylinder air-cooled radial engines

**Maximum speed:** 440 km/h (273 m.p.h.) at 5800 m (19,000 ft.)

**Initial climb rate:** 1850 m (6,070 ft.) in 9.8 min

**Range:** 6150 km (3,813 mi.)

**Service ceiling:** 6000 m (19,700 ft.)

**Weights:** normal loaded 40,970 kg (90,134 lb.); maximum take-off 44,970 kg (98,934 lb.)

**Armament:** one 20-mm (0.79-in.) MG 151 cannon in each of two dorsal turrets, the tail position, each waist position and the ventral gondola, plus one 13-mm (0.51-in.) machine-gun in the rear of the gondola

**Dimensions:**
| | |
|---|---|
| span | 42.00 m (137 ft. 8 in.) |
| length | 28.64 m (93 ft. 11 in.) |
| height | 6.83 m (22 ft. 5 in.) |
| wing area | 203.6 m² (2,213 sq. ft.) |

### Ju 290A-5

**Fernaufklärungsgruppe 5, with its force of no greater than 20 aircraft flying from Mont-de-Marsan, France, in 1944, constantly struggled to fulfil its commitments.**

The Ju 90, with its BMW 123 radials, had been underpowered, and so the Ju 290 was fitted with the 1268-kW (1,700 hp.) BMW 801D.

Being a large, heavy aircraft, the Ju 290 required a substantial undercarriage. When the Ju 390 was produced by adding extra sections to the wings and fuselage of the Ju 290, two extra main undercarriage units were added.

All aircraft from the Ju 90 V11 onwards had these distinctive angular fins. New windows and a redesigned wing were also introduced on this aircraft.

Using its nose-mounted FuG 200 search radar, the A-5 was able to detect a convoy at a distance of 80 km (50 mi.) from an altitude of 500 m (1,650 ft.), or at 100 km (60 mi.) from 1000 m (3,300 ft.). The aircraft would remain on station until it was relieved by another Ju 290.

The otherwise vulnerable underside of the aircraft was protected by a single, forwards-firing MG 151 cannon and a rearwards-firing MG 131 machine-gun. Both were mounted in the ventral gondola, which was offset to port.

All Ju 290A series aircraft retained the Trapoklappe. This was a hydraulically actuated ramp set into the underside of the rear fuselage. It could be opened in flight for paratrooping and was able to lift the aircraft into a horizontal position for easy loading when on the ground.

## A multitude of roles

■ **Ju 90B-1:** Two or three of the 10 production Ju 90B-1 airliners, in spurious Iraqi markings, were used by the Luftwaffe to ferry personnel and equipment to Iraq. Before the war the aircraft had belonged to Lufthansa.

■ **Ju 290A-5:** Typical of the most numerous variant, this A-5 shows the type's powerful defensive armament, which was improved as a result of operational experience with the A-4. The A-5 also introduced armour protection and fuel-dumping facilities.

■ **Ju 290A-6:** By 1945 all surviving Ju 290s were being used for agent-dropping and clandestine transport missions by KG 200. The single A-6, which was designed as a personal transport for Hitler, was in fact only used by this unit.

### COMBAT DATA

**RANGE**

The Ju 290's very long range was principal among the aircraft's excellent qualities. In addition to giving the aircraft a useful transport capability, long range also allowed crews to stay on station for extended periods at considerable distances from base when directing U-boats on to a convoy.

PB4Y-1 LIBERATOR 4764 km (3,207 mi.)
Ju 290A-5 6150 km (3,813 mi.)
Fw 200C-3/44 3560 km (2,953 mi.)

# JUNKERS

# Ju 188

● High-altitude reconnaissance bomber ● Ju 88 development

▲ A victim of the success of the Ju 88, the Ju 188 failed to be produced in sufficient numbers to have a significant effect on the Luftwaffe's fortunes. In fact, this was potentially a very effective aircraft, preferred by crews for its superior handling at high weights, its only real weakness being a lack of armament.

**G**ermany's air ministry (RLM) issued the 'Bomber B' requirement for a twin-engined replacement for the the He 111 and Ju 88 in 1939. Junkers' candidate was the Ju 288, a radical development of its earlier bomber design that was making its mark in the early years of the war in Europe. However, by late 1942, the ill-fated Ju 288 design was hopelessly delayed, leaving the Lutfwaffe with a need to urgently fill the bomber requirement. This paved the way for the more conventional Ju 188.

## JUNKERS Ju 188

### Captured Ju 388 high-altitude bomber ▶
This Ju 388K-0, captured in 1945, was extensively tested by the British Royal Aircraft Establishment until it was placed on display in 1948.

### ▼ SNCASE-built Ju 188
Based on a BMW 801-powered Ju 188F-1 reconnaissance variant, this is the third example of about a dozen Ju 188Es and Fs built by SNCASE for the French Aéronavale after 1945. Employed as the service's chief land-based bombers, these aircraft joined 30 ex-Luftwaffe Ju 188s.

### ▲ Reconnaissance Ju 188F-1
Over half the Ju 188s completed were for reconnaissance duties. Ju 188s were able to make better use of the power of the BMW 801 and Jumo 213 than was the Ju 88.

### ◀ Abandoned by retreating Luftwaffe
This was the sad fate of many unserviceable Ju 188s, caught by the advancing Allies. If not wrecked by retreating Germans, they were 'shot-up' by the Allied armies.

### Torpedo-bomber with Hohentwiel radar ▶
Sporting the distinctive arrays associated with the FuG 200 maritime search radar, this Ju 188E-2 torpedo-bomber also has the starboard fuselage bulge housing torpedo steering adjustment gear.

## FACTS AND FIGURES

➤ At least 30 ex-Luftwaffe and 12 SNCASE-built Ju 188Es and Fs were used by the the French Aéronavale after World War II.

➤ Ju 188s gained a reputation with crews for good handling.

➤ Ju 188R was a night-fighter version that failed to progress past evaluation.

➤ Fast high-altitude intruder Ju 188S and reconnaissance Ju 188T variants were proposed, giving rise to the Ju 388.

➤ At least one Ju 188E was converted to a fast staff transport for senior personnel.

➤ A remotely-controlled tail barbette was trialled in a Ju 188C, but was inaccurate.

**PROFILE**

# Ju 88 successor with unrealised potential

Official development of the Ju 88 had been effectively frozen for more than three years, although Junkers had continued trials with the Ju 88E-0 on a low-priority basis.

The first true Ju 188 (Ju 188 V1) was the Ju 88 prototype V44, a Ju 88E airframe with a new dorsal turret and 13-mm (0.51-in.) machine-gun, extended wingtips and a square tail fin. By January 1943, a second aircraft, Ju 188 V2, was under test. Production aircraft would be powered by Jumo 213 in-line or BMW 801 radial engines.

On 18 August 1943, French-based Ju 188s flew their first sortie, pathfinding for a bombing raid over northern England. By the end of 1943, 283 had been accepted by the Luftwaffe. In January 1944, 188s took part in Operation Steinbock, Germany's retaliatory 400-bomber raid on London.

The BMW-engined Ju 188Es (some of which were fitted with dive brakes) and Jumo-powered Ju 188As (which also sported a dorsal cannon in place of the machine-gun, and MW50 engine power boosting) were the initial variants – medium bombers with a 3000-kg (6,600-lb.) bombload.

However, 570 of the 1076 Ju 188s built were 188D and F reconnaissance marks. Some were fitted with FuG 200 radar for the maritime role, these aircraft seeing action in Russia and Scandinavia, often in concert with Ju 188A-3 and E-2 torpedo-bombers.

*Ju 188D-2s of 1.(F)/124 at Kirkenes in Arctic Norway. The nearest aircraft appears to have had its FuG 200 Hohentwiel radar removed.*

## Ju 188D-2

Serving with 1.Fernaufklärungsgruppe 124 at Kirkenes, Norway, was one of 17 Staffeln equipped with Ju 188D and F reconnaissance versions. 1.(F)/124 often provided sighting reports for III./KG 26 Ju 188A-3 torpedo-bombers.

### Ju 188D-2

**Type:** maritime reconnaissance/strike aircraft

**Powerplant:** two 1268-kW (1,700-hp.) (for take-off; 1671 kW/2,240 hp. with MW50 injection) Junkers Jumo 213A-1 12-cylinder inline engines

**Maximum speed:** 539 km/h (334 m.p.h.) at 6096 m (20,000 ft.)

**Range:** 3395 km (2,100 mi.) at 6096 m (20,000 ft.) with drop tanks

**Service ceiling:** 10,000 m (32,800 ft.)

**Weights:** empty 9900 kg (21,780 lb.); maximum loaded 15,195 kg (33,430 lb.)

**Armament:** one 20-mm (0.79-in.) MG 151 cannon in dorsal turret; one 13-mm (0.51-in.) MG 131 machine-gun in the rear cockpit; one 7.9-mm (0.31-in.) MG 81z twin machine-gun in ventral step, plus various camera fits for day and night missions.

**Dimensions:**
span 22.00 m (72 ft. 2 in.)
length 14.95 m (49 ft.)
height 4.44 m (14 ft. 7 in.)
wing area 56.00 m² (603 sq. ft.)

Luftwaffe Ju 188s suffered throughout World War II from a lack of defensive armament, the extreme rear of the aircraft being perhaps the most vulnerable. On reconnaissance variants, the redundant bomb bay could be fitted with an extra fuel tank.

MW50 methanol-water injection for the engines and extended wing tips gave improved altitude performance. Initially, the latter feature led to the aircraft being confused with the RAF's Mosquito.

Four hardpoints under the wing centre-section, available for two torpedoes on the Ju 188A-3 and E-2 variants, were often fitted with external fuel tanks on reconnaissance machines.

Unlike the four-man medium bomber variants, the Ju 188D-2 had only three crew – pilot, flight engineer and radar/wireless operator. The forward-firing 20-mm (0.79-in.) MG 151 cannon was also deleted from the cockpit. Intended for the maritime role, the Ju 188D-2 and BMW 801-engined Ju 188F-2 were equipped with FuG 200 search radar.

From the outset, the RLM demanded that the Ju 188 be able to accept either Jumo 213 liquid-cooled 12-cylinder or BMW 801 14-cylinder radial engine assemblies, or 'power eggs', interchangeably on the production line, minimising the effect of fluctuations in engine availability.

This aircraft carries a pale blue-grey *Wellenmüster* sprayed over the standard green camouflage scheme. *Balkenkrauz* and *Hakenkreuz* national markings are applied in outline form.

### COMBAT DATA

**MAXIMUM SPEED AT ALTITUDE**

Though endowed with good high-altitude speed, the Ju 188D-2 was still no match for the RAF's de Havilland Mosquito. However, the Arado Ar 234 reconnaissance jet was unbeatable.

Ju 188D-2   539 km/h (334 m.p.h.)
Ar 234B-2/b   742 km/h (460 m.p.h.)
MOSQUITO PR.Mk 34   684 km/h (424 m.p.h.)

**RANGE**

PR Mosquitos had excellent range performance, to match their speed. Although fast, the Ar 234 was, like many early jet designs, short on range. All three designs were also developed in the long-range bombing role.

Ju 188D-2 3395 km (2,100 mi.)
Ar 234B-2/b 1630 km (1,000 mi.)
MOSQUITO PR.Mk 34 5633 km (3,500 mi.)

---

## Junkers Ju 88 bomber family

**Ju 88:** There were few roles for which the Luftwaffe's Ju 88s were not adapted during World War II. More than 14,500 were built and carried out many tasks from bombing to tank-busting and night-fighting. The prototype flew in 1936.

**Ju 288:** The RLM's 'Bomber B' requirement called for a medium bomber able to take a 4000-kg (8,800 lb.) load at 600 km/h (370 m.p.h.) to Britain from anywhere in France or Norway. Unlike the Ju 188, 388 and 488, the ill-fated 288 was an entirely new design.

**Ju 388:** A high-altitude reconnaissance and bomber development of the Ju 188, the Ju 388 featured a pressurised cockpit section and boosted engines. Ju 388K bombers had a tail gun barbette. None entered service.

**Ju 488:** By 1944, the Luftwaffe was still without a reliable strategic bomber. Junkers suggested the quick production of the four-engined Ju 488 using existing tooling and components from the Ju 188, 288 and 388. None had flown by VE-Day.

# JUNKERS

# Ju 287

● Jet-powered bomber ● Forward-swept wing ● Only two built

▲ Again German
engineers had demonstrated their
innovation during the 1940s with an
unorthodox aircraft. Captured in 1945, the
new technology was tested in the USSR
post-war.

**A**mong a number of far-sighted designs initiated by the Luftwaffe during World War II, the Junkers Ju 287 was one of the most radical. It featured not only turbojet propulsion, but also a forward-swept wing. The wing was intended to alleviate the low-speed handling problems inherent in conventionally swept designs. The Luftwaffe wanted a high-speed bomber immune from Allied interception, but the Ju 287 came too late.

## JUNKERS Ju 287

▼ In flight
Seen here during trials in 1944,
Ju 287 V1 was a highly
unconventional aircraft for its day
and remained unique as an FSW
aircraft with podded engines.

▲ Ungainly prototype
Constructed from the components of a number of
different aircraft types and fitted with a fixed
undercarriage, Ju 287 V1 lacked finesse.

▼ Under construction
Ju 187 V1 nears completion at the Dessau factory
in the early summer of 1944.

▼ Forward-facing camera
A camera was fitted to a tripod in front of the tail
fin to record the aircraft's behaviour.

◄ Rocket boosters
A Walter 501 jettisonable rocket
booster was fitted beneath each
turbojet engine nacelle to assist
take-off. The low power of early jet
engines hampered development.

## FACTS AND FIGURES

➤ Post-war, Hans Wocke designed the HFB 320 Hansa business jet with forward-swept wings.

➤ A low-speed test aircraft, Ju 287 V1 still achieved speeds of 650 km/h (400 m.p.h.).

➤ Ju 287 V1 was badly damaged by Allied bombing in late 1944 or early 1945.

➤ After VE-Day, Ju 287s V1 and V2 were shipped to the Soviet Union, where the latter flew in 1947.

➤ Successive Ju 287 models were to have more, less powerful engines.

➤ Some sources say that Ju 287 V2 flew in the USSR with conventional swept wings.

# PROFILE

# Junkers' unorthodox jet bomber

Only one Ju 287 was completed and flown before the end of World War II – a prototype designated Ju 287 V1. Originally, Junkers designer Hans Wocke intended to build a conventional swept-wing jet, of the the type that would become a common sight from the 1950s, but he found undesirable low-speed handling characteristics that appeared insurmountable.

Wocke then proposed to reverse the wing configuration. This presented its own problems (including impaired control responses at higher speeds), but Wocke felt sure that they could be resolved. Ju 287 V1 first flew on 16 August 1944, powered by four 8.82-kN (1,984-lb.-thrust) Jumo 004B-1 turbojets. A testbed for the new wing, it consisted of a Heinkel He 177A fuselage with a Junkers Ju 388 tail and fixed tricycle undercarriage.

A further 16 flights were made, the aircraft exhibiting good flying characteristics. A high-speed prototype, Ju 287 V2, was ordered, but, as Germany urgently needed fighters, work was suspended.

However, a production prototype (Ju 287 V3) was ordered in early 1945. This and the second aircraft featured six BMW engines and retractable undercarriage. In addition, Ju 287 V3 would have had a pressure cabin and a bomb bay for 4000 kg (8,800 lb.) of bombs. The Junkers factory was overrun before either V2 or V3 had ever flown.

Two of the prototype's four engines were unusually mounted either side of the forward fuselage. Ju 287 V2 and V3 were to be powered by six wing-mounted BMW engines.

Defensive armament for Ju 287 V1 was restricted to a pair of remotely-controlled MG 131 13-mm machine-guns in the tail barbette.

Delays in the development of the intended engines meant that Ju 287 V2 and V3 were to have their six smaller engines, attached in two groups of three under the wings.

## Ju 287 V1

On 16 August 1944 the Ju 287 prototype (RS+RA) took to the air for the first time. Another 16 flights were made from Brandis before it was moved to Rechlin, where it was damaged in an Allied air raid.

Like the V1 prototype, the Ju 287A-0 (as the first production examples were to be known) would have featured a fully glazed nose for the crew of three.

The need for wing structural integrity during testing led to the use of fixed undercarriage on Ju 287 V1. Ju 287 V3 and subsequent aircraft were to have retractable gear.

Construction of production prototype V3 had begun by the time the war in Europe had ended. Its fuselage was essentially that of the aborted Ju 388 bomber, with a pressurised cabin and a more up-swept tail.

Fixed nose gear on the Ju 287 V1 was supported by nose wheels salvaged from a USAAF Consolidated B-24 Liberator and enclosed in a large fairing.

The main gear was fixed and shrouded in large fairings. Braced to the forward wing spars, it employed wheels designed for the Ju 352 transport.

A recessed wheel in the rear fuselage was a feature of Ju 287 V1. It was designed to prevent damage to the aircraft should the tail touch the ground during rotation.

## World War II Junkers projects

■ **Ju 252:** Designed for Deutsche Lufthansa in 1939, the Ju 252 was intended to replace the Ju 52/3m. A few were built for the Luftwaffe.

■ **Ju 288:** Though nominally related to the Ju 88, the Ju 288 was a new medium bomber design. Development snags led to cancellation.

■ **Ju 290:** The Ju 290 can trace its origins to the pre-war Ju 89 bomber. Derived from the Ju 90 airliner, it was adapted for maritime patrol.

■ **Ju 388:** Derived from the Ju 188, the Ju 388 was a produced in small numbers as a high-altitude reconnaissance aircraft.

# JUNKERS

# JU 322 MAMMUT

● Giant glider ● Flying wing ● Only one flown

▲ The Junkers Ju 49 monoplane was developed in 1927-28 for high altitude experiments. It claimed the world height record in 1929, reaching an altitude of 12735 m (41,770 ft.).

A mong the transport aircraft types to enter Luftwaffe service during World War II, the Ju 52/3m was the best known. Other Junkers transport designs to see service included the Ju 160 single-engined, high-speed airliner, the Ju 252 pressurised tri-motored airliner and the even bigger Ju 352. The Ju 352 was built mainly of wood, a feature shared with the most bizarre of the Junkers wartime transports, the Ju 322 Mammut glider.

## JUNKERS JU 322 MAMMUT

▼ High-altitude testplane
In 1936 Junkers developed the EF 61 research aircraft. It provided valuable data for the Ju 86P and Ju 86R reconnaissance aircraft.

▲ Parasol design
Developed from the H.21 of the early 1920s, the Junkers H.22 was a single-seat parasol design with unusual undercarriage fairings.

◄ Rare bird
Only one Ju 322 flew and it made just a few flights. This is believed to be the only existing picture of the Ju 322.

Wartime trainer ►
Developed in 1933-34 from the Ju 60 high-speed airliner, the Ju 160 was used by the Luftwaffe for communication/training.

▼ Tri-engined transporter
The Ju 252 was built to replace the Ju 52/3m in Lufthansa service; 15 were used by the Luftwaffe for transport duties.

## FACTS AND FIGURES

➤ Intended loads for the Ju 322 included 100 fully-equipped troops, a PzKw IV tank, or a towed 8.8-cm gun with crew.

➤ Two Ju 322s were completed; 98 production examples had been ordered.

➤ In all, 45 million Reichsmarks were spent on the unsuccessful Mammut project.

➤ For its first flight, Ju 322 V1 was towed aloft on an 8000-kg (17,600-lb.) trolley. When released, it disintegrated on impact.

➤ After cancellation, Ju 322s were used as fuel for wood-burning vehicles.

➤ The Ju 322 was based on the earlier Junkers G.38 and EF 94 designs.

**PROFILE**

# Junkers' mighty Mammoth

The Mammut (Mammoth) was built to the same specification as the Me 321, but was of all-wood construction. Both designs were required to deliver a 20-tonne load during the planned airborne assault on Britain.

The Ju 322 was effectively a 'flying wing' design. Its short fuselage supported only the tailplane, the bulk of the glider's payload being carried inside the wing. The use of wood caused a number of problems, not least of which was Junkers' inexperience with the material.

Sub-standard and rotten timber and defective glue meant that the airframe lacked sufficient strength; by the time the Ju 322 V1 prototype flew in April 1941, its design payload had slipped to 16 tonnes, then 11. The second payload reduction was necessitated by the need to strengthen the aircraft's cargo floor after a PzKw IV tank fell through it during loading trials.

On its first flight, towed by a Ju 90, the Mammut was unstable and began to climb above the tug aircraft. As the climbing Mammut began to pull the

The Mammut was basically a 'flying wing' with a rear fuselage section to carry the tail surfaces. The wing was of multi-spar wooden construction.

Ju 90's tail alarmingly upwards, the glider's pilot was fortunately able quickly to release the tow line and avert disaster. Though the Ju 322 made a perfect landing, modifications were carried out and further trials flown, the overwhelming weaknesses of the design led to development being abandoned in May 1941.

## EF 94

**The Junkers Ju 322 was largely based on the EF 94 project which never reached flying status, but would have looked something like this in service. The Ju 322 featured a revised armament.**

The pilot's cockpit was a raised, glazed gondola which was offset to the port side. The pilot had excellent forward vision from this raised position which would have been vital for landing in small fields.

The EF 94, like the Ju 322, was fitted with three turrets, each containing a single 7.9-mm machine gun. The turrets fitted to the wings of the EF 94 were moved forward to the front of the fuselage section on the Ju 322.

Although the tail surfaces on the EF 94 appear large, the surfaces on the final Ju 322 were actually quite small for an aircraft of this size. After the near-disastrous first flight the vertical tail surfaces were enlarged to improve stability.

The cargo hold was to carry a payload of 20000 kg (40,000 lb.). After a weakness in the main spar was recognised, this was reduced to 11000 kg (22,000 lb.).

The outer panels of the wing had dihedral on their undersides. The swollen centre-section formed the cargo hold and had a detachable leading edge for the loading of cargo.

For take-off a large jettisonable trolley constructed of lattice girders with eight pairs of wheels was to be used. Beneath the centre-section were four steel-sprung landing skids.

### Ju 322 V1 Mammut

**Type:** high-capacity experimental transport glider

**Glide angle:** 1:50

**Payload:** 11000 kg (22,000 lb.)

**Armament:** production versions were to receive three turrets each mounting a single 7.9-mm MG 15 machine gun

**Dimensions:** span 62.00 m (203 ft. 4 in.)
length 30.25 m (99 ft. 3 in.)
wing area 925 m² (9,953 sq. ft.)

*Above: Two prototypes of the EF 61 were constructed and were used in the development of pressurised cabins and turrets. They were powered by two Daimler-Benz DB 600 engines.*

### COMBAT DATA

**PAYLOAD**

Designed to the same specification, the Me 321 and the Ju 322 were to have had similar payloads. However, structural deficiencies with the Ju 322 reduced the payload by 45 per cent. British gliders such as the Horsa were much smaller and carried far less.

Ju 322 MAMMUT 11000 kg (22,000 lb.)  Me 321 GIGANT 21000 kg (46,200 lb.)  AS 58 HORSA 3200 kg (7,040 lb.)

**WINGSPAN**

With its 'flying wing' layout, the Ju 322 had a massive wingspan and wing area. This provided a tremendous amount of lift, allowing large loads to be carried. The Horsa with its smaller dimensions was able to use smaller landing grounds than the larger German gliders.

Ju 322 MAMMUT 62.00 m (203 ft. 4 in.)  Me 321 GIGANT 55.00 m (180 ft. 5 in.)  AS 58 HORSA 26.82 m (87 ft. 11 in.)

## German gliders of World War II

**BLOHM UND VOSS BV 40:** With a pilot in the prone position and heavy cockpit armour, the BV 40 was designed as a fighter and intended to make diving head-on attacks.

**DFS 331:** Designed during 1940, only one example of this cargo glider was flown. The cockpit was positioned on a raised platform to allow a large cargo door on the port side.

**GOTHA Go 242:** The only aircraft produced by Gotha to see large-scale service in World War II, the Go 242 was a successful assault glider. In all, 1528 examples were produced.

**MESSERSCHMITT Me 321 GIGANT:** This high-capacity, high-wing transport glider was usually towed by either a single Junkers Ju 290A-1 or a trio of Messerschmitt Bf 110Cs.

# KAWANISHI

# H6K 'MAVIS'

● Maritime reconnaissance/bomber ● Long range ● Transport

I t was a Japanese navy need for an aircraft which could cover the vast expanses of the Pacific that inspired Kawanishi to design the 'Mavis'. Powered by four engines, the H6K, first flown in July 1936, was one of the most reliable and efficient of the flying-boats used by Japan during World War II. It also had a very long range and an endurance of more than 24 hours, making it ideally suited to long overwater missions.

▲ Although the 'Mavis'
was undoubtedly one of the finest World War II flying-boats, it was notoriously difficult to service. Large platforms were erected by engineers for engine maintenance.

▼ **Allied evaluation**
*Many Japanese aircraft were captured as the Allies overran Japanese bases in the Pacific. This H6K flew with the Allied Technical Air Intelligence Unit (ATAIU) which tested the capabilities of enemy types.*

▲ **Early introduction**
*In 1938 the first H6K1s entered service with the Imperial Japanese Navy after 18 months of flying and sea trials with four prototypes.*

◀ **Transport version**
*Code-named 'Tillie' by the Allies, the H6K4-L was a transport version with additional cabin windows. Armament was removed and sleeping berths were provided.*

▼ **Offensive armament**
*In the attack role, the H6K could carry two 800-kg (1,760 lb.) torpedoes or up to 1000 kg (2,200 lb.) of bombs attached to the wing-supporting struts.*

▲ **Series prototype**
*Originally named the Kawanishi Navy Experimental 9-Shi Large-size Flying-Boat, the 'Mavis' prototype was first flown on 14 July 1936, with test pilot Katsuji Kondo at the controls.*

## FACTS AND FIGURES

➤ Powered by four Nakajima Hikari engines, the prototype first flew in 1936 after three years of design work.

➤ The H6K was regarded as a success during the Sino-Japanese War of 1938–39.

➤ Total production of the H6K reached 215, of which 127 were H6K4s.

➤ As well as for maritime patrol, H6K4s were used against land targets in the Dutch East Indies during 1942.

➤ Transport versions were fitted with mail, cargo and passenger compartments.

➤ H6Ks were vulnerable to fighters as they lacked self-sealing fuel tanks and armour.

# Reconnaissance for the Imperial Fleet

The initial production model of the 'Mavis', the H6K2, had a powered turret with a single machine-gun on top of the rear fuselage, plus manually operated guns in the nose and tail. The 10 built were delivered to the Japanese navy in 1939, but were subsequently converted for use as transports.

The main version was the H6K4, which had two blisters for machine-guns on the sides of the forward fuselage. There were 66 of this model in service at the time of the attack on Pearl Harbor, and during the Japanese conquests of early 1942 they were used widely both for bombing and maritime patrol.

In 1942 the H6K5 introduced 969.4-kW (1,300-hp.) engines, but by this time the 'Mavis' was proving too vulnerable to Allied fighters, and its H8K replacement, the fastest flying-boat of the war, was already in production.

Altogether, 215 H6Ks were built before production ended in 1943. They included some 18 transports used by the Kaiyo (Ocean) division of Greater Japan Air Lines until 1945. A few survivors were used by the republican Indonesian air force during the post-war fight for independence and the civil war which followed.

*Above: The final maritime reconnaissance version was the H6K5. Fitted with more powerful Mitsubishi Kinsei 53 radial engines, this version had a turret housing a 7.7-mm (.303 cal.) machine-gun aft of the flight deck.*

*Left: As Allied fighters improved during the course of the Pacific War, the lumbering H6Ks became easy targets. This example was downed in 1944 by Lieutenant John D. Keeling of VB-109, US Naval Reserve.*

## H6K5 'MAVIS'

As the final production version, the H6K5 was fitted with more powerful engines and improved armament. This example is seen in standard Imperial Japanese Navy colours.

### H6K4 'Mavis'

**Type:** long-range reconnaissance, bomber or transport flying-boat

**Powerplant:** four 745.7-kW (1,000-hp.) Mitsubishi Kinsei 43 14-cylinder radial engines

**Maximum speed:** 340 km/h (211 m.p.h.) at 4000 m (13,125 ft.)

**Climb rate:** 5000 m (16,400 ft.) in 13 min 31 sec

**Range:** 6080 km (3,778 mi.)

**Service ceiling:** 9610 m (31,530 ft.)

**Weights:** 21,545 kg (47,499 lb.) maximum take-off

**Armament:** four 7.7-mm (.303 cal.) machine guns (one each in nose, dorsal and fuselage-side mountings) plus one 20-mm (0.79-in.) cannon in tail; two 800-kg (1,760-lb.) torpedoes or 1000 kg (2,200 lb.) of bombs

**Dimensions:** span 40.00 m (131 ft. 3 in.), length 25.63 m (84 ft. 1 in.), height 6.27 m (20 ft. 7 in.), wing area 170.00 m² (1,830 sq. ft.)

Replacing the bow gun position, a turret containing a 7.7-mm (.303 cal.) machine-gun was added immediately aft of the flight deck. This position protected the aircraft from attack from above or head-on.

The final production versions were powered by Kinsei 51 or 53 radials which were 224 kW (300 hp.) more powerful than earlier versions.

Offensive armament was mounted on the parallel wing supporting struts and consisted of bombs or two torpedoes. The beam blisters on each side of the fuselage each contained a single, hand-held 7.7-mm (.303 cal.) Type 92 machine-gun.

After studying the American Sikorsky S-42, Kawanishi designed the H6K with a slender two-step hull. The parasol wing was mounted above the fuselage and a stabilising float was fitted to each wing.

The tail turret had a large glazed section giving the gunner good visibility. Armament comprised a hand-held 20-mm (0.79-in.) Type 99 Model 1 cannon.

In earlier versions of the 'Mavis' a 7.7-mm (.303 cal.) hand-held Type 92 machine-gun was mounted in an open bow position. This was removed in the H6K5 but observation windows remained.

After the first test flight the forward step of the hull was moved 50 cm (20 in.) rearwards. This modification was successful and the H6K had the best water-handling characteristics of any World War II flying-boat.

## COMBAT DATA

**RANGE**

All three of these types were respected for their highly impressive range and endurance. The H6K was capable of remaining aloft for 24 hours and crew fatigue was often the limiting factor, rather than the endurance of the aircraft. Long range was especially important in order to cover the vast area of the Pacific theatre.

H6K4 'MAVIS' 6080 km (3,778 mi.)
PBY-5A 3782 km (2,350 mi.)
SUNDERLAND Mk V 4329 km (2,690 mi.)

## Kawanishi Seaplanes

**E7K 'ALF':** Flying anti-submarine, convoy escort and reconnaissance patrols in 1941-43, many E7K2s ended up in *kamikaze* attacks.

**E8K:** Designed in 1933 as a reconnaissance seaplane, the E8K lacked manoeuvrability and lost out to the Nakajima E8N1 biplane.

**E15K SHIUN 'NORM':** Repeated failures of the float assemblies were the main downfall of the Shiun (Violet Cloud). Only 15 were built.

**N1K KYOFU 'REX':** An ambitious design, the N1K suffered from a protracted development and only 97 of these floatplane fighters were built.

# KAWANISHI

# H8K 'EMILY'

● Long-range flying-boat ● Maritime patrol bomber

**G**iven the allied reporting name of 'Emily', the Kawanishi H8K was one of the most outstanding and advanced flying-boats to be built during World War II. Heavily armed and armoured, it had a very long range and flew superbly. Yet it was a complex machine, and the 167 examples built never fully replaced the Sikorsky-influenced H6K 'Mavis' with which the Imperial Japanese Navy had been equipped at the start of World War II.

▲ The H8K was similar to Britain's Short Sunderland in layout and role, but although the Sunderland was better known, the Japanese aircraft had superior performance. It was also far better than its Kawanishi predecessor, the H6K.

**PHOTO FILE**

## KAWANISHI **H8K** 'EMILY'

▲ **Float trials**
The initial trials of the H8K showed some flaws in handling on water, but performance was otherwise very good and it was ordered into production.

**Under attack** ▶
This 'Emily' was shot up by an A-26 over Saipan in 1944. It made a hurried forced landing after the port inner engine caught fire.

▲ **Transport**
The H8K was turned into a transport capable of carrying up to 64 passengers. Mitsubishi MK4Q engines were installed and armament was reduced.

▲ **High power**
The main advantage of the H8K over the H6K was the amount of power. Top speed was markedly higher, and take-offs were shorter and much easier.

◀ **Hitting the sea**
Attacking even a stricken 'Emily' like this could be a hazardous business because of its heavy defensive armament of 20-mm (0.79-in.) cannon.

## FACTS AND FIGURES

➤ The H8K prototype flew for the first time in January 1941.

➤ The first operational mission took place in 1942, when two aircraft set off from Wake Island to bomb Pearl Harbor.

➤ An H8K trials version was built with retractable floats and dorsal turret.

➤ Radar-equipped H8Ks sank at least three American submarines north of the Philippines in 1945.

➤ As a VIP transport the H8K could seat 29 passengers in great comfort.

➤ The 'Emily' could fly further than any other operational flying-boat of the war.

# PROFILE

# A floating flying fortress

The H8K prototype was first flown in 1941. It was designed to meet a 1938 requirement for a four-engined maritime reconnaissance flying-boat superior in all respects to the British Sunderland, then the best in the world. After modification improved the initially poor water handling qualities, the type was put into production as the Navy Type 2 Flying Boat Model 11. With armour protection, self-sealing fuel tanks, an armament that included 20-mm (0.79-in.) cannon and a maximum speed

of over 430 km/h (267 m.p.h.), it represented a great advance over previous types. The further improved H8K2 had more power, greater speed and its armament increased to five 20-mm (0.79-in.) cannon and four 7.7-mm (.303 cal.) machine-guns. This made it unquestionably one of the toughest opponents faced by the Allies in the Pacific. It was also one of the first Japanese aircraft to be fitted with anti-surface vessel radar, and achieved some success against American submarines late in the war.

*Above: With an empire stretching across thousands of kilometres of the Pacific, the Japanese needed good flying-boats urgently. This need became acute when American naval supremacy began to deny Japanese shipping access to the sea lanes.*

*Left: Equipped with radar, the 'Emily' was one of the few serious threats to the US Navy submarines which were strangling Japan's seaborne lifelines.*

## H8K2 'Emily'

**Type:** long-range maritime reconnaissance flying-boat

**Powerplant:** four 1380-kW (1,850 hp.) Mitsubishi Kasei 22 14-cylinder radial piston engines

**Maximum speed:** 467 km/h (290 m.p.h.)

**Range:** 7180 km (4,461 mi.)

**Service ceiling:** 8760 m (28,740 ft.)

**Weights:** empty 18,380 kg (40,520 lb.); loaded 32,500 kg (71,650 lb.)

**Armament:** 20-mm (0.79-in.) cannon in bow, dorsal, tail turrets and on each beam; four 7.7-mm (.303 cal.) machine-guns from beam hatches; up to 2000 kg (4,400 lb.) of bombs or two 800-kg (1,760-lb.) torpedoes

**Dimensions:**
span 38.00 m (124 ft. 8 in.)
length 28.13 m (92 ft. 3 in.)
height 9.15 m (30 ft.)
wing area 106.00 m² (1,141 sq. ft.)

## H8K2 'EMILY'

The H8K2 was the major production version of the 'Emily', with 112 boats being completed and entering service between 1942 and 1944.

Unlike many Japanese aircraft, the H8K had excellent armour protection for the crew.

Prototypes were powered by the Mitsubishi Mars MK4A engine, but later aircraft used the 1380-kW (1,850 hp.) MK4Q engine, driving Hamilton propellers.

The wing structure was all-metal, with a metal covering. The wing had slight dihedral for enhanced stability during long patrols.

The dorsal turret was powered and mounted a single 20-mm (0.79-in.) cannon.

Normally flown with a crew of 10, the H8K's capacious fuselage could hold up to 64 passengers.

The nose gunner operated a 20-mm (0.79-in.) cannon from his position, which was retained in the H8K transport.

The bulk fuel tanks in the hull were self-sealing and had a carbon dioxide fire suppression system.

The tail gunner operated a 20-mm (0.79-in.) cannon from the rear turret.

## COMBAT DATA

### CRUISING SPEED

Flying-boats are not the most streamlined of machines, and none of the really heavy examples was particularly fast. The specification for the H8K called for it to be able to outperform the British Sunderland, which it did. Both cruised faster than the massive German Bv 222.

H8K 'EMILY' 295 km/h (183 m.p.h.)
SUNDERLAND 285 km/h (177 m.p.h.)
Bv 222 WIKING 250 km/h (155 m.p.h.)

### RANGE

Maritime reconnaissance requires the aircraft to stay in the air for long periods. The H8K was designed to operate over the vast expanses of the Pacific, and had a considerably longer range than its rivals. It could remain on patrol for an entire day and night, the only limiting factor being the endurance of the crew.

H8K 'EMILY' 7180 km (4,461 mi.)
Bv 222 WIKING 6000 km (3,728 mi.)
SUNDERLAND 4700 km (2,920 mi.)

### DEFENSIVE ARMAMENT

The Short Sunderland was not an easy target in a fight and was nicknamed 'the Flying Porcupine' by the Luftwaffe. But the British aircraft's armament paled in comparison with that of the H8K. It took strong nerves on the part of an American fighter pilot to get in close to the 'Emily', with its powerful all-round armament of 20-mm (0.79-in.) cannon.

H8K 'EMILY' 5 x 20-mm (0.79-in.) cannon 4 x 7.7-mm (.303 cal.) MGs
SUNDERLAND 8 x 7.7-mm (.303 cal.) MGs
Bv 222 WIKING 3 x 20-mm (0.79-in.) cannon 5 x 13-mm (0.51-in.) MGs

## Giants of the oceans

**SHORT SUNDERLAND:** Smaller and slower than the 'Emily', the British Sunderland performed a similar function and amassed a superb combat record.

**BLOHM & VOSS Bv 222 WIKING:** The huge six-engined Wiking served from the north of Norway to the Mediterranean. It carried huge loads, but was vulnerable to Allied fighters.

**LATÉCOÈRE 631:** This elegant flying-boat was completed in occupied France and was immediately confiscated by the Germans. After the war it flew Atlantic passenger routes.

**CONSOLIDATED PB2Y CORONADO:** Reliable but sluggish, the Coronado was used by the US Navy as a long-range patroller, 44-seat transport and ambulance.

**MARTIN JRM MARS:** Ordered in 1938, only five examples of the US Navy's largest flying-boat were built. They were used from the end of the war as long-range cargo transports.

# KAWASAKI

# KI-61 HIEN 'TONY'

● Single-seat fighter ● Liquid-cooled engine ● More than 3000 built

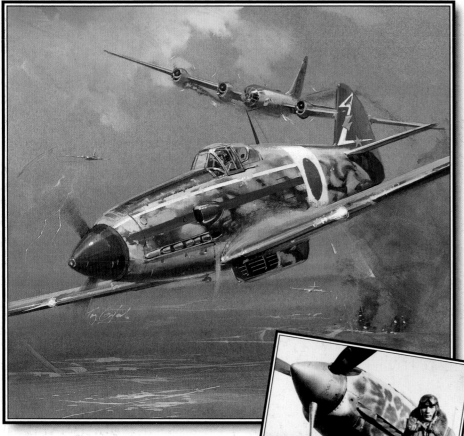

One of the better-looking fighters of World War II, the Kawasaki Ki-61 Hien (Swallow) was initially developed under the guidance of a German engineer and was powered by the Daimler-Benz DB 601A in-line piston engine. Japan produced this powerplant under licence from its designers, and called it the Kawasaki Ha-40. The Hien reached units in the Pacific from 1942 and served until Japan collapsed in 1945.

▲ The Ki-61 Hien did not face any real challenge until the P-51 Mustang appeared in the Pacific. Up until this time Allied pilots suffered at the hands of the Japanese in this high-performance machine.

## KAWASAKI KI-61 HIEN 'TONY'

### ▼ Improved Ki-61-II
With its larger engine and airframe changes, the initially troublesome Ki-61-II eventually entered production in September 1944.

### ▲ Camouflage schemes
Ki-61s wore a variety of camouflage patterns and high-visibility unit markings.

### ◀ Nationalist Chinese Hien
This Ki-61 was one of a number of Japanese aircraft to fall into Nationalist Chinese hands.

### ▼ Home defence units
Although most Ki-61s served in Japan, others saw combat in New Guinea, Rabaul and the Philippines.

### ▲ Three-bladed propeller
Both the Ki-61-I and Ki-61-II were fitted with a three-bladed, constant-speed propeller, in common with the Bf 109.

### Training School Hiens ▶
These Ki-61-Ias are seen at the Akeno Fighter Training School. Some Ki-61-Ias were equipped with two 20-mm (0.79-in.) cannon.

## FACTS AND FIGURES

➤ When production ended in 1945, a total of 3078 Kawasaki Ki-61 'Tony' fighters had been manufactured.

➤ The prototype Ki-61 was completed in December 1941.

➤ Ki-61-I KAIc production at Kagamigahara peaked at 254 per month in July 1944.

➤ The radial-engined Ki-100 was developed after the factory which produced the Ki-61-II's engine was bombed.

➤ There were several proposals for advanced Ki-61 versions, but none was built.

➤ An improved Ki-61-III mock-up was built, but the Ki-100 was put into production.

**PROFILE**

# Japan's only in-line-engined fighter

Americans in the Pacific often filed reports stating they had come up against Japanese pilots flying the Messerschmitt Bf 109 fighter. In fact, Japan never flew the Bf 109 operationally. The fighter in question was the Kawasaki Ki-61 Hien fighter, codenamed 'Tony' by the Allies. The Hien was a superb fighter of Japanese design and powered by a Japanese-built Daimler-Benz engine as fitted to the Messerschmitt.

A clean, streamlined, fast and manoeuvrable aircraft, the Ki-61

was the only liquid-cooled fighter to enter service with the Japanese air arms during World War II. The Hien scored many aerial victories against the Allies, and it also pioneered the use of armour and self-sealing fuel tanks that had been so useful in Europe.

Ironically, the engine that made the 'Tony' possible was also its biggest limitation. The licence-built Daimler DB 601A powerplant had little potential for further development. An attempt was made to improve the Ki-61 as the Ki-61-II, with an Ha-140

engine, but teething problems delayed its introduction. Thus, although the 'Tony' had an important role in the war, it never achieved the fame of the A6M 'Zero'.

*Below: The Ki-61-I was unable to match the American B-29's service ceiling and was outclassed by its P-51.*

*Above: After trials, an early production Hien was test-flown against a captured P-40E and an imported Bf 109E. The Ki-61 was the superior performer.*

## KI-61-I KAIC HIEN 'TONY'

This aircraft flew with the HQ Chutai, 244th Sentai, based at Chofu, Tokyo, during 1944/45. By the end of World War II 13 Sentais were equipped with the Ki-61, mainly in the defence of the Japanese mainland.

### Ki-61-I KAIc Hien 'Tony'

**Type:** single-seat fighter

**Powerplant:** one 880-kW (1,180-hp.) Kawasaki Ha-40 inverted-vee piston engine

**Maximum speed:** 590 km/h (366 m.p.h.) at 4260 m (14,000 ft.)

**Climb rate:** 7 minutes to 5000 m (16,400 ft.)

**Range:** 580 km (360 mi.)

**Service ceiling:** 10,000 m (33,000 ft.)

**Weights:** empty 2630 kg (5,786 lb.); maximum take-off 3470 kg (7,634 lb.)

**Armament:** two 20-mm (0.79-in.) Ho-5 cannon in the nose and 12.7-mm (.50 cal.) Type 1 (Ho-103)

**Dimensions:** 
| | | |
|---|---|---|
| span | 12.00 m | (36 ft. 4 in.) |
| length | 8.94 m | (29 ft. 4 in.) |
| height | 3.70 m | (12 ft. 2 in.) |
| wing area | 20.00 m² | (215 sq. ft.) |

Daimler-Benz's DB 601 inverted-vee, 12-cylinder, liquid-cooled engine that had powered the early Messerschmitt Bf 109 was licence-built by Kawasaki as the Ha-40. The first example was in operation by mid-1941.

After the Ki-61-I entered production, the factory immediately started development of a more powerful Ki-61-II with a 1118-kW (1,500-hp.) Ha-140 engine, an improved version of the Ha-40. This proved to be unreliable, as the crankshaft was prone to breakage.

The Ki-61-II featured improvements to the airframe, including a redesigned cockpit canopy and enlarged wings to enhance manoeuvrability at altitude. However, test-flights revealed handling problems.

The Hien's fuel capacity (one fuselage tank behind the cockpit able to carry 165 litres/44 gal.) could be augmented by fitting a 200-litre (53-gal.) drop-tank under each wing.

The Ki-61 did not have a gun fitted in the propeller hub, but was equipped with two machine-guns mounted above the nose and firing through the propeller.

The oil cooler radiator was positioned under the main wings, in a similar manner to that of the P-51 Mustang.

To reduce drag, the earliest Ki-61s had a retractable tailwheel. In later models, in order to simplify production, a fixed tail wheel was fitted.

### COMBAT DATA

#### MAXIMUM SPEED

While the Ki-61 was a high-performance machine that presented a major challenge to Allied fighters in 1943, the P-51 and P-38 were both superior and outclassed the Hien later in the war. If the Ki-61-II had not been trouble-plagued, the tables may have been turned.

| | |
|---|---|
| Ki-61-I KAIc HIEN | 590 km/h (366 m.p.h.) |
| P-51D MUSTANG | 716 km/h (437 m.p.h.) |
| P-38J LIGHTNING | 666 km/h (413 m.p.h.) |

#### ARMAMENT

Japanese fighter designers benefited from German advances in fighter armament, utilising 20-mm (0.79-in.) cannon in the Ki-61. The USAAF was slow to fit cannon to its aircraft, although the Lightning was equipped with one in addition to its four machine-guns.

| | |
|---|---|
| Ki-61-I KAIc HIEN | 2 x 20-mm (0.79-in.) cannon 2 x 12.7-mm (.50 cal.) machine-guns |
| P-51D MUSTANG | 6 x 12.7-mm (.50 cal.) machine-guns |
| P-38J LIGHTNING | 1 x 20-mm (0.79-in.) cannon 4 x 12.7-mm (.50 cal.) machine-guns |

#### RANGE

Without auxilliary fuel the range of the Ki-61-I KAIc Hien was much less than that of contemporary US aircraft. Drop-tanks could be fitted to the Hien and, although these improved range, they reduced its top speed by 80 km/h (50 m.p.h.).

| | |
|---|---|
| Ki-61-I KAIc HIEN | 580 km (360 mi.) |
| P-51D MUSTANG | 1207 km (750 mi.) |
| P-38J LIGHTNING | 724 km (450 mi.) |

## Japanese warplanes with inline powerplants

■ **AICHI M6A SEIRAN:** Intended as a submarine-borne attack aircraft, the M6A was almost operational when war ended in 1945.

■ **KAWASAKI Ki-32:** The last Japanese army bomber powered by a liquid-cooled engine, the Ki-32 took part in the bombing of Hong Kong.

■ **KAWASAKI Ki-60:** Kawasaki was instructed to build two designs for the licence-built DB 601 engine. Only three of this heavy fighter were built.

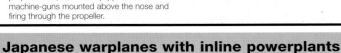

■ **YOKOSUKA D4Y SUISEI:** This two-seat dive-bomber initially saw service as a reconnaissance aircraft because of its speed.

# LAVOCHKIN

# LA-5 AND LA-7

● Soviet dogfighter ● Wooden construction ● Flown by aces

▲ The La-5 inspired confidence in those who flew it. Pavel Kocfelda of the Ist Fighter Regiment of the Red air force christened his personal machine 'Rene'.

**D**eveloped from the disappointing LaGG-3, the Lavochkin La-5 was one of the great fighters of World War II. It shared the earlier machine's wooden construction, but the new radial engine gave it vastly superior performance. The La-5 and its successors were amongst the best dogfighters of the war, especially at low level, and were flown by most leading Soviet pilots including Ivan Kozhedub, the Allied 'ace of aces'.

---

## LAVOCHKIN LA-5 AND LA-7

**Simple cockpit ▶**
The 'Lavochka' was basic, with a rough finish. There was no cockpit heating and the instruments and radios were often very poor, but it handled like a dream.

**▼ On the ground**
The La-5 was superb in the air, but it had bad manners on the ground. Landings were usually a bouncy, prolonged business.

**▲ Ready for battle**
The La-5 was simply and ruggedly constructed. Its structure was mostly built from wood rather than scarce light aircraft alloys.

**Forced down ▶**
The Lavochkin's basic construction was easy to repair after minor accidents like this.

**▼ Rugged radial**
The La-5's excellent radial engine and wooden bonded construction were ideal for service in Russia. Complex aircraft with tricky liquid-cooled engines like the Spitfires supplied by Britain proved harder to maintain in the field.

**▲ Tactical hideout**
The rapid advance across Russia in 1944 meant that the La-5 was usually based in remote strips. Russian airmen always hid their aircraft well.

### FACTS AND FIGURES

➤ Lavochkins were very successful at the battle of Kursk, where they escorted Il-2 Shturmovik rocket-firing tank-busters.

➤ About 12,000 radial-engine Lavochkin fighters were manufactured.

➤ The La-11, the last piston Lavochkin, still served with Communist forces in 1960.

➤ The La-5 was flown by the highest-scoring Allied ace, Ivan Kozhedub, who scored 62 kills against the Luftwaffe.

➤ The La-5 wing structure was made of plastic bonded wood veneer strips.

➤ A volunteer unit of Czech pilots fought with the Red air force using the La-5.

# PROFILE

# Wooden warrior of the Eastern Front

As the Soviet armies reeled back from the German invasion of 1941, there were frantic demands for the Soviet air force to be re-equipped with modern fighters. In October 1941, Semyon Lavochkin began work on an improved version of the heavy LaGG-3 fighter. The ensuing La-5, equipped with a powerful radial engine and cut-down rear fuselage, entered production in July 1942, and more than 1000 were built by the end of the year.

The first large-scale use of the La-5 came in 1942 over Stalingrad. Here, and at Kursk the following year, it proved to be a ferocious dogfighter, especially at low level. The lightweight La-5FN appeared that year, and was flown by many top Soviet aces.

The La-7 of 1944 had more power and many minor improvements, making it one of the most effective fighters of the war.

*The La-5 had excellent low-speed handling, assisted by the automatic slats on the leading edges of the wings, which are shown here in the operating position.*

## LA-5FN

This lightweight variant of the La-5 was used by hero of the Soviet Union P.J. Linkholetov, who shot down 25 enemy aircraft in 1944.

**The basic wing construction** was made of birch wood, cross-grained and impregnated with a resin mixture and covered in plywood.

**Twin 20-mm (0.79-in.)** cannon were mounted above the engine, and were synchronised to fire through the propeller disc.

**Most La-5s** wore the brown and green paint scheme, but winter white was also used, sometimes topped with dramatic red arrows and Cyrillic slogans.

**The La-5 control surfaces** were of fabric-covered light alloy construction, and were paired with large flaps. With a low wing loading, the La-5 had an exceptionally fast rate of roll.

**The elevator and rudder** were among the few metal parts, having an alloy frame and fabric covering.

**The success of the Lavochkin** series owed much to its ability to accept ever bigger engines. The later La-7's Shvetsov radial produced 1500 kW (2,000 hp.). These engines performed best at an altitude of around 2000 m (6,000 ft.).

**Five self-sealing fuel tanks** were contained in each wing. The two outer tanks were generally left empty, as their weight when filled limited manoeuvrability.

**This Cyrillic slogan** translates as 'for Vasek and Zhora'.

**The retractable tailwheel** often proved unreliable.

### La-5FN

**Type:** interceptor fighter

**Powerplant:** one 1231-kW (1,650-hp.) Shvetsov M-82FN (ASh-82FN) radial piston engine

**Maximum speed:** 650 km/h (403 m.p.h.)

**Climb rate:** 5 minutes to 5000 m (16,000 ft.)

**Range:** 765 km (475 mi.)

**Service ceiling:** 11,000 m (36,000 ft.)

**Weights:** empty 2605 kg (5,737 lb.); loaded 3360 kg (7,932 lb.)

**Armament:** two or three 20-mm (0.79-in.) ShVAK or 23-mm (0.9-in.) NS cannon plus provision for 158 kg (350 lb.) of bombs or four 82-mm (3-in.) rockets underwing

**Dimensions:**
| | | |
|---|---|---|
| span | 9.80 m (32 ft.) |
| length | 8.67 m (28 ft.) |
| height | 2.54 m (8 ft.) |
| wing area | 17.59 m² (189 sq. ft.) |

## COMBAT DATA

### MAXIMUM SPEED

The La-5 was considerably faster than the Messerschmitt Bf 109 at all levels below 6000 m (20,000 ft.), but the German fighter was better at high altitude. However, since combat on the Eastern Front was at low level, this was no real disadvantage to Russian pilots.

| | |
|---|---|
| La-5FN | 650 km/h (403 m.p.h.) |
| Bf 109G-6 | 620 km/h (384 m.p.h.) |
| P-39 | 612 km/h (379 m.p.h.) |

### SERVICE CEILING

Although the Lavochkin and the American-supplied Bell P-39 each had a reasonable service ceiling, neither was much good at extreme altitude. The P-39 was particularly bad, but like the Lavochkin it generally fought at lower levels, and both Soviet-operated fighters achieved considerable success.

La-5FN: 11,000 m (33,000 ft.)
Bf 109G-6: 11,500 m (37,700 ft.)
P-39: 10,700 m (35,000 ft.)

### ARMAMENT

The Lavochkin was relatively lightly armed, but this did not stop it becoming a highly successful dogfighter. The P-39 had a particularly heavy but slow-firing gun, which doubled as an effective ground-attack weapon. The Messerschmitt's standard armament was often heavily augmented by field conversions.

La-5FN
2 x 20-mm (0.79-in.) cannon

Bf 109G-6
1 x 30-mm (1.18-in.) cannon
2 x 13-mm (0.51-in.) machine-guns

P-39
1 x 37-mm (1.47-in.) cannon
2 x 12.7-mm (.50 cal)
machine-guns
4 x 7.62-mm (.30 cal.)
machine-guns

## Lavochkin development

■ **LaGG-3:** Developed by Lavochkin, Gorbunov and Gudkov in 1940, the LaGG was fast and reasonably agile, but it was a sluggish climber and pilots complained of very heavy controls.

■ **LAVOCHKIN La-5:** Fitting a more powerful radial engine to the LaGG-3 led to marginally increased drag, but much greater power meant that the La-5 gained more than 50 km/h (30 m.p.h.) in speed.

■ **LAVOCHKIN La-7:** More power and lower drag meant that the La-7 of 1944 had a top speed of 680 km/h (422 m.p.h.). This is the La-7 in which Ivan Kozhedub achieved the last of his 62 victories.

# LAVOCHKIN

# LaGG-3

● Wooden fighter ● More than 6000 built ● Early Soviet defender

▲ During the early stages of the Luftwaffe onslaught, the good reputation of the LaGG-3 owed more to its rugged construction and the courage of its pilots than to its design as a fighter.

**D**esigned by a new bureau and rushed into production as World War II was getting under way, the LaGG-3 was an improved version of Lavochkin's original LaGG-1. Although they had many shortcomings, the urgent need for new fighters meant that around 300 LaGG-3s were in service by the time Germany invaded the Soviet Union in June 1941. And by the time production ended just over a year later a further 6000 had been delivered.

## LAVOCHKIN LaGG-3

▲ **Early Lavochkin**
*The basic design of the LaGG-3 was progressively improved in production, with later aircraft having retractable tailwheels and heavier armament.*

▲ **Flying the LaGG-3**
*Reports vary with regard to the flying qualities of the LaGG-3. Some sources suggest it was as dangerous to its pilots as it was to the enemy.*

▲ **Finnish LaGG**
*Wearing Finnish markings, this LaGG-3 was probably captured after landing in Finland during World War II.*

◀ **LaGGs abroad**
*Another captured aircraft, this machine was flown in Japanese markings. Japan and the Soviet Union shared a long-running territorial dispute.*

**Finnish inspection ▶**
*At least two LaGG-3s were flown in Finland, since this aircraft does not have the leading-edge slats of the machine shown above right.*

### FACTS AND FIGURES

➤ Designers Lavochkin, Gorbunov and Gudkov used the initial letters of their names to produce the LaGG designation.

➤ Both the LaGG-1 and LaGG-3 were constructed of wood.

➤ The LaGG-3 was intended as a stop-gap fighter, but 6528 were built.

➤ The I-22 prototype of the LaGG-1 was later modified as the I-301 prototype of the LaGG-3.

➤ Late versions of the LaGG-3 were able to carry drop-tanks.

➤ Lavochkin developed the La-5 from an M-82-powered version of the LaGG-3.

# PROFILE

# Long-serving Soviet stop-gap

First flown as the I-22 in March 1939, the LaGG-1 was built largely of wood and armed with a 23-mm (0.9-in.) cannon plus two 12.7-mm (0.5 cal.) machine-guns in the nose. It proved short on performance, range and manoeuvrability and was difficult to control.

The need for a new fighter was urgent, however, and so the LaGG-1 was fitted with lighter weapons, had its control system improved and had additional fuel tanks installed to produce the

LaGG-3. This aircraft still suffered from a lack of power and had a very poor view from the cockpit.

Most units equipped with the type suffered heavy losses and the pressure of war meant that few of the improvements proposed were actually carried out. Instead, the heavier weapons of the LaGG-1 were often fitted so that the LaGG-3 could be used for close support missions against ground targets.

Modifications included three aircraft fitted with 37-mm

*Soviet forces relied heavily on the LaGG-3, flying it against far superior enemy fighters until the introduction of more advanced Soviet fighter designs.*

(1.47-in.) cannon and one with a 1230-kW M-10A engine. But it was the installation of the M-82 air-cooled radial to produce the La-5 that finally turned Lavochkin's design into a worthwhile fighter.

Both the LaGG-1 and -3 were poorly armed and tricky to fly. It was an air force joke that LaGG actually stood for *lakirovannii garantirovannii grob* – Russian for 'guaranteed varnished coffin'.

Lavochkin retained the best features of the LaGG-3 in subsequent designs. The tail and wing surfaces of the La-5 and -7, for example, owed much to the earlier fighter.

## LaGG-3

This LaGG-3 was assigned to an IAP (Independent Air Regiment) of the VVS KBF (Red Banner Baltic Fleet Air Force). It was shot down over Finland in March 1942.

A Hucks starter could be used for starting the engine via the shaft in the propeller spinner.

LaGG-3 armament varied considerably, according to mission. Typically, a LaGG-3 was armed with a single ShVAK cannon (with 120 rounds) firing through the propeller hub and two 12.7-mm (.50 cal.) BS machine-guns, each with 220 rounds, mounted above the engine.

The only parts of the LaGG-3's structure which were not made from wood were the control surfaces, which were light alloy with fabric covering, and the flaps, which were all-metal to avoid damage.

Both the LaGG-1 and -3 were powered by a Klimov M-105P in-line V-12 liquid-cooled piston engine. The LaGG-3's M-105PF developed 157 kW (210 hp.) more power and drove an improved propeller.

The birch plywood skinning was both impregnated and bonded with phenolformaldehyde resin. Radical at the time, this wood-bonding technique is now widely used.

Rare among contemporary monoplane fighters in not having metal stressed-skin construction, the LaGG-3 was built almost entirely of wood. Diagonal strips of plywood were bonded onto its internal wooden structure.

## Soviet World War II monoplane fighters

**LAVOCHKIN La-7:** Working on his own, Lavochkin produced the highly successful La-7, based on the LaGG-3 with a radial engine.

**LAVOCHKIN La-9:** Arriving late in the war, the La-9 was a truly exceptional fighter and several continued to serve after the war.

**MIKOYAN GUREVICH MiG-3:** Though an improvement over the earlier MiG-1, the MiG-3 was still no match for Luftwaffe fighters.

**POLIKARPOV I-16:** About 4000 I-16s fought against the Luftwaffe. Hopelessly obsolete, they were often used in deliberate ramming attacks.

# LOCKHEED

# P-38 LIGHTNING

● Twin-engine fighter ● Flown by top aces

**M**any believe the Lockheed P-38 Lightning was the finest American fighter of World War II. The twin-boomed P-38 was fast, heavily-armed and extremely versatile. While it had trouble matching single-engine fighters like the Messerschmitt 109 and Focke-Wulf 190, the Lightning was very manoeuvrable for such a big machine, and in capable hands it could hold its own. The P-38 more than held its own in the South West Pacific, where the aircraft was flown by Major Richard I. Bong and Major Thomas B. McGuire, America's top-scoring aces of all time.

▲ Lieutenant Murray J. Shubin was just one of the many aces to succeed in a Lightning. Shubin gained five kills in an hour in his P-38, which he named after his Australian girlfriend.

## PHOTO FILE

## LOCKHEED P-38 LIGHTNING

▼ **Photo fighter**
The F-5 reconnaissance Lightning performed dangerous lone missions without any armament.

▲ **Napalm attack**
Lightnings blast Japanese positions with napalm bombs near the Ipoh Dam in the Philippine Islands.

**Night Lightning ▶**
The P-38M was one of the fastest night-fighters of the war, despite the added weight of radar and a second crewmember.

◀ **Clothes line**
The Lightning served throughout the Solomons. It performed many tasks, including drying the clothes of 13th Air Force pilots!

**Caught napping ▶**
It wasn't all victories; this sad remnant of a P-38 at Tacloban was the result of Japanese bombing during the 1944 struggle for Leyte.

▲ **Outdoor factory**
Lightnings were built in the California sun while the Lockheed production line was modernised.

### FACTS AND FIGURES

➤ The P-38 Lightning prototype made its first flight on 27 January 1939.

➤ The Lightning produced for the Royal Air Force was at first named the Atlanta.

➤ Experimental Lightning variants included the high-altitude XP-49 and XP-58 Chain Lightning bomber escort.

➤ To overcome tail buffeting in early P-38s, an aluminium fillet was added to the wingroot.

➤ F-4 and F-5 photo-gathering Lightnings were among the best reconnaissance aircraft of the war.

➤ Production of all versions of this great Lockheed fighter totalled 9924 aircraft.

# PROFILE

# The fork-tailed devil in the sky

As late as 1944, when Mustangs were sweeping the skies clear of foes, a poll in flying classes showed that student pilots' 'most wanted' aircraft was the Lockheed P-38 Lightning, the design of which dated back to 1937.

The P-38 was rugged and versatile, and because of its low-drag aerodynamic shape and heavy weight it accelerated to high speeds faster than any previous warplane. A potent

fighter and a superb fighter-bomber, it also flew as a night-fighter, reconnaissance aircraft, ambulance, torpedo-bomber and target tug.

More than 100 US Army squadrons flew the P-38, which was produced in at least two-dozen versions. In the Pacific, P-38 pilots carried out the long-range intercept mission which downed and killed Japan's Admiral Isoroku Yamamoto, a planner of the Pearl Harbor

attack. In the Mediterranean, Luftwaffe pilots showed respect for the Lightning by calling it der gabelschwanz Teufel (the fork-tailed devil).

The ultimate P-38L model was flown by Dick Bong and Tommy McGuire, who with 40 and 38 victories, respectively, were the most successful American fighter pilots in history.

*RAF Lightnings were early aircraft with low-rated engines, and had all the faults and none of the advantages of later machines. They were not popular with British pilots.*

## P-38L Lightning

**Type:** single-seat fighter and fighter-bomber

**Powerplant:** two turbo-charged 1194-kW (1,600-hp.) Allison V-1710-111/113 in-line piston engines

**Maximum speed:** 666 km/h (414 m.p.h.) at 7620 m (25,000 ft.)

**Range:** 765 km (475 mi.) on internal fuel

**Service ceiling:** 13,400 m (44,000 ft.)

**Weights:** empty 5806 kg (12,800 lb.); loaded 9798 kg (21,600 lb.)

**Armament:** one 20-mm (0.79-in.) cannon and four 12.7-mm (.50 cal.) machine-guns, plus up to 1450 kg (3,197 lb.) of ordnance – usually two 454-kg (1,000-lb.) or 726-kg (1,600-lb.) bombs or 10 127-mm (5-in.) rocket projectiles under wings

**Dimensions:**
| | | |
|---|---|---|
| span | 15.85 m | (52 ft.) |
| length | 11.53 m | (37 ft. 10 in.) |
| height | 3.00 m | (9 ft. 10 in.) |
| wing area | 30.42 m² | (327 sq. ft.) |

One 20-mm (0.79-in.) cannon and four heavy machine-guns concentrated in the nose made the P-38 one of the hardest-hitting American fighters of the war. The battery of guns was also very useful in the ground-attack role.

## P-38J LIGHTNING

This Lockheed P-38J served with the 55th Fighter Squadron at Kingscliffe, Northamptonshire, and flew fighter escort for 8th Air Force bombers over Germany.

Unlike British twin-engine aircraft such as the Mosquito, the P-38 was built with 'handed' engines turning in opposite directions. This eliminated engine torque reaction, making take-off extremely simple.

Early Lightnings were notoriously uncomfortable, having a cramped cockpit that lacked proper heating. The first attempts at flying at high altitude resulted in pilots getting frostbite.

328430

N KI

The turbo-charged Allison in-line engines were never the P-38's best feature, being prone to over-heating.

The Lightning's nosewheel undercarriage was a very welcome new feature for pilots. It made engine maintenance easy for the engineers, as well as reducing accidents on take-off and landing.

Turbo-charged engines with boom-mounted radiators gave the P-38 superb high-altitude performance. Early examples for Britain were delivered without turbos, which virtually crippled the aircraft as a fighting machine.

Early Lightning prototypes suffered severe buffeting around the tail from the airflow over the wings, but this was cured in production versions.

## COMBAT DATA

### MAXIMUM SPEED

The P-38 was the first American Army Air Force fighter capable of more than 650 km/h. Its sensational high-altitude performance remained a feature of the type throughout its career, along with its superb climbing and diving ability.

| | |
|---|---|
| P-38L LIGHTNING | 666 km/h (414 m.p.h.) |
| A6M6 ZERO | 557 km/h (346 m.p.h.) |
| Bf 109G | 620 km/h (385 m.p.h.) |

### SERVICE CEILING

The P-38's twin turbo-charged engines gave it superb high-altitude performance, and at heights over 8000 metres it was one of the best fighters in the world. At medium altitudes, however, the big fighter had less of an advantage, and could get into trouble against more agile German or Japanese machines which could out-turn the P-38L.

P-38L LIGHTNING: 13,400 m (44,000 ft.)
A6M6 ZERO: 10,700 m (35,100 ft.)
Bf 109G: 11,500 m (37,730 ft.)

### ARMAMENT

Although on paper the P-38 had lighter armament than most of its opponents, the concentration of guns in the nose allowed it to bring an immense amount of fire to bear on targets at all ranges. Lightnings were known to 'saw Zeros in half' with a long burst of fire.

**P-38L LIGHTNING**
1 x 20-mm (0.79-in.) cannon
4 x 12.7-mm (.50 cal.) MGs
1450 kg (3,197 lb.) of bombs

**A6M6 ZERO**
2 x 20-mm (0.79-in.) cannon
3 x 13.2-mm (0.51-in.) MGs
1 x 250-kg (550-lb.) bomb

**Bf 109G**
1 x 30-mm (1.18-in.) cannon
2 x 20-mm (0.79-in.) cannon
1 x 454-kg (1,000-lb.) bomb

## The Lightning's prey

**KAWANISHI N1K2:** Developed from a floatplane, the N1K2 was one of the most manoeuvrable fighters ever, let down by unreliable engines.

**MITSUBISHI A6M ZERO:** The great Japanese fighter was far more agile than the Lightning, but it was considerably slower.

**MITSUBISHI G4M:** The Japanese navy's main bomber proved horribly vulnerable to being set ablaze by the P-38's concentrated firepower.

**NAKAJIMA Ki-43:** The Japanese army's equivalent of the Zero was regularly shot down by Lightning pilots in the South West Pacific.

**NAKAJIMA Ki-84:** This was the best Japanese fighter of the war. Although slower, in competent hands it could sometimes outfly the Lightning.

# LOCKHEED

# P-80 SHOOTING STAR

● Jet fighter ● European deployment ● Test flying

I n 1944 the US Army Air Force began gunnery trials in Nevada with the Lockheed P-80 Shooting Star; this design promised to revolutionise air warfare. The P-80 was the first fully operational type in the US to have a jet engine – an innovation already familiar to German and British scientists. The US rushed four P-80s to Europe – two each to England and Italy – and they were hours from entering combat when World War II ended.

▲ Proudly wearing
the Lockheed emblem on its nose, the P-80 Shooting Star was equipped with six forward-firing machine-guns, a typical armament fit for fighters of the era.

▼ Graceful lines
Before the addition of wingtip tanks and essential service equipment, the Shooting Star was one of the most elegant aircraft ever produced by Lockheed. Pilots marvelled at the design.

▲ Fighter testing
Known as Lulu Belle, this P-80 was flown against the conventionally powered fighters of the period to explore jet tactics.

▲ Future potential
With large test markings displayed on its fuselage, this particular P-80 undertook a series of developmental flights to try out future jet fighter equipment.

▲ Service entry
Seen high over California's foothills, this P-80A was assigned to the 412th Fighter Group at March Field in late 1945.

◄ Lakebed landings
Early flights were performed from the Muroc range in California, and made use of the many dry lakebeds.

## FACTS AND FIGURES

➤ The Shooting Star was designed from the start to be the United States Army Air Force's first operational jet fighter.

➤ One of the first examples of the P-80 was completed in just 143 days.

➤ Early aircraft were given names like The Grey Ghost and Silver Ghost.

➤ Lockheed hoped to deliver 450 Shooting Stars per month during World War II, but this was never accomplished.

➤ Richard Ira Bong, America's highest-scoring ace, was killed testing a P-80.

➤ Many pilots found it hard to adjust to the new demands of jet flying.

# PROFILE

# Shooting for success

Work on the P-80 began in 1943 when famous engineer Clarence L. ('Kelly') Johnson persuaded his bosses at Lockheed to attempt to build the USAAF's first operational jet fighter in just 180 days. They actually completed the pace-setting first P-80 in 143 days.

The P-80 was a clean design with straight wings and tail surfaces, and a tricycle landing gear. Air intakes positioned on the lower fuselage forward of the wing leading edge fed the British-designed de Havilland H.1B turbojet, which was replaced in production examples by the Allison/General Electric I-40 (J33).

Many pilots with propeller experience took to the jet-powered P-80 with enormous enthusiasm. An ambitious programme progressed toward the goal of getting the Shooting Star into combat. Several P-80s were lost in tragic mishaps, but the aircraft performed well, and the USAAF moved rapidly to finalise the configuration of this

*Above: After completing extensive test work, this Shooting Star was restored by ex-Lockheed employees.*

fighter and to develop a photo-reconnaissance version. Had World War II lasted weeks longer, it is certain that the P-80 Shooting Star would have done battle with the top fighters developed by the Axis, including Germany's much-vaunted Messerschmitt Me 262.

*Below: Having just completed another test flight, an early P-80 is seen parked on one of Muroc's dry lakebeds. A major debrief followed each flight.*

## XP-80 Shooting Star

**Type:** single-seat jet fighter

**Powerplant:** one 10.9-kN (2,450-lb.-thrust) de Havilland H.1B Goblin turbojet

**Maximum speed:** 808 km/h (557 m.p.h.); cruising speed 692 km/h (429 m.p.h.)

**Initial climb rate:** 914 m/min (3,000 f.p.m.) from sea level

**Range:** 1609 km (1,000 mi.)

**Service ceiling:** 12,497 m (41,000 ft.)

**Weights:** empty 2852 kg (6,274 lb.); maximum take-off 4498 kg (9,896 lb.)

**Armament:** six 12.7-mm (.50 cal.) nose-mounted machine-guns

**Dimensions:**
span 11.27 m (36 ft. 11 in.)
length 10.00 m (32 ft. 9 in.)
height 3.12 m (10 ft. 3 in.)
wing area 22.29 m² (240 sq. ft.)

## RF-80A SHOOTING STAR

Many early model Shooting Stars were built for, or converted to, the photo-reconnaissance role. This example saw service in Korea, where the aircraft operated with an escort of fighters.

The pilot enjoyed exceptional visibility through a teardrop sliding canopy. The cockpits of reconnaissance versions differed very little from fighter variants. The only additions were camera switches, film counters and blinker lights to replace the K-14 gunsight.

Despite the early success of the Shooting Star, it was quickly overshadowed by more advanced designs from rival manufacturers. The type was retained for second-line duties, in which the Shooting Stars remained for a number of years until fatigue problems caused their withdrawal.

Though the aircraft were initially flown in their peacetime natural colour scheme, some RF-80s adopted olive-drab upper surfaces when they went to war in Korea. Despite this the retention of the large 'buzz' numbers compromised the end result.

An enlarged forward section housed the reconnaissance camera suite. Access to the camera bay installation was by way of an upward-hinging nose section. Camera film could be replaced in a few minutes by experienced personnel.

Mounted low on either side of the fuselage were the small intakes. They were prone to ingesting foreign objects when the aircraft operated from semi-prepared runways.

To answer requests from USAF pilots for additional range, wingtip tanks were installed on the Shooting Star. They varied in size, and later models were fitted with additional fuel tanks under the wings.

A red fuselage band was painted on all early Shooting Stars. This denoted the turbine position within the engine. At this point the rear fuselage could be removed to allow maintenance personnel access to the engine.

## FIGHTING JETS

**BRITISH FIGHTERS:** Entering service with the Royal Air Force in late 1944, the Gloster Meteor (pictured above) saw limited use, often on ground attack duties. After the end of World War II, a host of specialised variants were introduced into service, such as night-fighters, target-tugs and tactical photo-reconnaissance models. Widely exported to European and Middle Eastern countries, the Meteor remained in limited service until the late 1970s when it was finally replaced by more modern types. The Meteor had the distinction of being the first jet fighter in RAF service.

**GERMAN GENESIS:** Widely regarded as the best fighter of World War II, the Messerschmitt Me 262 was introduced into (limited) operational service before its rivals. Allied pilots found the Me 262 had remarkable agility and was able to outperform anything the Americans or British could offer. Hampered by a dwindling fuel supply, the Germans initially used the aircraft as a light bomber before pilots saw the full potential of the fighter. After the end of hostilities, Allied pilots flight-tested the aircraft and were thoroughly impressed. It had only limited post-war service, but the aircraft's design influenced fighter design for years to come. Other variants constructed were two-seat trainers, night-fighters, and precision attack bombers which were equipped with a glazed nose-section for an additional crew member.

## Lockheed's adaptable lady

■ **T-33 SHOOTING STAR:** Developed into a highly successful trainer, the T-33 is operated by a number of countries. It provides the first experience of jet flight for many pilots.

■ **XF-90:** Offered to the USAF as a potential long-range bomber escort, the XF-90 was not successful and eventually lost out to the two-seat McDonnell F-101 Voodoo.

■ **F-94C STARFIRE:** A specialised variant of the T-33 was developed to intercept intruders at night. Fitted with an improved radar, the aircraft saw much service with the USAF.

# LOCKHEED

# PV-1 VENTURA/PV-2 HARPOON

● Light bomber/maritime patroller ● Built to an RAF requirement

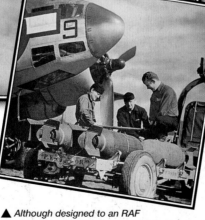

▲ Although designed to an RAF requirement for a light bomber, the Ventura was found to be more suitable for maritime patrol duties. When the US Navy took over ASW duties in spring 1942, it ordered the PV-1.

Its initial sorties as a light bomber with the RAF were not a success, but in the maritime role the Ventura proved invaluable. Impressed by this performance, the US Navy adopted the type as the PV-1 for Pacific service. A major redesign to increase range and load-carrying ability resulted in the PV-2 Harpoon. After war service, surplus aircraft flew with several air forces, while others were converted to crop sprayers and executive transports.

## LOCKHEED PV-1 VENTURA/PV-2 HARPOON

### ◀ RAF Ventura Mk II
The RAF took delivery of 394 Ventura light bombers, which entered service in 1942. By 1943 all were with Coastal Command units.

### ▼ Post-war conversions
Harpoons were among a number of wartime aircraft converted into executive transports after 1945.

### ▼ North Atlantic livery
This all-white colour scheme was usually used over the North Atlantic and made the black rubber de-icer boots very prominent. The underwing tanks carried 587 litres (150 gal.) each and bomb-bay tanks increased range further.

### ▼ Improved war load
Successive versions of the Ventura carried between 1134 kg (2,495 lb.) and 1362 kg (2,994 lb.) of weapons. The Harpoon increased this to 1816 kg (3,990 lb.) internally, with an extra 454 kg (1,000 lb.) under each wing.

### ▼ Post-war Reserve PV-2
This Harpoon, seen in post-war markings, has had its undernose 12.7-mm (.50 cal.) guns removed.

### FACTS AND FIGURES

➤ The first Marine Corps night-fighter unit, VMF(N)-531, scored its first kill with a radar-equipped PV-1 in November 1943.

➤ A failure as an RAF bomber, all Venturas went to Coastal Command in 1943.

➤ PV-2 Harpoons saw limited war service, being phased out by the US Navy in 1948.

➤ On Christmas Eve 1943, a No. 1 Squadron, RNZAF, Ventura crew shot down three Japanese 'Zero' fighters.

➤ Venturas built on British contract and taken over by the US Navy were PV-3s.

➤ US Marine Corps PV-1 night-fighters had six forward-firing guns and British AI radar.

**PROFILE**

# Lodestars in Allied uniforms

Pleased with the Hudson, the British Air Ministry was interested in Lockheed's proposal to modify the Lodestar in a similar way, as a replacement for both the Hudson (in the maritime reconnaissance role) and the Bristol Blenheim light/medium bomber.

The Ventura, as it was to be known, was larger than the Hudson, with more powerful engines, improved armament and a greater load-carrying capability. Large numbers went to the RAF, RAAF, RNZAF and SAAF. A few were retained by the USAAF for over-water patrols as B-34 and B-37 Lexingtons.

From 1942 the US Navy took over all ASW work from the army and obtained 1600 PV-1s. The improved PV-2 Harpoon followed, with major design changes to optimise it for the maritime role.

War surplus PV-1s and -2s were used after the war for a variety of roles. Some have been restored by warbird enthusiasts.

The Harpoon was a major redesign of the Ventura to optimise it for maritime patrol. It had longer span wings to improve take-off performance with a full fuel load and enlarged vertical tail surfaces.

Initial PV-2 operations revealed a serious wing wrinkling problem. Attempts to solve this by reducing the span failed and a complete wing redesign was required, which slowed down production.

The Harpoon differed from the Ventura in almost every detail except for small sections of the fuselage, inboard wing ribs and engine cowlings.

## PV-2 HARPOON

This PV-2 wears the markings of US Navy Patrol Bomber Squadron VPB-142 based in the Marianas Islands in 1945. Wartime deliveries to Allied air arms included five to the Brazilian air force and four to the RNZAF.

As a maritime patrol bomber the PV-2 had a crew of four or five, comprising a pilot, navigator/bomb aimer, radio operator/gunner and turret gunner. When operated solely as a patrol aircraft a fifth crewmember was carried.

This PV-2 carried eight 127-mm high-velocity aerial rockets (HVAR) below the wings as well as two 587-litre (150-gal.) drop-tanks. An internal bomb-bay held up to 1816 kg (3,990 lb.) of bombs.

Armament consisted of eight 12.7-mm (.50 cal.) machine-guns, including three in an undernose pack, two above the nose, two in a dorsal turret and one in the ventral position.

Harpoons (and most Venturas) were fitted with two Pratt & Whitney R-2800 Double Wasps, each rated at 1491 kW (2,000 hp.). These engines were also fitted to the Vought F4U and Douglas A-26.

## COMBAT DATA

### MAXIMUM SPEED

Based on the civil Lodestar, the Ventura was a relatively fast warplane, even with a typical weapon load aboard. The G4M 'Betty' first flew in 1939 and suffered at the hands of Allied fighters. Both the 'Betty' and Warwick were purpose-designed military aircraft.

PV-1 VENTURA — 518 km/h (321 m.p.h.)
G4M2 'BETTY' — 438 km/h (272 m.p.h.)
WARWICK B.Mk II — 483 km/h (300 m.p.h.)

### MAXIMUM RANGE

Although its speed was good, the range of the PV-1 Ventura could not match that of the 'Betty' naval bomber. To boost its range the Ventura could carry internal bomb-bay tanks and external drop-tanks under the wings. Because they were larger aircraft, the 'Betty' and Warwick had greater internal capacities.

PV-1 VENTURA 2670 km (1,650 mi.)
WARWICK B.Mk II 4575 km (2,837 mi.)
G4M2 'BETTY' 6059 km (3,756 mi.)

### INTERNAL BOMBLOAD

Although it was a bigger aircraft than the PV-1, the G4M had a limited load capacity. The Warwick carried over two and a half tonnes of bombs and was intended as a replacement for the Wellington in the maritime reconnaissance role.

PV-1 VENTURA 1362 kg (2,994 lb.)
G4M2 'BETTY' 1000 kg (2,200 lb.)
WARWICK B.Mk II 2608 kg (5,738 lb.)

---

## Disaster over Amsterdam

**1** OPERATION 'RAMROD 16': On 3 May 1943 twelve Venturas of No. 487 Squadron, a New Zealand-manned unit, set off on a daylight raid on Amsterdam. At 4.43 p.m. Squadron Leader Leonard Trent led his squadron skywards towards Amsterdam.

**2** GERMAN WOLFPACK: Unknown to the Ventura force, two crack Luftwaffe fighter units were alerted to the raid. The Venturas lumbered into the trap and most were ripped to shreds by the 70 enemy fighters.

**3** LONE SURVIVOR: Trent continued the bomb run with five remaining Venturas. Four of these were shot down, but Trent managed to release his bombs over the target before being shot down himself. He was awarded the Victoria Cross for his bravery.

# LOCKHEED

# HUDSON

● Maritime patrol ● Anti-submarine ● Light bomber transport

One of the few combat aircraft to have been developed from a civil transport, the Lockheed Hudson maritime patrol bomber (and navigator trainer) owes its basic design to the Lockheed Model 14 Super Electra of the late 1930s. The Hudson was a smooth-handling and popular aircraft which never quite had the performance needed in warfare. Nevertheless, it made a fine contribution to the Allies' war effort.

▲ Converted airliners often made rather indifferent warplanes, but the Hudson was an immediate success. Orders for it from Britain made Lockheed a big name in America's aircraft industry.

**▼ Rockets and radar**
For anti-submarine patrol work, the Hudson was fitted with eight rockets and simple radar.

**▲ Airliner lines**
The Hudson's airliner heritage made it a good warplane. The capacious but sleek fuselage gave the aircraft long range and high speed, and the broad wings made it very stable in flight.

**▲ Lifeboat carrier**
Hudsons also saved lives. This aircraft from No. 123 Squadron, Royal Canadian Air Force, carried a large lifeboat under the fuselage, which could be dropped to survivors at the scene of a disaster.

**▲ American patrol**
This immaculate Hudson, with the pre-1942 American markings and British camouflage, was one of the first A-29s repossessed by America.

**◄ Hudson down**
The crew walked away from this mishap in a Hudson Mk VI, which has a radio direction-finding loop aerial.

## FACTS AND FIGURES

➤ A Hudson directed British naval forces to the German prison ship *Altmark* in February 1940.

➤ The prototype for the Hudson made its maiden flight on 10 December 1938.

➤ A single Hudson was used by the Sperry Gyroscope Company as a test aircraft.

➤ No. 280 Squadron, RAF, was the first to use Hudsons to drop airborne lifeboats over the North Sea in 1943.

➤ Some Hudsons were based in Manaos, Brazil, to patrol the South Atlantic.

➤ A total of 2941 Hudsons had been built when production ended in May 1943.

## PROFILE

# Airliner turned patrol bomber

Based on the Super Electra civil transport, the Hudson was the first American-built aircraft to fly with the Royal Air Force during World War II. The airframe was instantly recognisable as a modified Electra, with more powerful engines, gun armament and internal bomb-bay. This bomber was rushed into production to meet Britain's requirement for a maritime patrol aircraft and navigation trainer. Search-and-rescue Hudsons were also built,

with a lifeboat stored under the fuselage.

After its early success in British use, the Hudson was employed by the US Army Air Forces in A-28 and A-29 attack variants, and as the AT-18 advanced trainer. The US Navy adopted the Hudson as a patrol bomber, and called it the PBO.

US Navy Hudsons sank two U-boats on 15 March 1942. This was the first of several such successes in combat. An A-29 sank the German submarine U-701 on 7 July 1942.

*Above: This highly polished Hudson is an AT-18 gunnery trainer. These aircraft allowed trainee gunners to fire shots realistically from the turrets in peacetime conditions.*

*Right: In US Army Air Force service, the A-28 and A-29 series was never officially known as the Hudson, reflecting the fact that the aircraft was first and foremost designed to serve the RAF.*

Hudsons were used by many Allied air forces, including the Soviet Union and South Africa. The aircraft continued to serve faithfully in support roles up until the end of the war.

### Hudson Mk I

**Type:** maritime patrol-bomber

**Powerplant:** two 820-kW (1,100-hp.) Wright GR-1820-G-102A radial piston engines

**Maximum speed:** 396 km/h (245 m.p.h.) at 1980 m (6,500 ft.)

**Range:** 3154 km (1,955 mi.)

**Service ceiling:** 7620 m (25,000 ft.)

**Weights:** empty 5275 kg (11,605 lb.); maximum take-off 7938 kg (17,464 lb.)

**Armament:** two 7.62-mm (.30 cal.) forward-firing machine-guns and two similar weapons in a dorsal turret, plus up to 635 kg (1,400 lb.) of bombs or depth charges in internal bomb-bay

**Dimensions:**
| | |
|---|---|
| span | 19.96 m (65 ft.) |
| length | 13.51 m (44 ft.) |
| height | 3.61 m (12 ft.) |
| wing area | 51.19 m² (551 sq. ft.) |

### HUDSON MK V

This Lockheed Hudson Mk V served with No. 48 Squadron of the Royal Air Force Coastal Command, based at Stornoway in the Outer Hebrides during 1941. Its main tasks were patrol and air-sea rescue.

The RAF's Hudson had provision for two forward-firing fixed machine-guns in the upper fuselage, ahead of the pilot.

The upper surface of the fuselage contained a Perspex astrodome for visual observation, a large aerial mast with cables to the horizontal tailfin and a bullet-shaped fairing for the D/F loop antenna.

The Hudson's Boulton Paul dorsal turret provided good visibility and two hard-hitting 7.62-mm (.30 cal.) machine-guns.

Standard accommodation was for a crew of four: pilot, navigator, bomb-aimer and radio operator.

The Hudson's fuselage was very similar to the Super Electra airliner it was developed from. The lower fuselage, however, contained a large bomb-bay with provision for up to 635 kg (1,400 lb.) of offensive weapons or rescue life-rafts.

The large internal space could be converted into a troop transport or for VIP work.

The tail unit featured twin vertical fins and rudders, enabling the gunner (generally the radio operator) to have an almost completely clear field of vision and the ability to engage fighters flying behind him.

OY·G

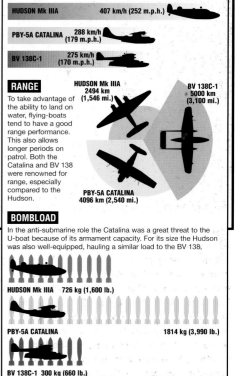

### COMBAT DATA

#### MAXIMUM SPEED

Flying-boats, carrying the extra weight of a strong hull, tend to have a lower top speed than equivalent landplanes. The Hudson design was based on that of a small airliner and had a fairly good speed compared to its contemporaries.

| | |
|---|---|
| HUDSON Mk IIIA | 407 km/h (252 m.p.h.) |
| PBY-5A CATALINA | 288 km/h (179 m.p.h.) |
| BV 138C-1 | 275 km/h (170 m.p.h.) |

#### RANGE

To take advantage of the ability to land on water, flying-boats tend to have a good range performance. This also allows longer periods on patrol. Both the Catalina and BV 138 were renowned for range, especially compared to the Hudson.

HUDSON Mk IIIA 2494 km (1,546 mi.)

BV 138C-1 5000 km (3,100 mi.)

PBY-5A CATALINA 4096 km (2,540 mi.)

#### BOMBLOAD

In the anti-submarine role the Catalina was a great threat to the U-boat because of its armament capacity. For its size the Hudson was also well-equipped, hauling a similar load to the BV 138.

| | |
|---|---|
| HUDSON Mk IIIA | 726 kg (1,600 lb.) |
| PBY-5A CATALINA | 1814 kg (3,990 lb.) |
| BV 138C-1 | 300 kg (660 lb.) |

## Coastal Command patrollers

■ **BRISTOL BEAUFORT:** Coastal Command's standard torpedo-bomber from 1940 to 1943, the prototype first flew in 1938.

■ **ARMSTRONG WHITWORTH WHITLEY:** Outmoded as bombers, Whitleys were the first to carry ASV.Mk II radar in Coastal Command.

■ **CONSOLIDATED LIBERATOR:** Late-model B-24s were used as VLR (very-long-range) patrol aircraft hunting for German U-boats.

■ **VICKERS WARWICK:** An enlarged variant of the famous Wellington, in the anti-submarine role the Warwick was just too late for war service.

# MACCHI
# MC.200 SAETTA

● Monoplane fighter ● Entered service 1939 ● Co-belligerent service

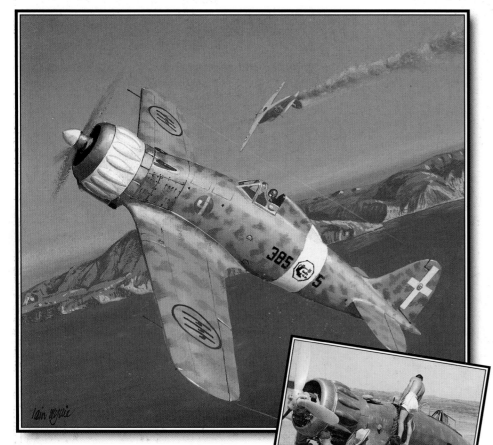

A s holder of the world speed, height and distance records in the late 1930s, the Regia Aeronautica (Italian air force) was perhaps blind to the fact that its service aircraft were lagging behind in terms of performance. During the Spanish Civil War, the success of Italian fighter and bomber types reinforced the air force's view of their aircraft. Consequently, the Macchi MC.200 was obsolete as soon as it entered service in 1939.

▲ Best known for its exploits in North Africa, the MC.200 was well-suited to desert operations, with its structural strength and short take-off run. Hurricanes and P-40s were its opponents.

## MACCHI MC.200 SAETTA

### ▲ Eastern Front
From August 1941 until the spring of 1942, 51 Italian MC.200s of 22º Gruppo and later 21º Gruppo operated over Russia, mainly on air-to-ground sorties.

### ▲ Defending Rome, 1940
This early production MC.200 of 371ª Squadriglia, 22º Gruppo, was based at Campino near Rome.

### ▼ Allied service
After the Italian surrender, the Aeronautica Cobelligerante del Sud (Southern Co-belligerent Air Force) operated around 23 MC.200s.

### ▲ Pre-war markings
Green, white and red stripes on this Saetta's tail were typical of the markings carried by the aircraft prior to Italy joining the fighting in 1940.

### Off the production line ▶
This aircraft was among the last batch of MC.200s built by Macchi. The fully enclosed cockpit was a feature of only the earliest production examples; Regia Aeronautica pilots preferred the traditional open cockpit to which they were accustomed.

## FACTS AND FIGURES

➤ The only Macchi MC.200s operated by the Allies were used as trainers by the co-belligerent air force.

➤ Eastern Front MC.200s flew over 6300 sorties; 88 Soviet aircraft were downed.

➤ Denmark ordered 12 MC.200s, but they were cancelled after the German invasion.

➤ Macchi developed a version with a new fuselage and engine, the MC.201, but it did not proceed beyond one prototype.

➤ MC.200 fighter-bombers fitted with bomb shackles were designated MC.200CBs.

➤ During raids on Malta in 1940, MC.200s escorted Luftwaffe Ju 87 dive-bombers.

## PROFILE

# Italy's under-powered Lightning

Known as the Saetta (Lightning), the MC.200 flew in prototype form for the first time on 24 December 1937. A cantilever, low-wing monoplane of all-metal construction (apart from fabric-covered control surfaces), the Macchi fighter had a retractable tail wheel and an enclosed cockpit. Pilots liked its light controls and all-round manoeuvrability. The design's main weak point was its 649-kW (870-hp.) Fiat A.74 RC.38 radial engine, which bestowed a top speed of just 502 km/h (312 m.p.h.) at 4500 m (14,800 ft.).

Fighter development in the late 1930s had moved on rapidly, resulting in aircraft like the Bf 109 and Spitfire. They were powered by in-line, liquid-cooled engines that offered more power and greater streamlining, and thus much higher speeds.

The MC.200's armament of two machine-guns was also inadequate – even when it was doubled to four in later aircraft.

Entering service in October 1939, Saettas numbered 150 when Italy entered World War II in June 1940. Their first combat

Below: This Regia Aeronautica Saetta is in the company of a tri-motored Italian bomber and a Romanian-built IAR.80 monoplane fighter. MC.200s saw service on the Eastern Front where they scored a number of victories.

Above: MC.200AS was the designation of aircraft fitted with dust filters for North African service.

came in the autumn, when Lightnings escorted bombers attacking Malta. Action over Greece and Yugoslavia followed; a few served on the Eastern Front during 1941–42. However, it was in the deserts of North Africa that the type saw the most use.

### MC.200 Saetta

**Type:** single-seat fighter/fighter-bomber

**Powerplant:** one 649-kW (870-hp.) Fiat A.74 RC.38 radial piston engine

**Maximum speed:** 502 km/h (312 m.p.h.) at 4500 m (14,800 ft.)

**Range:** 870 km (541 m.p.h.) with auxiliary fuel

**Service ceiling:** 8900 m (29,200 ft.)

**Weights:** empty 1895 kg (4,178 lb.); maximum take-off 2590 kg (5,710 lb.)

**Armament:** two fuselage-mounted Breda-SAFAT 12.7-mm (.50 cal.) machine-guns (and two wing-mounted Breda-SAFAT 7.7-mm (.303 cal.) machine-guns on later aircraft), plus up to 294 kg (648 lb.) of bombs on field-modified aircraft

**Dimensions:**
| | | |
|---|---|---|
| span | 10.58 m | (34 ft. 9 in.) |
| length | 8.19 m | (26 ft. 10 in.) |
| height | 3.50 m | (11 ft. 6 in.) |
| wing area | 16.80 m² | (181 sq. ft.) |

### MC.200 Saetta

This aircraft was among those of 90ª Squadriglia, 10º Gruppo, 4º Stormo at Crotone, Sicily in 1941. The squadron's emblem, a red elephant, was painted below the cockpit.

Regia Aeronautica pilots disliked the MC.200's original enclosed cockpit. Macchi redesigned the canopy, this semi-enclosed design being the result. Still unimpressed, some pilots discarded the side panels to improve visibility.

4º Stormo's famous 'Cavallino Rampante' emblem was applied to their aircraft on a white fuselage band. Regia Aeronautica aircraft were among the most colourfully adorned of the war.

Given Macchi's success with in-line engines in its Schneider Trophy-winning aircraft, the choice of a radial design for its new generation of fighters was surprising. Fiat's 14-cylinder A.74 radial powered the MC.200, as it did the Fiat CR.42 biplane fighter and G.50 monoplane.

Initially, the MC.200 was fitted with just two 12.7-mm (.50 cal.) Breda-SAFAT machine-guns mounted above and behind the engine. This armament fit was later doubled to four, with the addition of a gun in each wing, though the aircraft was still seriously under-armed by the standards of the day.

The MC.200's semi-monocoque fuselage structure and wings were all-metal save for fabric-covered control surfaces. Field modifications included the fitting of underwing hardpoints for two 147-kg (325-lb.) bombs or fuel tanks. Ground strafing and offensive sweeps became major roles for the Saetta as it became increasingly vulnerable in the fighter role.

### ACTION DATA

#### MAXIMUM SPEED

Faster than its contemporary, the Fiat G.50, the Macchi 200 was nevertheless still on the slow side and could not match the performance of the superb Spitfire or Messerschmitt Bf 109.

| | |
|---|---|
| MC.200 | 502 km/h (312 m.p.h.) |
| KITTYHAWK Mk IV | 552 km/h (343 m.p.h.) |
| G.50 | 472 km/h (293 m.p.h.) |

#### POWER

A major problem with the Saetta was its lack of power. Producing just 649 kW, the Fiat A74 hardly made the MC.200 a super-fighter, and it proved extremely vulnerable to attack. Like the Kittyhawk and the G.50, it was more suitable as a fighter-bomber.

| MC.200 | KITTYHAWK Mk IV | G.50 |
|---|---|---|
| 649 kW (870 hp.) | 895 kW (1,200 hp.) | 626 kW (840 hp.) |

#### ARMAMENT

None of these aircraft was known for its hard-hitting armament, though later versions of the Kittyhawk had six guns. A lack of heavy armament was yet another drawback of the Saetta, and battle experience showed that both it and the G.50 were obsolete.

| | |
|---|---|
| MC.200 | 2 x 12.7-mm (.50 cal.) machine-guns / 2 x 7.7-mm (.303 cal.) machine-guns |
| KITTYHAWK Mk IV | 6 x 12.7-mm (.50 cal.) machine-guns / 680-kg (1,5000 lb.) bombload |
| G.50 | 2 x 12,7-mm (.50 cal.) machine-guns |

## Fighters in North Africa

**CURTISS TOMAHAWK:** Members of the American P-40 family served the RAF in large numbers in North Africa. No. 112 Squadron became famous for its sharkmouth markings.

**FIAT G.50:** Powered by the same Fiat radial as the MC.200 – and bearing a strong resemblance to that aircraft – the G.50 served as a fighter-bomber in the North African campaign.

**HAWKER HURRICANE:** Gradually outmoded as interceptors, Hurricanes became bombers and 'tank-busters'. For the latter role Mk IVs were fitted with 40-mm (1.57-in.) cannon.

**MACCHI MC.202 FOLGORE:** The best fighter to serve with the Regia Aeronautica in large numbers during World War II, the Folgore (Thunderbolt) entered service in Libya in 1941.

# MACCHI

# M.C.202 AND M.C.205V

- Italy's finest dogfighter ● Tactical fighter-bomber

▲ Before the war, Macchi produced some of the world's fastest record breakers, and that experience was put to good use in the company's fine series of wartime fighters.

**T**he Macchi M.C.202 Folgore (Thunderbolt) was among the most beautiful fighters to fly with wartime Axis forces, reflecting the aerodynamic flair of designer Mario Castoldi – the genius behind most Macchi warplanes. Building upon the M.C.200 Saetta (Lightning) but offering cleaner lines and more power, the M.C.202 was rushed into production and fought from 1941 onwards. To many, this was the best Italian fighter of the war.

▼ **Nose down**
A little too hard on the brakes on a desert airstrip, and the result was a broken propeller.

▲ **Alfa power**
The Alfa Romeo RA.1000 was one of the finest aero engines which Italy built. Many other Italian fighters were underpowered.

◀ **Sleek lines**
Italian fighters were, like the early Soviet MiG fighters, reliant on light weight and clean lines. Fitted with neat inline engines for their speed, they emphasised agility at the expense of armament.

**Smashed Veltro** ▶
This M.C.205V crashed in 1986, after being lovingly restored. Examples of the aircraft are now rare, as few survived the war.

▲ **Inside**
The M.C.202 had a small cockpit with modern, well laid out instruments and controls.

## FACTS AND FIGURES

➤ The Folgore traces its heritage in part to the Macchi floatplanes that competed in the Schneider Trophy Races.

➤ The first flight of a Folgore took place on 10 August 1940.

➤ About 1500 M.C.202s were built, including 393 built by Macchi.

➤ Although agile, the M.C.202 was slower than the Bf 109 and the Spitfire.

➤ A specialised fighter-bomber version, the M.C.202CB, carried two 320-kg (700-lb.) bombs.

➤ A restored Macchi M.C.202 is displayed in the US National Air & Space Museum.

# PROFILE

# Italy's finest wartime fighter

Following Italy's military campaigns in East Africa, the Regia Aeronautica re-equipped with the Saetta (recognised by its radial engine) and later the M.C.202 Folgore and M.C.205V Veltro (Greyhound). Of the trio, the Folgore was the most pleasing to the eye. It introduced a new fuselage and improved engine but retained the tail unit, landing gear and similar wings to the Saetta.

Manufactured by Macchi, Breda and SAI-Ambrosini alongside the Saetta, the graceful Folgore was propelled by a German Daimler-Benz DB 601A-1 engine until a licence-built Alfa Romeo version became available. It had a dramatically better performance than its Saetta ancestor, but Italy was under bombardment and its aero industry could not produce enough engines.

MC.202 Folgores began fighting in Libya in November 1941 and on the Eastern Front in September 1942. Italian pilots regarded the Folgore as an excellent combat aircraft, and many fought superbly in it. It could easily outfly Hurricanes and P-40s in the desert, and was a match for the famous Spitfire.

*The M.C.205 Veltro was the ultimate Macchi fighter. With great agility, adequate speed and, in its final version at least, a powerful cannon armament, the Castoldi design team had produced a fighter to match the best produced in Britain, Germany or America.*

## M.C.202 Folgore

**Type:** single-seat fighter/fighter-bomber

**Powerplant:** one 876-kW (1,175-hp.) Alfa Romeo RA.1000 RC 41-I Monsone inverted V-12 piston engine (licence-built Daimler-Benz DB 601)

**Maximum speed:** 596 km/h (370 m.p.h.) at 4570 m (15,000 ft.)

**Range:** 765 km (272 mi.)

**Service ceiling:** 11,500 m (37,700 ft.)

**Weights:** empty 2350 kg (5,170 lb.); loaded 3010 kg (6,620 lb.)

**Armament:** two 12.7-mm (.50 cal.) machine-guns in engine cowling

**Dimensions:**
| | | |
|---|---|---|
| span | 10.58 m | (34 ft. 8 in.) |
| length | 8.85 m | (63 ft. 9 in.) |
| height | 3.04 m | (10 ft.) |
| wing area | 16.80 m² | (181 sq. ft.) |

## M.C.202

This MC.202 Folgore served with 22⁰ Gruppo, 369⁰ Squadriglia, based at Capodichino, Naples. The sparrow badge on the white band was the wing emblem, and '369' was the number of the squadron.

Its long nose meant that the M.C.202 was difficult to taxi on the ground, even though it was stunning in the air.

The tail unit was a metal monocoque unit with fabric-covered moving control surfaces. The tailwheel was retractable.

The Macchi design showed its racing heritage with a very thin wing. Cannon armament had to be fitted beneath later M.C.202s' wings rather than in them.

The fuselage and wing were of all-metal construction, with fabric covering for the moveable control surfaces.

A large sheet of armour protected the pilot – not always a feature of Italian fighters.

The secret of the M.C.202's success was in its engine, the German DB 601, built under licence as the Alfa RA.1000. The engine radiator was located underneath the engine, which drove a three-bladed variable-pitch airscrew.

The wing featured interconnected flaps and slats. When the pilot selected flap down, the ailerons also lowered, giving a more efficient wing at low airspeeds. The flaps were also hydraulically operated.

## COMBAT DATA

### MAXIMUM SPEED

Although the Macchi was faster than previous Italian fighters, it could not quite match the speeds possible in the Allied fighters which it faced in North Africa. But the difference was marginal, and its fine handling meant that it was better than a P-40 and a match for the Spitfire.

| | |
|---|---|
| M.C.202 FOLGORE | 595 km/h |
| SPITFIRE Mk V | 602 km/h |
| P-40N WARHAWK | 609 km/h |

### SERVICE CEILING

The Macchi could climb fairly high, just being able to outperform the standard Spitfire, and easily outstripping those assigned to the desert campaign with 'low-blown' engines. On paper the P-40 could fly even higher, but this was not its best altitude, where it was sluggish and difficult to manoeuvre.

| M.C.202 FOLGORE 11,500 m (37,700 ft.) | SPITFIRE Mk V 11,300 m (37,000 ft.) | P-40N WARHAWK 11,600 m (38,000 ft.) |
|---|---|---|

### ARMAMENT

Armament was a major weakness in Italian fighters. The M.C.202 was originally designed with only two guns at a time when British fighters were carrying eight and German fighters were armed with cannon. Later examples of the Macchi fighter were fitted with cannon under the wings, but increased drag meant lower performance.

**M.C.202 FOLGORE**
2 x 12.7-mm (.50 cal.) MGs, 2 x 7.7-mm (.303 cal.) MGs

**SPITFIRE Mk V**
2x 20-mm (0.79-in.) cannon, 4 x 7.7-mm (.303 cal.) MGs

**P-40N WARHAWK**
6 x 12.7-mm (.50 cal.) MGs

## Macchi fighter development

■ **M.C.200 SAETTA:** Light and extremely agile, the radial-engined M.C.202 with which Italy began the war was at a disadvantage when confronting British fighters like the Spitfire.

■ **M.C.202 FOLGORE:** Fitting a Daimler-Benz DB 601 engine into a Saetta airframe transformed the Macchi fighter into a much more capable machine, which fought with distinction in Africa.

■ **M.C.205 VELTRO:** The powerful DB 605 kept Macchi fighters competitive, but poor industrial performance meant that only 262 Veltros were produced before the Italian armistice.

# MARTIN

## 167 MARYLAND/187 BALTIMORE

● Desert operations ● Export only ● Reconnaissance

I n the late 1930s the Glenn L. Martin Company created the Maryland for the US Army (later selling it to France) and the Baltimore for Britain's RAF. Both were twin-engined light bombers with a modest bombload, defensive armament and performance that compared poorly with modern fighters like the Supermarine Spitfire and the Messerschmitt Bf 109. Although they were solidly designed aircraft, they were not advanced enough for World War II.

▲ All 400 Baltimores initially ordered by the RAF were sent to Egypt to help the Allied effort against Rommel's 1942 offensive. Escorted by Curtiss Kittyhawks, they excelled in the Battle of El Alamein.

▲ Maryland prototype
The prototype first flew on 13 March 1939 and was given the designation XA-22. It lost out to the Douglas A-20 in the US Army competition.

▲ Narrow fuselage
The Baltimore's narrow fuselage prevented the crew from moving about and stretching on long trips.

British Marylands ▶
Both the RAF and Royal Navy operated Marylands in the long-range reconnaissance role.

◀ Advancing through Italy
An RAF Baltimore Mk III drops its load over the railway station and sidings at Sulmona in northern Italy. British and South African Baltimores fought throughout the Italian campaign.

Turkish delight ▶
A number of Baltimores were supplied to Turkey during the later stages of World War II under the Lend-Lease arrangement. This is an ex-RAF aircraft.

## FACTS AND FIGURES

➤ Martin built 496 Maryland bombers, all but one for France; many of these were transferred to the RAF and Royal Navy.

➤ The Maryland was produced at what was the USA's largest aircraft factory in 1939.

➤ More than 20 Baltimores were lost during delivery by sea to Great Britain.

➤ In all, 1,575 Baltimores were built – more than any Martin aircraft except for the B-26 Marauder (5266).

➤ The Baltimore cost $120,000, compared with $78,000 for a B-26 Marauder.

➤ After the war a Baltimore was used by the US Navy to test experimental airfoils.

**PROFILE**

# Distinguished desert bomber

The Maryland was designed by Martin engineer James S. McDonnell, who later gave his name to the McDonnell Douglas Corporation. It was tested by the US Army as the XA-22 and performed better than attack bombers put forward by other manufacturers. The Army withheld a production contract, however, and the Maryland was exported instead to France. The first Marylands left the factory on 2 September 1939, the day before France and Britain declared war on Germany. They had little impact on the conflict, however.

The Maryland led to the Baltimore, which was known by the US Army as the A-30. Built to satisfy British requirements, the Baltimore was a somewhat more formidable attack bomber that was used extensively in North African fighting at El Alamein in June 1942. The Baltimore also achieved moderate success in Italy later in the war.

The last Baltimores served with the RAF in Kenya, performing aerial mapping and locust control duties until 1948.

*Above: Ordered before the prototype had even flown, France received 140 Marylands. A number of them served with the Free French forces until 1943.*

*Right: No. 13 Squadron re-equipped with the Baltimore in December 1943, and spent the next 10 months on day and night operations in northern Italy.*

## Baltimore Mk IV

**Type:** four-seat light bomber (Martin 187 Baltimore)

**Powerplant:** two 1238-kW (1,660-hp.) Wright R-2600-19 Cyclone 14 radial piston engines

**Maximum speed:** 491 km/h (304 m.p.h.) at 3505 m (11,500 ft.)

**Range:** 1741 km (1,080 mi.)

**Service ceiling:** 7100 m (23,300 ft.)

**Weights:** empty 7013 kg (15,429 lb.); maximum take-off 10,251 kg (22,550 lb.)

**Armament:** four 7.7-mm (.303 cal.) wing-mounted machine-guns, two or four similar guns in ventral position and provision for four 7.62-mm (.30 cal.) machine-guns in fixed, rear-firing position, plus a bombload of up to 907 kg (2,000 lb.)

**Dimensions:**
| | | |
|---|---|---|
| span | 18.69 m | (61 ft. 4 in.) |
| length | 14.78 m | (48 ft. 6 in.) |
| height | 5.41 m | (17 ft. 9 in.) |
| wing area | 50.03 m² | (538 sq. ft.) |

## BALTIMORE MK V

This example flew with No. 232 Wing, comprising Nos 55 and 223 Squadrons, of the North-west African Tactical Air Force in the Italian campaign during 1944.

With the narrow fuselage, communication between crewmembers was difficult. If the pilot was injured it was almost impossible for anyone else to reach the controls.

Early versions of the Baltimore had only poor protection from the mid-upper gun position. This made the aircraft extremely vulnerable to attacks from above and behind. The problem was solved in the Mk III with the introduction of a Boulton-Paul hydraulically-operated turret containing four Browning 7.7-mm (.303 cal.) machine-guns.

With a distinctive curved rudder and a low-mounted tailplane, the Baltimore had responsive controls which were necessary for a single pilot on long-range operations.

The rear fuselage was virtually a boom carrying the tail unit. The Baltimore featured a much deeper front fuselage than the Maryland.

Originally powered by two Wright R-2600-19 engines, the more powerful Mk V was fitted with two 1268-kW (1,700-hp.) R-2600-29 radials. These improved speed and climb performance.

Up to 907 kg (2,000 lb.) of bombs could be carried in the Baltimore's bomb-bay. The aircraft could bomb very accurately and on some occasions dropped bombs from more than 3000 m (12,000 ft.) on targets situated only 700 m (2,300 ft.) from Allied troops.

Much of the Baltimore's design was based on its predecessor, the Maryland. Its all-metal wing was practically identical and was similarly mounted in the low-mid position.

All Baltimores delivered to the RAF served in the Mediterranean theatre and were painted in a brown/sand desert camouflage scheme.

### COMBAT DATA

#### CRUISING SPEED
Although the Baltimore had more powerful engines than the Maryland, they had similar top speeds. The Maryland actually cruised faster than the Baltimore, thanks to its more aerodynamically streamlined shape. Both were slower than the Boston, however.

| | |
|---|---|
| **BALTIMORE Mk IV** | 362 km/h (224 m.p.h.) |
| **MARYLAND Mk I** | 399 km/h (247 m.p.h.) |
| **BOSTON Mk III** | 402 km/h (249 m.p.h.) |

#### POWER
The Boston and Baltimore had a distinct power advantage over the Maryland. This allowed them to carry more defensive armament and gave them a better rate of climb.

| | | |
|---|---|---|
| **BALTIMORE Mk IV** 2476 kW (3,320 hp.) | **MARYLAND Mk I** 1566 kW (2,100 hp.) | **BOSTON Mk III** 2386 kW (3,200 hp.) |

#### ARMAMENT
Later marks of the Baltimore had heavy defensive armament and could put up a stubborn defence against enemy fighters. The Maryland had poor defence against attack from behind. All three types carried a similar bombload.

**BALTIMORE Mk IV** 8 x 7.7-mm (.303 cal.) machine-guns 4 x 7.62-mm (.30 cal.) machine-guns, 907-kg (2,000-lb.) bombload

**MARYLAND Mk I** 4 x 7.62-mm (.30 cal.) machine-guns 2 x 7.7-mm (.303 cal.) machine-guns, 907-kg (2,000-lb.) bombload

**BOSTON Mk III** 7 x 7.7-mm (.303 cal.) machine-guns 4 x 20-mm (0.79-in.) cannon, 907-kg (2,000-lb.) bombload

## RAF Lend-Lease bombers

■ **BOEING FORTRESS:** Of 125 Lend-Lease Fortresses delivered to the RAF, 19 were Mk IIs (equivalent to the B-17F). Most were used by Coastal Command for maritime reconnaissance.

■ **CONSOLIDATED LIBERATOR:** Famous for helping to close the U-boat 'gap' in the middle of the Atlantic, Liberators also served with Bomber Command and in the Middle and Far East.

■ **MARTIN MARAUDER:** Around 525 Marauders were delivered to the RAF and SAAF under the Lend-Lease arrangement. They were used exclusively in the Mediterranean theatre.

■ **NORTH AMERICAN MITCHELL:** The Mitchell proved to be a capable close-support bomber for the RAF when operating with the 2nd Tactical Air Force during the Allied advances of 1944/45.

# MARTIN

# B-10

● **Medium bomber** ● **Pioneering construction** ● **Pacific warrior**

When the Martin B-10 joined the US Army in 1934, it was a revolution in every way. Suddenly, fabric-covered biplane bombers were replaced by a silvery, all-metal monoplane. And the bomber, once easy pickings for any enterprising fighter pilot, was now faster than any fighter. The B-10's moment of glory was brief, as other manufacturers followed its lead, but it stayed in service until the first days of the war in the Pacific.

▲ *Martin was determined to break back into the bomber market after years of domination by other manufacturers. It built medium bombers for many years, based on the success of the B-10 family.*

## MARTIN **B-10**

▼ **America's finest**
*The B-10 was seen as America's first line of defence by the bomber strategists of the mid-1930s. B-10s remained in service until the introduction of B-17s and B-18s in the late 1930s.*

▲ **First of a new breed**
*The prototype XB-10 had an open cockpit but no nose turret. It first flew in the summer of 1933, with the first production B-10s seen a year later.*

▼ **World's finest**
*The USAAC was the envy of the world in 1934 when it first took delivery of the B-10. Between mid 1936 and 1939, 189 were exported.*

▼ **Floatplane version**
*Martin produced the YB-12 floatplane for the Army for coastal defence, a responsibility previously held by the US Navy.*

▲ **Finished product**
*In service the B-10 looked very modern with its aggressive gun turrets and clean fuselage design.*

### FACTS AND FIGURES

➤ A total of 152 B-10 and B-12 bombers were delivered to the US Army, plus 190 to foreign allies.

➤ China flew its B-10 bombers on raids against Japan in 1938.

➤ Dutch pilots used their B-10 variant in action in the Dutch East Indies.

➤ In July/August 1934, 10 B-10s set a round-trip record from Washington to Alaska, flying a total of 13,341 km (8720 miles).

➤ The US Army's first order was for 48 B-10s costing a total of $2,440,000.

➤ The B-10 was not the first US all-metal bomber; this was the Boeing B-9.

# PROFILE

# Martin's metal wonder-bomber

Martin's B-10 (and similar B-12) were the forerunners of advanced World War II bombers. The B-10 was an all-metal, twin-engine, mid-wing monoplane with retractable landing gear.

The pilot sat in the cockpit, the radio operator and one gunner in the dorsal turret, and one other gunner positioned in the rotating nose turret. Winner of the 1932 Collier Trophy for achievement, the B-10 featured such refinements as internal bomb racks, Norden bombsight, enclosed crew stations and controllable pitch props. A prototype had a turbo-supercharger fitted which gave a maximum speed of 343 km/h (212 mph), faster than any fighter aircraft in the US arsenal.

Some B-12s were fitted with twin floats and used on coastal patrols. A Martin B-12 floatplane bomber was flown from Langley Field, Virginia, on 24 August 1935 to set three world payload-speed records. The aircraft also achieved considerable export success, with sales to Argentina, China, The Netherlands, Thailand, Turkey and the USSR.

By the time the war began the B-10 was obsolete, but a handful of the Dutch East Indies aircraft were among the first aircraft to see action in the Pacific in December 1941.

*Below: Despite the high performance of the standard B-10, the Army wanted more. It ordered the YB-10A, with turbosupercharged engines, and the YB-14, with powerful Twin Wasp engines.*

*Above: Aircraft design was moving at a tremendous pace in the 1930s. The B-10 looked far more modern than any aircraft in service in 1934, but was soon obsolete.*

## B-10B

**Type:** three-seat medium bomber

**Powerplant:** (B-10) two 578-kW (775-hp) Wright R-1820-33 Cyclone radial piston engines; (B-12) two 578-kW Pratt & Whitney R-1690-11 radial piston engines

**Maximum speed:** 343 km/h (212 mph)

**Range:** 1996 km (1240 miles)

**Service ceiling:** 7375 m (24,200 ft)

**Weights:** empty 4391 kg (9660 lb); maximum take-off 7439 kg (16,366 lb)

**Armament:** three 7.62-mm (.30-cal.) machine guns in nose and rear turrets and a ventral position, plus up to 1025 kg (2255 lb) of bombs in fuselage bomb-bay

**Dimensions:**
| | |
|---|---|
| span | 21.49 m (70 ft) |
| length | 13.64 m (45 ft) |
| height | 4.70 m (15 ft) |
| wing area | 62.99 m² (678 sq ft) |

# MODEL 139WH-1

The Martin 139WH was the export model of the B-10 bomber developed for The Netherlands. In all, 118 were produced in two versions and were among the very first aircraft to fight in the Pacific theatre against invading Japanese forces in December 1941.

The rear cockpit was modified to accommodate a radio operator and a gunner operating a 7.62-mm (.30-cal.) machine gun. The bomb-bay was in the bottom of the fuselage under the front cockpit, with a second gun firing through the floor of the rear cockpit.

In the late 1930s, when fighters seemed like a remote threat to high-flying fast bombers and the Dutch forces in the Pacific faced little threat of attack, high-visibility paint schemes were common.

The nose turret mounted a single machine gun. It was manually traversed, unlike the powered turrets in later bombers.

Martin B-10s were powered by a variety of Wright Cyclone engines, the prototype having the 503-kW (675-hp) R-1820-25. The YB-13 used the Pratt & Whitney Hornet engine.

The bomb-bay could accommodate an extra fuel tank to extend the impressive range even further. This was especially useful for operations in the Pacific. Total offensive armament was four 227-kg (500-lb) bombs, all of which were carried internally.

Among the many innovative features was a retractable tailwheel. A ski-wheel undercarriage was also tested.

# COMBAT DATA

## MAXIMUM SPEED

Although the B-10 was obsolete by the outbreak of war, it was still faster than some bombers in service, such as the SM.81, and when introduced it could outrun any fighter in the world.

| | |
|---|---|
| B-10B | 343 km/h (212 mph) |
| [WELLINGTON] Mk III | 411 km/h (255 mph) |
| SM.81 SERIES 5 | 336 km/h (208 mph) |

## RANGE

For the long-range bombing missions to attack an invasion fleet heading for America, the B-10 needed good range. This was one of the reasons the design was so popular with the Dutch East Indies air force, which had to fly long missions over the sea. The B-10 could carry extra fuel if required in the bomb-bay.

WELLINGTON Mk III 2478 km (1536 miles)

B-10B 1996 km (1238 miles)

SM.81 SERIES 5 2000 km (1240 miles)

## ARMAMENT

For its time the B-10 had respectable armament, especially considering that most fighters only had a pair of machine guns. By 1940 most bombers carried at least twice the B-10's payload.

| B-10B | WELLINGTON Mk III | SM.81 SERIES 5 |
|---|---|---|
| 3 x 7.62-mm (.30-cal.) machine guns 1025 kg (2255 lb) of bombs | 8 x 7.7-mm (.303-cal.) machine guns 2041 kg (4490 lb) of bombs | 4 x 7.7-mm (.30-cal.) machine guns 2000 kg (4400 lb) of bombs |

# Bombers from the Martin Company

■ **MARYLAND:** Rejected by the USAAC in its original form, the Martin 167 was ordered by France and ended up in the hands of the RAF following the French surrender. It was used as a light bomber and reconnaissance aircraft, and performed the pre-strike missions over Taranto harbour in November 1940.

■ **BALTIMORE:** Developed to a British specification, the Baltimore was used by the RAF in the Middle East, gaining a good record as a day and night medium-bomber and reconnaissance aircraft. Like the B-10, it had a narrow, deep fuselage that made it difficult for the crew to change positions.

■ **MARAUDER:** One of the fastest medium bombers of World War II, the B-26 suffered from a reputation as a dangerous aircraft when it was first introduced. However, when crews had gained experience with it, the Marauder went on to record the lowest loss rate of any bomber aircraft used in Europe.

# MARTIN
# B-26 MARAUDER

● Very fast ● Difficult to fly ● USAAF's most potent medium bomber

▲ Designed in 1939 for the US Army Air Corps, the sleek, fast, twin-engined Martin Model 179 Marauder was ordered straight into production without a prototype or trials.

**D**uring World War II the Martin B-26 Marauder was considered a 'hot' ship – high-powered, unforgiving and risky to fly. But in spite of unflattering nicknames like 'Widowmaker' and 'Flying Coffin', the Marauder was not as dangerous as was widely believed. In fact, it was a potent warplane – a silvery sleek bullet of a medium bomber which could carry a respectable bombload and outrun the opposition.

## MARTIN B-26 MARAUDER

▲ **Streamlined for speed**
The B-26 was designed with a very sleek, circular section fuselage, curving to the nose and tail cones. The cockpit windscreen was streamlined, and the wing was designed for speed rather than lift.

▲ **Medium bombload**
A stick of 114-kg (250-lb) bombs falls from the internal bomb-bay of a raiding B-26. The aircraft could carry a rather modest total weight of 2359 kg (5,200 lb.).

◀ **Fast targets**
Some Marauders were stripped of their armour and used as high-speed target tugs and trainers by the US Air Force and Navy.

▼ **Tactical bomber**
Flying with the US 9th Air Force from May 1943, the B-26 quickly became the hardest-worked Allied daylight medium bomber over Europe.

▲ **Shot down**
As crews got used to the B-26's performance it became less vulnerable. By VE Day it had the lowest loss rate of any US bomber in Europe.

## FACTS AND FIGURES

➤ The first flight of the B-26 took place at the Martin factory in November 1940.

➤ B-26s began service with the 22nd Bomb Group in Australia just after Pearl Harbor.

➤ Future American president Lyndon B. Johnson received a Silver Star for a Marauder mission in New Guinea.

➤ During an attack on Ijmuiden, Holland, in May 1943, an entire group of 10 B-26s was shot down by fighters, flak and collisions.

➤ The price of a B-26 was $261,000 in 1940, which had reduced to $192,000 by 1944.

➤ Of the 5157 Marauders built, 522 were supplied to the Royal Air Force.

## PROFILE

# The flying torpedo

The Martin Marauder went straight into production, the first aircraft to fly being a service model and not a prototype. It made an immediate impact, rumour giving the new medium bomber an (exaggerated) top speed of almost 600 km/h (370 m.p.h.), faster than most fighters then in service. Its engines were in streamlined nacelles underslung from a shoulder-mounted wing, enhancing the image of the Marauder as a silvery 'Flying Torpedo'.

Although employed to good effect for conventional and torpedo bombing, the Marauder never made its mark in the Pacific theatre where the more conventional, less challenging B-25 Mitchell was preferred.

In Europe the story was very different, with B-26s joining US squadrons in 1942. The initial deployment by the 319th Bomb Group was trouble-plagued. The Marauder landed at 210 km/h (130 m.p.h.) and could betray an unskilled pilot. But the B-26 soon made its mark over the continent, proving to be a rugged, accurate and extremely hard-hitting tactical weapon. Following their success in covering the invasion of Normandy, Marauders again proved successful in attacking the heavily defended German V-1 flying bomb launch sites during 1944.

*When it entered service the B-26 had the highest wing loading of any aircraft in the USAAF. The high-set, short-span wing and two large, powerful engines optimised it for high speed rather than bombload or handling.*

*The 525 Marauders that flew with the RAF and the South African air force replaced Blenheims in the Mediterranean theatre.*

### B-26B Marauder

**Type:** seven-seat medium day-bomber

**Powerplant:** two 1432-kW (1,920-hp.) Pratt & Whitney R-2800-43 Double Wasp radial piston engines

**Maximum speed:** 454 km/h (317 m.p.h.) at 4570 m (15,000 ft.)

**Climb rate:** to 4600 m (15,000 ft.) in 13 minutes

**Range:** 1851 km (1,148 mi.) with 1361 kg (2,994 lb.) of bombs

**Service ceiling:** 6400 m (23,500 ft.)

**Weights:** empty 10,886 kg (23,950 lb.); normal take-off 16,783 kg (36,923 lb.)

**Armament:** up to eight 12.7-mm (.50 cal.) machine-guns with 3950 rounds of ammunition, plus a maximum internal bombload of 2359 kg (5,170 lb.)

**Dimensions:**  
span late models 21.64 m (71 ft.)  
early models 19.12 m (63 ft.)  
length 17.75 m (58 ft.)  
height 6.55 m (21 ft.)  
wing area 61.13 m² (679 sq. ft.)

## B-26C MARAUDER

**This B-26C, nicknamed 'Baby Bumps II', was flown by the 557th Squadron of the 98th Wing based at Chipping Ongar.**

As a medium bomber the B-26 crew varied from five to seven. One gunner manually operated the nose machine-guns and others the electrically-operated dorsal turret, tail turret and the manually aimed waist guns.

When it entered service the Marauder had the highest wing loading of any USAAF aircraft. This gave it high take-off and landing speeds, which caused problems for inexperienced pilots.

In order to save weight, the Marauder's flying control surfaces (rudder, elevators and ailerons) were wooden ribbed and covered with doped fabric.

In order to improve handling performance on take-off and landing, the B-26's fin and rudder was extended and the wing span was increased.

The B-26C had a heavier armament and more powerful engines than the major production version, the B-26B, that preceded it.

The B-26 was powered by two 1432-kW (1,920-hp.) Pratt & Whitney R-2800-43 piston engines, which drove large four-blade propellers.

The engine nacelles housed the large, single wheels of the tricycle undercarriage. All three units had single strut legs, the nosewheel retracting rearwards into the lower fuselage below the cockpit.

This B-26 carries the black and white invasion stripes applied at the time of the Normandy landings of June 1944. It is in standard USAAF colours with the KS code letters of the 557th Squadron.

### COMBAT DATA

#### ARMAMENT

The B-26's defensive armament was better than its German or Japanese contemporaries. Having both fixed and mobile guns in the nose, dorsal and tail turrets, together with rear side-window guns, it had an all-round arc of fire.

**Ju 88A-4**  
3000 kg of bombs  
4 x 7.92-mm  
(0.31-in.) MGs

**B-26B MARAUDER**  
2359 kg of bombs  
8 x 12.7-mm  
(.50 cal.) MGs

**Ki-49-IIA 'Helen'**  
1000 kg of bombs  
5 x 7.7-mm  
(.50 cal.) MGs  
1 x 20-mm  
(0.79-in.) cannon

## Medium bombers: the rivals

**JUNKERS Ju 88:** One of the Luftwaffe's main bombers, the Ju 88 was designed as a medium-range tactical aircraft that was also used as a dive-bomber and night-fighter. It was nearly 100 km/h (60 m.p.h.) slower than the B-26, but could carry nearly double the weight of bombs. Total production of the Ju 88 was about 15,000.

**MITSUBISHI Ki-67 HIRYU 'PEGGY':** This Japanese army Type 4 was the country's fastest medium-range bomber of the war, with a top speed of 537 km/h, nearly 100 km/h (60 m.p.h.) greater than that of the B-26. The penalty for this was a small bombload of just 800 kg (1,760 lb.). Only 698 Ki-67s were built before the war ended.

**NORTH AMERICAN B-25 MITCHELL:** The USAAF's 'gull-wing' B-25 was developed at the same time as the Marauder. It carried a smaller bombload, was a good deal slower, but was more rugged and relatively easy to fly. Nearly twice as many B-25s were built (9816) than B-26s (5157).

# MARTIN
# PBM MARINER

● Flying boat ● Amphibian ● Anti-submarine and SAR aircraft

▲ The amphibious capabilities of the later Mariner versions made them versatile aircraft. The high-mounted engines, search radar and gull wing were distinctive features.

O ne of the truly great flying boats of all time, the Martin PBM Mariner was produced in seaplane and amphibian versions. It was the most important naval aircraft in its class during World War II. Largely used as a replacement for the Consolidated PBY Catalina, which was perhaps the only better-known flying boat, the big, sturdy PBM Mariner served in every combat theatre. Many other countries used the Mariner well into the 1950s.

## PHOTO FILE

MARTIN PBM MARINER

▲ Search and rescue
Used in the search and rescue role after World War II, the Mariner served on into the 1950s with the US Coast Guard and US Navy.

▼ Onto the ocean
Launched from a slipway at NAS Norfolk, Virginia, this Mariner is being prepared for a mission in late 1942. The aircraft is armed with eight machine guns.

▲ Rocket assistance
Rockets fixed to the fuselage sides helped heavily loaded aircraft get airborne. Drag from the water was a serious problem.

▼ Full power
The two huge Wright Cyclone engines haul the Mariner into the air on another long-range patrol mission.

Search radar ▶
Radar allowed the Mariner to hunt for submarines and ships. Later it was useful in the search and rescue role, operating far out to sea.

## FACTS AND FIGURES

➤ The prototype for the Mariner series completed its maiden flight on 18 February 1939.

➤ British Mariners were returned to the US without seeing operational service.

➤ Seven PBMs sank the submarine U-615 near Aruba on 6 August 1943.

➤ The Navy first used RATO (rocket-assisted take-off) boosters to fly a stranded PBM off the Colorado river.

➤ A 3/8 scale model of the Mariner was flown before the prototype PBM flew.

➤ The Martin 162-A scale model was manned and had Chevrolet engines.

## PROFILE

# US Navy patrol flying boat

The Mariner was designed in 1937 when the US Navy wanted a new patrol flying boat. The big, gull-wing Mariner was sturdy and tough, and featured weapons bays in its engine nacelles.

The pilots and crew of the Mariner had tremendous confidence in a ship that had been optimized to give them the strongest chance of surviving combat and getting home safely. There were numerous combat actions in which the PBM Mariner excelled, beginning on

30 June 1942, when a crew headed by Lieutenant Richard E. Schreder sank the German submarine U-158 near Bermuda. Exactly a dozen U-boats had been sent to the bottom of the sea by Mariners by the time the war ended.

In the Pacific, Mariners fought just about everywhere, but were particularly active at Saipan and in the liberation of the Philippines. In the post-war era, Mariners took part in atomic weapons tests in the Pacific and fought in the 1950–53 Korean

*Below: The Royal Air Force received 27 Mariners. Fitted with British equipment, they were never used operationally and were returned to the United States.*

*Above: Although the Mariner could reach an altitude of 6095 m (20,000 ft.), patrols were normally flown at low level. Attacks on submarines were made at wave-top height using bombs and depth charges.*

War. Production of the Mariner ceased in 1949, but the aircraft remained a mainstay of the US Coast Guard for many years.

### PBM-3D Mariner

**Type:** seven- or eight-seat patrol flying boat

**Powerplant:** two 1417-kW (1,900-hp.) Wright R-2600-22 Cyclone radial piston engines

**Maximum speed:** 338 km/h (210 m.p.h.) at 520 m (1,700 ft.)

**Cruising speed:** 303 km/h (188 m.p.h.) at 520 m (1,700 ft.)

**Ceiling:** 6095 m (20,000 ft.)

**Combat radius:** 1162 km (722 mi.)

**Range:** 3597 km (2,235 mi.)

**Weights:** empty 15,017 kg (33,106 lb.); maximum take-off 26,253 kg (57,878 lb.)

**Weapons:** eight 12.7-mm (.50 cal.) machine guns in nose, dorsal turrets, waist and tail; plus up to 1,646 lb.) of bombs, torpedoes or depth charges

**Dimensions:**
span 35.97 m (118 ft.)
length 24.38 m (80 ft.)
height 8.23 m (27 ft.)
wing area 130.71 m² (1,407 sq. ft.)

## PBM-5 Mariner

The PBM-5 variant was used post-war by the US Navy and Coast Guard, mainly in the search and rescue role. This aircraft carries a Pacific theatre paint scheme.

The large search radar was enclosed by a streamlined fairing, mounted above and behind the cockpit.

The two Wright R-2600 engines were mounted high on the gull wings to keep the propellers clear of corrosive saltwater spray.

A fixed float under each wing kept the wingtips clear of the water and allowed a stable take-off and landing in rough seas.

The large engine nacelles were each able to carry up to 1,811 kg (3,993 lb.) of bombs, depth charges or air-dropped rescue equipment.

The prototype mounted its twin fins and rudders on horizontal tailplanes. Those on production aircraft were angled upward, keeping them in line with the inboard section of the wings.

Nose, dorsal and tail turrets contained a total of six 12.7-mm (.50 cal.) machine guns. These were supplemented by two more guns in the waist positions.

The boat-shaped underside was the key to easy operations from any large area of water. Early aircraft had retractable wing floats, while the PBM-5 was amphibious, with retractable wheeled landing gear.

## U.S. Navy patrol aircraft

■ **LOCKHEED PV-2 HARPOON:** Developed from the Lodestar airliner, the PV-2 was a well-armed coastal patrol aircraft.

■ **CONSOLIDATED PBY CATALINA:** Hugely successful, the Catalina served throughout World War II in the long-range patrol mission.

■ **CONSOLIDATED PB4Y-2 PRIVATEER:** This was a long-range patrol version of the B-24 Liberator developed for the Navy.

■ **CONSOLIDATED PB2Y CORONADO:** Similar in size to the PBM, the PB2Y carried a heavier bomb load and had more power.

### ACTION DATA

#### WEAPONS

Carrying a heavier bombload, the Mariner was designed to replace the smaller Catalina. Although it carried fewer bombs, the Sunderland had more defensive guns.

SUNDERLAND GR.Mk 5 — 463-kg (1,021-lb.) bombload — 10 x 7.62-mm (.30 cal.) machine guns

PBM-5A MARINER — 1654-kg (3,646-lb.) bombload — 8 x 12.7-mm (.50 cal.) machine guns

PBY-5A CATALINA — 374-kg (824-lb.) bombload — 1 x 12.7-mm (.50 cal.) machine gun — 3 x 7.7-mm (.303 cal.) machine guns

#### RANGE

The Catalina was renowned for its excellent range. The Mariner comes a close second and both aircraft beat the Sunderland by almost 1000 km (620 mi.).

PBY-5A CATALINA — 3774 km (2,345 mi.)

PBM-5A MARINER — 3597 km (2,235 mi.)

SUNDERLAND GR.Mk 5 — 2482 km (1,766 mi.)

#### MAXIMUM TAKE-OFF WEIGHT

The Sunderland and Mariner are closely matched in weight. In the Mariner, however, far more of this weight consists of fuel and weapons. The lighter Catalina, although very successful, would have been more difficult to handle on open sea.

PBY-5A CATALINA 16,033 kg (35,347 lb.)

PBM-5A MARINER 26,218 kg (57,800 lb.)

SUNDERLAND GR.Mk 5 26,253 kg (57,878 lb.)

# MESSERSCHMITT

# BF 109

● 'Emil' in combat ● Bomber escort ● Fighter-bomber missions

## MESSERSCHMITT BF 109

**▼ Early action**
Crews soon applied dark mottling to cover the light blue sides of their aircraft.

**▲ Captive evaluation**
Several Bf 109Es fell into Allied hands before, during and after the Battle of Britain. This machine was tested by American analysts.

**▼ Out of combat**
This downed III./JG 26 aircraft shows the yellow nose colours which were used in the initial stages of the battle as a recognition feature.

**▼ Ace Galland**
By 24 September 1940 the rudder of Adolf Galland's aircraft had 40 kill markings applied.

**◄ Post-Battle honours**
By the end of the Battle of Britain, Werner Mölders had racked up an impressive score, as indicated by the rudder of his Bf 109. Like Galland, Mölders had led a unit during the Spanish Civil War.

**H**aving seen extensive service during the Spanish Civil War, early-model Bf 109s had given way to the Bf 109E by the spring of 1940. The Bf 109E series offered superior diving performance and various armament options, including the common layout of two cannon plus two machine-guns. The result was a highly effective fighter, but the operational circumstances of the Battle of Britain meant the odds were stacked heavily against it.

**▲** Conditions were harsh for all the combatants during the Battle of Britain. The Bf 109 stood up well to outdoor servicing in makeshift canvas hangars at forward airstrips.

## FACTS AND FIGURES

➤ Bf 109E-4 pilot Franz von Werra was the only German to escape a Western Allied prisoner of war camp and get home.

➤ Early Bf 109Es had arrived in Spain by the very end of 1938.

➤ A Bf 109E captured by the French was lost in a collision with a Hawk 75A.

➤ Captured Bf 109s were flown by the Royal Air Force in mock combat against Hurricanes and Spitfires.

➤ Cooling and vibration problems made the engine-mounted cannon troublesome.

➤ Late in the Battle, the Bf 109E-7 version introduced a 300-litre drop tank.

# Messerschmitts over Britain

By the time Germany launched its Eagle Day attack on Britain in August 1940, Bf 109Es (commonly known as 'Emils') had for a month been escorting bombers in attacks against coastal targets and shipping from bases in occupied France.

The German fighter pilots knew that their aircraft had an edge in performance over the British Hurricanes and Spitfires, and their twin cannon had proved highly effective. But

when they were forced to escort the Luftwaffe's bombers further inland, they began to lose their initial advantage.

As long as they were allowed to cross the Channel at altitudes of around 9000 m (29,000 ft.) and engage the British fighters in open combat, the 'Emils' more than held their own. Tied to the bomber formations, though, they lost their independence and, before the introduction of the drop-tank-equipped Bf 109E-7, they could

spend no more than 30 minutes over England.

Their pilots faced other disadvantages. British radar could detect the approaching formations, giving the RAF's fighters a tactical advantage. All missions involved long overwater flights, and the strain on the Luftwaffe fighter force proved too much. In September the Luftwaffe switched its efforts to night raids on London.

*As a source of great curiosity for the people of Eastbourne, this crashed 'Emil' is representative of the hundreds of aircraft lost by both sides during the Battle.*

## Bf 109E-3

**Type:** single-seat fighter

**Powerplant:** one 876-kW (1,175-hp.) Daimler-Benz DB 601A liquid-cooled inverted V-12 engine

**Maximum speed:** 560 km/h (347 m.p.h.) at 4440 m (14,500 ft.)

**Initial climb rate:** 1000 m/min (3,300 f.p.m.)

**Range:** 660 km (410 mi.)

**Service ceiling:** 10,500 m (34,400 ft.)

**Weights:** empty 1900 kg (4,180 lb.); maximum take-off 2665 kg (5,863 lb.)

**Armament:** one engine-mounted 20-mm (0.79-in.) MG FF cannon and four 7.9-mm (0.31-in.) MG 17 machine-guns

**Dimensions:** span 9.87 m (32 ft. 4 in.)
length 8.64 m (28 ft. 4 in.)
height 2.50 m (8 ft. 3 in.)
wing area 16.40 m² (176 sq. ft.)

Bf 109 pilots were accommodated in a small cockpit with poor forward view through the armoured windscreen. The cockpit's small dimensions allowed frontal area to be kept to a minimum, however.

## Bf 109E-4

Flown by Major Helmut Wick during October 1940 while he was Gruppenkommandeur of I./JG 2, this aircraft was based at Beaumont-le-Roger, France.

A 7.9-mm (0.31-in.) MG 17 machine-gun, synchronised to fire through the propeller, was mounted behind each of the troughs above the forward fuselage.

Even though the main landing gear was widely splayed, the Bf 109 still had a very narrow track. This meant that, like the Spitfire, the aircraft was tricky to handle on the ground.

A combination of initial air superiority and their long operational deployments allowed Luftwaffe fighter pilots to amass large scores. Shown here with 44 kills, Wick was to score 55 with this aircraft before it was shot down on 28 November 1940.

Easily distinguished from earlier Bf 109s by its lack of undernose radiator, the Bf 109E series introduced the DB 601 engine. The smaller undernose fairing housed an oil cooler.

A red 'R' on a white shield was proudly worn beneath the cockpit. This referred to Jagdgeschwader (JG) 2's heritage as the 'Richthofen' Geschwader. The marking was only worn during the early stages of the war.

A distinguishing feature of all early Bf 109s, up to and including the 'Emils', were the struts bracing each tailplane. They were deleted from the Bf 109F onwards; that type entered service with JG 2 from March 1941.

### COMBAT DATA

**MAXIMUM SPEED**

Faster than the Spitfire IA, the Bf 109E-3 was easily a match for the more numerous Hurricane Mk I. Rapid development work was necessary to give the Spitfire a new-found superiority over the Bf 109E-3.

| | |
|---|---|
| Bf 109E-3 | 560 km/h (347 m.p.h.) |
| SPITFIRE Mk IA | 557 km/h (345 m.p.h.) |
| HURRICANE Mk I | 520 km/h (322 m.p.h.) |

**CLIMB RATE**

A high rate of climb often allowed the Bf 109E-3 to get away from trouble or to climb above its adversaries for a high-speed, diving attack, a tactic which became impossible once the aircraft had been tasked with bomber escort.

Bf 109E-3 1000 m/min (3,300 f.p.m.)
SPITFIRE Mk IA 771 m/min (2,530 ft.)
HURRICANE Mk I 671 m/min (2,200 ft.)

**ARMAMENT**

Although they had a greater number of weapons, the British fighters with their machine-guns did not have the power or destructive capacity of the German cannon.

Bf 109E-3 1 x 20-mm (0.79-in.) cannon 4 x 7.9-mm (0.31-in.) machine-guns
SPITFIRE Mk IA 8 x 7.7-mm (.303 cal.) machine-guns
HURRICANE Mk I 8 x 7.7-mm (.303 cal.) machine-guns

## Battle of Britain aces

**BALTHASAR:** Having fought gallantly with the Condor Legion in Spain, Wilhelm Balthasar flew throughout the Battle of Britain, but was killed in 1941 when his Bf 109F shed a wing in combat.

**BÄR:** A veteran of the Battle of Britain and several other campaigns, Heinz Bär performed the difficult task of introducing the Heinkel He 162 into service early in 1945.

**GALLAND:** Wearing his personal Mickey Mouse badge and the S-marking of JG 26, Adolf Galland's Bf 109s, an E-3 and later this E-4, allowed him to score 40 victories by 24 September 1940.

# MESSERSCHMITT
# BF 110

● 'Destroyer' fighter ● Night-fighter ● Fighter-bomber

▲ Like so many
wartime German aircraft, the Bf 110 was
a good design that was kept in service too
long because its replacement (the Me 210)
was a failure. It was still in production
when the war ended.

**M**esserschmitt's Bf 110 was one of
the Luftwaffe's great hopes at the
start of World War II, but the
twin-engined Zerstörer (destroyer) proved
hopelessly vulnerable to single-engined
fighter opposition during the Battle of
Britain. Nevertheless, it was fast and
heavily armed, and as the war progressed
proved to be a solid fighting machine as a
long-range fighter and fighter-bomber, as
a bomber-destroyer and as a night-fighter.

## MESSERSCHMITT BF 110

▲ Firepower
The powerful cannon and
machine-gun nose was lethal to
ground targets and made short
work of enemy bombers.

▲ Desert destroyer
A Bf 110 kicks up sand as it
departs its desert base in north
Africa. Its powerful armament was
effective in the tank-busting role.

▼ Air supremacy
Operating over France in June 1940, the Bf 110s of ZG 52 were free
to carry out attacks on enemy airfields with near impunity.

▲ Photo mission
Bf 110s flew a variety of
missions. This Libyan-based
example is being loaded with
reconnaissance cameras.

Bomber buster ▶
Rocket-armed Bf 110s were
potent bomber-destroyers, but
were almost helpless against
Allied escort fighters.

### FACTS AND FIGURES

➤ During the invasions of Poland and
France, Bf 110s operated with great
success in support of the Wehrmacht.

➤ The Bf 110 also saw service on bombing
and reconnaissance missions.

➤ The prototype Bf 110 made its maiden
flight on 12 May 1936.

➤ In addition to its guns, the Bf 110 could
carry 1250 kg (2,750 lb.) of bombs or
rockets on underfuselage racks.

➤ The Bf 110 was used by Rudolf Hess to
fly to Britain in 1941.

➤ When production ended in March 1945,
about 6050 Bf 110s had been built.

# The Zerstörer fighter

The Bf 110 was without peer when it entered service in 1938 as a long-range heavy 'destroyer' fighter for the Luftwaffe. Development had been protracted due to problems with its DB 601 engines, but the Bf 110 was in action in time for the 1939 Polish campaign. That year, the Messerschmitt confirmed its worth as a 'bomber-destroyer' by shooting down nine of 22 RAF Wellington medium bombers on a single mission.

This twin-tailed, tailwheel-equipped fighter was rakish and nimble for its size and weight. Pilots found it adequate in combat, although interior space and outside vision left a little to be desired.

Even with a back-seat gunner, however, the Bf 110 could never cope with single-engine fighters, whether early Hurricanes or late P-51D Mustangs. But as a radar-equipped night interceptor, facing only bombers, the Bf 110 was capable of wreaking immense destruction. Even in this role, however, the Bf 110 was outclassed by later warplanes, but it pioneered nocturnal fighting with radar and air-to-air rockets.

Tactical air support was another role the Bf 110 was increasingly called on to perform as the war went on. This Bf 110, flying over Russia, carries the distinctive 'wasp' nose art of S.KG 210.

The main strength of the Bf 110 was its ability to accept armament such as the Bk 3.7 cannon. A single hit from this weapon was usually certain death to any Allied bomber.

### Bf 110C-4/B

**Type:** two-seat fighter-bomber/reconnaissance fighter

**Powerplant:** two 895-kW (1,200-hp.) Daimler-Benz DB 601N inverted V-12 piston engines

**Maximum speed:** 562 km/h (348 m.p.h.) at 7000 m (22,960 ft.)

**Range:** 850 km (527 mi.)

**Service ceiling:** 10,000 m (33,000 ft.)

**Weights:** empty 4500 kg (9,900 lb.); loaded 7000 kg (15,400 lb.)

**Armament:** two 20-mm (0.79-in.) Oerlikon MG FF cannon in belly and four 7.92-mm (0.31-in.) MG 17 machine-guns in nose; one 7.92-mm MG 15 machine-gun in rear cockpit; racks for four 250-kg (550-lb.) bombs under centre section

**Dimensions:** span 16.25 m (53 ft.); length 12.10 m (40 ft.); height 3.50 m (11 ft.); wing area 39.40 m² (424 sq. ft.)

## Bf 110C-4/B

The Bf 110C-4/B was a fighter-bomber variant. This example served in the Mediterranean with 9/ZG 26 'Horst Wessel', based at Palermo, late in 1940.

All Bf 110s were fitted with the Daimler-Benz DB 601 engine. The prototype had used the DB 600, which was plagued by reliability problems.

In theory, the single or twin 7.92-mm (0.31-in.) machine-guns carried in the rear cockpit of the Bf 110 provided some protection against attacks from the rear, but in practice it proved no match for a single-engined fighter's armament.

The oval-sectioned fuselage was of fairly standard all-metal stressed-skin construction, with the cantilevered tailplane mounted on the upper surface.

The small rear fins allowed the rear gunner a useful field of fire straight behind the aircraft. One unusual feature of the Bf 110 was that the tailplane incidence could be varied.

There were numerous variants of the Bf 110, with a variety of nose armament. Most early aircraft like this carried four machine-guns in the nose and a pair of belly-mounted 20-mm (0.79-in.) cannon.

A large fuel tank called a 'dachshund belly' could be fitted to extend range. They were vulnerable to enemy fire and were disliked by crews.

A direction-finding loop aerial was sometimes fitted under the fuselage.

The final variant, the Bf 110H, featured a strengthened rear fuselage.

### COMBAT DATA

#### MAXIMUM SPEED

Many nations developed twin-engined heavy fighters before World War II, and the various designs reflected different philosophies. The Bf 110 was much faster than the similar French Potez design, but could not match the smaller and lighter single-seat Westland Whirlwind.

Bf 110C — 562 km/h (348 m.p.h.)
WHIRLWIND Mk I — 580 km/h (360 m.p.h.)
POTEZ 63 — 440 km/h (273 m.p.h.)

#### RANGE

The Bf 110 was designed as a long-range fighter, and by contemporary German standards in the 1930s it had a fair performance. But it could not fly as far as its rivals, possibly because most German aircraft of the time were designed primarily for close support of the Wehrmacht.

Bf 110C 850 km (527 mi.)
WHIRLWIND Mk I 1300 km (800 mi.)
POTEZ 63 1500 km (930 mi.)

#### ARMAMENT

The Bf 110 had a powerful all-round armament, supplemented by the ability to carry a one-ton bombload. Later in the war, the aircraft proved capable of being significantly up-gunned, carrying 30-mm (1.18-in.) cannon or even 37-mm (1.47-in.) anti-tank guns.

Bf 110C
2 x 20-mm (0.79-in.) cannon
4 x 7.92-mm (0.31-in.) MGs
1 or 2 x 7.92-mm MGs in rear cockpit
1000 kg (2,200 lb.) of bombs

WHIRLWIND MK I
4 x 20-mm (0.79-in.) cannon
454 kg (1,000 lb.) of bombs

POTEZ 63
6 x 7.5-mm (0.3-in.) MGs
2 x 7.5-mm (0.3-in.) MGs in rear cockpit
600 kg (1,320 lb.) of bombs

## Messerschmitt's Zerstörer rivals

**HENSCHEL Hs 124:** Designed to meet the original Kampfzerstörer (bomber-destroyer) specification of 1934, the Henschel was a large, heavy and mediocre machine.

**FOCKE-WULF Fw 57:** Even larger than the Henschel, the Focke-Wulf Kampfzerstörer was grossly underpowered, and could not match the Bf 110's performance.

**MESSERSCHMITT Bf 162:** Based on the Bf 110, the Bf 162 featured an enlarged fuselage and was designed as a high-speed bomber. It was used for research.

**JUNKERS Ju 88:** Germany's premier 'Schnellbomber' was so agile that it was easy to convert as a heavy fighter, and was vastly more capable than the original Zerstörers.

**FOCKE-WULF Fw 187:** A superb performer which was faster than the Bf 109 single-seater, the Fw 187 was the victim of official indifference and never entered service.

# MESSERSCHMITT

# ME 209

● World speed record holder for 30 years ● Fighter developments

In November 1937 a Bf 109 fighter prototype set a new world air speed record for landplanes of 610.5 km/h(379 m.p.h.). By now Willy Messerschmitt was already working on a pure high-speed machine. Designated Me 209, it was intended to break the absolute speed record of 709 km/h (440 m.p.h.), held by a Macchi seaplane. What Messerschmitt did not know when he started was that his great rival, Ernst Heinkel, was aiming at the same target.

▲ Willy Messerschmitt (left) and his record-breaking test pilot Fritz Wendel: the Me 209's handling prompted Flugkapitän Wendel to describe it as a 'vicious little brute' and a 'monstrosity'.

## MESSERSCHMITT ME 209

▼ Snake markings on V4
With markings for propaganda photographs, Me 209 V4 was an attempt to utilise V1 experience to design a Bf 109 replacement.

▲ Messerschmitt's 'other' Me 209
Referred to as the Me 209 II or Me 209A, this was an attempt to build a replacement for the Bf 109.

Record breaker ▶
Designed from the outset as a high-speed aircraft, the Me 209 was not intended to serve operationally. Constraints centred around the DB 601 engine and the need to accommodate a pilot.

◀ Evaporative cooling
Like the racing seaplanes of the period, the Me 209 employed wing-mounted radiators to provide cooling for the powerful DB 601ARJ.

Me 209 V5 ▶
The first of the Me 209 IIs to fly, SP+LJ was known as Me 209 V5. Intended to use Bf 109G components, the aircraft would have been known as the Me 209A in production.

### FACTS AND FIGURES

➤ It was proposed eventually to install 30-mm cannon in the Me 209 fighter: one in the propeller hub and one in each wing.

➤ Me 209 V2 was written off in a landing accident after its engine failed.

➤ Originally, Me 209 V3 was to be used for the world record attempt.

➤ To give the impression that it was a variant of the Luftwaffe's fighter, the Me 209 was referred to as an 'Me 109R'.

➤ The V4 Me 209 fighter prototype in fact preceded the third machine into the air.

➤ Fritz Wendel noted that on landing the Me 209 swerved if brakes were applied.

## PROFILE

# Messerschmitt's 'vicious little brute'

With its small wings, a fuselage barely big enough to house the DB 601 engine and rear landing wheel mounted on the bottom of the tailfin, the Me 209 was much more compact than the Bf 109. Surface evaporation cooling, with condensers in the wings instead of conventional radiators, helped keep the airframe aerodynamically clean.

First flown in June 1938, the Me 209 proved extremely

difficult to control and prone to overheating. The second prototype was lost after the oil cooling system failed and the engine cut out suddenly.

Messerschmitt had intended to use the third prototype (V3) for the record attempt. The plan was changed at the end of March 1939, when a modified prototype of Heinkel's He 100 fighter reached a new absolute record of 746 km/h (463 m.p.h.).

Instead, Messerschmitt used the first prototype fitted with a boosted engine ordered for the attempt, which was capable of

delivering 1156 kW (1,550 hp.) with methanol injection and 1715 kW (2,300 hp.) in a one-minute burst. After a long wait for calm weather Flugkapitän Fritz Wendel finally succeeded in setting a new record of 755.138 km/h (469.22 m.p.h.) on 26 April 1939. This record stood for 30 years.

*Above: By the time the Me 209 had been modified for service use it was little faster than a Bf 109F.*

Me 209 V4 was fitted with a hub-mounted cannon and had twin machine-guns above the engine. Plans to fit guns in the wings were abandoned for lack of space.

### Me 209 V1
**Type:** single-seat high-speed aircraft
**Powerplant:** one 1156-kW (1,550-hp.) (1715-kW [2,300-hp.] with methanol injection) Daimler-Benz DB 601ARJ liquid-cooled piston engine
**Maximum speed:** 755 km/h (469 m.p.h.)
**Weights:** gross 2515 kg (5,533 lb.)
**Dimensions:** span 7.80 m (25 ft. 7 in.)
length 7.25 m (23 ft. 9 in.)
wing area 10.60 m² (114 sq. ft.)

### Me 209 V4
**Type:** single-seat high-speed fighter prototype
**Powerplant:** one 895-kW (1,200-hp.) Daimler-Benz DB 601N liquid-cooled piston engine
**Maximum speed:** about 600 km/h at 6000 m (372 m.p.h. at 19,700 ft.)
**Cruising speed:** 500 km/h (310 m.p.h.)
**Initial climb rate:** 1125 m/min (3,690 f.p.m.)
**Service ceiling:** 11000 m (36,080 ft.)
**Weights:** gross 2800 kg (6,160 lb.)
**Armament:** one 20-mm MG FF/M cannon and two 7.9-mm MG 17 machine-guns
**Dimensions:** span 10.04 m (32 ft. 11 in.)
length 7.24 m (23 ft. 9 in.)
wing area 11.07 m² (119 sq. ft.)

*Left: Me 209 V4 had little, other than its basic airframe, in common with the three earlier aircraft. As well as an entirely new wing, it had a larger tailfin.*

## ME 209 V4
First flown on 12 May 1939 carrying the civil registration D-IRND, Me 209 V4 was later adorned with these colourful snake markings, for propaganda photography purposes.

Among Fritz Wendel's complaints about the Me 209's handling were an excessive take-off run, 'vicious' take-off handling, instability during the climb and a tendency to roll on its back during banking.

In place of the methanol-injected Daimler-Benz DB 601ARJ racing engine, a standard DB 601N was fitted to Me 209 V4. This produced considerably less power than the racing powerplant and cooling proved problematic. Evaporative cooling was employed on V1, but this was clearly impractical for a fighter. Underwing radiators proved ineffective.

To improve handling and landing characteristics, an entirely new wing was fitted. The undercarriage legs were shortened.

Me 209 V4 was an attempt to apply the experience gained with the first machine to a potential service fighter to replace the Bf 109. The design compromises necessary in transforming a racing machine designed purely for high speed, into a viable fighter aircraft, proved insurmountable.

### ACTION DATA

**POWER**
The DB 603-powered V5 version had a power rating closer to that of the Me 209 racer than the Me 209 V4 fighter. Both types were considerably more powerful than the Heinkel He 100.

Me 209 V1 1715 kW (2,300 HP.) | Me 209 V5 1417 kW (1,900 HP.) | He 100 V1 670 kW (900 HP.)

**MAXIMUM SPEED**
Me 209 V1 set a new world speed record of just over 755 km/h (469 m.p.h.) in April 1939, beating the previous mark of 746 km/h (463 m.p.h.) set by the He 100. The Me 209 II (V5) was not as fast.

| Me 209 V1 | 755 km/h (469 m.p.h.) |
| Me 209 V5 | 745 km/h (462 m.p.h.) |
| He 100 V1 | 746 km/h (463 m.p.h.) |

**GROSS WEIGHT**
By maintaining a similar gross weight to that of the He 100, but increasing engine power, Messerschmitt was able to produce a faster aircraft. The Me 209 II (V5) was considerably heavier since it was equipped as a service fighter.

Me 209 V1 2515 kg (5,533 lb.) | Me 209 V5 4085 kg (8,987 lb.) | He 100 V1 2500 kg (5,500 lb.)

## Other Messerschmitt prototypes

**Me 261:** Designed to make non-stop flights from Germany to Japan, the Me 261 was considered for the maritime reconnaissance role.

**Me 263:** To address the shortcomings of the Me 163 Komet, Messerschmitt gave the Me 263 more fuel capacity and retractable landing gear.

**Me 264:** One of a number of aircraft put forward for the transatlantic bombing role, the 'Amerika-Bomber' first flew in 1942.

**P.1101:** Largely complete by VE Day, this swept-wing jet served as the basis for the Bell X-5 variable-geometry prototype.

# MESSERSCHMITT

# ME 262

● Pioneering jet fighter ● Revolutionised aircraft design

▲ The Me 262 pilot had under his control the world's first operational jet warplane. Had it been built earlier, it could have had a major impact on the course of the war.

**D**uring World War II the Me 262 was a high point of German scientific achievement. This shark-like craft with its epoch-making jet engines and potent firepower might have swept Allied bombers from the skies, had it been used properly. With the Me 262, Messerschmitt gave pilots a superb fighting machine for which the Allies had no equal, and a revolutionary portent of the future.

## MESSERSCHMITT ME 262

▼ Precision bomber
This trials aircraft had a position in the nose for a bomb-aimer, who lay face-down and peered through the glazed nose.

▲ Night-fighter
They could have been the best night-fighters of the war, but fewer than a dozen Me 262B-1a/U1s got into service. They had radar in the nose and a second crew member to operate the equipment.

◄ Air-to-air fighter
At full speed and altitude, nothing could catch the Me 262, but it was clumsy at low speeds and was vulnerable while landing and taking off: many were shot down by Allied fighters patrolling the Me 262 bases for returning jets.

Fighter or bomber? ▼
The Me 262 was designed as a fighter, but Hitler's insistence on it being a bomber is often believed to have impeded deliveries. In truth, it was the slow supply of engines which limited supply.

▼ First jet flight
Me 262 V3 first flew on jet power on 18 July 1942. It had a tailwheel, and when it landed unburned fuel ignited when the aircraft touched down.

## FACTS AND FIGURES

➤ From March 1944 to April 1945, the Luftwaffe received 1433 Me 262s.

➤ As a bomber the Me 262, with two 227- or 454-kg (500- or 1,000-lb.) bombs, had little impact on advancing Allied armies.

➤ An awesome Mauser 50-mm MK 214 cannon mounted on two Me 262A-1/U4 test ships was not used operationally.

➤ Five new Me 262s built by entrepreneurs in Texas, using American J85 engines, will begin flying in 1997.

➤ Though the Me 262 was a joy to fly at full power, it was sluggish and awkward at lower speeds.

➤ Me 262 two-seaters performed training and night-fighting duties.

# Germany's wonder jet

One of Germany's finest fighter pilots, Major Walter Nowotny, formed the Kommando Nowotny in late 1944 to combat Allied bombers and their fighter escorts. The result set off alarm bells in the USAAF. The graceful, potent Me 262 was easily the fastest fighter in the world: with guns and unguided R4M rockets, this fighter of the future had the potential to knock down Flying Fortresses almost with impunity. It was only the destruction of Germany's

industry by massive Allied raids that slowed the production of this incredible aircraft.

Other pilots flew the Me 262 as a bomber, a decision which may have squandered many of the technical advances offered by this new kind of warplane.

Too late and not always used in the best way, the Me 262 frightened the Allies but could not alter the outcome of the war. Afterwards, Allied experts studied the airframe and engine and determined that the

*An operational Me 262A takes off from its base at Lechfeld. In the spring of 1945 the Me 262 scored many victories over Allied aircraft.*

Messerschmitt Me 262 was years ahead of fighters of other nations. Its secrets helped the Americans, Russians and British to develop more advanced jet engines and airframes to the magic of Mach 1 and beyond over the ensuing years.

*The prototype of the Me 262 first flew as a tail-dragger. However, this caused problems on take-off, so the Messerschmitt engineers revamped their design and operational aircraft came equipped with a nosewheel.*

Handling and control of the Me 262 was surprisingly good, but it tended to snake at high speed, making accurate gun-firing difficult. If an engine failed at low speed (a common occurrence) the results were usually catastrophic.

## Me 262A-2

**Type:** single-seat air superiority fighter

**Powerplant:** two 8.82-kN (1,980-lb.-thrust) Junkers Jumo 004B-1, -2 or -3 axial-flow turbojets

**Maximum speed:** 870 km/h (540 m.p.h.)

**Range:** 1050 km (650 mi.) at 9000 m (30,000 ft.)

**Service ceiling:** 11,450 m (37,500 ft.)

**Weights:** empty 3800 kg (8,738 lb.); maximum 6400 kg (14,110 lb.)

**Armament:** four 30-mm (1.18-in.) Rheinmetall-Borsig MK 108A-3 cannon with 100 rounds for the upper pair and 80 rounds for the lower pair; 12 R4M air-to-air rockets; two 226-kg (500-lb.) bombs or one 452-kg (1,000-lb.) bomb

**Dimensions:**
| | | |
|---|---|---|
| span | 12.50 m | (40 ft. 11 in.) |
| length | 10.58 m | (34 ft. 9 in.) |
| height | 3.83 m | (12 ft. 7 in.) |
| wing area | 21.73 m² | (234 sq. ft.) |

## Me 262 'SCHWALBE'

Beautifully sleek for its time, the Me 262 also had acceptable handling qualities and blistering performance. Its one disadvantage was its sluggishness and lack of manoeuvrability in the airfield circuit.

Visibility from the Me 262's cockpit was considerably better than from the preceding Bf 109 piston-engined fighter, thanks to a relatively unobstructed canopy.

500491

Fighter Me 262s carried a heavy punch in the form of four 30-mm (1.18-in.) MK 108 cannon in the forward fuselage. Twelve R4M unguided air-to-air rockets could be carried under the wings.

The Me 262 was powered by a pair of Junkers Jumo 004B-1 turbojets, each giving about 9 kN (1,900 lb. thrust). These early engines had a life of only 25 hours, and needed major overhaul every 10 hours.

The Me 262's fuselage was of all-metal monocoque construction. The wings, tailplane and fin were also all-metal, and each had a moderate sweepback on the leading edge only.

### COMBAT DATA

#### MAXIMUM SPEED

| | |
|---|---|
| Me 262A-1 | 870 km/h (540 m.p.h.) |
| METEOR Mk III | 700 km/h (435 m.p.h.) |
| P-80 SHOOTING STAR | 898 km/h (556 m.p.h.) |

The Me 262 was considerably faster than its contemporary, the Gloster Meteor, and was almost as fast as America's Lockheed P-80 Shooting Star, which only became operational in the last week of conflict. However, early jet fighters had poor acceleration at low speeds.

#### SERVICE CEILING

Jet engines are much more efficient at high altitude than piston-engine-driven propellers, and all the early jets had considerably better high-altitude performance than other fighters of the day.

Me 262 11,450 m (37,500 ft.)
METEOR Mk III 12,250 m (40,200 ft.)
P-80 SHOOTING STAR 13,715 m (45,000 ft.)

#### ARMAMENT

The Me 262 was designed primarily as a bomber-destroyer, and was very heavily armed for the purpose, as well as cannon they could also carry unguided rockets. The Meteor was also cannon-armed, although less powerfully than the German jet. Like most American fighters of the period, the P-80 was underarmed by European standards carrying only machine-guns.

Me 262 4 x 30-mm (1.18-in.) cannon

METEOR Mk III 4 x 20-mm (0.79-in.) cannon

P-80 6 x 12.7-mm (.50 cal.) machine-guns

## The first jets

**HEINKEL He 178:** One of the most important aircraft in history, the He 178 was the first aircraft to fly under jet power, on 27 August 1939, paving the way for jet-powered fighters.

**HEINKEL He 280:** Heinkel flew the world's first twin jet in May 1941. Completely outclassing all piston-engined fighters, its development was stopped in favour of the Me 262.

**GLOSTER E28/39:** Britain had been ahead of Germany in engine design thanks to pioneer Frank Whittle, but due to official indifference the first British jet did not fly until 15 May 1941.

**GLOSTER METEOR:** Although it first flew in March 1943, nine months after the Me 262, the Meteor became operational a week before the Messerschmitt, in July 1944.

# MESSERSCHMITT

# ME 323 GIGANT

● Giant glider ● Multi-engine transport ● Huge cargo loads

**A** real weightlifter, the Me 321 Gigant was a huge glider intended for an invasion of England. With up to six engines, it became the Me 323 transport to get soldiers and equipment into battle areas. It had the perfect name: this incredible flying machine was one of the largest World War II aircraft, and had astonishing carrying capacity. But it was slow, and easy prey for fighters.

▲ In spite of its fragile-looking steel tube and canvas construction, the Me 323 Gigant carried some of the heaviest payloads of World War II.

## MESSERSCHMITT ME 323 GIGANT

◀ Outsize cargo carrier
The Gigant was one of the largest aircraft of its time. Even with the power of six engines it was a poor performer, and very hard to fly.

▲ Keeping the giant flying
Servicing the Gigant was a problem. Its six engines were more than 5 m (16 ft 5 in.) off the ground, so special work vehicles were developed to allow maintenance engineers access. But these were only available at airfields where the Gigants were based.

**Monster glider ▶**
The unpowered Me 321 glider was designed to carry heavy equipment and artillery for airborne troops. But it was so big that finding a suitable glider tug was a problem.

▼ Easy prey
The Gigant was slow and sluggish, and was easy meat for long-range fighters. Many were shot down over the Mediterranean as they tried to bring supplies to the beleaguered Afrika Korps.

▲ Power for the giant glider
The Gigant was never a viable proposition as a glider, so Messerschmitt decided to produce a powered variant using French-built Gnome-Rhône engines. These were in production in Vichy France and were available in some numbers.

### FACTS AND FIGURES

➤ Rocket boosters were needed to get a loaded Gigant into the sky.

➤ One Me 323 evacuated 220 soldiers from North Africa to Italy – 140 in the cargo compartment and 80 inside its wings!

➤ A weapons carrier Me 323 carried 11 automatic cannon and a crew of 17 men.

➤ The Gigant's cockpit was as high as a third-storey window.

➤ Me 323s saw service from the ice on the Eastern Front to the heat of the desert.

➤ The Gigant introduced many features now standard on cargo aircraft, including clamshell loading doors and high wings.

# PROFILE

# Messerschmitt's monster weight lifter

Germany dominated the world in the design of gliders, and the Gigant proved it. The Me 321 was so huge that a special aircraft had to be developed as a tow ship. To carry soldiers and vehicles into a combat landing zone, a real mammoth was needed, and the Gigant filled the bill.

The powered version, the Messerschmitt Me 323, was so big it required six engines. As a glider and as an aircraft, the Gigant carried three vehicles or 200 combat troops with equipment. The clamshell nose door and the ability to 'roll-on, roll-off' cargoes was a futuristic idea adopted on big transports today.

Size and capacity were not enough. The Me 323 Gigant was very slow and, even with gun turrets, almost unable to defend itself. Made of fabric-covered steel tubes, the Gigant was nevertheless immensely strong and Allied fighters sometimes expended their ammunition without downing the lumbering giant. This remarkable aircraft succeeded only in regions where it did not have to face Allied warplanes.

Left: Key to the Gigant's ability was its huge cargo capacity. Its outsize fuselage could hold loads of up to 20 tons.

Even with six engines, it was an effort to get the Gigant into the air. The Luftwaffe had a lot of experience with assisted take-off, however, and using rockets enabled the Me 323 to lift heavy loads into the air with relative ease.

## Me 323E Gigant

**Type:** heavy general-purpose transport

**Powerplant:** six 850-kW (1,140-hp.) Gnome-Rhône 14N 48/49 radial air-cooled engines

**Maximum speed:** 253 km/h (157 m.p.h.) at 1500 m (4,900 ft.)

**Range:** 1100 km (682 mi.)

**Service ceiling:** 4500 m (18,730 ft.)

**Weights:** empty 29,060 kg (69,932 lb.); loaded 45,000 kg (99,000 lb.)

**Armament:** one 20-mm (0.79-in.) cannon in each of two turrets (one on each wing), two 13-mm (0.51-in.) machine-guns in nose doors, and five 13-mm machine-guns firing from the flight deck

**Dimensions:**
| | | |
|---|---|---|
| span | 55.00 m | (180 ft.) |
| length | 28.50 m | (93 ft.) |
| height | 9.60 m | (31 ft.) |
| wing area | 300 m² (3,228 sq. ft.) | |

Gigants were powered by French Gnome-Rhône radial engines, which were available in large numbers after the fall of France.

Armament varied greatly, but most Gigants carried five machine-guns in the flight deck, together with mounts for five or six infantry machine-guns in beam windows. More guns were added in the field.

The Me 323 had the then-novel feature of clamshell nose doors, which allowed vehicles to be rolled directly into the capacious cargo hold.

The low bed of the cargo hold and the wide-opening front doors made it simple to load outsize cargoes. This effective feature has been copied many times since the 1940s.

## ME 323E-2 GIGANT

Fitted with a Mediterranean white theatre band this Me 323 was rushed into service on the Eastern Front serving with 1 Gruppe, Transportgeschwader 54, late in 1943.

The Gigant was difficult to fly, since flaps and rudders required very high control forces to operate.

Structure of the Gigant was brutally simple: a strong framework of steel tubes mated with wooden-framed wings, and covered in fabric.

Early gliders took off with jettisonable main wheels, landing on skids. The powered version had a pioneering multi-wheeled undercarriage for use on rough fields.

## WEAPONS DATA

### ME 323E-2/WT

In an attempt to provide protection against fighters, one Me 323 was heavily armed to serve as escort to other Gigants.

The Waffenträger carried 11 MG 151 cannon. Added to the machine-guns fired from the beam windows, they made the Me 323WT one of the most heavily armed aircraft ever flown.

Beam gun positions were protected by 90 mm (3½ in.) of armoured glass and 20 mm (¾ in.) of steel plate.

The Waffenträger concept was never really put to the test: extensive trials showed that conventional escort fighters provided more effective protection.

## Gigant cargo loads

■ **TROOP CARRIER:** At a time when most tactical transport aircraft could carry about 20 troops the Gigant could seat 120, three or four abreast on two decks. During the evacuation of North Africa Gigants were pushed to their limits. The lack of transport aircraft forced them to carry up to 200 troops, some in the wings.

■ **ARTILLERY CARRIER:** Gigant was the only aircraft which could carry an artillery piece, its tractor and its crew in a single load. Gigant's large nose doors meant that it could also carry trucks, fuel bowsers, ambulances or other assorted cargo up to 20 tons with a minimum of preparation.

# MIKOYAN-GUREVICH

# MiG-1 AND MiG-3

● Interceptor fighter ● First of the MiGs ● Tactical reconnaissance

▲ The MiG-3 was a fast fighter but had poor handling and light armament. At the time of the invasion in 1941, over a third of the Soviet fighter force was equipped with MiG-1 and MiG-3 fighters.

I f they had not used the scarce Mikulin AM-35 engine, the MiG-1 and MiG-3 fighters might have served the USSR for much longer than they actually did. Unusually for wartime Soviet fighters, they performed better at altitude than at low level, and for this reason were often used as high-flying reconnaissance aircraft. More importantly, these warplanes launched the Mikoyan-Gurevich design bureau, the first to bear the immortal MiG name.

## MIKOYAN-GUREVICH MiG-1 AND MiG-3

▼ Radial engine
The I-211 was an attempt to match a radial M-82 engine to a MiG-3 airframe. It proved successful, but by this time the rival La-5 was in mass production and required these radial engines.

▲ First service
Many Soviet fighter units were still converting to the MiG-3 as war struck the USSR. These pilots of 12 GvIAP are swearing allegiance to the flag.

◀ Victim of the Luftwaffe
Below 5000 metres, the MiG-3 was inferior to the Bf 109 and Fw 190, and many were downed by the Luftwaffe in 1941. The machine-guns on top of the engine cowling have been exposed in this crashed aircraft.

▼ Caught on the ground
Because the Soviets hoped to contain German forces in the western USSR, many MiGs were based in this area. Consequently, hundreds were destroyed in the initial assault in June 1941. A final batch of 50 were built in 1942 from old spare parts.

◀ Design genius
Artem Mikoyan was half of the design team that produced the MiG fighters. Between 1940 and 1970, this outspoken and open-minded Armenian was the inspiration behind some of the world's finest fighters.

### FACTS AND FIGURES

➤ Pilots of the 401st Fighter Squadron, one of the first MiG-3 units, included test pilot and fighter ace Stepan Surprun.

➤ A. N. Yekatov first flew the I-200 prototype for the MiG-1 on 5 April 1940.

➤ MiG tried the AM-39 engine in a revised MiG-3 airframe, called the I-231.

➤ Alexandr Pokryshkin gained his first kill, a Bf 109E of Jagdgeschwader 77, on 23 June 1941 while flying a MiG-3.

➤ The rear fuselage skin was made of Bakelite plywood bonded with glue.

➤ Test pilot Yekatov was killed in a MiG-3 when the supercharger exploded.

**PROFILE**

# Genesis of the MiG fighters

MiG's first fighters were capable machines that fell foul of the requirement for an inline engine. The basic design was fairly capable, and the prototype (I-200), powered by a Mikulin AM-35 engine, was the equal of a Spitfire or early Bf 109.

The urgent demand for modern fighters to replace the Polikarpov I-16 set production going in 1940, despite some early handling problems. The first units were operational by the time of the invasion in 1941.

The weakness of the MiG-3

was that it shared the Mikulin AM-35 engine with Ilyushin's Il-2 Shturmovik. Stalin and his generals decreed that the Il-2 had absolute priority, and sent threatening telegrams to factory managers who continued to produce MiGs instead of Il-2s. Consequently, production was terminated in 1942, after only 3120 aircraft had been built.

Attempts to fit radial engines proved unsuccessful as they only added to the MiG's unforgiving reputation. This resulted in many MiGs being promptly replaced by Yak and Lavochkin fighters.

Despite its failure, the MiG proved useful in combat, giving a good account of itself when fighting above heights of 5000 metres. At lower altitudes, where much of the fighting took place, it was not quite the equal of the Fw 190 or Bf 109F.

*Left: By the time of the German invasion in June 1941, 13 fighter units had been fully equipped with the MiG-3.*

*Below: Demand for modern fighters was such that the I-200 prototype was built in just 100 days from first drawings.*

## MiG-3

**Type:** single-seat fighter

**Powerplant:** one 1007-kW (1,350-hp.) Mikulin AM-35A V-12 piston engine

**Maximum speed:** 640 km/h (397 m.p.h.) at 7800 m (25,600 ft.)

**Range:** 1195 km (743 mi.)

**Service ceiling:** 12,000 m (39,400 ft.)

**Weights:** empty 2595 kg (5,709 lb.); maximum take-off 3350 kg (7,370 lb.)

**Armament:** one 12.7-mm (.50 cal.) Beresin and two 7.62-mm (.30 cal.) ShKAS machine-guns, plus up to 200 kg (440 lb.) of bombs or six RS-82 rocket projectiles on underwing racks

**Dimensions:**
| | | |
|---|---|---|
| span | 10.20 m | (33 ft. 9 in.) |
| length | 8.25 m | (20 ft. 9 in.) |
| height | 3.50 m | (11 ft. 6 in.) |
| wing area | 17.44 m² | (188 sq. ft.) |

## MiG-3

**Between December 1940 and December 1941, just over 3100 MiG-3s were built. The badge on this aircraft reads 'for the motherland'.**

In the long nose section the Mikulin AM-35 engine with two 110-litre (29-gal.) fuel tanks was fitted. The MiG-3 had a second oil cooler and improved engine cooling compared to the MiG-1. The engine was quite heavy, at 830 kg (1,826 lb.) compared to the Bf 109's DB 601 of 575 kg (1,265 lb.). The exhaust pipes were made of EYa1-TL-1 heat-resistant steel.

All armament was grouped above the engine. It consisted of a UBS 12.7-mm machine-gun with 300 rounds and two 7.62-mm ShKAS machine-guns with 375 rounds each.

Like most Soviet aircraft the MiG-3 had a very austere cockpit fit, with only 13 instruments and no radio. The pilot sighted his weapons through a PBP-1 gunsight.

Са родину

The engine drove a 3-m (10-ft.) diameter VISh-22Ye propeller made of a magnesium alloy known as electron.

Although the forward fuselage was made of steel tubing with an alloy stressed skin, the rear fuselage consisted of four pine longerons with a 0.5-mm (⅟₅₀-in.) plywood and calico skin.

## COMBAT DATA

### ARMAMENT

Perhaps the biggest failure of the MiG-3 was its weak armament. The weight of a salvo from the MiG was more than doubled with the addition of two more of the heavy Beresin guns.

| | |
|---|---|
| **MiG-3** | 1 x 12.7-mm (.50 cal.) machine-gun<br>2 x 7.62-mm (.30 cal.) machine-guns |
| **Yak-1** | 1 x 20-mm (0.79-in.) cannon<br>1 x 12.7-mm (.50 cal.) machine-guns |
| **Bf 109F** | 1 x 20-mm (0.79-in.) cannon<br>2 x 7.92-mm (0.31-in.) machine-guns |

### MAXIMUM SPEED

Supercharging the engine and the MiG's beautiful streamlined shape gave it very high speed, but without the AM-35 the MiG was useless, and no replacement engine was forthcoming.

| | |
|---|---|
| **MiG-3** | 628 km/h (397 m.p.h.) |
| **Yak-1** | 531 km/h (329 m.p.h.) |
| **Bf 109F** | 589 km/h (365 m.p.h.) |

### CEILING

Another benefit of the supercharger was the MiG's high ceiling. Performance at altitude was so good that German pilots always avoided combat with MiGs above an altitude of 5000 m (16,000 ft.). The reconnaissance MiGs were very hard to catch.

MiG-3 12,000 m (39,400 ft.)
Bf 109F 11,930 m (39,130 ft.)
Yak-1 10,500 m (34,440 ft.)

## Exploits of the MiG aces

**ALEXANDR LUBOV:** A pilot of the crack 16th Guards Polk, Lubov was never afraid to attack against superior odds. On one occasion, he flew his MiG-3 against a force of six Bf 109s, destroying two in seconds.

**ALEXANDR POKRYSHKIN:** On 20 November 1941, Pokryshkin volunteered to fly a lone tactical reconnaissance mission near Rostov. He discovered a large force of Von Kleist's tanks approaching the town in a snow storm, and managed to warn the defenders in time to improve preparations for the town's defence.

CLASSIC MILITARY AIRCRAFT

# MITSUBISHI
# A5M 'CLAUDE'

● Naval fighter ● Open cockpit ● Successful in China

*Pilots of the 'Claude' had to face the elements as it was the last Japanese naval fighter to be fitted with an open cockpit. However, they did have an exceptional field-of-view.*

**W**hen it entered service at the beginning of 1937, the A5M 'Claude' represented a giant leap forwards in carrier-based fighters. Replacing antiquated biplane aircraft, it was the fastest naval fighter in the world and would remain so for almost two years. The A5M was the dominant fighter in the Sino-Japanese conflict, and built up an enviable reputation for strength and agility. By 1942, however, A5Ms were relegated to training duties.

---

## PHOTO FILE
## MITSUBISHI A5M 'CLAUDE'

**▲ Action over China**
*With superior training and high morale, pilots flying A5M2s devastated the Chinese air force, including its faster Polikarpov I-16s.*

**▲ Long-legged 'Claude'**
*To improve effective range the A5M4 was fitted with a 160-litre ventral drop-tank, which gave increased patrol endurance.*

**Dominant fighter ▶**
*When the 12 and 13 Kokutais entered the Sino-Japanese war in 1937, the A5M2 quickly gained complete air superiority.*

**▲ Small but strong**
*After early handling problems were solved the A5M was a joy to fly, although landing accidents still occurred on rough strips. The 'Claude' could take considerable battle damage; one aircraft made it home despite losing a third of its port wing.*

**▼ A5M1 roll-out**
*With its sleek lines and a flush-rivetted aluminium stressed-skin covering, this was the first A5M from the Sasebo Naval Factory. A total of 1094 'Claudes' had been built when production ended in 1940.*

## FACTS AND FIGURES

➤ Originally called the Ka-14, the 'Claude' easily exceeded the demands of the strict naval 9-Shi specification.

➤ The aircraft first flew at Kagamigahara on 4 February 1935.

➤ The first A5M aerial victories were three Curtiss Hawks of the Chinese air force.

➤ Seven A5M pilots became aces in the Sino-Japanese conflict; Lt Tetsuzo Iwamoto was the top ace with 14 'kills'.

➤ After May 1942 remaining A5Ms were relegated to training duties in Japan.

➤ A number of A5Ms ended their days in kamikaze attacks on Allied shipping.

# Champion fighter over China

Despite decimating supposedly superior Chinese opposition in 1938, the A5M and the other rapid advances in Japanese aviation went largely unnoticed in the West. By the time Japan entered World War II the 'Claude' was being replaced by the superb A6M 'Zero', but it continued to serve in secondary roles throughout the war.

The strict 9-Shi specification of 1934 requested a fighter that was small enough to fit on an aircraft-carrier, but which was fast and

manoeuvrable. Mitsubishi proposed the Ka-14, and production commenced with the A5M1, which proved in operations that the Japanese had a world-beating fighter. Development led to the more powerful A5M2 and A5M4 which were very impressive in the Sino-Japanese War.

Carrier-based A5M4s saw action at the start of World War II in Malaya and the Dutch East Indies. However, many A5Ms were used for last-ditch kamikaze raids in 1945.

## A5M4 'CLAUDE'

Based on the aircraft-carrier *Soryu* during the blockade of the East China Sea in November 1939, this A5M4 was flown by Lieutenant Tamotsu, leader of the *Soryu* fighter element.

*Work on a two-seat advanced trainer version, designated A5M4-K, began in 1940. A turn-over pylon was fitted between the cockpits to improve safety.*

Two 7.7-mm (.303 cal.) Type 89 machine-guns were the standard armament for all operational versions of the 'Claude' except the A5M1a which had two 20-mm (0.79-in.) Oerlikon cannon.

To replace the biplane fighters in service, Mitsubishi's team designed the A5M as a low-wing gull monoplane.

The 'Claude' had an open cockpit. The pilot often had a gunsight extending from the centre of the windshield.

Japanese fighters were generally colourfully decorated in their squadron markings. Many aircraft were funded by public subscription and carried the inscription 'Hokokugo' (patriotism).

The Nakajima Kotobuki 41 KAI nine-cylinder radial engine drove a three-bladed propeller. To improve forward visibility from the cockpit a NACA (National Advisory Committee for Aeronautics) cowling with cooling flaps was fitted.

As the Chinese retreated beyond the range of the A5M2, the A5M4 was developed with a 160-litre (42-gal.) drop-tank.

At the design stage great attention was given to minimising the cross-section of the airframe to reduce drag. The metal structure was covered in an aluminium stressed skin.

## A5M4 'Claude'

**Type:** single-seat carrier-borne fighter

**Powerplant:** one 529-kW (710-hp.) Nakajima Kotobuki 41 nine-cylinder air-cooled radial engine

**Maximum speed:** 440 km/h (270 m.p.h.)

**Initial climb rate:** 3000 m (9,800 ft.) in 3 min 35 sec

**Range:** 1200 km (750 mi.)

**Service ceiling:** 9800 m (32,200 ft.)

**Weights:** empty 1216 kg (2,675 lb.); maximum take-off 1705 kg (3,751 lb.)

**Armament:** two 7.7-mm (.303 cal.) Type 89 machine-guns fitted in the upper fuselage, plus two 30-kg (66-lb.) bombs

**Dimensions:**
| | | |
|---|---|---|
| span | 11.00 m | (36 ft. 1 in.) |
| length | 7.57 m | (24 ft. 10 in.) |
| height | 3.27 m | (10 ft. 9 in.) |
| wing area | 17.80 m² | (192 sq. ft.) |

## COMBAT DATA

### MAXIMUM SPEED

When it entered service the A5M was the fastest naval fighter in the world. However, by the time of the Sino-Japanese War it had been overtaken by land-based fighters such as the I-16 and D.XXI.

**A5M4 'CLAUDE'** 440 km/h (270 m.p.h.)

**I-16 TYPE 24** 490 km/h (304 m.p.h.)

**D.XXI** 460 km/h (258 m.p.h.)

### ARMAMENT

One of the major deficiencies of the A5M was its lack of firepower. By the mid to late 1930s most fighters had four, six or even eight machine-guns, which were much more destructive than two.

**A5M4 'CLAUDE'** 2 x 7.7-mm (.303 cal.)machine-guns 60-kg (132-lb.) bombload

**I-16 TYPE 24** 4 x 7.62-mm (.30 cal.) machine-guns 200-kg (440-lb.) bombload

**D.XXI** 4 x 7.9-mm (0.31-in.) machine-guns

### RANGE

With its ventral drop-tank the 'Claude', like its replacement the A6M 'Zero', had far superior range over its contemporaries. This allowed it to harass opponents deep into enemy territory, as well as mounting patrols of great endurance. Land planes generally required less range than their naval equivalents.

**A5M4 'CLAUDE'** 1200 km (750 mi.)

**I-16 TYPE 24** 600 km (370 mi.)

**D.XXI** 950 km (590 mi.)

## 'Claude' colour schemes

■ **TRAINING SQUADRONS:** After the B-25 Doolittle raid on mainland Japan in April 1942, training aircraft were camouflaged with dark green upper surfaces and orange underneath.

■ **14 KOKUTAI:** Typical of the colour schemes worn by aircraft of the 14 Kokutai operating from China, this particular A5M4 was flown by Lieutenant Motonari Suho from Wichow Island in 1940.

■ *SORYU* **AIRCRAFT-CARRIER:** The 'W' prefix on the fin of this A5M4 clearly identifies it as being from the aircraft-carrier *Soryu*. The black auxiliary tank and fuselage bands were not standard.

# MITSUBISHI

# A6M ZERO

● Carrier fighter ● Highly agile dogfighter

▲ The A6M Zero in the hands of the highly trained pilots of the Imperial Japanese Navy could match any fighter in the world in the first two years of the Pacific war.

**W**hen Imperial Japanese forces burst like a tidal wave across the Pacific in December 1941, they were spearheaded by the amazing Mitsubishi Zero. It was not new even then, but Western experts had shrugged off reports that Japan possessed a world-class warplane. No American fighter matched the Zero in firepower, agility or range, and in the early stages of the war it was absolutely dominant.

## MITSUBISHI A6M ZERO

▲ **Wonder fighter**
The Zero gained a reputation as an invincible opponent in the first two years of the Pacific war. Very much a 'pilot's aeroplane', it was one of the most agile aircraft ever built.

▲ **Range and performance**
With a drop-tank, the lightly-built Zero's combat endurance was an astonishing eight hours. Early versions had a range of more than 3000 km (1,900 mi.).

▲ **Floatplane fighter**
The Zero's excellent range and adaptable airframe made it a successful seaplane fighter. It was given the codename 'Rufe'.

▲ **Pearl Harbor attack**
Zeroes aboard the carrier Shokaku prepare to take off as Japan launches the surprise attack on Pearl Harbor which marked the start of World War II in the Pacific.

◀ **Jungle relic**
The remnants of a Zero lie rotting on a jungle airstrip. Such aircraft were still being discovered in remote Pacific islands as late as the 1970s, often in fair condition.

### FACTS AND FIGURES

➤ The Reisen or 'zero fighter', named for the Japanese year 2600 (1940), was called 'Hamp' and 'Zeke' by the Allies.

➤ Early Sakae radial engines were superb, but quality declined sharply in the war.

➤ More Zeroes were manufactured than any other Japanese aircraft of the war.

➤ Of 125 Zeroes which participated in the 7 December 1941 raid on Pearl Harbor, only nine failed to return.

➤ More Zeroes were used in kamikaze attacks than any other Japanese aircraft.

➤ Only two airworthy Zeroes out of the 10,499 built exist today.

# From Pearl Harbor to kamikaze

*The A6M1 prototype flew on 1 April 1939. Built to an exacting Imperial Navy specification, it performed better than almost any fighter in the world in every area except speed.*

The notion that Japan could produce a superb combat craft was so alien to the West that ordinary fighters like the Nakajima Ki-43 'Oscar' were mistakenly called 'Zeroes' and overestimated by besieged Americans. Colonel Claire Chennault's 'Flying Tigers' in China never saw a Zero but their combat reports fuelled growing alarm as the Japanese navy swept across the Pacific with squadrons of the real thing: the A6M, designed by Mitsubishi's Jiro Horikoshi.

The early successes of the Zero were due in part to its light weight, power, armament and manoeuvrability – but also partly to its brilliant and courageous pilots, many of whom fell along the way and proved difficult to replace.

The initial success was not to last for long. Within two years, Japan's adversaries developed new warplanes like the hard-hitting Grumman F6F Hellcat, while only minor improvements were made to the Zero. The tide turned, Japan's situation deteriorated, and in the end, as defeat closed in, this great fighter was reduced to the role of kamikaze – suicide – aircraft.

Although it had space for two, the A6M5c usually carried a single heavy machine-gun over the engine.

## A6M5c ZERO

By the end of 1943 the original Zero was being outfought by new American fighters. The improved A6M5 was introduced to try to close the gap, and was built in greater numbers than any other model.

The biggest weakness of the Zero was a total lack of armour plate. The A6M5 introduced armoured glass in the cockpit, but the fighter was still horribly vulnerable.

Zeroes had three fuel tanks, one in each wingroot and a fuselage tank just in front of the pilot. This usually meant death for the pilot if a bullet hit the aircraft.

The A6M5c carried a 20-mm (0.79-in.) cannon inboard and a 13.2-mm heavy machine-gun outboard in each wing.

The Zero wing had combat flaps fitted, which helped give the aircraft its phenomenal manoeuvrability.

### A6M3 Zero

**Type:** single-seat carrier-based fighter-bomber

**Powerplant:** one 843-kW (1,130-hp.) Nakajima NK1F Sakae 21 radial engine

**Maximum speed:** 565 km/h (350 m.p.h.)

**Range:** 1800km (1,200 mi.) with drop-tank

**Service ceiling:** 11,740 m (38,500 ft.)

**Weights:** empty 1876 kg (4,000 lb.); loaded 2733 kg (6,025 lb.)

**Armament:** two 7.7-mm (.303 cal.) machine-guns with 600 rounds above the engine and two 20-mm (0.79-in.) Type 99 cannon with 100 rounds each in the wings, plus two 60-kg (130-lb.) bombs under wings (suicide mission, one 250-kg/550-lb.) bomb)

**Dimensions:**
span 11.00 m (36 ft. 1 in.)
length 9.12 m (29 ft. 11 in.)
height 3.60 m (11 ft. 6 in.)
wing area 21.30 m² (230 sq. ft.)

The Sakae radial was not very powerful when compared to the huge American engines, but was fine for this very small and light machine.

Like every good carrier plane, the Zero had a wide, strong and stable undercarriage.

The Zero had exceptionally long range, and the carriage of a drop-tank extended its endurance even further. But the lack of self-sealing fuel tanks was a very grave tactical weakness.

The rear fuselage contained a large canvas flotation bag in case the aircraft was ditched.

## COMBAT DATA

### RANGE

The Zero's light weight and highly efficient engine meant that it had a longer range than almost any other single-seat fighter of World War II. This made it ideally suited to the long-range war over the Pacific, but less suited to actual combat, where the lack of protection made it vulnerable to enemy fire.

P-40C WARHAWK 975 km (605 mi.)
A6M2 ZERO 3110 km (1,900 mi.)
F6F-1 HELLCAT 1750 km (1,080 mi.)

### CLIMB RATE

One rule which successful American pilots followed was to never get into a dogfight with a Zero. At low speeds the lightly-built Japanese machine could easily out-turn its heavier American opponents, and in the early days of the war it could climb twice as fast as heavy machines like the Curtiss P-40.

A6M2 ZERO 1370 m/min (4,500 f.p.m.)
F6F-1 HELLCAT 990 m/min (3,200 f.p.m.)
P-40C WARHAWK 750 m/min (2,400 f.p.m.)

### ARMAMENT

Although the Zero's designers sacrificed protection to save weight, they decided from the very beginning to equip their nimble fighter with heavy cannon. Although slow-firing, these hard-hitting weapons gave the Zero a decided advantage over American fighters armed only with machine-guns.

A6M2 ZERO
2 x 20-mm (0.79-in.) cannon
2 x 7.7-mm (.303 cal.) machine guns

P-40C WARHAWK
6 x 12.7-mm (.50 cal.) machine guns

F6F-1 HELLCAT
6 x 12.7-mm (.50 cal.) machine gun

## Attack on Pearl Harbor

**DRAGGED INTO THE WAR:** The Japanese assault came as a complete surprise to the American Pacific Fleet. At 6 a.m. on the morning of 7 December 1941, Zero fighters took off from the six aircraft-carriers of Japan's First Air Fleet, followed by Aichi 'Val' dive-bombers and Nakajima 'Kate' torpedo-bombers. Their destination: Pearl Harbor.

**FIRST WAVE**
Wheeler
Kaneohe
Ewa
Bellows
Hickam
Pearl Harbor

**FIRST WAVE:** The first wave reached Oahu at 7.53 a.m. The fighters and dive-bombers concentrated on Wheeler Field, Bellows Field and Kaneohe, while level bombers and torpedo-bombers hit Pearl Harbor and the airfields on Ford Island, Ewa and Hickam Field.

**SECOND WAVE**
Wheeler
Kaneohe
Ford Island
Hickam

**SECOND WAVE:** Taking off at 7.15, the second wave arrived 30 minutes after the end of the first attack. The main bulk of the attack concentrated on port facilities and the battleships at Ford Island, although some fighters and bombers diverted to make further strikes at airfields.

# MITSUBISHI
# F1M 'PETE'

● Observation ● Advanced trainer ● Floatplane

**D**esigned to meet a 1934 Japanese naval requirement, Mitsubishi's F1M was to be the only observation seaplane in its class built in quantity for the navy. Highly manoeuvrable, the F1M2 production variant was used as an interceptor, dive-bomber, convoy escort and coastal patrol aircraft during World War II, such was its versatility. It was to earn a commendable reputation. The F1M2 was known as 'Pete' to the Allies.

▲ Production
of the F1M2 was initially undertaken by Mitsubishi Jukogyo K.K. Later on production was switched to the Dai-Nijuichi K.K. (21st Naval Air Arsenal) at Sasebo.

## MITSUBISHI F1M 'PETE'

◀ **Ground-attack duties**
Although mainly employed for coastal patrol and reconnaissance, the F1M2's three machine-guns and 120-kg (264-lb.) bomb load were also used for ground attack.

▼ **Major production**
The F1M2 was undoubtedly the most important Japanese observation floatplane of the war, with more than 1000 built.

▲ **South Seas base**
Two F1M2s are moored at an island base in the South Pacific ready for another sortie.

▼ **On dry land**
For servicing the 'Pete' was ferried from the water using a three-wheeled trolley.

◀ **Singapore scrapyard**
Like many Japanese aircraft, this F1M2 ended its days on the scrapheap at RAF Seletar.

## FACTS AND FIGURES

➤ The F1M2 was officially known to the Japanese navy as the Navy Type 0 Observation Seaplane Model 11.

➤ A small number of F1M2s were delivered to Thailand for coastal patrol duties.

➤ A total of 1118 F1Ms were built, including the four F1M1 prototypes.

➤ Apart from Mitsubishi and Aichi, Kawanishi was also asked to build a seaplane prototype, but declined.

➤ The F1M was of all-metal construction with fabric-covered control surfaces.

➤ Experiments were carried out in which an F1M2 carried a 250-kg (550-lb.) bomb.

# Imperial navy spotter

Mid-1936 saw the first flight of the F1M prototype, the first of four F1M1s. This flew alongside an Aichi design built to the same specification; both aircraft were powered by a Nakajima Hikari 1 nine-cylinder radial rated at 611 kW for take-off.

A remarkably 'clean' design, the F1M was a two-seat, single-bay biplane with a central float and stabilising floats beneath its wings. These features gave the aircraft excellent performance, but the F1M was far from perfect. Its biggest problems were a tendency to 'porpoise' on the water and a lack of directional stability in flight.

Mitsubishi then set about redesigning the aircraft to cure these problems and re-powered the F1M with a 652-kW (875-hp.) Mitsubishi Zuisei 13, 14-cylinder radial in a longer cowling. The tail fin, rudder and wings were also altered.

This variant was ordered into production as the F1M2. Mitsubishi built 524 examples then Dai-Nijuichi Kaigun KoKusho (21st Naval Air Arsenal) added another 590.

Serving aboard seaplane tenders, cruisers and from shore bases, F1M2s were primarily reconnaissance, coastal patrol and convoy escort aircraft but performed various other combat and support roles, including training as the F1M2-K.

Two forward-firing 7.7-mm (.303 cal.) Type 97 machine-guns were sufficient for the observation role, but left the F1M under-armed when it was used as a fighter.

*Above: Although it was a pre-war biplane design, the F1M2 served the Japanese throughout World War II.*

*Below: Seen after the war at RAF Seletar in Singapore, this F1M2 'Pete' (background) was captured in airworthy condition. It was, however, never flown again and was later scrapped.*

Little protection was afforded the pilot, who was sheltered only by a windscreen. A large cut-out in the upper wing centre section gave the pilot an acceptable view upwards, however.

A single 7.7-mm (.303 cal.) Type 92 machine-gun was provided for the observer. Flexibly mounted, the weapon allowed the rear crew member to protect the aircraft's rear hemisphere from attack.

A 652-kW (875-hp.) Mitsubishi Zuisei 13 engine drove the three-bladed propeller of the F1M2. Earlier F1M1 versions featured a two-bladed propeller and a 611-kW (820-hp.) Nakajima Hikari 1 nine-cylinder radial piston engine.

In a style typical of Japanese floatplanes, the F1M featured a large central float, with a smaller float beneath each wing providing stability on the water.

## F1M2 'PETE'

This F1M2 carries a typical Imperial Japanese Navy colour scheme of green over light grey. Japanese aircraft often carried a minimum of markings.

A rudder fitted at the extreme trailing edge of the central float allowed the pilot to steer the aircraft on water. Early F1M1 aircraft had shown a tendency to porpoise on the surface.

### F1M2 'Pete'

**Type:** single-engined observation or training floatplane

**Powerplant:** one 652-kW (875-hp.) Mitsubishi Zuisei 13 14-cylinder radial engine

**Maximum speed:** 370 km/h (229 m.p.h.)

**Range:** 740 km (460 mi.)

**Service ceiling:** 9440 m (31,000 ft.)

**Weights:** empty 1928 kg (4,242 lb.); loaded 2550 kg (5,610 lb.)

**Armament:** two fixed forward-firing 7.7-mm (.303 cal.) Type 97 machine-guns and one flexible rear-firing 7.7-mm Type 92 machine-gun plus a normal bombload of two 60-kg (1320lb.) bombs

**Dimensions:**
| | |
|---|---|
| span | 11.00 m (36 ft. 1 in.) |
| length | 9.50 m (31 ft. 2 in.) |
| height | 4.00 m (13 ft. 2 in.) |
| wing area | 29.54 m² (316 sq. ft.) |

## COMBAT DATA

### SERVICE CEILING

The two Japanese floatplanes had a big advantage over their American counterpart as far as ceiling was concerned. High altitude flight allowed a larger field of view but also made the aircraft vulnerable to fighters.

F1M2 'PETE' 9440 m (31,000 ft.)

N1K 'REX' 10,560 m (34,600 ft.)

OS2U-3 KINGFISHER 3960 m (13,000 ft.)

### MAXIMUM SPEED

A later and more powerful design, the Kawanishi N1K vastly out-performed the two older aircraft. Despite being of biplane design, the F1M2 had good performance for an aircraft in its class. The slow speed of the OS2U-3 left it at the mercy of enemy fighters.

F1M2 'PETE' 370 km/h (229 m.p.h.)

OS2U-3 KINGFISHER 264 km/h (164 m.p.h.)

N1K 'REX' 490 km/h (304 m.p.h.)

### RANGE

For operations over the vastness of the Pacific Ocean range was the most important consideration. The 'Pete' with its less impressive range was mainly confined to patrolling coastal waters. The longer-ranged N1K was more versatile.

F1M2 'PETE' 740 km (460 mi.)

OS2U-3 KINGFISHER 1296 km (804 mi.)

N1K 'REX' 1665 km (1,032 mi.)

## World War II Japanese floatplanes

■ **AICHI E16A ZUIUN 'PAUL':** This twin-float reconnaissance aircraft entered service in 1944 and suffered heavy losses to Allied fighters.

■ **AICHI E13A 'JAKE':** This all-metal reconnaissance floatplane was built in large numbers and had an impressive endurance.

■ **NAKAJIMA E8N 'DAVE':** Operating as a catapult-launched reconnaissance aircraft the E8N saw service from battleships and cruisers.

■ **MITSUBISHI A6M2-N:** A floatplane version of the famous 'Zero' fighter was developed although the float markedly reduced performance.

# MITSUBISHI

# G4M 'BETTY'

● Bomber ● Missile carrier ● Transport

▲ Mitsubishi's G4M was a very modern design when it appeared in 1941, and it was modified considerably with extra guns, more powerful engines and propellers and a laminar-flow wing.

**M**itsubishi's G4M 'Betty' bomber made its name by sinking two battleships in a day in 1941. Although the 'Betty' was not a perfect design, lacking in protection, this twin-engine warplane had respectable performance and bomb-carrying capacity. This much admired aircraft was the backbone of Japan's bomber force all the way through to the end of World War II, by which time it was used for carrying missiles.

## MITSUBISHI G4M 'BETTY'

▼ **Best bomber**
For all its faults, the G4M was one of the best bombers Japan owned, and was built in larger numbers than any other Japanese bomber.

▲ **Glazed nose**
The distinct glazed nose housed a 7.7-mm (.303 cal.) machine-gun and the bomb-aimer's seat. The nose also contained anti-surface vessel radar in a small number of modified 'Bettys'.

**Long range** ▼
For duties in Japan's vast Pacific empire, the G4M had exceptional range.

▲ **Dorsal turret**
In an effort to increase defence, the G4M2 was fitted with a dorsal gun turret containing a 20-mm (0.79-in.) Type 99 cannon. The gunner reached the weapon by standing on a platform inside the fuselage.

▼ **Dead 'Betty'**
Like many Japanese aircraft, the G4M had long range but little armour protection. It did not take much attention from enemy fighters to destroy one.

▲ **More power**
Another improvement to the G4M2 was to fit bigger engines with four-bladed propellers, namely the Kasei 21 radial with water injection.

## FACTS AND FIGURES

➤ In April 1943, P-38s downed a 'Betty' carrying Admiral Yamamoto, killing Japan's top commander.

➤ The prototype G4M bomber first took to the skies on 23 October 1939.

➤ Though primarily a bomber, the G4M existed in trainer and transport versions.

➤ The first mission to launch Okha missiles from G4Ms was a disaster, as all were shot down before releasing the weapon.

➤ In 1944 many G4M bombers were converted to carry Okha suicide aircraft.

➤ G4Ms helped sink the British battleships *Prince of Wales* and *Repulse*.

## PROFILE

# Bombing with the 'Betty'

*The G4M was a sound design, but too much was asked of it, especially at the end of the war. It was very successful during early operations in China.*

Nicknamed 'Betty' by the Allies, this bomber did not have enough defensive armament and was susceptible to a fiery doom if its fuel was ignited. Some American pilots called the G4M the 'flying cigarette lighter'. Even so, Japan threw 2000 Mitsubishi G4Ms into the Pacific battle. The practical qualities of this aircraft, including its reliability and long range, frequently overcame its shortcomings, leaving a trail of

destruction in its wake.

Designed in 1937 and becoming operational in 1940, the 'Betty' had an unremarkable record with the Japanese army, but became one of the strongest weapons in Japan's naval force. Manufactured in greater numbers than any other Japanese aircraft, the G4M achieved considerable success in long-range bombing duties.

Mitsubishi engineers improved the 'Betty' as the war progressed, adding a better

tailgun and other features, but even though pilots liked the aircraft it was a creature of the past, not the future. Ironically, after years of war, the G4M's final duty was to carry the Japanese surrender delegation to the island of Ie Shima four days after the fighting ended.

Kiro Honjo, the G4M designer, had envisaged a longer span wing for greater range, but for structural strength he eventually decided on this design with four fuel tanks in the leading edge of the wings.

The two pilots sat side-by-side in the cockpit, which had an emergency roof escape hatch. The navigator sat below and to the rear.

### G4M 'BETTY'

This G4M Model 11 served on the Rabaul front in 1942 with the first Chutai of the Takao Kokutai, which suffered very heavy losses in action. This model does not have the dorsal turret of the G4M2.

Early 'Bettys' had distinct blisters on the fuselage sides for the waist gunners, who each operated a 7.7-mm (.303 cal.) machine-gun. These were deleted in the G4M2 in favour of a further gun position with 20-mm (0.79-in.) cannon.

The low-set tailplane was aerodynamically very clean and had a glass tailcone for a rearwards observer. Later versions possessed a 20-mm (0.79-in.) cannon in a rear turret for additional defensive armament.

Kasei 21 two-row radial engines were fitted to the early G4Ms, followed by Kasei 25s in the G4M2.

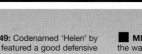

Unusually, the G4M bomb-bay did not have conventional hinged doors but fixed ones which could be removed before a mission to accommodate the weapon load.

The tail gunner's position gave the fuselage its distinct cigar shape. It also housed a 20-mm (0.79-in.) Type 99 cannon with a 60-round ammunition drum.

### G4M2 'Betty'

**Type:** twin-engined seven-seat land-based naval medium-bomber

**Powerplant:** two 1343-kW Mitsubishi Kasei 25 radial engines

**Maximum speed:** 438 km/h (270 m.p.h.) at 4600 m (15,000 ft.)

**Climb rate:** 32 minutes to 8000 m (26,250 ft.)

**Range:** 4335 km (2,694 mi.)

**Weights:** empty 8160 kg (17,952 lb.); loaded 12,500 kg (27,500 lb.)

**Armament:** one 20-mm (0.79-in.) cannon in tail, two 7.92-mm (0.31-in.) machine-guns in nose and one in each beam position; 1000 kg (2,200 lb.) of bombs or one 800-kg (1,760-lb.) torpedo

**Dimensions:**
| | |
|---|---|
| span | 25.00 m (82 ft.) |
| length | 20.00 m (66 ft.) |
| height | 6.00 m (20 ft.) |
| wing area | 78.12 m² (841 sq. ft.) |

### ACTION DATA

#### MAXIMUM SPEED

The G4M was a fast, twin-engined bomber that could outrun many fighters at the start of the war. However, with the introduction of newer fighters, such as the F6F Hellcat and P-51 Mustang, lightly armed G4Ms became easy prey.

G4M2 'BETTY' **438 km/h (270 m.p.h.)**

WELLINGTON **378 km/h (230 m.p.h.)**

He 111H **365 km/h (225 m.p.h.)**

#### BOMBLOAD

The Wellington could carry more than twice the weight of bombs of its two contemporaries. The G4M sacrificed a heavy bombload for increased speed and range. By 1943 all three of these aircraft were outclassed by the massive British and American four-engined bombers of the war.

G4M2 'BETTY' **1000 kg (2,200 lb.)**

WELLINGTON **2041 kg (4,490 lb.)**

He 111H **1000 kg (2,200 lb.)**

#### RANGE

Designed for operations over the vast areas of the Pacific Ocean, G4Ms possessed excellent range allowing them to strike far from their bases. Both the Wellington and He 111 operated in the more confined European theatre and therefore did not need such long reach. Later in the war long-range versions of the Wellington were used for maritime patrol and strike.

G4M2 'BETTY' **4334 km (2,694 mi.)**

WELLINGTON **2500 km (1,550 mi.)**

He 111H **1950 km (1,200 mi.)**

## Japanese bombers of World War II

■ **MITSUBISHI G3M:** Also possessing very long range, the G3M was used in the attacks on HMS *Prince of Wales* and *Repulse*. Most G3Ms were used for secondary roles by 1945.

■ **MITSUBISHI Ki-21:** Another medium-bomber design that was approaching obsolescence, the Ki-21 was used on suicide commando attacks on US bases in 1944.

■ **NAKAJIMA Ki-49:** Codenamed 'Helen' by the Allies, the Ki-49 featured a good defensive armament and fuel protection, but carried only a light bombload over a fairly short range.

■ **MITSUBISHI Ki-67:** Produced at the end of the war, the Ki-67 was a fast design with good armament. By the time it was in production massive American air raids hindered delivery.

# MORANE-SAULNIER

# M.S.406

● Interceptor ● Used by Finland ● Also built in Switzerland

▲ *This Finnish M.S.406 is seen next to a captured Soviet Yak-1, its opponent which provided the Klimov engines which the Finns fitted in their Morane-Saulnier aircraft.*

**F**rench experts developed the M.S.406 while the Messerschmitt Bf 109 was entering service in Germany. Unfortunately, the Morane-Saulnier aircraft looked better than it flew. It lacked power and was never the equal of the Bf 109. After suffering heavy losses in France, the M.S.406 was relegated to serving with a single unit of the Vichy air force. Ironically, M.S.406s with Russian engines were used with some success by Finland's air force.

## PHOTO FILE

## MORANE-SAULNIER M.S.406

### ▲ Prototype test
This M.S.405, forerunner to the M.S.406, was used for early trials. Pilots liked the aircraft, but immediately recognised the limitations of its design.

### ▲ Colonial base
Many M.S.406s were deployed to North Africa before the German invasion of France and saw no action. A few French aces, such as Robert Wuilliame, downed aircraft over France, usually Ju 87 Stukas.

### ▲ Nose in the grass
The majority of the M.S.406s that fought ended up like this aircraft. Although some gained kills, tangling with a Messerschmitt was a dangerous occupation.

### ▼ Swiss defender
Switzerland built almost 290 of the EFW D-3800 fighter, based closely on the M.S.406 airframe.

### ▲ Lebanese gold
France deployed the M.S.406 to its Middle Eastern bases in March 1940. This aircraft of G.C.1/7, number 805, was off-loaded in Beirut by the seaplane carrier Commandant Teste. The M.S.406 had little more success here than in Europe.

## FACTS AND FIGURES

➤ Only 572 of the planned 1,000 M.S.406s had been delivered to the French air arm when the war began.

➤ Switzerland manufactured 289 fighters in two models based on the M.S.406.

➤ The first production M.S.406 flew on 24 January 1939.

➤ On the first day of the Battle of France 37 M.S.406s were destroyed by the Luftwaffe on the ground.

➤ The limited production run of the M.S.406 occupied three factories over 14 months.

➤ Some French aircraft ended up in Finland and Croatia during the occupation.

## PROFILE

# France's failed fighter

Developed from the M.S.405 of 1934, the M.S.406 was a sleek monoplane but had features which were soon out of date, including a braced tailplane and significant fabric construction.

Although the aircraft was well-behaved in the hands of a capable pilot and was not difficult to fly, it lacked power for the aerial combat that was to become routine in the 1940s. During the first year of the war, the M.S.406 claimed 175 kills

but for the loss of over 400 of its kind.

Versions of the M.S.406 for China, Lithuania and Yugoslavia were never delivered, although others flew with Finland and Switzerland. The Vichy French regime kept some of these planes flying, but by then it was too late for the M.S.406 to mount the effective defence for which it had been intended. Germany gave the captured French aircraft to its Croat and Finnish allies, and the Finns

*Above: The pre-production M.S.405 was produced as a testbed for the mass-produced M.S.406 fighter.*

made the M.S.406 a success by installing the powerful 820-kW (1,100-hp.) Klimov engine. With this powerplant the aircraft proved quite successful, and served until the end of the war.

*Below: Poland was one of several customers that ordered the M.S.406 but did not receive it in time. It was then used by the French air force.*

### M.S.406C-1

**Type:** single-engine fighter

**Powerplant:** one 641-kW (860-hp.) Hispano-Suiza 12Y-31 V-12 piston engine

**Maximum speed:** 485 km/h (300 m.p.h.) at 5000 m (16,500 ft.)

**Range:** 1100 km (680 mi.)

**Service ceiling:** 9400 m (31,000 ft.)

**Weights:** empty 1900 kg (4,180 lb.); maximum take-off 2470 kg (5,434 lb.)

**Armament:** one engine-mounted 20-mm (0.79-in.) cannon firing through propeller hub and two wing-mounted 7.5-mm (0.3-in.) machine-guns

**Dimensions:**
| | | |
|---|---|---|
| span | 10.60 m | (23 ft. 9 in.) |
| length | 8.15 m | (26 ft. 9 in.) |
| height | 2.80 m | (9 ft. 3 in.) |
| wing area | 16.00 m² | (172 sq. ft.) |

One of the best features was the engine-mounted 20-mm (0.79-in.) Hispano cannon, which fired through the propeller hub.

The tubular gunsight in front of the cockpit was a throwback to the 1930s.

### M.S.406C

**The most numerous fighter in service with the Armée de l'Air in 1940, only half of the 1000 M.S.406s ordered reached the squadrons. By the end of July 1940, 400 of these had fallen to the Luftwaffe.**

The majority of the rear fuselage was fabric-covered. The tailplane had large bracing struts for support.

Most of the failings of the M.S.406 were caused by lack of power from the Hispano-Suiza 12Y engine. When Finland replaced this with the Klimov powerplant the resultant aircraft (known as Morko Moraani) was greatly improved.

Secondary armament of two 7.5-mm (0.3-in.) machine-guns was housed in the wings. These fired outside the propeller disc.

Early M.S.406s had only a tailskid, but later aircraft were fitted with a retractable tailwheel.

## COMBAT DATA

### MAXIMUM SPEED

French fighters of 1939 were slower than their German and British contemporaries. Although the D.520 was deemed adequate, taking on a Bf 109 in an M.S.406 or a Bloch 152 was disastrous.

| | |
|---|---|
| **M.S.406C-1** | 485 km/h (300 m.p.h.) |
| **D.520** | 535 km/h (331 m.p.h.) |
| **BLOCH 152** | 482 km/h (298 m.p.h.) |

### ARMAMENT

With only a single cannon and two machine-guns the M.S.406 was underarmed. The D.520, however, had superior firepower and could match the Bf 109 in weaponry during 1940.

| | |
|---|---|
| **M.S.406C-1** | 1 x 20-mm (0.79-in.) cannon<br>2 x 7.5-mm (0.3-in.) MGs |
| **D.520** | 1 x 20-mm (0.79-in.) cannon<br>4 x 7.5-mm (0.3-in.) MGs |
| **BLOCH 152** | 2 x 20-mm (0.79-in.) cannon<br>2 x 7.5-mm (0.3-in.) MGs |

### RANGE

The French warplanes of the period had relatively small, but economical, engines. The Hispano-Suiza 12Y gave the M.S.406 excellent range allowing it to dogfight for longer than its opponents.

**BLOCH 152** 955 km (592 mi.)

**D.520** 890 km (552 mi.)

**M.S.406C-1** 1100 km (680 mi.)

## French fighters in 1940

**BLOCH 152:** Another design that reflected the sorry state of French aircraft design in the 1930s, it was difficult for the Bloch 152 to catch a Dornier 17, let alone a Bf 109.

**CURTISS HAWK:** Purchased from America, the Curtiss 75 claimed some victories against the Luftwaffe, but was inferior to the Bf 109; many French Hawks were given to Finland by Germany.

**DEWOITINE 520:** The best fighter available to France in 1940, the D.520 was only in service with a few units. Unlike the M.S.406, it could take on the Bf 109 with a reasonable chance of success.

# NAKAJIMA

# KI-43 HAYABUSA 'OSCAR'

● Interceptor ● Air defence ● Kamikaze aircraft

▲ The Hayabusa might not have been produced if the Japanese army had adopted the superior Mitsubishi A6M, but the rivalry with the navy meant that the service had to have its own fighter despite the inferiority of the design.

**N**amed Hayabusa (peregrine falcon) by the Japanese army, the Ki-43 was ordered in December 1937 as a replacement for the Ki-27 'Nate'. The aircraft had a retracting undercarriage, but its performance was not much better than that of the earlier fighter. Even so, the Hayabusa was more than a match for the Allied fighters in the early stages of the Pacific War, and in terms of numbers it became the Imperial Army's most important fighter.

---

▼ Big wing
The prototype Hayabusa had poor manoeuvrability, so a new wing was designed with increased area and combat flaps. This gave the aircraft an excellent ceiling as well as improved agility.

▲ On test
The Allies tested a Hayabusa and discovered its lack of armour protection and limited armament. In many ways the Ki-43 was a poor performer, but it could outmanoeuvre most Allied fighters.

▼ Fighter mission
Most Ki-43s were used on fighter missions in a vain attempt to stop American bomber raids, but by 1944 a shortage of other aircraft meant that it was used for ground-attack duties.

▲ Hucks starter
Like many fighter aircraft of the day, the Hayabusa required mechanical starting. The Sakae radial engine was one of the plane's best features.

More guns ▶
In an attempt to give the Hayabusa more effective firepower, it was fitted with two 20-mm (0.79-in.) cannon but still lacked punch.

## FACTS AND FIGURES

➤ Hayabusas were used in theatres of war as far apart as Burma, China, Japan, the Philippine Islands and Thailand.

➤ The Ki-43-IIIb interceptor with cannon armament never entered service.

➤ By 1945 Hayabusas were often used as kamikaze aircraft on suicide missions.

➤ The Hayabusa was designed to replace Nakajima's own Ki-27 to a specification from the Imperial Japanese army.

➤ Production of the Ki-43 totalled 5,919, including 3239 by Nakajima.

➤ When it entered service the Ki-43 was said to be the army's most agile fighter.

## PROFILE

# Japan's peregrine falcon

With a top speed of less than 500 km/h (310 m.p.h.) and armed with only a pair of light 7.7-mm (.303 cal.) machine-guns, the Ki-43-I-Hei was almost obsolete by the time it entered service in 1941. It was highly agile, though, and the 40 in service by December of that year faced little opposition during the invasions of Burma and Malaya.

More powerful engines improved performance, however, and the Ki-43-II-Ko was used

widely as a fighter-bomber, carrying a 250-kg (550-lb.) bomb under each wing. In September 1943 the Allies captured several damaged 'Oscars' on an airfield in New Guinea. They were able to build a complete example from the wreckage, and after testing it they worked out how to counter its outstanding low-speed manoeuvrability.

But its replacement, the P-51 Mustang-beating Ki-84, was late, and the more powerful Ki-43-III-Ko had to remain in production

until the end of the war. Nearly 6000 Ki-43s had been completed by then, and the Hayabusa was still in widespread service, even though it was clearly outclassed by the modern fighters it faced. One of the Hayabusa's last roles was as a kamikaze aircraft, frequently loaded up with underwing bombs for additional effect.

*Although it was a capable performer in 1941, the Hayabusa was not in the same league as later Allied fighters and losses were very high in 1944.*

### Ki-43IIb Hayabusa 'Oscar'

**Type:** single-seat land-based radial-engined interceptor fighter

**Powerplant:** one 858-kW (1,150-hp.) Nakajima Ha-115 radial piston engine

**Maximum speed:** 530 km/h (329 m.p.h.)

**Climb rate:** 5000 m (16,400 ft.) in 5.8 min

**Maximum range:** 1760 km (1,090 mi.)

**Service ceiling:** 11,200 m (36,750 ft.)

**Weights:** empty 1910 kg (4,202 lb.); loaded 2925 kg (6,435 lb.)

**Armament:** two 12.7-mm (.50 cal.) machine-guns and up to two 250-kg (550-lb.) bombs underwing

**Dimensions:**
span 10.84 m (35 ft. 6 in.)
length 8.92 m (29 ft. 3 in.)
height 3.27 m (10 ft. 9 in.)
wing area 21.40 m² (230 sq. ft.)

## KI-43 HAYABUSA 'OSCAR'

**Built between 1939 and 1945, the Ki-43 was the most numerous fighter in Japanese army service. By 1945 most aircraft had been withdrawn to the home islands for defence against daylight B-29 bomber raids.**

The Hayabusa was powered by a Nakajima 14-cylinder air-cooled radial engine. The final interceptor variant would have used the Ha-112 version of this engine if it had ever been put into production.

Unlike most single-seat Japanese fighters, the Ki-43 had some cockpit armour and fuel tank protection.

The Ki-43 was superseded in production by the Ki-43-IIa. This featured a Ha-115 engine and additional pilot armour, as well as innovative self-sealing fuel tanks.

The wing hardpoints were repositioned in the Ki-43-IIb, as some early aircraft had taken off their own propellers when dropping their bombload.

A pair of fuel tanks could be fitted under the wings to extend the Hayabusa's impressive range.

The main armament was two 12.7-mm (.50 cal.) machine-guns in the wings. This had originally been two 7.7-mm (.303 cal.) weapons, later changed to one 7.7-mm and one 12.7-mm gun in the Ki-43-1b variant.

Two underwing 250-kg (550-lb.) bombs could be carried for ground attack or kamikaze missions.

Combat flaps were fitted to the wings to enhance turning performance in a dogfight.

The Japanese forces frequently painted their fighters with gaudy unit markings, like the red lightning strikes on the tail of this aircraft and the blue spinner and stripes shown in the plan view.

## COMBAT DATA

### MAXIMUM SPEED

The lightweight Ki-43 had a good power-to-weight ratio, making it one of the best performers in its class. Although quicker than the less aerodynamic MC.200, the Ki-43 was slower than the big P-40.

**Ki-43IIb HAYABUSA** 530 km/h (329 m.p.h.)
**MC.200** 502 km/h (311 m.p.h.)
**P-40N WARHAWK** 552 km/h (378 m.p.h.)

### SERVICE CEILING

In terms of altitude, the Ki-43 was superior to both the P-40 and MC.200. However, by the time the American Hellcat and Mustang were on the scene it was firepower and agility that counted most.

**Ki-43IIb HAYABUSA** 11,200 m (36,750 ft.)
**MC.200 SAETTA** 8900 m (29,200 ft.)
**P-40N WARHAWK** 9450 m (38,000 ft.)

### FIXED ARMAMENT

The small Ki-43 was let down by its light armament, especially when compared to the Italian MC.200 and the P-40N, which are in a class of their own. However, the Ki-43 could carry additional bombs.

**Ki-43IIb HAYABUSA** 2 x 12.7-mm (.50 cal.) machine-guns
**MC.200** 2 x 12.7-mm (.50 cal.) and 2 x 7.7-mm (.303 cal.) machine-guns
**P-40N WARHAWK** 6 x 12.7-mm (.50 cal.) machine-guns

## Nakajima fighters

■ **Ki-27 'NATE':** Production of the pre-war vintage Ki-27 ended in 1942, after nearly 4000 had been delivered. For most of the war it served only in less-important theatres and as a trainer.

■ **Ki-44 SHOKI 'TOJO':** Nakajima began designing the Ki-44 immediately after the Ki-43, and the new machine featured an uprated engine, and increased manoeuvrability and top speed.

■ **Ki-84 HAYATE 'FRANK':** Entering service late in the war, the Ki-84 was superior to the P-51H Mustang and P-47N Thunderbolt. It was deployed in small numbers, however, so its impact was reduced.

# NAKAJIMA
# KI-84 'FRANK'

● Single-seat fighter/fighter-bomber ● Agile defender of Japan

▲ The Ki-84 was by many accounts Japan's best fighter of World War II. Adding performance to the extreme agility of earlier Japanese fighters, it was an immensely potent war machine. But for Japan it was too little, too late.

**N**o fighter ace of World War II was deadlier than the pilot of the powerful Nakajima Ki-84 Hayate ('gale' – nicknamed 'Frank' by the Allies). One of the few entirely new fighters developed by Japan once hostilities were under way, the potent Ki-84 climbed faster and was more manoeuvrable than the American P-51D Mustang and P-47N Thunderbolt. Unfortunately for Japan, this impressive warplane came too late to turn the tide.

## PHOTO FILE
## NAKAJIMA KI-84 'FRANK'

▲ **Raw pilots**
The Ki-84 might have performed better if Japan had better pilots, but many of the experts had been killed in the early war years.

**Wasted potential ▶**
Poor reliability and Allied air superiority meant that most Ki-84s undeservedly ended up as scrap metal on Pacific Islands.

▲ **Powerful performer**
With a large engine and a four-bladed propeller, the Ki-84 was in the same league as the large Allied designs that it faced. It also maintained the startling manoeuvrability of earlier Japanese fighters.

▼ **American 'Frank'**
The US Technical Air Intelligence Command evaluated the Ki-84 after the war, prompting admiration from American test pilots. One Ki-84 was rebuilt in the USA in 1963, and was eventually returned to its homeland in 1973.

▲ **Air defender**
The Ki-84 ended up flying desperate defence missions against B-29 bombers attacking the Japanese homeland. This was less than ideal for the Ki-84, which performed better at low altitudes.

## FACTS AND FIGURES

➤ Delivery of 373 Ki-84s in December 1944 marked the highest monthly production rate for any Japanese army fighter.

➤ Nakajima and Mansyu delivered 3382 Ki-84s in 17 months.

➤ Three Ki-106 all-wood fighters based on the 'Frank' design were built.

➤ The Ki-113 with strengthened structure and the Ki-116 with a lightweight engine were 'one-off' experimental Hayates.

➤ The planned Ki-117 interceptor version never reached service.

➤ Although slower, the 'Frank' could outmanoeuvre late-model Mustangs.

## PROFILE

# Japan's greatest fighter

Given the codename 'Frank' by the Allies, the Nakajima Ki-84 Hayate entered service in the summer of 1944. Had it come earlier, this excellent warplane would have posed serious problems for them: it was clearly the best Japanese fighter to serve in large numbers.

The prototype flew at Ojima in April 1943, and was rushed into service while the Allies pursued their relentless advance toward the Japanese home islands. In early clashes in the Philippines the 'Frank' proved a superior combatant, but was outnumbered from the start.

Production aircraft were plagued by inferior workmanship. Fuel and hydraulic problems were never fully solved but the Ki-84 performed effectively anyway, proving a fierce opponent in the final battle for Okinawa. Later models used wooden rear fuselage, fittings and wingtips to conserve strategic materials, but performance remained superb, an impression confirmed by American tests conducted after the war.

By the close of the conflict, underground factories were being readied to produce 200 Ki-84s per month.

The Ki-84 was a dangerous opponent against even the latest Allied types. When pitted against Curtiss P-40s in China and slower US Navy Hellcats, it proved deadly.

### Ki-84-Ia 'Frank'

**Type:** single-seat interceptor fighter/fighter-bomber

**Powerplant:** one 1416-kW (1,900-hp.) Nakajima Ha-45-23 18-cylinder radial piston engine

**Maximum speed:** 631 km/h (391 m.p.h.) at 6120 m (20,000 ft.)

**Range:** 2168 km (1,350 mi.)

**Service ceiling:** 10,500 m (34,500 ft.)

**Weights:** empty 2660 kg (5,830 lb.); loaded 3890 kg (8,558 lb.)

**Armament:** two 12.7-mm (.50 cal.) Ho-103 synchronised nose machine-guns and two wing-mounted 20-mm (0.79-in.) Ho-5 cannon (later models had four cannon), plus underwing racks for two 250-kg bombs or two 190-litre (50-gal.) drop-tanks

**Dimensions:**
| | |
|---|---|
| span | 11.24 m (36 ft. 10 in.) |
| length | 9.92 m (32 ft. 6 in.) |
| height | 3.39 m (11 ft. 1 in.) |
| wing area | 21.00 m² (226 sq. ft.) |

## KI-84-IA 'FRANK'

This 'Frank' was a home defence fighter serving with the 74th Sentai at Naruhatsu, Japan, in the summer of 1945.

The main fuselage tank carried up to 217 litres (60 gal.) of fuel. The provision of self-sealing tanks was a major improvement for Japanese fighters.

The bubble canopy gave the Ki-84's pilot superb all-round combat visibility.

The four-bladed propeller was a constant-speed electrically-operated variable-pitch unit.

A long-wing version of the Ki-84 was planned to counter high-flying B-29 bombers, but it never saw combat.

A pair of 190-litre (50-gal.) fuel tanks could be carried under the wings. The internal wing tanks had a capacity of 173 litres (45 gal.).

The handling of the Ki-84 was almost faultless, although test pilots complained that the elevators felt heavy at high speed and the rudder felt mushy at low speed.

The radio was fitted in a bay behind the cockpit, which had a large sheet of armour protecting the pilot's back.

The Ha-45-23 radial proved more reliable than previous Japanese engines. Later variants were turbo-supercharged.

The bomber-destroyer Ki-84-Ic variant carried a pair of 30-mm (1.18-in.) cannon mounted in the wingroots.

The white panel behind the national markings indicated a 'home defence' aircraft.

### COMBAT DATA

#### MAXIMUM SPEED

Although the Ki-84 was faster than most other Japanese fighters, it could not match its American opponents for sheer speed. But at combat speeds it could accelerate very quickly, and its agility was superior.

| | |
|---|---|
| Ki-84-Ia | 631 km/h (391 m.p.h.) |
| P-51D MUSTANG | 700 km/h (438 m.p.h.) |
| P-38J LIGHTNING | 666 km/h (412 m.p.h.) |

#### CLIMB RATE

The Japanese army and navy both emphasised climbing ability in their fighter specifications, and the Ki-84 was no exception. It could outclimb faster and more powerful types such as the P-51 Mustang and the P-38 Lightning.

Ki-84-Ia 'FRANK' 1100 m/min (3,600 f.p.m.)
P-51D MUSTANG 1000 m/min (3,280 f.p.m.)
P-38J LIGHTNING 870 m/min (2,854 f.p.m.)

#### SERVICE CEILING

If the Ki-84 had a weakness, it was in its lack of ability at high altitude. That was no problem early in the war when its design was fixed, but by the end of the conflict bombers like the B-29 routinely operated at high altitudes that the 'Frank', with its radial engine, struggled to reach.

13,410 m (44,000 ft.)
12,750 m (42,000 ft.)
10,500 m (34,500 ft.)

| Ki-84-Ia 'FRANK' | P-51D MUSTANG | P-38J LIGHTNING |

# Defending Japan's home islands

**■ NAKAJIMA Ki-44 'TOJO':** The first Japanese fighter designed as an interceptor, the Ki-44's limited manoeuvrability made it unpopular when introduced in 1940. But late in the war it was to prove reasonably effective against high-level bombers.

**■ KAWASAKI Ki-61 'TONY':** The Ki-61 was powered by a Japanese copy of the German DB 601 inline engine. It was a capable fighter in the Messerschmitt Bf 109 mould, but maintenance problems meant that it could not be relied upon.

**■ MITSUBISHI J2M 'JACK':** Designed by the team which produced the Zero, the Raiden was a very different machine. An out-and-out interceptor it climbed fast and was heavily armed, but like most late-war Japanese fighters it was unreliable.

# NIEUPORT

# TYPE 17

● Scout fighter ● Favourite of aces ● Highly manoeuvrable

▲ France produced some of the finest fighters of World War I. The experience gained in producing pre-war aircraft was reflected in the success of Nieuports, which were loved by pilots.

T he Nieuport Type 17 was the first of the truly great fighters to carry its famous name into the skies of World War I. Derived from a series of light fighter scouts, the Nieuport was so successful that it was supplied to most of the Allied powers, including Russia and America. Many of the great aces of the war flew the type, which had particularly fine manoeuvrability and rate of climb. Nieuports were still flown after the war.

## NIEUPORT TYPE 17

▲ Swing start
The Le Rhône rotary could be hand-swung into action, with care and by a strong pilot.

▲ America's fighter
A lack of indigenous designs meant that the American forces purchased many French planes, including 298 Nieuport 28s. This model was flown by Eddie Rickenbacker, the top-scoring American ace.

◀ Lewis gun
Many Nieuports had a Lewis gun on top of the wing, fitted with the distinct flat magazine. This was reloaded by swinging the gun down on a rack, which was an awkward feature of the design.

▼ Large numbers
The demand for Nieuports was great, and huge numbers were produced. At many Allied air bases the Nieuports were the most numerous aircraft.

▲ Trusty design
Based on the proven Nieuport 11, the 17 had a more powerful Le Rhône or Clerget rotary and synchronised Vickers gun.

## FACTS AND FIGURES

➤ At first the Type 17's gun fired above its propeller; a synchroniser enabled the gun to fire through the propeller.

➤ In 1910 Edouard de Nieuport began the company that made these fine planes.

➤ Canadian Major 'Billy' Bishop claimed many of his 72 kills in a Nieuport 17.

➤ The success of the Type 17 led to more Nieuport aircraft, including the famous Type 28 supplied to America in 1918.

➤ Earlier Nieuports included monoplanes, which could even perform loops.

➤ Nieuport 11s were built under licence in Italy and flown by 12 squadrons in 1917.

# Nieuport's great fighter scouts

By the time war clouds loomed over Europe in 1914, Nieuport had been making innovative aircraft for half a decade. The first fighters were the Nieuport 11s, which gave the Allies a brief return to air superiority in 1915, as a result of their excellent manoeuvrability and climb rate. The Nieuport 17 was the next single-seater. It was stronger than the previous Model 11

and had more powerful Clerget or Le Rhône engines. The success of the type attracted much attention from abroad and the type was ordered by Belgium, Britain, Italy, Russia and the United States. With larger ailerons and a 60-kW (110-hp.) Le Rhône engine, the Type 21 was introduced in late 1917, and the Type 28 appeared in 1918.

Some of the famous aces of the war, among them

Nungesser, Ball and Bishop, flew the Nieuport Type 17. Like any aircraft made of wood and fabric, the plane could become a death trap if things went wrong. But in the right hands this aircraft was a real winner, as evidenced by its long list of successful aerial victories.

*Left: The long slats on the struts of this Nieuport are the Le Prieur rocket rails used against airships. Eight of these weapons were carried, inclined to fire upwards, and were electrically triggered.*

*Right: American pilots liked the Nieuport 17, often decorating their aircraft with colourful artwork, like this Indian's head. The US pilots also flew other French fighters such as the SPAD.*

## Type 17

**Type:** single-seat fighter

**Powerplant:** one 89-kW (110-hp.) Le Rhône (Type 17) or one 97-kW (120-hp.) Clerget rotary piston engine (Type 17bis)

**Maximum speed:** 170 km/h (105 m.p.h.) at 1980 m (6,500 ft.)

**Range:** 250 km (155 mi.)

**Service ceiling:** 5350 m (17,550 ft.)

**Weights:** empty 374 kg (822 lb.); maximum take-off 560 kg (1,232 lb.)

**Armament:** one fixed forward-firing 7.7-mm (.303 cal.) Vickers or Lewis machine-gun

**Dimensions:**
| | |
|---|---|
| span | 8.20 m (27 ft.) |
| length | 5.96 m (20 ft.) |
| height | 2.44 m (8 ft.) |
| wing area | 14.75 m² (159 sq. ft.) |

## TYPE 17C

The Imperial Russian Flying Corps used large numbers of Nieuport fighters. This Nieuport 17C was flown by No. XIX Gruppe, No. 1 Ostryad, and was subsequently captured by the Austrians.

Like all World War I fighters the Nieuport 17 had an open cockpit, which made flying at high altitude very uncomfortable.

The tails of the Nieuport 11, 17, 21 and 23 had a similar, distinct shape; the tail profile was more rounded in the Nieuport 24. The tail structure was wood, with fabric covering, and wire bracing helped to strengthen it. The large elevators and rudder helped give the Nieuport its legendary agility.

Distinct V-shaped struts were a recognition feature of the Nieuport 17. In the Nieuport 28, parallel struts were used. The 28 was not as popular as the 17 as it tended to shed its upper wing fabric in long dives and had engine problems.

One unusual feature of the Nieuport was the small width of its lower wing, only half as wide as the upper. The Nieuport 11 was even fitted with Le Prieur rockets to the wing struts, which were used for attacking balloons and airships.

Like their successors in World War II, Russian pilots in 1917 were fond of decorating their machines, and were glad to show their opponents who they were taking on.

## COMBAT DATA

### MAXIMUM SPEED

Both the Nieuport and Sopwith Pup were powered by Le Rhône engines, giving them a good turn of speed. The later Albatros D.V had even greater speed.

| | |
|---|---|
| **NIEUPORT 17** | 170 km/h (105 m.p.h.) |
| **SOPWITH PUP** | 180 km/h (112 m.p.h.) |
| **ALBATROS D.III** | 165 km/h (102 m.p.h.) |

### ARMAMENT

Most German fighters had two machine-guns by 1916, giving them a decisive advantage in firepower. Pilots often chose the mix of ammunition that was used in their guns in World War I.

**NIEUPORT 17**
1 x 7.7-mm (.303 cal.) machine-gun

**SOPWITH PUP**
1 x 7.7-mm (.303 cal.) machine-gun

**ALBATROS D.III**
2 x 7.92-mm machine-guns

### SERVICE CEILING

Pilots often mounted their offensive patrols at around 5000 m (16,500 ft.), despite the lack of heating or oxygen in their aircraft, which made flying in these open-cockpit fighters very uncomfortable. The Nieuport was particularly fast-climbing, which allowed it to gain a height advantage over its opponents.

**NIEUPORT 17**
5350 m (17,500 ft.)

**ALBATROS D.III**
5500 m (18,000 ft.)

**SOPWITH PUP**
5335 m (17,000 ft.)

## Nieuport fighter scouts

■ **NIEUPORT 27:** Derived from the Type 17bis, the Nieuport 27 had a more powerful (89-kW (120-hp.)) Le Rhône engine and a circular-section fuselage. It was also purchased by Sweden.

■ **NIEUPORT 28:** The Type 28 had new wings, which were of almost equal size compared to the Type 17's unequal wings. The US Navy launched Type 28s from battleship gun turrets.

■ **NIEUPORT-DELAGE Ni-D 29:** This single-seat fighter made its first flight in 1918, and served with French forces throughout the 1920s. It was also built by SABCA of Belgium.

■ **NIEUPORT-DELAGE Ni-D 52:** Constructed largely of metal, the Ni-D 52 first appeared in 1927 and was used by Spain in the Civil War. The aircraft was developed into the Ni-D 62.

# NIEUPORT-DELAGE

# NI-D 29

● Inter-war biplane fighter ● World speed record holder ● Air racer

▲ In spite of a tendency to spin out of control the Ni-D 29 was regarded as an excellent fighter. The Nieuport-Delage aircraft served faithfully with the French Aviation Militaire and after a single example was sent to Japan as a pattern aircraft, Nakajima built 608 for the Imperial Japanese Army.

**A**fter producing a series of outstanding fighters during World War I, the Nieuport company added the name of chief designer Gustave Delage to its model designations. The Ni-D 29, the first aircraft to carry the new designation, was too late to see combat during the war. In the years immediately after the war, however, racing versions set new world records for speed and altitude as well as winning several of the main air races.

▲ Wartime ancestry
Nieuport built a range of superb fighters during World War I. The Ni-D 29 clearly owed much to these earlier designs, but the adoption of an in-line engine considerably altered the contours of the forward fuselage.

▲ Clean racing machine
Several racing Ni-D 29s were cleaned up aerodynamically and flown without weapons. In addition, a few had shorter span wings, with only one set of interplane struts on each side.

▲ Ungainly fighter
With full military equipment and protruding exhausts, the Ni-D 29 was not a graceful aircraft.

▲ Pilot protection
A pronounced headrest protected the pilot in the event of the aircraft overturning on the ground.

Slim waist ▶
The fuselage tapered towards the rear, giving the aircraft a streamlined appearance.

## FACTS AND FIGURES

➤ The first Ni-D 29s were delivered to French Aviation Militaire squadrons serving in Germany.

➤ Although the Ni-D 29 was popular with pilots, it did have a tendency to flat-spin.

➤ Nakajima Ko-4s flew during the Japanese occupation of Manchuria.

➤ Spain flew 30 Ni-D 29s, Belgium 108, Italy 181, Japan 609 and Sweden nine; Argentina also operated a few.

➤ French aircraft fought Rif insurgents in Morocco, alongside Spanish Ni-D 29s.

➤ An Ni-D 29G floatplane took part in the 1920 Monaco seaplane meeting.

## PROFILE

# Classic French fighter

With its in-line, rather than rotary, engine, the Ni-D 29 differed from the earlier Nieuports. Its achievements in 1920, when it pushed the world speed record beyond 300 km/h (185 m.p.h.), plus its high rate of climb and good handling won Nieuport-Delage an order to supply the French air force with the new fighter. Two-thirds of the 30

French fighter squadrons were equipped with the Ni-D 29C1 by 1923, and another five were using it by 1925. The type remained in service until 1928.

Nieuport's test pilot Sadi Lecointe, flying in the 1925 Moroccan campaign, formed an experimental flight of three machines which were modified with bomb racks for use as ground attack aircraft. In

November and December these aircraft dropped 5600 kg (12,320 lb.) of light bombs during 70 sorties.

The Ni-D 29 was also widely built under licence, especially in Japan, where Nakajima built the aircraft as the Ko-4.

Left: One of the more highly modified racing variants was the Ni-D 29V, which won the 1919 Coupe Deutsche and 1920 Gordon Bennet Trophy races. The aircraft had a span of only 6 m (20 ft.) and a boosted engine of 239 kW (320 hp.).

Above: This standard fighter variant shows the two-bay wings and extensive cable bracing. The two machine-guns were covered by streamlined fairings.

### Ni-D 29

**Type:** biplane fighter

**Powerplant:** one 224-kW (300-hp.) Hispano-Suiza 8Fb liquid-cooled V-8 piston engine

**Maximum speed:** 235 km/h (146 m.p.h.)

**Climb rate:** 4000 m (13,120 ft.) in 9 min 44 sec

**Range:** 580 km (360 mi.)

**Service ceiling:** 8500 m (27,900 ft.)

**Weights:** empty equipped 760 kg (1,672 lb.); maximum take-off 1150 kg (2,530 lb.)

**Armament:** two fixed forward-firing 7.7-mm (.303 cal.) machine-guns

**Dimensions:**
| | | |
|---|---|---|
| span | 9.70 m | (31 ft. 10 in.) |
| length | 6.49 m | (21 ft. 3 in.) |
| height | 2.56 m | (8 ft. 5 in.) |
| wing area | 26.70 m² | (287 sq. ft.) |

---

Twin, fixed 7.7-mm (.303 cal.) machine-guns were mounted on the upper forward fuselage and fired through the propeller. This aircraft carries a tubular gunsight.

When first flown on 21 August 1921, the Ni-D 29 met all performance requirements except that of ceiling. In order to increase operational altitude, slightly longer wings were introduced.

### Ni-D 29

Eight companies, including Nieuport-Delage, delivered a total of 250 Ni-D 29s to the French air force. This aircraft served with 'La Fayette' squadron during the 1920s.

Apart from his headrest, the only protection for the pilot came from a small windscreen and glazed side panels.

Wartime Nieuport designs used rotary engines, whereas the Ni-D 29 was powered by a V-8 in-line engine. This allowed a slimmer forward fuselage to be used.

To provide maximum agility, the prototype had ailerons fitted to the upper and lower wings. On production aircraft the upper set was eliminated and the lower set enlarged.

During World War I US volunteers formed the 'La Fayette' squadron as part of the French air force. The Sioux Indian's head badge has been used by the squadron ever since, most recently on the Mirage 2000N.

France's national colours were usually carried on the rudder of its air force fighters. Data, including the aircraft designation and weight details, were applied over these colours.

---

### COMBAT DATA

#### MAXIMUM SPEED

Nieuport-Delage produced a fighter which was much faster than most of its rivals and which had sufficient performance to keep it in service into the late-1920s. Compared to the principal fighter of the RAF, the Snipe, the Ni-D 29 was very impressive.

| | |
|---|---|
| Ni-D 29 | 235 km/h (146 m.p.h.) |
| SNIPE Mk I | 195 km/h (121 m.p.h.) |
| WAGTAIL | 209 km/h (130 m.p.h.) |

#### POWER

With its powerful Hispano-Suiza engine, the Ni-D 29 was able to offer greater performance than contemporary fighters. As one of the most developed late-World War I fighters, the aircraft became one of the most important 1920s fighters.

| Ni-D 29 | SNIPE Mk I | WAGTAIL |
|---|---|---|
| 224 kW (300 hp.) | 172 kW (230 hp.) | 127 kW (170 hp.) |

#### ARMAMENT

Fighter armament remained at a standard requirement of two fixed, forward-firing machine-guns for several years after World War I. The Snipe was a more versatile aircraft, being able to carry light bombs in the close support role.

| Ni-D 29 | 2 x 7.7-mm (.303 cal.) machine-guns |
|---|---|
| SNIPE Mk I | 2 x 7.7-mm (.303 cal.) machine-guns / 2 x 11.3-kg (25-lb.) bombs |
| WAGTAIL | 2 x 7.7-mm (.303 cal.) machine-guns |

---

## Nieuport-Delage designs

**Ni-D 52:** This fighter development of the Ni-D 42 appeared in 1927 in response to a Spanish requirement. In addition to the 34 aircraft that were bought, 92 were built under licence.

**Ni-D 62:** Representing a refined Ni-D 42, the 62 represented the most important French fighter in the 1930s. In May 1940, 143 of the outdated fighters were still on strength.

**Ni-D 82:** Revising the upper-wing planform of the Ni-D 52, Nieuport-Delage produced the single Ni-D 82. It was later modified, as seen here, to the parasol monoplane form.

**Ni-D 122:** First flown in the early 1930s, the Ni-D 122 fighter featured a graceful, elliptical wing and streamlined wheel spats. The aircraft was lost during a demonstration flight in 1933.

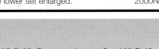

# NORTH AMERICAN

# TEXAN/SNJ/HARVARD

● Allied aircrew trainer ● Thousands built ● Licence-production

▲ Derived from the privately financed NA-16 prototype, the Texan was adopted by a USAAC which was looking for an aircraft with performance close to that of combat types.

**M**ore than 300,000 American and Allied student pilots earned their wings in this renowned aircraft. So important was it to the Allied effort during World War II that it was dubbed 'the pilot maker'. A conventional low-wing 'tail-dragger', the aircraft was a forgiving 'classroom' for trainee pilots, providing a bridge between initial flight training and operational duties. Texans served widely in wartime; some air forces continue to train pilots in them to this day.

▼ Captured French NA-57
France took delivery of 230 NA-57s pre-war. After the German invasion these AT-6 forerunners, with fixed landing gear, were used by the Luftwaffe.

▲ Pre-war US Navy SNJ
In 1936 the US Navy ordered four NJ-1s, derived from the USAAC's BT-9. The SNJs that followed, from 1938, became the Navy's standard trainer.

▼ Wartime camouflage
In wartime camouflage, this AT-6 shows off the squarer wingtips that characterised this and subsequent members of the Texan family. Wartime demand led to the establishment of a second production line in Dallas to assist the California factory.

▲ Non-strategic materials
Low-alloy steel and plywood were used in the AT-6C variant to save 565 kg (1246 lb) of aluminium alloy.

RAF's first American type ▶
Harvard Mk Is, the first of which were delivered in late 1938, were the RAF's first US-built aircraft. Total deliveries to Commonwealth air forces exceeded 5000.

## FACTS AND FIGURES

➤ More than 17,000 trainers in this series were manufactured before, during and after World War II.

➤ The prototype NA-16 that led to the AT-6 Texan made its initial flight in April 1935.

➤ One AT-6D was fitted with a Ranger V-770 inline engine, as the XAT-6E.

➤ Australia's Commonwealth Aircraft Corporation built NA-33s as Wirraway armed multi-role combat aircraft.

➤ Some air forces maintained ex-wartime Texan/Harvard fleets into the 1970s.

➤ A few US Navy SNJs were equipped with arrester hooks for deck landing training.

# Aircrew trainer extraordinaire

North American's AT-6 Texan was known by many other designations and names, perhaps the most well-known of which were Harvard (in the RAF and Commonwealth air forces) and SNJ (in the US Navy). One of the most famous of flying machines, and the most extensively used trainer of all time, the AT-6 family trained the majority of Allied pilots and other aircrew during World War II.

Developed from the original NA-16 of 1935, the design was first ordered as the BT-9 basic trainer, with fixed undercarriage, a fabric-covered fuselage and a 298-kW Wright R-975 radial engine. With the aim of producing a trainer to reproduce the characteristics of operational aircraft, various airframe changes were made and a new engine with 50 per cent more power installed. The result was the BC-1 basic combat trainer, the BC-1A variant of which was later redesignated the AT-6.

With the onset of World War II, thousands of AT-6s were built for the Allies' flying training schools, a significant number under licence in Canada. Small numbers train pilots to this day.

*Above: Although early examples were built by North American, most of Canada's Harvards were constructed by Noorduyn. The RAF received 900.*

## AT-6A Texan

**Type:** two-seat advanced pilot trainer

**Powerplant:** one 447-kW (600-hp) Pratt & Whitney R-1340-47 radial piston engine

**Maximum speed:** 330 km/h (205 mph) at 1525 m (5000 ft)

**Initial climb rate:** 7.4 minutes to 3048 m (10,000 ft)

**Range:** 1207 km (750 miles)

**Service ceiling:** 7376 m (24,200 ft)

**Weights:** empty 1769 kg (3900 lb); maximum take-off 2338 kg (5154 lb)

**Armament:** one fixed forward-firing 7.62-mm (.30-cal.) machine gun and one flexible rear-mounted 7.62-mm machine gun

**Dimensions:**
| | |
|---|---|
| span | 12.80 m (42 ft) |
| length | 8.84 m (29 ft) |
| height | 3.58 m (11 ft 9 in) |
| wing area | 23.60 m² (254 sq ft) |

## HARVARD MK I

**Equivalent to the USAAC's BC-1 of 1937, the Harvard Mk I entered RAF service in December 1938. This aircraft flew with No. 2 Flying Training School at RAF Brize Norton during the early years of World War II.**

Pratt & Whitney's reliable nine-cylinder R-1340-49 Wasp radial powered the Harvard family. A two-bladed propeller was fitted, the high-speed tips of which produced the well-known 'rasping' note familiar to pilots.

As a dual-control trainer, the Harvard was equipped to accommodate the student in the front cockpit and the instructor in the rear seat. USAAF gunnery trainers had a rear-mounted machine gun.

Harvard Mk Is, in common with the BC-1, had a steel tube rear fuselage structure with fabric covering. Most later marks had a light alloy monocoque with metal skinning, apart from the Mk IIB, which had a plywood rear fuselage.

RAF Harvards carried this semi-camouflaged colour scheme during the early war years. Later, camouflage was extended to cover all the upper surfaces. The undersides remained yellow for safety reasons.

A curved rudder was fitted to the BC-1 and Harvard Mk I. On later versions this had a straight trailing edge.

N 7033

## ACTION DATA

### POWER

Compared to contemporary trainer types, the Texan was moderately powered. The RAF's Miles Master, in Wasp radial-engined form, was more powerful than the Texan/Harvard and equipped advanced flying schools in the same way as the Harvard. The Luftwaffe equivalent was the Arado Ar 96.

| AT-6D TEXAN 447 kW (600 hp) | MASTER Mk II 649 kW (870 hp) | Ar 96B-2 347 kW (465 hp) |
|---|---|---|

### MAXIMUM SPEED

The USAAF's Texan was faster than the biplane trainers of the late 1930s, having been produced to simulate more closely the flying characteristics of combat aircraft. The Miles Master, with its larger engine, was faster, while the less powerful Ar 96 was able to maintain a top speed similar to that of the Texan.

| AT-6D TEXAN | 330 km/h (205 mph) |
|---|---|
| MASTER Mk II | 389 km/h (242 mph) |
| Ar 96B-2 | 330 km/h (205 mph) |

### RANGE

An area in which the AT-6 Texan performed well was range. Good range (around 1200 km/746 miles) meant that the aircraft was able to stay aloft on a training sortie for a longer time. The more powerful Miles Master had only half the range ability, and the Arado Ar 96 fell between the two in endurance.

AT-6D TEXAN 1207 km (750 miles)
Ar 96B-2 990 km (615 miles)
MASTER Mk II 632 km (393 miles)

## Texan evolution from NA-16 to P-64

■ **NA-16:** The privately funded NA-16 prototype had a 298-kW (400-hp) engine, open cockpits, fixed gear and a fabric-skinned fuselage.

■ **BT-9:** This 'basic trainer' was the first NA-16 variant to enter US service in 1935. Changes were few, but included enclosed cockpits.

■ **BC-1/BC-1A/YALE:** A short step from the AT-6 was the 'basic combat' BC-1 trainer, still with a 298-kW (400-hp) engine and fixed undercarriage.

■ **P-64:** In 1939, NAA developed this fighter version of the AT-6. A few were sold to Peru and Siam, but the Siamese ones were not delivered.

# NORTH AMERICAN
# B-25 MITCHELL

● Medium bomber ● Devastating low-level attacker ● Gunship

▲ After the USAAF, the Royal Air Force was the most important B-25 user, taking 910 of nearly 10,000 built. Russia was also given 870 aircraft for the war on the Eastern Front.

**R**ushing in at low level with guns blazing, this twin-engine medium bomber was the most fearsome sight of World War II. The North American B-25 Mitchell sent bombs screaming earthward from high in the sky, but it also attacked with speed and surprise down on the deck, strafing ships and troops with its lethal nose guns. The B-25 was a hard-hitter, a superb weapon, and a great aircraft.

## NORTH AMERICAN B-25 MITCHELL

▼ **Long-lived B-25**
Mitchells fought in all theatres, including Italy, where this famous B-25 racked up an incredible 103 missions in a theatre in which air and ground defences were fierce.

▲ **Low-level gunship**
When the USAAF realised that most B-25 missions were at low level, they took out the bombardier and replaced him with a battery of guns in the nose and on the fuselage sides.

◀ **Mitchell with a message**
This B-25 carries the rousing legend 'Finito Benito, next Hirohito' along its wings – a reference to the defeat of the Italian dictator and the anticipated battle for Japan.

▼ **Shipping strikes**
In the Far East the B-25s were used to devastating effect against Japanese shipping, their low-level attacks being accurate and deadly.

▲ **Parachute bomber**
Attacking airfields at low level was no easy task because standard bombs would explode beneath the aircraft. Using bombs on parachutes allowed the B-25 to escape the blast.

## FACTS AND FIGURES

➤ The Mitchell's American combat debut came on Christmas Eve 1941, when a B-25 sank a Japanese submarine.

➤ In the early years of the war, the B-25 was faster in a dive than many fighters.

➤ Mitchells often skip-bombed, bouncing bombs from low level across the water.

➤ The bombardier was not needed at low level, so many Mitchells were fitted with solid noses bristling with guns.

➤ A B-25H sank a Japanese destroyer with just seven shots from its 75-mm (2.95-in.) cannon.

➤ Mitchells were still flying as multi-engine trainers in the 1950s.

**PROFILE**

# First of the gunships

The first bomber from North American, the graceful and deadly B-25 was named after the outspoken champion of US air power, General 'Billy' Mitchell. The B-25 is best remembered for the April 1942 bombing of Tokyo led by Lieutenant Colonel James Doolittle, which was launched from the carrier *Hornet*. At the time, the Allies were being defeated in the Pacific and this first strike on Japanese soil boosted American morale.

The Mitchell bomber fought all over the world. Pilots praised its speed, brute strength and quick control response. Some Mitchells carried nose 75-mm (2.95-in.) cannons to increase their firepower during low-level raids on Japanese shipping.

Mitchells flew with the Marines in tough Pacific fighting and were called PBJs. The B-25 also flew with a dozen other nations in Russia, North Africa and throughout Europe. It was frightening to be on the

*With a hard-hitting 75-mm (2.95-in.) cannon in the lower left fuselage, the B-25H was one of the most heavily armed aircraft of World War II.*

receiving end of a B-25 attack, but to the Allies the aircraft was a great warrior and a triumph of weaponry.

*The B-25's best-known exploit was the daring raid in April 1942 when Lt Col Jimmy Doolittle led 16 Mitchells from the deck of USS* Hornet *on the first strike against the Japanese mainland.*

### B-25H Mitchell

**Type:** five-seat medium bomber

**Powerplant:** two 1268-kW (1,700-hp.) Wright R-2600-92 Cyclone 14-cylinder radial piston engines

**Maximum speed:** early versions 500 km/h (275 m.p.h.); armed and armoured aircraft (typically) 438 km/h (240 m.p.h.) at 4000 m (13,125 ft.)

**Range:** 2200 km (1,300 mi.) with bombload

**Service ceiling:** 7375 m (23,800 ft.)

**Weights:** empty 8836 kg (19,400 lb.); loaded 15,876 kg (36,000 lb.)

**Armament:** one 75-mm (2.95-in.) cannon or up to 16 x 12.7-mm (.50 cal.) machine-guns, plus eight 127-mm (5-in.) rocket projectiles and up to 1360 kg (3,000 lb.) of bombs

**Dimensions:**
| | | |
|---|---|---|
| span | 20.60 m | (67 ft. 7 in.) |
| length | 16.13 m | (51 ft.) |
| height | 4.98 m | (15 ft. 9 in.) |
| wing area | 56.67 m² | (610 sq. ft.) |

## B-25J 'BETTY'S DREAM'

'Betty's Dream' flew in the south-west Pacific with the famed 499th Bomb Squadron, otherwise known as the 'Bats Outa Hell'. The whole front-end was adorned with a massive bat figure with teeth and wings.

The dorsal turret was used as protection against fighters, but could be locked forwards to add extra weight to the nose guns.

All but the first few Mitchells had this characteristic 'inverted gull' wing. This modification made the B-25 much more manoeuvrable than when it had a standard straight wing.

The B-25J had a fearsome armament of 12 heavy machine-guns in the nose and on the sides of the fuselage.

Solid-nosed Mitchells generally flew with a crew of five. Pilot, co-pilot and gunner occupied the flight deck, while two more gunners manned the waist and tail guns.

Quite apart from the heavy gun armament, the B-25 could also lift 1360 kg (3,000 lb.) of bombs in its two vertical bomb-bays.

The crew boarded the aircraft through hatches in the lower fuselage.

By far the most colourful of all the wartime Mitchells were those assigned to the 345th Bomb Group (Medium), which flew this solid-nosed B-25J in the Far East. The group was known as the 'Air Apaches', and its aircraft carried a large Indian's head on their tails.

### M43 227-kg (500-lb.) General-Purpose Bomb

American GP bombs were generally of thin case construction, giving a high-explosive filling-to-weight ratio of around 51 per cent. There were two fuses, in the nose and tail.

The B-25 carried a maximum bombload of 1360 kg (3,000 lb.) internally, increased by underwing racks in some models to 2360 kg (5,000 lb.). A 907-kg (2,000-lb.) weapon could be carried, but four 227-kg (500-lb.) or two 454-kg (1,000-lb.) bombs were more usual.

**3 GETTING CLEAR:** At the last minute the aircraft lifted up and over the ship, an instant before the bomb hit.

## Skip-bombing in the Pacific

Leading on from trials with a B-17, the USAAF honed the concept of skip-bombing to a fine art with the B-25.

**2 FLAK SUPPRESSION:** After bomb release the Mitchell continued its run towards the ship, with up to 14 guns blazing to keep Japanese heads down.

**1 BOMB RUN:** Releasing the bomb at low level and high speed caused it to bounce or 'skip' across the water, greatly increasing its range and accuracy against ship targets.

# NORTH AMERICAN

# P-51 EARLY VERSIONS

● Initially Allison-engined ● RAF service ● High speed at low level

▲ P-51A, B and C
aircraft served in large numbers until the end of World War II. All performed exceptionally well, flying close-support, reconnaissance and escort missions.

Though designed to a World War II RAF requirement, the Mustang was destined to become the finest of the USAAF's fighters and, arguably, the finest such machine of the war. With an Allison V-1710 liquid-cooled engine, the Mustang's performance at altitude was limited, the P-51 thus being initially employed as a ground-attack and reconnaissance aircraft (as the A-36 in the former role). The British Merlin engine was to transform the type.

▼ Asian combat service
These P-51As were operated by the 1st Air Commando Group in Burma during 1944.

▲ US Army Air Force service
Although it received its Mustangs some time after the RAF, the USAAF was to operate the type in huge numbers. This trio of P-51As carries tanks to disperse smoke screens and tear gas, the latter only for training.

▲ First of the thoroughbreds
AG345 was the first production Mustang Mk I for the RAF and made its first flight on 23 April 1941. The aircraft features the early, short carburettor air intake above the nose.

▲ British Malcolm hood
This rocket-armed Mustang Mk III demonstrates the blown 'Malcolm' hood, for improved visibility.

'Ski Fifty-One' ▶
Two P-51As were tested with retractable skis in Alaska. Although few problems were found, no further use was made of this special undercarriage.

## FACTS AND FIGURES

➤ It reportedly took the personal intervention of General 'Hap' Arnold for the USAAF to accept the P-51.

➤ A-36A ground-attack aircraft sported wing-mounted dive brakes.

➤ Camera-equipped USAAF Mustangs were designated F-6s.

➤ The USAAF's first P-51s differed from RAF Mustangs in having wing-mounted cannon armament.

➤ The first USAAF Mustangs in action were A-36As in the invasion of Sicily and Italy.

➤ Mustangs were built by North American at plants in California and Texas.

**PROFILE**

# Flying thoroughbred for the RAF

After the end of World War II, Reichsmarschall Hermann Goering, supreme commander of the mighty Luftwaffe, declared, 'When I saw Mustangs over Berlin, I knew the war was lost.' The aircraft he was describing was conceived with haste in 1940 and proved to be arguably the finest piston-engined fighter of World War II.

Starting life with an Allison engine, the Mustang was designed in early 1940 in response to an RAF requirement for a new fighter which would benefit from experience gained in Europe the previous year.

Flown in 1941, the Mustang Mk I entered RAF service in 1942 in the armed tactical reconnaissance role, because of the Allison engine's poor performance at altitude. After some convincing the USAAF ordered Mustangs in 1942, initially as the A-36 ground-attack aircraft (sometimes referred to as the Apache).

In an attempt to address the altitude performance problem, the RAF proposed the installation of the Rolls-Royce

*Carrying serial number 43-6013, this aircraft was one of the first P-51As of an order for 310. The RAF received 50 of these aircraft, designated Mustang Mk II, while a further 35 were converted to F-6B standard for photo-reconnaissance duties.*

Merlin engine, the result being the P-51B and C fighters. Delivery of the first B models in 1943 immediately gave the USAAF the ability to escort its bombers over Germany.

No fewer than eight machine guns armed the Mustang Mk I. A pair of 12.7-mm (.50-cal.) M2 Brownings was mounted in the nose. Synchronised to fire through the propeller blades, they were canted over so that they could be fed from magazines fitting neatly into the bottom of the nose.

A single F24 oblique camera was fitted behind the pilot's seat, facing to port. No. 26 Squadron also flew photo-recce missions, dubbed 'Poplars', over the French coast.

A heavily framed canopy gave the pilot poor visibility, even when compared with other contemporary fighters. Later versions had bulged clear-vision hoods and the P-51D had a bubble canopy.

### MUSTANG MK I

AM101 served with No. 26 Squadron, based at Gatwick in East Sussex, from early 1942. The unit's main tasks were flying 'Rhubarbs' (fighter sweeps over German-occupied northern France) and reconnaissance sorties.

The Mustang Mk I was powered by a single Allison V-1710-39 in-line liquid-cooled piston engine, rated at 857.6 kW (1150 hp). This gave the aircraft excellent performance at low altitude, but at higher level the early Mustangs were disappointing.

The Mustang was fitted with a laminar flow wing to reduce drag and improve performance. This was a major innovation at the time.

## From NA-73X prototype to Mustang

**NA-73X:** Registered NX19998, this was the first member of the Mustang family. The prototype flew on 26 October 1940. The RAF had already ordered 320 examples the previous May.

**MUSTANG Mk I:** Depicted in the markings of No. 613 Squadron, RAF, Mustang Mk I AG522 was delivered in mid-1942 and employed on 'Poplar' reconnaissance missions over France.

**F-6B:** Malcolm hood-equipped 43-6163 began life as a P-51A but was converted to F-6B standard for service with the Ninth Air Force's 107th Tactical Reconnaissance Squadron.

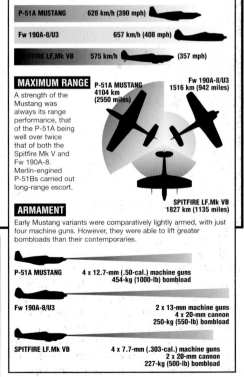

### P-51B Mustang

**Type:** single-seat long-range escort fighter

**Powerplant:** one 1029-kW (1380-hp) Packard (Rolls-Royce) V-1650 Merlin piston engine

**Maximum speed:** 708 km/h (440 mph) at 9144 m (30,000 ft)

**Cruising speed:** 583 km/h (362 mph)

**Initial climb rate:** 12.5 minutes to 9144 m (30,000 ft)

**Range:** 3347 km (2080 miles)

**Service ceiling:** 12,741 m (41,800 ft)

**Weights:** empty 3168 kg (6984 lb); gross 5352 kg (11,799 lb)

**Armament:** four 12.7-mm (.50-cal.) machine guns plus up to 907 kg (2000 lb) of bombs

**Dimensions:**
| | | |
|---|---|---|
| span | 11.28 m (37 ft) |
| length | 9.83 m (32 ft 3 in) |
| height | 3.70 m (12 ft 2 in) |
| wing area | 21.90 m² (236 sq ft) |

### COMBAT DATA

**MAXIMUM SPEED**

Initially the Allison-engined P-51 was employed in the ground-attack role. It compared favourably with other ground-attack types of the period, like the marginally faster Focke-Wulf Fw 190A-8 and Supermarine Spitfire Mk V.

| | |
|---|---|
| P-51A MUSTANG | 628 km/h (390 mph) |
| Fw 190A-8/U3 | 657 km/h (408 mph) |
| SPITFIRE LF.Mk VB | 575 km/h (357 mph) |

**MAXIMUM RANGE**

A strength of the Mustang was always its range performance, that of the P-51A being well over twice that of both the Spitfire Mk V and Fw 190A-8. Merlin-engined P-51Bs carried out long-range escort.

P-51A MUSTANG 4104 km (2550 miles)
Fw 190A-8/U3 1516 km (942 miles)
SPITFIRE LF.Mk VB 1827 km (1135 miles)

**ARMAMENT**

Early Mustang variants were comparatively lightly armed, with just four machine guns. However, they were able to lift greater bombloads than their contemporaries.

| | |
|---|---|
| P-51A MUSTANG | 4 x 12.7-mm (.50-cal.) machine guns / 454-kg (1000-lb) bombload |
| Fw 190A-8/U3 | 2 x 13-mm machine guns / 4 x 20-mm cannon / 250-kg (550-lb) bombload |
| SPITFIRE LF.Mk VB | 4 x 7.7-mm (.303-cal.) machine guns / 2 x 20-mm cannon / 227-kg (500-lb) bombload |

# NORTH AMERICAN
# P-51D MUSTANG

● Long-range escort fighter ● Most Allied kills ● 281 Mustang aces

▲ One of the great Mustang heroes, Major Don Gentile, with his favourite machine 'Shangri-La' during 1943. He made 15 kills in Mustangs – half of them in one month!

A s the bombers of the Eighth Air Force fought their way deep into Hitler's German heartland, it was the Mustang that cleared the skies of Luftwaffe fighters. No other combat airplane of the war could fly as high, go as far and fight as hard as the mighty Mustang. In the skilled hands of young USAAF pilots, it took on all comers and accounted for more kills than any other Allied aircraft.

# NORTH AMERICAN P-51D MUSTANG

◄ All the way!
With underwing tanks, Mustangs had enough range to be able to escort their charges more than 1200 km (746 m.p.h.) to the target and were agile enough to beat all comers when they got there.

▼ High flyer
The Mustang's phenomenal range and performance made it ideal for escorting high-flying B-29s across the vast Pacific.

◄ Mud movers
The Mustang's hard-hitting and accurate guns made it an excellent ground-attack aircraft, which could also deliver air-to-ground rockets or bombs.

Powerpack ►
The early Mustang was transformed into a superb high-level fighter by the British-designed, Packard-built Rolls-Royce Merlin engine, which could deliver 1186 kW (1,590 hp.).

▼ Flying veterans
The Mustang's impeccable handling characteristics, bubble canopy and performance make it a popular rich man's toy; many of them are still flying. This example even carries a passenger!

## FACTS AND FIGURES

➤ Ordered by the British, the prototype Mustang was proposed, designed, built and flown in an incredible 117 days.

➤ That initial aircraft was the first of 15,586 examples of the P-51 produced.

➤ The Mustang was flown by 11 Allied air forces in addition to the USAAF.

➤ A total of 281 Allied Mustang pilots were to qualify as 'Aces', with five or more kills.

➤ The P-51H was, at 760 km/h (472 m.p.h.), one of the fastest piston-engined fighters.

➤ In October 1944, Mustang pilot Lieutenant Urban L. Drew managed the astonishing feat of shooting down two Me 262 jets.

**PROFILE**

# Top Gun to the bomber force

Faced with imminent invasion in 1939 and desperately short of fighters, the Royal Air Force asked North American Aviation to produce urgently the existing but obsolete P-40 Warhawk. But instead the company designed, built and flew a new airplane in just 117 days – the Mustang.

Using an existing Allison engine and the latest laminar-flow wing, the new fighter immediately went into service with the RAF. In December 1941 America joined the war, and it too needed good fighters fast. So the USAAF took the basic RAF Mustang, re-armed it with four machine-guns, and added an uprated engine. It was a good performer, but couldn't operate well alongside the high-flying long-range bomber.

By 1944 the aircraft used the Rolls-Royce Merlin engine, had a new bubble cockpit and

*Mustangs were flown by more aces than any other Allied fighter. Their prey even included the Me 262 jet.*

increased firepower to six 12.7-mm (.50 cal.) machine-guns. It was now the best fighter in the war and fought superbly in all theatres, as fighter, fighter-bomber and reconnaissance platform. It was loved by its aircrews, and no fewer than 281 Mustang pilots became aces by scoring five kills apiece.

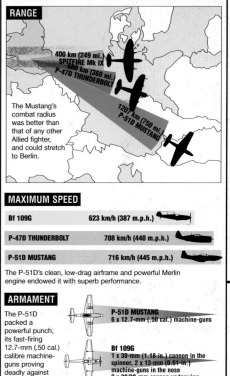

The low-drag laminar-flow wing was largely responsible for the Mustang's combination of agility and long-range capability, and accommodated six 12.7-mm (.50 cal.) machine-guns.

## P-51K MUSTANG 'NOOKY BOOKY IV'

This shortened propeller version of the P-51D was flown by Major Leonard 'Kit' Carson (left) of the 362nd Fighter Squadron, based at Leiston, Suffolk, during 1944. Carson was one of the top-scoring Mustang aces, with 18½ air-to-air victories.

The bubble canopy and cut-down rear fuselage of the P-51D gave the pilot an unsurpassed all-round view.

MAJ. KIT CARSON

Nooky Booky IV

G4 ★ C

411622

The P-51 was transformed by the adoption of the Merlin engine. The original Allison engine delivered plenty of power at low altitude, but was disappointing at higher altitude.

Even without optional underwing fuel tanks, the Mustang had a good radius of action: with tanks fitted it could escort bombers all the way to Berlin. These tanks could be jettisoned if the Mustang had to engage in manoeuvring combat.

Despite having an inline, liquid-cooled engine and a prominent and vulnerable ventral (underfuselage) radiator, the P-51D was remarkably tolerant of battle damage.

Initially painted with olive drab camouflaged top surfaces, paint was soon stripped off to save weight, and the bare skin was highly polished to reduce drag.

### P-51D Mustang

**Type:** single-seat long-range escort fighter, fighter-bomber

**Powerplant:** one 1186-kW (1,590-hp.) Packard V-1650-7 (US-built Rolls-Royce Merlin 61) inverted-vee 12-cylinder inline water-cooled piston engine

**Maximum speed:** 716 km/h (445 m.p.h.) at 7620 m (25,000 ft.)

**Combat radius:** 525 km (326 mi.) on internal fuel; 1210 km (752 mi.) with two 491-litre (108-gal.) tanks

**Service ceiling:** 12,770 m (41,900 ft.)

**Weights:** empty 3232 kg (7,125 lb.); loaded 5265 kg (11,607 lb.)

**Armament:** six 12.7-mm (.50 cal.) Browning machine-guns in wings; two 227-kg (500-lb.) bombs or eight 75-mm rockets in place of long-range drop-tanks

**Dimensions:**

| | |
|---|---|
| span | 11.29 m (37 ft.) |
| length | 9.83 m (32 ft. 3 in.) |
| height | 3.71 m (12 ft. 2 in.) |
| wing area | 21.83 m² (235 sq. ft.) |

### COMBAT DATA

**RANGE**

400 km (249 mi.) SPITFIRE Mk IX
580 km (360 mi.) P-47D THUNDERBOLT
1207 km (750 mi.) P-51D MUSTANG

The Mustang's combat radius was better than that of any other Allied fighter, and could stretch to Berlin.

**MAXIMUM SPEED**

| | |
|---|---|
| Bf 109G | 623 km/h (387 m.p.h.) |
| P-47D THUNDERBOLT | 708 km/h (440 m.p.h.) |
| P-51D MUSTANG | 716 km/h (445 m.p.h.) |

The P-51D's clean, low-drag airframe and powerful Merlin engine endowed it with superb performance.

**ARMAMENT**

The P-51D packed a powerful punch, its fast-firing 12.7-mm (.50 cal.) calibre machine-guns proving deadly against enemy fighter targets, although they lacked the stopping power of a 20- or 30-mm cannon.

P-51D MUSTANG
6 x 12.7-mm (.50 cal.) machine-guns

Bf 109G
1 x 30-mm (1.18-in.) cannon in the spinner, 2 x 13-mm (0.51-in.) machine-guns in the nose
2 x 20/30-mm cannon underwing

SPITFIRE Mk IX
4 x 7.7-mm (.50 cal.) machine-guns
2 x 20-mm (0.79-in.) Hispano cannon

## Mustang: the all-the-way escort fighter

■ **THE BOMBERS:** Eighth Air Force bombers left their British bases an hour ahead of the Mustangs, escorted in the first part of the mission by shorter-ranged P-38s and P-47s.

■ **HAND OVER:** The faster Mustangs would catch the formation over the Dutch/German border, where they would relieve the P-47 and the Thunderbolts high above the B-17s.

■ **ESCORT:** Some fighters flew close escort. Their nearness boosted the morale of the bomber crews, who had been so severely mauled over Germany the year before.

■ **DOGFIGHTER:** The Mustang had more than long range. It was fast and it was a ferocious dogfighter, as the pilot of this Messerschmitt Bf 109G shot down by a P-51 discovered to his cost.

■ **CONTROL OF THE SKIES:** It was the appearance of swarms of these graceful fighters in the skies over Germany that was to signal the death knell of the Luftwaffe.

# NORTHROP

# P-61 BLACK WIDOW

● Enormous but agile ● Powerful ● Complex fighter

▲ Long in development, the
P-61 only saw service in the last year of
the war. It was the biggest, heaviest and
most powerful night-fighter of the war, but
was also agile and fast.

**N**orthrop's P-61 Black Widow was
a creature of the night. This large,
powerful, twin-engined craft was
the first American combat plane designed
from the beginning as a night-fighter and
optimised for air-to-air combat during
the nocturnal hours. Beneath its slick
coat of black paint, the P-61 proved
itself a deadly foe in the dark, invisibly
approaching Japanese aircraft and
blasting them from the sky.

◀ Heavily armed
The P-61's dorsal barbette was
fitted with four 12.7-mm (.50 cal.)
Colt-Browning M-2 machine-guns.
In addition, it had four 20-mm
(0.79-in.) cannon in the fuselage.

▲ Pacific theatre
Ten squadrons of Black Widows
operated in the Central Pacific
theatre as the standard USAAF
night-fighter from June 1944.

Slow development ▶
The original XP-61
prototype was flown on 26
May 1942 with most of its
features mocked-up while
awaiting the real parts.

▲ Good night-fighter
Once the strict initial flight
limitations were lifted, P-61s
became highly regarded.

Long range ▶
This P-61B carries four
drop-tanks, which increased
fuel capacity by 4692 litres
(1,110 gal.) and provided
for an impressive range.

## FACTS AND FIGURES

➤ On 26 May 1942 famous test pilot Vance
Breese flew the P-61 on its first flight.

➤ On 6 July 1944, the P-61 racked up its
first air-to-air victory, a Japanese
Mitsubishi G4M 'Betty' bomber.

➤ Production of the Black Widow totalled
706 aircraft of all variants.

➤ P-61 Black Widows shot down nine
German V-1 'buzz' bombs.

➤ Design and development of the P-61's
SCR-720 search radar involved
172,000 man-hours of work.

➤ Three P-61 pilots became aces, with two
of them including kills flying other types.

# Killer of the night

The P-61 Black Widow was the largest, heaviest and most powerful fighter of World War II. It resulted from efforts by designer Jack Northrop to create a night-fighter able to use air-to-air radar to destroy enemy warplanes after dark.

The Black Widow was deceptively agile, and challenged and defeated smaller fighters. More than a twin-engine, twin-boomed aircraft of great size and strength, the Black Widow was truly a fighter, and it produced an impressive number of air-to-air kills.

The Black Widow looked like a strange, menacing machine. In fact, it was easy to fly and responsive to the touch. The unusual cockpit layout placed the radarman/forward gunner above and behind the pilot (the third crewman was behind both), and pilots disliked having the propellers in line with their cockpit position. But once P-61s reached night-fighter squadrons in Europe and the Pacific in 1944, they achieved an impressive combat record.

This XF-15A conversion of a P-61C was the second Black Widow adapted for the photographic reconnaissance role, fitted with six cameras in the lengthened nose. It had a long, clear-view canopy over the tandem cockpits. Only 36 F-15As were built, although 175 were ordered.

Twin tailbooms extended aft from the engine nacelles. The fins were built integral with the tailbooms and the tailplane was located between the fins. The crew of three was housed in the large central pod.

The all-metal, shoulder-mounted wing had a broad chord and straight leading edge. It had a span of 20.11 m (66 ft.) and a wing area of 61.53 m² (662 sq. ft.), giving a low wing loading and agile performance.

## P-61B BLACK WIDOW

The Northrop P-61 Black Widow was the first USAAF night-fighter designed for this role. This aircraft was called 'Time's a'Wastin' and was one of the most famous Black Widows of the Pacific theatre.

Additional firepower was provided by a General Electric dorsal barbette with four 12.7-mm (.50 cal.) Colt-Browning machine-guns, each with 560 rounds.

The nose-mounted SCR-720 radar scanner was covered by a painted dielectric nose cone.

Underwing drop-tanks extended the P-61's range to 2172 km (1.350 mi.).

P-61s were powered by two Pratt & Whitney R-2800-65 Double Wasp radial engines, powering Curtiss Electric propellers.

The unique twin-boom configuration housed a crew of three in a large pod mounted onto a sturdy centre section. The fuselage nacelle also housed the radar and most of the armament.

Built as an early P-61B, 'Time's a'Wastin' was one of only two of the first 200 P-61Bs that retained the dorsal barbette. This was not revived until buffeting problems from the guns were solved.

### P-61B Black Widow

**Type:** three-seat night-fighter

**Powerplant:** two 1491-kW (2,000-hp.) Pratt & Whitney R-2800-65 Double Wasp 18-cylinder radial engines

**Maximum speed:** 589 km/h (365 m.p.h.) at 6096 m (20,000 ft.)

**Range:** 1513 km (940 mi.) (2172 km/1,350 mi. with drop tanks)

**Service ceiling:** 12,445 m (40,800 ft.)

**Weights:** empty 9654 kg (21,239 lb.); loaded 13,471 kg (29,636 lb.); maximum overload 16,420 kg (36,124 lb.)

**Armament:** four 20-mm (0.79-in.) M-2 cannon each with 200 rounds; dorsal barbette with four 12.7-mm (.50 cal.) machine-guns each with 560 rounds; pylons for 454 kg (1,000 lb.) of bombs, rockets or other weapons

**Dimensions:**
span 20.11 m (66 ft.)
length 15.11 m (50 ft.)
height 4.47 m (15 ft.)
wing area 61.53 m² (662 sq. ft.)

## COMBAT DATA

### MAXIMUM SPEED
The bigger and much heavier Black Widow was only slightly slower than the nimble Rolls-Royce Merlin-engined Mosquito night-fighter variant. The Ki-45 was appreciably slower.

P-61B BLACK WIDOW **589 km/h (365 m.p.h.)**
MOSQUITO NF.Mk II **595 km/h (370 m.p.h.)**
Ki-45 'NICK' **547 km/h (340 m.p.h.)**

### ARMAMENT
After development problems had been cured, the P-61B was equipped with four cannon and four powerful machine-guns, giving it superb firepower. The Ki-45 had a 37-mm (1.47-in.) fixed forward-firing cannon which was a very powerful weapon, but had a slow rate of fire.

P-61B BLACK WIDOW 4 x 20-mm (0.79-in.) cannon 4 x 12.7-mm (.50 cal.) MGs
MOSQUITO NF.Mk II 4 x 20-mm (0.79-in.) cannon 4 x 7.7-mm (.50 cal.) MGs
Ki-45 'NICK' 2 x 20-mm (0.79-in.) cannon, 1 x 37-mm (1.47-in.) cannon 1 x 7.92-mm (0.31-in.) MGs

### RANGE
The maximum range achieved by the Mosquito when fitted with two underwing drop-tanks was 2993 km (1,856 mi.), some 25 per cent greater than the P-61B with its four additional tanks. The ranges were similar on internal tanks only. The Ki-45 had the shortest range of the three night-fighters.

Ki-45 'NICK' 2000 km (1,240 mi.)
P-61B BLACK WIDOW 2172 km (1,350 mi.)
MOSQUITO NF.Mk II 2993 km (1,856 mi.)

## Twin-engined night-fighters

**DE HAVILLAND MOSQUITO NF.Mk II:** The Mosquito night-fighter was developed throughout the war, the first NF.Mk IIs entering service in March 1942. Later versions had the same SCR-720 radar as the P-61, but were less heavily armed.

**JUNKERS Ju 88G-7B:** The Luftwaffe's definitive night-fighter, the Ju 88G entered service in the summer of 1944, becoming Germany's night fighter by the end of the war. It was used effectively for home defence in the final months.

**KAWASAKI Ki-45 'NICK':** The Japanese contemporary of the P-61, the Ki-45 Model C had good speed and performance but failed to receive its centimetric nose radar. It was successful against B-29s for home defence during the last year of the war.

# PETLYAKOV

# PE-2

● Dive-bomber ● Tactical reconnaissance ● Heavy fighter

▲ In common with the majority of the best twin-engined multi-role aircraft of the 1940s, the Pe-2 was designed as a long-range fighter like the Bf 110 but spent most of the war in tactical air support.

**S**econd in importance only to the Tupolev Tu-2 for its wartime role, the Petlyakov Pe-2 was a superb Russian light bomber. It was actually a close Soviet counterpart to Britain's de Havilland Mosquito, although the Mosquito was constructed of wood and the Pe-2 of metal. Designed as a high-altitude fighter, the Pe-2 entered service as a tactical support dive-bomber, proving a huge success in a role it was not intended for.

## PETLYAKOV PE-2

### Defensive formation ▶
*Fighter escort was a rare luxury for Soviet fighter-bombers, with Pe-2 pilots relying on mutual protection. The ventral gun can be seen on the nearest Pe-2.*

### ▼ Dive-bomber
*For its new found dive-bombing role the Pe-2 was fitted with special automatic divebrakes.*

### ▲ Reconnaissance patrol
*A special Pe-2R variant was built for long-range reconnaissance. It had no divebrakes or bombs, but carried extra fuel and three BS machine-guns.*

### ▼ Polish squadron
*In 1945 units of the new Polish army began receiving Pe-2s, which assisted in the liberation of the country. This is a 'UT' trainer version, with a second cockpit positioned behind the standing pilot.*

### ▲ Equipment testbed
*The versatility of the Pe-2 meant that it was used for trials of a large amount of new equipment being tested, such as ejection seats. The RD-1 rocket motor and special heavy cannon were also tested.*

### FACTS AND FIGURES

➤ In the late-1950s, many years after it was in service, the Pe-2 was given the NATO codename 'Buck'.

➤ The prototype Pe-2 series first appeared in the 1940 May Day flypast.

➤ The Pe-2Sh was a ground-attack version with oblique-firing gun batteries.

➤ On 12 January 1942 a test Pe-2 caught fire and all on board, including bureau chief Vladimir M. Petlyakov, were killed.

➤ Prototype Pe-2 versions were built for long-range bombing and as fighters.

➤ Post-war experimental versions used rocket engines and German pulse-jets.

## PROFILE

# Fighter turned dive-bomber

Soviet designer Vladimir M. Petlyakov is really known for only one aeroplane, but his Pe-2 was such a success that it assures immortality. First conceived as a high-altitude fighter, the Pe-2 was ordered into production as a light bomber in 1940.

The Pe-2 became the backbone of the Soviet light bomber force after Germany invaded Russia in 1941. Flying with wheels, or skis in the severe Russian winter, Pe-2 pilots

used the speed and flexibility of this twin-engine aircraft to fly bombing missions and carry out reconnaissance duties.

Usually the Pe-2 was fast enough to evade fighters if challenged, but when lightly loaded it was manoeuvrable enough to fight any Bf 109 or Fw 190 that caught up. In fact, because the Pe-2 was so nimble, its two gunners had the ride of their lives in the midst of battle.

Although the demand for attack aircraft gave the Pe-2

a new role, some fighter versions were still completed, such as the Pe-2VI high-altitude fighter. The majority of the 11,400 aircraft built were used in support of the Red Army.

Above: Although designed to fight at high altitude, the Pe-2 usually operated below 3000 metres, and often very much lower than that.

Below: Bombs away – a formation release their weapons together at medium altitude. The Red air force seldom had much success with these tactics, preferring low-level strikes.

### Pe-2

**Type:** three-seat bomber

**Powerplant:** two 939-kW (1,260-hp.) Klimov VK-105PF 12-cylinder piston engines

**Maximum speed:** 449 km/h (278 m.p.h.)

**Range:** 1315 km (815 mi.)

**Service ceiling:** 8800 m (28,900 ft.)

**Weights:** empty 6200 kg (13,640 lb.); maximum 8520 kg (18,744 lb.)

**Armament:** four 100-kg (220-lb.) bombs in bay plus two in rear of engine; four 250-kg (550-lb.) bombs under centre section; two forward-firing 7.62-mm (.30 cal.) ShKAS machine-guns; MV-3 dorsal turret with single 12.7-mm (.50 cal.) UBT; one ShKAS in ventral position plus one at rear beam

**Dimensions:** span 17.11 m (56 ft. 2 in.)
length 12.78 m (41 ft. 11 in.)
height 3.42 m (11 ft. 3 in.)
wing area 40.50 m² (436 sq. ft.)

## PE-2

**One of the finest twin-engined aircraft of the war, over 11,400 Pe-2s were built and served as light bombers and reconnaissance aircraft.**

The radio operator, seated in the cockpit back-to-back with the pilot, could get into the prone bomb-aiming position in the nose by crawling under the pilot's seat.

The wide track undercarriage gave good stability for operating from rough Russian airstrips. However, the aircraft had a notorious reputation for bouncing heavily on landing.

Defence was provided by a rear gunner, who fired a hand-held gun in the cockpit as well as the ventral weapon. The gunner would also call out the movements of enemy fighters to the other crewmembers.

The twin-fin tail allowed the gunner a good field of fire, as well as allowing the pilot some measure of control authority if one fin was shot off.

Eleven fuel tanks were installed in the wings and fuselage, feeding small header tanks above each engine. Inert exhaust gases were fed to the tanks as a fire-suppressant measure.

The Pe-2 was powered by two VK-105 12-cylinder Vee liquid-cooled engines with electrically-driven two-speed superchargers.

The cockpit was well laid-out, offering an excellent view for the crew. High-altitude variants had special pressurised cabins.

Offensive armament was carried in an internal bomb-bay and on external racks inboard of the engine nacelles. Normal load was four FAB-100 bombs in the bomb-bay and one in each nacelle, with four FAB-250s under the wings.

The ventral rear gun was sighted by a periscope and controlled remotely. It was of more use for strafing overflown targets than fighting off a determined fighter attack.

The tail section was constructed of metal alloy with fabric-covered tabbed control surfaces.

### COMBAT DATA

#### MAXIMUM SPEED
Although slower than a Mosquito or Bf 110, the Pe-2 was still capable of shaking off a fighter attack, and was faster than the RAF's Blenheims and the Luftwaffe's Ju 88 bombers.

| | |
|---|---|
| Pe-2 | 449 km/h (278 m.p.h.) |
| Bf 110C | 560 km/h (347 m.p.h.) |
| MOSQUITO B.Mk XVI | 668 km/h (471 m.p.h.) |

#### SERVICE CEILING
Although designed as a high-altitude fighter, the Pe-2 had an inferior ceiling to the Mosquito and Bf 110. This mattered little, as most Pe-2s carried out attacks from very low level.

MOSQUITO B.Mk XVI 12,192 m (37,500 ft.)
Bf 110C 10,000 m (35,000 ft.)
Pe-2 8800 m (28,900 ft.)

#### BOMBLOAD
The Pe-2 had a hefty bombload, but generally carried a large number of small bombs. The Mosquito had a smaller bombload which it generally used for precision attacks.

| Pe-2 | MOSQUITO B.Mk XVI | Bf 110C |
|---|---|---|
| 3000 kg (6,600 lb.) of bombs | 1814 kg (3,000 lb.) of bombs | 1000 kg (2,200 lb.) of bombs |

## Twin-engined fighter-bombers

■ **DE HAVILLAND MOSQUITO:** Capable of outrunning most fighters of its day, the all-wooden Mosquito was one of the finest aircraft of the war. It was used in the fighter-bomber, reconnaissance, night-fighter and pathfinder roles.

■ **LOCKHEED P-38 LIGHTNING:** Originally a high-altitude long-range fighter like the Pe-2, the P-38 was eventually found to be better suited to low-level attack and reconnaissance missions but also flew the early escort missions over Germany.

■ **MESSERSCHMITT Bf 110:** Designed specifically as a heavy fighter, the Bf 110 was also used as a light bomber, a night-fighter equipped with Schräge Musik cannon and radar, and for daylight air defence duties armed with air-to-air rockets.

# PFALZ

# D.III – D.XII

● Biplane fighter family ● Western Front service ● Diverse designs

S tarting out by building the French Morane L and H monoplanes under licence, Pfalz moved on to production of the D.I and D.II biplanes, which were licence-built versions of Roland designs. Their first original biplane design was the D.III of 1917. Within a year, however, Pfalz had progressed to the D.XII, a fighter built only in limited numbers, but one which was able to hold its own against the British Camel and SE5a.

▲ Among a variety of biplane designs from Pfalz Flugzeug-Werke which did not enter service was the the D.VI. Those designs that did reach the squadrons were highly successful.

## PFALZ D.III – D.XII

**▲ Successful D.XII**
Pfalz entered the D.XII in fighter trials in June 1918. The aircraft equipped 10 units on the Western Front.

**▲ Improvements to the D.III**
The D.IIIa of 1918 differed from the D.III in having an increased tailplane area and a more efficient lower wing with rounded tips.

**▲ Captured D.III**
Seen in winter snow 'somewhere in France', this 1917-built D.III has fallen into Allied hands.

**▲ D.VIII with rotary engine**
The D.VIII fighter was built only in small numbers; a few had reached the Front for evaluation by August 1918.

**Not for service ▶**
With either a Oberursel U.III or Siemens-Halske Sh III of 119 kW, the D.VII suffered from a poor rate of climb, as did the smaller single-seat D.VI which preceded it.

### FACTS AND FIGURES

➤ Some 600 D.III and D.IIIa fighters were delivered; by August 1918, 350 were in front-line service.

➤ Allied evaluation of a D.III noted that it handled better than the Albatros D.V.

➤ German aces Ernst Udet and Hans Weiss are thought to have favoured the D.XII.

➤ Such was the reputation of the Fokker D.VII, that the Pfalz D.XII was not welcomed by pilots.

➤ Pfalz biplane fighters were armed with twin Spandau forward-firing guns.

➤ The robust D.XII was unpopular with ground crews as it had complex rigging.

# PROFILE

# Unsung Western Front fighters

Less manoeuvrable than the Albatros and Fokker fighters of 1917, the Pfalz D.III was still a useful combat aircraft and around 600 were produced in the original and improved D.IIIa variants. It proved particularly suitable for diving attacks on Allied balloons and airships.

From a series of nearly a dozen subsequent designs, four prototypes were tested in the first round of fighter trials early in 1918. One of them, the rotary-engined D.VIII, was built in small numbers, but Pfalz was already working on the D.XII.

In May and June, five versions of the D.XII were evaluated in a second series of trials. The BMW.IIIa-engined version had the best rate of climb, but this powerplant was reserved for the Fokker D.VII, so the version ordered used Mercedes engines.

The D.XII entered service alongside the Fokker D.VII, an aircraft with which it was always compared. The Pfalz proved faster in a dive, although it was slower in a turn, and prone to stalling without warning. Nevertheless, it was an important aircraft which operated at a crucial stage of the war.

*Above: The D.XII was a very different aircraft from the D.III, showing many design influences from the Fokker D.VII.*

*Left: Powered by a de Havilland Gipsy Major engine, this Pfalz D.III was one of two replicas built in the 1960s for the film* Blue Max.

The well-respected and widely used Mercedes D.111 six-cylinder, water-cooled, in-line engine powered the Pfalz D.III, rated at 119 kW (160 hp.), and driving a two-bladed propeller. The later D.IIIa used a more powerful 134-kW (180-hp.) Mercedes D.IIIa engine.

## D.III

**Flown by Vizefeldwebel Barth of Jasta 10, this D.III was based at Heule in the summer of 1917. Jasta 10's staffel marking was a yellow nose.**

Apart from metal panelling around the engine, the remainder of the fuselage was a wooden semi-monocoque structure. The framework was of spruce and plywood with a plywood skin. The latter was then fabric-covered and doped.

The tailplane structure was wooden with a fabric covering. It employed an inverted aerofoil section to aid dive recovery. The rudder was of welded steel tube.

Most D.IIIs were finished in *Silbergrau* aluminium dope. Each Jasta applied its own colourful staffel markings. Vizefeldwebel Barth added a personal dumb-bell marking to his aircraft.

A conventional vee-type undercarriage was fitted, the axle and spreaders between the wheels being encased in a streamlined fairing. The tailskid was sprung with elastic cord.

## COMBAT DATA

### ENGINE POWER

Employing the tried-and-tested Mercedes D.III six-cylinder in-line engine, the Pfalz D.III had a reliable and reasonably powerful powerplant. While aircraft like the Sopwith Camel had comparatively small engines, they also had lighter airframes.

| D.IIIa | S.XIII | F.1 CAMEL |
|---|---|---|
| 134 kw (180 hp.) | 164 kw (220 hp.) | 97 kw (130 hp.) |

### SERVICE CEILING

The Pfalz had a lower service ceiling than other comparable fighters over the Western Front. The D.III was an unstable aircraft which contributed to its good manoeuvrability, but its lack of ceiling meant that it could not seize an altitude initiative as easily as Allied fighters during dogfights. The Spad S.XIII had a 1500-m (4,800-ft) service ceiling advantage.

| D.IIIa | S.XIII | F.1 CAMEL |
|---|---|---|
| 5180 m (17,000 ft.) | 6650 m (21,800 ft.) | 5790 m (19,000 ft.) |

### ENDURANCE

Endurance values of around two to two and a half hours were typical of fighters of the period. Such values varied greatly depending upon a number of factors, including the fuel load carried and the flying conditions encountered.

| D.IIIa | S.XIII | F.1 CAMEL |
|---|---|---|
| 2.5 hours | 2 hours | 2.5 hours |

## Pfalz fighter family

■ **Dr.I:** Starting life as a smaller, refined D.III called the D.VI, the Dr.I had an extra wing surface added to improve its climb rate.

■ **E.II:** Based on the Morane-Saulnier Type H, the E.I and E.II were armed single-seat scouts, powered by Oberursel rotary engines.

■ **E.III:** With Fokker gun synchronisation gear fitted, the E.II became the E.III. Built in small numbers, it was followed by the E.IV.

■ **E.V:** While the E.IV was a more powerful E.III, reliability problems saw it re-engined with a Mercedes rotary, but this was too late for the war.

# PIPER

# L-4 GRASSHOPPER

● Liaison role ● Artillery spotting and observation ● Military lightplane

▲ Many Piper L-4 Grasshoppers and Cubs remain airworthy around the world as a testimony to the quality of Gilbert Taylor's original design.

The Piper L-4 Grasshopper was an important aircraft for the infantryman. On the battlefield, the soldier wanted a quick, reliable way to guide artillery fire. The L-4 Grasshopper could take up position 100 to 200 m (328 to 656 ft) in front of troops, look down on the enemy and call in a devastating barrage of shellfire. Artillery spotting, however, was only one of the many military jobs assigned to the famous Grasshopper.

## PIPER L-4 GRASSHOPPER

◀ Still flying
An L-4 wearing the black and white stripes added for identification when the Allies invaded Europe.

▼ Rosie the Rocketeer
Aircraft which are admired by their crews often acquire 'nose-art'. This L-4 carries rocket tubes strapped to the wing struts.

▲ Cabin glazing
Compared with the basic civilian L-4 Cub, the Grasshopper provided its crew with brilliant all-round visibility.

▼ High-flying Grasshopper
Over the battlefield, Grasshopper pilots would keep low, using natural cover to hide the aircraft – especially from groundfire. L-4s operated in many theatres.

◀ Muddy tyres
With large 'balloon-type' tyres, the L-4 could operate from the roughest of muddy fields.

## FACTS AND FIGURES

➤ General Douglas MacArthur was taken for several flights in an Australian military L-4 in the Philippines.

➤ Between 3 February 1942 and 22 August 1945, 5424 Piper L-4s were built.

➤ Grasshoppers were sometimes known by the nickname 'L-Birds'.

➤ A typical US Army combat division operated six to eight Piper L-4 Grasshoppers for spotting duties.

➤ The US Marine Corps operated L-4s in the New Britain campaign in the Pacific.

➤ After World War II many L-4s were used for primary training.

# PROFILE

# Piper's amazing Grasshopper

In 1930 C. Gilbert Taylor designed the E-2 Taylor Cub. William L. Piper took over production of the aircraft as the J-3C-65 Cub in 1935, and the civil J-3 Cub became a popular sporting aircraft in the years just before World War II.

Four machines were acquired by the US Army Air Corps in 1941 for evaluation in the role of artillery spotting and front-line liaison. Having more than satisfied the army, the Cub became the military Grasshopper by the expedient of cutting away fabric and replacing it by transparent Pyralyn to give the back-seat observer the best possible visibility.

The Cub was a peppy, energetic aircraft which was propelled through the sky by ordinary automobile gasoline. Because it was small and lightweight, it could operate near the front lines where its spotting capabilities were most needed. And because it was so much slower than Luftwaffe fighters, the aircraft was also relatively immune to fighter attack, although groundfire was a constant threat.

The L-4 Grasshopper was produced in greater numbers than any other liaison aircraft of World War II. More advanced models were used by the military for spotting and training duties in the post-war years and were not retired until the late 1950s.

Left: Many air forces used the Grasshopper after the war. With many restored aircraft flying, most enthusiasts recognise the classic high-wing design.

Above: Showing the elastic chord shock absorbers on the main undercarriage and wing-strut arrangement to advantage, this L-4 wears typical US Army Air Corps markings.

## L-4 Grasshopper

**Type:** two-seat liaison and observation aircraft

**Powerplant:** one 48-kW (64-hp) Continental O-170-3 flat-four piston engine

**Maximum speed:** 148 km/h (92 mph); cruising speed 120 km/h (75 mph)

**Range:** 416 km (258 miles)

**Service ceiling:** 2835 m (9301 ft)

**Accommodation:** pilot and observer in tandem in two-seat cockpit; dual controls standard, observer on swivelling seat

**Weights:** empty 331 kg (730 lb); maximum take-off 533 kg (1175 lb)

**Dimensions:**
| | |
|---|---|
| span | 10.73 m (35 ft 2 in) |
| length | 6.78 m (22 ft 1 in) |
| height | 2.03 m (6 ft 8 in) |
| wing area | 16.54 m² (178 sq ft) |

## L-4 GRASSHOPPER

Finished in the olive-drab over neutral grey camouflage that was typical of many US Army Air Corps and Air Force types, this aircraft also carries D-Day invasion stripes.

Cables or struts braced the tailplanes and wings. These allowed the necessary strength to be built in without resorting to a heavy structure. Rough-field operations exert a lot of stress on airframes.

All Allied aircraft operating during and after D-Day were painted with distinctive stripes to avoid confusion with Luftwaffe aircraft. In the event, very few Luftwaffe machines operated over the beaches of Normandy.

Mounted semi-exposed, the Continental flat-four engine powered the majority of more than 5000 L-4s delivered to the Army. Several J-4 Cubs owned by civilians were pressed into service.

Structurally, the L-4 was quite simple and had a fabric-covered wooden framework. The wing had no slats or flaps, but was equipped with large, long-span ailerons. Internally the wing was braced with wire.

For solo flights the pilot sat in the rear seat, which had a full set of controls but was normally used by the observer. The Grasshopper was also equipped with a map table and the radio fit varied between models.

## COMBAT DATA

### MAXIMUM CRUISING SPEED

Although speed is not an important factor for the artillery spotting role, it may be useful for liaison tasks and for some secondary duties such as casualty evacuation.

| | |
|---|---|
| L-4 GRASSHOPPER | 120 km/h (75 mph) |
| AUSTER Mk V | 180 km/h (112 mph) |
| Fi 156C STORCH | 130 km/h (81 mph) |

### ENGINE POWER

Small and lightweight, the Grasshopper had little need for extra power. More power would have required a heavier engine, and would have decreased range and only slightly improved performance.

| L-4 GRASSHOPPER | AUSTER Mk V | Fi 156C STORCH |
|---|---|---|
| 48 kW (64 hp) | 97 kW (130 hp) | 179 kW (240 hp) |

### RANGE

Being a much larger aircraft the Storch carried more fuel and therefore had a longer range. Large aircraft present large targets, however, and the L-4 boasted good range for its compact size.

| | |
|---|---|
| L-4 GRASSHOPPER | 416 km (258 miles) |
| AUSTER Mk V | 402 km (250 miles) |
| Fi 156C STORCH | 467 km (290 miles) |

## US Army Air Corps observation aircraft

**TAYLORCRAFT L-2 GRASSHOPPER:** Designed by the man who started the Piper L-4 line, 1866 Taylorcraft L-2s were built.

**AERONCA L-3 GRASSHOPPER:** Using more metal in its structure than the L-4, at least 1475 L-3s were manufactured.

**STINSON L-5 SENTINEL:** L-5s served mostly in the Pacific and later in Korea. A total of 3590 were built for the army.

**INTERSTATE L-6 GRASSHOPPER:** Outward angled windows on the 250 L-6s built allowed an excellent downwards view.

# POLIKARPOV

# I-15/I-153

● Fighter biplane ● Fought in Spain and China ● Highly manoeuvrable

▲ Polikarpov fighters fought with distinction in the late 1930s, taking on aircraft like the CR.32 and Ki-27.
The I-15 was so manoeuvrable that it broke records, turning through 360° in only eight seconds. The design formed the basis of the later I-16 monoplane.

**D**esigned by Polikarpov while he was in prison, the biplane I-15 'Chaika' (Seagull) was involved in many air battles in the 1930s from Mongolia to Spain. The aircraft was continually improved; the final I-153 was one of the most capable biplane fighters ever built. Displaying excellent manoeuvrability, the I-15 was still in service in large numbers in 1941, by which time it had been rendered obsolete.

## POLIKARPOV I-15/I-153

▼ **Hidden in the woods**
The Soviets were masters of camouflage, but that did not save these I-15s from destruction in 1941. Luftwaffe fighters decimated the Soviet biplanes.

▲ **Still fighting**
The I-153 was still in action as late as 1943 dropping light bombs in the close support role. The type was flown by aces Grigory Rechkalov and Alexander Klubov before they flew MiG-3s.

◄ **Fighting the invader**
Finland's forces used 14 captured 'Chaikas' fitted with German radios and Browning machine-guns. With the advantage of having better pilots and the fact that they were often mistaken as friendly, the Finns wrought havoc against the Soviets.

▼ **Starting up**
These bomb-armed 'Chaikas' are being started up by trucks using a Hucks starter.

▲ **Spanish tour**
The 'Chaika' was the main Republican fighter in the Spanish Civil War, fighting Nationalist Fiat CR.32s. The two types were closely matched, although the I-15 had better firepower.

## FACTS AND FIGURES

➤ More than 550 I-15s were supplied to the Spanish Republicans; they were known as 'Chato' (flat nose) to their opponents.

➤ I-153s were cleared to fire six RS-82 underwing rockets for ground attack.

➤ The 'Chaika' was flown by the Spanish ace Miguel Zamudio in the Civil War.

➤ A single I-15 variant was produced with rubber-sealed pressurised cockpits for high-altitude work.

➤ Two I-152s were rebuilt as 'Shturmovik' dedicated ground-attack prototypes.

➤ In October 1940 an I-153/DM-4 reached 440 km/h (274 m.p.h.) in a ramjet test flight.

**PROFILE**

# Dogfighting in the 'Seagull'

When he designed a replacement for the earlier I-5, Polikarpov retained the biplane formula but created a gull-wing shape, leading to the nickname Seagull. Early versions were powered by an American Wright Cyclone engine driving a Russian propeller. First flown in 1933, the aircraft displayed astonishing agility.

Production began in 1934 and the armament was doubled to four guns with a high reserve of ammunition. The I-15 had an active combat life, fighting the Japanese at the battle of Khalkin Gol and in China. The aircraft also served the Republican cause in Spain, and fought on both sides in the Finnish campaign in 1940.

The Soviets tried to prolong the life of the I-15 with various improvements, such as revised cowlings and more powerful engines, for the I-15bis, I-152 and I-153 models. Even with turbocharged engines, however, the performance was not vastly improved, and Polikarpov turned to the monoplane I-16 which was very similar. Over 1000 'Chaikas' were still in service with the USSR in 1941.

*Above: The bizarre I-153/DM-4 was an experimental version used to test ramjet-assisted propulsion.*

*Left: Fitting a Cyclone engine in such a short airframe gave the I-15 its distinctive portly lines. The Soviet M-62 engine was used in the I-153 version.*

## I-15

One of the most successful biplane fighters ever, the I-15 was the main Spanish Republican fighter.

The 'Chaika' gained its nickname from the distinct shape of its upper wing. Many pilots disliked the gull-wing, saying the view was worse.

At an early stage in its production, the I-15 was equipped with seat armour. PV-1 guns were fitted in the fuselage sides in addition to the pair in original versions.

The multicoloured tail was the emblem of the Spanish Republican air force. The black cross of the Nationalists was later painted over this.

Such was the demand for the I-15 that the first examples had the original American engines, but most had Russian licence-built M-25 versions of the Wright Cyclone.

One outstanding feature was the undercarriage legs; the lower portion slid up and down inside the upper portion through an internal slot to provide wheel suspension.

The fuselage was constructed of KhMA gas-welded tube with light-alloy removable skin panels forwards of the windscreen and fabric covering behind.

### 'Chaikas' at war

**OUTSMARTING THE JAPANESE:** During the Sino-Japanese War, which began in 1937, Chinese Nationalists flew their manoeuvrable I-15s against more advanced Japanese fighters.

**WITH REPUBLICAN FORCES:** Spanish Republican forces equipped with I-15s came up against Nationalist and Condor Legion fighters from Germany during the Spanish Civil War.

**CAPTURED CHAIKAS:** During World War II, Finland used 14 captured examples fitted with Browning guns and German radio to bomb Soviet positions.

## I-15

**Type:** single-seat radial-engined biplane fighter and ground-attack aircraft

**Powerplant:** one 528-kW (708-hp.) Wright Cyclone F-3 radial piston engine

**Maximum speed:** 367 km/h (228 m.p.h.) at 3000 m (9,840 ft.)

**Initial climb rate:** over 900 m/min (2,953 f.p.m.)

**Combat radius:** 550 km (342 mi.)

**Service ceiling:** 9800 m (32,150 ft.)

**Weights:** empty 1130 kg (2,491 lb.); loaded 1390 kg (3,064 lb.)

**Armament:** four PV-1 7.62-mm (.30 cal.) machine-guns with 3000 rounds; provision for four 20-kg (44-lb.) bombs or (I-153) six rockets

**Dimensions:**
| | |
|---|---|
| span | 9.75 m (32 ft.) |
| length | 6.10 m (20 ft. 1 in.) |
| height | 2.19 m (7 ft. 2 in.) |
| wing area | 23.55 m² (253 sq. ft.) |

### COMBAT DATA

#### MAXIMUM SPEED

By the end of the 1930s fighters were approaching the feasible maximum speeds for biplane design. Even the first all-metal monoplane fighters which were entering service were at least as fast.

| | |
|---|---|
| I-15 | 367 km/h (228 m.p.h.) |
| CR.32 | 375 km/h (233 m.p.h.) |
| GLADIATOR Mk I | 410 km/h (255 m.p.h.) |

#### ARMAMENT

Four-gun armament was a vital improvement in the last biplane fighters, as a lethal shot was less easy to attain due to the increasing speed and armour protection of enemy aircraft.

| | |
|---|---|
| I-15 | 4 x 7.62-mm (.30 cal.) machine-guns |
| CR.32 | 2 x 7.7-mm (.303 cal.) machine-guns |
| GLADIATOR Mk I | 4 x 7.7-mm (.303 cal.) machine-guns |

#### SERVICE CEILING

The I-15 had a good climb rate and ceiling, and against a CR.32 pilots often had the edge in diving and climbing. With its pressurised cockpit the I-152GK could routinely operate at high altitudes.

| | | |
|---|---|---|
| I-15 9800 m (32,150 ft.) | CR.32 8800 m (28,900 ft.) | GLADIATOR Mk I 10,060 m (33,000 ft.) |

# POLIKARPOV

# I-16

● Early monoplane fighter ● Spanish war veteran ● Dogfighter

▲ Polikarpov's I-16 was something of a compromise design, accepted into service for all its faults in an attempt to match rival designs that outperformed the earlier (biplane) I-15 in Spain. This I-16 is shown at Jerez airfield in Spain prior to acceptance by the Republican 22 Rgt.

**W**hen Hitler invaded the USSR in 1941, the open-cockpit I-16 was the most numerous fighter in service with the Soviet. Designed to replace biplane fighters, the I-16 was a fast machine when it first appeared in 1934, and was the first low-wing cantilever monoplane with a retractable undercarriage. It is best remembered for fighting with government forces in Spain and China against desperate odds, and facing the invasion of the USSR.

## POLIKARPOV I-16

### ▲ Fighting for the enemy
During the war with Finland, numerous I-16s were captured by the Finns and restored to use against their former owners. This example is a Type 12 with a tubular sight in the windshield. Soviet I-16 pilots had a hard time flying against Finnish pilots.

### ▲ Ski champion
For operations in the ferocious Russian winter, the I-16 was often fitted with skis. These could be retracted to lie flat against the wing in flight.

### Fighting fly ▶
Known as 'Mukha' (Russian for fly) in Spain the I-16 was the best Government fighter aircraft.

### ▼ Spanish warrior
Nationalist forces inherited the I-16s previously used by the Republican side in Spain's civil war.

### ◀ No more flying
Hundreds of I-16s were destroyed in June 1941, when the Luftwaffe attacked Soviet airfields. Even those that took off in time were soon shot down.

## FACTS AND FIGURES

➤ Although outmoded by 1941, the I-16 equipped about 65 per cent of the Soviet fighter force when the Germans invaded.

➤ The I-16 was the first monoplane fighter to enter service in 1935.

➤ Production of the I-16 exceeded 8000 single- and two-seat examples.

➤ I-16 ace Grigori Ravchenko shot down three Japanese aircraft in China and later led an I-16 unit with success in Mongolia.

➤ The I-16 type 5 SPB was a fast dive-bomber variant with special dive brakes.

➤ At least one I-16P was tested with a powerful four-cannon installation.

## PROFILE

# Dogfighting in the mighty 'fly'

Polikarpov began planning a successor to the biplane I-15 series while he was in a Soviet labor camp. In 1933, he designed a rival monoplane to the ANT-31, and the result was the I-16, with its wooden fuselage and metal wing. First prototypes used Soviet M-22 engines, but by 1934 licence-built Wright Cyclone engines were

fitted, giving a dramatic increase in performance and making the I-16 one of the fastest machines of its day. Although hard to fly, the Soviet forces ordered thousands of them.

The I-16 really made its mark in the Spanish Civil War, where government forces pitted the I-16 against the Fascists. The I-16 was built under license there by

Hispano-Suiza. In China, Soviet I-16s flew well in overwhelming air battles with Japanese pilots, repeating this again in 1939 in battles on the Manchurian border. Huge numbers of I-16s were destroyed in the invasion of the USSR, but the aircraft remained in service until 1943, by which time it was obviously obsolete.

*Flying the I-16 called for considerable skill, because it was prone to stalling and spinning, stability was marginal and the aircraft would easily drop a wing if the pilot allowed speed to bleed off during landing. Without trimmers to take back pressure forces off the controls, it was exhausting to fly.*

### I-16

**Type:** single-seat interceptor fighter

**Powerplant:** one 578-kW (775-hp.) Shvetsov M-25 air-cooled radial

**Maximum speed:** 489 km/h (304 m.p.h.)

**Service ceiling:** 8268 m (27,125 ft.)

**Weights:** empty 1347 kg (2,970 lb.); loaded 1711 kg (3,773 lb.)

**Armament:** four 7.62-mm (.30 cal.) Shpital'ny-Komaritsky ShKAS machine guns in upper fuselage and wings; up to six RS-82 rocket projectiles, six Der-31 bomb containers or two 100-kg (220-lb.) bombs (I-16P); and two 20-mm (0.79-in.) ShVAK cannon in wings

**Dimensions:** span 9.14 m (30 ft.)
length 5.79 m (19 ft.)
height 2.44 m (8 ft.)
wing area 14.49 m² (156 sq. ft.)

## I-16 (TYPE-17)

The Type-17 variant carried two ShKAS machine guns and two ShVAK cannon and was the first version to fire RS-82 rockets. Many saw action against Japanese forces in August 1939.

Best feature of the I-16 was its armament of two ShVAK cannon in the wings. Two ShKAS machine guns were carried in the upper fuselage.

Foreign pilots often complained about the narrow cockpit with its folding sidewall exit. The lack of trim tabs meant that constant stick and rudder forces had to be suffered by the pilot. After the type 4, thick rear armor, over 6mm (¼ in.), was fitted.

Early I-16s were powered by Wright Cyclone radials imported and built under license, driving Hamilton two-pitch propellers. After the type 6, I-16s used M-25A engines, later types having M-62 and M-63 engines with superchargers.

Undercarriage retraction was another failing of the early I-16. It took no less than 44 progressively harder turns of a crank to raise the gear, which often jammed half way when lowered. Pilots were even issued cable shears to free jammed undercarriages.

Slogans painted on aircraft were much loved by Soviet pilots. This one reads 'For the USSR'.

The tail structure was made of D6 alloy with a fabric covering for lightness. There was no counterweighted or aerodynamic balancing, making the controls rather heavy.

### ACTION DATA

**SPEED**

The first generation of monoplane fighters that began to appear in the early 1930s had a significant speed advantage over their biplane rivals. The Ki-27 and I-16 were evenly matched.

I-16 489 km/h (304 m.p.h.)
P-26 377 km/h (234 m.p.h.)
Ki-27 468 km/h (291 m.p.h.)

**RANGE**

Fighters of the 1930s had notoriously short range. Designed to operate close to their bases, they traded extra fuel capacity for speed and agility. All three had similar ranges.

I-16 599 km (372 mi.)
P-26 579 km (360 mi.)
Ki-27 624 km (388 mi.)

**WEAPONS**

The P-26 and the Ki-27 possessed the standard fighter armament of the time consisting of two machine guns. The I-16 was one of the few more heavily armed fighters with four machine guns.

I-16 4 x 7.62-mm (.30 cal.) MGs
P-26 2 x 12.7-mm (.50 cal.) MGs
Ki-27 2 x 7.7-mm (.303 cal.) MGs

## Fighters in the Spanish Civil War

■ **Bf 109B:** The finest fighter of the war, the Bf 109 totally outclassed machines like the I-16 and earlier biplanes.

■ **HAWKER FURY:** Supplied to the Government side, the Fury was an obsolete design that performed adequately.

■ **POLIKARPOV I-15:** Predecessor to the I-16, 550 biplane I-15s were used in Spain with some success against Fiat CR.32s.

# POLIKARPOV

# Po-2/U-2

● Multiple variants ● Massive production ● Built pre- and post-war

▲ Having been built in massive numbers in the Soviet Union and in Poland between 1948 and 1953, it is not surprising that examples of this tough, versatile biplane remain airworthy.

**D**esigned originally as a trainer to replace the U-1 Soviet-built version of the Avro 504, the U-2 and its derivatives were produced from 1928 until 1944. Production was resumed after World War II, when thousands more were built in Poland. Designated 'Mule' by NATO in 1954, Russian troops nicknamed the aircraft 'Kukuruzhnik' ('corn-cutter'). In 1944 the U-2's designation was changed to Po-2 in recognition of Polikarpov's role in its creation.

## POLIKARPOV Po-2/U-2

◀ **Preserved Polikarpov**
Wearing the markings of the former Yugoslavia, this Po-2 has been displayed at air shows in France.

▼ **Soviet service**
Serving in a multitude of roles, the Po-2/U-2 was highly respected by Soviet forces.

▲ **Wartime trainer**
When it first flew in 1928 as a basic trainer design, the U-2 already appeared obsolete. Its simple structure proved to be the basis for success, however.

◀ **Civilian roles**
This aircraft, wearing CCCP codes, represents one of the many thousands of civilian Po-2/U-2s used in roles as diverse as training, transport (with open and enclosed cabins), crop-dusting and flying ambulance.

**Still flying** ▶
A strong cross-axle undercarriage unit with comprehensive shock-absorbing gave good airfield handling. The U-2 was originally designed with interchangeable, rectangular wing panels for ease of maintenance and repair, but this resulted in very poor flight characteristics.

### FACTS AND FIGURES

➤ Deliveries of the Po-2 began in 1928 and by the time of the 1941 German invasion 13,000 had been built.

➤ U-2s flew low-level, night-time nuisance raids against German forces.

➤ An incredible 80 different factory-built variants of the U-2 were produced.

➤ Continuing its nuisance raider role, the Po-2 flew 'bed-check Charlie' raids against UN positions in the Korean War.

➤ A Po-2SKF variant could carry two stretcher patients in underwing pods.

➤ One experimental aircraft was tested with a 'butterfly' tail.

# Prolific Polikarpov

A great number of variants of the Po-2/U-2 have been identified. Military versions were used for training, observation and light attack, as close-support aircraft with rockets and bombs, and as black-painted night-bombers carrying two 100-kg (220-lb.) bombs. Two aircraft were even equipped with transmitters and loudspeakers for psychological warfare.

Several ambulance versions were produced. The first carried a single stretcher and attendant, but later medevac models had an enclosed rear cockpit for two stretchers. Another variant carried a cylindrical container for a stretcher on each lower wing.

One of the first non-military uses was crop-dusting, and large numbers were built for this task both before and after the war. A tank for chemicals replaced the rear cockpit. There were other versions with three seats, some of which had enclosed cabins, and one 1944 model had five seats for military liaison.

There was also a series of floatplane versions, including one fitted with a 537-kW (720-hp.) Wright Cyclone engine, which set new altitude records for seaplanes in 1937, as well as many one-off and experimental conversions.

Left: Polish-built aircraft had the basic designation CSS-13, but like their Soviet equivalents they were produced in many forms, often with different designations.

Above: Although it was widely used and often modified, the U-2 airframe remained largely unchanged. Features such as the tailskid were retained throughout the extended production run.

No attempt was made to streamline or protect the engine installation. This seems to have caused few problems since the engine remained uncowled on most variants.

Having rejected the original wing design, Polikarpov adopted this more conventional staggered wing layout. A single set of interplane struts braced the wings on each side, making this a single-bay biplane.

This ring-mounted 7.7-mm (.303 cal.) ShKAS machine-gun gave the U-2LSh a limited self-defence and ground strafing capability.

A windscreen was provided for the pilot and rear-seat occupant, in this case a gunner. Some aircraft were given enclosed cabins, with the Po-2ShS accommodating the pilot and three passengers.

Ailerons were fitted to each wing, with the upper and lower surfaces on each side connected by cables. The tips of the lower wings were protected in the event of a rough landing by underwing skids.

Cables running along the fuselage side connected the elevators to the control column and the rudder to the pedals. One aircraft was built with all the controls connected to the control column.

A large, tall rudder of broad chord was typical of the Po-2/U-2. Like all of the control surfaces, it was linked to the cockpit controls by a series of cables.

## U-2LSʜ

Soviet forces flew these aircraft in a light Shturmovik role. Many pre-war aircraft were modified for these light-attack duties and saw action from 1941 onwards. Flying at low level, they were very successful.

# World War II trainers

**AVRO TUTOR:** Used by the RAF as a basic trainer during World War II, the Tutor wore the standard yellow training colour scheme.

**BOEING STEARMAN KAYDETT:** Built in huge numbers, the Kaydett provided basic training for US Army and Navy pilots throughout the war.

**BÜCKER Bü 131 JUNGMANN:** This aerobatic trainer was used to teach many of the Luftwaffe's best pilots the art of flying.

**NIHON TYPE 93 K5Y1:** The two-seat K5Y1 was among a number of Japanese aircraft used to train naval pilots.

# Potez

# 25

● **More than 4000 built** ● **General-purpose biplane** ● **Numerous variants**

Built in large numbers and used by the air forces of more than 20 countries, the Potez 25 was developed from the earlier models 15S and 24, and flew for the first time early in 1925. During the following 10 years more than 4000 were built, several hundred of them under licence for export customers, in over a dozen different versions. The Potez's career with the French air force ended in the mid-1930s, but some served elsewhere into the 1940s.

▲ *In addition to its military applications, the Potez 25 found useful employment as a mail plane in South America during the 1930s. Aéropostale and its associated companies made regular mail flights, frequently taking the aircraft on hazardous routes over the Andes with considerable loads.*

## Potez 25

**▲ Swiss 25 A.2**
*This Potez 25 A.2 observation aircraft was powered by a Lorraine-Dietrich 12Eb liquid-cooled engine.*

**▲ Potez 25 'Jupiter'**
*Switzerland operated a mixture of aircraft with liquid- and air-cooled engines. This aircraft has a 313-kW (420-hp.) Gnome-Rhône 9Ac Jupiter radial installed.*

**▲ Unequal-span wings**
*A common feature of all 25s was the design's unequal span mainplanes. Tail shapes varied; the Salmson radial-engined machines had an extended rudder.*

**▲ Salmson engine**
*A distinctively shaped engine cowling was a feature of the 388-kW (520-hp.) Salmson radial-powered Potez 25 versions.*

**Clean lines ▶**
*The clean lines of the 25 are evident in this view, though they are spoilt slightly by the radial engine.*

## FACTS AND FIGURES

➤ Licence production was undertaken in factories in Poland, Yugoslavia, Romania and Portugal.

➤ Apart from Potez, ANF Les Mureauz and Hanriot built 25s in France.

➤ China employed Potez 25s in action against the Japanese.

➤ A dozen countries, including the Soviet Union, took delivery of Potez 25s for test purposes.

➤ Ethiopian 25s saw action against the invading Italian troops in 1935.

➤ Civil-operated 25s were used by Hanriot and Caudron flying schools in France.

# PROFILE

# Widely used French design

Basic models of the Potez 25 built for the French Armée de l'Air were the A.2 reconnaissance aircraft, the B.2 bomber and the TOE for operations in overseas theatres. The B.2's bombload consisted of 12 12-kg (26-lb.) or four 50-kg (110-lb.) bombs under the fuselage, plus six 12-kg (26-lb.) bombs under the wings.

There were also civil derivatives of the aircraft. Some were used to carry mail in South America, and two were built with metal fuselages and extra fuel tanks as part of an unsuccessful attempt to make the first non-stop flight from Paris to New York. Designated 25-O (for Océan), they were designed to jettison their undercarriage after take-off and land on a strengthened skid on the underside of the fuselage. The 25H was a floatplane variant built in two forms, one with a large central float, the other with twin floats. Many engine types, both in-line and radial, were used with power ratings in the 298- to 447-kW (400- to 600-hp.) range. Other operators were the air arms of Afghanistan, Algeria, Argentina, Brazil, China, Estonia, Ethiopia, Finland, Guatemala, Indo-China, Japan, Madagascar, Morocco, Poland, Portugal, Romania, Switzerland, Turkey, Uruguay, the USSR, and Yugoslavia.

*Above: Like its other aircraft, Switzerland's large fleet of French-built Potez 25s was long-serving, the last flying until 1940.*

*Below: This Potez 25 TOE was among 2,270 examples of this general-purpose variant built. They were designed for colonial use but many saw home service with the French air force.*

## 25 A.2

During the Gran Chaco War of 1932-35, this aircraft operated from Isla Poi with 2º Escuadrón de Reconocimiento y Bombardeo, Paraguayan air force. In this conflict Paraguay disputed the sovereignty of Chaco Boreal with neighbouring Bolivia.

A variety of engine types was fitted to Potez 25s, to drive a wooden fixed-pitch propeller.

Pilot and observer were accommodated close together in tandem cockpits beneath a cut-out in the trailing edge of the upper wing centre-section.

Twin Lewis 7.7-mm (.303 cal.) machine-guns were mounted on a TO 7 ring in the observer's cockpit. Another was fixed to fire forward.

Designed by Louis Coroller, the Potez 25 was derived from the Potez 24 A.2-category fighter aircraft.

Potez 25s were fitted with a new cross-axle landing gear with specially designed shock absorbers. The undercarriage wheels were formed with metal spokes and fitted with rubber tyres.

Bombloads of around 200 kg (440 lb.) could be carried by the Potez 25 on underfuselage racks, further enhancing the type's versatility. The 25 B.2 variant was specifically designed for the role.

A refined 25 prototype was flown for the first time from the new Méaulte factory in early 1925.

## 25 TOE

**Type:** two-seat general-purpose biplane

**Powerplant:** one 335-kW (450-hp.) Lorraine-Dietrich 12Eb liquid-cooled piston engine

**Maximum speed:** 208 km/h (129 m.p.h.) at sea level

**Range:** 1260 km (783 mi.)

**Service ceiling:** 5800 m (19,000 ft.)

**Weights:** empty equipped 1510 kg (3,329 lb.); maximum take-off 2500 kg (5,512 lb.)

**Armament:** one fixed forward-firing 7.7-mm (.303 cal.) Vickers machine-gun and two 7.7-mm Vickers machine-guns on trainable single mounting in observer's cockpit, plus 200 kg (440 lb.) of bombs

**Dimensions:**
| | |
|---|---|
| span | 14.14 m (46 ft. 5 in.) |
| length | 9.10 m (29 ft. 10 in.) |
| height | 3.67 m (12 ft.) |
| wing area | 47.00 m² (506 sq. ft.) |

## COMBAT DATA

### MAXIMUM SPEED

Compared to other general-purpose types of the inter-war period, the Potez 25 had a good top speed. With a bombload this would be considerably reduced.

| | |
|---|---|
| 25 TOE | 208 km/h (129 m.p.h.) |
| WAPITI Mk IIA | 217 km/h (135 m.p.h.) |
| IIIF Mk IV | 193 km/h (120 m.p.h.) |

### POWER

Engines of varying power were fitted to Potez 25s, the 25 TOE having a Lorraine rated at 335 kW. Westland's Wapiti had a larger engine, while that of the Fairey IIIF was of a similar rating.

| 25 TOE | WAPITI Mk IIA | IIIF Mk IV |
|---|---|---|
| 335 kW (450 hp.) | 373 kW (500 hp.) | 339 kW (455 hp.) |

### RANGE

The Potez 25's range figure fell between those of the Fairey IIIF and Westland Wapiti. The Wapiti was a modest performer at 579 km (360 mi.), while the Fairey type was designed for maritime patrols over long distances of almost 2500 km (1,550 mi.) (though this would be considerably reduced with a full weapons load).

25 TOE 1260 km (783 mi.)

WAPITI Mk IIA 579 km (360 mi.)

IIIF Mk IV 2446 km (1,520 mi.)

# Aircraft of the Chaco War

**BREDA Ba.44:** This transport design, bearing a remarkable resemblance to the de Havilland DH.84, served the Paraguayan forces.

**FIAT CR.30:** A small number of these Italian biplane fighters served with the Paraguayan air force, opposing Bolivian Curtiss Hawk IAs.

**CURTISS TYPE 18T:** Designed for the US Navy, one example of this two-seat triplane was imported by Bolivia in 1919.

**JUNKERS W.34:** Transport aircraft like this one were converted to bombers by the Bolivian air force. Many pilots were mercenaries.

# PZL

# P.11

● Interceptor fighter ● Light attack ● Poland's last line of defence

▲ The P.11 fell in large numbers to the superior German fighters, but scored an impressive number of kills for such a dated machine, thanks to the aggression of its pilots.

**A**lthough heavily outnumbered by superior fighters, Polish air force pilots flying P.11s and P.7s put up a heroic resistance during the German invasion of their country in September 1939. By then their fighters, among the fastest in the world a few years earlier, were slower than any of the opposing machines except for the Hs 126 and Ju 87. Yet they scored the first Allied aerial victories of World War II, and shot down 126 German aircraft.

## PZL P.11

◀ **Revolutionary design**
At a time when others were still using biplane wings, Poland's Zygmunt Pulawski pioneered the gull-wing monoplane fighter.

◀ **Imported engines**
The P.11 first flew with a French Gnôme-Rhône radial engine, later replaced by a licence-built British Mercury VIS.

▲ **Poland's defender**
At the time of the German invasion in 1939 the obsolete P.11 made up the majority of the small Polish air arm. In battle they were outclassed.

▼ **P.11 exported**
The tough P.11 fighter was used by several smaller air forces, notably the Romanians whose aircraft fought against the Allies.

▲ **Gallant defeat**
Poland's 128 P.11s were arranged into six defence regiments, who fought bravely against the invading German forces in 1939. They lost a total of 46 aircraft in the first three days of the short conflict.

## FACTS AND FIGURES

➤ Romania produced 120 of its own P.11f version, which went on to fight with the German Luftwaffe.

➤ The prototype PZL P.11 first flew in September 1931.

➤ The first production variant, the two-gun P.11b, entered service in 1935.

➤ A total of 50 P.11b models with indigenous engines and instruments were exported to Romania.

➤ In all, a total of 330 PZL P.11s of all types had been built when production ended.

➤ Three hundred of the improved P.24 series were made solely for export.

# PROFILE

# Poland's gull-winged defender

The P.11's distinctive gull wing helped it to set new standards of performance in the age of biplane fighters. The wing was intended to partner a V-type engine, but after being used on a series of prototypes it was combined with a radial engine on the production P.7 and its successor, the P.11.

The P.11a had a 373-kW (500-hp.) Bristol Mercury engine and two fuselage-mounted machine-

guns. It was followed by the more powerful P.11c, which carried an extra machine-gun in each wing. The P.11c's top speed of 390 km/h (242 m.p.h.) was impressive in the early 1930s. By 1939, though, its two-blade propeller, open cockpit and fixed under-carriage were clearly outmoded.

Romania bought 50 P.11bs, with Romanian engines and instruments, and IAR in Bucharest built 120 P.11fs.

These participated in the war against the Soviet Union. The 12 squadrons of Polish P.11s claimed the destruction of 126 Luftwaffe aircraft in 1939, losing 114 of their own aircraft.

*The P.11c model was by far the most modern fighter asset available to the Poles in any number. It was comparable to the British Gloster Gladiator or German Heinkel 51, and although it was less heavily armed it featured a more advanced monoplane wing.*

## P.11c

**Type:** single-seat monoplane interceptor and light-attack fighter

**Powerplant:** one 373-kW (500-hp.) Skoda-built Bristol Mercury VIS.2 radial piston engine

**Maximum speed:** 390 km/h (242 m.p.h.) at 5500 m (18,000 ft.)

**Initial climb rate:** 5000 m (16,400 ft.) in 6 min

**Combat radius:** maximum loaded range 700 km (435 mi.)

**Service ceiling:** 8000 m (26,250 ft.)

**Weights:** maximum take-off weight 1800 kg (3,960 lb.)

**Armament:** two 7.7-mm (.303 cal.) machine-guns

**Dimensions:**
span     10.72 m (35 ft. 2 in.)
length    7.55 m (24 ft. 9 in.)
height    2.85 m (9 ft. 4 in.)

---

*The P.11c was equipped with two KM Wz33 machine-guns in the forward fuselage sides and light bombs under each wing.*

*Power came from a Skoda-built Bristol Mercury VIS.2 radial piston engine.*

## P.11c

**This aircraft wears the markings of No. 113 'Owls' Squadron, Polish Air Force. The aircraft was used by the 1st Air Regiment, during the invasion of September 1939.**

*The single pilot sat in a modestly sized cockpit. This did not have a canopy, was unarmoured and had only a small windscreen.*

*Of sturdy construction and using primitive cable controls, the P.11 could survive a fair degree of gunfire.*

*The undercarriage was fixed, but the double bracing and heavy-duty wheels made it exceptionally strong.*

*Its high parasol wing was revolutionary for the time and enabled the aircraft to outmanoeuvre, if not outrun, the less agile aircraft of the German invasion, notably the Dornier Do 17, Junkers Ju 87 Stuka and the Henschel Hs 126.*

*The P.11 shown here carries the colourful unit markings of No. 113 Squadron: a black owl on either side of the fuselage. Four weeks into the fighting P.11 squadrons were instructed to paint over the markings to reduce the planes' visibility.*

*A simple spring-loaded tail skid was fitted.*

---

## COMBAT DATA

### ARMAMENT

As speeds increased in the late 1930s designers realised that more firepower was needed, as pilots would only have a target in their sights for a few seconds. Earlier twin-gun designs like the P.11 and He 51 were replaced by four- or six-gun types.

| | |
|---|---|
| P.11C | 2 x 7.7-mm (.303 cal.) MGs |
| He 51 | 2 x 7.92-mm (0.31-in.) MGs |
| GLADIATOR | 4 x 7.7-mm (.303 cal.) MGs |

### MAXIMUM SPEED

Although the P.11 was a fast aircraft compared to most of the biplanes of its day, it presented little problem for the monoplanes that appeared soon after, like Germany's Bf 109 which were 50 per cent faster.

| | |
|---|---|
| P.11C | 390 km/h (242 m.p.h.) |
| He 51 | 330 km/h (205 m.p.h.) |
| GLADIATOR | 410 km/h (254 m.p.h.) |

### SERVICE CEILING

The P.11 could outclimb most biplane fighters, but compared to its adversary, the Bf 109 monoplane with its fuel injection and more advanced airframe, it was a poor performer and an easy victim.

P.11C
8000 m
(26,250 ft.)

He 51
7700 m
(25,250 ft.)

GLADIATOR
10,000 m
(32,800 ft.)

---

## Poland's air force in the 1930s

**ANSALDO BALILLA A-1:** An Italian design built under licence, the Balilla was used by both sides during the Russo-Polish war.

**PZL P.37 LOS:** This bomber was the best aircraft used by Poland in the war. Romania operated the P.37 against the Soviet Union.

**BREGUET 19:** This multi-role French design was used by many air forces in Europe, including the Spanish republican air force.

**PZL P.23 KARAS:** This single-engined army co-operation aircraft was heavily committed during the invasion in 1939.

# REGGIANE

# RE.2001/5

● German power ● Built in small numbers ● Late-war fighter

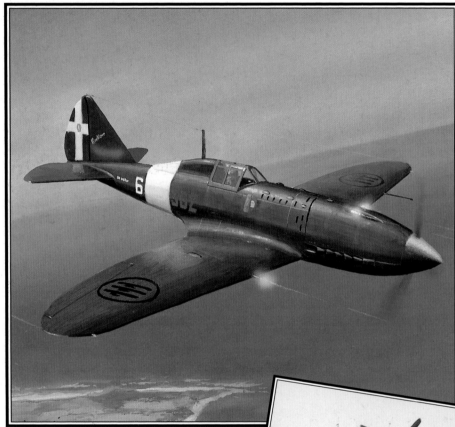

T hough Reggiane attempted to address the worst of the Re.2000's weaknesses – its lack of power – by introducing an in-line engine, the change made little impact. The Re.2001's performance was hardly improved and engine supplies were limited. The ultimate member of the family – the Re.2005 Sagittario – was one of the finest Italian fighter designs of World War II, but was built in only small numbers.

▲ Disappointing
performance by the Re.2000 led to the marriage of the Daimler-Benz DB.601 to the Falco airframe. The result was an improvement over its predecessor.

---

# REGGIANE RE.2001/5

### ▼ One-off
One Re.2001 was fitted with a Fraschinin Delta IV engine. Performance was even worse than that of other Falcos.

### ▲ Good handling
Only 252 Re.2001s were built, though a handful did see combat over Malta in 1942. They proved to be extremely agile against the Allied fighters.

### ▼ Last and best
Having little in common with the Falco II, the Re.2005 Sagittario was truly outstanding and was arguably the best Italian fighter of the war. Only a handful ever became operational.

### ▲ Falcons by night
Most numerous of all variants was the Re.2001CN night-fighter. This featured a 20-mm (0.79-in.) cannon under each wing and was designed to confront the Allies' nocturnal bombing raids over northern Italy.

### Low production ▶
Of the 48 Sagittarios actually completed, the majority ended up in the hands of the 22º Gruppo de Cacci, which was tasked with the defence of Rome and Naples during the last months of the war in Europe. A further 300 were almost completed.

## FACTS AND FIGURES

➤ Proposed Re.2001 versions included a two-seat trainer, tank-buster and torpedo-fighter.

➤ Of the 252 Re.2001s built, 150 were completed as Re.2001CN night-fighters.

➤ Towards the war's end in Italy, plans were advanced for an all-wooden Re.2001.

➤ Reggiane planned to build a 730-km/h Re.2005R with a centrifugal compressor powered by an additional piston engine.

➤ After Italy surrendered, the Co-Belligerent Air Force continued to operate Re.2001s.

➤ Two Re.2001s were fitted with arrester hooks for deck-landing trials.

## PROFILE

# In-line Falcons and Archers

*Left: Only the wing of the Re.2001 was retained, the fuselage being extensively redesigned.*

Without doubt an excellent design, the Re.2000 Falco was underpowered. The Piaggio radial fitted to the first example developed just 649 kW (870 hp.), providing a top speed of only 529 km/h (328 m.p.h.). Believing that an in-line engine would improve top speed, Reggiane next developed the Re.2001, known as the Falco II.

This was fitted with a licence-built Daimler-Benz DB.601A-1 (Alfa Romeo RA.1000 RC.41-1a Monsonie) rated at 876 kW

(1,175 hp.). However, its maximum speed was just 542 km/h (336 m.p.h.). Re.2001s entered the war with the Regia Aeronautica over Malta in 1942. Only 252 were built, for most RA.1000 engines were earmarked for Macchi M.C.202 production.

The second in-line Re.2000 variant was the last of the line – the Re.2005 Sagitarrio (Archer). It retained the basic configuration of earlier aircraft, but was considerably redesigned, with outward-retracting undercarriage and a licence-built DB.605A-1

*Right: A few Sagittarios took part in the defence of Bucharest and Berlin alongside the Luftwaffe.*

engine (the Fiat RA.1050 R.C.58 Tifone) rated at 1100 kW (1,475 hp.). Only 48 of these 630-km/h (390-m.p.h.) aircraft were completed before Italy's collapse, seeing combat during the defence of Sicily, Naples and Rome. A few later served in the defence of Bucharest and Berlin.

### Re.2005 Sagitarrio

**Type:** single-seat fighter/fighter-bomber

**Powerplant:** one 1100-kW (1,475-hp.) Fiat RA.1050 R.C Tifone (Daimler-Benz DB.605A-1) in-line liquid-cooled piston engine

**Maximum speed:** 630 km/h (390 m.p.h.)

**Range:** 1250 km (775 mi.)

**Service ceiling:** 12,000 m (39,400 ft.)

**Weights:** empty 2600 kg (5,720 lb.); loaded 3560 kg (7,832 lb.)

**Armament:** three Mauser MG 151 20-mm (0.79-in.) cannon, one engine- and two wing-mounted, plus two 12.7-mm (.50 cal.) machine-guns with 350 rounds, and up to 630 kg (1,390 lb.) of bombs

**Dimensions:** span 11.00 m (36 ft. 1 in.)
length 8.73 m (28 ft. 8 in.)
height 3.15 m (10 ft. 4 in.)
wing area 20.40 m² (220 sq. ft.)

### RE.2001 FALCO II

Wearing an interesting colour scheme, this Re.2001 was on the strength of the 82ª Squadriglia, 21º Gruppo, 51º Stormo of the Co-Belligerent Air Force, based at Puglia towards the end of 1943.

Compared to Allied fighters such as the Spitfire and P-51, the cockpit of the Falco II was cramped and visibility was rather poor.

All Re.2000 series fighters were cantilever stressed-skin monoplanes. The basic airframe bore a strong resemblance to the Seversky P-35. This was no coincidence, as the chief engineers of the design, Alessio and Longhi, had worked for Seversky prior to World War II.

A very broad fin made the Re.2000 series instantly recognisable and contributed significantly to its excellent handling.

Powering the Falco II was a 12-cylinder Alfa Romeo RA.1000. Essentially a copy of the DB.601, this engine offered only a slight performance gain over the Piaggio P.XI radial of the earlier Re.2000.

Most Re.2001s were built as night-fighters and were fitted with a 20-mm (0.79-in.) cannon under each wing, mounted in a gondola. They proved quite effective against medium- and heavy-bombers.

A feature unique to the Re.2001 variant was the fixed tailwheel. Both the radial-engined Falco and the later Re.2005 Sagitarrio featured fully-retractable tailwheels.

### COMBAT DATA

#### MAXIMUM SPEED

Both the Bf 109K and Re.2005 were powered by essentially the same engine, but superior aerodynamics made the Italian machine discernably quicker. Neither was a match for the Spitfire, however.

Re.2005 630 km/h (390 m.p.h.)
Bf 109K-4 608 km/h (377 m.p.h.)
SPITFIRE FR.Mk XIVe 721 km/h (447 m.p.h.)

#### RANGE

Throughout World War II, short range remained the Achilles heel of the Spitfire and Bf 109. Italian fighters, in particular late-war types such as the Re.2005, had much greater endurance and could loiter for longer periods.

Re.2005 SAGITTARIO 1250 km (775 mi.)
Bf 109K-4 573 km (355 mi.)
SPITFIRE FR.Mk XIVe 845 km (525 mi.)

#### ARMAMENT

Armed with two and three 20-mm (0.79-in.) cannon respectively, both the Spitfire and Sagitarrio were formidable opponents in battle; despite their heavy armament, they retained excellent agility.

Re.2005 SAGITTARIO
3 x 20-mm (0.79-in.) cannon, 2 x 12.7-mm (.50 cal.) machine-guns

Bf 109K-4
1 x 30-mm (1.18-in.) cannon, 2 x 15-mm (0.59-in.) machine-guns

SPITFIRE FR.Mk XIVe
2 x 20-mm (0.79-in.) cannon, 2 x 12.7-mm (.50 cal.) machine-guns

## Falcos in service with the Regia Aeronautica

■ **REGGIANE Re.2000:** Prior to the Armistice, Regia Aeronautica aircraft wore distinctive white recognition bands.

■ **REGGIANE Re.2001 2º GRUPPO:** Among the last Falco IIs fighting with the Regia Aeronautica were those of 2º Gruppo.

■ **REGGIANE Re.2001 22º GRUPPO:** Painted in the standard dark green, this Falco II served with one of the most famous units.

# REPUBLIC

## P-47 THUNDERBOLT (RAZORBACK)

● Fighter-bomber ● Heavy and powerful ● European service debut

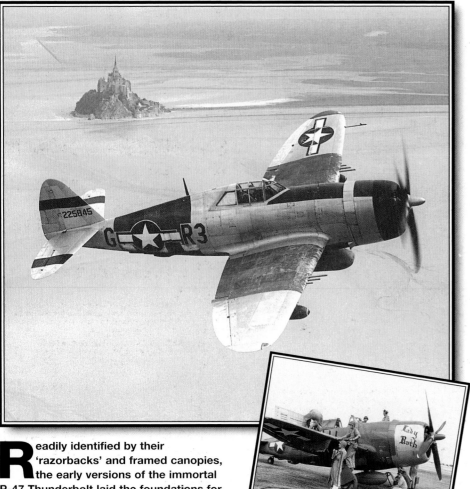

**R**eadily identified by their 'razorbacks' and framed canopies, the early versions of the immortal P-47 Thunderbolt laid the foundations for what was to become an unrivalled fast and immensely robust aircraft. 'Razorback' Thunderbolts were built by Republic and Curtiss-Wright and had a dominant role in the USAAF from 1943, firstly as a fighter, then as a fighter-bomber making sweeps over occupied Europe.

▲ *If the 'razorback' early P-47s had a weakness it was the 20° blindspot behind the cockpit. This was rectified in the late-production P-47Ds and other 'bubble'-canopied variants.*

# REPUBLIC P-47 THUNDERBOLT (RAZORBACK)

**▼ RAF Thunderbolt Mk I**
*In the RAF the P-47B (pictured below) and the P-47D were known as the Thunderbolt Mk I and Mk II, respectively. Most were deployed in the Far East.*

**▲ First 'Juggernauts' in combat**
*These P-47Bs were among the first delivered to a fighting unit, the 56th Fighter Group. They arrived in England in late 1942 to prove the type in combat.*

**▼ Carrier-borne in the Pacific**
*USAAF P-47s were delivered from Hawaii to the Marianas aboard USS Manila Bay in June 1944.*

**▲ Built at three factories**
*Thunderbolts were produced by Republic at factories in Evansville, Indiana, and Long Island, New York, and by Curtiss-Wright in Buffalo, New York.*

**Preserved 'warbird' example ▶**
*A number of 'razorback' P-47s, including this P-47G, have been restored to airworthy condition.*

## FACTS AND FIGURES

➤ Like the P-51 Mustang, the P-47 was conceived, tested and put into service entirely during the war years.

➤ The first P-47 was accepted by the USAAF on 21 December 1941.

➤ 'Razorback' P-47Ds were also supplied to the air forces of France and the USSR.

➤ The 56th Fighter Group, the first unit to take the P-47 into combat, was the top-scoring US fighter group with 674½ kills.

➤ A fully-loaded P-47D weighed more than 2.5 times as much as a Bf 109.

➤ The P-47's massive four-bladed propeller had a diameter of 3.76 m (12 ft 4 in).

**PROFILE**

# Brute force of the 'Juggernaut'

Thunderbolts reached England just before Christmas 1942. The first operational sweep over Europe was made by the 4th Fighter Group on 10 March 1943 and was the beginning of an incredible success story.

The first known combat occurred on 15 April 1943 when the 4th Group came up against Focke-Wulf Fw 190s. P-47 pilot Major Donald Blakeslee intercepted a flight of three and was able to shoot one down over Ostend, Belgium, to claim the Thunderbolt's first aerial victory.

'Razorback' P-47s were flown by many of the best-known American air aces, including Francis Gabreski, Robert Johnson and 'Bud' Mahurin.

Unable to escort bombers far into Europe (until later versions were fitted with external fuel tanks), the P-47 gained a greater reputation as a fighter-bomber, sharing the role of train- and tank-buster with the British Typhoon. Like the Typhoon, P-47s were fitted with bombs and rockets.

The first version to enter service was the P-47B, of which 171 were built. This was followed

*Below: This aircraft was one of two TP-47G trainers converted from Curtiss-Wright-built P-47Gs. The front seat displaced a fuel tank.*

*Above: On 4 August 1944, this XP-47J, powered by a 1566-kW (2100-hp) R-2800-57 engine, reached a record speed of 811 km/h (504 mph).*

by the C model (602 built), with a lengthened fuselage and provision for a 227-kg (500-lb) bomb or drop-tank. The most widely produced version was the P-47D, which had increased power and bombload.

The 'razorback' of the early Thunderbolts was a feature of the earlier Kartveli designs, the Seversky P-35 and the Republic P-43 Lancer.

## P-47D THUNDERBOLT

42-22490 'Beetle' was serving with the 358th Fighter Squadron, 355th Fighter Group on escort and attack missions when it force-landed at Caen, France, on 7 November 1943. It was soon flown by the Luftwaffe from their Rechlin test centre.

The P-47 was originally conceived as a lightweight fighter, but it was redesigned as the XP-47B to improve top speed. The prototype first flew on 6 May 1941. Weighing in at 6059 kg (13,358 lb), it was the heaviest single-seat fighter adopted by the USAAF.

P-47Bs entered service in Europe in early-1943 in the bomber escort role. Early experience revealed an inadequate climb rate and poor manoeuvrability, but dive performance was good. Its ability to survive battle damage became legendary.

Based on Alexander Kartveli's earlier P-44 design, the P-47 was built around one of the most powerful engines then available, the Pratt & Whitney R-2800 18-cylinder, two-row radial. The variant used in the P-47D employed water injection to boost performance at altitude.

The R-2800 engine's turbocharger was positioned in the rear fuselage, fed by a duct from below the engine. Here it could be adequately cooled and allowed a more aerodynamic engine cowling arrangement. A waste gate either expelled the hot air to the atmosphere or diverted it to the turbo.

## Pre-war Seversky/Republic aircraft

**■ SEV-3:** This three-seat, twin-float aircraft first flew in June 1933. Seversky's first aircraft, the SEV-3M-WW version, was built for Colombia.

**■ BT-8:** This two-seat basic trainer for the US Army Air Corps was powered by a 335-kW Pratt & Whitney Twin Wasp. Thirty were built.

**■ P-35:** Flown in 1935, this fighter, with retractable landing gear, was built in limited numbers for the USAAC. Sweden received 60.

**■ P-43 LANCER:** By the time the P-43 appeared, Seversky had become Republic. This 580 km/h (360 mph) fighter was the basis for the P-47.

# REPUBLIC

# P-47D/M/N THUNDERBOLT

● Tactical fighter-bomber ● Long-range escort ● Train-buster

▲ While the P-47 will always be remembered as an escort fighter, the beefy warplane was perhaps even more effective as a fighter-bomber.

**M**ore Republic P-47 Thunderbolts were built than any other US fighter. The 'Jug', named for its bulky shape, was a monster of a machine, yet it was fast and manoeuvrable. The pilot had enormous power at his fingertips and knew that if his aircraft was hit by gunfire, he had an excellent chance of getting home safely. From the early XP-47B to the final P-47N, the 'T-bolt' was a real winner.

## REPUBLIC P-47D/M/N THUNDERBOLT

### ▼ Pacific island-hopper
*Two Thunderbolts power into the air from a temporary coral air strip on a Pacific island. P-47s were employed in every theatre of the war, flying air-to-air and air-to-ground missions.*

### Rocket launcher ▶
*Tube-launched rockets were a fearsome addition to the Thunderbolt's armoury. The fighters decimated German armour in France in 1944 using this weapon, flying precision low-level attack missions.*

### ▲ Air superiority
*The P-47N was the ultimate Thunderbolt. It had an immensely powerful engine which made it the fastest piston-engined fighter in the world, and had increased fuel capacity to enable it to accompany B-29 bombers over the Pacific.*

### ▼ Crash and burn
*Thunderbolts were famed for their enormous strength and ability to survive damage, but this aircraft did not fly again after crash-landing.*

### ▲ French dive-bomber
*France was one of many countries that used the P-47 into the 1950s. The aircraft were used as dive-bombers in French Indochina, often dropping napalm tanks.*

## FACTS AND FIGURES

➤ The first Thunderbolt was the XP-47B, which flew on 6 May 1941.

➤ According to designer Alexander Kartveli, the layout of the P-47 was drawn on the back of an envelope at a meeting in 1940.

➤ 15,683 Thunderbolts were built between 1940 and 1945, with more 'D' models than any other aircraft sub-type in history.

➤ With a fully loaded weight of 9390 kg, a late-model P-47N was heavier than a bombed-up Dornier Do 17 bomber.

➤ On 5 August 1944, a specially prepared Thunderbolt attained a speed of 811 km/h (504 m.p.h.), a record for WWII fighters.

➤ 'Jugs' flew over 500,000 combat sorties between March 1943 and August 1945.

## PROFILE

# Biggest, fastest and meanest

Never beautiful like the Spitfire, not as agile as the Bf 109, nor as long-legged as the P-51 Mustang, the big Republic P-47 Thunderbolt nevertheless was one of the most successful and best-loved fighters of all time. With its huge R-2800 engine driving a colossal 3.71-m (12-ft.) propeller, the Thunderbolt was well suited to long-distance escort operations. With its ability to haul bombs and absorb punishment, it was equally well suited to ground attack.

The P-47 is remembered for ranging over European skies, where aces like those of Colonel Hubert 'Hub' Zemke's 56th Fighter Group valiantly fought the Luftwaffe. But the 'Jug' was widely used elsewhere. Among Allied forces during World War II, Thunderbolts were flown by the Brazilian, British, French, Mexican and Russian pilots. The long-range P-47N fought in the Pacific, where it was a potent weapon against the Japanese. Another service variant was the 'hot-rod' P-47M, which was quickly produced in the summer of 1944 to counter the V-1 flying bombs.

*The P-47 was an excellent fighter, but gained its legendary reputation flying hard-hitting ground-attack missions.*

### P-47D Thunderbolt

**Type:** single-seat fighter and fighter-bomber

**Powerplant:** one 1715-kW (2,535-hp.) Pratt & Whitney R-2800-59 Double Wasp 18-cylinder radial engine

**Maximum speed:** 697 km/h (430 m.p.h.)

**Range:** 3000 km (1,860 mi.) with drop-tanks

**Service ceiling:** 13,000 m (42,000 ft.)

**Weight:** empty 4853 kg (10,660 lb.); loaded 7938 kg (17,500 lb.); later versions: loaded 9390 kg (20,700 lb.)

**Armament:** eight 12.7-mm (.50 cal.) Browning M2 machine-guns with 267 to 500 rounds; plus provision for maximum external load of 1134 kg (2,500 lb.) including bombs, napalm or eight rockets

**Dimensions:**  span 12.42 m (40 ft. 9 in.)
length 11.02 m (36 ft. 2 in.)
height 4.30 m (14 ft. 2 in.)
wing area 27.87 m² (300 sq. ft.)

## P-47D THUNDERBOLT

This 'D' model P-47 was flown by the 527th Fighter Squadron, 86th Fighter Group, serving in North Africa, Sicily and Italy in the close-support role.

Early P-47s were known as 'Razorbacks' to pilots. Cutting down the rear fuselage and fitting a bubble canopy greatly improved rear views.

Thunderbolts were fitted with eight 12.7-mm (50-cal.) machine-guns. Although lightly gunned by British or German standards, they proved highly effective.

Drop-tanks greatly increased the P-47's already impressive range.

The P-47's paddle-bladed propeller gave it an exceptional climb rate.

The huge fuselage of the P-47 was the cause of many jokes when the fighter entered service. A fully loaded 'Jug' was about three times heavier than an early Spitfire.

The massive R-2800 engine was the most powerful fitted to a single-engine fighter in the war. With turbocharging, late variants delivered 2090 kW (2,535 hp.). An experimental P-47 touched 800 km/h (497 m.p.h.) in 1946, thanks to the power of this engine.

Tactical support missions were usually flown with an underwing armament of a pair of 500-kg (1,100-lb.) bombs or eight rockets.

### COMBAT DATA

#### MAXIMUM SPEED

| | |
|---|---|
| Bf 109G | 690 km/h (428 m.p.h.) |
| P-47D THUNDERBOLT | 697 km/h (430 m.p.h.) |
| Ki-84 | 624 km/h (388 m.p.h.) |

The P-47D was introduced in 1943, and immediately proved itself at least as fast as anything else in the sky in Europe, until the advent of the powered Me 163 Komet rocket in 1944. It had considerably greater performance than the best of its Pacific opposition, although Japanese aircraft like the Nakajima Ki-84 'Frank' were much more agile.

#### RANGE

Nothing could be more striking than the difference between fighters intended for a close-range European war, such as the Bf 109, and those like the P-47 and the Ki-84, whose designers had the vast operational distances of the Pacific in mind. It was the Thunderbolt's range which made it such a capable escort fighter.

P-47D THUNDERBOLT 3000 km (1,860 mi.)

Bf 109G 700 km (435 mi.)

Ki-84 'FRANK' 2900 km (1,800 mi.)

#### SERVICE CEILING

American bombers were designed to attack from high altitude, so American fighters had to be equally capable at great heights. The P-47's immensely powerful Double Wasp engine pulled the 'T-bolt' higher than most of its rivals. The Messerschmitt was also good near its slightly lower altitude limits, but Japanese fighters simply could not compete.

Ki-84 'FRANK' 10,500 m (34,400 ft.)

Bf109G 11,600 m (38,000 ft.)

P-47D THUNDERBOLT 13,000 m (42,000 ft.)

## All-the-way bomber escort

The P-47 Thunderbolt and the P-51 Mustang changed the war in the air. American bombers could now attack anywhere in the Reich, secure in the knowledge that they were being escorted all the way.

**TEAMWORK DEFENCE:** The P-47 originally lacked the range to go all the way to Berlin with the bombers. It was used to protect the B-17s and B-24s on the outward and homeward legs of the flight, handing over responsibility to the long-range P-51 for the central portion of the mission.

**TARGET: BERLIN**

1. 8th Air Force bombers form up over the English coast
2. P-47 Thunderbolts provide escort to the German border
3. P-47s are relieved by P-51 Mustangs
4. Mustangs escort the bombers all the way to the target and back
5. Fresh P-47s escort the bombers home

# ROYAL AIRCRAFT FACTORY

# B.E.2

● **Two-seat reconnaissance** ● **Western Front light bomber**

▲ *The inherent stability of the B.E.2, an important feature in the reconnaissance role, proved to be the type's downfall, especially during the 'Fokker Scourge' of 1915/16.*

**D**eveloped at the Farnborough home of the Royal Aircraft Factory, the original B.E.2 was flown for the first time in February 1912 and remained in service until the end of World War I. By the start of the war at least three Royal Flying Corps squadrons were using the unarmed B.E.2a, and later versions, armed but still lacking in manoeuvrability, were operational on the Western Front in 1917.

## ROYAL AIRCRAFT FACTORY B.E.2

▼ **Wartime service**
*In service throughout World War I, the B.E.2 served initially as a spotter aircraft, Zeppelin interceptor and light bomber until its vulnerability forced remaining aircraft to be redeployed to a training role.*

▲ **B.E.12 fighter**
*The B.E.12a was an attempt to build a single-seat fighter based on the B.E.2's airframe. A bigger engine was fitted but its agility was still poor.*

▼ **In the bomber role**
*This RFC B.E.2c 'Tasmania' carries a small load of bombs.*

◄ **Post-war service**
*After 1918 many B.E.2s, like other wartime RFC types, found their way into Britain's fledgling civil aviation market.*

◄ **Artillery spotter**
*B.E.2s made their mark as reconnaissance aircraft during the first months of 1915.*

▲ **A gift from Imperial lands**
*This B.E.2c carries the wording 'Presented by the Indian Nobles'. Presentation aircraft such as this were paid for by wealthy benefactors.*

### FACTS AND FIGURES

➤ Geoffrey de Havilland, later a famous manufacturer himself, flew the first B.E.2 in trials.

➤ The first B.E.2, a development of the earlier B.E.1, was built and flown in 1912.

➤ Two B.E.2s are in British museums; one is at the Imperial War Museum.

➤ B.E. stood for 'Blériot Experimental', as the B.E.1 was rebuilt from a damaged Blériot monoplane.

➤ Most B.E.2s were built under subcontract in factories other than Farnborough's.

➤ B.E.2s made the first reconnaissance flight by an RFC aircraft in World War I.

**PROFILE**

# RFC's vulnerable two-seat spotter

After the outbreak of war in August 1914, B.E.2as were the first British aircraft to land in France. Like the B.E.2bs that followed, they had no defensive armament but were used for bombing with a single 45-kg (100-lb.) bomb or up to three smaller bombs.

The B.E.2c was a more stable aircraft, making it suitable for reconnaissance and bombing

but limiting its manoeuvrability. It proved a good interceptor of Zeppelin airships, and it claimed to have downed at least four. But against the Fokker Eindecker, with its forward-firing armament, the B.E.2 suffered heavy losses over the Western Front in 1915.

The B.E.2c was also handicapped by having only a trainable gun in the front

cockpit. The B.E.2d of 1916 reversed the crew positions to seat the observer in the rear and added a forward-firing gun. The later B.E.2e reverted to the original arrangement, however.

More than 3,000 B.E.2s were built by more than 20 manufacturers. They served in the Aegean, North Africa and the Middle East, as well as in France.

*Above: Built by Denny and Brothers in Dumbarton, Scotland, this B.E.2e was flown by Australian airline QANTAS.*

*Below: Blackburn was among several firms that built more than 3000 B.E.2s during World War I.*

### B.E.2c

**Type:** two-seat reconnaissance and light-bombing aircraft

**Powerplant:** one 67-kW (90-hp.) RAF 1a eight-cylinder air-cooled inline engine

**Maximum speed:** 138 km/h (86 m.p.h.) at sea level

**Climb rate:** 1066 m (3,500 ft.) in 10 mins

**Service ceiling:** 3050 m (10,000 ft.)

**Weights:** empty 621 kg (1,366 lb.); loaded 1077 kg (2,370 lb.)

**Armament:** one trainable 7.7-mm (.303 cal.) machine-gun, up to 100 kg (220 lb.) of bombs or rockets

**Dimensions:** span 11.30 m (37 ft.); length 8.30 m (27 ft. 3 in.); height 3.40 m (11 ft. 2 in.); wing area 34.47 m² (371 sq. ft.)

A number of World War I designs featured tall, upturned exhaust pipes. These kept potentially harmful, hot, exhaust gases away from the fragile fuselage sides and cockpit area.

Most B.E.2s were fitted with eight-cylinder Royal Aircraft Factory 1a engines, although the first examples had a Renault powerplant of the same configuration.

Although 'B.E.' originally stood for Blériot Experimental, these letters were applied to a number of early RAF designs, the letters later standing for 'Bomber Experimental'.

In most of the two-seat B.E.2s the pilot sat in the rear cockpit with the observer/gunner in the front armed with one or two Lewis 7.7-mm (.303 cal.) machine-guns.

### B.E.2c

One of a batch of 100 B.E.2c aircraft built by Ruston, Proctor and Company Limited, 2713 was fitted with a 67-kW (90-hp.) Royal Aircraft Factory 1a engine.

National markings were usually prominently displayed on military aircraft of the Great War period. Note the large roundels under the wings and the brightly painted rudder markings. The aircraft's serial number is displayed on the forward section of the tailfin.

The relatively flimsy construction of the B.E.2 was a reflection of its early design and the fact that it was intended as a slow and stable observation platform.

### COMBAT DATA

**MAXIMUM SPEED**

Speed was not a strongpoint of the B.E.2 or any of the other early reconnaissance types of the Great War. Stability and endurance were seen as more important attributes. This, however, counted against these machines when fast, agile and well-armed fighters began to appear in the skies over France.

| | |
|---|---|
| B.E.2e | 145 km/h (90 m.p.h.) |
| ALBATROS C.I | 140 km/h (87 m.p.h.) |
| AVIATIK C.I | 142 km/h (88 m.p.h.) |

**ENDURANCE**

The B.E.2 had excellent endurance, which made it a very useful type in its intended reconnaissance and artillery spotting roles. This was also useful in the training role, allowing long flights. Both the German types also had useful endurance, with the Aviatik being the better of the two.

| B.E.2e | ALBATROS C.I | AVIATIK C.I |
|---|---|---|
| 4 hours | 2½ hours | 3 hours |

**ARMAMENT**

In common with other observation aircraft of the period, the B.E.2 had a single machine-gun for self-defence which was operated by the observer. B.E.2 crews also used them in an offensive role against Zeppelins. When up against fighters with forward-firing guns this armament fit was to prove extremely inadequate.

| B.E.2e | 1 x 7.7-mm (.303 cal.) machine-gun |
| ALBATROS C.I | 1 x 7.92-mm machine-gun |
| AVIATIK C.I | 1 x 7.92-mm machine-gun |

## World War I Royal Aircraft Factory designs

■ **F.E.2b:** Entering service in France in 1915, the F.E.2b was an interim solution to the problem of providing forward-firing armament.

■ **R.E.7:** Introduced in 1916 and judged to be unsuitable for reconnaissance, R.E.7s became light bombers and could carry a 152-kg bombload.

■ **R.E.8:** Popularly known as the 'Harry Tate', this aircraft was in many ways a scaled-up B.E.2. Unfortunately it was just as ungainly.

■ **S.E.5:** The S.E.5 and S.E.5a both entered service in France in 1917 and became formidable fighters after early teething problems.

# ROYAL AIRCRAFT FACTORY

# F.E.2

● Pusher engine design ● Two-seat fighter ● Night bomber

**A**s a companion to the Airco DH.2, the Farman Experimental 2b (F.E.2b) pusher-fighter was a vital component of the Royal Flying Corps' scout force over the Western Front in 1916. The German Fokker Eindekker had been taking a terrible toll of Allied aircraft and the introduction of the F.E.2b helped redress the balance. With an excellent field of fire and an ability to carry a useful bombload, the F.E.2 also served as a day and night bomber.

▲ *This F.E.2b*
*built by Weir was used for experiments in the use of airborne searchlights for home defence at night. A generator-powered light was attached to two 7.7-mm (.303 cal.) Lewis guns.*

## ROYAL AIRCRAFT FACTORY F.E.2

**Under repair▶**
*The simple construction of World War I fighters meant that many could be repaired after serious crashes. This F.E.2 from No. 18 Squadron, RFC, is seen after a landing accident in France.*

**◀ Tandem seating**
*The pilot sitting in the rear cockpit had a good view over the gunner.*

**Coastal patrol ▶**
*Based at the Isle of Grain at the mouth of the Thames for anti-submarine patrols, this F.E.2b is seen with flotation bags.*

**◀ F.E.2d prototype**
*The F.E.2d was fitted with a bigger Rolls-Royce Eagle engine.*

**F.E.2b at war ▶**
*Without the obstruction of an engine and propeller in front of them, the pilot and observer had an excellent all-round view. Although the aircraft did not have remarkable performance, it proved to be effective against the Fokker Eindekker.*

## FACTS AND FIGURES

➤ The revised F.E.2 of 1913 was destroyed in a fatal crash in February 1914 when the pilot, R. Kemp, lost control in a dive.

➤ On 18 June 1916 a No. 25 Squadron F.E.2b claimed the German ace Max Immelmann.

➤ Most of No. 20 Squadron's record 600 kills from 1914 to 1918 were made by the F.E.2b.

➤ After withdrawal from daylight operations, the F.E.2b became the RFC's standard night bomber until August 1918.

➤ On 31 May 1918 a coastal patrol F.E.2b sank U-boat *UC 49* with two 45-kg bombs.

➤ In 1916-17 816 F.E.2s were allocated to fighter duties and 395 to bomber duties.

## PROFILE

# The RFC's finest pusher fighter

Uniquely among Royal Aircraft Factory machines, the F.E.2 existed in two entirely dissimilar forms. The first F.E.2 was actually a rebuilt F.E.1 and first flew in 1911. In 1913 this aircraft was entirely redesigned and rebuilt, and was the first in the successful series of wartime F.E.2 fighters.

The first major production version was the F.E.2b which featured twin-Lewis gun armament and entered operational service with No. 6 Squadron, RFC, in September 1915. The arrival of these aircraft in France throughout the autumn of 1915 marked the beginning of the Eindekker's decline.

Although slower than other types, the F.E.2b proved to be an excellent gun platform and the introduction of the larger 119.3-kW (160-hp.) Beardmore engine kept the aircraft competitive until the spring of 1917.

Other versions included the specialist F.E.2c night-fighter, in which the positions of the pilot and observer were reversed to give the pilot the best possible view forward for night landings, and the F.E.2d powered by a Rolls-Royce Eagle engine.

*Left: During 1917-18 the F.E.2b became an important ground-attack type. This No. 149 Squadron example is being loaded with a 50.8-kg (112-lb.) high-explosive bomb beneath the fuselage*

*Below: Night bombing raids were carried out by the F.E.2b. This one is fully 'bombed-up' for another sortie.*

### F.E.2b

**Type:** two-seat fighter and fighter-bomber

**Powerplant:** one 119.3-kW (160-hp.) Beardmore liquid-cooled in-line engine

**Maximum speed:** 147 km/h (91 m.p.h.)

**Initial climb rate:** 39 min 44 sec to 3048 m (10,000 ft.)

**Endurance:** 3 hours

**Service ceiling:** 3353 m (11,000 ft.)

**Weights:** empty 935 kg (2,057 lb.); maximum take-off 1378 kg (3,032 lb.)

**Armament:** one or two 7.7-mm (.303 cal.) Lewis machine-guns plus up to 235 kg (517 lb.) of bombs carried externally

**Dimensions:**
| | | |
|---|---|---|
| span | 14.55 m | (47 ft. 9 in.) |
| length | 9.83 m | (32 ft. 3 in.) |
| height | 3.85 m | (12 ft. 8 in.) |
| wing area | 45.89 m² | (494 sq. ft.) |

---

On the F.E.2b the pilot sat in the rear cockpit with the observer/gunner in the front. The observer fired either a trainable Lewis gun mounted on the front of the cockpit or one mounted on a pillar between the cockpits, which he fired by standing up and facing backwards.

The wooden structure of the biplane wings was covered with doped fabric. The first F.E.2bs had wings of R.A.F.6 section, which were later replaced by R.A.F.14 section wings with a larger angle of incidence.

### F.E.2B

F.E.2bs were used by 16 Royal Flying Corps squadrons on the Western Front in France, along with six home defence squadrons. Other RFC F.E.2bs were used for coastal patrol and night training.

A number of different powerplants were fitted to the F.E.2 series. The F.E.2b was initially powered by an 89.5-kW (120-hp.) Beardmore engine; later F.E.2bs used a 119.3-kW (160-hp.) unit. The F.E.2d was powered by the much larger 186.4-kW (250-hp.) Rolls-Royce Eagle.

The tail empennage was fabric-covered and was mounted at the end of two pairs of converging wooden booms. A wooden tailskid prevented damage to the rear of the aircraft.

A5448

---

### COMBAT DATA

#### MAXIMUM SPEED

Pusher designs were generally slower than their tractor-engined counterparts, but this drawback was overcome in the F.E.2 by its excellent field of fire and manoeuvrability. The later F.E.2 and DH.2 were far faster than the earlier F.B.5.

| | |
|---|---|
| F.E.2b | 147 km/h (90 m.p.h.) |
| DH.2 | 150 km/h (93 m.p.h.) |
| F.B.5 'GUNBUS' | 113 km/h (70 m.p.h.) |

#### ARMAMENT

The F.E.2b is the only one of the types which was extensively used for bombing. It would usually carry Cooper bombs beneath the wings and could also carry a high explosive bomb beneath the fuselage. The F.E.2 had double the firepower of the other types.

| | |
|---|---|
| F.E.2B | 2 x 7.7-mm (.303 cal.) machine-gun 235-kg (517-lb.) bombload |
| DH.2 | 1 x 7.7-mm (.303 cal.) machine-gun |
| F.B.5 'GUNBUS' | 1 x 7.7-mm (.303 cal.) machine-gun |

#### SERVICE CEILING

Flying at high altitudes was extremely uncomfortable in open-cockpit aircraft because of the cold. However, it was important to gain tactical advantage over enemy aircraft and height could be converted to speed. The DH.2 was a lighter single-seat design and had the best ceiling. The F.B.5 was at a disadvantage.

F.E.2b — 3353 m (11,000 ft.)
DH.2 — 4265 m (14,000 ft.)
F.B.5 — 2743 m (9,000 ft.)

---

## Piston pusher fighters

**■ AIRCO DH.1:** Geoffrey de Havilland's first design after joining Airco was this two-seat reconnaissance fighter which served until 1917.

**■ RAF F.E.8:** More than 180 F.E.8s served with the Royal Flying Corps from 1916, but were quickly declared obsolete.

**■ VICKERS F.B.5 'GUNBUS':** The Fighting Biplane No. 5 (F.B.5) was designed specifically as a fighter and entered service in 1915.

**■ VICKERS TYPE 161:** In 1929 the Air Ministry was looking for designs to carry the 37-mm C.O.W. gun. The Type 161 first flew in 1931.

# ROYAL AIRCRAFT FACTORY

# R.E.8

● Reconnaissance bomber ● World War I ● Europe and Middle East

▲ As they replaced the B.E. series two-seaters, it was hoped that the new R.E.8s would improve the fortunes of the RFC's reconnaissance units and their crews. However, losses were still high.

**M**ore than 4000 R.E.8s were produced during World War I. Like other aircraft produced by the Royal Aircraft Factory (which became the Royal Aircraft Establishment in 1918 to avoid confusion with the newly formed RAF), they were designed to be stable in flight, but were thus short on manoeuvrability. However, with a useful gun armament and light bombs, they were to be the RFC's most widely used reconnaissance type.

▼ **Presentation aircraft**
*Lamberhurst was a late production R.E.8 built by the Siddeley-Deasy Motor Co. Ltd, at Coventry. Apart from the Royal Aircraft Factory, five companies built R.E.8s.*

▲ **Defensive machine-guns**
*The R.E.8 had much better armament than the B.E.2. It was fitted with forward-firing Vickers and rear-mounted Lewis machine-guns.*

**'Somewhere in France'** ▶
*Surrounded by friendly troops, this No. 9 Squadron, RFC, aircraft has come to grief, possibly after a tangle with the enemy or an engine failure.*

▼ **Mesopotamia, 1918**
*As well as the Western Front, R.E.8s served in the Middle East and Italy during World War I. These No. 63 Squadron, RAF aircraft are seen in Mesopotamia, where the unit remained until 1920.*

▲ **Widely employed**
*The most widely used of the RFC's reconnaissance types, the R.E.8 was employed by only one Allied country. Belgium took delivery of 22 in July 1917. Replacement began after 10 months.*

## FACTS AND FIGURES

➤ In a pun on the aircraft's designation, the R.E.8 was nicknamed the 'Harry Tate' after a music-hall comedian of the day.

➤ Two R.E.8s have survived; one is at the Imperial War Museum, Duxford.

➤ Night bombing was undertaken by R.E.8s at the Battle of Ypres.

➤ After the two prototypes, 4430 R.E.8s were ordered; by late 1918, 4077 had been delivered and the others were cancelled.

➤ During August 1917, a number of RFC R.E.8s shot down German single-seaters.

➤ Plans to fit Rolls-Royce Eagles to R.E.8s were cancelled due to engine shortages.

**PROFILE**

# 'Harry Tate' on the Western Front

After the R.E.8 prototype had been tested in France in mid-1916, large-scale production was ordered. R.E. stood for Reconnaissance Experimental, but the aircraft was actually used in a host of roles, including artillery spotting, ground strafing, light bombing and supply-dropping to troops.

The first squadron equipped with the type arrived on the Western Front in November 1916. By the end of 1917 there were 18 R.E.8 squadrons. Early models tended to spin easily, but a bigger tailfin cured the problem.

More than 2000 were used in France, while another 300 served in the Middle East. They bombed the Turkish forces in Palestine, and carried supplies in Mesopotamia. Others were used in Italy and Russia and by the Belgian air force.

Although it equipped 19 RAF squadrons in 1918, the R.E.8 was retired quickly once the fighting was over. Although an easy target for German fighters, it had become a standard type because of the sheer numbers built.

*Below: Evidently under repair, this R.E.8 carries the markings of No. 34 Squadron, RFC, based at Villers-Brettoneux during the spring of 1917.*

*Above: Named* Spitfire, *this unarmed R.E.8 was with No. 35 Reserve Squadron, based in Britain.*

## R.E.8

**Type:** reconnaissance, artillery and light bombing aircraft

**Powerplant:** one 112-kW (150-hp.) RAF 4a air-cooled V-12 piston engine

**Maximum speed:** 164 km/h (102 m.p.h.) at 1980 m (6,500 ft.)

**Endurance:** 4 hours 15 min

**Service ceiling:** 4115 m (13,500 ft.)

**Weights:** empty 717 kg (1,577 lb.); maximum take-off 1301 kg (2,862 lb.)

**Armament:** two or three 7.7-mm (.303 cal.) machine-guns plus up to 116 kg of bombs, made up of two 51-kg (112-lb.), four 29-kg (64-lb.) or eight 9-kg (20-lb.) bombs

**Dimensions:**
| | | |
|---|---|---|
| span | 12.98 m | (42 ft. 7 in.) |
| length | 8.50 m | (27 ft. 10 in.) |
| height | 3.47 m | (11 ft. 4 in.) |
| wing area | 35.07 m² | (389 sq. ft.) |

A prominent feature of the R.E.8 was its exhaust system, which directed smoke and fumes above the top wing and away from the aircraft's crew.

Having apparently forgotten the lessons learned during the service life of the B.E.2, the R.E.8 was an inherently stable aircraft, ideal for artillery spotting, but vulnerable to attack by agile enemy fighters.

## R.E.8

C5048 was one of a batch of 100 'Harry Tates' built by Coventry Ordnance Works Limited. This aircraft was operated by No. 16 Squadron, RFC, in France during 1917/18.

Defensive armament consisted of two machine-guns: a fixed, synchronised, forward-firing 7.7-mm (.303 cal.) Vickers controlled by the pilot, and a pivoting 7.7-mm Lewis mounted on a Scarff ring in the observer's cockpit. On some aircraft the latter carried twin Lewis guns.

After the type was introduced in small quantities in France in 1916, a number were lost in accidents. Investigations revealed a tendency to spin, which was rectified by increasing the area of the tail fin. This aircraft has the revised fin.

Standard R.E.8s were fitted with an air-cooled 12-cylinder Royal Aircraft Factory 4a engine rated at 112 kW (140 hp.) and driving a four-bladed propeller. A small number of aircraft were fitted with a 149-kW RAF 4d engine; a few others had Hispano-Suiza powerplants.

RFC R.E.8s had a bombload capacity of 102 kg (224 lb.), made up of two 51-kg (112 lb.) bombs or more lighter bombs.

The airframe was a conventional wire-braced, fabric-covered wooden structure. The mainplanes were of unequal span. Military equipment included a camera and a wireless transmitter.

**ACTION DATA**

**SERVICE CEILING**

Compared to other designs like the Rumpler C.1a and Breguet 14A.2, the R.E.8 had a limited service ceiling of just over 4115 m (13,000 ft.). This made the aircraft more vulnerable to attack from high-flying enemy fighters approaching from 'out of the sun' to surprise their quarry.

R.E.8 4115 m (13,500 ft.)
C.1a 5000 m (16,400 ft.)
14A.2 6000 m (19,700 ft.)

**ENDURANCE**

R.E.8s had a good endurance, useful for the reconnaissance and artillery spotting roles. This allowed sorties over greater distances with longer 'loiter' times over the target.

R.E.8 4 hours 15 min
C.1a 4 hours
14A.2 3 hours

**ARMAMENT**

'Harry Tates' compared well with other reconnaissance and light bomber types, having a defensive armament of two (or three in some cases) machine-guns and a 102-kg bombload.

R.E.8 2 x 7.7-mm (.303 cal.) machine-guns 102-kg (224-lb.) bombload

C.1a 3 x 7.7-mm (.303 cal.) machine-guns 40-kg (88-lb.) bombload

14A.2 2 x 7.92-mm machine-guns 100-kg (220-lb.) bombload

## Warplanes over Palestine

■ **ALBATROS C.III:** Once the C.III was outclassed over the Western Front in 1917, this reconnaissance type was sent to Palestine.

■ **AIRCO DH.2:** The RFC's first true single-seat fighter, the pusher-prop DH.2 was among more types sent to Palestine from 1916.

■ **RAF B.E.2:** Predecessors of the R.E.8, B.E.2s were among the first British aircraft committed to the Middle East in 1915.

■ **RUMPLER C.IV:** A few C.IV reconnaissance aircraft were sent to Palestine in 1917 to 'spot' for Turkish artillery forces.

# ROYAL AIRCRAFT FACTORY

# S.E.5A

● Single-seat scout biplane fighter ● Flown by Britain's top aces

▲ The S.E.5a was easy to fly, without the handling vices of more agile scouts. This was vital in an era when as many pilots were killed in accidents as in air combat.

**D**esigned by H.P. Folland at the Royal Aircraft Factory in Farnborough, the S.E.5a was one of the finest scout aircraft to fly in World War I. Despite early teething troubles, it went on to achieve great success in the hands of aces like William 'Billy' Bishop, Ray Collishaw and Edward 'Mick' Mannock. Beautifully proportioned in spite of its angular lines, the S.E.5a was very fast and provided a very stable gun platform, qualities which more than compensated for its slight lack of agility.

## ROYAL AIRCRAFT FACTORY S.E.5A

▲ **Replica pair**
Precise in every detail, these two S.E.5as are in fact replicas. They were flown in Canada and the United States in the 1970s.

▲ **The Aces' favourite**
Although not the best dogfighter of the time, the S.E.5a was fast. This made it the preferred aircraft of the aces, most of whom achieved success by stalking their targets from behind.

**Kill record ▶**
A pilot proudly records his squadron's grim tally of victims. The S.E.5 gave the Allies an aircraft capable of taking on and beating Germany's best.

▲ **Still flying after 80 years**
This immaculate S.E.5a is part of the Shuttleworth Trust collection at Old Warden in England, and is one of the few original aircraft still flying.

▼ **Squadron on show**
Posing for a photograph, a squadron shows off its new machines. The S.E.5 was an aircraft to be proud of, and together with the Sopwith Camel did much to regain Allied air superiority during late 1917.

▲ **Bad landing**
American pilots flew the S.E.5 as well as various French aircraft. They suffered an equally appalling loss rate as their Allies.

## FACTS AND FIGURES

➤ The S.E.5 entered service on the Western Front in March 1917, followed by the more reliable S.E.5a in June.

➤ Major 'Mick' Mannock racked up 50 of his 73 aerial victories flying the S.E.5a.

➤ Elliott Springs became an early American ace flying S.E.5 scouts.

➤ The tough little S.E.5 was so rugged that one pilot flew it through the side of a house and emerged unhurt.

➤ By 1918 the S.E.5a was flown by 21 British and two American squadrons.

➤ Production of the S.E.5 and S.E.5a totalled 5205 aircraft.

## PROFILE

# The saviour of the Royal Flying Corps

The S.E.5 was one of the classic fighters of World War I. Though less manoeuvrable than Britain's other World War I 'great', the Sopwith Camel, the S.E.5 was much faster. It reached the Front in France during 'bloody April' 1917, the blackest month of the war in terms of casualties for the Royal Flying Corps. The S.E.5 was more than a match for the German Albatross, which until then had ruled the skies.

The improved S.E.5a was plagued by problems of an inadequately developed engine and other difficulties, but once these shortcomings were wiped away it excelled in battle, being both fast and an extremely stable gun platform. Flown by most of the top British and Commonwealth aces of World War I, the S.E.5a also equipped units of the American Expeditionary Force.

### S.E.5A

**The S.E.5, together with the Sopwith Camel, turned the tide of the air war at a time when Allied losses had risen to truly catastrophic levels. This aircraft was flown by Major Edward Mannock, Britain's most successful ace.**

The S.E.5a was unusual in having only a single fixed forward-firing weapon. The Vickers machine-gun was mounted above the engine on the starboard side, synchronised to fire through the propeller.

The 149-kW (200-hp.) Hispano-Suiza engine gave the S.E.5a its superior speed. It had teething problems however, and most aircraft had the less temperamental Wolseley Viper engine fitted instead.

As with all aircraft in the early years of flying, the S.E.5a was equipped with a sturdy fixed undercarriage.

The Lewis gun mounted on the wing was magazine-fed, and could be swung down on a rail to change its magazine. It could also fire upwards.

Visibility from the S.E.5's cockpit was excellent, although the long in-line engine obscured the view ahead more than in its snub-nosed contemporary, the Sopwith Camel.

All RFC aircraft carried large and vivid national markings, but like their counterparts in World War II they still found that 'friendly' ground troops would shoot at them.

Aircraft in World War I were built as light as possible to save weight, the skeleton usually being of wood with a fabric skin.

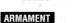

The in-line engine and beautifully-proportioned wing made the S.E.5a an inherently more stable airframe than the Camel, which gained a reputation as a killer of inexperienced young pilots.

Wood and fabric construction meant that the S.E.5 was as much of a death trap as its contemporaries if it caught fire, but it did have exceptional structural strength.

The wedge-shaped tail, which was much more modern-looking than those of its contemporaries, was a key recognition feature of the S.E.5.

### S.E.5a

**Type:** single-seat fighter

**Powerplant:** one 149-kW (200-hp.) Hispano-Suiza V-8 piston engine

**Maximum speed:** 218 km/h (135 m.p.h.)

**Endurance:** 2 hours and 30 minutes

**Service ceiling:** 6705 m (22,000 ft.)

**Weights:** empty 635 kg (1,397 lb.); loaded 887 kg (1,951 lb.)

**Armament:** one forward-firing synchronised 7.7-mm (.303 cal.) Vickers machine-gun and one 7.7-mm Lewis gun mounted over the centre section of the upper wing, plus up to four 18.6-kg (40-lb.) bombs

**Dimensions:**
| | |
|---|---|
| span | 8.12 m (26 ft. 7 in.) |
| length | 6.38 m (20 ft. 11 in.) |
| height | 2.90 m (9 ft. 6 in.) |
| wing area | 22.67 m² (244 sq. ft.) |

### COMBAT DATA

#### MAXIMUM SPEED

The development of aircraft during World War I was rapid, with fighters like the S.E.5a of 1917 being twice as fast as those which had gone to war less than three years before. The S.E.5 was one of the fastest fighters of its time.

| | |
|---|---|
| S.E.5a | 218 km/h (135 m.p.h.) |
| SPAD XIII | 218 km/h (135 m.p.h.) |
| FOKKER DVII | 195 km/h (121 m.p.h.) |

#### ENDURANCE

British warplanes almost invariably conducted long, aggressive patrols deep behind enemy lines. They needed much greater endurance than their German opponents, which were more defensive, rarely crossing into hostile territory.

| S.E.5a | SPAD XIII | FOKKER DVII |
|---|---|---|
| 2.5 hours | 2 hours | 1.5 hours |

#### ARMAMENT

The machine-gun was as much of an influence in the air as it was in the muddy battles on the ground. Most top-class scouts had a pair of guns synchronised to fire through the propeller. The S.E.5 was unusual in that one of its guns was mounted above the wing, and could be aimed upwards into the belly of an enemy aircraft.

**S.E.5a**
1 x Vickers 7.7-mm (.303 cal.)
1 x Lewis 7.7-mm (.303 cal.) machine-gun

**Fokker DVII**
2 x 7.92-mm machine-guns

**SPAD XIII**
2 x 7.7-mm (.303 cal.) Vickers machine-guns

## Aces high in the S.E.5

**ALBERT BALL:** The first British pilot to become nationally known as an ace, Ball switched from Nieuports to the S.E.5 early in 1917, scoring 34 of his 44 victories on the type. An intensely religious loner, Ball disappeared on 7 May 1917. His death remains a mystery, although some experts think that he was shot down by Lothar von Richthofen.

**JAMES McCUDDEN:** Originally a non-commissioned aircraft mechanic, McCudden became a pilot in 1916. Commissioned in January 1917, he joined the famous No. 56 Squadron flying S.E.5s, and was an immediate success. Like Ball, he was a loner, preferring to stalk his prey unaccompanied. He was killed in an accident when his score stood at 57.

**EDWARD MANNOCK:** Mannock transferred to the Royal Flying Corps in 1916 despite being all but blind in one eye. A ruthless fighter, he was an inspiring leader who made sure his pilots received the best possible combat training. He was shot down by ground fire in July 1918 when his score stood at 73, the highest by a British pilot. His body was never found.

# RUMPLER

# C.I

● First of the C-types ● Service on all fronts ● Photo reconnaissance

▲ *Thanks to its unusual construction, the C.I offered both crew members an excellent field of view. It performed some of the first photographic reconnaissance missions.*

I n the early stages of World War I, the Rumpler B.I biplane was widely used as an unarmed scout and reconnaissance aircraft. By 1915, it was becoming obvious that armament was essential for survival over the Western Front. Accordingly, Rumpler developed the C.I – the C-type designation being applied to armed two-seat biplanes with an engine of 112 kW (150 hp.) or more – with a single ring-mounted Parabellum machine-gun in the rear cockpit.

# RUMPLER C.I

**Two-spar wing ▶**
*Sunlight streaming through the canvas covering of this Rumpler's wings throws the internal structure into silhouette. Each wing had two spars and a series of plywood ribs.*

**▼ Exhaust installation**
*A feature of the C.I and C.Ia was the tall exhaust installation. This fed the exhaust gases upwards and over the upper wing, keeping the cockpit free of noxious fumes.*

**▲ Captured Rumpler**
*Several aircraft from both sides fell into enemy hands. This C.I carries British roundels.*

**▼ Field improvements**
*This C.I has been fitted with crude skis. Simply attached to the wheels, the skis would have been easily removable, but tricky to use.*

**Wing cut-outs ▶**
*Experience had shown that the observer often had a less than ideal view from the rear cockpit. Hence, Rumpler put large cut-outs in the wing centre-sections, improving the view considerably.*

## FACTS AND FIGURES

➤ During the 1917 battle for Gaza, a white cloth was laid on the ground whenever a C.I was required to land for instructions.

➤ British prisoners reported the devastation caused by C.I bombing.

➤ Bayerische Rumpler-Werke took responsibility for the trainer version.

➤ Photo reconnaissance was difficult in Gaza, since the heat damaged photographic plates.

➤ After World War I, some C.Is were converted into passenger aircraft.

➤ The German navy received 98 6B 1 and 6B 2 aircraft, based on the C.I.

# Multi-role Rumpler

*Right: Twin floats distinguished the 6B 1 floatplanes, which were otherwise similar to the C.I. The 6B 2 introduced the tail surfaces of the Rumpler C.III.*

After the C.I's service entry in 1915, it soon became clear that the single ring-mounted Parabellum machine-gun in the observer's cockpit offered insufficient firepower. Thus, in common with most C-types, a forward-firing Spandau machine-gun was mounted on the left side of the forward fuselage.

Increasingly accurate Allied anti-aircraft defences meant that greater altitude was required of the C-types. In response, Rumpler introduced the C.Ia, with a 134-kW (180-hp.) Argus As.III engine, which was otherwise almost identical to the C.I. Both types were built by several German manufacturers, and were widely used, serving in Macedonia, Salonika and Palestine as well as over the Western Front.

By the autumn of 1916, there were approximately 250 C.Is and C.Ias in squadron service. They earned a reputation for being very difficult to shoot down, and were the first German aircraft to be used for photographic reconnaissance. Some were still in service 18 months later, although mostly in the training role. In 1918 Rumpler also produced a specialised dual-control trainer, powered by a 112-kW (150-hp) Bz.III engine, with all armament deleted.

*Below: Although it was no great performer in the air, the C.I had a good reputation and was considered a difficult adversary.*

## C.Ia

**Type:** two-seat reconnaissance/general-purpose aircraft

**Powerplant:** one 134-kW (180-hp.) Argus As.III 6-cylinder water-cooled in-line piston engine

**Maximum speed:** 150 km/h (93 m.p.h.) at sea level

**Endurance:** 4 hours

**Service ceiling:** 5000 m (16,200 ft.)

**Weights:** empty 793 kg (1,745 lb.); maximum take-off 1300 kg (2,860 lb.)

**Armament:** one fixed forward-firing 7.92-mm LMG 08/15 machine-gun and one 7.92-mm Parabellum machine-gun in the rear cockpit, plus 100 kg (220 lb.) of light bombs

**Dimensions:**
| | | |
|---|---|---|
| span | 12.15 m | (39 ft. 10 in.) |
| length | 7.85 m | (25 ft. 9 in.) |
| height | 3.05 m | (10 ft.) |
| wing area | 35.70 m² | (356 sq. ft.) |

The tall chimney exhaust became a feature of several Rumpler designs. Engine installation differed according to the powerplant manufacturer and the company building the airframe. All C.I engines were six-cylinder units, fitted with the cylinder heads exposed.

The simple open cockpits afforded the crew little protection. Rumpler was one of the first companies to introduce a frontal engine radiator, mounted in the leading edge of the upper wing. Known as the Stirnkuhler, this installation caused less drag than traditional systems and allowed the pilot a better forward view.

Only the upper wings had ailerons fitted. The surfaces were controlled by a wire which ran through the lower wing and vertically upwards to connect with the aileron.

The fuselage consisted of box-girders, covered by ply sheeting forwards and fabric to the rear. Steel was employed for the framework forward of the cockpit.

Rumpler adopted this style of tail assembly, using it for several later designs. The surfaces were of welded steel tube with fabric covering and all had a triangular shape in plan view.

## C.I

Poland had 21 C.Is on strength in 1919, carrying the red and white shield markings which were used prior to the familiar checkerboard design. Some C.Is, which were used as trainers, survived into 1920.

## ACTION DATA

### MAXIMUM SPEED

Rumpler was one of the first companies to introduce a successful C-type into service. Hannover introduced the CL.IIIA late in the war, which offered greater performance than the earlier types.

| | | |
|---|---|---|
| **RUMPLER C.Ia** | 150 km/h (93 m.p.h.) | |
| **AVIATIK C.I** | 142 km/h (88 m.p.h.) | |
| **CL.IIIA** | 165 km/h (102 m.p.h.) | |

### ENDURANCE

On reconnaissance missions, endurance was important if a number of targets were to be covered or if the progress of a campaign was to be monitored.

**RUMPLER C.Ia** 4 hours    **AVIATIK C.I** 3 hours    **CL.IIIA** 3 hours

### SERVICE CEILING

Flying at a high altitude was the only method of reducing the danger posed by anti-aircraft artillery. Most C-types received more powerful engines during their careers. The C.Ia was moved from the Western Front in the later stages of the war because of its vulnerability and the availability of more advanced types.

**RUMPLER C.Ia** 5000 m (16,200 ft.)    **AVIATIK C.I** 3500 m (11,500 ft.)    **CL.IIIA** 7498 m (24,600 ft.)

## Wartime Rumplers

■ **C.V:** Developed from the C.III, the C.V acted as an intermediate type before the C.VII was introduced. This machine fell into Allied hands.

■ **6A 2:** Powered by a 119-kW (160-hp.) Mercedes engine, the 6A 2 of 1916 was a two-seat experimental fighter.

■ **7D 7:** Developed from the 7D 4, the 7D 7 was one of several prototypes developed to test systems for the D.I.

■ **D.I:** Marking the culmination of a series of Rumpler single-seat fighter designs, the D.I was not adopted for service.

# SAVOIA-MARCHETTI

# S.M.79 SPARVIERO

● Bomber ● Torpedo aircraft ● Three-engined design

▲ The Sparviero crews of the Regia Aeronautica and Aerosiluranti were Italy's best, delivering highly effective blows against British shipping in the Mediterranean in daring torpedo attacks.

**W**ith its robust tri-motor shape and extensive fabric covering, the Savoia-Marchetti S.M.79 Sparviero was very much a creature of the 1930s. Designed for a long-distance air race, it became famous as Italy's most successful bomber. Contrary to wartime propaganda, its British and American foes found the Sparviero an effective and very tough adversary that proved difficult to shoot down.

◀ **Spanish Sparviero**
The Aviazione Legionara of the Italian air force took the S.M.79 into combat during the Spanish Civil War. Against the meagre fighter opposition of the Republican forces, it did well.

**Record breaker** ▶
Civil S.M.79s took the first three places in the 1937 Istres-Damascus-Paris race, beating the 'MacRobertson' race winner, the DH.88 Comet, into fourth place.

▲ **Luftwaffe prize**
After the Armistice in 1943, the Luftwaffe took over all the S.M.79s using them mainly as transport aircraft.

**Three engines** ▶
Italy's lack of suitable powerplants led to the three-engined configuration, which aided survival in combat conditions.

◀ **Gunner's view**
Looking back at another S.M.79 in close formation, the forward-mounted machine-gun bulge above the cockpit is clearly visible. This unusual feature earned the S.M.79 the nickname 'Il Gobbo' ('The Hunchback').

## FACTS AND FIGURES

➤ The prototype S.M.79, built as a commercial airliner, made its first flight in October 1934.

➤ The first S.M.79 made a record flight from Milan to Rome in June 1935.

➤ Production of the S.M.79 totalled 1,330 in Italy and about 80 in Romania.

➤ Sparvieri sank four British destroyers and damaged a battleship and three carriers.

➤ When Italy surrendered, 36 airworthy S.M.79s survived at Capodichino, Littoria, Pisa and Siena; most flew again.

➤ Three surviving S.M.79s were sold as transports to the Lebanon in 1950.

# Three-engined 'Hunchback'

Before war clouds loomed, Italy's brilliant Alessandro Marchetti proposed the high-speed, eight-passenger S.M.79 for an England–Australia air race. Too late for this event, the S.M.79 racked up other long-distance records. A twin-engine 'no-frills' version was quite advanced when delivered to Romania (which also produced it), Brazil and Iraq.

Italian pilots flew S.M.79 bombers with success in the Spanish Civil War, and they were to repeat the success in World War II. Well-armed and carrying a respectable payload, the S.M.79 made plenty of trouble for the Allies. Given Italy's reputation in torpedo warfare, the Sparviero (Sparrow) inevitably served as a potent torpedo bomber.

The Sparviero was a great aircraft which never reached full potential because Allied bombing of Italy disrupted supplies and production. Ethyl injection improved the performance of the Sparviero's engines but wore them out, leaving most of them unserviceable by the time the Allies invaded Sicily in 1943. A few Sparvieri survived the war as transports, but this was an aircraft whose time came and went quickly.

*In the course of the Mediterranean air–sea war, Sparvieri severely damaged the battleship HMS Malaya and the carriers HMS Indomitable, Victorious and Argus. Successful pilots such as Cimicchi, Di Bella and Melley together with Capitano Buscaglia, commanding the 132° Gruppo, became national heroes in Italy.*

## S.M.79-I Sparviero

**Type:** four-/five-crew medium bomber and torpedo-bomber

**Powerplant:** three 582-kW (780-hp.) Alfa Romeo 126 RC.34 nine-cylinder air-cooled radial piston engines

**Maximum speed:** 430 km/h (267 m.p.h.) at 4000 m (13,000 ft.)

**Range:** 1900 km (1,178 mi.)

**Service ceiling:** 6500 m (21,000 ft.)

**Weights:** empty 6800 kg (14,960 lb.); loaded 10,500 kg (23,100 lb.)

**Armament:** one 12.7-mm (.50 cal.) machine-gun firing forward over the cabin roof, 12.7-mm guns in dorsal and ventral positions, one 7.7-mm (.303 cal.) machine-gun for beam defence, plus five 250-kg (550-lb.) bombs or one 45-cm (18-in.) naval torpedo

**Dimensions:**
| | | |
|---|---|---|
| span | 21.20 m | (69 ft. 6 in.) |
| length | 15.60 m | (51 ft. 2 in.) |
| height | 4.60 m | (15 ft.) |
| wing area | 61.70 m² | (664 sq. ft.) |

*The crew had access to each other in the S.M.79. This, and good armour protection, made the aircraft popular in service.*

*The S.M.79 had a wooden wing structure with a fabric covering, with all the trailing edge consisting of flaps and ailerons and the leading edge having Handley Page slots.*

## S.M.79 SPARVIERO

The S.M.79 served Italy throughout the war in the bombing, transport and torpedo attack roles. Sparvieri fought in the Balkans and North Africa as well as the Mediterranean.

*The SM.79 was no easy meat for attacking fighters, with thick armour in the cockpit.*

**205-1**

*Performance of the S.M.79 was much improved when the Alfa Romeo radials were replaced by more powerful Piaggio radials.*

*The wireless operator doubled as a rear gunner. His position gave a good field of fire for the Breda 12.7-mm (.50 cal.) machine-gun.*

*All of the S.M.79's bombs were contained in its internal fuselage bomb-bay. Torpedoes were mounted under the fuselage.*

*Because the nose was occupied by an engine, the S.M.79's bomb-aimer occupied the front of the ventral gondola. A rearward-firing machine-gun was added to all military aircraft after the prototype.*

*The tail unit was constructed of tubular steel, covered in fabric. Its unusual curved outline and the three-engined layout made the Sparviero easy to recognise.*

## COMBAT DATA

### MAXIMUM SPEED

| | |
|---|---|
| S.M.79-I SPARVIERO | 430 km/h (267 m.p.h.) |
| WELLINGTON | 378 km/h (234 m.p.h.) |
| He 111 | 365 km/h (226 m.p.h.) |

Designed from the outset as a racing machine, the Sparviero showed a good turn of speed and was considerably faster than its British and German contemporaries. It could even outpace fighters when it first flew, but it was no match for the new generation of monoplane fighters which were soon to appear.

### RANGE

The monoplane bombers of the mid-1930s were far more capable than their biplane predecessors. Their lower-drag airframes and more efficient engines meant that they could travel much further on a load of fuel, greatly increasing strike ranges.

| | |
|---|---|
| S.M.79-I SPARVIERO | 1900 km (1,178 mi.) |
| WELLINGTON | 2500 km (1,550 mi.) |
| He 111 | 1950 km (1,209 mi.) |

## Savoia-Marchetti's Sparviero family

■ **PROTOTYPE:** Although not completed in time to take part in the air race for which it was designed, the prototype S.M.79 flew for the first time in October 1934.

■ **BOMBERS:** The second prototype was completed as a bomber, and from 1936 the aircraft saw service in the Spanish Civil War with the Stormi Bombardamento Veloce.

■ **TWIN ENGINES:** Twin-engined Sparvieri achieved some export success, being sold to Iraq, among other nations. Licence-built Romanian aircraft saw action in Russia.

■ **MARITIME BOMBER:** The S.M.79 was a fast and stable low-level striker and, armed with torpedoes, achieved considerable success against the British in the Mediterranean.

■ **THE LAST SPARVIERO:** Upgraded with more powerful Piaggio engines, the ultimate S.M.79 was entering service just as the Armistice of 1943 took Italy out of World War II.

### ARMAMENT

| S.M.79-I SPARVIERO | WELLINGTON | He 111 |
|---|---|---|
| 3 x 12.7-mm (.50 cal.) MGs, 1 x 7.7-mm (.303 cal.) MG 1250 kg (2,750 lb.) of bombs | 8 x 7.7-mm (.303 cal.) MGs 2000 kg (4,400 lb.) of bombs | 1 x 20-mm (0.79-in.) cannon, 1 x 13-mm (0.51-in.) MG, 3 x 7.92-mm (0.31-in.) MG 1000 kg (2,200 lb.) of bombs |

The Sparviero was a good compromise between speed and bombload, but its defensive armament was not as good as it might have been.

# SEVERSKY

# P-35

● Single-seat fighter ● All-metal ● Retractable undercarriage

▲ *After beating the Curtiss Hawk Model 75 in a US Army Air Corps (USAAC) fighter competition, the P-35 initially represented a great advance in US fighter design.*

**A**merica's first modern all-metal fighter, the P-35 proved to be lacking in performance when delivered to the USAAC in 1938. It was underarmed and difficult to handle in comparison with more modern Allied fighters and was quickly obsolete. Consequently, it suffered badly during its brief operational career when pitted against the Mitsubishi and Nakajima fighters in the initial Japanese onslaught against the Philippines.

---

## PHOTO FILE

## SEVERSKY P-35

▲ **Export version**
*EP-106 was the designation given by Seversky to the 60 aircraft supplied to Sweden. Orders amounted to 120, but deliveries ceased in 1939.*

▲ **Twin Wasp**
*One very neat feature of the P-35 was its closely cowled Twin Wasp radial engine.*

▼ **Thin wings**
*The elegant elliptical wings of the P-35 were very thin and allowed only partial gear retraction.*

▲ **Last of the line**
*Seversky completed the last P-35 with an 895-kW R-1830-19 turbo-charged engine. Designated XP-41, this aircraft was further improved by Seversky and acted as the prototype for the Republic P-43 Lancer, which in turn led to the P-47.*

**Into combat ▶**
*When designed the P-35 was under-gunned, and in combat the aircraft suffered dreadfully. Of the 48 P-35As in the Philippines, 40 were lost during the first two days of the Japanese offensive.*

### FACTS AND FIGURES

➤ The P-35 introduced refinements such as an enclosed cockpit, a constant-speed propeller and a retractable undercarriage.

➤ The P-35 was America's first modern all-metal monoplane fighter.

➤ Three squadrons of the 1st Pursuit Group received P-35s in 1938.

➤ When Japan attacked Pearl Harbor, P-35As constituted the entire air defence of the Philippines.

➤ P-35As were supplied to the Ecuadorean air force and the Philippines.

➤ An export version was sold to the Royal Swedish Air Force.

# PROFILE

# Seversky's out-classed fighter

Although a robust aircraft, the P-35 lacked performance, and by the time that the last one was delivered in August 1938 it was already considered obsolete.

The initial P-35 was withdrawn from front-line service in 1941, but undelivered Swedish examples continued to serve with the US Army Air Force as the P-35A. They were severely mauled by the Japanese when deployed in the Philippines, and only eight of 48 of the aircraft remained airworthy after the first two days of enemy attack. This was the first and last time that the type was used operationally.

The P-35's armament was completely inadequate for a 'modern' fighter, especially when compared with the contemporary British Spitfire and Hurricane or the Luftwaffe's Messerschmitt Bf 109. Deliveries of the aircraft were extremely slow and in 1938 the USAAC was already beginning to have second thoughts about the P-35. Consequently, the USAAC placed an order for 210 Curtiss P-36s, the aircraft that had been placed second in the competition won by the P-35.

*Left: This pre-war photograph shows P-35s of the 27th Pursuit Squadron. The aircraft are wearing the flamboyant markings which were typical of the period.*

*Right: The two-seat Seversky 2PA-L, based on the P-35, was acquired by the Soviet Union in March 1938 and was powered by a 746-kW (1000-hp) Wright R-1820 engine.*

## P-35A

**Type:** single-seat fighter

**Powerplant:** one 783-kW (1050-hp) Pratt & Whitney R-1830-45 14-cylinder, air-cooled radial piston engine

**Maximum speed:** 499 km/h (310 mph) at 4359 m (14,300 ft)

**Initial climb rate:** 585 m/min (1919 fpm)

**Maximum range:** 1529 km (950 miles)

**Service ceiling:** 9571 m (31,400 ft)

**Armament:** two 12.7-mm (.50-cal.) and two 7.62-mm (.30-cal.) machine guns plus up to 159 kg (350 lb) of bombs

**Weights:** empty 2075 kg (4575 lb); maximum take-off 3050 kg (6724 lb)

**Dimensions:**
| | | |
|---|---|---|
| span | | 10.97 m (36 ft) |
| length | | 8.18 m (26 ft 10 in) |
| height | | 2.97 m (9 ft 9 in) |
| wing area | | 20.44 m² (220 sq ft) |

## EP-106

Sweden's aircraft, known as the J9 in service, were redesignated P-35A when diverted to the USAAF. This aircraft served with Flygflottilj 8 during 1942/43.

Two 7.62-mm (.30-cal.) synchronized machine guns were mounted within troughs in the upper section of the engine cowling.

Even though it was considerably modified, the P-35 still resembled the earlier SEV-2XP design. This was especially true of the cockpit glazing, which extended some way behind the cockpit.

The only non-metal components of the fighter were the control surfaces, all of which were fabric-covered. The fin and rudder shape was carried over to the P-43 and eventually to the P-47 Thunderbolt after Seversky became Republic.

Most of the P-35's airframe was constructed of metal. The elliptical wings were reminiscent of those of the Spitfire and were of the cantilever type.

The tailwheel of the P-35 was fully retractable and when stowed it was covered by a pair of doors. Seversky produced a hooked variant for the US Navy, but its appalling performance discouraged production.

As rival fighters had retractable undercarriages, Seversky designed a rather crude system for the P-35. The wheels remained semi-exposed when retracted.

## Seversky developments

■ **SEV-3:** Seversky's first project was the three-seat SEV-3 amphibian. It set the world speed record for amphibians in 1935.

■ **SEV-3XAR:** A two-seat landplane was developed from the SEV-3. The USAAC took 30 of a developed version as the BT-8 trainer.

■ **SEV-2XP:** This aircraft was Seversky's original entrant in the USAAC competition. It was damaged in transit and repaired as the P-35.

■ **AT-12:** A number of SEV-2PAs were diverted from USSR and Swedish orders and used as AT-12 trainers with the USAAC.

## COMBAT DATA

### MAXIMUM SPEED

Although the P-35A was faster than the early Bf 109, it would have been no match for the Bf 109E, which was fighting over Europe while the P-35A was being mauled by 'Zeros' over the Philippines.

| | |
|---|---|
| **P-35A** | 499 km/h (310 mph) |
| **Bf 109B-2** | 465 km/h (289 mph) |
| **A6M2 'ZERO'** | 533 km/h (331 mph) |

### RANGE

Long range is desirable in any fighter and here the P-35A performed admirably. In the event, the aircraft was only to see combat during last-ditch attempts at defence, where speed, manoeuvrability and firepower were more important.

**P-35A** 1529 km (950 miles)

**Bf 109B-2** 692 km (430 miles)

**A6M2 'ZERO'** 1897 km (1235 miles)

### ARMAMENT

Compared to the early Bf 109B-2, the P-35A was well armed. Messerschmitt had the problem well in hand, however, unlike Seversky whose P-35A had no answer to the A6M2's cannon.

**P-35A** 2 x 12.7-mm (.50-cal.) machine guns / 2 x 7.62-mm (.30-cal.) machine guns / 159-kg (350-lb) bombload

**Bf 109B-2** 2 x 7.9-mm machine guns

**A6M2 'ZERO'** 2 x 7.7-mm (.303-cal.) machine guns / 2 x 20-mm cannon

# SHORT

# SINGAPORE

● Maritime patrol ● Long range ● Excellent safety record

▲ The Singapore's unusual engine arrangement consisted of four Rolls-Royce Kestrels in tandem tractor-pusher pairs. This design principle was stated by Horace Short in 1911.

Typical of flying-boats of the 1930s, the Short Singapore was a large, sturdy and functional machine with enormous potential for both civil and military use. It never lived up to its promise, however. The Singapore biplane is best known for demonstrating the ability of aircraft in its class to make marathon long-distance flights. Less well remembered is that it also achieved modest success as an armed military reconnaissance craft.

## PHOTO FILE

## SHORT SINGAPORE

▲ Patrolling the Empire
With its excellent range, the Singapore Mk III was regarded as the most suitable aircraft to patrol the main trade and shipping routes of the British Empire. This example later served in Singapore.

▲ Biplane boat
The Singapore was the last biplane flying-boat to see operational service with the RAF.

▲ Scandinavian cruise
The only Singapore I first flew in 1926. It performed well on the RAF's Scandinavian cruise of 1927 and was later used by Alan Cobham on his flight around Africa.

▲ Operational trials
The first true production aircraft, K4577, underwent armament and equipment trials with the Marine Aircraft Experimental Establishment at Felixstowe.

Rochester works ▶
The Singapore II, seen on No. 3 slipway at Rochester, first flew in March 1930.

### FACTS AND FIGURES

➤ Despite the Air Ministry specification calling for a three-engined design, Short's four-engined Singapore eventually won.

➤ The first production Singapore Mk III made its initial flight in March 1935.

➤ Singapore production included three prototypes and 33 service aircraft.

➤ Singapore flying-boats served with Nos 203, 205, 209, 210 and 230 Squadrons of the RAF.

➤ Nineteen Singapore aircraft remained in service at the start of World War II.

➤ The Japanese used design features from the Singapore in their own flying-boats.

# Patrolling the British Empire

Even some experts have difficulty in recognising the Short Singapore flying-boat of the 1930s. But the aircraft made a mark in history in a modest way and contributed to aviation knowledge.

Short Brothers had great hopes for the Singapore prototype, but its main claim to fame was that it was used by adventurer Alan Cobham for his 37,015-km (22,950-mi.) survey flight around the African continent.

The Singapore II, which came on the scene in 1930, was also the subject of ambitious hopes that were essentially unfulfilled. The Mk III, which appeared

soon afterward, was more successful and resulted in an Air Ministry order for four developmental aircraft.

Testing led to a production order, and nearly three dozen Singapore flying-boats joined British military service in the mid-1930s. The aircraft, although representing outdated technology, combined reliability with the ability to undertake impressive long-distance patrol missions. Despite its obsolescence, Japan thought the

Singapore was a practical design which was worth copying. New Zealand purchased four ex-RAF Mk IIIs, which served faithfully on patrol missions from Fiji until April 1943.

*Below: The Singapore Mk II was originally fitted with a single tailfin. This arrangement was found to be inadequate after the loss of one engine, and a triple-fin arrangement was used.*

*Above: The first Singapore Mk III was K3592, which flew development and acceptance trials. It later served with No. 205 Squadron at Seletar, Singapore.*

## SINGAPORE MK III

K4578 was coded '4' when it served with No. 203 Squadron. The squadron was based first at Aden and then Basrah before returning to Aden in 1939.

### Singapore Mk III

**Type:** six-seat reconnaissance flying-boat

**Powerplant:** four 418-kW (560-hp.) Rolls-Royce Kestrel Mk VIII/IX V-12 piston engines (two tractor/two pusher)

**Maximum speed:** 233 km/h (145 m.p.h.)

**Range:** 1610 km (1,000 mi.)

**Service ceiling:** 4570 m (15,000 ft.)

**Weights:** empty 8355 kg (18,381 lb.); maximum take-off 12,474 kg (27,443 lb.)

**Accommodation:** crew of six, consisting of two pilots, navigator, radio operator/gunner and two gunners

**Armament:** three 7.7-mm (.303 cal.) Lewis machine-guns, including nose and tail guns, plus up to 908 kg (2,00 lb.) of bombs or survey equipment

**Dimensions:**
| | | |
|---|---|---|
| span | 27.43 m | (90 ft.) |
| length | 23.16 m | (76 ft.) |
| height | 7.19 m | (23 ft. 6 in.) |
| wing area | 170.38 m² | (1,833 sq. ft.) |

The Singapore II flew with Rolls-Royce F.XII engines. The definitive Mk III was powered by four Kestrel Mk IX in-line engines.

The crew entered the aircraft via a large door on the starboard side. The original open cockpit was later enclosed by a glass 'greenhouse'.

The biplane wings created a great deal of lift. Drag was reduced by strengthening the wingroots which negated the need for extensive bracing.

The Singapore Mk III was of all-metal construction. The planing hull was so strong that it could withstand impacts of up to 9g.

The dorsal gun position housed a 7.7-mm (.303 cal.) Lewis gun, with 485 rounds of ammunition, mounted on a Scarff ring.

The triple-fin arrangement allowed the installation of a gunner's cockpit with a 7.7-mm (.303 cal.) machine-gun in the extreme rear of the hull.

The Singapore Mk III was modified from the Singapore II by the introduction of a deeper hull which featured a pointed step.

When brought onto land via a slipway, the Singapore sat on either detachable wheels or a trolley.

## COMBAT DATA

### POWER

Not surprisingly, the amount of power each aircraft produced was proportional to the number of engines. The four-engined Singapore had more than twice the power of the smaller twin-engined Scapa.

**SINGAPORE Mk III** 1672 kW (2,240 hp.)
**SCAPA** 783 kW (1,049 hp.)
**RANGOON** 1208 kW (1,619 hp.)

### ARMAMENT

Typical defensive armament for British flying-boats of the period was three 7.7-mm (.303 cal.) Lewis guns usually mounted on Scarff rings. The larger Singapore could carry the greatest bombload.

**SINGAPORE Mk III** 3 x 7.7-mm (.303 cal.) machine-guns 908-kg (2,000-lb.) bombload

**SCAPA** 3 x 7.7-mm (.303 cal.) machine-guns 454-kg (1,000-lb.) bombload

**RANGOON** 3 x 7.7-mm (.303 cal.) machine-guns 454-kg (1.000-lb.) bombload

### RANGE

Long range is vital for a maritime patrol craft. The Singapore and Scapa both had impressive range and endurance, allowing them to cover large expanses of ocean. The Rangoon had shorter reach and tended to patrol smaller stretches of water such as the North Sea.

**SINGAPORE Mk III** 1610 km (1,000 mi.)
**SCAPA** 1770 km (1,100 mi.)
**RANGOON** 1046 km (650 mi.)

## Short biplane flying-boats

**N.3 CROMARTY:** The Cromarty was the first flying-boat of Short Brothers' design and took to the air in April 1921. Only one example was built and it was scrapped in 1922.

**CALCUTTA:** Designed primarily for long-distance Empire sea routes flown by Imperial Airways, this three-engined flying-boat had accommodation for 15 passengers.

**RANGOON:** This was a naval reconnaissance version of the Calcutta. Six were built for the RAF and entered service in 1931. Defensive armament consisted of three machine-guns.

**SARAFAND:** With a similar engine layout to the Singapore, but having three instead of two tractor/pusher combinations, the single Sarafand was said to have been trouble-free and viceless.

# SHORT

# STIRLING

● RAF heavy bomber ● Glider tug ● Paratroop carrier

▲ The Stirling stands tall on its stalky undercarriage designed to improve take-off performance with a full bombload. Its usefulness was limited by the size of bombs it could carry in its bomb-bay.

**S**hort's Stirling is one of the unsung heroes of the war. This large aircraft was Britain's first four-engine monoplane bomber to enter service. It became a stalwart of the night bombing campaign over Europe, even though it was never given as much credit as the better known Lancaster and Halifax. First entering service with No. 7 Squadron in February 1941, the Stirling flew on Bomber Command's major raids until September 1944.

## SHORT STIRLING

▲ **Bombing-up**
Stirling Mk I of No. 7 Squadron, the first unit to equip with the heavy bomber, receives its load of bombs.

▲ **Limited ceiling**
With a top speed of 435 km/h (269 m.p.h.) and a maximum all-up weight of 31,751 kg (69,938 lb.), the Stirling was handicapped by its low service ceiling.

▲ **Short-span wings**
The Stirling's wing span was limited so that it could fit into RAF hangars. This gave a very low aspect ratio wing and the need for a stalky undercarriage.

▼ **MacRobert's Reply**
This Short Stirling Mk 1 of No. XV Squadron was named 'MacRobert's Reply' in honour of Lady MacRobert's sons when it was delivered to the RAF in 1941. It is painted matt-black for night bombing.

▲ **Mass production**
The RAF received a grand total of 2,374 Stirlings comprising four marks – I, III and IV (bombers) and the Mk V transport. They were built at three factories, with most produced by Short & Harland in Belfast.

## FACTS AND FIGURES

➤ No. 7 Squadron became the RAF's first four-engined bomber squadron when it received Stirlings in August 1940.

➤ The prototype Stirling flew on 14 May 1939, but was destroyed on landing.

➤ In total, 162 Stirlings were built as transport aircraft.

➤ An advantage of the Stirling's internal layout was the absence of a wing spar to impede crew movement.

➤ The last bombing raid by Stirlings was on 8 September 1944 against Le Havre.

➤ Stirlings played a major part in the D-Day landings as glider tugs and for air supply.

# PROFILE

# Short's lofty Stirling bomber

A bulky, four-engine bomber, the Stirling was especially heavy for its tailwheel landing gear. It became an important participant in the war over the European continent.

The Stirling has been called the 'ugly duckling' of Royal Air Force bombers, and is deemed by many not to have reached its full potential. Facing flak and fighters, many Stirling crews feared their plane was a firetrap. This negative reputation was exaggerated: many crewmembers had great confidence in what was, in most respects, a fine aircraft.

After bloody battles on bombing sorties against ferociously defended targets, from early 1944 the Stirling's primary role changed to glider tug and transport.

Towing troop-carrying gliders, Stirlings had an important role in the Normandy invasion. Thereafter, Stirlings hauled gliders for the failed airborne operations at Arnhem and the March 1945 crossing of the Rhine.

By March 1946, most Stirling squadrons had been disbanded or had converted to other aircraft and the last Stirling was retired from Royal Air Force service.

Stirlings were operated by 11

Bomber Command squadrons, made 18,440 sorties, dropping 28,268 tonnes (27,821 tons) of bombs and laid about 20,000 mines. Of the 2369 production Stirlings, 769 were lost, including 641 in action. During 1947 two dozen Stirling Mk Vs were converted as cargo and passenger aircraft for a Belgian operator.

*Above: With its long, narrow fuselage bomb-bay that was divided into four sections, the Stirling was not able to carry a worthwhile bombload on very long-range missions.*

*Right: The Stirling V was a dedicated transport version with no armament. The first was flown for the first time in August 1944, and entered service in January 1945 with Transport Command.*

## Stirling B.Mk III

**Type:** seven-place heavy bomber with a crew of seven or eight

**Powerplant:** four 1230-kW (1,650-hp.) Bristol Hercules VI or XVI radial piston engines

**Maximum speed:** 435 km/h (270 m.p.h.) at 4420 m (14,500 ft.)

**Range:** 950 km (590 mi.)

**Service ceiling:** 5180 m (17,000 ft.)

**Weights:** empty 19,595 kg (43,109 lb.); maximum take-off 31,751 kg (69,938 lb.)

**Armament:** eight 7.7-mm (.303 cal.) Browning machine-guns in Frazer-Nash FN.5A nose turret (two), FN.7A dorsal turret (two) and FN.20A tail turret (four), plus up to 6350 kg (14,000 lb.) of bombs

**Dimensions:**
| | | |
|---|---|---|
| span | | 30.20 m (99 ft.) |
| length | | 26.59 m (87 ft. 3 in.) |
| height | | 6.93 m (22 ft. 9 in.) |
| wing area | | 135.63 m² (1,482 sq. ft.) |

---

## STIRLING MK I

This Stirling Mk I of No. 7 Squadron Pathfinder Force, fitted with top secret H2S radar, attacked Hamburg on 30/31 January 1943.

The Stirling was powered by four 1230-kW (1,650-hp.) Bristol Hercules 14-cylinder air-cooled sleeve-valve radial engines driving three-bladed de Havilland constant-speed propellers. It contained self-sealing fuel tanks within the wing spar trusses.

Armament consisted of two 7.7-mm (.303 cal.) Browning machine-guns in the nose (FN.5) and dorsal (FN.50) turrets and four 7.7-mm Browning machine-guns in the FN.20A rear turret.

The centre section above the bomb-bay was braced to allow the crew to pass through. Aft of the centre section were the main flare chutes and a walkway through to the tail turret. Crew entered via a door on the port side.

A crew of seven was normally carried, comprising two pilots, navigator/bomb-aimer, front gunner/wireless operator, two air gunners and a flight engineer/air gunner.

The main fuselage bomb-bay was 13 metres long and divided into six cells by longitudinal girders with arched members, each section with a hinged door. Also internal bomb racks inboard of the engine nacelles.

The tail unit was of cantilever construction with the single fin and rudder and tailplane of similar shape and size. It was based on the previous Empire flying-boat design.

---

# Four-engined RAF bombers

**HANDLEY PAGE HALIFAX:** Powered by the same Bristol Hercules engines, the Halifax B.Mk III was faster than the Stirling, had a higher service ceiling, carried more bombs and had better defensive armament.

**AVRO LANCASTER:** With its four Rolls-Royce Merlin 24 engines, unrestricted bomb-bay carrying 8165-kg (17,963-lb.) bombs, good service ceiling and huge range, the Lancaster was superior to the Stirling and Halifax in most respects.

**CONSOLIDATED LIBERATOR:** The American B-24 was flown by RAF Bomber and Coastal Commands. Although it had a better performance than the British bombers it carried a significantly smaller bombload.

---

## COMBAT DATA

### MAXIMUM SPEED

One feature of the Stirling that did not endear it to its crews was its lack of speed. Pilots preferred Lancasters and Halifaxes as they had an edge in performance that often proved vital.

| | |
|---|---|
| STIRLING B.Mk III | 435 km/h (270 m.p.h.) |
| B-17F FLYING FORTRESS | 475 km/h (295 m.p.h.) |
| HALIFAX B.Mk III | 454 km/h (281 m.p.h.) |

### BOMBLOAD

The Stirling could carry a slightly smaller bombload than the Halifax, which was one reason why it was more suitable for transport duties. The B-17F was a far more powerful bomber.

| | |
|---|---|
| B-17F FLYING FORTRESS | 7983 kg (17,600 lb.) |
| STIRLING B.Mk III | 6350 kg (14,000 lb.) |
| HALIFAX B.Mk III | 6577 kg (14,500 lb.) |

### ARMAMENT

Like most British bombers, the Stirling had good power turrets. These 7.7-mm machine-guns were no answer to the Ju 88's 20-mm (0.79-in.) cannon and there was no protection from fighters below.

| | |
|---|---|
| STIRLING B.Mk III | 8 x 7.7-mm (.303 cal.) machine-guns |
| B-17F FLYING FORTRESS | 12 x 12.7-mm (.50 cal.) machine-guns |
| HALIFAX B.Mk III | 9 x 7.7-mm (.303 cal.) machine-guns |

# SHORT

# SUNDERLAND

● Maritime patrol ● Anti-submarine ● Long-range flying-boat

▲ The rugged Sunderland was one of the finest flying-boats of the war. Its vital role in fighting the U-boat blockade around Britain made it one of the most important weapons in the RAF's arsenal.

**D**erived from the pre-war Empire flying-boat, the Sunderland became a legend in World War II as the main patrol flying-boat of British Commonwealth forces. It was tough and reliable, performing just about any maritime task including U-boat hunting, air-sea rescue and transport. Adversaries found the Sunderland a prickly customer and nicknamed it 'The Flying Porcupine'.

## SHORT SUNDERLAND

### ▲ Maritime heritage
Short Brothers' expertise in flying-boat design was perfected with 'Empire'-type boats before the war. The Sunderland first flew in October 1937, and the type was operational by 1938.

### ▼ Run ashore
The Sunderland, as a flying-boat, had no undercarriage. Repair work on land meant that it had to be beached on a landing trolley and fitted on chocks.

### ▲ Coastal patrol
Sunderlands operated from some of the most remote areas in Europe and Asia. The crew had the comfort of knowing that they could always land on the sea if the engines failed.

### ▲ In the hull
The huge interior allowed space for weapon and flare stowage, crew rest areas, a galley, radio and radar, and plenty of fuel.

### ◄ On the slipway
The addition of radar to the Sunderland Mk II was a key turning point in the war against the U-boats, giving Royal Air Force Coastal Command the ability to hunt by day or by night. This new Mk II was the first built by Shorts in Belfast. The four radar aerials are visible along the aircraft's spine.

### ▲ Depth-charged
This attack in the Bay of Biscay in 1943 sent a U-boat to the bottom. Radar-equipped Sunderlands forced U-boats to cross the bay submerged.

## FACTS AND FIGURES

➤ The prototype Sunderland made its maiden flight from the River Medway on 16 October 1937.

➤ One Sunderland won a battle with eight Ju 88 fighters, shooting down two.

➤ The Sunderland was the first flying-boat to have power-operated gun turrets.

➤ Shorts produced 721 Sunderlands between 1937 and 1945, and 17 Royal Air Force squadrons flew them.

➤ Sunderlands delivered 4877 tonnes (4,800 tons) of supplies during the Berlin Airlift.

➤ France was the last country to fly military Sunderlands, retiring them in 1960.

# PROFILE

# The flying porcupine

When the Short Sunderland entered service in 1938, this big seaplane gave the RAF the endurance for gruelling 20-hour patrols. During the war Sunderlands undertook many dangerous missions, including evacuating Crete by making trips with up to 82 armed passengers plus a 10-man crew. As the war progressed, improved Sunderlands introduced search radar with huge antennas atop

the rear fuselage; no other aircraft was more capable at stalking and attacking U-boats.

The Sunderland carried bombs and depth charges internally, then cranked them out on underwing pylons when preparing to attack. Its gunners could rake the deck of an enemy submarine, preventing its crew from manning their own weapons.

Some Sunderlands became stripped, high-speed transports for British Overseas Airways

Corporation. During the 1948 Berlin Airlift Sunderlands lifted almost five million kilograms of freight flying hazardous mercy missions.

The final Sunderland introduced Pratt & Whitney R-1890-90B Twin Wasp engines to replace the reliable but somewhat underpowered Pegasus. This impressive aircraft remained the standard RAF ocean flying-boat until its retirement in 1959.

## Sunderland Mk III

**Type:** long-range reconnaissance and anti-submarine flying-boat

**Powerplant:** four 794-kW (1,064-hp.) Bristol Pegasus XVIII nine-cylinder radial piston engines

**Maximum speed:** 341 km/h (211 m.p.h.)

**Range:** 4828 km (2,993 mi.)

**Service ceiling:** 5300 m (17,930 ft.)

**Weights:** empty 15,663 kg (34,459 lb.); loaded 26,308 kg (57,878 lb.)

**Armament:** eight 7.7-mm (.303 cal.) Browning machine-guns in nose, dorsal and quad tail turrets; some fitted with four fixed forward-firing 7.7-mm and twin 12.7-mm (.50 cal.) Brownings in waist; 2250 kg (4,950 lb.) of bombs, depth charges, mines or pyrotechnics

**Dimensions:**
| | |
|---|---|
| span | 34.38 m (113 ft.) |
| length | 26.01 m (85 ft.) |
| height | 9.79 m (32 ft.) |
| wing area | 138.14 m² (1,486 sq. ft.) |

*On land, the Sunderland looked clumsy and heavy. But its performance in the air surprised many enemy pilots, who learned to treat this aircraft with respect.*

## SUNDERLAND MK III

This Sunderland Mk III is seen in the markings of No. 228 Squadron RAF during its deployment to the Mediterranean in 1940 and 1941.

The powered Frazer-Nash nose turret mounted two 7.7-mm (.303 cal.) machine-guns. It could be retracted into the nose.

Most Sunderlands were powered by Bristol Pegasus nine-cylinder radial engines, replaced in the final variant by more powerful Pratt & Whitney R-1890 14-cylinder radials.

The mid-upper turret replaced the single hand-held guns fired from beam windows of the Mk I.

The aft section of the fuselage contained the crew's quarters, bomb stowage and galley area.

The aerials of the ASV Mk II surface-search radar were mounted on the upper fuselage.

The fin and tailplane were metal-framed and skinned, with fabric-covered control surfaces.

The rear gunner's turret mounted four 7.7-mm (.303 cal.) machine-guns. Unlike tail gunners in other aircraft, he had easy access to the main hull.

NJ188

WH●C

## Royal Air Force flying-boats of the 1930s

■ **SHORT SINGAPORE Mk III:** Developed from the Singapore Mk I of 1926, the Singapore Mk III patrol boat served from 1935 to 1941. With a speed of 230 km/h (143 m.p.h.), it could carry a tonne of bombs over a range of 1600 km (994 mi.).

■ **SUPERMARINE STRANRAER:** The last of Supermarine's classic series of biplane flying-boats, the twin-engined Stranraer was operational from December 1936 to 1940. Smaller than the Singapore, it had a 454-kg (1,000-lb.) bombload.

■ **SARO LONDON:** Ordered to a 1931 maritime reconnaissance requirement, the London was Britain's last front-line biplane, serving in home waters and the Mediterranean until late 1941. It had a range of 2800 km (1,736 mi.).

## COMBAT DATA

### ENDURANCE

Although it served all over the world, the Sunderland's main area of operations was the Atlantic, where it partnered the American-built Catalina and where its great German rival was the Focke-Wulf Fw 200 Condor. All three aircraft were well suited to maritime patrol, where the prime performance requirement was to be able to monitor large areas of ocean for extremely long periods of time.

| SUNDERLAND | CONDOR | CATALINA |
|---|---|---|
| 20 hours | 14 hours | 21.5 hours |

# SIKORSKY
# R-4/R-5

● First production helicopter ● Successful design ● Wartime service

**M**any people believe the role of the helicopter in World War II was restricted to experimental flights. The USAAC took it far beyond the test phase and Sikorsky's diminutive R-4 performed some of the most significant flights of the entire war. Pilots found themselves confronted with an entirely new era of flight, and the potential of the military helicopter was quickly seen. As a search and rescue platform, it was a life-saver.

▲ Sikorsky's R-4 can rightly be considered as the world's first true production helicopter. First flying in 1939, it entered service with the USAAF, the USN, the RAF and the Royal Navy.

## SIKORSKY R-4/R-5

**Natural progression ▶**
Following on from the R-4 was a slightly larger machine, the R-5. It is seen here in early configuration with a tailwheel undercarriage.

**◀ Production gets underway**
With flight trials having been conducted successfully, the R-4 was put into production at Stratford, Connecticut in early 1942.

**Workhorse forerunner ▶**
Although the R-5 was successful, redesigning it resulted in the S-51, which did more to establish the concept of rotary-winged flight than any other helicopter.

**◀ Distinctive looks**
Compared to later designs, the R-4 was an ungainly machine featuring a boxed spar fuselage covered in fabric.

**British helicopter evaluation ▶**
After the R-4 had been ordered by the US armed services, a handful found their way overseas. The Royal Air Force and Fleet Air Arm evaluated the type during the closing months of World War II. In UK service, they were given the designation Hoverfly Mk I.

### FACTS AND FIGURES

➤ On 21 April 1945 a single Canadian R-4 became the first helicopter to rescue a downed crew in the Arctic.

➤ Thirty production machines (YR-4As and YR-4Bs) were ordered in total.

➤ US Army Air Force R-4s were used to rescue downed crews in the Pacific.

➤ By the time production switched to the improved R-5/S-51 series, a total of 130 Sikorsky R-4s had been built.

➤ A Sikorsky R-4 was the first true helicopter to make a landing at sea.

➤ On 17 May 1942, the XR-4 flew a distance of 1224 km (760 mi.).

## PROFILE

# Rotary-winged warriors

Igor Sikorsky finally managed to fly his first successful rotary-winged craft in 1939. Known as the VS-300, it was instrumental in the development of the world's first true production helicopter, the amazing Sikorsky R-4. With the VS-300 flying at speeds of up to 113 km/h (70 m.p.h.) by 1941, it was obvious that a more practical machine was viable.

The resulting XR-4 featured an enclosed cockpit with dual, side-by-side seating and a single Warner R500 piston engine. After successful trials, an order for 30 production aircraft (three YR-4As and 27 YR-4Bs) was placed by the

United States Army Air Force. They were later augmented by 100 more R-4Bs which featured more powerful engines. R-4s were pioneers in the development of the helicopter and, on 6 May 1943, an early production machine became the first helicopter to land successfully aboard a ship, touching down on the aircraft carrier, USS *Bunker Hill*.

Using the R-4 as a basis, Sikorsky developed the larger R-5, which featured an all-metal fuselage and other improvements. It first flew in 1943, but did not enter service until after World War II. Nevertheless, it proved tremendously successful and

some 379 of these aircraft, later called S-51, were built.

*Above: This photograph is unique, showing the Sikorsky R-4, R-5 and R-6 together. The evolution of the helicopter can already be seen.*

*Left: Col Frank Gregory, who helped to bring about the R-4, was the first person to land a helicopter on board ship.*

Tests were conducted in which the tail rotor was mounted horizontally, with the hub pointing skyward. Although the aircraft could get airborne with few problems, stability and directional control were still difficult. The XR-4 reverted to the more familiar layout.

All R-4s were fitted with three-bladed main rotors. To reduce weight, they were constructed from spruce wood, which proved a problem during rescue operations in the Pacific theatre.

At the time, the cockpit of the R-4 was quite unusual for many pilots. The aircraft commander sat in the right-hand seat. It was not a difficult machine to fly and pilots could go solo in just a few hours.

The XR-4 was powered by a 123-kW Warner R-500 piston engine. From pre-production machines onward, this was substituted by a 138-kW (180-hp.) R-550.

Despite its appearance, the fuselage was extremely strong, with diagonally mounted spars increasing stiffness and strength. The rear section was uncovered.

Another feature pioneered by the R-4 was the interchangeable undercarriage. R-4Bs in service with the US Navy aboard ships were often fitted with floats.

Because of the extreme upward tapering of the fuselage, a very long tail wheel was necessary to keep the R-4 level while on the ground.

## R-4

During initial trials the Sikorsky R-4 wore an overall silver dope scheme with full colour insignia. Wartime operations saw the adoption of a drab green colour scheme to offer some form of camouflage to the vulnerable R-4.

### GETTING IT RIGHT

**MULTIPLE ROTORS:** Igor Sikorsky's most successful testbed before the R-4 was the VS-300. This strange-looking machine made its maiden flight on 14 September 1939. Sikorsky had been experimenting with the idea of rotary-winged aircraft for many years, but until the late 1930s the technology was not sufficient to warrant a full working example. This tri-rotored layout was just one configuration tested on the VS-300.

**FURTHER IDEAS:** After experimenting with many configurations, Sikorsky discovered that stability and directional control problems could be solved by adopting an anti-torque rotor on the tail. This configuration has been adopted by the vast majority of helicopters since; the design is similar to that which ultimately emerged on the R-4 itself.

## Early Sikorsky helicopters

■ **SIKORSKY R-6:** Installing the R-4's engine and gearbox in a new, much more streamlined fuselage resulted in the R-6. They were delivered to the RAF as Hoverfly Mk IIs.

■ **SIKORSKY S-52:** This little helicopter has the distinction of being the first of its type to feature all-metal rotor blades. It also established national helicopter records for speed and altitude.

■ **SIKORSKY S-55:** Entering service in 1952, the S-55 served with the US Army and Air Force in large numbers as the H-19. It was built under licence in France and the United Kingdom.

# SIKORSKY

# ILYA MUROMETS

● Heavy bomber ● Record-breaker ● Numerous variants

▲ One of the most innovative designers of all time, Sikorsky developed combat aircraft for Russia before emigrating to the USA and designing flying-boats and helicopters.

I gor Ivanovitch Sikorsky was born in Kiev in 1889 and became one of Russia's most famous aircraft designers of the pre-revolution era. In 1909, he experimented with unsuccessful rotary-wing aircraft. By 1910, he had developed his first fixed-wing aircraft and the success of these early types led to his appointment as chief engineer of the Russo-Baltic Wagon Works (RBVZ). By 1913, he had developed the Ilya Muromets series of bombers which saw service in World War I.

---

## SIKORSKY ILYA MUROMETS

▼ Great War bomber
The size of the Ilya Muromets allowed it to carry a large bombload. Igor Sikorsky is seen standing next to the man with the clipboard.

▲ Ahead of their time
In their day, the Ilya Muromets were very advanced aircraft and demonstrated some features that would become a hallmark of later heavy bombers.

◄ Piggy-back ride
The first Ilya Muromets is seen here on its maiden flight carrying two brave passengers on its fuselage. A similar escapade five days earlier ended in near disaster because of poor lift from the wings.

▼ Extra endurance
To increase the aircraft's range, two fuel tanks were fitted above the top wing on this variant.

▲ Multiple versions
The Ilya Muromets was produced in more than 25 versions. This one features a fully-glazed nose, improving visibility.

### FACTS AND FIGURES

➤ On 12 February 1914, the aircraft broke the world height-with-payload record, carrying 16 people to 2000 m (6,560 ft.).

➤ The Russkii Vityaz recorded 53 flights before being damaged on the ground.

➤ The Ilya Muromets was the first aircraft with an enclosed cabin, nose to tail.

➤ After the 1917 revolution, Sikorsky fled to the USA where he suffered great hardship until he formed a new company in 1924.

➤ The type's first combat mission was flown on 15 February 1915.

➤ In September 1916, an Ilya Muromets shot down three German fighters on one sortie.

# PROFILE

# First of the giant Soviet bombers

When RBVZ took on young designer Igor Sikorsky, he had already designed a number of experimental types (S-1 to S-6A), achieving his first flight in the S-3 biplane in November 1910.

Once the RBVZ had formed an aircraft division, Sikorsky became instrumental in shaping its new designs. After designing a number of moderately successful types, many of which he flew himself, Sikorsky began work on a large strategic reconnaissance biplane named the Russkii Vityaz (Russian

Knight). Also known as 'Le Grand', this twin-engined machine was the largest aircraft in the world when it first flew on 15 March 1913. In May of that year the aircraft was fitted with two additional engines to become the first four-engined aircraft to fly.

This remarkable aircraft formed the basis of the Ilya Muromets series of heavy bombers which were used by the Imperial Russian army during World War I. Bristling with guns, 80 of these aircraft were produced in dozens of

*Above: The Ilya Muromets was flown with wheels and skis in 1913. In the spring of 1914, the aircraft was evaluated as a floatplane.*

different variants including floatplane and ski-equipped versions.

Named after a legendary hero from Kiev, only two Ilya Muromets were shot down during the war and a number of the surviving craft went on to serve into the 1920s as Bolshevik trainers and transports.

*Above: First flown by Sikorsky in March 1913, the* Russkii Vityaz *was originally named* Bolshoi Baltiiskii. *The aircraft was fitted with a sofa, table and toilet.*

## Ilya Muromets E2

**Type:** four-engined biplane heavy bomber

**Powerplant:** four 164-kW (220-hp.) Renault piston engines

**Maximum speed:** 137 km/h (85 m.p.h.)

**Take-off run:** 450 m (1,475 ft.)

**Range:** 560 km (348 mi.)

**Service ceiling:** 3200 m (10,500 ft.)

**Weights:** empty 5000 kg (11,000 lb.); loaded 7460 kg (16,450 lb.)

**Armament:** up to six machine-guns of various makes including Maxim, Lewis, Madsen and Browning

**Dimensions:**
| | | |
|---|---|---|
| span | 34.50 m | (113 ft. 2 in.) |
| length | 18.80 m | (61 ft. 8 in.) |
| wing area | 220 m² (2,368 sq. ft.) | |

An identifying feature of the Ilya Muromets was an extremely snub nose and extensive cockpit glazing which wrapped around the sides.

Most of the rear fuselage consisted of four main spars, two on the top and two along the bottom. Connecting them were a series of diagonally-mounted spars which increased the strength of the airframe and reduced flexing. Fabric covered most of the skeletal frame.

In an effort to generate as much lift as possible, the IM-V featured a huge tailplane, which was greater in chord than the main wing. It was a complex design and featured extensive bracing. Mounted just forward of the tail unit was an enormous tail skid.

To cope with the rough state of Soviet airfields at the time, the IM-V was fitted with wheels and skis. Dual tyres were necessary for effective weight distribution.

Powerplants differed, depending on the variant. The Type V, featured four in-line liquid-cooled Sunbeam engines, each producing up to 167 kW (224 hp.). Others could be fitted with Salmson radials or the powerful Renault V-12 in-line engines.

Production of these giant aircraft eventually totalled 80. They were originally built as reconnaissance aircraft, but were later converted for other roles. A large bombload could be carried, but because of the size and shape of the fuselage, only small bombs could be accommodated.

**This particular aircraft, actually an IM-V variant, is typical of the Ilya Muromets in use as long-range bombers. By 1918, they were becoming obsolete and were soon withdrawn from front-line service.**

## ACTION DATA

### MAXIMUM SPEED

Compared to other heavy bombers of the period, the Ilya Muromets were blessed with surprising performance, although this depended on the type of engines fitted. The IM-V, with its four Sunbeam engines, could fly at speeds of up to 137 km/h (85 m.p.h.).

| | |
|---|---|
| ILYA MUROMETS-V | 137 km/h (85 m.p.h.) |
| 0/100 | 122 km/h (76 m.p.h.) |
| R.IV | 125 km/h (78 m.p.h.) |

### WINGSPAN

Although it had a wing which spanned a gigantic (for the time) 34.5 m (113 ft. 2 in.), the Ilya Muromets were not the longest-spanned aircraft of the World War I era, the R.IV featuring a much larger wing.

| | |
|---|---|
| ILYA MUROMETS-V | 34.50 m (113 ft. 2 in.) |
| 0/100 | 30.50 m (100 ft.) |
| R.IV | 42.20 m (138 ft. 5 in.) |

### ARMAMENT

Both the Ilya Muromets and the R.IV could be heavily armed, with machine-guns, making them difficult to shoot down. One of the Soviet machines actually managed to shoot down three German fighters. The Handley Page 0/100 had only light armament.

| ILYA MUROMETS-V 6 machine guns | 0/100 4 machine guns | R.IV 7 machine guns |
|---|---|---|

## Sikorsky's early designs

■ **S-1:** Sikorsky's first attempts at building flying machines were the S-1 and S-2 co-axial helicopters. On its first attempt to fly, the S-1 lifted but toppled over. The S-2 never managed to leave the ground. After these two unsuccessful attempts Sikorsky turned to fixed-wing aircraft. In the 1940s he returned to work on helicopters and produced some of the world's greatest designs.

■ **S-3:** Sikorsky's first fixed-wing design was the S-3. In November 1910 he completed a number of short flights.

■ **S-29A:** After his emigration to the US, Sikorsky's first design was the S-29A. This twin-engined transport first flew in May 1924.

# SOPWITH

# PUP

- RFC fighter ● Home defence ● Synchronised machine-gun

J ust as the Hurricane has been overshadowed by the Spitfire, so the Pup has been pushed into second place by its illustrious successor, the Camel. Sopwith's Pup was a fine fighting scout, however, and it revolutionised Royal Flying Corps (RFC) tactics by introducing machine-gun armament synchronised to fire through the propeller disc. Principally a naval aircraft, the Pup equipped three squadrons of the RFC in France.

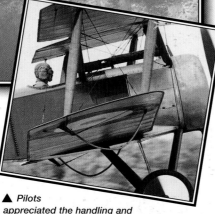

▲ Pilots
*appreciated the handling and synchronised armament of the Pup, which allowed them to gain an advantage over contemporary German fighters and two-seat C-type scouts.*

## SOPWITH PUP

◀ **Pup preservation**
*Many veteran and vintage aircraft are flown by The Shuttleworth Collection in the UK, including this original Pup.*

**Post-war prototype** ▶
*Photographed in 1925, the Pup prototype survived World War I. The Dove, a two-seat civil version of the Pup, sold badly.*

▼ **Lightweight elegance**
*Despite its low power, the Pup offered good performance and manoeuvrability. This was largely because of its lightweight but strong internal structure.*

▲ **Naval dominance**
*More Pups entered service with the RNAS than with the beleaguered RFC.*

**Shipboard modifications** ▶
*Several Pups suffered failures of their narrow wheels, leading to replacement with skids on some ship-based aircraft.*

## FACTS AND FIGURES

- ➤ Most Pups were built by one of three companies: Whitehead Aircraft, William Beardmore or Standard Motors.

- ➤ On its 9 February 1916 first flight, the Pup was piloted by Harry Hawker.

- ➤ No. 54 Squadron, the first RFC Pup unit, arrived in France on 24 December 1916.

- ➤ In the home defence role, the Pup was used to intercept Gotha G IV bombers attacking southeast England.

- ➤ Some home defence Pups received 74.6-kW (100-hp.) Gnome Monosoupape engines.

- ➤ Pup production reached a total of 1770 airframes from all sources.

# PROFILE

# Turning the German tide

A t the close of 1915, Germany's fighting scouts were more than a match for any Allied aircraft. In recognition of the enemy's superiority, design of the Pup was initiated.

T.O.M. Sopwith's new fighter was officially known as the Scout, but its similarity to a scaled-down version of the same company's 1½ Strutter led to the aircraft being nicknamed 'Pup'. The type's major innovation was its employment of Sopwith-Kauper synchronising equipment. This enabled the

pilot to aim the whole aircraft at an enemy machine, greatly simplifying combat and allowing the Pup to gain ascendancy over its German rivals. While other Allied types were easy prey, Pups were strenuously avoided.

Since Sopwith was committed to production of the 1½ Strutter, Pup production was handled by three sub-contractors, with first deliveries to the Royal Naval Air Service (RNAS) occurring in September 1916. Pups were slow to reach the RFC, in spite of mounting losses, since

Sopwith was traditionally an RNAS supplier and the government was unwilling to divert its designs to the RFC. Hence, only three squadrons of RFC Pups fought in France, with others serving at home. Perhaps if more had been delivered, the return to ascendancy of the German scouts early in 1917 would have been avoided.

*Appearing here during the late 1990s as N6181, the Shuttleworth Collection's Pup is a regular air show performer.*

Metal sheeting covered the forward part of the fuselage aft of the engine. The neat fairing was also of metal and closely faired the Le Rhône engine. All aircraft employed a twin-bladed wooden propeller.

While its synchronised machine-gun initially represented a major advance, the Pup was soon to find itself too lightly armed. The Camel rectified this with its twin-gun armament.

Using conventional wood and fabric construction, Sopwith gave the Pup an unusually strong structure. This helped it perform tight manoeuvres, while its light weight allowed reasonable performance with little power. The split axle main undercarriage was of a type used widely by Sopwith.

During missions of up to three hours duration, the pilot was given minimum protection by the Pup's cockpit. Pilots found the aircraft easy to fly and highly effective in combat, however.

In common with the majority of World War I combat aircraft, the Pup employed a simple tail skid. This was easier to maintain than a tail wheel and kept weight to a minimum.

## PUP

This brightly marked aircraft was on the strength of No. 46 Squadron, RFC during 1917. The machine was based at Izel-le-Hameau, France, and typifies the finish of the few that reached the RFC.

## Pup

**Type:** single-seat fighter

**Powerplant:** one 60-kW (80-hp.) Le Rhône rotary piston engine

**Maximum speed:** 180 km/h (112 m.p.h.) at sea level

**Climb rate:** climb to 4907 m (16,100 ft.) in 35 min

**Service ceiling:** 5335 m (17,500 ft.)

**Weights:** empty 357 kg (785 lb.); maximum take-off 556 kg (1,223 lb.)

**Armament:** one fixed forward-firing, synchronised 7.7-mm (.303 cal.) Vickers machine-gun and up to four 11.3-kg (25-lb.) Cooper bombs

**Dimensions:**
| | | |
|---|---|---|
| span | 8.08 m | (26 ft. 6 in.) |
| length | 6.04 m | (19 ft. 10 in.) |
| height | 2.87 m | (9 ft. 5 in.) |
| wing area | 23.60 m² | (254 sq. ft.) |

## COMBAT DATA

### MAXIMUM SPEED

At sea level the Pup could not match the excellent speed of the SPAD S.VII. It was far more agile, however, and had a great advantage in speed over the Halberstadt D.II which was a close German contemporary of the Sopwith type.

| | |
|---|---|
| SPAD S.VII | 192 km/h (119 m.p.h.) |
| PUP | 180 km/h (112 m.p.h.) |
| D.II | 145 km/h (90 m.p.h.) |

### SERVICE CEILING

Although it suffered from an inferior service ceiling, the Pup more than compensated with its impressive agility. Attacking from altitude usually gives an advantage in combat, but German aircraft were very wary of the Pup at all heights.

SPAD S.VII 6550 m (21,500 ft.)
D.II 5974 m (19,600 ft.)
PUP 5335 m (17,500 ft.)

### ARMAMENT

Utilising its limited bomb capacity, the Pup was able to take on a secondary ground-attack role. This made it a more versatile aircraft than either the SPAD or D.II. With its synchronised machine-gun, the Pup was a formidable fighter.

SPAD S.VII — 1 x 7.7-mm (.303 cal.) machine-gun

PUP — 1 x 7.7-mm (.303 cal.) machine-gun / 4 x 11-kg (25-lb.) bombs

D.II — 1 x 7.92-mm machine-gun

## Fighting Scouts of late 1916

■ **ALBATROS D.I:** Having done much to assert the superiority of German aircraft, the D.I was a serious adversary for the Pup.

■ **HALBERSTADT D.II:** By late 1916, the D II was becoming obsolete and was no match for the Sopwith Pup.

■ **NIEUPORT 17:** Originally fitted with a single machine-gun firing above the propeller, the Type 17 was the mount of many Allied aces.

■ **SPAD S.VII:** A powerful engine and streamlined airframe guaranteed the success of the S.VII from its appearance in late 1916.

# SOPWITH

## PUP NAVAL FIGHTER

● Carrier fighter ● Scout ● Navy pioneer

▲ *The pioneers of naval flight were brave and enthusiastic men, who took considerable risks to prove the concept of launching from ships. The value of carrier-launched aircraft was not realised at the time, but the future of naval warfare was to be totally changed by it.*

**N**aval aviation began when a handful of adventurers went to sea in the wood and fabric Sopwith Pup, perfecting the technique of operating from ships' decks. Techniques for launch included take-off from platforms mounted on top of battleship gun turrets, and the first experiments were also made with deck landings. Although these were a success, leading to the first real aircraft-carrier, early naval pilots often paid the ultimate price for their daring challenges.

## SOPWITH PUP

**▲ Splash down**
*Before aircraft began landing on the decks of ships pilots had no choice but to ditch, which was extremely dangerous.*

**Platform launch ▶**
*Trials were carried out with launching platforms on cruisers, but turbulence from the ship's funnel was a major problem.*

**▲ Over the edge**
*The pilot was killed when this Pup ran off the edge of the deck during a trials flight. The crew dashed after the aircraft in an attempt to catch it.*

**▼ Pup in America**
*The US Navy took a keen interest in ship-launced aircraft. This aircraft was flown in Guantanamo Bay in Cuba from the USS Ohio. The launch was made from the ship's 355-mm (14-in.) gun turret.*

**▲ 1¹/₂ Strutter**
*This Sopwith 1¹/₂ Strutter was launched from a cruiser using launch rails on the bow. The skid undercarriage was a new feature.*

### FACTS AND FIGURES

➤ By the end of World War I ten Pups were flying from aircraft-carriers and 13 from battleships and cruisers.

➤ About 1770 Pups were manufactured, many for home defence of Great Britain.

➤ A two-seat civil version of the Pup, the Sopwith Dove, was unsuccessful.

➤ On 28 June 1917 Flt Cdr Rutland flew a Pup from a 5.95-m (19-ft. 6-in.) platform protruding from the light cruiser *Yarmouth*.

➤ Flying a Pup from the *Yarmouth*, Flt Sub. Lt B. A. Smart shot down the Zeppelin L-23.

➤ The Pup was known officially as the Sopwith Scout.

## PROFILE

# First of the carrier fighters

*Although it looked strange, launching from gun turrets was actually quite useful because the aircraft could take off into wind regardless of the ship's course.*

One of the most exciting areas of aviation involved the Sopwith Pup – the first aircraft ever to land on a ship at sea. It happened on 2 August 1917 when Squadron Commander E. H. Dunning matched the speed and path of his aircraft with that of the steaming aircraft-carrier *Furious*, and touched down on the ship.

Thus the Royal Naval Air Service (RNAS) began pioneering the operation of aircraft from vessels on the ocean.

The Sopwith Pup was ideal for this challenging effort. An elegant little biplane with wings of equal span, the Pup entered service with Britain's flying corps and navy in 1916. The Pup is remembered today as a true gem of a fighter aircraft,

almost totally devoid of faults and effective with its forward-firing, synchronised machine-gun. At the time of its introduction, the Pup was able to remain manoeuvrable and responsive at a greater height than any other fighter.

Flying at sea was hazardous, and the trials killed many men. Naval aviators were as much an elite then as today.

Pups used a 60-kW (80-hp.) Le Rhône rotary engine, a relatively low-powered engine even by the standards of 1916.

In common with aircraft of the period, the Pup was largely of wooden construction and fabric covered.

As the first naval Pups were required to ditch in the sea after a sortie, flotation bags were fitted under the wings to aid recovery of the aircraft.

### PUP

This Royal Flying Corps (RFC) Pup is one of a batch of 350 delivered during 1917/18. About 290 Pups served with the RNAS, including a number diverted from RFC contracts.

Squadron Commander Dunning's third attempt to land an aircraft on the forward flight deck of a ship resulted in his death.

One of the advantages of the fabric-covered fuselage was that damage from hostile machine-gun fire was easily and quickly repaired.

Its low wing loading meant the Pup could hold its height better than any Allied or enemy aircraft of the period and was still manoeuvrable at altitudes of around 4500 m (14,760 ft).

Certain standard British markings of the period were common to RFC and RNAS aircraft, namely the fuselage roundel and striped rudder. Naval aircraft tended to carry their serial number on the fuselage, however, under the leading edge of the tailplane.

Skid undercarriages were fitted to early naval Pups. A system of fore-and-aft wires on the ship's deck engaged 'dog-lead' clips on the Pup's undercarriage to stop the aircraft.

While RFC Pups used a synchronised Vickers machine-gun firing through the propeller, those flying from ships had a single Lewis machine-gun firing upwards and eight strut-mounted Le Prieur rockets.

### Pup

**Type:** single-seat fighter

**Powerplant:** one 60-kW (80-hp.) Le Rhône rotary engine or one 75-kW (100-hp.) Gnome Monosoupape rotary engine

**Maximum speed:** 180 km/h (112 m.p.h.)

**Service ceiling:** 5335 m (17,500 ft.)

**Endurance:** 3 hours

**Weights:** empty 357 kg (785 lb.); maximum take-off 556 kg (1,223 lb.)

**Armament:** one forward-firing synchronised 7.7-mm (.303 cal.) Vickers machine-gun, plus up to four 11.3-kg (25-lb.) bombs

**Dimensions:** span 8.08 m (26 ft. 6 in.)
length 6.04 m (19 ft. 10 in.)
height 2.87 m (9 ft. 5 in.)
wing area 23.60 m² (254 sq. ft.)

### COMBAT DATA

#### MAXIMUM SPEED

Compared to other scout aircraft of the period the Pup had a slight edge in top speed and therefore climb rate. This and the ability to maintain height were important in dogfight situations.

| | |
|---|---|
| PUP | 180 km/h (112 m.p.h.) |
| ALBATROS D.III | 165 km/h (103 m.p.h.) |
| NIEUPORT 17 | 170 km/h (105 m.p.h.) |

#### ARMAMENT

The German Albatros family was well-armed. Later Allied aircraft had better armament – usually two machine-guns. Naval Pups could also carry rockets for attacking Zeppelins.

PUP 1 x 7.7-mm (.303 cal.) machine-gun
ALBATROS D.III 2 x 7.92-mm machine-guns
NIEUPORT 17 1 x 7.7-mm (.303 cal.) machine-gun

#### SERVICE CEILING

All three types had comparable service ceilings, although the important factor was not how high the aircraft could fly but how the aircraft performed at altitude. The Pup was acknowledged as having good handling above 4500 m (14,760 ft.) due to low wing loading.

PUP 5335 m (17,500 ft.)
ALBATROS D.III 5486 m (18,000 ft.)
NIEUPORT 17 5350 m (17,550 ft.)

## Sopwith naval aircraft of World War I

**TABLOID:** One of the outstanding aircraft produced before 1914, the land-based Tabloid entered naval service that year and was used by the RNAS to bomb Zeppelin sheds in 1914.

**TYPE 860 SEAPLANE:** One of a family of large single-engined seaplanes built for the RNAS, the torpedo-armed Type 860 patrolled home waters during 1915 and 1916.

**BABY:** Delivered between 1915 and 1916, Babies operated from seaplane-carriers in the North Sea and Mediterranean. Bombing raids were carried out using two 30-kg bombs.

**CUCKOO:** The first landplane torpedo-carrier able to operate from a flight deck, the Cuckoo entered service aboard the *Argus* just before the Armistice and was too late to see action.

# SOPWITH

# CAMEL

● Fighter scout ● Close support fighter ● Flown by aces

▲ The Camel at last
gave Allied fighter pilots an aircraft that could take on the German Albatros and Fokker scouts, and did much to restore morale.

It was a wicked, snub-nosed killer. The Sopwith Camel gave Britain a fighter capable of defeating any adversary in the 'Kaiser's War'. But the Camel was not for the faint-hearted, and was mastered only with the most superb flying skills. The Camel's bad habits were also its strength: because propeller, engine and armament were concentrated up front, the Camel was difficult to fly but was also incredibly manoeuvrable in a dogfight.

## SOPWITH CAMEL

▲ **Deck launch**
The Camel was used in carrier trials by HMS Pegasus in November 1919. The sailors watching from the lower deck obviously doubted whether the experiment would work.

▲ **Supreme dogfighter**
Combining a good climb rate with twin-gun firepower and immense agility, the Camel helped restore Allied fortunes in the sky after the disastrous defeats of April 1917.

**Airborne take-off** ▶
This Camel was dropped from the airship R.23 as part of a bizarre experiment to give airships defence against enemy fighters.

▲ **Camel replica**
Although 5490 Camels were completed in the last two years of World War I, none have survived in flying condition. The only Camels to be seen in the air today are replicas.

◀ **Down in no-man's land**
This Camel crashed between the Canadian and German lines at Villers le Roye in August 1918. The belts of machine-gun ammunition have been dragged clear of the aircraft for use by the soldiers. Although the Camel was a tough opponent, it was also a tough aircraft to fly, and many novice pilots died in spinning incidents.

## FACTS AND FIGURES

➤ The Camel prototype was first flown by Harry Hawker in January 1917.

➤ Camel production totalled 5,490, with 1325 produced in 1917 and 4165 in 1918.

➤ Sopwith Camels destroyed 1294 enemy aircraft during World War I, more than any other aircraft of the conflict.

➤ The Camel pilot sat in a wicker chair without a restraining seat belt.

➤ The US Navy tested the Sopwith Camel as a ship-borne fighter aboard the battleships Texas and Arkansas.

➤ The Camel was flown by Canadian ace pilots 'Billy' Barker and Roy Brown.

# PROFILE

# Sopwith's finest fighting scout

The Camel was introduced in 1917, initially as a fighter for the Royal Naval Air Service and soon afterward for the Royal Flying Corps. From its first appearance at the Battle of Ypres, the Camel proved itself to be an agile and potent pursuit craft.

Many rotary engines were flown in the Camel and numerous versions were built, including a night-fighter with a pair of Lewis guns mounted above the top wing centre section.

Most Camels lifted off noisily from grass strips to fly to the Front and beyond, to engage Fokker, Pfalz and other German warplanes. Some of these high-performing Sopwiths had special tasks, however: several went to sea aboard the aircraft-carriers HMS Furious and Pegasus or were catapulted from atop turrets on other warships. Two Camels were modified for trials as parasite fighters, carried aboard the airship R.23.

Camels served in several foreign air forces, including those of Belgium and Greece as well as with the American Expeditionary Force.

Britain led the world in taking aircraft to sea. This Camel was launched during trials in the Forth estuary from the carrier HMS Furious.

## CAMEL

This Camel served on the Western Front in 1918 with 'B' flight, 210 Squadron RAF, previously 10 (Naval) Squadron RNAS.

The Camel got its (unofficial) name from the small 'hump' fairing over the twin Vickers guns.

In common with most aircraft of the time, the Camel was driven by a simple fixed-pitch wooden propeller.

Camels used a number of different engines including the Clerget, Le Rhone 9J and Gnome Monosoupape.

The forward fuselage contained the engine, fuel, pilot and guns. This concentration of weight and the high torque led to the tricky handling that made Camels infamous.

Twin ammunition feed chutes led from stowage bins to the guns, which were cocked by large levers. Although the Vickers guns were generally reliable, many pilots kept a hammer in the cockpit to enable them to clear jams.

The outer fuselage skin was aluminium around the engine, plywood around the centre section and fabric around the rear section.

Part of the upper wing was cut out to give the pilot better upwards visibility.

The elevator had a large 'notch' cut in it to allow free movement of the rudder.

Mastering rudder control was all-important to Camel pilots, for it allowed them to make violent turns without producing spectacular and often fatal spins.

A simple tailskid was fitted, with an elastic cord shock-absorber.

### Camel F.I

**Type:** single-seat fighting scout

**Powerplant:** one 97-kW (130-hp.) Clerget nine-cylinder air-cooled rotary piston engine

**Maximum speed:** 188 km/h (117 m.p.h.) at sea level

**Climb rate:** 10 min to 3000 m (9,850 ft.)

**Endurance:** 2 hr 30 min

**Service ceiling:** 5790 m (19,000 ft.)

**Weights:** empty 421 kg (926 lb.); maximum take-off 659 kg (1,450 lb.)

**Armament:** two 7.7-mm (.303 cal.) Vickers machine-guns on nose synchronised to fire through the propeller, plus four 11.35-kg (25-lb.) bombs carried on external racks beneath the fuselage

**Dimensions:**
span 8.53 m (28 ft.)
length 5.72 m (19 ft.)
height 2.60 m (9 ft.)
wing area 21.46 m² (231 sq. ft.)

## COMBAT DATA

### MAXIMUM SPEED

The Camel was reasonably fast and had a speed advantage over the Albatros D.V which appeared at the same time. Other Allied fighters like the SPAD and the S.E.5 were considerably quicker, but lacked the Camel's incredible agility.

| | |
|---|---|
| CAMEL | 188 km/h (117 m.p.h.) |
| ALBATROS D.V | 165 km/h (102 m.p.h.) |
| SPAD XIII | 215 km/h (133 m.p.h.) |

### ENDURANCE

British fighters were generally more aggressive than their opponents, and scouts usually operated over enemy territory. They needed to be able to stay in the air longer than German machines which, with a few notable exceptions, patrolled close to their home airfields.

| CAMEL | ALBATROS D.V | SPAD XIII |
|---|---|---|
| 2 hours 30 minutes | 2 hours | 2 hours |

### ARMAMENT

Most fighters of 1916 had a single machine-gun synchronised to fire through the propeller blades. The Camel's generation of scouts invariably carried two guns, which was to remain the standard fighter armament for the next 15 years.

CAMEL 2 x 7.7-mm (.303 cal.) machine-guns

ALBATROS D.V 2 x 7.92-mm machine-guns

SPAD XIII 2 x 7.7-mm (.303 cal.) machine-guns

## Sopwith single-seat scouts

**SOPWITH PUP:** Entering service in 1916, the Pup was underpowered but reasonably fast. It had a good climb rate and was very agile, and was very much a pilot's aircraft.

**SOPWITH TRIPLANE:** The Sopwith Triplane appeared in 1916 as a variant of the Pup. It had an extra wing for added lift and increased climb performance.

**SOPWITH SNIPE:** A development of the Camel with more power, more speed and more forgiving handling, the Snipe entered service in the last months of the war.

# SOPWITH

# SNIPE

● World War I ● RAF fighter of the early 1920s ● Camel successor

**A**lthough it was involved in combat for only the last few weeks of World War I, the Snipe was, however, clearly the best Allied fighter of the conflict. Designed in 1917 to use a new 171.5-kW (230-hp.) rotary engine, it resembled the Sopwith Camel but was not as difficult to handle. It became the RAF's standard fighter in the early-1920s, serving in Egypt, Iraq and India as well as with home-based air-defence squadrons.

▲ *Joining combat only briefly at the end of World War I, the Snipe still managed to impress with its exceptional handling qualities. Many experts consider it to have been the greatest single-seat fighter of the conflict. Snipes went on to form the backbone of the post-war RAF.*

## SOPWITH SNIPE

◀ **Restored Snipe**
*Pilots had a degree of upwards visibility through the large cut-out in the upper wing. This was important to see attacks from above.*

▲ **Camel origins**
*Although the Snipe shared the Camel's manoeuvrability, it did not have the earlier fighter's tricky handling qualities. The Snipe had more power and two sets of wing struts on each side.*

◀ **Starting the Snipe**
*The Huck's starter consisted of a long spindle chain-driven from the car's engine and attached to the Snipe's propeller boss.*

**Service into the 1920s** ▶
*Snipes served as front-line RAF fighters until 1926. During this period many of the squadrons adopted flamboyant unit markings.*

◀ **Vickers armament**
*The Snipe was armed with twin forward-firing 7.7-mm (.303 cal.) machine-guns, aimed by the sight between the guns of this restored aircraft.*

### FACTS AND FIGURES

➤ Major W. G. Barker received the Victoria Cross for destroying four enemy aircraft in one action, even though he was wounded.

➤ After the war, No. 25 Squadron took its Snipes to Constantinople for a year.

➤ Snipes continued to serve as trainers for some time after 1926.

➤ Due to the B.R.2 engine not being ready, the prototype Snipe flew with the B.R.1 as fitted to the Camel.

➤ An attack aircraft, the Salamander, was developed from the Snipe.

➤ An A.B.C. Dragonfly I-powered Snipe, called the Dragon, was not successful.

**PROFILE**

# Top World War I fighter design

Although it retained the humped forward fuselage that had earned the Camel its name, the 7F.1 Snipe's larger engine meant that the fuselage was deeper and on the third prototype longer wings were added.

Its combat career may have been brief, but Major W. G. Barker earned the Victoria Cross while flying a Snipe.

On 27 October 1918, in a series of dogfights with a total of 15 Fokker D.VIIIs, he shot down four of the enemy aircraft.

As well as the standard single-seater, there was a long-range bomber escort version, the 7F.1A, which had an endurance of 4½ hours.

A small number of Snipes were fitted with arrestor hooks and flotation bags for deck landing trials. There were also about 40 two-seat trainer conversions, five of which formed the RAF's first formation aerobatic team flown by instructor pilots.

*Above: Decorated with the colourful markings of the time and demonstrating exceptional performance, the Snipe was a popular performer at 1920s RAF pageants.*

*Left: Showing obvious similarities to the Camel, the Snipe was an all-round better performer. It retained the two-gun Vickers armament, as shown on this American museum replica.*

Like most fighters of the time, the Snipe had a two-bladed wooden propeller. The propeller of Major Barker's aircraft was shattered when the aircraft 'nosed-over' on landing.

Internally the Snipe had an all-wooden structure. This was covered by a combination of plywood, fabric and sheet metal.

This unusual fin and rudder arrangement was used on the second prototype and early production machines; all other Snipes had a Camel-like tail.

E8102

Flying initially with a Bentley B.R.1 engine, the first prototype looked almost identical to a Camel. All later Snipes used the B.R.2 as their powerplant and were the RAF's last rotary-engined fighters.

It was not until the third prototype that two-bay wings were fitted. The lower wing was staggered backwards to give the pilot a better view downwards, which was especially important during trench bombing missions.

The tail of Major Barker's aircraft was seriously damaged, probably when it overturned.

### SNIPE MK I
Major W. G. Barker, a Canadian temporarily on attachment to No. 201 Squadron, won the Victoria Cross flying this aircraft. Barker managed to cross back into friendly territory at very low level before he crash-landed his Snipe.

## Snipe Mk I
**Type:** single-seat biplane fighter

**Powerplant:** one 171.5-kW (230-hp.) Bentley B.R.2 nine-cylinder air-cooled rotary engine

**Maximum speed:** 195 km/h (121 m.p.h.)

**Climb rate:** climb to 3048 m (10,000 ft.) in 27.3 min

**Endurance:** 3 hours

**Service ceiling:** 6248 m (20,500 ft.)

**Weight:** 914 kg (2,010 lb.) maximum take-off

**Armament:** two 7.7-mm (.303 cal.) machine-guns in forward fuselage, one 51-kg (112-lb.) or four 9-kg (20-lb.) bombs

**Dimensions:** span 9.47 m (31 ft.)
length 6.05 m (19 ft. 10 in.)
height 2.90 m (9 ft. 6 in.)
wing area 25.08 m² (270 sq. ft.)

### COMBAT DATA

**MAXIMUM SPEED**
The SPAD was respected for its exceptional speed, but the Snipe was not far behind and was far more manoeuvrable. The Albatros represented one of the final developments of a long line.

| | |
|---|---|
| SNIPE Mk I | 195 km/h (121 m.p.h.) |
| SPAD S.XIII | 224 km/h (139 m.p.h.) |
| ALBATROS D.V | 186 km/h (115 m.p.h.) |

**ENGINE POWER**
A powerful Bentley engine gave the Snipe a good rate of climb and enough power to carry light bombs in a secondary attack role. The SPAD and Albatros did not serve long after the war.

| SNIPE Mk I | S.XIII | D.V |
|---|---|---|
| 171.5 kW (230 hp.) | 164 kW (220 hp.) | 149 kW (200 hp.) |

**SERVICE CEILING**
A high-flying aircraft is able to dive on the enemy, attacking at great speed and maintaining momentum throughout the engagement. High initial altitude was crucial to Barker's successful attack.

SNIPE Mk I 6248 m (20,500 ft.) — S.XIII 6650 m (21,800 ft.) — D.V 5700 m (18,700 ft.)

## Victoria Cross winners' aircraft

**ROYAL AIRCRAFT FACTORY B.E.2:** Rhodes-Moorhouse of No. 2 Squadron, Royal Flying Corps, was honoured for a 1915 raid.

**BRISTOL SCOUT:** Major Lanoe G. Hawker was awarded the VC for a successful combat in which he was armed only with a cavalry rifle.

**NIEUPORT 17 SCOUT:** Captain Albert Ball was one of the Allies' most successful single-seater pilots, receiving the VC posthumously.

**ROYAL AIRCRAFT FACTORY S.E.5A:** Major Edward Mannock achieved 61 victories and was posthumously honoured in 1919.

# SOPWITH

# TRIPLANE

● Agile dogfighter ● First combat triplane ● Naval service

▲ Making its combat debut in France during February 1917, the Triplane was feared by the enemy. Manfred von Richthofen stated that the Triplane was 'the best Allied fighter at that time'.

**S**opwith's Triplane flew for the first time in May 1916, just as the Sopwith Pup was joining the action on the Western Front. Six months later the first Sopwith Camel flew. As a result of appearing between these two famous fighters, the Triplane was built in only limited numbers. Even so, it made quite an impact on the fighting in France in spring 1917, claiming a large number of victories and inspiring several German fighter triplane designs.

## SOPWITH TRIPLANE

▲ Hispano-Suiza power
N509 was built with a 112-kW (150-hp.) Hispano-Suiza engine.

▲ High climber
With three wings providing vast amounts of lift, the Triplane could climb faster than its contemporaries.

Small-scale production ▶
Despite its superb flying qualities only 150 Triplanes were built. The majority flew with the RNAS.

▲ Airworthy again
The only Triplanes that are still flying are replicas. This example is owned by the Fighter Collection at Duxford.

▲ Lone survivor
The only authentic Triplane still in existence is preserved at the RAF Museum, Hendon.

Respected fighter ▶
The Triplane was highly regarded by the Germans and led Fokker to build a triplane known as the Dr.1.

## FACTS AND FIGURES

➤ The structure of the Triplane was very similar to its highly successful predecessor, the Sopwith Pup.

➤ Harry Hawker looped the Triplane just three minutes into its first flight.

➤ The 150 Triplanes produced were built by three different companies.

➤ One of the 16 victories Raymond Collishaw claimed in June 1917 was the famous German ace Allmenroder.

➤ Despite being successful the Triplane saw only seven months of front-line service.

➤ Five Triplanes were delivered to France and one to Russia.

# World's first fighting triplane

The purpose of the Triplane's triple wings was to give pilots a better view than they had from the Pup's cockpit while retaining the earlier fighter's manoeuvrability. The wings were shorter and much narrower than those of the Pup, with the central wing level with the top of the fuselage and the top wing high above it.

No more than 150 Triplanes were built and in British service all were flown by the Royal Naval Air Service (RNAS). The RNAS had formed its own land-based fighter units to help meet the urgent need for more fighter squadrons on the Western Front, and exchanged its Spad VIIs for Triplanes ordered by the Royal Flying Corps.

By the spring of 1917, five squadrons were equipped with the Triplane on the Western Front. No. 10 Squadron was particularly successful, with 'B' Flight managing to down 87 enemy aircraft in just 55 days. All five squadrons re-equipped with Camels later in the year.

Away from the Western Front, one Triplane operated with RNAS forces in the Aegean and another was fitted with skis for service in Russia. One version was fitted with bigger wings and a Hispano-Suiza V-8 engine, but only two were built.

The triplane design was regarded with much suspicion when first introduced. However, pilots soon found the 'extra wing' gave the aircraft a superb rate of climb and good agility. The wood and fabric wings were supported by continuous broad-chord wooden interplane struts. Ailerons were fitted to all three wings.

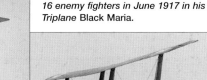

Below: Raymond Collishaw, one of the most famous Triplane pilots, shot down 16 enemy fighters in June 1917 in his Triplane Black Maria.

Above: Triplanes were well-liked by Royal Navy pilots. Their front-line career was shortened by the disproportionate amount of repair work required for minor damage.

Most production Triplanes were powered by the 96.9-kW (130-hp.) Clerget 9B engine which gave the aircraft excellent performance. Several airframes were tested with a Le Rhône 9J engine, but this was not successful.

A single Vickers machine-gun was mounted centrally in front of the cockpit. It was intended that Triplanes constructed by Oakley & Co. would have twin Vickers guns, greatly increasing firepower, but none of these machines saw operational service.

On the first prototypes the entire tail assembly was identical to that of the Sopwith Pup, but the Triplane had the refinement of an adjustable tailplane. However, in February 1917 a smaller tailplane and elevators were fitted which improved the Triplane's control response and enabled the aircraft to be dived vertically.

Like most World War I combat aircraft, the Triplane was constructed from wood and doped fabric, which gave a light, but strong, airframe. The pilot sat in an open cockpit with the middle wing level with the pilot's eyes.

## TRIPLANE

N533 was one of batch of six Sopwith Triplanes built by Clayton & Shuttleworth. 'N'-prefixed serial numbers were allocated to RNAS aircraft between 1916 and 1930.

## Triplane

**Type:** single-seat fighting scout

**Powerplant:** one 96.9-kW (130-hp.) Clerget 9B nine-cylinder air-cooled rotary engine

**Maximum speed:** 188 km/h (116 m.p.h.) at 1830 m (6,000 ft.)

**Endurance:** 2 hr 45 min

**Initial climb rate:** 10 min 35 sec to 3050 m (10,000 ft.)

**Service ceiling:** 6250 m (20,500 ft.)

**Weights:** empty 450 kg (20,500 ft.); maximum take-off 642 kg (1,412 lb.)

**Armament:** one 7.7-mm (.303 cal.) nose-mounted Vickers machine-gun

**Dimensions:**
| | | |
|---|---|---|
| span | 8.08 m | (26 ft. 6 in.) |
| length | 5.94 m | (18 ft. 6 in.) |
| height | 3.20 m | (10 ft. 6 in.) |
| wing area | 21.46 m² (231 sq. ft.) | |

## COMBAT DATA

### MAXIMUM SPEED

The Sopwith Triplane possessed excellent speed characteristics and was faster than the later Fokker Triplane. The slower Nieuport Type 11 was in service when the Triplane was introduced and lacked the power, and therefore the speed, of the later Triplanes.

| | |
|---|---|
| **TRIPLANE** | 188 km/h (117 m.p.h.) |
| **Dr.1 TRIPLANE** | 165 km/h (102 m.p.h.) |
| **TYPE 11** | 155 km/h (96 m.p.h.) |

### ENDURANCE

The Triplane's Clerget engine was economical and gave the aircraft excellent endurance, which was vital for long patrols over enemy lines. The Type 11 was also a good performer in this respect. Dr.1s, like many German designs, lacked endurance.

| TRIPLANE | Dr.1 TRIPLANE | TYPE 11 |
|---|---|---|
| 2 hours 45 min | 1 hour 30 min | 2 hours 30 min |

### SERVICE CEILING

Both Triplane designs had an impressive service ceiling thanks to powerful engines and the high lift generated by three wings. The earlier Nieuport could not reach these altitudes. However, by 1917 ceiling was dictated by the cold temperatures and lack of oxygen and their effects on the pilots at altitude, rather than the aircraft's performance.

TRIPLANE 6250 m (20,500 ft.)

TYPE 11 4500 m (14,800 ft.)

Dr.1 TRIPLANE 6095 m (20,000 ft.)

---

## Great War naval fighters

**■ MORANE PARASOL:** The most famous feat by a naval Parasol fighter was by F./Sub-Lt Warneford of No. 1 Squadron, RNAS, who downed Zeppelin L.Z. 37 in this machine.

**■ NIEUPORT TYPE 11:** Entering service in 1915, the Type 11 saw much combat. RNAS pilot Sqn Cdr Bell Davies won the V.C. for rescuing a downed pilot under fire.

**■ SOPWITH 2F.1 CAMEL:** The Camel 2F.1 was designed specifically as a shipboard fighter and saw action against Zeppelins from aircraft-carriers such as HMS Furious.

# SPAD

# S.VII & S.XII

● World War I fighter ● Sturdy construction ● Flown by aces

## SPAD **S.VII & S.XII**

**▲ Braving the weather**
*Operating conditions on the Western Front were harsh, especially in winter.*

**◄ Built tough**
*Appearances were not at all deceptive; the S.VII was as sturdy as it looked.*

**Key to success ▶**
*What made the S.VII special was its powerful Hispano-Suiza in-line V8 engine and its streamlined airframe.*

**▼ International popularity**
*The S.VII was such an improvement over earlier fighters that it found favour with other nations. The Royal Flying Corps used the little machine once initial problems had been solved.*

**▲ American fliers**
*In France, the American Expeditionary Force acquired a handful of SPAD S.VIIs, though they were primarily used to train new pilots for the later S.XIII which was supplied in larger numbers. Some went across the Atlantic after the Armistice.*

**M**any consider the SPAD S.VII and S.XII to have been the best Allied fighters of the late stages of World War I. Previous fighter scouts had often been flimsy and prone to breaking up during aerial manoeuvres, but the sturdy SPAD was different. Flown by aces such as the Frenchman Georges Guynemer and Italian Francesco Barraca, the S.VII played a crucial part in helping to wrest supremacy in the air from the Germans.

*▲ SPAD first made its mark building two-seat pusher biplanes, though in 1915 the company turned its attention to fighters. What emerged was the S.VII, one of the best fighters of World War I.*

## FACTS AND FIGURES

➤ SPAD was originally the name of an aircraft manufacturing company. When Blériot took it over, the initials remained.

➤ Some 300 of all S.XII variants were built, a small number of them as float-planes.

➤ Armand Pinsard was the first pilot to score a 'kill' in a S.VII on 23 August 1916.

➤ After a series of fatal crashes caused by weak airframes, the Royal Flying Corps initially refused to accept S.VIIs.

➤ S.VIIs were built under licence at Brooklands, near Weybridge in the UK.

➤ Several examples of this famous fighter are preserved in Europe and the USA.

# PROFILE

# A new fighter for a new war

Taking to the air in April 1916, the arrival of the SPAD S.VII could not have been better timed. The 'war of attrition' was living up to its name as thousands were killed on the battlefield. In the air pilots battled constantly, but the Germans enjoyed an advantage with their Albatros and Fokker scouts. The arrival of the SPAD S.VII on the Western Front gave the Allied flyers an aircraft with which they could meet the enemy on equal terms.

The first unit to receive the S.VII was Escadrille (Squadron) N. 26 in August 1916, with one of its pilots making the first recorded victory in the little machine later the same month.

In combat, the S.VII soon established itself and was blessed with an excellent rate of climb, but most of all it gained celebrity as a steady gun platform enabling pilots to score many 'kills'. An improved variant, the S.XII, was built under the encouragement of the French ace

*Above: Aircraft flown by the aces, especially the Americans and the French, often wore bright markings.*

Georges Guynemer and entered service in 1917. Guynemer scored four victories in the new machine, but it did not prove popular, and only 300 were delivered. Later development culminated in the S.XIII.

*Below: Seen wearing the markings of Captain Eddie Rickenbacker's famous mount, this is actually a replica of an S.XIII, a much improved S.VII. This variant became the most famous.*

## S.VII

This colourful S.VII is a post-war aircraft, assigned to the commanding officer of XIII Grupo, Regia Aeronautica (Italian air force) in 1924.

### S.VII

**Type:** single-seat fighting scout

**Powerplant:** one 134-kW (180-hp.) Hispano-Suiza 8Ab V8 in-line piston engine

**Maximum speed:** 212 km/h (132 m.p.h.)

**Endurance:** 1 hr 30 min

**Initial climb rate:** 421 m/min (1,381 f.p.m.)

**Range:** 350 km (217 mi.)

**Service ceiling:** 6550 m (21,500 ft.)

**Weights:** empty 500 kg (1,100 lb.); loaded 705 kg (1,554 lb.)

**Armament:** one fixed forward-firing 7.7-mm (.303 cal.) machine-gun with 500 rounds

**Dimensions:**
span 7.82 m (25 ft. 8 in.)
length 6.08 m (19 ft. 11 in.)
height 2.20 m (7 ft. 3 in.)
wing area 17.85 m² (192 sq. ft.)

---

For the time, the wing had a remarkably thin aerofoil section and, unlike many other designs, featured ailerons on the upper wing only. Two sets of struts were mounted between the wings on each side, with a third set acting as tie struts for the bracing and flying wires. Construction was entirely of wood.

Underneath the smooth exterior was a very strong airframe with four major box sections. The S.VII was heavier than some of its contemporaries but it was soon discovered that S.VIIs could be sent up to meet the opposition time and again, and be able to engage in dogfights without the risk of breaking up in the air.

In common with most Allied fighter scouts of World War I, SPAD S.VIIs often wore bright colours on their rudders, usually representing the national flag of the service that used them. Even after the war, Italian examples, such as this one, continued to wear the Tricolore.

Powering the SPAD S.VII was a 134-kW (180-hp.) Hispano-Suiza 8Ab V8 engine. A powerful and initially reliable engine, it made a perfect marriage with the sleek airframe. On the front line, however, SPADs were often plagued by overheating engines, something which was never rectified during their service careers.

Apart from the forward fuselage panelling, the airframe was covered in doped fabric. This particular machine is actually unpainted, the beige finish being the natural colour of the fabric material.

## COMBAT DATA

### POWER

At the time of its appearance in 1916, the power of the SPAD S.VII was heartily welcomed. It at last put Allied pilots on an equal footing with their German adversaries.

| S.VII | F.1 CAMEL | D.VII |
|---|---|---|
| 134 kW (180 hp.) | 97 kW (130 hp.) | 138 kW (185 hp.) |

### ENDURANCE

With many of the aerial battles taking place over enemy-held territory, Allied aircraft such as the S.VII and the Sopwith F.1 Camel needed greater endurance in order to engage in combat.

S.VII 1 hr 30 min
F.1 CAMEL 2 hr 30 min
D.VII 1 hr 30 min

### ARMAMENT

If there was a drawback to the SPAD S.VII it lay in its lack of powerful armament. The Camel was harder hitting, but also more difficult to fly. The Fokker D.VII also sported two guns.

S.VII 1 x 7.7-mm (.303 cal.) machine-gun
F.1 CAMEL 2 x 7.7-mm (.303 cal,) machine-guns
D.VII 2 x 7.92-mm machine-guns

---

## European SPAD S.VIIs

**FINLAND:** After the end of World War I, S.VIIs continued in service for a few years, particularly with nations such as Finland.

**GREAT BRITAIN:** This particular S.VII was a French machine acquired by the RFC in 1917.

**ITALY:** Some SPADs in post-war Italian service were painted in this dark green colour scheme with a white band on the tail.

# SPAD
# S.XIII

● **Best of the SPADs** ● **Flown by aces** ● **Biplane fighter**

▲ *One of the most flamboyant units of World War I, the Escadrille Lafayette gained considerable success with its SPAD S.XIIIs. The aircraft was not as agile as many contemporaries, but gained a reputation for its high speed and strength.*

O ne of the finest fighters of World War I, the SPAD S.XIII was the culmination of a long line of SPAD fighters. Heavy, fast and very rugged, the S.XIII was immediately successful, taking on the best German designs over the Western Front. It saw action with the new American squadrons in 1918, and became the favoured mount of many aces. The S.XIII was so good that it remained in service after the war.

---

## SPAD S.XIII

▲ **Crashed SPAD**
The SPAD had a reputation as a rugged aircraft, but no fighter could survive a crash like this.

▲ **Adornments**
American pilots adorned their aircraft with bold emblems, including the Indian's head of the *Escadrille Lafayette*.

▼ **SPAD seven**
The similar S.VII was actually a much less powerful aircraft with a single gun.

▲ **Museum piece**
A few SPADs remain as museum exhibits as a testimony to the design. A flying full-size replica is also on display in the United States.

**Bull nose** ▶
Pilots loved the SPAD for its performance and also for its solid, threatening appearance. The success of the aircraft owed a great deal to the very powerful Hispano-Suiza engine.

---

## FACTS AND FIGURES

➤ The top-scoring American ace of World War I was Eddie Rickenbacker, who gained many of his 26 kills in a S.XIII.

➤ SPAD was an abbreviation of Societé Pour L'Aviation et ses Dérives.

➤ SPADs were also used by the British Royal Flying Corps and Royal Air Force.

➤ Orders for S.XIIIs at the end of the war amounted to 10,000 aircraft; these were cancelled after the Armistice.

➤ After the war SPAD S.XIIIs were exported to Czechoslovakia, Japan and Poland.

➤ The SPAD was also flown by French aces like Fonck, Guynemer and Nungesser.

# PROFILE

# Biggest and fastest SPAD

Louis Bleriot took over the SPAD company when it went bankrupt and went on to produce a highly acclaimed family of fighter aircraft. After experimenting with radical and unsuccessful designs with a gunner in front the propeller, the company produced the SPAD S.VII, a conventional design with an eight-cylinder Vee engine. First flown in 1916, this aircraft was widely used by the Allies, including the American forces.

The success of the S.VII led to the much more powerful S.XIII with a longer-span wing and improved ailerons. The prototype first flew in April 1917, a time when the Allies were suffering badly from the latest German aircraft. It was rushed into service quickly and met with instant success; the aircraft was required in great numbers and sub-contractors began producing them in the thousands.

A single-seat photo-reconnaissance version, the SPAD S.XVII, was produced just

*Below: The S.XX was a two-seat spotter-scout aircraft. It failed to live up to the reputation of the single-seat SPAD designs.*

*Above: After the war SPADs were highly popular for sport flying because of their good performance. This aircraft was flown in the Detroit races in 1922.*

as the war ended. It had two cameras and only a single machine-gun. The projected S.XXI was cancelled as the war came to an end.

## S.XIII

**Type:** single-seat Vee-engined fighter biplane and scout aircraft

**Powerplant:** one 164-kW (220-hp.) Hispano-Suiza 8Be eight-cylinder Vee engine

**Maximum speed:** 224 km/h (130 m.p.h.)

**Endurance:** 2 hr

**Range:** 400 km (250 mi.) (estimated)

**Service ceiling:** 6650 m (21,800 ft.)

**Weights:** maximum take-off 845 kg (1,859 lb.)

**Armament:** two Vickers 7.7-mm (.303 cal.) water-cooled machine-guns

**Dimensions:**
| | | |
|---|---|---|
| span | 8.10 m | (26 ft. 7 in.) |
| length | 6.30 m | (20 ft. 8 in.) |
| height | 2.35 m | (7 ft. 8 in.) |
| wing area | 20.00 m² | (199 sq. ft.) |

## S.XIII

**Probably the finest French fighter of the war, the S.XIII was the favoured aircraft of the Escadrille Lafayette.**

The S.XIII was better armed than most Allied fighters, having two Vickers machine-guns instead of the single gun of earlier types. The cockpit was very close to the upper wing surface.

The Lafayette Escadrille was an American-staffed squadron consisting of volunteer pilots fighting for the French air force. The unit included aces such as Raoul Lufbery, who shot down 17 enemy aircraft.

Like the S.VII, the S.XIII had a long, sloping fin with a ribbed trailing edge. The aircraft had large, powerful rudder and elevator surfaces.

The S.XIII's success was mainly due to the power of the Hispano-Suiza engine. The previous two-seat SPAD had an unreliable engine.

Many aircraft had tailwheels by 1917, but the S.XIII retained a simple skid. The fuselage structure was very strong; this was one of the reasons that the American Skyraider pilots in Vietnam nicknamed their similarly rugged aircraft the 'SPAD'.

## COMBAT DATA

### MAXIMUM SPEED

With its closely cowled fuselage and very powerful engine, the S.XIII could outrun almost any other fighter. The Camel and D.VII had lower all-out speed, but both were more agile. This was an important factor as most combat degenerated into turning dogfights.

| | |
|---|---|
| S.XIII | 224 km/h (140 m.p.h.) |
| CAMEL | 185 km/h (115 m.p.h.) |
| D.VII | 200 km/h (124 m.p.h.) |

### ARMAMENT

By 1917 fighter designers on the Allied side had caught up with their German counterparts who had been arming their fighters with twin guns for a long time. The Vickers guns fitted to the Camel and S.XIII were highly effective and reliable.

| | |
|---|---|
| S.XIII | 2 x 7.7-mm (.303 cal.) machine-guns |
| CAMEL | 2 x 7.7-mm (.303 cal.) machine-guns |
| D.VII | 2 x 7.9-mm machine-guns |

### ENDURANCE

Endurance was less important to these dedicated air combat machines than to patrol and observation aircraft. It was still a vital commodity, however; a pilot who had to break off combat for lack of fuel was vulnerable as he turned towards base. Long endurance also meant that a fighter could fly further over enemy territory, denying more of the front-line to their observation balloons. Two hours' combat flying was sufficient for most pilots.

| | |
|---|---|
| S.XIII | 2 hours |
| CAMEL | 2 hours |
| D.VII | 1 ½ hours |

## Best fighters of World War I

**SPAD VII:** The VII was probably the second-best SPAD fighter after the model S.XIII. It was fitted with only one gun, but had similar handling and ruggedness and a high top speed.

**FOKKER D.VII:** A good claimant for the title of best fighter of World War I, the D.VII was such a good performer that the Allies specifically ordered their confiscation after the war.

**SOPWITH CAMEL:** Fast and extremely agile, the twin-gun Camel was a tricky aircraft for novice pilots, gaining a reputation for spinning easily. It was highly successful in combat, however.

# SUKHOI

# Su-2

● Close-support bomber ● Heavy losses ● Wooden construction

**A**long with Germany, Great Britain and the USA, in the mid-1930s the Soviet Union saw the need to develop a multi-purpose tactical bomber. The resulting Su-2 never achieved the air superiority enjoyed by the Germans and suffered terrible losses at the hands of Messerschmitt Bf 109 and Focke-Wulf 190 fighters. These losses resulted in the Su-2's premature relegation to second-line tasks in 1942.

▲ Many of the 500 Su-2s that were hastily constructed to provide the Soviet air force with a close-support bomber were lost in the first few months of Operation Barbarossa. A large number, like this example, were damaged on the ground and could not be repaired before being taken by advancing German soldiers.

## SUKHOI **Su-2**

**▲ Sukhoi on skis**
*For winter operations in the snow and ice that cover much of Russia during the winter, the Su-2w/M-82 could be fitted with non-retractable skis.*

**▲ Molotov production**
*Production of the Su-2w/M-82, also referred to as the Su-4, was based in the town of Molotov.*

**High attrition ▶**
*Because of the heavy losses suffered, only one Su-2 (mostly replica parts) survives today at Monino, Moscow.*

**▼ Heavy losses**
*Even when fitted with the more powerful M-88 engine, the Su-2's performance was inadequate. Losses to German fighters were prohibitively high.*

**▲ German onslaught**
*As the German forces rapidly advanced through western Russia during the summer of 1941, many Soviet aircraft were destroyed or damaged on the ground, such as this hastily camouflaged Su-2.*

## FACTS AND FIGURES

➤ Three factories – Kharkov, Tananrog and Aircraft Factory No. 207 near Moscow – built production Su-2s (BB-1s).

➤ Fifteen Soviet air regiments operated the Su-2 during World War II.

➤ During 1941, several Su-2s were pressed into emergency action as fighters.

➤ In September 1941, Yekaterina Zelenko, flying an Su-2, made the only ramming attack in history by a female pilot.

➤ A camera located in a special photo turret could be fitted on the starboard side.

➤ The BB-1 designation stood for *Blizhny Bombardirovshick* (short-range bomber).

## PROFILE

# First Sukhoi to see combat

Pavel Osipovich Sukhoi was undoubtedly one of the greatest Soviet aircraft designers of all time. However, his first design to see combat, the Su-2, suffered greatly at the hands of German fighters in 1941 and 1942.

Developed from the ANT-51, the first production Su-2 (then designated BB-1) flew in April 1940 and, by September 1941, five aircraft were being produced every day. With its two-man crew, cockpit armour and robust, mainly wooden construction, the

aircraft was initially successful, carrying out short-range bombing, reconnaissance and artillery-spotting missions in the first weeks of the German invasion. However, once the Su-2 encountered the Bf 109 fighters, losses rapidly began to mount.

Desperate fighting in 1942, when some Su-2s were converted into makeshift fighters, resulted in severe attrition rates. By the end of the year, the surviving Su-2s had been withdrawn and assigned to second-line duties.

*Below: This ski-equipped Su-2 is fitted with a removable machine-gun, attached to the rear-fuselage escape hatch.*

*Above: Built only in prototype form, the aerodynamically improved ShB strike bomber was based on the Su-2. Its modifications enhanced performance.*

Throughout the Su-2's service life, a number of different variants were produced, including a version carrying eight unguided rockets, and the more powerful Su-4 with an M-82 engine.

### Su-2 (BB-1)

**Type:** two-seat armed close-support bomber and reconnaissance aircraft

**Powerplant:** one 820.3-kW (1,100-hp.) Tumanskii M-88B radial piston engine

**Maximum speed:** 455 km/h (282 m.p.h.)

**Climb rate:** 4000 m (13,120 ft.) in 8 min

**Range:** 850 km (525 mi.)

**Service ceiling:** 8900 m (29,200 ft.)

**Weights:** empty 2875 kg (6,325 lb.); maximum take-off 4150 kg (9,130 lb.)

**Armament:** up to four 7.62-mm (.30 cal.) ShKAS machine-guns in wings and one 7.62-mm ShKAS machine-gun in turret, plus up to 600 kg (1,320 lb.) of bombs

**Dimensions:**
| | | |
|---|---|---|
| span | 14.30 m | (46 ft. 11 in.) |
| length | 10.25 m | (33 ft. 8 in.) |
| height | 3.94 m | (12 ft. 11 in.) |
| wing area | 29.00 m² | (312 sq. ft.) |

### Su-2 (BB-1)

Like many Soviet combat aircraft flying over snow-covered terrain, this example was camouflaged by being painted white. Production of Su-2s reached 889.

A raised sliding canopy covered the pilot. Cockpit heat was fed through to the pilot's seat via a special pipeline running along the starboard side of the fuselage.

The navigator/gunner was covered by a canopy comprising both a fixed and hinged section. He was protected by 9-mm (⅓-in.) armour located in the front and bottom of the seat.

The monocoque fuselage was of all-wood construction with a load-bearing skin. Four main spars supported 20 frames with associated stringers.

The all-metal horizontal stabiliser was designed in two pieces for ease of assembly. The fin was of wooden construction.

Power was provided by the 14-cylinder M-88B radial engine. A three-bladed VISh-23 variable-pitch propeller was usually fitted.

The cantilever, two-spar wing was of all-metal construction. The outer sections were flush-riveted to reduce drag. Up to 250 kg (550 lb.) of bombs could be carried beneath the wings.

Ordnance was attached on bomb racks within the fuselage bomb bay. Bombs, each ranging from 8 to 100 kg (18 to 220 lb.) (up to a maximum of 600 kg/882 lb.), could be carried.

An emergency escape hatch made from a Duralumin sheet was positioned underneath the rear fuselage. If necessary, a gun mount could be fitted to the hatch to provide some protection from the rear.

### COMBAT DATA

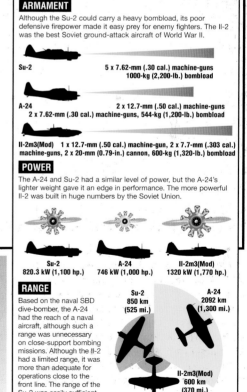

**ARMAMENT**

Although the Su-2 could carry a heavy bombload, its poor defensive firepower made it easy prey for enemy fighters. The Il-2 was the best Soviet ground-attack aircraft of World War II.

**Su-2** 5 x 7.62-mm (.30 cal.) machine-guns 1000-kg (2,200-lb.) bombload

**A-24** 2 x 12.7-mm (.50 cal.) machine-guns 2 x 7.62-mm (.30 cal.) machine-guns, 544-kg (1,200-lb.) bombload

**Il-2m3(Mod)** 1 x 12.7-mm (.50 cal.) machine-gun, 2 x 7.7-mm (.303 cal.) machine-guns, 2 x 20-mm (0.79-in.) cannon, 600-kg (1,320-lb.) bombload

**POWER**

The A-24 and Su-2 had a similar level of power, but the A-24's lighter weight gave it an edge in performance. The more powerful Il-2 was built in huge numbers by the Soviet Union.

**Su-2** 820.3 kW (1,100 hp.)  **A-24** 746 kW (1,000 hp.)  **Il-2m3(Mod)** 1320 kW (1,770 hp.)

**RANGE**

Based on the naval SBD dive-bomber, the A-24 had the reach of a naval aircraft, although such a range was unnecessary on close-support bombing missions. Although the Il-2 had a limited range, it was more than adequate for operations close to the front line. The range of the Su-2 was easily sufficient.

**Su-2** 850 km (525 mi.)  **A-24** 2092 km (1,300 mi.)  **Il-2m3(Mod)** 600 km (370 mi.)

## Early Sukhoi designs

**Su-3:** The high-altitude Su-1/Su-3 fighters were the first designs to bear Sukhoi's name. Despite excellent performance, they were not put into production because of the unreliable turbochargers.

**Su-5:** Designed as an interceptor, the Su-5 featured a piston/jet engine combination. Although able to reach a speed of 793 km/h (492 m.p.h.), it was abandoned in 1945 in favour of pure-jet designs.

**Su-6:** The Su-6 was superior to the Il-2/Il-10 Shturmovik in most respects, but was not selected for production as a ground-attack aircraft. The programme ended in 1944.

**Su-8:** This superb attack aircraft never entered production despite having the heaviest forward firepower of any World War II aircraft. It also handled very well.

# SUPERMARINE
# SPITFIRE MK I-V

● Air defence interceptor ● Tactical fighter-bomber

▲ No. 303 (Polish) Squadron notch up their 178th kill. Many RAF Spitfire squadrons were crewed by foreign pilots, including Czechs, French, Belgians and the famous American Eagle squadron.

**T**he Spitfire is the most famous British aircraft of all time. Although less numerous than the Hawker Hurricane during the Battle of Britain, it is nevertheless remembered as the sleek, thoroughbred fighting machine that turned the tide during that campaign. The Spitfire is among the fastest and most manoeuvrable fighters of World War II, and served in every combat theatre.

---

## SUPERMARINE SPITFIRE MK I-V

### Flying to fight ▼
Pilots loved the Spitfire cockpit, which was roomy and had an excellent view. The sliding canopy was later replaced by a bubble canopy.

### ▶ Instant recognition
The Spitfire's performance was in part due to its efficient and beautiful elliptical wing.

### ▼ Prototype
The first Spitfire to fly had a twin-bladed propeller and a tailskid. Its Merlin engine had only half the power of the massive Griffon engines of later Spitfires.

### In the factory ▶
Spitfires were hand-built by craftsmen, but took up to three times as long to assemble as their main adversary, the fearsome German Messerschmitt Bf 109.

### ▼ Rhubarb patrols
After the Battle of Britain, Spitfires were sent on patrols over France known as 'rhubarb' missions, to attack such opportune targets as trains or convoys.

### ▲ Tactical air strike
Armed with a pair of 110-kg (243-lb.) bombs, the Spitfire was a very useful fighter-bomber, serving with distinction in North Africa and Europe. The weapon load was doubled in the later Spitfires, and could also include eight rocket projectiles.

## FACTS AND FIGURES

➤ The Spitfire prototype made its initial flight on 5 March 1936.

➤ More than 600 Spitfires were flown by the US Army Air Force during World War II.

➤ The Spitfire will always be compared to its adversary, the Messerschmitt Bf 109; both were among the best of their day.

➤ By 1941 Spitfires were being fitted with cannon in place of machine-guns.

➤ Spitfires intended for low-level combat had 'clipped' wings for extra agility.

➤ 22,890 Spitfires and Seafires were built between 1936 and 1947. Merlin engines powered 20,017 of them.

**PROFILE**

# Victorious in the Battle of Britain

Supermarine designer Reginald Mitchell created a small, graceful fighter with elliptical wing and eight guns in the wings, able to fire without being hindered by the propeller. The immortal Spitfire thus became not merely one of the best-performing fighters of all time, but also one of the best-looking. Although never a long-ranged aircraft, the Spitfire was a champion in an air-to-air duel. Spitfires were routinely dived at velocities approaching the speed of sound, faster than any of the German jets.

Merlin engines were used in the early versions of the Spitfire, later supplanted by the more powerful Griffon. Late Spitfires introduced a bubble canopy which made one of history's most beautiful aircraft even more appealing. The carrier-based Seafire, derived from the Spitfire Mk V, made a vital contribution to British naval air power until new American carrier fighters appeared later in the war. The Spitfire also found a new role as a tactical fighter-bomber.

*Few airworthy Spitfires survive; those that do are the stars of any air show at which they appear.*

The ejector exhaust stubs were designed to add thrust to the Spitfire's propellers; designers claimed they added 5 km/h (3 m.p.h.) to the fighter's maximum speed.

The Spitfire's instantly identifiable elliptical wing combined low drag with huge strength.

Mk I Spitfires were armed with eight 7.7-mm (.303 cal.) Browning machine-guns in the wings, but in later models some or all of the guns were replaced by two or four 20-mm (0.79-in.) cannon.

## Spitfire Mk VA

**Type:** single-seat fighter/interceptor

**Powerplant:** one 1103-kW (1,440-hp.) Rolls-Royce Merlin 45 Vee piston engine

**Maximum speed:** 594 km/h (374 m.p.h.) at 5945 m (13,000 ft.)

**Range:** 1827 km (1,135 mi.)

**Service ceiling:** 11,125 m (37,000 ft.)

**Weights:** empty 2267 kg (5,000 lb.); loaded 2911 kg (6,400 lb.)

**Armament:** eight 7.7-mm (.303 cal.) Browning machine-guns with 350 rounds per gun

**Dimensions:**
| | | |
|---|---|---|
| span | 11.23 m | (36 ft. 10 in.) |
| length | 9.12 m | (29 ft. 11 in.) |
| height | 3.02 m | (11 ft. 5 in.) |
| wing area | 22.48 m² | (242 sq. ft.) |

### SPITFIRE MK IA

The Mk I Spitfire was introduced in May 1938, and fought in the desperate battles over Britain and France in 1940. Production of Mk Is ceased in 1941, when cannon-armed versions were introduced.

Behind the cockpit was a thick sheet of armour, fitted as a result of early air battles over France. Pilots were very glad to have it.

The radio aerial ran from a mast behind the cockpit to the top of the tailfin.

The Spitfire's success owed much to its engine. The Rolls-Royce Merlin was constantly modified to give more power, keeping it ahead of the Fw 190 and Bf 109. Power almost doubled during the war years.

One weakness in the Spitfire, which it shared with the Bf 109, was its narrow-track outward-retracting undercarriage. This made it prone to accidents on the ground or on carrier decks.

While not as effective as the teardrop hoods which later became standard, the bulged cockpit canopy gave the Spitfire pilot much better visibility than his German counterpart in the Bf 109.

The prototype Spitfire was equipped with a tailskid, which was replaced by a castoring tailwheel in the production Mk I.

## COMBAT DATA

### MAXIMUM SPEED

The Spitfire and the Bf 109 were comparable in performance: the Spitfire was fractionally quicker at some altitudes, while the Messerschmitt was faster in a dive. The Hurricane was considerably slower than the other two fighters, but was very tough and manoeuvrable.

| | |
|---|---|
| **SPITFIRE Mk I** | 580 km/h (360 m.p.h.) |
| **Bf 109E** | 570 km/h (354 m.p.h.) |
| **HURRICANE Mk I** | 511 km/h (318 m.p.h.) |

### ARMAMENT

The standard British fighter armament of eight machine-guns was considered heavy before the war. But although they could pump out a lot of ammunition, the machine-guns were not as effective as the heavy cannon carried by German fighters.

**SPITFIRE Mk I**
8 x 7.7-mm (.303 cal.) MGs

**Bf 109E**
2 x 20-mm (0.79-in.) cannon
2 x 7.92-mm (0.31-in.) MGs

**HURRICANE Mk I**
8 x 7.7-mm (.303 cal.) MGs

### CEILING

The Messerschmitt's engine had direct fuel injection, which gave it an advantage over the Spitfire at high altitudes. But for much of the Battle of Britain that advantage was negated by the need for the German fighter to stay down and protect the bombers. The Bf 109's ceiling advantage was important when tackling US daylight raids from 1942.

| SPITFIRE Mk I | Bf 109E | HURRICANE Mk I |
|---|---|---|
| 10,000 m (32,800 ft.) | 11,000 m (36,000 ft.) | 10,500 m (34,500 ft.) |

## Defence of the Kingdom

**SECTOR CONTROL:** RAF fighters were controlled from centralised nerve centres. These collated all information from radar stations, observers and fighters in contact with the enemy. They assigned units to deal with specific threats, ensuring the most efficient use of scarce fighter resources.

**CHAIN HOME DEFENCE RADAR:** A chain of radar stations along the south and east coasts ensured that no air raid approached undetected.

**INCOMING AIR RAIDS:** German aircraft were often detected by radar as they formed up over their French bases, so that by the time they had crossed the Channel the RAF's fighters were already in the air and in a position to intercept.

# SUPERMARINE

# WALRUS

● Naval spotter ● Air-sea rescue ● Catapult launched

▲ Air-sea rescue was vital during the Battle of Britain as Fighter Command's pilot resources were becoming desperately low. Many grateful pilots were rescued by the trusty Walrus.

**L**ike a dinosaur stepping through a time warp, the Supermarine Walrus was a piece of history caught up in World War II. Resembling an aircraft of the 1920s (except for its enclosed cockpit), the biplane had fabric surfaces, a wooden hull (on the Mk II version) and a single pusher engine. It was an anachronism, but to a pilot downed at sea, suffering from cold and hunger, it was a welcome sight.

## SUPERMARINE WALRUS

▲ **Catapult launch**
Ship-based Walruses were launched from a catapult. Australia operated the aircraft under the name Seagull Mk V.

▲ **Back onboard**
After a sortie the Walrus would be hoisted aboard its mothership by crane and securely tied down to avoid damage in heavy seas.

▲ **Watertight hull**
After taking off from land the wheels retract into wells in the wing allowing the aircraft to operate on water.

▲ **'Shagbat' rescue**
More than 2000 survivors were rescued by Walruses. Landings were often made in mine-infested enemy waters.

◄ **Ugly duckling**
Although not an elegant aircraft, the sedate Walrus established a reputation for reliability and an ability to withstand damage.

## FACTS AND FIGURES

➤ One Walrus based aboard a Royal Navy cruiser completed 16 separate rescues in one day.

➤ The name Walrus was allocated when the RAF ordered it in May 1935.

➤ The Walrus first flew in June 1933 and was called the Seagull Mk V.

➤ The Walrus was used by seven home and four Middle East rescue squadrons and a single mine-spotting squadron.

➤ Walrus production totalled 746, of which 461 were built by Saunders-Roe.

➤ The Anson and Lysander often worked with the Walrus in air-sea rescues.

# PROFILE

# Picked up by a 'Shagbat'

Supermarine was an expert manufacturer of seaplanes, and the Walrus was a great aircraft, although it was out-of-date by the time World War II began.

The earlier Seagull amphibian was developed into a version powered by the Bristol Pegasus engine, 24 of which were ordered by Australia. Evaluation of this aircraft led to it being adopted for service with Britain's Fleet Air Arm as the Walrus.

Supermarine-built Walruses had metal hulls, but more than half of the total number built were produced by Saunders-Roe which manufactured them with wooden surfaces.

Entering service with the Fleet Air Arm in 1936, the Walrus, which was stressed for catapult launching, equipped battleships and cruisers of the Australian, British and New Zealand navies, and was operational in practically every theatre of the war.

The Walrus, known to wartime servicemen as the 'Shagbat', also played an important air-sea rescue role in Royal Air Force service, rescuing many downed aircrew.

Left: Powered by a pusher engine and fitted with biplane wings, the Walrus was no faster than a World War I fighter. However, its ability to land on water and pick up survivors made it ideal for air-sea rescue.

Above: Walruses served wherever the Royal Navy was active. Here the crew paddle their aircraft towards a crane aboard HMS Belfast in the freezing conditions of an Icelandic fjord.

## Walrus Mk II

**Type:** four-seat spotter reconnaissance amphibian

**Powerplant:** one 578-kW (620-hp.) Bristol Pegasus VI radial piston engine

**Maximum speed:** 217 km/h (135 m.p.h.) at 1524 m (5,000 ft.)

**Range:** 966 km (600 mi.)

**Service ceiling:** 5210 m (17,100 ft.)

**Weights:** empty 2223 kg (4,890 lb.); maximum take-off 3266 kg (7,185 lb.)

**Armament:** one 7.7-mm (.303 cal.) Vickers 'K' gun in bow and one or two similar weapons amidships, plus up 272 kg (600 lb.) of bombs carried beneath the wings, or two Mk VIII depth charges

**Dimensions:**

| | | |
|---|---|---|
| span | 13.97 m | (45 ft. 10 in.) |
| length | 11.35 m | (37 ft. 3 in.) |
| height | 4.65 m | (15 ft. 3 in.) |
| wing area | 56.67 m² | (610 sq. ft.) |

## WALRUS MK I

As well as RAF land-based squadrons the Walrus was also operated by the Royal Navy from cruisers and battleships. This example of No. 700 Squadron served aboard HMS Belfast in the early 1940s.

The open bow cockpit contained a 7.7-mm (.303 cal.) Vickers 'K' or Lewis machine-gun mounted on a Scarff ring. Marine rescue gear was also stored in the cockpit together with the bow mooring line.

The enclosed cockpit housed the pilot in the left seat with the co-pilot/observer on the right. Between and behind the pilots seats was the navigator's compartment.

The equal-span, single-bay biplane wings folded around the rear spar hinges on the centre section and hull. Ailerons were fitted to all four wings and bomb racks for carrying up to 345 kg (760 lb.) of bombs or depth charges were incorporated beneath the lower wing.

The Mk I was fitted with a 462-kW (620-hp.) Bristol Pegasus IIM2 engine. The later Mk II was fitted with the more powerful Pegasus VI.

Supermarine built the Mk I versions which all had an anodically-treated aluminium alloy hull. The Mk IIs were built by Saunders-Roe and had wooden hulls.

ROYAL NAVY X9556

The aft-gunner's cockpit, with a machine-gun fitted on a flexible mount, was positioned behind the wings.

A large rudder was necessary to provide good manoeuvrability on the water when retrieving survivors.

## COMBAT DATA

### MAXIMUM SPEED

Speed was not a factor in the design of these aircraft and all three were easy prey for patrolling fighters. Despite its slow speed the Walrus could operate from a short runway.

| | |
|---|---|
| WALRUS Mk II | 217 km/h (135 m.p.h.) |
| He 59B-2 | 220 km/h (135 m.p.h.) |
| E7K2 'ALF' | 275 km/h (170 m.p.h.) |

### RANGE

Designed for coastal patrol the Walrus only had the range for rescuing crew close to the UK coastline. The Kawanishi and He 51 had the range to patrol greater areas of ocean.

| | |
|---|---|
| WALRUS Mk II | 966 km (600 mi.) |
| He 59B-2 | 1750 km (1,085 mi.) |
| E7K2 'ALF' | 1480 km (918 mi.) |

## Walrus rescue in the Channel

During the Battle of Britain RAF rescue procedures were shambolic. However, after a review in 1941 co-ordinated rescue operations saved the lives of many aircrew.

**1 SHOOTDOWN:** If an English pilot was downed in the Channel he would either ditch his aircraft or parachute into the water. He would already be wearing a life jacket and would inflate his life raft once in the water.

**2 SPOTTING SURVIVORS:** When the pilot was spotted in the sea a Walrus was summoned to pick him up. The survivor used sea dye and launched flares to attract the attention of the crew.

**3 PICK UP:** The Walrus pilot landed his aircraft as close to the downed pilot as possible, often having to avoid mines and enemy fire. A line was then thrown to the dinghy which was towed to the aircraft. The survivor was pulled aboard the Walrus, which then left the area as quickly as possible.

### BOMBLOAD

The more powerful He 59 could carry over twice the weight in bombs compared to the Walrus. It was also used for mine-laying. The E7K2 could only carry four small bombs beneath its wings.

| WALRUS Mk II | He 59B-2 | E7K2 'ALF' |
|---|---|---|
| 345 kg (760 lb.) | 1000 kg (2,200 lb.) | 120 kg (264 lb.) |

# TAYLORCRAFT

# AUSTER SERIES

● Battlefield observation ● Communications ● D-Day veteran

**O**riginally designed pre-war in the USA as lightplanes for the growing civilian private pilot market, the Auster series provided some of Britain's most important light observation aircraft of World War II. Although the Auster was slow and appeared old-fashioned, it was an ideal mount for artillery spotting and provided the pilots with an excellent field of view. It was also agile enough to dodge enemy fighters and operate from tiny grass airstrips.

▲ *The Auster Mk I-V series was built in large numbers and served in every combat theatre, throughout the war, with the RAF's Air Observation Post (AOP) Squadrons.*

## TAYLORCRAFT AUSTER SERIES

**▼ Basic interior**
*Inside, the Auster Mk IV variant was spartan to say the least. The flying controls were mounted on the left side. This example carries a wireless system in place of the right-hand seat.*

**▲ Powerplant exposed!**
*One of the only two Auster Mk IIs built sits with its engine cowling removed, revealing the compact Lycoming engine.*

**High-mounted wing ▶**
*In common with other light observation aircraft, the Auster series featured a single high-mounted wing, which provided an unobstructed view of the ground and generated tremendous lift.*

**◀ Built tough**
*Knowing that these little observation machines would spend most of their lives operating from primitive airstrips out in the open, Taylorcraft kept the design very simple and made it strong.*

**Enter the Auster Mk III ▶**
*Looking externally very similar to the Cirrus Minor-powered Auster Mk I, the Mark III variant differed in being fitted with a 97-kW (130-hp.) Gipsy Major. This was one of the most widely produced of the early Auster variants with 470 examples built.*

### FACTS AND FIGURES

➤ In 1938 Taylorcraft Aeroplanes (England) Ltd was established to build the parent company's light aircraft under licence.

➤ Austers played an important part during the Allied invasion of France in 1944.

➤ Only one unit, No. 656 Squadron, operated the Auster in the Far East.

➤ Only two examples of the Auster Mk II were built, because of a severe shortage of American Lycoming engines.

➤ Experiments with a floatplane version, the Auster Mk V, were conducted in 1945.

➤ Austers were used for air photography duties in the closing stages of the war.

**PROFILE**

# Supreme artillery spotter

Following on from the success of the Taylorcraft series of lightplanes in the USA, licence production was established at Thurmaston, in Leicestershire, under the name of Taylorcraft Aeroplanes (England) Ltd.

Several civilian variants were produced and with the outbreak of World War II these were evaluated for the airborne observation role. The Taylorcraft Plus C was selected for production under the military designation Auster Mk I.

The suitability of the aircraft was quickly appreciated and the design was developed into the Mk III. Powered by a 97-kW Gipsy Major I engine, 470 of this version were produced.

Next major production variant was the Mk IV which was fitted with an American Lycoming O-290 engine and had a larger cabin to accommodate a third seat. The most common wartime Auster was the Mk V, which introduced blind-flying instrumentation and other improvements. About 800 of this variant were built.

Auster series aircraft gave invaluable service in North Africa and, later in the war, in southern and northern Europe. At their peak, Austers equipped 19 squadrons, often using their remarkable short-field performance to operate very close to the front line.

*Left: Outward visibility was not particularly good on the early Auster variants, especially to the side and rear.*

*Above: MZ 105 was one of the prototype Auster Mk IIs and illustrates the unique snub-nose profile of this rare variant.*

---

## Auster Mk V

**Type:** light liaison and observation/reconnaissance aircraft

**Powerplant:** one 97-kW (130-hp.) Lycoming O-290-3 horizontally opposed four-cylinder engine

**Maximum speed:** 209 km/h (130 m.p.h.)

**Maximum cruising speed:** 180 km/h (112 m.p.h.)

**Range:** 402 km (250 mi.)

**Service ceiling:** 5639 m (18,500 ft.)

**Weights:** empty 499 kg (1,098 lb.); loaded 839 kg (1,846 lb.)

**Accommodation:** one pilot and observer, sitting side by side

**Dimensions:**
| | | |
|---|---|---|
| span | 10.97 m | (36 ft.) |
| length | 6.83 m | (22 ft. 5 in.) |
| height | 2.44 m | (8 ft.) |
| wing area | 15.51 m² | (167 sq. ft.) |

---

The engine was enclosed underneath two upward-lifting hatches for easy maintenance with the minimum of equipment in the field.

The high-set wing was fitted with large-trailing edge flaps allowing for an extremely low speed, this was particularly useful during missions when targets on the ground needed to be observed and recorded.

A large rudder allowed the Auster exceptional turning ability when operating at low speed. Positioned above this was a mass balancing weight.

## AUSTER MK IV

Operating near the front line of every major battlefield in Europe, the Auster allowed Allied commanders to observe enemy movements. This camouflaged example was in operation after the D-Day landings.

Because of the requirement to operate from rough landing strips the Auster had large wheels and tyres. Specialised variants were equipped with skis or floats for operations from snow-covered airfields or lakes.

Enclosed in a fully glazed cockpit, the pilot and his observer were afforded excellent visibility from the Auster. The rear of the cockpit could be utilised for urgent cargo if required for particular flights.

**MT134**

---

## COMBAT DATA

### MAXIMUM SPEED

Though equipped with a rather low-powered engine, the Auster was faster than Germany's Fieseler Storch. Because of its reasonable speed the Auster was often used for courier duties.

| | |
|---|---|
| AUSTER Mk V | 209 km/h (130 m.p.h.) |
| Fi 156C-2 STORCH | 175 km/h (108 m.p.h.) |
| O-49 VIGILANT | 196 km/h (122 m.p.h.) |

### RANGE

The ability to fly great distances for observation purposes was a requirement for all light reconnaissance aircraft. The Auster compared favourably to the German Storch but offered slightly less range than the American Stinson Vigilant.

AUSTER Mk V 402 km (250 mi.)

Fi 156C-2 STORCH 385 km (240 mi.)

O-49 VIGILANT 451 km (280 mi.)

### MAXIMUM TAKE-OFF WEIGHT

Its low take-off weight helped the Auster to operate from small forest clearings or similar front-line locations and respond quickly when a reconnaissance or artillery spotting mission was needed.

| AUSTER Mk V | Fi 156C-2 STORCH | O-49 VIGILANT |
|---|---|---|
| 839 kg (1,846 lb.) | 1325 kg (2,915 lb.) | 1542 kg (3,392 lb.) |

---

## British military light aircraft

**DE HAVILLAND DH. 82 TIGER MOTH:** One of the most famous British aircraft of all time, the Tiger Moth served as the RAF's basic trainer from February 1932 and was finally retired as late as 1955.

**MILES M.38 MESSENGER:** Evaluated as a potential three-seat observation aircraft, the distinctive Messenger was never adopted by the RAF, but was successful on the civilian market.

**PERCIVAL PRENTICE T.MK 1:** Incorporating many features learned during the war, the Prentice T.Mk 1 was a far more powerful and advanced training aircraft, though it did not enter service until 1947.

# THOMAS-MORSE
# SCOUT

● Purpose-built ● Pursuit trainer ● Movie star

▲ The Thomas-Morse Scout, a single-seat scout aircraft for training pursuit pilots bound for the Western Front, appeared on the eve of the USA's entry into World War I.

**T**homas-Morse produced the highly praised Scout throughout the Great War, culminating in the S4C. This was a sprightly, nimble aircraft which was once intended to spy on the enemy, but which was actually used to train pilots. The S4C Scout was one of the most successful US-developed aircraft of the 1914–1918 era and remained a familiar sight at civilian air shows throughout the 1930s.

## ▲ Tricky handling
Despite its primary role as a trainer, the S4 was tail-heavy and was difficult to control. It could prove quite a handful for a novice.

## ▼ World War I Kaydet
The Thomas-Morse Scout was the 1917 equivalent of the later Boeing PT-13 and was also built in huge numbers.

## ▲ Purpose-built trainer
A characteristic of the 'Tommy' was that it was designed especially for training pursuit pilots. Previous trainers were often tired, or surplus, front-line aircraft. The S4C variant (shown above) was produced in the greatest numbers.

## ◄ Totally new
When the first S4 took to the air in June 1917, nothing like it had ever been built before in the United States. A 74.57-kW (100-hp.) Gnome rotary engine powered the first prototype.

## Sopwith style cues ►
The chief designer of the Scout, Douglas Thomas, had previously worked for Sopwith. It was, therefore, not surprising that the American aircraft bore a strong resemblance to Sopwith designs, notably the Tabloid.

## FACTS AND FIGURES

➤ The Scout was an 'equal' biplane, with upper and lower wings of exactly the same span.

➤ Float-equipped S5s had to have their floats repaired after each flight.

➤ Scouts starred in several films, including *Hell's Angels* and *Dawn Patrol*.

➤ A popular modification to privately-owned 'Tommies' was to turn them into two- or three-seat sport aircraft.

➤ The S9, with side-by-side seating, was the last Scout; only one was built.

➤ Only one Scout in 10 was test-flown before being delivered to a unit.

# PROFILE

# Super abundant Scout

The Thomas-Morse Scout was initially designed as a combat aircraft, but was used instead as an advanced solo trainer. The US Army's training programme was not well organised during World War I and not all pilots received proper instruction. A large number were fortunate enough to progress to the Scout, however, and sharpened their

flying skills on a fine aircraft that performed well and was similar to warplanes that were being used in action over the Front.

Although designed by Douglas Thomas for combat, the Scout was quickly converted for use in the rapidly expanding effort to train young cadets. In general, the Scout was a pleasant aircraft to fly, although

it had a tendency to bounce on landing and was difficult to loop. Nevertheless, it provided pilots with good preparation for the Front.

Although the Armistice signalled an end of production, the Scout was durable and remained on the aviation scene for decades after the war.

Left: Floats were tested on the S4 prototype and the US Navy acquired six S5s. Performance of the S5 was inferior to that of its land-based counterparts.

Right: The rudder control on the ground was so ineffective that the ailerons were used for directional control during take-off and landing.

Simplicity was the key to the S4's success and the fuselage was built from solid spruce and covered in fabric. At the height of production, 30 aircraft were being delivered per week.

### S4C

**Type:** single-seat pursuit trainer and scout aircraft

**Powerplant:** one 60-kW (80-hp.) Le Rhone C-9 (built under licence by Union Switch & Signal)

**Maximum speed:** 152 km/h (94 m.p.h.)

**Initial climb rate:** 138 m/min (450 f.p.m.)

**Service ceiling:** 4876 m (16,000 ft.)

**Fuel weight:** 73.02 kg (161 lb.)

**Weights:** empty 437 kg (961 lb.); loaded 623 kg (1,371 lb.)

**Armament:** one 7.7-mm (.303 cal.) forward-firing Marlin machine-gun or a gun camera, smokescreen or radio equipment

**Dimensions:**
| | | |
|---|---|---|
| span | 8.07 m | (26 ft. 5 in.) |
| length | 6.05 m | (19 ft. 10 in.) |
| height | 2.69 m | (8 ft. 10 in.) |
| wing area | 21.73 m² | (234 sq. ft.) |

## OTHER THOMAS-MORSE DESIGNS

**MB-7:** After the Scout, Thomas-Morse turned its attention to building successors. Three different prototypes, designated MB-1, MB-2 and MB-3, were built for evaluation purposes. The MB-3 was the most successful during flight tests due, in part, to its powerful 224-kW Wright-Hispano in-line engine. About 200 MB-3s were built and other variants, such as the MB-3M advanced trainer, the MB-6 and MB-7 (above) racing aircraft, were developed from it.

The landing gear consisted of steel tube struts streamlined with spruce wood. The axle-bearer was constructed of ash and was slotted to hold the axle assembly. In common with contemporary practice, high-pressure tyres were fitted.

One difference between the S4B and S4C variants was a change from cable-operated ailerons to a torque tube system inside the rear fuselage.

Because of the immense torque of the rotary engine, Scouts were notorious for being tiring aircraft to fly over long distances. Considerable rudder input was required during take-off to counteract the torque. Sometimes the pilot would have to brace his arm between his stomach and the cockpit wall.

### S4C SCOUT

This anonymous-looking aircraft was typical of the S4Cs that equipped the Signal Corps in 1917–18. The standard finish was overall olive drab green. Military serial numbers were carried in black on both sides.

**XP-13:** During the 1920s, Thomas-Morse continued as a small aircraft manufacturer, whose efforts also centred on adopting new materials for aircraft construction. This culminated in a series of biplanes which made extensive use of aluminium alloy. One such aircraft was the XP-13 Viper single-seat fighter. Powered by a 447-kW Wright-Hispano engine, it offered superb performance, but was destroyed in a crash.

## Other scout aircraft of World War I

■ **A.E.G D-I:** This little fighter was A.E.G's first single-seat scout aircraft and was distinguished by its 'ear'-type radiators.

■ **ROYAL AIRCRAFT FACTORY B.E. 2C:** These were in service by the time World War I began and were easy targets for the Germans.

■ **BRANDENBURG KDW:** Only a small number of these single-seat seaplane scouts were built, between late 1917 and early 1918.

■ **BRISTOL SCOUT:** Similar in concept to the S4C, the early Scouts were simple aircraft that were also powered by Gnome radial engines.

# TUPOLEV
# TB-3

● TB-1 successor ● First modern four-engined bomber

I n 1926 the Tupolev design bureau, under Vladimir Petliakov, was given the task of designing the world's first monoplane bomber with engines mounted on the leading edge of the wing. So challenging was the project that the aircraft did not fly until 1930. What finally emerged was the ANT-6, a tremendously capable long-range bomber. It entered VVS (Soviet air force) service in 1932 as the TB-3. It was truly an aircraft ahead of its time.

▲ At the time of its first flight, nothing like the ANT-6 had ever been seen before. It proved to be a tough and reliable aircraft, though early variants suffered from weak engines.

## TUPOLEV TB-3

▼ Air force assets
Introduction of the TB-3 significantly improved the capabilities of the VVS (Soviet air force). These bombers were among the first Soviet aircraft employed to drop paratroops.

▲ Tupolevs at the North Pole
Two ANT-6s (as civilian TB-3s were known) were used as support aircraft on a survey party to find a suitable base for an Arctic expedition.

▼ World renown
During its early years, the giant Tupolev earned international recognition because of its size.

▼ Heavyweight bomber
Early tests illustrated the need to beef up the structure and production machines were very heavy by the standards of the time.

▲ Ahead of its time
Even by the mid-1930s few aircraft were capable of matching the capabilities of the TB-3.

## FACTS AND FIGURES

➤ When tests were conducted on the first production TB-3, it was found to be 1000 kg (2,200 lb.) heavier than the prototype.

➤ Nine aircraft embarked upon a series of goodwill flights over the summer of 1935.

➤ A single TB-3 was used as a mother ship for Zveno (link) trials with I-16 fighters.

➤ In September 1936 pilot A Yumashev set an international altitude record, reaching 8116 m with a five-ton load in a TB-3.

➤ Sadly, no TB-3s still exist. All had been scrapped by the mid-1950s.

➤ An ANT-6, SSSR-N169 flew on the last pre-war Soviet Polar expedition in 1941.

## PROFILE

# Soviet bombers come of age

Taking to the air for the first time on 22 December 1930, the ANT-6 at first seemed little more than a scaled up Tupolev TB-1. True, it did retain many features of the older design, including the landing gear, engines and propellers, but it was destined to be of far greater importance.

A massive production programme was instigated and the first ANT-6 (TB-3s) began to roll off the assembly lines in 1930, with deliveries to the VVS beginning soon after. Amazingly

few problems were met, although early aircraft were fitted with unreliable Mikulin M17 engines and had poor build quality. Once these problems had been rectified, the TB-3 proved itself to be the most modern and capable bomber in the world and did more than any other aircraft to give the Soviet Union a long-range strike capability.

Besides bombing, TB-3s were also used for paratroop drops, and the unorthodox Zveno (link) experiments, in which the aircraft acted as

mother ship for Polikarpov I-5 and I-16 fighters.

By the late 1930s the aircraft were approaching obsolescence and began to be withdrawn from service, though a handful were still active by the outbreak of World War II in 1939.

*Above: Zveno experiments were conducted for several years. The combination actually saw combat, attacking a bridge in August 1941.*

*Right: A logical step from the earlier TB-1, the TB-3 truly established the Soviet Union as a major builder of heavy bombers. Later versions, with M-34 engines, were able to reach speeds of 288 km/h (179 m.p.h.).*

### TB-3/M34R

**Type:** five-seat long-range bomber and transport aircraft

**Powerplant:** four 615-kW (825-hp.) Mikulin M-34 water cooled in-line V-12 piston engines

**Maximum speed:** 288 km/h (179 m.p.h.)

**Initial climb rate:** 227 m/min (745 f.p.m.)

**Maximum operating radius:** 960 km (595 mi.)

**Normal range:** 1400 km (868 mi.)

**Service ceiling:** 7740 m (25,400 ft.)

**Weights:** empty 12,585 kg (27,687 lb.); loaded 18,877 kg (61,917 lb.)

**Armament:** six DA machine guns, in pairs

**Dimensions:**
| | |
|---|---|
| span | 41.85 m (137 ft. 3 in.) |
| length | 25.10 m (82 ft. 4 in.) |
| height | 5.60 m (18 ft. 4 in.) |
| wing area | 234.50 m² (2,523 sq. ft.) |

## TB-3/M34

This machine is an M34 variant, which featured more powerful engines with revised cooling, including repositioned radiators, and a slightly redesigned forward fuselage with a gondola for the bombardier.

The wing, one of the largest built up to that time, was based extensively on that used for the TB-1. It was built in five sections, all of which could be conveniently dismantled for transport by rail.

Armament was also similar to that of the earlier TB-1 with twin batteries of DA machine guns mounted in the nose and two mounted in tandem in the rear fuselage. A tail turret was later introduced on the TB-3/M34R.

Early aircraft were powered by Mikulin M17 V12 in-line engines. These had a complex cooling system and were prone to overheating. They were later replaced by more powerful M34s which featured Allison superchargers.

More of an evolutionary rather than a revolutionary design, the TB-3 retained many proven components of the TB-1, including the landing gear. To cope with the extra weight of the four-engined aircraft, the oleos were strengthened and tandem tyres fitted on bogies.

Pilots who had gained experience on TB-1s, found the new bomber little different and the TB-3 also retained some traits of its predecessor, notably the heavy handling. The elevators were especially hard work, and in-flight vibration could be quite severe, especially towards the rear of the aircraft.

### ACTION DATA

#### MAXIMUM SPEED

With more power available from its four engines, the TB-3 was faster than its predecessor, but was still heavy and lumbering. Later aircraft such as the Hendon were more advanced and faster.

| | |
|---|---|
| TB-3/M-17 | 226 km/h (140 m.p.h.) |
| TB-1 | 178 km/h (110 m.p.h.) |
| HENDON | 249 km/h (154 m.p.h.) |

#### SERVICE CEILING

During the late 1920s, few aircraft were capable of reaching the same altitude as the TB-3. The Hendon was conceived later and although it could climb to 6553 m, it did not prove successful in RAF service.

| TB-3/M-17 | TB-1 | HENDON |
|---|---|---|
| 5100 m (16,700 ft.) | 4830 m (15,800 ft.) | 6553 m (21,500 ft.) |

#### BOMBLOAD

Operational TB-3s could carry more bombs than any other aircraft during their heyday and set several records for altitude with a full bombload. A major drawback of inter-war British bombers such as the Hendon was their inability to carry substantial bombloads.

| | |
|---|---|
| TB-3/M-17 | 2000 kg (4,400 lb.) |
| TB-1 | 1000 kg (2,200 lb.) |
| HENDON | 753 kg (1,660 lb.) |

## Soviet bombers of World War II

■ **TUPOLEV TU-2R 'BAT':** A twin-engined attack bomber and reconnaissance aircraft, the Tu-2 entered service in 1944.

■ **TUPOLEV SB-2:** Built in huge numbers, the SB-2 was one of the most numerous Soviet aircraft of World War II.

■ **ILYUSHIN IL-4:** Know initially as the DB-3F, this was one of Ilyushin's most successful designs in the bureau's early years.

# TUPOLEV

# Tu-2

● Medium bomber ● Ground and torpedo-attack ● Reconnaissance

F ew great aircraft have been designed in a prison cell. Andrei Tupolev was ordered to produce a versatile aircraft 'better than the Luftwaffe's Ju 88' on his drawing board in the Butyrkii prison. He did just that. The Tupolev Tu-2 family was one of the most varied and successful aircraft of World War II. It remained in production until 1948, by which time 2527 had been delivered for service.

▲ With its exceptionally aerodynamic design and inherent versatility, the Tu-2 gave long and distinguished service to the Soviet air force and was widely exported.

---

## TUPOLEV Tu-2

▲ **Crew accommodation**
The pilot, radio operator/gunner and bombardier/navigator were accommodated forward of the wing.

▲ **UTB trainer**
Designed by P.O.Sukhoi, the UTB was a simplified and lighter Tu-2 airframe with lower powered engines. The Polish air force had 100 delivered.

▲ **Jet testbed**
A Tu-2 was fitted with a Russian version of the Rolls-Royce Nene 1 turbojet engine for flight test development work as the Tu-2N.

▲ **Tu-2 Paravan**
Two aircraft had a giant 6-m (20-ft.) probe on the nose. This carried wires attached to the wingtips, where cable cutters were installed to cut balloon cables.

▲ **Fighter prototype**
This much modified variant, the ANT-63P, was a heavily armed fighter first flown in December 1946. It had provision for radar.

◄ **Special service**
With a GAZ-67B cross country vehicle in its bomb-bay, this Tu-2 was used for special missions.

---

## FACTS AND FIGURES

➤ Designed for tactical attack, the Tu-2 was also an effective dive-bomber, torpedo bomber and armored strike fighter.

➤ The first prototype was flown on 29 January 1941, but production was slow.

➤ Tu-2s first went to the front line in November 1942 and were well received.

➤ With two forward-firing 20-mm (0.79-in.) cannon, the Tu-2 proved to be an effective fighter when attacking bombers from the rear.

➤ Only 1111 were built during the war with 1416 more built post-war.

➤ Tu-2s served in Bulgaria, China, Hungary, North Korea, Poland and Romania.

# Tupolev's tactical masterpiece

By mid-1938 Tupolev had a full team of designers and engineers working for him. All were held prisoner by the Soviet authorities and none could have imagined the excellence of the design they were producing.

After a number of delays, the ANT-58 design, which was to become the Tu-2, was finally approved on 1 March 1940. Unfortunately, the prototype had to wait until 1941 before its engines were ready, but when it eventually flew on 29 January 1941, it proved to be an exceptional performer in every respect. Further testing refined the aircraft and it entered series production in 1943. The first machines went into combat in the spring of 1944.

Such was its success that Tupolev and his team were released from prison and Tupolev himself was awarded the Stalin Prize. Continuous development, mostly centred on the engine installations, resulted in the Tu-2 remaining a viable combat aircraft in the post-war era and it was produced in quantity until 1948.

Late production Tu-2Ss had four-blade propellers, more powerful engines and equipment improvements. Given the NATO codename 'Bat', it saw combat in the Korean War and served with Communist air forces until the late 1950s.

A tall radio mast was mounted on the left side above the bullet-proof windscreen. Wires ran to the port fin and down to the left side of the nose.

The aircraft was aerodynamically outstanding, due to the low drag, stiff sandwich wing skins and flush riveting. It had detachable wingtips.

## TUPOLEV TU-2S

This aircraft is typical of Soviet Tu-2s. Pilots were impressed by the aircraft's handling, which was said to be fighter-like. Such was the success of the airframe that several postwar versions were built.

Giving the Tu-2 good ground clearance, the stalky main landing gear retracted to the rear, as did the single tailwheel. The fuselage nose was plywood with a near conical shape. The pilot sat high above the nose had a good forward view, even while on the ground.

The high-mounted, fixed, fabric-covered tailplane had an eight degree dihedral with balanced, trim-tabbed elevators. The oval-shaped twin fins and rudders remained standard on all variants.

Two 1,850-hp. ASh-82FN 14-cylinder radial piston engines powered the Tu-2S. Some had enlarged carburetor intakes and shorter exhausts.

Armament comprised two 20-mm (0.79-in.) ShVAK cannon in the wing roots and three single 12.7-mm (.50 cal.) UBT guns, aimed by three crewmembers: one behind the pilot, another in a ventral turret and the third in a dorsal turret, all rearward facing.

## ACTION DATA

### SPEED

Tupolev paid great attention to the aerodynamic qualities of the Tu-2. This resulted in an impressive top speed, and the aircraft remained fast even with the addition of more equipment.

| | |
|---|---|
| Tu-2S | 547 km/h (339 m.p.h.) |
| Ju 88A-4 | 468 km/h (291 m.p.h.) |
| B-25J | 438 km/h (272 m.p.h.) |

### WEAPONS

The Tu-2S carried a much heavier bomb load than its major contemporaries. The North American B-25J was optimized as a ground-attack aircraft with heavy forward fire-power.

| | |
|---|---|
| Tu-2S | 3 x 12.7-mm (.50 cal.) machine guns, 2 x 20-mm (0.79-in.) cannon, 4000-kg (8,800-lb.) bombload |
| Ju 88A-4 | 3 x 7.92-mm (0.31-in.) machine guns, 2 x 20-mm (0.79-in.) cannon, 2000-kg (4,400-lb.) bombload |
| B-25J MITCHELL | 18 x 12.7-mm (.50 cal.) machine guns, 1358-kg (2,994-lb.) bombload |

### RANGE

As one of the great Soviet combat aircraft of World War II, the Tu-2S also offered good range and was on a par with its American rival. The Junkers Ju 88A-4 was used in the long-range role, but had been designed for medium range. It was not as versatile as the Tu-2S.

Tu-2S 1400 km (870 mi.)
Ju 88A-4 2728 km (1,695 mi.)
B-25J MITCHELL 2173 km (1,350 mi.)

## Soviet twin bombers

**ILYUSHIN Il-4:** With its 2694-kg (5,940-lb.) bomb load and 3581-km (2,225-mi.) range, the Il-4 was a useful medium- to long-range bomber. It was not as versatile as the Tu-2.

**PETLYAKOV Pe-2:** A range of Pe-2 variants was built, serving as light- and dive-bombers and ground attack aircraft. The Pe-2m bomber had a maximum bomb load of 2000 kg (4,400 lb.).

**POLIKARPOV NB, T:** An exceptionally advanced night-bomber, the NB, T was designed under mysterious circumstances and never entered series production.

**TUPOLEV SB-2:** One of the most important bombers of the 1930s, the SB-2 was developed from the ANT-20. The aircraft was still in production at the beginning of World War II.

# VICKERS

# VIMY

● Strategic bomber ● Middle East service ● Pioneer flights

▲ In the later years of World War I, controversy raged over the merits and morality of strategic bombing. However, once German bombers appeared over Britain in 1917, the RAF was prompted to order more than 1000 Vimys.

**N**amed after a famous World War I battle, the Vimy achieved a dramatic 'first' when Britain's Alcock and Brown flew one eastward on the first crossing of the Atlantic. The Vickers Vimy bomber arrived too late for World War I, but served with the RAF, mainly in the Middle East, from 1918 to 1931. A flight to Australia and a semi-successful expedition to Cape Town in February 1920 capped off a number of achievements by this great aircraft.

## VICKERS VIMY

### ▼ Vimy ambulance
Built in 1921 for the RAF in the Middle East, the Vimy Ambulance was a Vimy Commercial equipped to carry four stretchers or eight sitting casualties.

### ▲ Home-based Vimy
Most Vimy bomber units were based in the Middle East. No. 9 Squadron, however, flew Vimys for 14 months from RAF Manston during 1924/25.

### Replica recreates flight ▶
In 1994 this replica re-enacted the trail-blazing flight made in 1919 from England to Australia.

### ▼ Vimy Mk II prototype
The Mk II's Eagle engines gave the new bomber reliability.

### To South Africa...just ▶
In early 1920 two South African air force pilots attempted to fly civil Vimy G-UABA Silver Queen from England to Cape Town. After crashing in North Africa, they borrowed an RAF Vimy, but engine failure forced them to complete the flight in a DH.9.

## FACTS AND FIGURES

➤ To help to establish civil aviation in China, 40 Vimy Commercials were imported; most appear not to have flown.

➤ Total Vimy production is believed to have reached 232 between 1917 and 1924.

➤ Vimy production was sub-contracted to firms like Westland and Morgan.

➤ Vickers designed the Vimy with the help of the world's first commercially owned wind tunnel, in St Albans, Hertfordshire.

➤ An RAF Vimy reached France in 1918 but arrived too late to make raids on Berlin.

➤ Vimys built during 1918 were fitted with torpedoes for anti-submarine duties.

## PROFILE

# Strategic reach for the RAF

Although made famous by the transatlantic flight of 1919, the Vimy was designed during World War I as a strategic bomber for the Royal Flying Corps (RAF from 1918).

Bombing of this nature was the subject of much debate during the later years of the war. However, British hesitation to commit itself to this new type of warfare was soon overcome when German air force bombers appeared over London in 1917. Bombers like the

Handley Page O/400 were ordered into production, as were new prototypes like the Vickers FB.27.

Able to lift heavier loads than the much bigger and more powerful O/400, large numbers of Vimy aircraft were planned. But, by the time the Armistice had been signed in 1918, only one had reached France. The end of the war brought many cancellations; just over 200 were built, most powered by the ever-reliable Rolls-Royce Eagle engine.

Most Vimy bombers served in the Middle East, but by the end of the 1920s training was their main role.

*Above: The Smith brothers and their mechanics pose in front of a Vimy at Brooklands before their 1919 flight to Australia.*

*Below: The RAF continued to employ the Vimy for training long after its retirement as a bomber. It was used to train searchlight crews until 1938.*

## VIMY MK IV

One of 25 of a batch of 75 ordered from Westland Aircraft Works, Vimy H5066 and the rest of the fleet were intended to be fitted with Liberty engines, but were built with Rolls-Royce Eagles.

### Vimy Mk IV

**Type:** heavy bomber

**Powerplant:** two 269-kW (360-hp.) Rolls-Royce Eagle VIII V-12 water-cooled engines

**Maximum speed:** 166 km/h (103 m.p.h.) at sea level

**Range:** 1464 km (900 mi.) at 130 km/h (80 m.p.h.); more on record flights

**Service ceiling:** 2135 m (7,000 ft.)

**Weights:** empty 3221 kg (7,086 lb.); loaded 5670 kg (12,474 lb.)

**Armament:** two to four 7.7-mm (.303 cal.) Lewis Mk III machine-guns with twelve 97-round ammunition drums in nose, dorsal and ventral positions, plus bombload of 1123 kg (2,476 lb.)

**Dimensions:**
| | |
|---|---|
| span | 20.75 m (68 ft. 1 in.) |
| length | 13.27 m (43 ft. 6 in.) |
| height | 4.76 m (15 ft. 7 in.) |
| wing area | 123.56 m² (1,330 sq. ft.) |

Four prototype Vimys were built, each with a different type of engine. Those fitted to the first three aircraft were underpowered and, in some cases, unreliable. Rolls-Royce's liquid-cooled, 12-cylinder Eagle of 269 kW (360 hp.), fitted to the fourth example, was the most promising and was fitted to most production aircraft.

The Vimy had four crew: a pilot and observer/bomb aimer/nose gunner, a rear gunner and a ventral gunner. As the ventral gun was not always fitted, the latter was sometimes not carried.

In production form the Vimy followed conventional design practice of the time, with a wire-braced biplane structure and rear stabiliser arrangement. The front fuselage structure was of steel tube, the rear of wood.

Three 7.7-mm (.303 cal.) Lewis machine-guns were generally fitted to RAF Vimy bombers: one in the nose and dorsal positions, each mounted on Scarff rings, and a third in a ventral mounting.

The Vimy was able to lift a heavier load than the much larger Handley Page O/400. Maximum bombload was 1123 kg (2,476 lb.), typically made up of 18 x 51-kg (112-lb.) bombs under the wings and 2 x 104-kg (230-lb.) bombs under the fuselage.

A small window was fitted on either side of the lower fuselage for the ventral gunner, so that he could see to change the gun's ammunition drums. The Lewis machine-gun was fired through an opening in the bottom of the fuselage.

Late production Vimys with Eagle engines were originally referred to as Mk IVs (as was the fourth Vimy prototype, also fitted with the Rolls-Royce powerplants). In 1923 most surviving Eagle-engined Vimys were redesignated Mk IIs.

## COMBAT DATA

### MAXIMUM SPEED

The Handley Page V/1500 and de Havilland DH.10 Amiens were contemporaries of the Vimy, the former being a larger, heavier aircraft and the latter considerably smaller. The DH.10 had more powerful engines than the larger Vimy and was therefore faster.

| | |
|---|---|
| **VIMY Mk IV** | 166 km/h (103 m.p.h.) |
| **V/1500** | 159 km/h (99 m.p.h.) |
| **DH.10 AMIENS Mk II** | 185 km/h (115 m.p.h.) |

### ARMAMENT

Each of these bombers carried a bombload in keeping with its size, with the V/1500 being able to carry over three tonnes (three tons) of bombs. The larger aircraft required more protection against fighters and were therefore fitted with extra machine-guns.

| | |
|---|---|
| **VIMY Mk IV** | 2 x 7.7-mm (.303 cal.) machine-guns / 1123-kg (2,476-ln.) bombload |
| **V/1500** | 4 x 7.7-mm (.303 cal.) machine-guns / 3402-kg (7,485-lb.) bombload |
| **DH.10 AMIENS Mk II** | 2 x 7.7-mm (.303 cal.) machine-guns / 408-kg (900-lb.) bombload |

### POWER

The V/1500 had four Rolls-Royce Eagle engines in paired, push-pull configuration. The Amiens used two Liberty engines with slightly more power than the Eagles fitted to the Vimy. Both types were among the most widely used liquid-cooled engines of the period.

| VIMY Mk IV | V/1500 | DH.10 AMIENS Mk II |
|---|---|---|
| 538 kW (720 hp.) | 1119 kW (1,500 hp.) | 984 kW (1,320 hp.) |

# Vickers Vimy variants

■ **VIMY Mk I:** After their withdrawal from front-line units in the 1920s, many Vimys were relegated to flying and parachute training. A number were re-engined with air-cooled radials.

■ **VIMY (CIVIL):** There were at least six civil-registered Vimy 'bombers', including those used on the pioneering flights of 1919 and 1920. G-EAOU was originally an RAF aircraft.

■ **VIMY COMMERCIAL:** A spacious new fuselage allowed the Commercial to carry up to 10 passengers or 2,200 kg (4,900 lb.) of freight. This example spent five years on European routes.

# VICKERS

# WELLINGTON

● Medium bomber ● U-boat destroyer ● Mine hunter

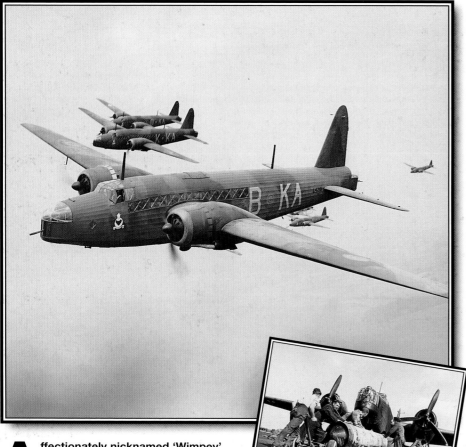

**A**ffectionately nicknamed 'Wimpey' after a wartime cartoon character, the Wellington was one of the most popular aircraft used by RAF Bomber Command. Designed to deliver bombs over medium ranges, its twin-engined performance prevented the Wellington from reaching targets deep in Germany. It was ultimately employed in many other roles throughout World War II, including anti-submarine warfare and mine hunting.

▲ Wellingtons made the first RAF attacks on German targets in 1939 and were the mainstay of Royal Air Force Bomber Command until the advent of the four-engined heavy bombers. It was the first bomber type to drop the 4000-lb. (1814-kg) 'blockbuster' bomb, in 1941.

## VICKERS WELLINGTON

### ▲ Six crewmembers
Wellington bombers carried a crew of six. The wireless operator manned a machine-gun position if the aircraft was attacked.

### ▲ Night camouflage
Bomber Command Wellingtons had a matt-black fuselage and lower surfaces.

### Geodetic strength ▶
The Wellington's designer, Barnes Wallis, devised the immensely strong geodetic structure which was unique to the Wellington and the earlier Vickers Wellesley light bomber.

### ◀ Various engines
Wellingtons were fitted with a number of different types of engine, including the Bristol Hercules, Bristol Pegasus, Pratt & Whitney Twin Wasp and Rolls-Royce Merlin. The aircraft in this photograph contains a Hercules engine.

### ▲ Flying testbeds
The Wellington served as a test aircraft for various types of new equipment. One series of trials involved mounting a Vickers 40-mm (1.57-in.) gun in a dorsal turret and replacing the single fin by two smaller ones to ensure adequate rudder control.

## FACTS AND FIGURES

➤ The Wellington prototype, the Vickers Type 271, first flew as an unarmed prototype on 15 June 1936.

➤ Coastal Command Wellingtons sank or damaged 51 U-boats during the war.

➤ Wellingtons were built in 16 marks and 11,461 were completed by 1945.

➤ Special high-flying Wellingtons (Mks V and VI) fitted with a pressure cabin reached an altitude of 11600 m (38,000 ft.).

➤ The last Wellingtons in RAF service were withdrawn in 1953.

➤ Wellingtons equipped no less than 57 Royal Air Force squadrons.

**PROFILE**

# Barnes Wallis' 'Wimpey'

Built on the then-advanced principle of aerodynamic construction known as geodetic (inherently self-supporting), the Wellington prototype was the brain-child of Dr Barnes Wallis, later to win fame for his 'Dam Buster' bouncing bomb.

The Wellington's long wartime service showed that the 'basket weave' method of interlaced metal sections bolted together for high strength was very sound. This often enabled 'Wimpeys' to return to base with huge holes torn in them by flak and fighter attack. Wellingtons were first used as day-bombers, but their vulnerability was exposed in several disastrous raids.

After British night bombing passed to larger aircraft such as the Lancaster and Halifax in 1943, Wellingtons saw sterling service with Coastal Command as maritime reconnaissance aircraft. A number became successful U-boat hunters by both day and night. Sometimes fitted with Leigh Lights to illuminate submarines, the aircraft carried a fearsome array of depth charges and bombs to destroy them. One of the Wellington's most unusual roles was to destroy magnetic mines. The aircraft were fitted with a huge metal ring that released echoes powerful enough to trigger the mines, enabling aircrew to 'sweep' ports and coastal waters sown with such weapons. After the war the Wellington was used as a crew trainer.

*More than 600 Wellingtons were involved in the first 1000 bomber raid of the war, which targeted Cologne on the night of 30/31 May 1942. In all, 1042 aircraft took part in the raid.*

The only Victoria Cross awarded to a Wellington crewmember was won by a New Zealander, Sergeant J. A. Ward, flying as second pilot with No. 75 Squadron, RAF, after he climbed onto the aircraft's wing to put out an engine fire.

## Wellington B.Mk III

**Type:** medium-bomber

**Powerplant:** two 1119-kW (1,500-hp.) Bristol Hercules radial piston engines

**Maximum speed:** 410 km/h (254 m.p.h.) at 3810 m (12,500 ft.)

**Range:** 3540 km (2,195 mi.) with 680 kg (1,500 lb.) of bombs; 2478 km (1,535 mi.) with 2041 kg (4,500 lb.) of bombs

**Service ceiling:** 5790 m (19,000 ft.)

**Weights:** empty 8417 kg (18,517 lb.); maximum take-off 13,381 kg (29,438 lb.)

**Armament:** two 7.7-mm (.303 cal.) machine-guns in nose turret, four in tail turret and one in each rear fuselage beam position; up to 2041 kg (4,500 lb.) of bombs

**Dimensions:**
| | |
|---|---|
| span | 26.26 m (86 ft. 2 in.) |
| length | 18.54 m (60 ft. 10 in.) |
| height | 5.31 m (17 ft. 5 in.) |
| wing area | 78.04 m² (840 sq. ft.) |

## WELLINGTON B.Mk IC

R1492 was one of 2,685 Vickers Wellington B.Mk IC bombers constructed. It was delivered to an Operational Training Unit from Vickers' Chester factory in 1941.

Training versions of the Wellington often had their machine-gun armament removed and the nose turret faired over. Operational aircraft had two 7.7-mm (.303 cal.) guns in the turret.

Unlike other RAF types, especially those designed later in the war, all Wellington's were built by the company which designed the aircraft. Vickers used three factories at Weybridge, Chester and Blackpool.

Lacking a dorsal turret, the Wellington was somewhat vulnerable to attacks from the beam. Some aircraft had an improvised gun armament in the beam to remedy this.

The Bristol Hercules was a reliable and efficient engine that was able to survive considerable battle damage. Rolls-Royce Merlins were tried as an alternative powerplant in the Wellington Mk II.

Early Wellington B. Mk I aircraft required modification to carry the 1814-kg (4,000-lb.) 'blockbuster' bomb.

Early examples of the Wellington bomber were fitted with a 'dustbin' machine-gun turret which was lowered amidships when required.

The rear gunner was armed with four 7.7-mm (.303 cal.) Browning machine-guns, and many Wellington gunners shot down Bf 109s that strayed too close.

### COMBAT DATA

#### MAXIMUM SPEED

For a medium-bomber the Wellington was very fast by pre-war standards, but fighter design evolved rapidly as the war began and the Wellington could not outrun fighters. The G4M had a higher speed, but lacked the Wellington's armour and power turrets.

WELLINGTON B.Mk III 410 km/h (254 m.p.h.)
He 111H-6 271 km/h (168 m.p.h.)
G4M2 'BETTY' 438 km/h (271 m.p.h.)

#### ARMAMENT

RAF bombers were well armed by contemporary standards, and the Wellington carried a fair bombload and defensive armament. Despite its gun armament, it was vulnerable to enemy fighters.

**G4M2 'BETTY'**
3 x 7.7-mm (.303 cal.) MGs
2 x 20-mm (0.79-in.) cannon
1000 kg (2,200 lb.) of bombs

**He 111H-6**
1 x 13-mm (0.51-in.) MG
2 x 7.2-mm (0.28-in.) MGs
2 x 7.9-mm (0.31-in.) MGs
1 x 20-mm (0.79-in.) cannon
2000 kg (4,400 lb.) of bombs

**WELLINGTON B.Mk III**
8 x 7.7-mm (.303 cal.) MGs
2041 kg (4,500 lb.) of bombs

#### RANGE

Wellingtons had a reasonable range. Japanese aircraft had to fly over long distances in the Pacific and had greater range, gained at the expense of armour and offensive load.

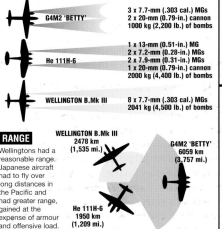

WELLINGTON B.Mk III 2478 km (1,535 mi.)
G4M2 'BETTY' 6059 km (3,757 mi.)
He 111H-6 1950 km (1,209 mi.)

## Leigh Light Wellington versus the U-boat

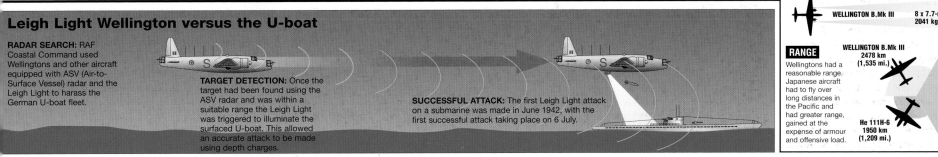

**RADAR SEARCH:** RAF Coastal Command used Wellingtons and other aircraft equipped with ASV (Air-to-Surface Vessel) radar and the Leigh Light to harass the German U-boat fleet.

**TARGET DETECTION:** Once the target had been found using the ASV radar and was within a suitable range the Leigh Light was triggered to illuminate the surfaced U-boat. This allowed an accurate attack to be made using depth charges.

**SUCCESSFUL ATTACK:** The first Leigh Light attack on a submarine was made in June 1942, with the first successful attack taking place on 6 July.

# VOUGHT
# F4U CORSAIR

● Carrier fighter ● Potent ground-attacker ● Dominant in the Pacific

▲ Flying in May 1940, the XF4U-1 was the smallest possible airframe mated with the most powerful engine then available. It was the first of more than 12,500 Corsairs built over the following 13 years.

**V**ought's F4U Corsair was one of the finest fighters ever built. At first thought too powerful to fly from carrier decks, the Corsair weaved a path of destruction in battle after battle during World War II, totally outclassing the much-feared Japanese Zero. With its instantly recognisable gull-wing shape and its great speed and firepower, the Corsair was still coming off the production line in 1953, one of the last of the great piston-engined fighters.

▲ **Gull wing**
The kinked wing allowed short landing gear to be fitted while lifting the huge propeller clear of the deck.

▲ **Into the air**
With a self-generated vapour trail spiralling around the propeller, a radar-equipped F4U night-fighter runs down the deck of a 'Midway'-class aircraft-carrier.

◀ **Raw power**
The massive 18-cylinder Pratt & Whitney Double Wasp radial engine was the key to the Corsair's superb performance.

▼ **Super performer**
From its earliest test flights in 1940, the Corsair showed that it could exceed 650 km/h (400 m.p.h.) in a straight line. This was faster than any other American aircraft, a unique achievement for a naval fighter designed for carrier operations.

▲ **Pacific killer**
Superb as a dogfighter or ground-attack platform the Corsair helped the Allies sweep through the western Pacific in 1944-45.

## FACTS AND FIGURES

➤ The F4U's propeller was one-third larger than that of the Messerschmitt Bf 109.

➤ The final F4U-7 Corsair was delivered to France in 1953, just as the last attack Corsairs were reaching the US Marines.

➤ The 'ultimate' Corsair was the Goodyear F2G, fitted with a P&W R-4360 engine delivering 2685 kW (3,600 hp.) of power.

➤ Charles Lindbergh demonstrated Corsair tactics during a Pacific tour in 1943.

➤ A US Navy Corsair night-fighter pilot was the only Allied ace of the Korean War who did not fly the F-86 Sabre.

➤ Except for Yugoslavia's S-49 and Spain's Ha 1112, the 12,571 Corsairs were the last piston fighters produced.

# PROFILE

# The mighty Corsair

The fighter which took shape on designer Rex Beisel's drawing board in 1938 was a monster. The prototype Vought F4U Corsair, flown on 29 May 1940, was the heaviest shipborne fighter built to that time. It was tough, fast and very manoeuvrable, but early pilots encountered handling problems at low speeds, and the restricted view made carrier landing very tricky. As a result, the first Corsairs in combat were flown with

enormous success by land-based Marines.

Modified with a raised seat and bulged canopy, Corsairs were flying from British carriers in 1943 and from US Navy carriers by 1944, and racked up an impressive score of aerial victories against Japan's best fighters. Corsairs using bombs and rockets paved the way for the final battles at Iwo Jima and Okinawa. The Royal Navy also used the Corsair to great effect in the Pacific, attacking Japanese oil

refineries and airfields.

Vought's remarkable fighter, also manufactured by Brewster and Goodyear, was still an important component in US naval air power during the Korean War. One Corsair even shot down a MiG-15 jet fighter.

*As the Corsair's place as a fighter was taken by jets, the tough Vought warbird was turned into a highly effective ground-attack machine.*

The most instantly recognisable feature of the Corsair was its inverted gull wing. In addition to giving the huge propeller extra ground clearance, it also ensured that the wing met the fuselage at right-angles, causing minimum interference drag.

## F4U-1A Corsair

**Type:** single-seat, carrier-operable fighter-bomber

**Powerplant:** one 1492-kW (2,000-hp.) Pratt & Whitney R-2800-8 Double Wasp 18-cylinder radial piston engine

**Maximum speed:** 671 km/h (417 m.p.h.) at 6605 m (20,000 ft.)

**Range:** 1650 km (1,010 mi.)

**Service ceiling:** 11,247 m (37,000 ft.)

**Weights:** empty 4074 kg (9,000 lb.); loaded 6350 kg (14,000 lb.)

**Armament:** six 12.7-mm (.50 cal.) Browning M2 machine-guns with 400 rounds (outboard) and 375 rounds (inboard) per gun; up to 1800 kg (4,000 lb.) of bombs or rockets

**Dimensions:**
| | | |
|---|---|---|
| span | 12.49 m | (41 ft.) |
| length | 10.16 m | (33 ft. 5 in.) |
| height | 4.90 m | (15 ft. 1 in.) |
| wing area | 29.17 m² | (314 sq. ft.) |

## F4U-1A CORSAIR

This aircraft was flown by Lieutenant Ira C. Kepford, the US Navy's leading ace in 1944. He was one of 15 aces from VF-17, the first Navy Corsair squadron.

Much of the Corsair's long nose was occupied by a single self-sealing fuel tank holding 896 litres (237 gal.).

Early Corsairs had the standard American fighter armament of six 12.7-mm (.50 cal.) machine-guns. Later variants carried four cannon.

Structure of the Corsair was conventional all-metal, although extensive spot welding rather than riveting gave it a very smooth skin.

The 18-cylinder Pratt & Whitney Double Wasp engine drove a three-bladed Hamilton Standard propeller. At 4.04 m (13 ft.) across, it was easily the biggest fitted to a fighter of the time.

The cockpit was set well back along the fuselage. Visibility ahead and down was poor, which contributed to the type's early carrier landing problems.

## COMBAT DATA

### MAXIMUM SPEED
The Corsair remained one of the fastest fighters of the war. Far superior to hasty improvisations like the Seafire, it was also much faster than late-war Japanese interceptors like the Raiden, which had been designed to try to match American fighter performance.

- **F4U-1A CORSAIR** 671 km/h (417 m.p.h.)
- **J2M RAIDEN** 612 km/h (380 m.p.h.)
- **SEAFIRE Mk III** 570 km/h (354 m.p.h.)

### RANGE
Air warfare at sea is generally fought at longer ranges than on land, especially when the sea is the Pacific Ocean. Aircraft designed for Pacific operations generally had far greater range than those like the Seafire, which were intended for more confined areas of operation.

- **J2M RAIDEN** 1000 km (621 mi.)
- **F4U-1A CORSAIR** 1650 km (1,010 mi.)
- **SEAFIRE Mk III** 750 km (470 mi.)

### ARMAMENT
The Corsair carried a heavy bombload at great speed. It was more lightly armed than some of its contemporaries, although superior American pilot training meant that this was not too much of a handicap during a dogfight. The big '50-calibre' machine-gun still packed quite a punch, with the ability to sink small warships.

- **F4U-1A CORSAIR** 6 x 12.7-mm (.50 cal.) machine-guns, 1800 kg (4,000 lb.) of bombs
- **J2M RAIDEN** 2 x 20-mm (0.79-in.) cannon, 2 x 7.7-mm (.303 cal.) machine-guns
- **SEAFIRE Mk III** 2 x 20-mm (0.79-in.) cannon, 4 x 7.7-mm (.303 cal.) machine-guns, 227 kg (500 lb.) of bombs

## A combat record second to none

**1943 – FIRST COMBAT:** The first F4U users were the Marines of Guadalcanal's 'Cactus Air Force', who revelled in its speed and power.

**1944 – AIR SUPERIORITY:** Going to sea with the US Navy in early 1944, the Corsair established domination over Japanese fighters.

**1945 – NIGHT-FIGHTER:** By the end of WWII, night-fighting Corsairs carried airborne intercept radar with a wing-mounted antenna.

**1951 – ATTACK BOMBER:** With rockets and up to 2000 kg (4,400 lb.) of bombs, the Corsair was a mainstay of US Korean War attack capability.

# VOUGHT

# OS2U KINGFISHER

● Two-seat observation/scout aircraft ● Search-and-rescue

▲ Some 1500 Kingfishers were built, 300 of these by the Naval Aircraft Factory in Philadelphia as the OS2N. The last examples left the production line in 1942.

**H**undreds of Allied airmen owe their lives to Vought OS2U Kingfisher crews who made many rescues in World War II. Before the advent of the helicopter, a downed flier regarded the sight of an OS2U Kingfisher with a sigh of relief. The Kingfisher, operated on wheeled landing gear or floats, was valuable to the Allies in anti-submarine and reconnaissance roles, but it is as a search-and-rescue aircraft that it is most widely remembered.

## VOUGHT OS2U KINGFISHER

### ▲ Stable platform

*Kingfishers were renowned for their stability at sea, a valuable attribute for an aircraft of its type. Engine reliability and range were also important.*

### ▼ Fleet Air Arm bird

*Supplied under Lend-Lease arrangements, 100 OS2Us were delivered to the British Fleet for use onboard cruisers and as trainers.*

### ▲ OS2Us at Pearl Harbor

*Of the six Kingfishers that reached the Pearl Harbor Battle Force by the end of 1940, a number were destroyed on December 7, 1941.*

### ◀ Preserved Kingfisher

*Here an OS2U is preserved onboard the battleship USS Alabama, which would have carried up to three in service.*

### ▲ Over 1000 OS2Us

*The main production model was the OS2U-3, which featured extra fuel tanks in the wings and better armor protection for the pilot and observer.*

## FACTS AND FIGURES

➤ On entering service in 1940, OS2Us were the U.S. Navy's first catapult-launched monoplane observation aircraft.

➤ One hundred Kingfishers served with the Royal Navy between 1941 and 1947.

➤ The Kingfisher first flew as a landplane in March 1938 and on floats in May.

➤ Several battleships preserved as museums in the United States have restored OS2Us onboard.

➤ OS2Us were used in the Aleutians as dive-bombers against Japanese targets.

➤ Some Fleet Air Arm Kingfishers were based in the West Indies for training use.

# Sharp eyes of the Navy

Designed to replace a biplane, the Vought OS2U Kingfisher was modern for the late 1930s, employing spot-welding and other advanced construction techniques.

The US Navy needed a reliable aircraft that could be launched from a ship's catapults on rescue and reconnaissance missions, and in designing the Kingfisher Vought drew on their wealth of experience in observation aircraft. OS2Us were also useful as anti-submarine craft flown by inshore patrol squadrons.

The pilot and observer/gunner had a high perch with excellent visibility. Though slow and somewhat underpowered, the Kingfisher was stable and thoroughly reliable. On at least one occasion, a Kingfisher outmaneuvered and shot down a Japanese Zero fighter. During fighting at the island of Yap, an OS2U rescued a three-man bomber crew within eyesight of Japanese shore gunners, then taxied five miles to take the men to a ship.

Other users included the Royal Navy, the forces of Australia and several South American countries.

*The bulk of OS2Us built were mounted on floats for service from catapult-equipped cruisers.*

## OS2U-3 Kingfisher

**Type:** two-seat observation aircraft

**Powerplant:** one 336-kW (450-hp.) Pratt & Whitney R-985-AN-2 radial piston engine

**Maximum speed:** 264 km/h (164 m.p.h.) at 1767 m (5,500 ft.)

**Range:** 1287 km (800 mi.)

**Service ceiling:** 396 m (1,300 ft.)

**Weights:** empty 1867 kg (4,115 lb.); max take-off 2716 kg (5,988 lb.)

**Weapons:** two .303 cal. (7.62-mm) machine guns, with one forward-firing and one on trainable mount in rear cockpit; plus two 100-lb. or 325-lb. bombs on underwing racks.

**Dimensions:**
| | | |
|---|---|---|
| span | 10.97 m (36 ft.) |
| length | 10.36 m (34 ft.) |
| height | 4.57 m (15 ft.) |
| wing area | 24.34 m² (262 sq. ft.) |

## KINGFISHER Mk I

**En route to the Netherlands East Indies when these islands were over-run by the Japanese, 18 of 24 Vought VS-310s were absorbed by the Royal Australian Air Force as Kingfisher Mk Is.**

The two crew in the OS2U were the pilot and observer/radio operator/gunner. A large area of plexiglass in the cockpit canopies provided a good all-round view.

Two defensive 7.62-mm (.303 cal.) machine guns were usually fitted to Kingfishers; one flexibly-mounted in the rear cockpit, the other fixed to fire forward. Underwing racks were fitted for up to 295 kg (650 lb.) of bombs.

The Australian markings on A48-4 are based on Fleet Air Arm camouflage and feature early-style British national markings. Later in the Pacific war, RAAF aircraft adopted a blue and white roundel and fin flash.

Pratt & Whitney's reliable R-985 Wasp Junior rated at 336 kW (450 hp.) powered most Kingfishers. This well-known engine also powered the Beech Model 18 (C-45) twin-engine trainer/transport.

A48-4

Intended to replace the land-based O3U Corsair biplane, the OS2U introduced a number of new construction techniques, including spot welding of metal components.

The large centerline float was stabilized by the outboard floats; one under each wing. When returning to a USN cruiser after a catapult launch, OS2Us taxied on to a recovery sled towed by the ship and were then hoisted aboard by crane.

### RANGE

One of the outstanding floatplanes of the war, Aichi's E13A1 'Jake' had good range and speed performance. Its range (and therefore endurance) was almost twice that of the Ar 196 and considerably more than the Kingfisher. Most were operated at sea.

OS2U-3 KINGFISHER 1287 km (800 mi.)
Ar 196A-3 1067 km (663 mi.)
E13A1a 'JAKE' 2086 km (1,296 mi.)

### SPEED

The Kingfisher was perhaps the slowest of the comparable World War II floatplanes. The 'Jake' had a margin of 110 km/h (70 m.p.h.) over the OS2U, largely due to its much larger engine, which was rated almost three times that of the latter.

OS2U-3 264 km/h (164 m.p.h.)
Ar 196A-3 309 km/h (192 m.p.h.)
E13A1a 'JAKE' 375 km/h (233 m.p.h.)

### WEAPONS

By far the best armed of these types was the Arado Ar 196, with its two cannon and machine guns. The Kingfisher, however, was able to carry a much larger bomb load – almost three times as much as the Ar 196 – but about the same load as the 'Jake'.

OS2U-3 KINGFISHER
2 x 7.62-mm (.30 cal.) MGs
295-kg (650-lb.) bomb load

Ar 196A-3
2 x 20-mm cannon
2 x 7.92-mm MGs
100-kg (220-lb.) bomb load

E13A1a 'Jake'
1 x 7.7-mm (.303 cal.) MG
250-kg (550-lb.) bomb load

## Kingfisher deployment

**LAND BASED:** The option of wheeled undercarriage allowed the Kingfisher to be shore based. The Royal Navy used these aircraft for training purposes.

**ON FLOATS:** Kingfishers were in their element on the water. Their floats allowed them to be deployed from catapult-equipped cruisers. After a sortie, the OS2U simply alighted on the water next to the ship and was lifted aboard again by crane. Floats also allowed the Kingfisher to land during a sortie, to pick up a downed pilot for example.

**CATAPULT LAUNCH:** Special catapults were fitted to U.S. Navy and Royal Navy ships intending to use the Kingfisher. These were swung out from the side of the vessel and the aircraft launched over the water.

# VOUGHT

# SB2U VINDICATOR

● US Navy scout-bomber ● Pacific 1942 ● Royal Navy trainer

▲ The Battle of Midway of 1942 was one of the few engagements in which the Vindicator saw combat in World War II. Its lack of performance against fighters like the Japanese Zero meant it was replaced by the Douglas SBD Dauntless.

**B**uilt in 1935, while the service still favoured biplanes, Vought's SB2U Vindicator was the US Navy's first monoplane scout bomber. This two-seat, all-metal combat plane was a step forward in the 1930s, but by the time World War II began it was inferior to other fighting machines in its class. Vulnerable to fighter attack, the SB2U actually saw relatively little combat service, although it performed admirably in the training role.

---

## VOUGHT SB2U VINDICATOR

◀ **Improved variants**
Carrying bright pre-war markings, nine SB2Us formate. Later versions carried more fuel, armament and armour.

▲ **Fleet Air Arm Chesapeake**
The V-156 proved unsuitable for the Royal Navy's escort carriers due to its long take-off run, and was relegated to a land-based training role.

▲ **Prototype**
This is the first XSB2U-1 seen shortly after completion. The Vindicator was relatively lightly constructed compared to later dive-bomber types.

▲ **Based aboard USS Saratoga**
These three SB2U-1s are seen on 23 May 1939 in the full markings of bomber squadron VB-3.

◀ **SB2U-3 of VS-1**
The US Navy did not officially adopt the name Vindicator until the SB2U-3 version was delivered.

### FACTS AND FIGURES

➤ In 1936, tests at Anacostia Naval Station, Washington, showed the SB2U to be superior to its SB3U biplane competitor.

➤ The prototype for the SB2U series made its maiden flight on 4 January 1936.

➤ The first SB2Us went to US Navy unit VB-3 from 20 December 1937.

➤ Captured French V-156s are reputed to have been used to bomb Dover, although this was never confirmed.

➤ Two Marine Corps squadrons flew Vindicators in action in the Pacific.

➤ In 1939 a single SB2U-1 had floats added and flew as a seaplane XSB2U-3.

**PROFILE**

# Diving pioneer monoplane

Configured much like other scout and torpedo-bombers of the 1930s, the Vought SB2U Vindicator was designed to fly from aircraft-carrier decks. However, once in the air it lacked the speed, manoeuvrability or defensive armament to survive against the nimble, single-seat fighters emerging in the late 1930s.

In the mid-1930s, it took the US Navy many months to choose the Vindicator in preference to a competing biplane design. Once production Vindicators began to emerge

from Vought Sikorsky's Stratford, Connecticut, factory in 1937, it was very clear that the monoplane was the wave of the future. Designers kept improving the Vindicator. Even so, it was at best only an equal for the Navy's other scout bomber of the era, the Douglas SBD Dauntless. US Navy and Marine Corps SB2Us were active against the Japanese in the Pacific, including the Battle of Midway, during World War II, but were soon replaced by other types.

Vought built and delivered 24 of 40 planned aircraft to France

under the designation V-156. Some of these fell into German hands after the French capitulated. Fifty more, called Chesapeakes, went to the British Fleet Air Arm, which used them in an operational training role serving with two squadrons.

*Left: Bomber squadron VB-3 'Top Hatters' equipped with SB2U-1s in 1939. The squadron was still active in 1990, serving in the Gulf War as fighter squadron VF-14 with F-14 Tomcats.*

*Above: In 1938 France's naval air service ordered the SB2U under the Vought company designation V-156-F3.*

## SB2U-3 Vindicator

**Type:** carrier-based scout/bomber

**Powerplant:** one 615-kW (825-hp.) Pratt & Whitney R-1535-02 Twin Wasp Junior radial piston engine

**Maximum speed:** 391 km/h (242 m.p.h.) at 2895 m (9,500 ft.)

**Range:** 1802 km (1,117 mi.)

**Service ceiling:** 7195 m (23,600 ft.)

**Weights:** empty 2556 kg (5,623 lb.); loaded 4273 kg (9,400 lb.)

**Armament:** two 12.7-mm (.50 cal.) machine-guns (one forward-firing and one in rear cockpit), plus up to 454 kg (1,000 lb.) of bombs

**Dimensions:**
| | | |
|---|---|---|
| span | 12.80 m | (42 ft.) |
| length | 10.36 m | (34 ft.) |
| height | 3.12 m | (10 ft. 3 in.) |
| wing area | 28.33 m² | (305 sq. ft.) |

## CHESAPEAKE MK I

In Royal Navy service the Vought V-156 was known as the Chesapeake. AL924 was one of 50 V-156-B1s ordered, and the first entered service in 1941 with No. 811 Squadron at Lee-on-Solent.

Pratt & Whitney's R-1535 Twin Wasp Junior engine powered the SB2U and V-156. This drove a two-bladed metal propeller.

The Chesapeake had provision for four forward-firing machine-guns in the wings, with a further free-mounted gun in the rear cockpit. American SB2U-3s had one forward- and one aft-firing 12.7-mm (.50 cal.) machine-gun.

A Fleet Air Arm three-tone grey colour scheme was applied to the Chesapeake. This aircraft also carries early-style national markings as displayed at the start of World War II.

A 'trapeze' below the cockpit was fitted to a bomb on the centreline pylon. This pulled the bomb downwards and clear of the aircraft.

The undercarriage on the Vindicator retracted to the rear and rotated through 90°, with the wheels fitting into a recessed bay in each wing.

Maximum ordnance load for Fleet Air Arm Chesapeakes was 680 kg (1,500 lb.) of bombs: either three 227-kg (500-lb.) bombs or a dozen 53-kg (117-lb.) bombs. US Navy Vindicators were restricted to 454 kg (1,000 lb.) of bombs.

The arrester hook can be seen in the retracted position on this aircraft. The arrester gear on British aircraft was of a different design to the American.

*ROYAL NAVY AL924 K*

## COMBAT DATA

### BOMBLOAD
Even though it was an improvement over that of the SBU-1, the bombload carried by the Vindicator was still inferior to that of the Dauntless, the Navy's main wartime scout/bomber.

| SB2U-3 VINDICATOR | SBD-5 DAUNTLESS | SBU-1 |
|---|---|---|
| 454 kg (1,000 lb.) | 1021 kg (2,240 lb.) | 227 kg (500 lb.) |

### MAXIMUM SPEED
Top speed performance of the Dauntless was only marginally better than that of the Vindicator. However, other more marked performance improvements made the SBD the superior aircraft.

| | |
|---|---|
| SB2U-3 VINDICATOR | 391 km/h (242 m.p.h.) |
| SBD-5 DAUNTLESS | 406 km/h (251 m.p.h.) |
| SBU-1 | 330 km/h (198 m.p.h.) |

### ENGINE POWER
Power ratings climbed steadily to take advantage of better engines. SBDs introduced a significantly more powerful engine which improved flight performance and load-carrying capability.

| SB2U-3 VINDICATOR | SBD-5 DAUNTLESS | SBU-1 |
|---|---|---|
| 615 kW (825 hp.) | 895 kW (1,200 hp.) | 522 kW (700 hp.) |

## Naval dive-bombers of World War II

■ **AICHI D3A:** Known as 'Val' to the Allies, the D3A was a major participant in the Pearl Harbor attack of 1941. Over 1400 were built.

■ **DOUGLAS SBD DAUNTLESS:** Entering service in 1940, the SBD served with the Navy and Marine Corps, and replaced the SB2U.

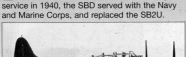

■ **FAIREY BARRACUDA:** First flown in 1940, this aircraft was employed as a dive-bomber by the Royal Navy in the Atlantic and the Pacific.

■ **JUNKERS Ju 87:** The Ju 87C-1 variant of the 'Stuka' was intended for the German carrier *Graf Zeppelin* before construction was halted.

# VULTEE

# A-31/A-35 VENGEANCE

● Dive-bomber ● Gunnery trainer ● Unique wing structure

O ften vilified as an inferior warplane that should not have been produced in large numbers, the Vengeance was, in truth, a robust, fast aircraft with good flying characteristics. It was built for a military tactic – dive-bombing – that was rapidly falling out of favour. A true vertical dive-bomber, the Vengeance proved quite effective when used against targets that required its special capability, such as Japanese jungle positions in Burma and New Guinea.

▲ Despite harsh jungle operating conditions, the Vengeance had the best targets destroyed per loss of aircraft record of any RAF type in the Far East.

## VULTEE A-31/A-35 VENGEANCE

◄ **Training the French**
*This A-35B was one of 36 ex-USAAF examples delivered to the French during 1943.*

▼ **Official disapproval**
*Throughout World War II the British Air Ministry insisted that dive-bombers were out-moded despite their success in the Far East.*

**Wing structure ►**
*The Vengeance's unique 'cranked' wing design was immensely strong, which was necessary to withstand the regular high g forces involved in dive-bombing.*

**Australian service ►**
*This Vengeance Mk II, diverted to the RAAF from a British order, flew with No. 12 Squadron in 1943.*

◄ **Bombing Burma**
*In June 1943 No. 45 Squadron Vengeances started striking back at advancing Japanese forces in Burma. Attacking communications and troop positions, they combined accuracy and reliability with a low loss rate.*

### FACTS AND FIGURES

➤ Like the Ju 87 Stuka, the Vengeance began as a twin-tailed design, but flew with a single tail.

➤ The initial contract price for the RAF was $17,042,640 for 200 aircraft.

➤ A Vengeance 'warbird' has been restored to flying condition in Australia.

➤ The Vengeance had a unique 'cranked' wing shape which enhanced its dive-bombing capability.

➤ Total Vengeance production was 1931 aircraft, including 1529 built in Nashville.

➤ Heavy control surfaces resulted in one pilot calling his aircraft the *Flying Cow*.

# PROFILE

# Wreaking vengeance in the Far East

Vultee designed the Vengeance dive-bomber initially for France's Armée de l'Air, which was seeking an equivalent to the dreaded Junkers Ju 87 Stuka. As the war progressed, the Vengeance flew for Britain, India, Australia, and the US.

After production began in Downey, California, most Vengeances were built at the maker's plant in Nashville, Tennessee.

In the US, some Vengeances were used to train dive-bomber

pilots, but most simply languished at American bases, with little effort made to exploit their potential.

In the Far East, four RAF, two Indian, and five Australian squadrons operated Vengeances resourcefully under difficult conditions during the period May 1942–July 1944. The Indian-based squadrons saw action in Burma, while the Australians made perilous attacks on New Guinea and other islands until B-24 Liberators could take over the job at higher altitude.

*Below: Despite early problems, mainly with the powerplant, the Vengeance had a distinguished career with the RAF as a low-level bomber and dive-bomber.*

*Above: The US judged the Vengeance unsuitable for front-line operations. Its duties included training in gunnery and dive-bombing.*

The US Army experimented with improved versions of the Vengeance, including one model which had the same engine as the B-29 Superfortress. The Vengeance was used by both France and Great Britain as a gunnery trainer and target tug in the latter stages of the war.

## A-35B Vengeance

**Type:** two-seat dive-bomber

**Powerplant:** one 1268-kW (1700-hp) Wright R-2600-13 Cyclone 14-cylinder radial engine

**Maximum speed:** 449 km/h (279 mph) at 4115 m (13,500 ft)

**Cruising speed:** 370 km/h (230 mph)

**Range:** 3701 km (2300 miles)

**Service ceiling:** 6800 m (22,310 ft)

**Weights:** empty 4672 kg (10,300 lb); maximum take-off 7439 kg (16,400 lb)

**Armament:** four fixed forward-firing 7.62-mm (.30-cal.) or 12.7-mm (.50-cal.) machine guns in wings plus two flexible rear-firing 7.62-mm machine guns in gunner's position; two 227-kg (500-lb) bombs in fuselage bay and two 113-kg (250-lb) bombs under the wings

**Dimensions:**
| | |
|---|---|
| span | 14.63 m (48 ft) |
| length | 12.11 m (39 ft 9 in) |
| height | 4.67 m (15 ft 4 in) |
| wing area | 30.84 m² (332 sq ft) |

## VENGEANCE MK III

**Although dive-bombers were dismissed by the British Air Ministry as unsuitable, Vengeances such as this example served with distinction with four RAF squadrons in the Far East.**

Early problems with the Wright R-2600 engine were largely solved by a series of modifications on the British aircraft. French machines without these modifications were judged to be unreliable and uneconomical.

The pilot was protected by 8-mm thick armour plating covering an area of 1.35 m² (14½ ft). The gunner was protected by bullet-proof glass shields. The pilot was provided with a stainless steel 'relief tube' for long sorties.

The wing structure comprised a very heavy skin reinforced with U-shaped stringers, allowing a large space for the bulletproof fuel tanks. Large perforated dive-brakes made of aluminium alloy gave the aircraft excellent stability when dive-bombing.

After tests the British found the American 12.7-mm (.50-cal.) machine guns unsuitable, and modified all their aircraft to carry 7.7-mm (.303-cal.) Browning machine guns. Up to 907 kg (2000 lb) of bombs could be carried beneath the wings.

Although aileron controls were light, pilots found that rudder and elevator controls were extremely heavy, especially when recovering from a dive. However, the large flying surfaces gave the aircraft good stability, which is vital for accurate bombing.

FB922

Built in three sections, with crew and bomb-bay in the deep forward section, the fuselage was riveted together on final assembly.

## COMBAT DATA

### MAXIMUM SPEED

As an early version of the P-51 Mustang powered by an Allison engine, the Apache was faster than the purpose-built A-35 and Ju 87 dive-bombers, which traded speed for strength and bombload.

| | |
|---|---|
| **A-35B VENGEANCE** | 449 km/h (279 mph) |
| **Ju 87D-1** | 410 km/h (255 mph) |
| **A-36A APACHE** | 499 km/h (254 mph) |

### ARMAMENT

Able to carry a far larger bombload than the two US designs, the Ju 87 delivered its ordnance with great accuracy. However, its lack of speed and armament made it more vulnerable to enemy fighters.

| | |
|---|---|
| **A-35B VENGEANCE** | 6 x 7.62-mm (.30-cal.) machine guns / 680-kg (1500-lb) bombload |
| **Ju 87D-1** | 3 x 7.9-mm machine guns / 1800-kg (3968-lb) bombload |
| **A-36A APACHE** | 6 x 12.7-mm (.50-cal.) machine guns / 454-kg (1000-lb) bombload |

### RANGE

The Vengeance's impressive range made it ideally suited to the vast Pacific theatre. The Ju 87 and A-36 could only operate fairly near to the front line and generally flew close air support missions in co-operation with ground forces.

A-35B VENGEANCE 3701 km (2300 miles)

Ju 87D-1 1535 km (954 miles)

A-36A APACHE 499 km (310 miles)

## Vengeances around the world

■ **FREE FRENCH AIR FORCE:** This A-35B of GB I/35 served briefly as a pilot and gunnery trainer in North Africa before economy and reliability problems led to early retirement.

■ **ROYAL AUSTRALIAN AIR FORCE:** After retiring as bombers, a number of Vengeances were converted for use as target tugs. This example served with No. 7 Operational Training Unit in 1944.

■ **US ARMY AIR FORCE:** Most A-35s intended for US Forces were exported and few saw operational duties. This example was used as a station 'hack' in the UK during 1944.

# WESTLAND

# LYSANDER

● Army co-operation ● Clandestine spyplane ● Air–sea rescue

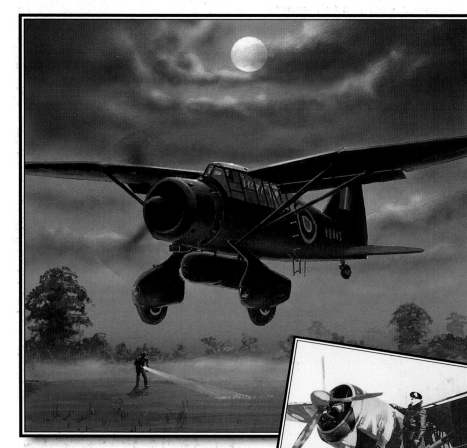

When Westland created its most famous aircraft, the immortal Lysander, in 1935, no one dreamed that this high-winged craft would fly into occupied territory, at night, on secret missions vital to the outcome of World War II. The Lysander introduced STOL (short take-off and landing) capability, crucial to today's military, long before the term was coined. As a flagship for spying missions behind the lines, it had no equal.

▲ With a wide range of speed, short-field take-off and landing capability and a strong undercarriage, the Lysander was well suited to clandestine flights into the fields of Belgium, France and Holland.

PHOTO FILE

## WESTLAND LYSANDER

**▲ Field operations**
The winter of 1939/40 was very difficult for the Army co-operation Lysanders in France. Wheel covers were removed to prevent the mud from clogging the inside of the spats when flying from fields.

**▲ Air-sea rescue**
Lysanders were flown by RAF air-sea rescue squadrons. The Mk IIIA had a good range and slow-flying qualities for dropping dinghies to aircrew in the sea.

**▼ Easy access**
Almost all of the starboard side of the Lysander's fuselage panels could be removed for inspection and access to internal equipment.

**◄ Ground attack**
The first Lysander had a 20-mm (0.79-in.) Oerlikon cannon mounted above each of the wheel fairings for a possible army ground-attack support role.

**Gunner down ►**
The first production Lysander, nicknamed 'The Pregnant Perch', was fitted with a ventral gun position with two cannon for strafing trials. Here it has come to grief after suffering engine failure.

### FACTS AND FIGURES

➤ The prototype for the Lysander series made its first flight on 15 June 1936.

➤ First entering RAF service in May 1938, the Lysander went on to fly with more than 30 squadrons during World War II.

➤ Total production of all models of the Lysander was 1652 aircraft.

➤ Lysanders saw service in Burma, Egypt, Greece, India and Palestine.

➤ A total of 225 Lysanders were manufactured by National Steel Car Corporation of Canada.

➤ A remarkable 21 Lysanders survive today as display aircraft or in flying condition.

## PROFILE

# Westland's Lysander spyplane

The Westland Lysander entered service in 1938 and served throughout the war. A versatile, solid performer useful for a wide range of duties, the aircraft earned a special place in history for its ability to land in unbelievably short spaces and drop off, or retrieve, secret agents working far behind enemy lines. The Lysander's broad wing and huge flight surfaces enabled it to land in unpaved fields, often with as little as 200 m (650 ft.) of taxi space. This was a treacherous job for its pilot – in many ways, riskier than the more glamorous task of flying fighters – but these covert missions were of paramount importance.

The Lysander is best-remembered for its use by confidential agents of British Intelligence and of the American Office of Strategic Services, but it also carried out many other tasks. Although less than ideal as an observation craft, the Lysander carried out reconnaissance missions and served as a spotter for Allied warplanes and artillery. Some aircraft functioned as VIP transports at battlefields where paved runways were unavailable. The Lysander made a unique contribution to World War II.

*Right: RAF Lysander Mk IIIAs completed over 400 special operations between August 1941 and December 1944. They supplied the Resistance and flew agents in and out.*

*Above: This Lysander wears the markings of the Finnish air force early in 1940. Nine aircraft were obtained for Army co-operation duties, being fitted with removable stub winglets/bomb racks on each undercarriage leg for up to six 9-kg high-explosive bombs.*

## LYSANDER MK II

The high-winged Westland Lysander is most famous for its many night missions into mainland Europe, using its short take-off and landing capabilities to maximum advantage.

### Lysander Mk III

**Type:** army co-operation aircraft

**Powerplant:** one 649-kW (870-hp.) Bristol Mercury XX radial piston engine

**Maximum speed:** 341 km/h (211 m.p.h.) at 1525 m (5,000 ft.)

**Range:** 966 km (600 mi.)

**Service ceiling:** 6655 m (21,800 ft.)

**Weights:** empty 1980 kg (4,356 lb.); maximum take-off 2866 kg (6,305 lb.)

**Armament:** four 7.7-mm (.303 cal.) Browning machine-guns (one in each wheel spat and two on trainable mount in rear cockpit); up to 227 kg (500 lb.) of flares, rocket projectiles or bombs

**Dimensions:**
| | | |
|---|---|---|
| span | | 15.24 m (50 ft.) |
| length | | 9.30 m (30 ft. 6 in.) |
| height | | 4.42 m (14 ft. 6 in.) |
| wing area | | 24.15 m² (260 sq. ft.) |

Lysander Mk IIIs were powered by a nine-cylinder Bristol Mercury XX air-cooled radial engine, developing 649 kW (870 hp.) at 4160 m (13,653 ft.). It had a front edge exhaust collector ring.

The pilot sat high in the cockpit, which took him level, and in front of, the wing leading edge. It had transparent sliding roof and deep glazed side windows.

The high wing was a distinctive shape with a single main spar. Leading-edge slats were positioned along the full span, in two sections. Handley-Page flaps were fitted between the elevators and the fuselage.

The all-metal framed fin and rudder was fabric covered. The tailplane was metal-framed and covered, although the elevators had fabric covering.

The propeller was a three-bladed, pitch-controllable de Havilland type with a medium-sized spinner. A Rotax electric engine starter was normally fitted.

The main fixed landing gear was machined aluminium alloy, bent into shape, with Dowty internally sprung wheels.

The front fuselage consisted of square, light-alloy tubing, while the rear fuselage was welded steel tube. It was covered by fabric over wooden stringers with detachable metal panels.

The non-retractable Dunlop 'Ecta' tailwheel was fully castoring. A message hook could be provided at the rear.

## Clandestine mission

**1 UNARMED:** Using dead-reckoning the pilot flies his black-painted Lysander by moonlight to a secret landing site in France. It is identified by coded torch flashes.

**2 FIELD LANDING:** With only portable lights marking the strip the pilot makes a steep approach and a short field landing.

**3 RAPID PICK-UP:** In real danger of discovery the pilot releases a rope ladder from the side of the cockpit and the agent climbs quickly into the Lysander.

**4 SHORT TAKE-OFF:** Now much heavier, with an extra person on board, the pilot has to take-off from the field and clear obstacles, before setting course back home.

## COMBAT DATA

### ARMAMENT

The Lysander carried more defensive armament and a higher bombload than either the Henschel Hs 126 or the Fieseler Fi 156 Storch. For self-defence it had two pairs of Browning machine-guns, compared with the Hs 126's two singles and just one gun fitted to the Storch. Lysanders could also carry over 200 kg (500 lb.) of bombs while the Henschel only manage half that weight.

Fi-156 STORCH
1 x 7.9-mm (0.31-in.) MGs

LYSANDER Mk III
4 x 7.7-mm (.303 cal.) MGs

Hs 126
2 x 7.9-mm (0.31-in.) MGs

# WESTLAND

# WAPITI

● RAF general-purpose type ● Indian and Iraqi service ● Radial engine

▲ Although defence budgets were cut after 1918, the RAF needed a replacement for a number of wartime models. Wapitis became the mainstay of the RAF's overseas deployments.

With World War I at an end, the newly formed RAF found the idea of a general-purpose aircraft very attractive – defence spending had been cut, so a new aircraft needed to be 'multi-role'. In 1918 the RAF was saddled with wartime designs and by 1926 the DH.9A needed replacing. To complicate matters, however, Air Ministry Specification 26/27 required that the new aircraft use as many DH.9A parts as possible – another economy measure.

## WESTLAND WAPITI

▲ **Australian Wapiti Mk IA**
In early 1929 the RAAF took delivery of the first of 28 Wapitis, some for use as trainers. RAAF Director of Training, Sqn Ldr Smart, said: 'The Wapiti is ideal for desert flying in Australia'.

▲ **'Bombed up'**
Although a general-purpose type for overseas use, the Wapiti also gave valuable service as a day-bomber for the Auxiliary Air Force.

**External fuel ▶**
To extend the Wapiti's endurance and range, trials were undertaken with external fuel tanks. Each tank had a propeller-driven pump.

**◀ On floats**
A number of Wapiti Mk IIAs were fitted with Short's-built floats for trials. Wapitis could also be adapted for a ski undercarriage.

**Civil-registered Wapiti Mk V ▶**
In 1930 the Wapiti Mk V prototype was registered G-AAWA, fitted with floats and shipped to Buenos Aires for the 1931 British Exhibition and a sales tour of a number of South American states.

## FACTS AND FIGURES

➤ An RAF Wapiti Mk IIA was used as a receiver aircraft during the in-flight refuelling trials of 1934.

➤ From 1929 the Prince of Wales used a specially equipped VIP Wapiti Mk IA.

➤ Wapiti Mk Vs were still employed in the army co-operation role as late as 1940.

➤ Wapiti prototype J8495 was mistakenly built with a fuselage that was 0.61 m (2 ft.) shorter than was originally intended.

➤ Wapitis served the air forces of Australia and South Africa.

➤ Heavily modified Wapiti Mk V/VII G-AAWA was later redesignated as a Wallace Mk I.

# Biplane with a general purpose

Seven companies put forward eight different designs to meet the 1926 specification for a new general-purpose aircraft. All were to employ an all-metal airframe and use the Napier Lion engine.

Westland's Wapiti design actually used neither (at least initially), although it did incorporate de Havilland DH.9A components. Powered by a more modern 313-kW Bristol Jupiter radial, the prototype flew on 7 March

1927 and took part in trials with five other designs. In late 1927, 25 Wapiti Mk Is were ordered for service trials at home and with No. 84 Squadron in India. This marked the beginning of an almost 10-year association with the RAF's 'policing' squadrons in Iraq and on the Northwest Frontier.

An all-metal structure was finally introduced in the Mk II. Ten of these were built for No. 84 Squadron, before 430 Mk IIAs, with a 358-kW (480-

hp.) Jupiter engine, were ordered. The first was delivered in 1930 and served in the bombing, supply-dropping and army co-operation roles.

*Wapiti prototype J8495 used a set of virtually unaltered DH.9A wings and a modified DH.9A tailfin.*

*Below: The main Wapiti variant in RAF service was the Mk IIA. Of the 558 Wapitis built, 430 were Mk IIAs. These three aircraft from No. 55 Squadron, RAF, were among the Wapitis serving over the Northwest Frontier of India.*

*Above: Pictured in the 1930s, a Wapiti Mk IIA of No. 30 Squadron flies over the city of Mosul, Iraq.*

## Wapiti Mk IIA

**Type:** two-seat general-purpose biplane

**Powerplant:** one 358-kW (480-hp.) Bristol Jupiter VIII or VIIIF nine-cylinder radial piston engine

**Maximum speed:** 217 km/h (135 m.p.h.) at 1525 m (5,000 ft.)

**Cruising speed:** 177 km/h (110 m.p.h.)

**Range:** 580 km (360 mi.)

**Service ceiling:** 6280 m (20,600 ft.)

**Weights:** empty 1728 kg (3,802 lb.); loaded 2454 kg (5,400 lb.)

**Armament:** one fixed forward-firing Vickers Mk II 7.7-mm (.303 cal.) machine-gun and one Lewis Mk III 7.7-mm (.303 cal.) machine-gun in the rear cockpit, plus up to 263 kg (580 lb.) of bombs under the wings and fuselage

**Dimensions:** span 14.15 m (46 ft. 5 in.)
length 9.65 m (31 ft. 8 in.)
height 3.96 m (13 ft.)
wing area 45.34 m² (488 sq. ft.)

## WAPITI MK IIA

From 1929 Wapiti Mk IIAs replaced the de Havilland DH.9As of No. 30 Squadron, RAF, on 'policing' duties in Iraq. Based at Mosul, the unit flew Wapitis until 1935, when they were replaced by the Hawker Hardy.

No. 30 Squadron's badge featured a date palm tree, which also adorned the tail of its aircraft. The unit was formed in 1914 for service in Egypt and remained in the Middle East until 1942.

Two 7.7-mm (.303 cal.) machine-guns were fitted for defence. A Lewis gun was mounted on a Scarff ring in the rear cockpit, while a fixed Vickers gun was controlled by the pilot and fired forward through the propeller arc.

Despite the requirement that the RAF's new aircraft should employ the Napier Lion engine, the majority of Wapiti production machines were fitted with the Bristol Jupiter, a newer design with more development potential. The Wapiti Mk III built for the South African air force employed an Armstrong Whitworth Jaguar 14-cylinder, two-row radial, while two civil-registered Mk Vs and four Chinese Mk VIIIs used AW Panther engines.

Universal carriers under the wings and fuselage could hold various combinations of 51-kg (112-lb.), 104-/113-kg (229-250-lb.) or 9-kg (20-lb.) bombs up to a total of 263 kg (580 lb.).

Wapiti Mk IIs differed from Mk Is in having a detachable control column in the rear cockpit (but no rudder bar) for use in emergencies.

### COMBAT DATA

#### POWER

A contemporary of the Wapiti, the Heinkel He 46 army co-operation aircraft had a much more powerful engine, but it was of similar weight and carried a smaller bomb load. It was, however, a slightly faster machine.

| WAPITI Mk IIA 358 kW (480 hp.) | He 46C-1 485 kW (650 hp.) | Ro.37bis 418 kW (560 hp.) |

#### MAXIMUM SPEED

Compared to other biplane types of the inter-war years, the Wapiti was relatively slow; more than 113 km/h (70 m.p.h.) slower than the Meridionali Ro.37 reconnaissance fighter.

WAPITI 217 km/h (135 m.p.h)
He 46C-1 250 km/h (155 m.p.h.)
Ro.37bis 330 km/h (205 m.p.h.)

## Specification 26/27 competitors

**BEAVER:** With a Napier Lion engine, Bristol's design was derived from the Type 93 Boarhound and did not use DH.9A parts. Another design was submitted, but was never built.

**GORAL:** Powered by a Bristol Jupiter engine, Gloster's design also used DH.9A wings. Although the Goral was rejected, Gloster went on to build the all-metal wings for the Wapiti Mk II/IIA.

**HOUND:** de Havilland's DH.65 suffered from a lack of internal stowage space and unacceptable handling on the ground. It was, however, the fastest of the trialists and used the Napier Lion.

**VALIANT:** Test pilots at RAF Martlesham Heath preferred the Vickers Valiant, but as it used no DH.9A parts (like the Fairey Ferret III) more expensive than the other designs.

# WESTLAND

# WHIRLWIND

● Long-range fighter ● Ground attack ● Heavily armed

A sound design let down by unreliable engines, the Whirlwind was a bold attempt to give the RAF a fighter with greater range than single-engined types. With four cannon grouped in the nose, it was able to bring a heavy weight of fire to bear on ground targets. Only two squadrons were issued with Whirlwinds, but the aircraft was greatly appreciated by its pilots. If it had been fitted with better engines, the Whirlwind's career might have taken a different turn.

▲ Although designed as a fighter, the Whirlwind was a very capable light-bomber. On anti-shipping patrols in the Channel or attacking German airfields in northern France the Whirlwind proved a success. The squadrons even developed a dive-bombing technique for the aircraft, achieving good results against the E-boats.

## WESTLAND WHIRLWIND

▲ **Low-level striker**
Carrying bombs on the wing pylons, Whirlwinds made low-level dashes across the Channel before attacking German-held airfields. The success of these missions depended on the element of surprise.

▲ **Capable dogfighter**
With good speed and excellent handling the Whirlwind could match the Bf 109 in a dogfight. They notched up a number of kills in 1942.

▲ **Production problems**
Deliveries of Whirlwinds from the Westland factory were painfully slow due to a shortage of engines.

▲**Powerful punch**
The Whirlwind was fitted with four 20-mm (0.79-in.) cannon, making it the most powerfully armed fighter in the RAF. However, early problems with these reduced serviceability and a mixed armament may have been a better option.

▲ **Fast fighter**
The key to the Whirlwind's impressive performance was its highly streamlined shape.

## FACTS AND FIGURES

➤ The Whirlwind was the first single-seat twin-engined fighter to enter RAF service.

➤ The Whirlwind was so secret that the first public mention of it in Britain was in a German magazine article.

➤ In August 1941 Whirlwinds escorted a force of Blenheims all the way to Cologne.

➤ Whirlwind production ran to 112 aircraft before the final service delivery to the RAF was made in December 1941.

➤ Bomb-laden Whirlwinds were usually nicknamed 'Whirlibombers' by pilots.

➤ Whirlwinds attacked the *Scharnhorst* and *Gneisenau* battleships in February 1941.

# PROFILE

# Westland's wonder

During the early part of World War II, Britain was very short of twin-engined fighters with the endurance to fly operational sorties across the English Channel and attack targets well inside occupied France. The Westland Whirlwind seemed to be the answer.

Entering service with No. 263 Squadron in December 1940, the Whirlwind was well armed for the ground-attack role and few pilots had ever seen such a concentrated weight of fire from four closely grouped 20-mm (0.79-in.) cannon.

The main problem was the engines, which were sometimes quite a liability. The Rolls-Royce Peregrine gave trouble both on the ground and in the air and the decision was taken – after No. 137 Squadron had also received Whirlwinds in September 1941 – not to develop it further. Installation of better engines would have meant a major and time-consuming redesign, and in view of the steady availability of Beaufighters and Mosquitoes, the Whirlwind became one of the war's potential outstanding aircraft that had to be left on the sidelines.

Before it was withdrawn, however, the Whirlwind gave a good account of itself on cross-Channel fighter operations. This attractive twin made short work of German ground targets, E-boats and other enemy shipping. Bombs supplemented the Whirlwind's cannon and for a time, the two squadrons were the scourge of the Germans.

*Above: Despite the engine problems, No. 263 Squadron achieved some success with the Whirlwind. A profitable month was August 1941, when they destroyed four Bf 109s and an E-boat.*

*Left: If the Whirlwind had been fitted with the superlative Merlin engine it could have been a great fighter with a top speed of 680 km/h (422 m.p.h.). Unfortunately, the Merlin was needed for the single-engined fighters and the heavy bombers.*

## Whirlwind Mk I

**Type:** single-seat fighter/fighter-bomber

**Powerplant:** two 660-kW (885-hp.) Rolls-Royce Peregrine liquid-cooled piston engines

**Maximum speed:** 580 km/h (360 m.p.h.)

**Range:** 1290 km (800 mi.)

**Service ceiling:** 9144 m (30,000 ft.)

**Weights:** empty 3770 kg (8,294 lb.); loaded 5166 kg (11,365 lb.)

**Armament:** four 20-mm (0.79-in.) Hispano cannon in fuselage nose, plus up to 454 kg (1,000 lb.) of bombs under wings

**Dimensions:**
| | |
|---|---|
| span | 13.72 m (45 ft.) |
| length | 9.98 m (32 ft. 9 in.) |
| height | 3.52 m (11 ft. 6 in.) |
| wing area | 23.22 m² (250 sq. ft.) |

## WHIRLWIND MK I

**Deliveries of the Whirlwind began in June 1940 when the first machine was delivered to No. 263 Squadron. This machine also served with No. 263 Squadron in the winter of 1941/42 from Charmy Down.**

This aircraft carries the markings of No. 263 Squadron. The only other squadron to fly the Whirlwind operationally was No. 137 which flew anti-shipping sorties.

The tailplane was mounted mid-way up the tall tailfin, which gave the Whirlwind good stability. This was especially useful when dive-bombing.

The Whirlwind carried its armament in the nose. It was heavily armed for the early stages of the war with four 20-mm (0.79-in.) cannon.

The single-seat cockpit bulged high above the fuselage giving the pilot excellent visibility.

Despite being an excellent design with superb low-altitude performance, the Whirlwind was never built in large numbers. The main reason was the unreliability of its Rolls-Royce Peregrine engines.

The Whirlwind's rudder extended to the bottom of the fin, allowing the pilot to line up the aircraft very accurately during a bomb run.

## COMBAT DATA

### MAXIMUM SPEED

At the start of the war the Whirlwind was the fastest twin-engined fighter in the world. The later P-38 was exceptionally fast and proved the equal of most single-engined fighters.

| | |
|---|---|
| WHIRLWIND Mk I | 580 km/h (360 m.p.h.) |
| P-38 LIGHTNING | 666 km/h (413 m.p.h.) |
| Bf 110C | 560 km/h (347 m.p.h.) |

### RANGE

Designed from the start as a long-range fighter, the Whirlwind could escort the early British bombing raids well inside enemy territory. The P-38 could double its range by carrying drop-tanks.

| | |
|---|---|
| WHIRLWIND Mk I | 1290 km (800 mi.) |
| P-38 LIGHTNING | 724 km (450 mi.) |
| Bf 110C | 775 km (480 mi.) |

### ARMAMENT

The Whirlwind was very heavily armed for RAF fighters of the time, but it experienced some problems with its cannon. German aircraft were always well armed and the Bf 110 was no exception.

| | |
|---|---|
| WHIRLWIND Mk I | 4 x 20-mm (0.79-in.) cannon |
| P-38 LIGHTNING | 1 x 20-mm (0.79-in.) cannon, 4 x 12.7-mm (.50 cal.) MGs |
| Bf 110C | 2 x 20-mm (0.79-in.) cannon, 5 x 7.92-mm (0.31-in.) MGs |

## Twin-engine day-fighters of World War II

■ **LOCKHEED P-38 LIGHTNING:** The P-38 was particularly effective as a long-range fighter in the Pacific War. P-38s were credited with more Japanese aircraft than any other type.

■ **MESSERSCHMITT Bf 110C:** At the start of World War II the Bf 110 was Germany's primary long-range fighter. It performed well in Poland and France, but suffered in the Battle of Britain.

■ **PETLYAKOV Pe-2:** Often referred to as the 'Russian Mosquito', the Pe-2 was a versatile combat aircraft. The interceptor version was fast and heavily armed.

# YAKOVLEV

# YAK-1 & YAK-7

● Fighter ● Ground attack ● Trainer

▲ These Soviet pilots
on the Kharkov front shot down 15 enemy
aircraft in a week in May 1942. The Yaks
gave the USSR air superiority after the
appalling defeats inflicted in 1941.

**F**irst of the modern Yak fighters, the
Yak-1 came into service just in time
to meet the German invasion in
1941. Agile and fast, the Yak was the best
of the new Soviet fighters and could equal
a Bf 109 or Fw 190 in a dogfight, in
addition to being a useful ground
attacker. The Yak-7, originally designed as
a trainer, was hastily converted for fighter
duties. Both aircraft evolved into better
designs, the later Yak-3 and Yak-9.

## YAKOVLEV YAK-1 & YAK-7

◀ **Ramjet Yak**
The DM-4S ramjet engine was tested on
a few Yak-7UTI trainers. Despite the
success of the trials, the system was
not adopted for operational use.

▼ **Best of the Yaks**
Finest of the Yak-1s was the Yak-1M,
which soon evolved into the Yak-3.
Reduced weight helped give agility,
although oil cooling was problematic.

▲ **Trainer variant**
Best of the trainers was the Yak-7V
with a fixed undercarriage and full
dual controls, but no armament, radio
or self-sealing fuel tanks.

◀ **Enemy colours**
This Yak-7 was seized by the Germans
and tested. Most German pilots thought
the Yak rather crude and simple, but
respected its combat performance.

**Mass production** ▶
More than 8700 Yak-1s and 6300 Yak-7s were produced
in total. Yaks were by far the most important fighters
in the Soviet arsenal.

### FACTS AND FIGURES

➤ Test pilot Piontkovskii was killed in
January 1940 while flying the prototype,
which had manufacturing defects.

➤ Naval aviation units of the Black Sea
Fleet used the Yak-1 over Crimea.

➤ The Yak-7DI long-range fighter version
ultimately became the Yak-9.

➤ Female ace Lilya Litvak claimed 13
victims in a year of flying the Yak-1 over
Rostov and Stalingrad.

➤ The 728th Polk replaced its old I-16s
with Yak-7Bs only in mid-1943.

➤ Stepan Suprun was made a Hero of the
Soviet Union for test flying the Yak-1.

## PROFILE

# First of the new Yak fighters

Yak began the project for a single-seat lightweight fighter before the war, and the prototype I-26 first flew in January 1940. Emphasis was on the use of cheap materials (using composite wooden skins and fabric covering) and integral armament, with a nose-mounted cannon. The aircraft showed immediate promise, and was rushed into production even before trials were complete. By March 1942, the Yak-1 was being produced in a lightened form for increased agility.

The acute shortage of fighters meant that the trainer Yak-7 was converted to combat use, including artillery spotting and fighter duties. The aircraft was also fitted with rockets for ground attack and tank-busting, and cameras for reconnaissance. The Yak-7R even mounted a rocket engine in the tail. Best of the Yak-1s was the Yak-1M, which was quickly redesignated the Yak-3. This aircraft gave its pilots a much improved field of vision, and was one of the war's most agile fighters.

The early Yaks were a vital stopgap between obsolete designs like the I-16 and the excellent later Yaks and Lavochkin La-5s with which the Soviet Union won the air war on the Eastern Front.

*Left: The prototype I-26 proved to be a winner immediately. Few modifications were made to the production fighter, the main ones being a strengthened wing and better armour protection. The prototype was known as the Krasavyets (Beauty).*

*Right: The Yak-1M was a far better dog-fighter, thanks to its new wing, bubble canopy and new gunsight.*

### Yak-1

**Type:** single-seat fighter and fighter-bomber

**Powerplant:** one 782-kW (1,050-hp.) Klimov M-105 V-12 liquid-cooled engine

**Maximum speed:** 530 km/h (329 m.p.h.)

**Initial climb rate:** 7 min to 5000 m (16,400 ft.)

**Turning time:** 360° in 17.6 sec

**Range:** 700 km (435 mi.)

**Service ceiling:** 9000 m (29,500 ft.)

**Weights:** empty 2550 kg (5,610 lb.); loaded 3130 kg (6,886 lb.)

**Armament:** 1 x 20-mm (0.79-in.) ShVAK cannon, one or two ShKAS 12.7-mm (.50 cal.) machine-guns; wing racks could carry six RS-82 rockets

**Dimensions:** span 10.00 m (32 ft. 10 in.)
length 8.48 m (27 ft. 9 in.)
wing area 17.15 m² (185 sq. ft.)

---

### YAK-1M

The ultimate Yak-1, the Yak-1M was soon to become the Yak-3, the most feared foe of Luftwaffe pilots at low level. First flown on 20 September 1943, the Yak-1M's fuel tanks were fitted with a nitrogen fire-suppression system.

One of the biggest improvements to the Yak-1M was the upgraded jettisonable hood, which gave all-round vision and was less prone to jamming than those of the first models. A sheet of 9-mm (⅓-in.) back armour protected the pilot from enemy fire.

A slogan painted on the fuselage was a common feature of Soviet fighters. This one reads: 'To the pilot of the Stalingrad front B.N. Yeremin, from the farmers of Stakhanov collective farm'. Wooden bonded skin materials were cheaper than aluminium, and easier to repair after combat damage.

Летчику Сталинградского фронти
Гвардии Майору тов Еремину В.Н.
От колхозника колхоза „Стаханова„
тов Головатова

Armament comprised a single 20-mm (0.79-in.) ShA-20M cannon firing through the spinner (replacing the heavier ShVAK of earlier Yak-1s) and two UBS 12.7-mm (.50 cal.) machine-guns in the upper fuselage.

The Yak-1M used the all-metal wing fitted to the Yak-9, which could be more easily replaced in the field. Oil coolers were mounted in the wingroots.

The radiator was cooled by air from a long ventral intake. The 30-kg (66-lb.) central fuselage fuel tank supplemented two larger wing tanks.

Another improvement to the Yak-1M was the addition of an elevator mass balance to lighten control forces. The rear fuselage skin was 2-mm (⅛-in.) plywood. The tailwheel retracted, unlike that of the early Yak-1s.

### COMBAT DATA

#### MAXIMUM SPEED

The Yak-1 was slower than most of its adversaries, mainly because of its higher drag. However, its agility more than made up for its lack of all-out speed, and most combat occurred at low level where the Yak was at least as good as its German adversaries.

YAK-1   530 km/h (329 m.p.h.)

Bf 109F   624 km/h (387 m.p.h.)

HURRICANE Mk IIB 541 km/h (335 m.p.h.)

#### SERVICE CEILING

Most Soviet fighters performed best at low level, and the Yak was no exception. German pilots were even ordered to avoid combat with the later Yak-3 at heights below 5000 m. The rival MiG-3, however, flew better than the Yak at altitude.

YAK-1 9000 m (29,500 ft.)

Bf 109F 10,668 m (35,000 ft.)

HURRICANE Mk IIB 10,850 m (35,600 ft.)

#### RANGE

The Yak achieved its performance and agility at the expense of reduced fuel capacity. Since Soviet fighters usually flew from bases close to the front line, this was not a problem. The Yak-9 was fitted with long-range fuel tanks.

YAK-1 700 km (435 mi.)

Bf 109F 700 km (435 mi.)

HURRICANE Mk IIB 740 km (460 mi.)

---

## Wartime Russian interceptors

■ **La-5:** Almost as agile as the Yak-3, the La-5 was relatively lightly armed and had fuselage skins made of wooden composite. It was produced in vast numbers, and updated variants like the La-7 and La-9 flew in Korea.

■ **MiG-3:** Very fast and possessing excellent high-altitude performance, the MiG-3 was doomed to a short life by its need for the AM-35 engines used by the Il-2 Shturmovik attack aircraft, which was deemed by Stalin to have production priority.

■ **Yak-9D:** Filling the need for a long-range escort fighter, the Yak-9 proved the equal of the Bf 109G and Fw 190D. This was also the most numerous of the 37,000 Yaks produced in the war; some were flown by the French Normandie-Niemen squadron.

# YAKOVLEV

# YAK-9

● Dogfighter supreme ● Long range ● Soviet fighter

▲ Widely regarded as the
most important fighter of the Great
Patriotic War, the Yak-9 was the mount
of many of the top-scoring Soviet aces
of World War II.

**B**ased on the Yak-7, the Yak-9 had
metal wing spars to make room for
additional fuel. Deliveries started in
August 1942, and by October the type was in
action at Stalingrad. The new fighter proved
popular with its pilots, despite its limited
armament of one 20-mm (0.79-in.) cannon and
a single 12.7-mm (.50 cal.) machine-gun. By
mid-1944 there were more Yak-9s in Soviet
service than all other fighters put together,
and the final variant fought in the Korean War.

## YAKOVLEV YAK-9

▼ **Proven design**
Although its makers studied British and
German fighter designs, the Yak-9 relied
on the proven layout of wooden wings
with a welded steel fuselage.

▲ **Constant combat**
Having been produced in larger numbers than any
other Russian fighter, the Yak-9 saw continuous action
against German Fw 190s and Bf 109s and always
gave an excellent account of itself.

**Russia's defender** ▶
Lined-up on a grass airfield, rows
of Yak-9s wait for the signal to
attack the German army in
another of the great battles which
took place on the Eastern Front.

▲ **Source of pride**
Preserved Yak-9s are displayed throughout the former
Warsaw Pact countries as a reminder of the war.

**Feared foe** ▶
German pilots were given orders to avoid combat with
any Yakovlev fighter fitted with an air scoop because of
the superior handling of such designs in a dogfight.

## FACTS AND FIGURES

➤ A variant of the Yak-9 was fitted with a
37-mm (1.47-in.) cannon which, on firing,
made the aircraft pitch up violently.

➤ The 'D' variant was developed to meet a
request for a fighter with more range.

➤ By 1944 the Yak-9 outnumbered all other
fighters in the Soviet air force.

➤ Yakovlev developed a long-range courier
variant, stripped of all excess weight, for
use over the battlefield.

➤ A batch of aircraft was supplied to
Bulgaria in late 1944.

➤ One aircraft factory produced 20 Yak-9
fighters per day.

**PROFILE**

# Fighter of the Eastern Front

Compared with the earlier Yak-7B, the Yak-9 had a retractable tailwheel and just a single 12.7-mm (.50 cal.) machine-gun in the forward fuselage, where the previous model had two. The cockpit was moved slightly aft and the radiator was moved forward, but otherwise it was externally similar. However, there were frequent later modifications to meet operational requirements.

The Yak-9D had fuel capacity increased to 650 litres (172 gal.)

and was powered by a 1014-kW (1,360-hp.) M-105PF-3 engine, while the -9DD had its fuel capacity increased to 880 litres (233 gal.) for operations over Romania and Yugoslavia. The -9T carried a 37-mm (1.47-in.) cannon for anti-tank missions.

A more radical change was the all-metal Yak-9U, which flew for the first time early in 1943. Powered by a 1230-kW (1,650-hp.) engine, it was capable of 670 km/h (415 m.p.h.), but development was delayed by

the loss of the prototype on an early test flight and it did not become operational until late 1944.

The all-weather Yak-9P did not appear until after the war. It was to be Yakovlev's last piston-engined fighter, and it was exported to several Soviet-allied countries.

*The immense pride in what was achieved with the Yak-9 is demonstrated by the numerous preserved examples displayed at various military installations in Russia.*

## YAK-9D

This Yak-9 was one of those equipping the Free French Normandie-Niemen regiments in 1944; this example survived until the end of the war.

A feature of the Free French aircraft was the spinner painted in the three colours of the French flag.

Despite its intended role as a fighter, the Yak-9D carried no armament in its wings. These were of a mainly wooden construction with later variants incorporating metal ribbing.

Positioned in the nose spinner was the 20-mm (0.79-in.) ShVAK cannon with 120 rounds of ammunition; to the right of this on the upper cowling was a single 12.7-mm (.50 cal.) machine gun, supplied with 200 rounds.

Visibility for the pilot from the Yak-9 cockpit was exceptional, especially when later variants were produced with a cut-down rear fuselage allowing the pilot all-round vision.

Many colour schemes were used by the front-line Soviet fighter squadrons; this example displays the summer camouflage. In winter a rough coat of white would be applied over the entire aircraft.

After the enlargement of the oil tank a larger oil cooler was installed in the nose of the aircraft. German fighter pilots were ordered by their superiors not to engage in combat with Soviet fighters with this feature.

The wide track undercarriage of the Yak-9 was adopted from earlier Yakovlev fighters. This allowed the aircraft to operate from rough fields alongside the advancing Soviet army. Very few landing accidents were encountered with the aircraft.

### Yak-9D

**Type:** single-seat long-range fighter/ground attack aircraft

**Powerplant:** one 940-kW (1,260-hp.) Klimov VK-105PF-1 liquid-cooled piston engine

**Maximum speed:** 533 km/h (330 m.p.h.) at sea level; 597 km/h (370 m.p.h.) at 3650 m (12,000 ft.)

**Range:** 1360 km (843 mi.); operational range 1329 km (824 mi.)

**Service ceiling:** 10,000 m (33,000 ft.)

**Weights:** empty 2420 kg (5,324 lb.); maximum take-off 3115 kg (6,850 lb.)

**Armament:** one 20-mm (0.79-in.) ShVAK cannon mounted in the spinner; one 12.7-mm (.50 cal.) machine-gun installed in the engine cowling

**Dimensions:**
span 9.74 m (31 ft. 11 in.)
length 8.50 m (27 ft. 10 in.)
height 2.60 m (8 ft. 6 in.)
wing area 17.15 m² (185 sq. ft.)

## COMBAT DATA

### MAXIMUM SPEED

Though not the fastest of the Russian fighters of World War II (that was Lavochkin's La-5FN), the Yak-9D was able to compete and win in dogfights with German fighters. The advent of the Fw 190D to the theatre saw the Russian fighters pushed to their limit.

| | |
|---|---|
| Yak-9D | 597 km/h (370 m.p.h.) |
| La-5FN | 648 km/h (402 m.p.h.) |
| MiG-3 | 640 km/h (397 m.p.h.) |

### OPERATIONAL RANGE

In response to requests from the Russian army for a fighter with more range, the Yakovlev design team incorporated additional fuel tanks in the wings into the design. This development allowed the Yak-9D to perform better for strike missions than both the MiG-3 and La-5FN.

Yak-9D 1329 km (824 mi.)

La-5FN 764 km (474 mi.)

MiG-3 1195 km (740 mi.)

### TAKE-OFF WEIGHT

The take-off weight of the Yak-9D was surprisingly small compared to other similar Soviet fighters. Both the MiG-3 and La-5FN were more often used in the ground-attack role, while the Yaks provided air cover and performed air interception duties.

Yak-9D 3115 kg (6,850 lb.)
MiG-3 3350 kg (7,370 lb.)
La-5FN 3402 kg (7,484 lb.)

## Stalin's air power

■ **MIG-3:** Developed from the MiG-1 the MiG-3 was found to have extremely poor performance and was quickly relegated to secondary tasks in 1942.

■ **Pe-2:** The most outstanding tactical bomber of World War II, this versatile twin-engined aircraft continued to serve with the Soviet air force after the war.

■ **P-39 AIRACOBRA:** Offered to the Soviet air force under the terms of the Lend-Lease agreement, the P-39 was used as a ground attack aircraft.

# ZEPPELIN

# STAAKEN R

● Four-engined pioneer ● Heavy bomber ● Raids over Britain

▲ Staaken R.VI 30/16 is prepared for flight, with Oberleutnant Meyer in the foreground. The Staaken crews developed tactics for long-range night bombing that were a completely new mode of warfare.

I n aviation no ordeal can compare with the demands of a seven-hour flight aboard the collosal Zeppelin Staaken R-series bomber; the boldest design of the Great War. The name of Count von Zeppelin is usually associated with dirigible airships, but this heavier-than-air warplane was just as striking as anything else made by the company. In long-range flights over Britain, the Staaken made history conducting the first strategic bombing missions.

## ZEPPELIN STAAKEN R

▲ **Modified version**
The Staaken R.IV was a modified VGO.III. The name changed to Staaken after the factory moved.

**Inside the giant ▶**
The enclosed cockpit contained radio and advanced equipment for navigation.

▲ **Long range**
Missions over Britain from bases in Belgium took several hours and were highly demanding, but these were also the safest. The short-range attacks over France were more dangerous due to better defence there.

▼ **Ready for action**
In 1916 the smaller VGO.III was already heavily committed to action over the Eastern Front, carrying out raids on railway installations near Riga.

▲ **Gunner's seat**
Staakens had excellent gun positions, and fighters attacking them usually received a curtain of accurate return fire. By the end of hostilities the addition of a Becker 20-mm cannon was considered.

## FACTS AND FIGURES

➤ The final R-series, built after the war, was banned by the Allied Control Commission and scrapped in 1922.

➤ Zeppelin's first heavy bomber made its maiden flight on 11 April 1915.

➤ A final R-plane raid against Britain planned for August 1918 was cancelled.

➤ The R.IV was so much bigger than other aircraft that British pilots often opened fire on them from too far away.

➤ R-planes dropped 27,190 kg (59,818 lb.) of bombs on Britain.

➤ Only three Staakens were shot down over Britain, all by anti-aircraft guns.

**PROFILE**

# Zeppelin's giant night-bomber

When the Great War began, Count von Zeppelin developed heavy bombers which he expected to strongly influence the conflict. Zeppelin worked on three aircraft, all with distinctive slab sides and biplane tail, before turning to the R-series (R for Riesenflugzeug). The first production R series aircraft was delivered in June 1917.

The distinctive lines of Zeppelin's bombers were unforgettable. Several companies turned their industrial prowess toward constructing these giant bombers, and even a two-float

seaplane version was built.

The Zeppelin carried out missions over France and Russia in support of the German army, but its most famous missions were the 11 raids over Britain, often accompanied by Gotha bombers. The Staaken crews developed new navigation techniques, including the use of radio, and dropped huge 1000-kg (2,200-lb.) bombs, never seen before. The British had to divert large numbers of guns and fighters to face the new threat. This caused more disruption than the actual bombing, which

did little damage. The Allies were highly impressed by the Staakens, and hurriedly developed similar aircraft like the Handley Page series of bombers.

*Above: The ultimate R-plane was the R.VI, of which 18 were built. The R.VI squadrons carried out bombing missions on the Western Front, suffering high losses.*

*Below: Construction of the VGO.III began in October 1915, using Mercedes D.III engines in place of the less reliable Maybach units. Two engines in the nose drove one propeller through a central combining gearbox.*

## Staaken R.IV

**Type:** seven-crew heavy bomber

**Powerplant:** two 119-kW (160-hp.) Mercedes D.III and four 164-kW (220-hp.) Benz Bz.IV inline piston engines

**Maximum speed:** 125 km/h (78 m.p.h.)

**Endurance:** 6 or 7 hours

**Service ceiling:** 3700 m (12, 150 ft.)

**Weights:** empty 8772 kg (19,298 lb.); maximum take-off 13,035 kg (28,677 lb.)

**Armament:** up to seven 7.92-mm Parabellum machine-guns, plus a maximum short-range bombload of 2123 kg (4,670 lb.)

**Dimensions:** span 42.20 m (138 ft. 5 in.)
length 23.20 m (76 ft. 1 in.)
height 6.80 m (22 ft. 4 in.)
wing area 332 m² (3,572 sq. ft.)

### STAAKEN R.IV

Assigned to Rfa 501 stationed near Ghent, the R.IV took part in raids on targets including London, the Thames Estuary, Calais, Morville and Bolougne. Rfa 500 also operated the R.IV, which saw service over the Eastern Front just before Russia surrendered in 1917.

The wing engines were fitted in a pusher-type configuration, with radiators mounted above the engines. The R.IV was the only R-plane with coupled engines to see service on both fronts up to the end of the war.

A great deal of thought went into the defence of the R.IV. Guns were fitted in the upper wing, accessible by a ladder, and in the rear fuselage where two gunners sat side by side.

One improvement over the R.III was to move the tail surfaces above the line of the fuselage. Tail damage almost inevitably occurred in any accident of the R.III.

The nose contained a forward engineer's compartment to allow inflight maintenance.

Almost the same wing structure was used in the R.IV as in the R.III, with the exception that the lower wing dihedral was decreased.

The ventral gun was useful for firing at enemy searchlight positions during night raids.

The lower tail spars extended under the top fuselage longeron, a feature retained on later R-series aircraft. The whole airframe (except around the engines) was covered in fabric, with the distinct polygon pattern common to German aircraft at the time. Occasionally this pattern was overpainted. Although the aircraft had a nosewheel, a tail skid was retained to prevent damage during take-off.

## COMBAT DATA

### MAXIMUM SPEED

Large and ungainly biplane designs like the Staaken were very slow. The primary requirements for the design were to obtain sufficient power and wing area to lift a useful load. This required large span wings and big engine radiators, which created large amounts of drag.

STAAKEN R.IV   125 km/h (78 m.p.h.)
MOUROMETS   137 km/h (85 m.p.h.)
0/100   122 km/h (76 m.p.h.)

### WING AREA

The size of the R.IV is vividly illustrated by comparing its wing area to that of its contemporaries. The need for lift meant that designers had to produce aircraft with large wing areas to compensate for lack of power. High speed was not a realistic requirement.

| STAAKEN R.IV 332 m² (3,572 sq. ft.) | MOUROMETS 220 m² (2,367 sq. ft.) | 0/100 153 m² (1,646 sq. ft.) |

### ARMAMENT

Fighter pilots who took on a Staaken were taking their lives in their hands, and many were driven back or killed by the accurate and powerful fire of the aircraft's gunners. The Ilya Mouromets gave similar problems to German and Austrian pilots.

STAAKEN R.IV 7 x 7.92-mm machine-guns | MOUROMETS 6 x 7.62-mm machine-guns | 0/100 4 x 7.7-mm (.303 cal.) machine-guns

## Long-range bombers of the Great War

■ **ILYA MOUROMETS:** Designed by Igor Sikorsky, the Ilya Mouromets was used for bombing by the Imperial Russian Air Service. One shot down three German fighters.

■ **CAPRONI Ca.36:** This twin-engined design was a derivative of the wartime Ca.3, which first flew in 1914. Over 150 large Capronis were built, and the Ca.36 was still in production after the war.

■ **GOTHA G.V:** A twin-engined design much smaller than the R-planes, the Gothas formed the backbone of the bomber fleet against Britain, and took part in raids alongside the R.IVs.

■ **VICKERS VIMY:** The British equivalent to the Gotha, the Vimy would have taken part in raids against Germany if the war had continued, but only three were ready by October 1918.

# Glossary

**Aileron:** an aerofoil used for causing an aircraft to roll around its longitudinal axis, usually fitted near the wingtips. Ailerons are controlled by use of the pilot's control column

**All-Up Weight:** the total weight of an aircraft in operating condition. Normal maximum AUW is the maximum at which an aircraft is permitted to fly within normal design restrictions, while overload weight is the maximum AUW at which an aircraft is permitted to fly subject to ultimate flying restrictions

**Altimeter:** instrument that measures altitude, or height above sea level

**Angle of Attack:** the angle between the wing (airfoil) and the airflow relative to it

**Anhedral:** The downward angle of a wing in relation to a horizontal cross-section line

**Apron:** The hard-surfaced or paved area around a hangar

**Aspect Ratio:** the ratio of wing span to chord

**Basic Weight:** the tare weight of an aircraft plus the specified operational load

**Ceiling:** the maximum height above sea level attainable by an aircraft

**Centre of Gravity:** point in a body through which the sum of the weights of all its parts passes.

**Centre of Pressure:** point through which the lifting force of a wing acts

**Chord:** cross-section of a wing from leading edge to trailing edge

**Coaming:** A padded, protective rim around an open cockpit

**Constant-speed Propeller:** A propeller that governs an engine at its optimum speed by the blade pitch being increased or decreased automatically

**Cowling:** a circular fairing around an aircraft engine for streamlining or cooling

**Drag:** The resisting force exerted on an aircraft in its line of flight in the opposite direction to its motion

**Elevator:** a horizontal control surface used to control the upward or downward inclination of an aircraft in flight. Elevators are usually hinged to the trailing edge of the tailplane

**Empennage:** An aircraft's tail group, includes rudder and fin, and stabilizer and elevator

**Ferry flight:** A flight for the purpose of either returning an aircraft to base; delivering an aircraft from one location to another or moving an aircraft to and from a maintenance base.

**Flap:** A movable, usually hinged airfoil set in the trailing edge of an aircraft wing, designed to increase lift or drag

**Fuselage:** An aircraft's main body structure

**Hangar:** An enclosed structure for housing aircraft

**Jet propulsion:** method of propulsion in which an object is propelled in one direction by a jet, or stream of gases, moving in the other

**Laminar Flow:** airflow passes over an aircraft's wing in layers, the first of which, the boundary layer, remains stationary while successive layers progressively accelerate; this is known as laminar flow. The smoother the wing surface, and the more efficient its design, the smoother the airflow

**Landing Weight:** the AUW of an aircraft at the moment of landing

**Maximum Landing Weight:** the maximum AUW, due to design or operational limitations, at which an aircraft is permitted to land

**Maximum Take-Off Weight:** the maximum AUW, due to design or operational limitations, at which an aircraft is permitted to take off

**MG:** Machine gun

**Monocoque:** type of fuselage design with little or no internal bracing other than bulkheads, where the outer skin bears the main stresses

**Operational Load:** The weight of equipment necessarily carried by an aircraft for a particular role

**Rotary Engine:** a powerplant that rotates on a stationary propeller shaft

**Rudder:** movable vertical surface or surfaces forming part of the tail unit, by which the yawing of an aircraft is controlled

**Seaplane:** a water-based aircraft with a boat-hull fuselage, often amphibious.

**Spin:** a spin is the result of yawing or rolling an aeroplane at the point of a stall

**Stall:** condition that occurs when the smooth flow of the air over an aircraft's wing changes to a turbulent flow and the lift decreases to the point where control is lost

**Yaw:** the action of turning an aircraft in the air around its normal (vertical) axis by use of the rudder. An aircraft is said to yaw when the fore-and-aft axis turns to port or starboard, out of the line of flight

# Index

With detailed features on more than 220 combat aircraft from the first 40 years of war in the air, **Classic Military Aircraft** is a comprehensive guide to the world's fighting aircraft, from the earliest World War I fighters to the end of World War II.

Densely packed with information, this book covers an array of biplane, triplane and monoplane designs, from the SPADs and Fokkers of World War I, through the dead ends and unusual prototypes of the interwar years, to high-powered World War II warbirds such as the P-51 Mustang and Supermarine Spitfire.

Each aircraft is covered in detail, with feature boxes outlining its development, technical specifications, performance data, and variants. Unique graphics allow the reader to compare specific features firepower, troop-carrying capacity, and bombload to those of other aircraft of the same type.

Published by
Amber Books Ltd
Bradley's Close
74–77 White Lion Street
London N1 9PF
United Kingdom
www.amberbooks.co.uk

ISBN: 978-1-907446-39-9

Printed in China

Cover images:
Front: Republic P-47 Thunderbolt (Alamy/David Gowans); Back: Focke-Wulf Fw 190 (Courtesy IMP AB)

ISBN 978-1-907446-39-9

9 781907 446399